*Introduction to*
# PLANT GEOGRAPHY

Other Books by the same Author:

*Russian Waters*, London: Arnold (1931)

*The Isle of Auks*, London: Arnold (1932)

*Botany of the Canadian Eastern Arctic*:

Part I, *Pteridophyta and Spermatophyta*, Ottawa: King's Printer (1940)

Part II, *Thallophyta and Bryophyta* (*ed.*), Ottawa: King's Printer (1947)

Part III, *Vegetation and Ecology*, Ottawa: King's Printer (1948)

*Arctic Unfolding*, London, etc.: Hutchinson (1949)

*Circumpolar Arctic Flora*, Clarendon Press, Oxford (1959)

*Arctic Botany* (3 vols.), Clarendon Press, Oxford (1960)

---

Editor of *Plant Science Monographs*, London: Leonard Hill; New York: Interscience.

General Editor of *World Crops Books*, London: Leonard Hill; New York: Interscience.

# INTRODUCTION TO PLANT GEOGRAPHY

## *and Some Related Sciences*

by

NICHOLAS POLUNIN

M.S. (Yale), M.A., D.Phil., D.Sc. (Oxon.)

*Guest Professor, University of Geneva; lately Professor of Plant Ecology and Taxonomy, Head of the Department of Botany, and Director of the University Herbarium, etc., Faculty of Science, Baghdad, Iraq. Formerly Fielding Curator and Keeper of the University Herbaria, University Demonstrator and Lecturer in Botany, and Senior Research Fellow of New College, Oxford; Macdonald Professor of Botany, McGill University; Research Associate, etc., of Harvard and Yale Universities.*

LONGMANS

LONGMANS GREEN AND CO LTD
London and Harlow

*Associated companies, branches and representatives throughout the world*


*First published 1960*
*New impression with minor corrections 1960*
*New impression 1964, 1967 and 1969*



Printed in Great Britain by Butler & Tanner Ltd., Frome and London

Dedicated To
THE AMERICAN
GEOGRAPHICAL SOCIETY
OF NEW YORK

*who inspired and first*
*commissioned this book*

# CONTENTS

# LIST OF ILLUSTRATIONS

# ACKNOWLEDGEMENTS

To one who considers that personal friendship and generosity in sharing the fruits of scholarship are among the very best things of life, it gives great pleasure to acknowledge indebtedness to the many *savants* who have contributed of their knowledge or store of illustrations to the benefit of this work. They must not, however, be held responsible for any shortcomings it may have—such as, perhaps, in some views, omission of discussion of certain controversial issues which seemed best by-passed at least at the time of writing. Notable among these are Dr. C. W. Thornthwaite's work on evapotranspiration and the classification of climates, Professor Eric Hultén's views on the history of arctic and boreal species, and various ideas about the places of origin of plant forms and the possibilities of their being multiple (polytopic).

The book owes its inception to the foresight of Dr. George H. T. Kimble, who, when Director of the American Geographical Society, was instrumental in my being invited and generously commissioned to prepare it for a new series of ' readers ' on geographical subjects.

Early on, the general plan was improved from time to time following discussion with colleagues at Oxford, Yale, and Harvard Universities, in its near-final form being approved by a seminar at the last-named. The plan also derived benefit from many individuals elsewhere; among these my former teacher and chief, the late Professor Sir Arthur G. Tansley, and my former pupils, Professor John H. Burnett and Dr. John Warren Wilson, were particularly helpful. Yet others who made valuable suggestions, most of which were gladly adopted, include Professor Hugh M. Raup of Harvard University, Professor Paul B. Sears of Yale University, Professor Joseph Ewan of Tulane University, and Drs. Raymond F. Fosberg and Henry K. Svenson, both of Washington, D.C. The then Directors of the two main botanical gardens of the United Kingdom, the late Professor Sir William Wright Smith of Edinburgh and Sir Edward J. Salisbury of Kew, also gave freely of their advice, as did the former Director of the New York Botanical Garden and of the Arnold Arboretum, the late Professor Elmer D. Merrill. The book, moreover, derives much from the able (and direct) teaching of two others who are unfortunately no longer with us, namely the late Professors George E. Nichols of Yale (in ecology) and Merritt L. Fernald of Harvard (in taxonomy).

Colleagues or friends who have been kind enough to read and give helpful advice about particular chapters or groups of chapters have included Professors G. E. Hutchinson, Harold J. Lutz, Paul B. Sears, and Mr. Albert F. Burke, all of Yale University, Professors Kenneth V. Thimann and Hugh M. Raup, and Drs. A. F. Hill and Richard E. Schultes, all of Harvard University, Drs. W. O. James, F.R.S., and F. H. Whitehead, both of Oxford University, Drs. H. Hamshaw Thomas, F.R.S., and Harry Godwin, F.R.S., both of Cambridge University, the late Professor Sir Arthur G. Tansley, F.R.S., of Grantchester, Cambridge, Professor Paul W. Richards of the University College of North Wales, Bangor, Dr. John Hutchinson, F.R.S., of the Royal Botanic Gardens, Kew, Mr. F. T. Walker of the Institute of Seaweed Research, Inveresk, Musselburgh, Scotland, Messrs. Robert Ross and W. T. Stearn, both of the British Museum (Natural History), Dr. Richard S. Cowan of the New York Botanical Garden, Professor G. W. Prescott of Michigan State University, Professor George L. Church of Brown University, Professor Valentine J. Chapman of Auckland University College, New Zealand, Professor G. Einar Du Rietz, of Uppsala, Professors Gunnar Erdtman of Stockholm and Karl H. Rechinger of Vienna (while Visiting Professors in my department at Baghdad, Iraq), Professor Thorvald Sørensen, of Copenhagen, Professor John H. Burnett, now of the University of St. Andrews, Dr. Frank E. Egler of Aton Forest, Norfolk, Conn., and Dr. Edward H. Graham, Director of Plant Technology in the Soil Conservation Service of the United States Department of Agriculture, Washington, D.C. Whereas the choice of these kind mentors was naturally governed largely by their specialist interests, to mention who ' passed ' what might leave them open to being held responsible for errors of commission or omission which are in fact my own. Most of the substance of this book was earlier presented in a full-year graduate course at Yale University—a circumstance which, at the instance of some senior participating students, has led to further constructive comment and, surely, improvement.

In the matter of illustration, so vitally important to a work of this kind, the greatest debt is to Ginn and Company, of Boston, Massachusetts, and Mrs. William H. Brown, for their loan of, and permission to use freely, so many of the fine drawings and photographic prints made for the late Professor William H. Brown's *The Plant Kingdom*, published in 1935. This was not only a great convenience but also a great privilege, these illustrations being often of unsurpassed excellence. Acknowledgment is also due to the National Museum of Canada for permission to reproduce many of my photographs of arctic regions that are now in their possession. Other sources of illustrations, where not contributed by myself, are acknowledged individually.

NICHOLAS POLUNIN

Faculty of Science,
Baghdad, Iraq
Spring, 1957[1]

[1] Since this was written it has not been possible to incorporate extensively any new ideas or to consider subsequent works, though some details of publication have been brought up to date. The proofs have kindly been read by Professor John H. Burnett and Dr. A. D. Q. Agnew (now of my Department in Baghdad), while in connection with their correction warm thanks are due to my secretary, Miss Christine Wright. Acknowledgment is also made to Dr. B. Barnes for his valued part in the preparation of the Index.

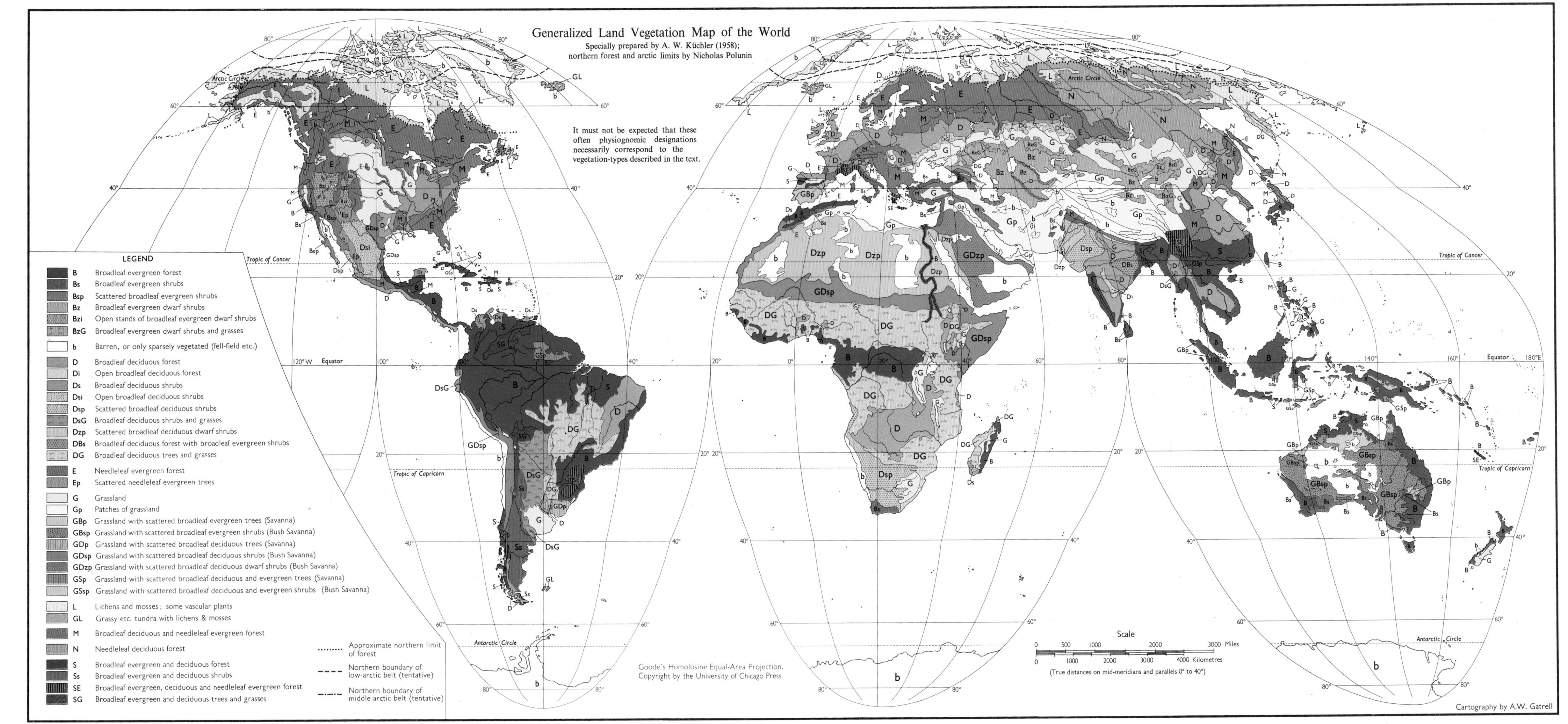
Generalized Land Vegetation Map of the World
Specially prepared by A. W. Küchler (1958);
northern forest and arctic limits by Nicholas Polunin
It must not be expected that these often physiognomic designations necessarily correspond to the vegetation-types described in the text.
LEGEND
B Broadleaf evergreen forest
Bs Broadleaf evergreen shrubs
Bsp Scattered broadleaf evergreen shrubs
Bz Broadleaf evergreen dwarf shrubs
Bzi Open stands of broadleaf evergreen dwarf shrubs
BzG Broadleaf evergreen dwarf shrubs and grasses
b Barren, or only sparsely vegetated (fell-field etc.)
D Broadleaf deciduous forest
Di Open broadleaf deciduous forest
Ds Broadleaf deciduous shrubs
Dsi Open broadleaf deciduous shrubs
Dsp Scattered broadleaf deciduous shrubs
DsG Broadleaf deciduous shrubs and grasses
Dzp Scattered broadleaf deciduous dwarf shrubs
DBs Broadleaf deciduous forest with broadleaf evergreen shrubs
DG Broadleaf deciduous trees and grasses
E Needleleaf evergreen forest
Ep Scattered needleleaf evergreen trees
G Grassland
Gp Patches of grassland
GBp Grassland with scattered broadleaf evergreen trees (Savanna)
GBsp Grassland with scattered broadleaf evergreen shrubs (Bush Savanna)
GDp Grassland with scattered broadleaf deciduous trees (Savanna)
GDsp Grassland with scattered broadleaf deciduous shrubs (Bush Savanna)
GDzp Grassland with scattered broadleaf deciduous dwarf shrubs (Bush Savanna)
GSp Grassland with scattered broadleaf deciduous and evergreen trees (Savanna)
GSsp Grassland with scattered broadleaf deciduous and evergreen shrubs (Bush Savanna)
L Lichens and mosses; some vascular plants
GL Grassy etc. tundra with lichens & mosses
M Broadleaf deciduous and needleleaf evergreen forest
N Needleleaf deciduous forest
S Broadleaf evergreen and deciduous forest
Ss Broadleaf evergreen and deciduous shrubs
SE Broadleaf evergreen, deciduous and needleleaf evergreen forest
SG Broadleaf evergreen and deciduous trees and grasses
Approximate northern limit of forest
Northern boundary of low-arctic belt (tentative)
Northern boundary of middle-arctic belt (tentative)
Goode's Homolosine Equal-Area Projection.
Copyright by the University of Chicago Press
Scale
0 500 1000 2000 3000 Miles
0 1000 2000 3000 4000 Kilometres
(True distances on mid-meridians and parallels 0° to 40°)
Arctic Circle
Tropic of Cancer
Equator
Tropic of Capricorn
Antarctic Circle
Cartography by A.W. Gatrell

## Chapter I

# WHAT IS PLANT GEOGRAPHY?

Let us begin with a few basic definitions and follow them with some general explanations.

Biology is the science of life, the study of living things, and it has two main branches—botany, which deals with plants, and zoology, which deals with animals. But whereas every one of us must surely be clear about the differences between the typical plant (which is static, green, and does not ingest solid food) and the typical animal (which is motile, not green, and ingests elaborated food), there remain many 'border-line cases' that are apt to be claimed by both botanists and zoologists. Indeed, each of the characteristics mentioned for one of these primary groups (kingdoms) of living organisms is exhibited by some members of the other, which prevents the drawing of any hard and fast line between all animals and all plants. And even if we add the stipulation that the greenness of plants shall be due to chlorophyll, and that they shall contain the carbohydrate cellulose, there remain many organisms which possess neither feature but still in other ways seem to be plants, and are usually treated as such.

Consequently it seems best in this case not to attempt precise definition but rather to visualize the typical plant as a living organism that is fixed, possessed of cellulose cell-walls, and dependent for its main food-supply upon simple, gaseous or liquid substances (principally carbon dioxide and water). With the aid of chlorophyll in the light, the organism builds up these substances into sugars and other complex materials. The green plant is thus responsible for the fundamental chain of reactions on which almost all life depends. But this partial description excludes many organisms (such as Yeasts and other small Fungi) which are commonly considered to be plants. These 'exceptions' often form major groups although, as we shall see in the next chapter, they may exhibit none of the stipulated main plant characteristics. The description also leaves behind a basic 'hub' of organisms, chiefly of microscopic types, that seem to belong almost as much to one kingdom as to the other. Among the more important of these are the Bacteria, which cause so many of our worst diseases but in other instances benefit us greatly. These and other 'border-line cases', which include many of the most primitive organisms living today, will be considered as within our immediate sphere of interest.

Fig. 1 illustrates some cases of plant-like animals; several animal-like plants will be described and illustrated in the next

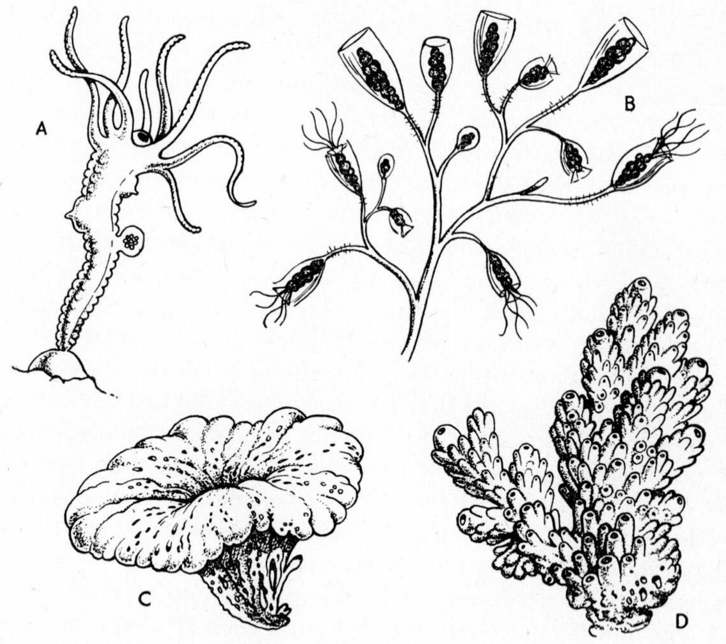


FIG. 1.—Some plant-like animals. A, *Hydra* (× 20); B, *Obelia* (× about 12); C, a Sponge (× about $\frac{1}{3}$); D, a Coral (× $\frac{1}{3}$).

chapter. Defining and classifying such nebulous groups is one of the trials and at the same time one of the fascinations of biology.

Geography is the study and description of the differentiation and distribution of earthly phenomena, embracing all that composes or affects the earth's surface—including its physical features, climates, and products whether living or inert. A major branch is biological geography, or biogeography, which for practical purposes is usually subdivided along the main line of division of living things into two kingdoms, so yielding plant geography and animal geography. Our main subject, plant geography, also called phytogeography (from the Greek word φύτον, a plant) accordingly deals with the plant cover of the world—with its composition, its local productivity, and particularly its distribution. This matter of distribution should be tackled both on the separate basis of individual species, etc., and collectively by dealing with their various and complex assemblages that make up vegetation. Our object will be to describe and interpret all we can of the manifestations of plant geography, paying special attention to the differences and similarities existing between the various floras and vegetations of the world. The continued increase in total human population makes such a study vitally significant, Man being dependent on plants for the very wherewithal of his existence.

The economic importance of our subject stems from the fact that green plants alone, on any substantial scale, are able to build, from simple raw materials and energy derived from sunlight, the complex substances on which animals as well as the plants themselves all depend for food. This food constitutes the main source of material used in body-building, and in it is locked the energy required for the various processes of life. Animals, with their usually active existence, commonly need this energy in abundance. In them, as in plants, it is liberated by the process of respiration, which is a kind of slow burning that takes place in living matter and gives to Mammals and Birds their bodily heat. Green plants provide food for us directly, when we eat them or their products, or indirectly, when we eat animals that fed on plants or were at least ultimately dependent upon some form of plant life, as indeed all are.

Plants also provide us with much of our clothing and housing as well as industrial raw materials, while in the world as a whole they largely condition our environment—forests, for example, being clearly different to live in from grassy plains or desert oases. Indeed, many of the major migrations of Man and other animals have been primarily due to plant distribution. Plants constitute for mankind the main inexhaustible source of fuel and industrial supplies and are of fundamental importance in many different branches of industry: in drug production, brewing, pulp and paper making; in lumbering, in the textile industries, in tanning, dyeing, and curing; in the production of plastics, animal feedstuffs, scent, oil, rubber, resin, gum, wax, and fibres; and, of course, in the wider fields of agriculture, horticulture, forestry, fish-culture, and the direct uses of their innumerable products.

It can be seen from the contents of the earlier works listed at the end of this chapter that authorities have differed greatly in the past as to the bounds and, in their view, legitimate content of the science of plant geography. In the present introductory work it will be interpreted in a much wider sense than usual, as including not only all geographical manifestations of plants whether single or collective (and hence a good deal of economic and some morphological botany), but also the reasons behind these manifestations. This will presuppose some consideration of the *bases* of distributions in space and time, and consequently of the relationship to environment (ecology), of the classification and systematic arrangement of different kinds of plants particularly through their external form (taxonomy and systematy), of the study of their internal workings (physiology), of their economic importance, and of other disciplines that are not normally thought of as plant geographical—hence in part the reference to ' some related sciences ' in the sub-title of this book, to certain of which in some modest degree it may also serve as a general introduction.

The ultimate purpose of geography is the study of the differences in the areas which make up the world. Yet when the plant populations are taken into consideration it comes as no surprise, in view of their extreme variability, to find that one of the main results of such a study is the realization that each area is unique. Once we leave the ' systematic ' study of particular phenomena, such as the relationship of individual kinds of plants to different areas, and enter the ' regional ' sphere of correlation of the various manifestations which point to these differences in area, the problem of organizing our study becomes almost overwhelming. With any set of phenomena as infinitely variable as vegetation (in both time and space, as we shall see), the areal integration desired in their geography is rendered practicable only by ignoring variations within the smaller unit-areas, which may then be studied together and ' lumped ' into larger ones.

Plant geography attempts to integrate these floristic and vegetational features as far as possible on a world basis, and for recording and illustration makes use of maps as one of its main tools. But the very construction of these maps presupposes the utmost care in the comparison of the entities whose ranges they indicate. Lack of such care is one of the greatest limitations with which the plant geographer is faced. Another is the still fragmentary state of Man's knowledge of the distribution of the vast majority of the many hundreds of thousands of different kinds of plants inhabiting the world—not to mention their proper delimitation and description. Yet another limitation is the extreme difficulty of collating such complex and often distant 'entities' as vegetation-types, with all their infinite variation and intricate intergradation. Even so, when no more research than has already been accomplished along these lines is brought together, we have a very impressive volume of material from which it seems permissible to make some useful generalizations, and on which we can build further our edifice of plant geography.

## Plan of the Book

As plants are our chief concern, we shall, after the present introductory chapter, first describe the main groups into which the myriad forms comprising the plant kingdom (in the wide sense) are classified. For each group we shall give some account of how its members live and reproduce, with mention of their habitats, distributions, and individual importance, and illustrations of examples. Then we shall have at least some conception of what we are dealing with, and, if previously uninitiated, have an opportunity of becoming familiar with our tools.

Our other main concern being with geographical phenomena and particularly with area, we shall deal next with the physiological attributes and external features that enable particular plants to grow, or prevent them from living, in particular circumstances. In this third chapter we shall also touch on the subject of plant classification by means of the various 'life-forms' which are brought about largely by the nature of the environment. This is particularly important because the reactions of plants to the environments in which they exist (*see* pp. 8–9) constitute one of the main 'keys' to their geographical ranges. In the fourth chapter we shall consider the means by which plants disperse themselves and migrate—with the kinds of aids they employ and, incidentally, some of the hindrances they meet in attaining their present-day distributions. The following chapter, our fifth, will deal with the early evolutionary development of plants, and the sixth will be concerned particularly with those developments in recent geological ages which have most profoundly influenced plant distributions as we see them nowadays.

In Chapter VII we shall go on to consider examples of the main *types* of distribution and consequent areas recognized today, where possible interpreting them in the light of information contained in the earlier chapters. This consideration of ' natural ' distributions will be followed by a chapter on man-made ones—both intentional (of crops) and unintentional (of weeds, etc.). And as the crops, or potential crops, of the various parts of the world introduce some of the greatest problems of mankind today, the next chapter will emphasize the economic, and basic, significance of plant life. For the geographical ranges of plants important to Man are often largely determined by him, on whom their very existence may depend.

In these initial chapters we will be dealing chiefly with special kinds or systematic groups of plants and their distributions. This is little more than a prelude to consideration of the *natural* groupings, the complex and variable assemblages of different plant communities each composed of more or less numerous and diverse kinds of plants, that make up collectively what we term vegetation. Before actually beginning our study of vegetation we must consider the environmental conditions (the ecological factors) which largely control its distribution and form : such consideration will occupy Chapter X. Some attention will also be given to physiological make-up, which primarily determines the reaction of a plant to its environment.

The ecological factors at a point collectively constitute the habitat, or ' habitat conditions '. The habitat, the place where an organism, or commonly many organisms, live, may vary greatly from place to place but tends to recur in at least comparable form in many different places. Particular habitats are often relatively uniform over considerable areas, as in the cases of salt-marshes, shallow ponds, and sandy plains. Moreover, when a bare or disturbed area is left alone, the vegetation inhabiting it tends to change, exhibiting a series of vegetational types ranging from the first lowly colonists to a relatively stable community which is ultimately the highest the area can support, the advancing series being called a ' succession ' or ' sere ', and its outcome the ' climax '. Chapter XI will deal in a general way with the main types of plant habitats, successions, and climaxes to be distinguished.

The next five chapters will outline and illustrate the chief vegetational types of the world, starting with those to be observed in temperate and adjacent lands as being most familiar and comprehensible to the greatest number of us. Following an account of the vegetational types of polar lands and high altitudes elsewhere, will be a chapter on tropical and adjacent lands, and thereafter one on the plant communities of fresh and inland saline waters, wherever they may be located, and another (Chapter XVI) on the communities of the oceans and seas.

Landscapes are often notable for peculiarities which concern the vegetation more than the actual surface of the land, and in Chapter XVII we will consider how landforms, which make up landscapes, tend to be characterized in this way. The study of vegetation, especially of the more established communities, generally gives a better indication of the combined action of environmental factors than all manner of measurements. Consequently the plant geographical and ecological evidence afforded by an area can be of the greatest practical value in interpreting local conditions and in planning the best use of land—particularly for agriculture and afforestation.

The concluding chapter deals with (1) some natural adaptations and (2) man-made adjustments, both in (*a*) individual plants and (*b*) vegetation. This consideration gives us by cross-inference four sets of topics, all of great interest and importance. Examples of these are (1*a*) evolution and its mechanisms, (1*b*) successional change in vegetation, (2*a*) plant-breeding, and (2*b*) combating erosion (itself usually brought on by Man's desecration of vegetation). The final paragraphs survey some of the more useful methods of study of plant geography, and give further indication of the values and future possibilities of the subject—both academically and in the service of Man. Despite vast advances in recent decades, there remain whole hosts of unsolved problems ; and, indeed, it is to be questioned whether this last chapter can ever be brought to a satisfactory closure. For such is biological science—an unending frontier.

Most chapters conclude with some indication, in smaller type, of how further pertinent information may be obtained through recommended *books* which are cited for the purpose. Shorter contributions are ignored in this connection as being too numerous and difficult to select, as well as usually unavailable to the layman, although naturally much of the material presented in this book has been drawn from such specialist ' papers '.

## Geographical Patterns

The botanical aspects of what may be termed geographical or areal patterns constitute much of plant geography. Such plant-distributional patterns are partly based on physiological reaction to ecological factors and, consequently, to a considerable extent on climate (*see* next section). An understanding of them is fundamental to our main subject, so some consideration of them seems desirable at this stage.

Just as the land-masses of the world, for example, make up a definite (if seemingly unorganized) pattern on the surface of the globe, so do other features, that are likewise definable in area, make up their own special patterns. Such pattern-forming features include the various factors of the environment, with which we shall deal in Chapter X. Thus, certain ranges of temperature, for example, obtain only within certain areas, and the same is true especially of other climatic features (*see* next section).

In the simplest case it might be supposed that a particular kind of land-plant, needing land to live on, could occupy all of the water- and ice-free land of the globe. But in actual fact quite numerous, often interdependent and overlapping, environmental and other factors prevent this, and no known kind of plant, however wide its habitat tolerance, occupies more than a very small proportion of the world's surface. At the other extreme are the numerous species which appear to inhabit only one limited tract of the globe or even a single spot. Each and every species has its particular area, its geographical distribution, whether this be small or large, and whether continuous or broken up into a more complicated pattern. And the pattern will be related to some particular factor or factors of the environment, to some migrational ability the plant may possess, and/or to evolutionary and geological or more recent history.

These migrational tendencies, together with the historical aspects of distribution, will be discussed in Chapters IV, V, and VI, and it will be found that such aspects may greatly affect the areas at present occupied by particular plants. But the factors of the environment are apt immediately to limit and circumscribe the area that *can be* occupied by a plant and, although treated in fair detail in a later chapter, require some explanation here before we can proceed.

Any condition of the habitat, whether climatic, physiographic, edaphic (concerned with the soil), or biotic (concerned with living organisms), may limit the area occupied by a plant, and usually many of these conditions do come into play. A simple instance is that a tropical plant requires warm conditions—or at least, it cannot grow in the cold. Usually, however, matters are far more complicated than this, in that such a plant commonly requires also environmental conditions within a certain range of moisture, light, soil type, etc. As the world affords, usually over considerable areas, practically every conceivable combination of habitat factors, the area occupied by a particular plant will, *inter alia*, depend upon its physiological make-up and reaction to the component factors. Herein lies the close connection between particular plants and their favoured habitats.

Whereas probably no two situations or even areas of a seemingly uniform habitat are exactly identical, we must in practice accept them as being alike, even as they appear to be so accepted by plants. Accordingly the similar habitats of the world may be grouped together to form recognizable patterns ; and, looking at things the other way, we find that there usually is a pattern of areas occupied by each kind of plant. Often a single habitat factor underlies such a pattern of plant distribution and may readily be recognized as doing so. But, unfortunately for those who crave simple monistic explanations, the area potentially inhabitable by a particular kind of plant, as prescribed by suitable habitat conditions, and that area which it actually occupies in the world today, are rarely if ever identical or even similar. Yet although the area which might be occupied is of both interest and importance to the scientist and to mankind, the plant geographer's immediate concern is with the fact, *i.e.* the actual area occupied.

In the same way, the many different types of *vegetation* form geographical patterns of their own, but here again the plant geographer is concerned more with the effects, *i.e.* the actual patterns, than with the causes which properly belong to the historical side of his studies. The vegetation pattern is to a considerable extent the sum of the overlapping distributions of the component plants ; but it commonly has a form of its own, for in biology the sum total of the components does not necessarily constitute the expected whole. The organisms' interrelationships and reactions add much that is new to the system and form an integral part of the end result.

## Climate the Master

As climate tends to supply the most important over-all factors determining plant distribution, it behoves us to give at this stage some outline of the main 'world' types of climate and related vegetational features. Further details on climatic factors will be found in Chapter X, with accompanying figures indicating temperature and precipitation in different parts of the globe, and in such recognized works as W. G. Kendrew's *Climatology*, second edition (Clarendon Press, Oxford, pp. xv + 400, 1957). The main vegetational types occurring on land are dealt with particularly in Chapters XII, XIII, and XIV.

Climate is the most far-reaching of the natural 'elements' controlling plant life, and its study, climatology, is accordingly fundamental to plant geography and related disciplines. In the words of Kendrew (*l.c.*), ' "Climate" is a composite idea, a generalization of the manifold weather conditions from day to day throughout the year. . . . In the study of climatology the primary interest lies in the facts of the climates of the earth in themselves, and as elements in the natural environment of life.' To the phrase 'throughout the year' the 'historical' plant geographer might wish to add 'and through the ages'.

Climatology deals with the atmospheric conditions which affect life—particularly light, temperature, precipitation, evaporating power, and wind. Additional factors include radiation, cloudiness, and storms. These components are often interdependent, their various combinations giving us the characteristic climates of different parts of the world which for our purposes may be divided broadly into three. These are the polar, temperate, and tropical regions, and they are primarily temperature zones. For convenience, the temperate areas lying north and south of the equator are considered together, as are the north and south polar areas in their turn. In this book the temperate regions are purposely treated first, for reasons already mentioned, and are followed by the polar regions. Besides these three primary categories there are the more localized climates of high altitudes (whose land vegetation, being largely comparable, we shall consider with that of the polar regions), of 'monsoon' and 'Mediterranean' types with warm and damp seasons alternating with dry ones, and of equable 'oceanic' and widely-extreme 'continental' types (*see* pp. 11–12). To the three primary climatic groupings the main vegetational belts of the world largely correspond, with local variations engendered by localized climatic and other features.

The climates of temperate and adjacent lands are mostly fairly warm and moist, at least in the favourable periods. They exhibit rather marked seasonal and diurnal fluctuations, and also vary greatly from place to place. The mean of the warmest month each year is normally above 10° C. (50° F.) and the annual precipitation is widely more than 762 mm. (30 inches). There is a marked difference between winter and summer light-climates and temperatures, and, often, precipitation. The vegetation tends to be fairly luxuriant at least in favourable situations, with trees and shrubs widely dominating but herbaceous plants usually exceeding them in number and variety. Most areas having a 'Mediterranean' type of climate, with hot and dry summers but with other seasons that are damp and not too cold for plant growth, are included here, their vegetation being often dominated by leathery-leafed shrubs but including many bulbous and ephemeral herbs. The main vegetation-types of temperate and adjacent lands are dealt with in Chapter XII.

The climates of polar lands and high altitudes are mostly rigorous, with the mean of the warmest month usually below 10° C. Precipitation is mostly in the form of snow and widely less than 254 mm. (10 inches) per annum, though owing to the prevailingly low temperatures the relative humidity may be high and the evaporating power low. There are wide seasonal fluctuations in most polar regions and wide diurnal ones in most alpine areas. In the higher latitudes there is continuous light in summer and darkness in winter. The vegetation is mostly low and scant—of dwarf shrubs, herbs (including many of grass habit), Lichens, and Mosses. The main vegetational types of polar lands and high altitudes are dealt with in Chapter XIII.

The climates of tropical and adjacent lands are warm and widely humid, with the mean temperature of the *coldest* month usually above 17·8° C. (64° F.) and the rainfall often heavy (*e.g.* 200–400 cm.). Frost and snow are usually unknown, the conditions being torrid and widely equable, with often little or no seasonal variation. The vegetation ranges from the world's most luxuriant rain forest to various scrub, grassland, and desert communities as the available water decreases. Most 'monsoon' areas of alternating wet and dry seasons, commonly dominated by deciduous trees and shrubs which lose their leaves to conserve water during dry periods, are included here. The main vegetational types of tropical and adjacent lands are dealt with in Chapter XIV.

It should be noted that the distinction between even 'oceanic' ('maritime', or 'insular') and uneven 'continental' climates is largely one of degree, being irrespective of latitude or temperature-relationships and consequently found in all of the above three primary climatic groupings. In general the oceanic extreme occurs on land where the prevailing winds come off the sea and are consequently moist and cloudy; its areas tend to be well vegetated, often with broad-leafed forests or verdant pastures. The continental extreme, on the other hand, is usually found far inland from the ocean and tends to have low relative humidity and precipitation, though exhibiting wide seasonal and daily fluctuations especially of temperature. The summer here is commonly sunny and warm but dry, the winter being relatively cold, so that vegetation tends to be limited, often consisting of drought-resistant Grasses, Heaths, or desert plants.

## The Ideal Plant

At this point will be given a brief account of the structure and adaptation of a multicellular 'higher' plant, such as a member of the Angiosperms which top the 'evolutionary tree' and are dealt with at the end of the next chapter. Such flowering plants make up most of the bulk of modern vegetation, give us very many of our foods and other necessities of life, and consequently loom largest in our plant geographical and allied studies.

Our ideal plant, as we may thus conceive it, will consist of (1) roots for anchoring in the ground and absorption from it of water and soluble nutrients, (2) a stem to hold the leaves and reproductive parts aloft, (3) green leaves to manufacture food substances in the light, and (4) flowers to produce seeds and so effect reproduction. Such features are too familiar to require illustration.

Each main portion of a higher plant is composed of 'cells', which are minute and often box-like structural units that are variously adapted to cover different needs. Cells of one kind are commonly aggregated together to form 'tissues' of particular form and function. Thus some cells are for conduction—particularly of water and dissolved salts upwards from the roots and of elaborated materials downwards from the leaves—and are consequently elongated and often pipe-like. Other cells have greatly thickened walls and give tensile strength to roots and rigidity to aerial parts of the plant—especially in the latter instance when aggregates of them are situated near the periphery, as they commonly are in stems. Many cells on the other hand remain thin-walled and serve the purpose of aeration, food-storage, or mere 'packing', while some may perform more than one function either concurrently or consecutively. All kinds of cells are produced from undifferentiated thin-walled 'meristematic' ones which divide actively, for example in the growing-points (meristems) situated near the apices of stems and roots. Fig. 19 (B and C) shows stem-sections of higher plants with the main types of tissues and examples of their disposition.

The above references are chiefly to the more or less solid walls of plant cells. But all these cells are alive, at least in youth—for they contain a viscous and very heterogeneous fluid known as protoplasm, which is the living matter of the plant. It is in the protoplasm that occur the extremely complex sequences of events which integrate into what we know as life, and which include the processes enabling the protoplasm to increase itself. This increase forms the basis of growth, which normally involves increase in size of the cell until it reaches a maximum and thereupon divides into two daughter cells. The daughters then repeat the process, and as a result of numerous repetitions of this activity the plant as a whole grows in size. Another activity going on in all living cells is the slow oxidative 'burning' known as respiration, which gives to living organisms the energy required for their life-processes.

Besides the apical meristems by which plant organs grow in length, there is, in the stems and roots of many long-lived higher plants, a layer of actively dividing cells (the 'cambium') which add daughters radially on either side and so lead to growth in girth. When this takes place year after year in regions of fluctuating climate, where cells of different sizes are produced at different seasons, annual 'growth-rings' are formed which may easily be seen in most timbers. In addition there are meristems in buds whose behaviour—varying from dormancy to active elongation—greatly affects the ultimate shape of the plant. These and other growth phenomena are largely controlled by special chemical substances produced by the plant, and in ways which are only nowadays being elucidated. These plant growth substances, for example, may stimulate the elongation of cells in some tracts while inhibiting that of others—resulting in curvature of an organ in relation to a directional stimulus, such as light, which itself affects the production or availability of the chemical stimulant. Other substances inhibit growth, an example being produced by many terminal buds; accordingly it is only when such inhibitors are removed that the lateral buds grow out actively (hence the sprouting of a hedge after clipping, and of pasturage after close grazing). For a general survey of this fascinating and important subject, *see* Professor L. J. Audus's *Plant Growth Substances*, second edition (Leonard Hill, London, pp. xxii + 553, 1959).

Plants cannot exist without water, though different kinds require it in very different amounts. Our ideal plant must be well adapted in its water economy to the prevailing conditions ; thus if water is scarce, it must have some means of keeping down the loss which takes place continuously from its aerial parts in the process known as transpiration. This economy may be effected by such devices as a thick and impervious bark or waxy or hairy covering, by protection of the ' breathing pores ', or by reduction of the total surface. Often more than one method is employed by a plant, which at the same time will have to be adapted to other factors of the environment. Through long processes of evolution, involving among other things the elimination of unsuitable features, different kinds of plants have become adapted to different environments, and this, as we shall see for example in Chapter III, is one of the most fundamental bases of their distribution and consequently of plant geography.

## Plant Sociology

Although opinions vary as to what constitutes a species (broadly speaking, a kind), we all have some conception of how similar individuals, whether plants or animals, make up such an entity. The numerous individuals comprising a particular species, while by no means all exactly identical, nevertheless are closely comparable in most respects, and normally have the appearance of belonging to the same kind. We have already observed that different plant species and other entities, often of many and various groups, become associated together in nature to compose what we term vegetation. This is made up of more or less definite plant communities, related at least in part to local conditions. Each of these communities is characterized by its own particular form (physiognomy), and in most cases also by one or more predominant species.

Plant sociology, also called phytosociology, is, strictly speaking, the study of the plant communities that make up vegetation—including their inception and formation, their structure, and, above all, their composition. Accordingly some parts of this subject, and particularly the composition of plant communities, are of vital interest to the plant geographer, even as the distribution of these communities forms an important part of his study. But in spite of a wide overlap of material, students of the two disciplines approach their problems and subjects from different angles of interest, and so it is not proposed to consider plant sociology here, except in so far as it may help us to understand our own problems.[1]

## The Animal Side

As animals are so largely dependent upon plants for food, shelter and other requisites of life, their geography and ecology tend to be less fundamental than those of plants, or at all events less closely related to the physical environment. Nevertheless the animal side of the picture of life (and in particular, Man's influence) must be vividly borne in mind by students of plant geography. Thus we shall see in Chapter IV how numerous plants depend upon animals, in many and various ways, for the dispersal of their seeds and fruits. Later on, in the chapters on vegetation-types, we shall be repeatedly reminded of how animals modify vegetation during their feeding and other activities, often favouring the growth, or very existence, of one species while discouraging that of another, and profoundly affecting the vegetation locally. In these and other ways, Man is apt to have the greatest influence of all. Many plants, too, depend on animals for pollination and hence fertilization of their flowers; here, at least in the absence of vegetative means of propagation, reproduction will not normally take place without animal aid. All of these features can, and frequently do, affect the spreading and ultimate distribution of plant species. It is therefore not surprising that many areas, such as Australia and South Africa, have both a floristic and faunistic character and identity of their own, their (often peculiar) plants and animals going hand in hand, so to speak. Furthermore, animal geography often corroborates the conclusions of plant geography, and offers splendid evidence of evolutionary trends in its fossil record. It also appears to corroborate migrational tendencies in its suggestion of certain 'land-bridges' and 'refuges'.

In view of the closeness with which the two are linked in nature, there is much to be said for the study, which has increased in popularity in recent decades, of plants and animals as they exist together in joint 'biotic' communities. But whereas the particular physical conditions in an area are more or less vividly expressed in the local plant cover, which forms, as it were, a living framework

[1] Interested readers are referred to the standard work on the subject by Dr. J. Braun-Blanquet (*Plant Sociology*, McGraw-Hill, New York & London, pp. xviii + 439, 1932), or the second German edition (*Pflanzensoziologie : Grundzüge der Vegetationskunde*, Springer, Wien, pp. xi + 631, 1951).

it is only secondarily that this in turn largely conditions the animal population—which thus becomes a subordinate characteristic of the locality and is usually less evident and immediately significant than the vegetation, at least on land. Indeed, where there are no suitable plants there can be no animals living normally. As M. D. Haviland puts it in the work cited at the end of Chapter XVII,

> 'It is the faithful correlation of plant growth with the physical environment, especially to the important factor, or complex of factors, called "climate", that leads us naturally to define the main types of land environment in terms of plant life as Woodland, Grassland and Desert . . . for vegetation is the apparel of scenery. As Darwin wrote: "A traveller should be a botanist, for in all views plants form the chief embellishment." But when the zoologist, forsaking botanical terms, tries to classify environments in the language of his own science, he cannot construct a workable scheme . . . he finds that he must fall back on the language of the botanist or geologist.'

In general, zoologists have not been very successful in recognizing definite animal communities of a complex nature, and their study in individual species of adaptive response to particular environments tends to be of less immediate significance than that of botanists with plants. Thus, whereas the marked dwarfing of many arctic and alpine plants is related directly to exposure to harsh physical environments, many similarly striking animal characteristics, such as broad teeth for grinding seeds and special organs for climbing trees, are related to the climatic conditions only indirectly through plant response. Nevertheless, as pointed out by Professor G. E. Hutchinson (*in litt.*), there are a number of known cases of warm-blooded animals responding directly to climate. For example, boreal Mammals not only have under-fur but also are of larger absolute size, and have shorter ears and tails, than their southern counterparts, while almost all desert Mammals and Birds are pale even if nocturnal, and insular races of Birds have relatively large beaks and feet. But in spite of such exceptions, and others which involve plants responding to animals (*e.g.* the striking adaptations of many flowers to insects in relation to pollination), plant response to climate is usually direct whereas that of animals tends to be indirect. Then again, animals are usually mobile, and individuals may wander or migrate vast distances. Consequently, apart from such connections as those mentioned above, animals tend to be of less geographical significance than plants, in the sense that they do not characterize areas to the same extent, and for our present purpose seem best considered as a mere factor of the environment.

This recognition of the more fundamental role of plants does not seem to be weakened by the realization that, often, plants and animals have evolved together and are necessary for one another's existence. For even in the case of flesh-eating animals, sooner or later, as we trace back the food-chain, we come to the ultimate point of dependence upon green plants. Furthermore, the animal geographer is not necessarily of much help to us, for the areas and boundaries which he recognizes (*e.g.* Fig. 2, A) are often very different from ours (*e.g.* Fig. 2, B), and he is prone to take for granted that the vegetation (which he considers simply as part of the environment) is a mere response to local conditions. Yet a plant community, quite apart from its historical implications, gives us many clues to the nature of the environment because its component members exhibit recognizable responses to physical features. No such general virtue is displayed by animal communities, if indeed these can be satisfactorily recognized.

Recent books on animal geography, with useful bibliographies suggesting further reading, include R. Hesse, W. C. Allee, & K. P. Schmidt's *Ecological Animal Geography*, second edition (Wiley, New York, pp. xiii + 715, 1951), F. L. de Beaufort's *Zoogeography of the Land and Inland Waters* (Sidgwick & Jackson, London, pp. viii + 208, 1951), Sven Ekman's *Zoogeography of the Sea*, translated by Elizabeth Palmer (Sidgwick & Jackson, London, pp. xiv + 417, 1953), and Philip J. Darlington's *Zoogeography : the Geographical Distribution of Animals* (Wiley, New York, pp. xiii + 675, 1957).

## Some Earlier Works on Plant Geography

*In English :*

Anonymous and other early works include *The Geography of Plants* (The Religious Tract Society, London, pp. vi + 7–192, undated), J. Barton's *A Lecture on the Geography of Plants* (Harvey & Darton, London, pp. 1–94 and index, etc., 1827), and R. B. Hinds's *The Regions of Vegetation ; being an analysis of the distribution of vegetable forms over the surface of the globe in connection with climate and physical agents* (Palmer, London, pp. 1–140, 1843).

Meyen, F. J. F. (1846) : *Outlines of the Geography of Plants : with particular enquiries concerning the native country, the culture, and the uses of the principal cultivated plants on which the prosperity of nations*

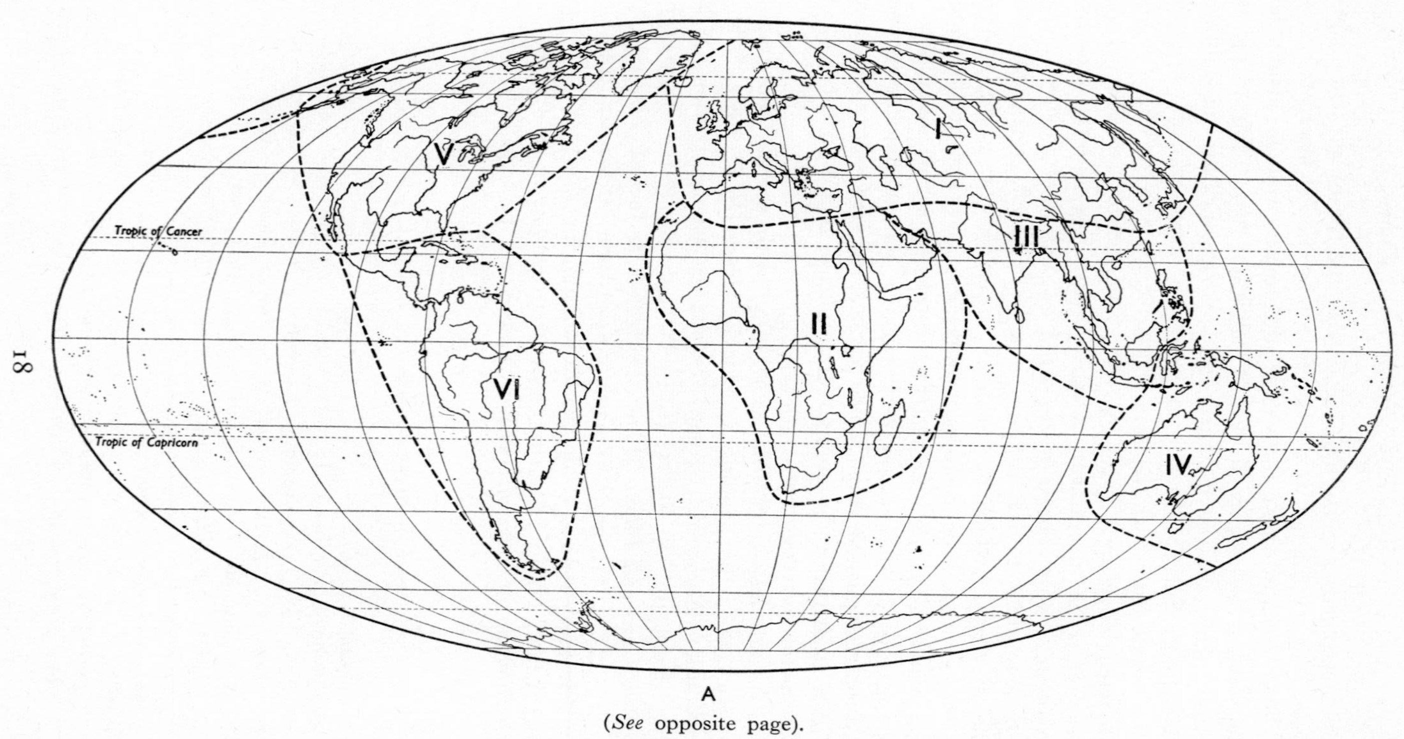


A

(*See* opposite page).

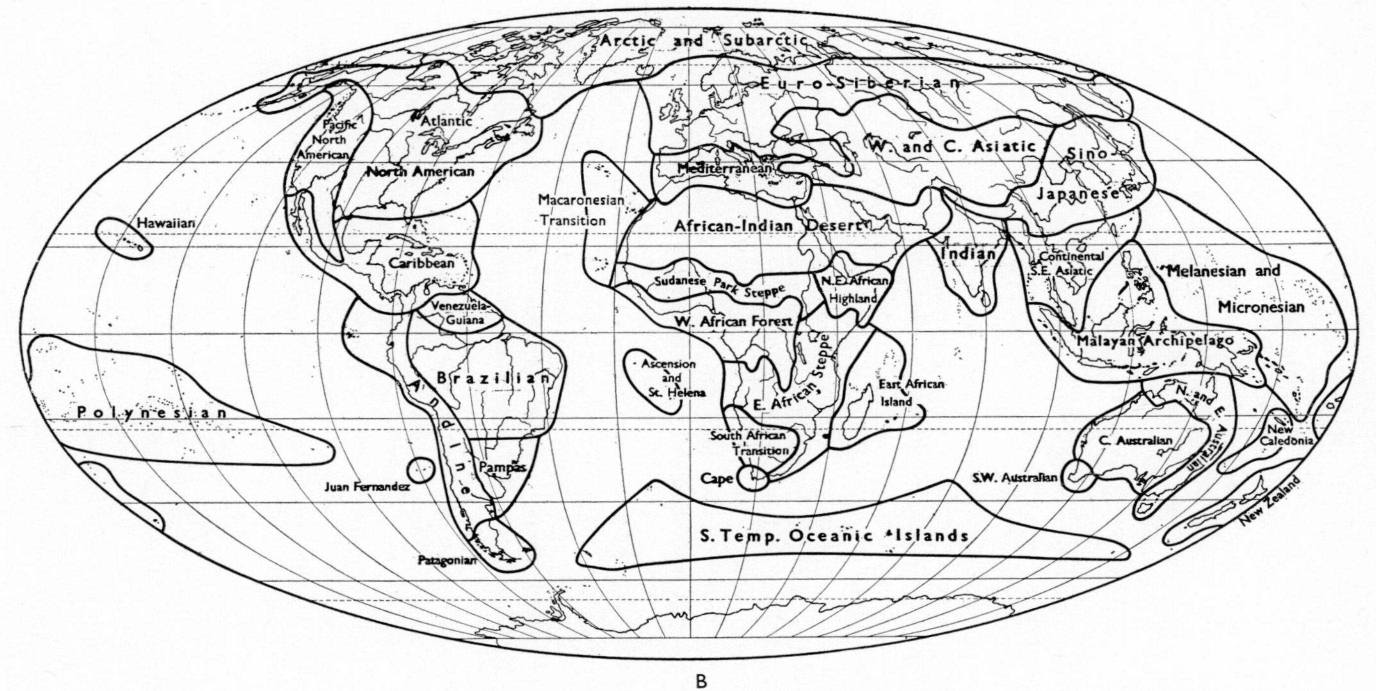


FIG. 2.—Zoogeographical realms and floristic regions of the world. A, zoogeographical realms, after Beaufort (1951). B, floristic regions, after Good (1953), modified.

*is based*, translated by M. Johnston (Ray Society, London, pp. x + 422). Follows the German edition, published in Berlin in 1836. Of historical interest as indicating the teachings of the day, including Man's dependence upon plants, but with over-emphasis on latitude as the limiting factor in plant distribution.

Daubeny, Charles, *ed.* (1855): *Popular Geography of Plants; or, a botanical excursion around the world* (Lovell Reeve, London, pp. xl + 370). A very readable illustrated account following Meyen's arrangement and, although often unreliable, of historical interest as indicating the type of work apparently favoured by the intelligent layman of a century ago: by 'E.M.C.', with a well-written and penetrating preface by its eminent editor.

Pickering, Charles (1876): *The Geographical Distribution of Animals and Plants. Part II. Plants in Their Wild State* (Naturalists' Agency, Salem, Mass., pp. 1–524 and additional maps). A sumptuous but evidently rare publication of some interest and foresight.

Schimper, A. F. W. (1903): *Plant-geography upon a Physiological Basis*, translated by W. R. Fisher, revised and edited by Percy Groom and I. B. Balfour (Clarendon Press, Oxford, pp. xxx + 839 and 4 additional maps). Still the great reference book on the subject in English, profusely illustrated and a commendable feat for its time, though in places unreliable and now largely outdated. A detailed up-to-date work in English, planned along modern lines and executed in the light of the latest knowledge, is badly needed to supersede it.

Warming, E., *et. al.* (1909): *Oecology of Plants* (Clarendon Press, Oxford, pp. xi + 422). For many years a standard source-book mainly on the ecological side but also describing the main vegetation-types.

Hardy, M. E. (1913): *A Junior Plant Geography* (Clarendon Press, Oxford, pp. 1–192). A light-weight but useful discourse on some aspects of the subject—like the next work, illustrated and readable though outdated and not always reliable. Some copies have been seen entitled 'An Introduction to Plant Geography'.

Hardy, M. E. (1920): *The Geography of Plants* (Clarendon Press, Oxford, pp. xii + 327). Consists chiefly of a discursive account of the more obvious vegetational features of the main land-masses and climatic regions (*cf.* above), largely ignoring aquatic habitats. Reprinted up to 1952.

Campbell, D. H. (1926): *An Outline of Plant Geography* (Macmillan, London [and New York], pp. ix + 392). Illustrated and readable: concerned chiefly with climatic zones and areas and their land flora and vegetational characteristics, but loosely written and frequently inaccurate, and omitting many topics which might with advantage have been treated.

Newbigin, M. I. (1936): *Plant and Animal Geography* (Methuen, London, pp. xv + 298). *See* also the practically identical 'second edition' (Dutton, New York, pp. xv + 298, 1948). A stimulating and usually reliable outline of many aspects of biogeography. The so-called second edition, although recent, is practically a reprint that, unfortunately, fails to remedy some misconceptions and to correct errors particularly in those chapters for which the original author was not responsible.

Wulff, E. V. (1943): *An Introduction to Historical Plant Geography*, translated by E. Brissenden (Chronica Botanica, Waltham, Mass., pp. xv + 223). Useful in elucidating the origin and development of floras as opposed to their composition, ecology, and other aspects. A succeeding volume was published later in Russia (*see* below).

Cain, S. A. (1944): *Foundations of Plant Geography* (Harper, New York & London, pp. xiv + 556). An important though rather technical survey of the history and interpretation of many phenomena of vascular plant distribution on land. Does not deal with aquatic habitats or lower groups of plants, and is professedly not a descriptive plant geography.

Croizat, L. (1952): *Manual of Phytogeography* (Junk, The Hague, pp. viii + 587 and 106 additional illustrations). Considers plant geography simply the study of plant dispersal, being 'that branch of botany which integrates plant-migrations in time and space'. A large part (pp. 68–399) is occupied by treatment of the 'intercontinental dispersal' of various (mainly tropical) Angiosperms. Often opinionated and sometimes crotchety: nor is the coverage in accordance with the subtitle which claims the work to be 'an account of plant-dispersal throughout the world'.

Good, Ronald (1953): *The Geography of the Flowering Plants*, second edition (Longmans, London etc., pp. xiv + 452). An illustrated manual of the distributions of flowering plants and the factors controlling them; does not deal with vegetation or with lower plants. Nevertheless a valuable work, and widely considered the standard one on the floristic side of the subject. The second edition should be used rather than the first, which was published in 1947.

Turrill, W. B. (1953): *Pioneer Plant Geography: the phytogeographical researches of Sir Joseph Dalton Hooker* (Nijhoff, The Hague, pp. xii + 267). Readable and instructive, with up-to-date comments, as well as historically interesting.

*In other languages:*

Humboldt, A., & A. Bonpland (1805): *Essai sur la Géographie des Plantes; accompagné d'un tableau physique des régions équinoxiales* (Paris, pp. i–xii + 13–155 and map.) One of the main foundations of our subject, followed by a German edition in 1807, and also by kindred works in various languages; of great historical interest.

Schouw, J. F. (1822): *Grundtraek til en almindelig Plantegeographie*

(Kjøbenhavn, pp. x + 463 and 4 additional illustrations). Followed the next year by a German edition entitled *Grundzüge einer allgemeinen Pflanzengeographie* (Berlin, pp. xix + 528 and 4 additional illustrations). Of historical interest.

RUDOLPH, L. (1853): *Die Pflanzendecke der Erde* (Berlin, pp. xiv + 416 and additional plates; also 'Supplementheft' of 34 pages, published in Berlin in 1859). An early semi-popular treatment.

DECANDOLLE, ALPHONSE (1855): *Géographie Botanique Raisonnée ou exposition des faits principaux et des lois concernant la distribution géographique des plantes de l'époque actuelle* (Paris & Genève, vol. I, pp. xxxii + 606 and additional maps, and vol. II, pp. 607–1366). An early detailed synthesis of much of our subject, now chiefly of historical interest.

GRISEBACH, A. (1877–8): *La Végétation du Globe d'après la disposition suivant les climats* . . ., translated by P. de Tchihatchef (Baillière, Paris, vol. I, pp. xvi + 765 and additional map, 1877, and vol. II, pp. vi + 905, 1878). Discursive but interesting, at least historically.

ENGLER, A. (1879–82): *Versuch einer Entwicklungsgeschichte der Pflanzenwelt, insbesondere der Florengebiete seit der Tertiärperiode* (Engelmann, Leipzig, vol. I, pp. xviii + 202 and additional map, vol. II, pp. xiv + 386 and additional map). Includes suggested explanations of plant distribution but was soon in part superseded. Vol. I, published in 1879, deals with the extratropical regions of the northern hemisphere, and vol. II, published in 1882, with the tropical regions and the remainder of the southern hemisphere.

GRISEBACH, A. (1880): *Gesammelte Abhandlungen und kleinere Schriften zur Pflanzengeographie* (Engelmann, Leipzig, pp. vii + 628). Various contributions including the general and lengthy 'Berichte über die Fortschritte in der Geographie der Pflanzen' (pp. 335–556).

CONTEJEAN, C. (1881): *Géographie Botanique; influence du terrain sur la végétation* (Baillière, Paris, pp. 1–144). Deals chiefly with habitat differences and their effect on local flora.

GOEZE, E. (1882): *Pflanzengeographie für Gärtner und Freunde des Gartenbaues* (Ulmer, Stuttgart, pp. xiv + 476). A general treatment, primarily but by no means exclusively for horticulturists.

DRUDE, O. (1890): *Handbuch der Pflanzengeographie* (Engelhorn, Stuttgart, pp. xvi + 582 and additional map). A general manual, illustrated chiefly by maps, of the subject as then developed, by a renowned investigator of the time. Followed in 1897 by a French edition entitled *Manuel de Géographie Botanique* (Klincksieck, Paris, pp. xxiii + 552).

SOLMS-LAUBACH, H. ZU (1905): *Die leitenden Gesichtspunkte einer allgemeinen Pflanzengeographie* (Felix, Leipzig, pp. ix + 243). A briefer, unillustrated account of much of the subject, with some novel ideas.

GRAEBNER, P. (1910): *Lehrbuch der allgemeinen Pflanzengeographie nach entwicklungsgeschichtlichen und physiologisch-ökologischen Gesichtspunkten mit Beiträgen von Paul Ascherson* (Quelle & Meyer, Leipzig, pp. viii + 303). A general, illustrated account of the history and composition of various floras and vegetation-types, paying due regard to their ecological bases.

HAYEK, A. (1926): *Allgemeine Pflanzengeographie* (Borntraeger, Berlin, pp. viii + 409 and 2 additional maps). A more modern account along similar general lines to the last, but illustrated by only a very few diagrams and maps.

DIELS, L. (1929): *Pflanzengeographie*, third edition (Grunter, Berlin & Leipzig, pp. 1–159 and additional map). Useful as presenting a largely modern account in outline of many aspects of the subject in handy pocket form. Later editions (not seen) have since appeared.

RUBEL, E. (1930): *Pflanzengesellschaften der Erde* (Huber, Bern-Berlin, pp. viii + 464 and map). Describes and illustrates the main plant communities and vegetation-types of the world.

WARMING, E., & P. GRAEBNER (1933): *Lehrbuch der ökologischen Pflanzengeographie*, fourth edition (Borntraeger, Berlin, pp. viii + 1158). A valuable illustrated work dealing particularly with ecological and vegetational aspects.

SCHIMPER, A. F. W. (1935): *Pflanzengeographie auf physiologischer Grundlage*, ' third ' edition, revised by F. C. von Faber (Fischer, Jena, vol. I, pp. xx + 588, and vol. II, pp. xvi + 589–1613 and 3 additional maps). An illustrated, extensive work weighing about 10 lb. and dealing mainly with the natural flora and vegetation of different zones and regions, after some consideration of ecological factors and principles. Generally reliable in those aspects of our subject with which it deals. Although called (in German) the third edition, this was in reality the second, as the so-called second edition was merely a reprint of the first edition.

ALEKHIN, V. V. (1944): [*Geography of Plants*], in Russian only (State Publisher, Moscow, pp. 1–455 and 2 maps). An illustrated account of many of the distributional and ecological aspects of the subject.

WULFF, E. V. (1944): [*Historical Plant Geography: history of the floras of the world*], in Russian only (Akademiya Nauk SSSR, Moscow-Leningrad, pp. xix + 546). This is the second volume, mainly on the origins of the floras of the different regions of the world, of a projected three-volume work of which the first was translated into English (*see* above) and the third was apparently never completed, the author being killed in 1941 during the siege of Leningrad.

GAUSSEN, H.: *Géographie des Plantes*, second edition (Colin, Paris, pp. 1–224, 1954). Gives a brief but useful account of many aspects of the subject.

## Chapter II

# THE VARIOUS GROUPS OF PLANTS AND HOW AND WHERE THEY LIVE

### Classification and Nomenclature

To enable us to name and deal effectively with the almost infinite variety of plants inhabiting the world, it is necessary to sort into groups those which seem to have the closest affinity or, at least, the greatest outward similarity. These groups in turn have to be aggregated into larger groupings, and so on, to create a hierarchical system of classification which we also like to think bears a close relation to evolutionary history. Thus the members of a group which look closely alike probably bear a ' blood relationship ' in being descended from a common ancestor at no very remote period of geological time ; indeed in some instances such a relationship has been experimentally demonstrated. Biologists, and this includes botanists, may in some cases disagree about the definitions, names, and limits of this hierarchy of groups, but for general purposes (and in descending order, from large to small) these groupings[1] may be listed as follows :

*Divisions* or *phyla* (sing. *phylum*) : the major (highest) groupings used in classifying plants, with names normally ending in *-phyta*, those commonly recognized being the Schizophyta, Thallophyta, Bryophyta, Pteridophyta, and Spermatophyta, and each consisting of one or more

*Classes :* the next commonly recognized units, plentifully exemplified below, and each consisting of one or more

*Orders :* each of which has its name ending in *-ales*, and in turn consists of one or more

*Families :* these, except in a few long-established instances, have their names ending in *-aceae*. Usually the members of a family all have some recognizable characteristic or characteristics, some common ' stamp ' ; they are grouped into one or more

[1] Also called *taxa* (singular *taxon*), regardless of rank.

*Genera* (sing. *genus*) : the members of each genus usually look alike in a number of features and constitute one or more

*Species* : these represent the smallest unit of classification in general use, being those whose members show a broad similarity. Biologists differ in their conception of what constitutes a species, and indeed the term is scarcely capable of satisfactory definition. However, for the great majority of animals and many plants a species is, roughly speaking, constituted by all those individuals which are able to interbreed among themselves but are unable to breed, at least at all freely, with members of other groups. The individuals of a species are by no means identical but form a more or less variable population in which some entities are often recognizable as *subspecies* (written subsp. or ssp.), or as still more subordinate *varieties* (written var.) or *formae* (written f.).

Even as species are divisible into subspecies, so are the major groups often divided into subphyla, subclasses, etc. The individual is the ultimate unit, but inasmuch as no two individual plants can be exactly identical, any more than two individual persons can be, the smallest recognizable unit of classification is the *biotype*, consisting of all those individuals which have the same genetical make-up. Thus most species consist of a large number of biotypes that differ slightly in their inheritance.

The scientific name of each species is normally made up of two Latin or latinized words of which the first is the name of the genus to which it belongs and the second is its own specific epithet, usually having some descriptive or historical connotation. The initial letter of the first, or generic, name is always capitalized, that of the specific epithet nowadays being customarily left 'small'. Unfortunately, English or other 'popular' names are too unreliable to employ at all widely, particularly because the same name is apt to be used for different plants in different places or by different people, and also because it is undesirable to have the same plant known under different names in different places or sometimes even in the same place. Moreover, it is confusing to have more than one combination of names in use for a single entity, and so the Latin one is agreed upon and employed internationally by scientists.

We will now consider briefly what seem for our purpose to be the main *classes* of the plant kingdom, each being treated under the primary heading of the phylum (division) to which it belongs. The sequence followed is probably indicative of evolutionary history in broad outline. After a brief general account of the characters of each of our chosen classes, we will deal with its modes of nutrition and reproduction and also, in the broadest terms, with its main habitats, distribution, and importance—both economically and as a component of natural vegetation.

## Schizophyta

Bacteria: These are very simple, exceedingly minute, and virtually ubiquitous organisms. Most types consist of single spherical, rod-shaped, branched, or variously curved cells, with or without delicate superficial thread-like processes known as flagella (*sing.* flagellum), through the action of which they may attain a fair

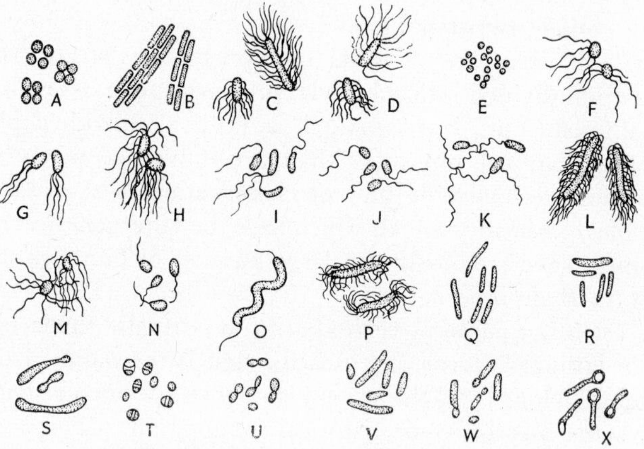


Fig. 3.—Various types of Bacteria. Among those causing serious human diseases are B, anthrax; H, typhoid fever; N, cholera; Q, tuberculosis; R, leprosy; S, diphtheria; T, meningitis; U, pneumonia; V, dysentery; X, tetanus. (Mostly × 1000, but Q and V considerably more magnified.)

degree of motility in liquid media. In other types the cells may adhere together in small groups or chains, or remain attached by the ends to form regular filaments. Various types of Bacteria are shown in Fig. 3, most of them being magnified about 1,000 times. Bacteria are found in vast numbers almost everywhere: in soils and the atmosphere, in fresh and salt waters, and in many of the most unlikely and unsavoury ' habitats '. Normal soils with a fair percentage of organic matter contain on the average from 2,000,000 to 200,000,000 Bacteria per gram, while manure and sewage may contain greater numbers still.

Bacteria multiply principally by simple cell division, sometimes as frequently as every twenty minutes—but only for a time, the chief limitation being their food supply. They may also form spores which in some cases are highly resistant. Recently, convincing evidence of a sexual process has been obtained in some Bacteria, but it is not known how frequent such a process may be in nature.

In their modes of nutrition Bacteria vary greatly: for although commonly they are either (1) *saprophytic*, deriving their energy and materials for life and growth from dead and usually decaying organic matter, or (2) *parasitic*, depending similarly on living organisms; there are also (3) many forms which can build up their bodies and live from carbon dioxide obtained from the air or water and energy liberated in the oxidation of inorganic compounds or even elements. Such organisms are said to be *chemosynthetic*, and examples of the substances oxidized by them are sulphur, hydrogen sulphide, nitrites, ammonia, hydrogen, and, apparently, iron and manganese compounds. The members of one interesting group of sulphur-oxidizing Bacteria, known as the Purple Bacteria, contain pigments enabling them to absorb radiant energy from light, and they appear to practise some kind of photosynthetic process which may be a prototype of that occurring in 'normal' green plants. Other types that seem properly referable to the Bacteria are green, through the inclusion of chlorophyll of a kind. But it seems improbable that the earliest living organisms possessed real chlorophyll or obtained their energy through such an elaborate series of reactions as are involved in photosynthesis (*cf.* p. 32). Rather is it considered likely that some of these peculiar Bacteria indicate means by which elementary organisms obtained their energy and other requisites of life before either chlorophyll or any form of photosynthesis was evolved. Consequently it seems most reasonable to start our sequence with this group.

Certain Bacteria are of major importance in causing diseases—particularly of animals, and including some of those most deadly to Man—while various other Bacteria cause the decay and breakdown of dead matter, or make available food-substances for higher plants, or produce chemical ions of many kinds. With their infinitesimal size and often resistant spores, they are among the most widespread of living organisms, being carried by air or water currents or in the bodies of animals practically everywhere in the world and its surrounding atmosphere. Nevertheless, as they are so minute, they play only a very minor direct role as components of most types of vegetation. Exceptions are afforded by some aquatic muds, in which

Bacteria may dominate, and also, of course, in diseased or decaying systems. They may also be the pioneers in the colonization of some bare areas.

CYANOPHYCEAE: These are the so-called 'Blue-green Algae', or Schizophyceae, but they seem to have their closest relationship with the Bacteria, which they resemble particularly in their lack of a

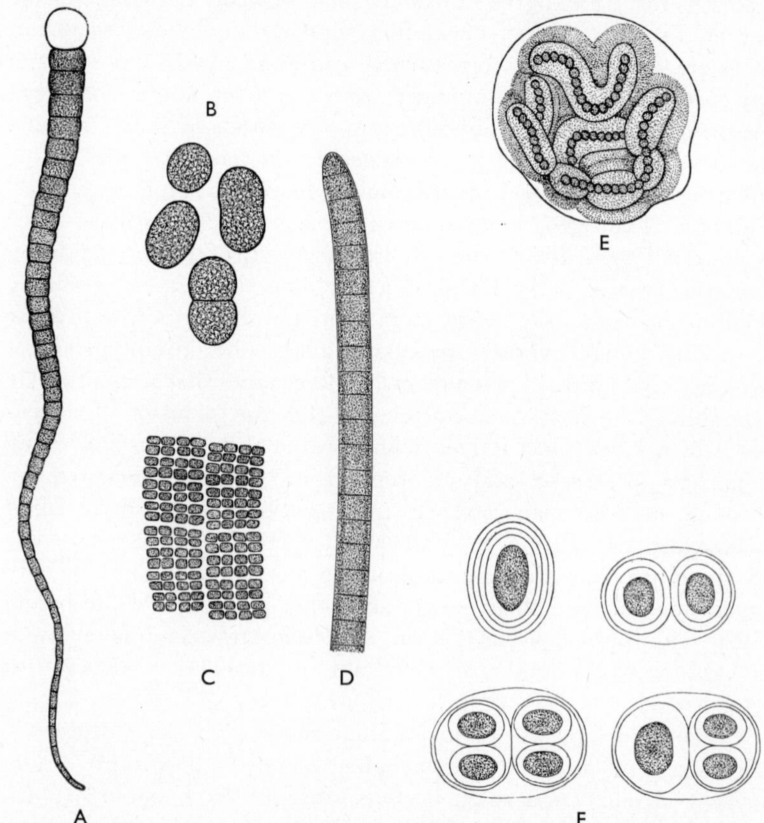


FIG. 4.—Various Blue-green Algae (Cyanophyceae). A, *Rivularia* (× about 600); B, *Aphanothece* (× about 1500); C, *Merismopedia* (× about 200); D, *Oscillatoria* (× about 800); E, a species of *Nostoc*, consisting of filaments embedded in a gelatinous matrix (× about 300); F, *Gloeocapsa*: a single-celled individual and colonies of two, three, and four cells (× 1285).

typically organized nucleus in the cell, in their method of cell division, and in the obscurity at all events of any sexual reproduction. They consist either of single cells, of cells joined end-to-end to form filaments, or of colonies in which either individual cells or filaments are held together in gelatinous masses. Examples, variously magnified, are shown in Fig. 4; but whereas the individual cells are microscopic and often exceedingly minute, the colonies may be many centimetres in diameter and of considerable bulk.

The Cyanophyceae contain chlorophyll of a sort and mostly live by photosynthesis although some appear to be at least partly saprophytic. The chlorophyll is diffused through the outer layers of protoplasm instead of being accumulated in special bodies as it is in higher plants. Cyanophyceae also contain bluish and/or reddish pigments, the former of which, with the chlorophyll, gives to many a blue-green coloration—hence their popular name. Others, however, are very differently coloured. Multiplication is by simple cell division or the formation of spores. The filaments or parts of filaments of many exhibit motions of various but characteristic kinds, including glidings and oscillations, the mechanisms of which are not understood.

Cyanophyceae are very widespread, occurring especially in a range of freshwater and damp to marshy habitats. However, though often abundant, they make relatively little showing as components of vegetation—except sometimes in lakes or ponds, where they may form a 'bloom', or on stones in fairly rapid streams where they provide a mucilaginous mat, in which other organisms such as Diatoms thrive. They tend to be important in arctic regions where they often form dark colonies on damp soil, in marshes, and about the margins of tarns. Ecologically they may be of some importance as the initial colonists (pioneers) on bare rock and other surfaces. They have little economic significance except as nuisances in fouling water supplies—to which they may impart a disagreeable odour and taste, sometimes killing fish or even cattle.

## Thallophyta

Chlorophyceae: These are a large and diverse group of Algae (seaweeds, aquatic 'slimes', etc.) having chlorophyll located in well-defined bodies called chloroplasts and not normally masked by other pigments. Consequently the plants are usually green in colour and the group is called the Green Algae. Characteristically they have cellulose cell-walls and store food in the form of starch. What appear to be the more primitive forms are microscopic, unicellular, and either motile by flagella or non-motile, the cells occurring singly

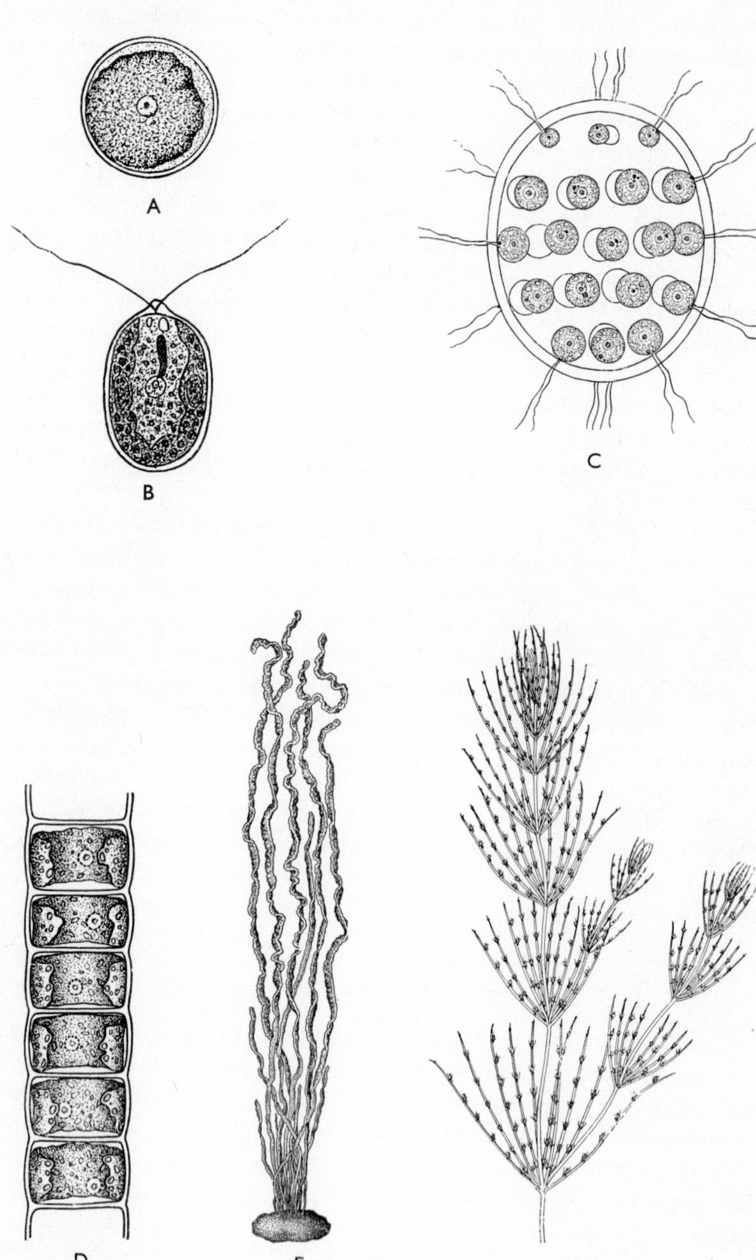
A
B
C
D
E
F

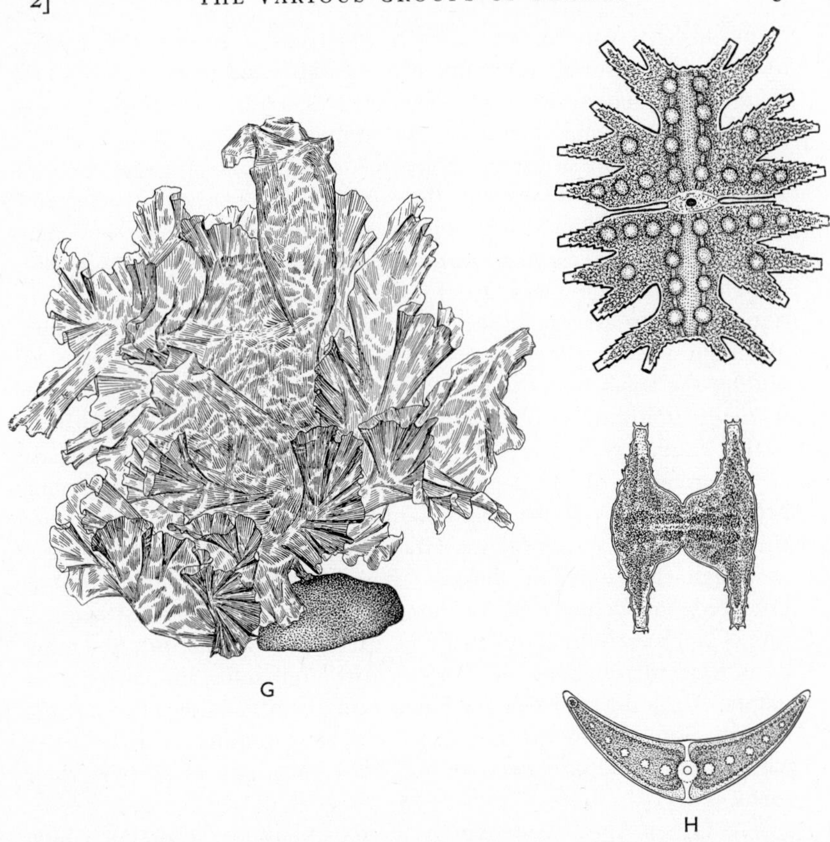


FIG. 5.—Some forms of Green Algae (Chlorophyceae). A, *Pleurococcus*—unicellular, non-motile (× 2470); B, *Chlamydomonas*—unicellular, motile (× about 500); C, *Pleodorina*, colonial, motile (× 250); D, cells from a filament of *Ulothrix* (× 462); E, *Enteromorpha intestinalis*, a relative of *Ulva* (*see* G) (× $\frac{1}{3}$); F, *Chara*, a highly organized Stonewort (× 1); G, *Ulva lactuca*, a Sea-lettuce (× about $\frac{2}{3}$); H, various Desmids (× 220).

or grouped into colonies. Advanced types are commonly attached to some object and consist of filaments or more substantial branched structures, or have the form of a flattened thallus (simple vegetative body lacking differentiation into true root, stem, and leaf) that may be several inches in diameter. Fig. 5 shows a range of different Chlorophyceae; they are not merely extremely diverse but also appear to have undergone evolution along a number of different lines, most of which have proved to be ' dead ends '. Here are included the Desmids, which are freshwater forms consisting usually of a single cell that is sharply marked off into two symmetrical (and often complicatedly lobed) halves by a constriction around the centre. Also included are a wide range of freshwater and marine slimes and scums, the sometimes bulky Sea-lettuces, and, according to most students, the peculiar and fir-like Stoneworts.

Different kinds of Green Algae are to be found in a vast array of habitats including damp soil, the surfaces of rocks, and the bark of trees. Here and on such objects as posts and palings they may form a green investment most typically on the pole-facing side, which tends to be less dried by the sun. But mainly they are aquatic, being especially abundant in freshwater lakes and streams, although numerous types occur in the sea. Many Green Algae are among the most widespread of plants, the group as a whole being virtually ubiquitous. Their nutrition is mainly by photosynthesis—that fundamental series of reactions on which they and practically all other forms of life depend, directly or indirectly. In this vital process, chlorophyll absorbs radiant energy from light and catalyzes the building up of simple materials into complicated carbohydrates in which the energy is locked—there to remain stored until it is liberated, for example by burning or the slower process of respiration. Such carbohydrates made by green plants constitute the main basic food materials of the world. Although some simulate higher plants, Algae do not need (or have) roots or other special absorbing organs, but take in the raw materials they require (chiefly water with certain salts and gases in solution) more or less all over their surfaces.

The Green Algae reproduce by various methods, several of which may be practised by the selfsame species. The chief types are asexual reproduction by cell division, fragmentation of the thallus, or the liberation of spores—which may swim actively by means of flagella. Or there may be sexual reproduction following conjugation or, more often, the fusion of special bodies (gametes) which are frequently differentiated into large female and small male ones. In some cases both of the gametes and in others only the male ones are motile. In spite of their great diversity and virtual ubiquity, the Green Algae are of rather little importance except as food for aquatic animals ; but they are of great interest in indicating some of the lines along which evolution to higher plants may have taken place. They are widely important constituents of aquatic vegetation and are often dominant in freshwater pools, though as constituents of human or domestic animals' food they are at best minor.

BACILLARIOPHYCEAE: These are the Diatoms, familiar to all microscopists, and comprise a large and important class of Algae that are all unicellular and microscopic, occurring singly or attached in filaments or chains, or grouped into colonies. The form is extremely various, as may be seen from Fig. 6, which shows a range of different types. The cell-wall is composed of two 'valves', overlapping one another like the halves of a pill-box, and is impregnated with silica. Its surface is finely and often beautifully sculptured, with extraordinary regularity and precision. The chloroplasts contain a brown pigment in addition to the all-important chlorophyll, and accordingly the colour of Diatoms both individually and *en masse* is usually a shade of brown or olive-green.

The nutrition of Diatoms is primarily by photosynthesis, food being stored in the form of oil. Their reproduction is normally by cell division, though occasionally sexual conjugation takes place, followed by the production of special 'auxospores', or these latter may be produced apomictically; alternatively, small flagellated gametes or spores may be formed. Diatoms are abundant in both marine and fresh waters in practically all climates, forming a significant, and often the main, constituent

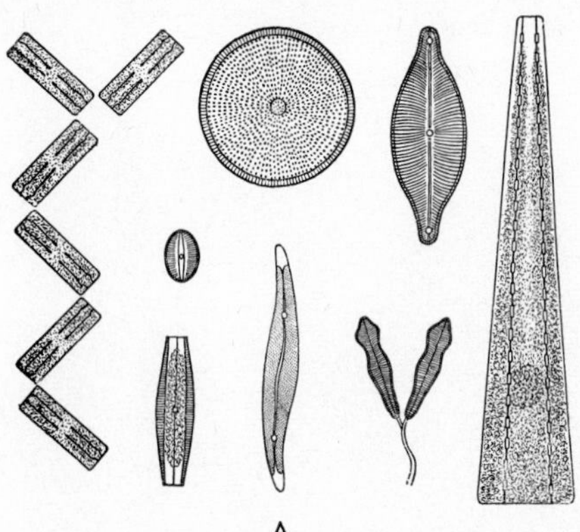


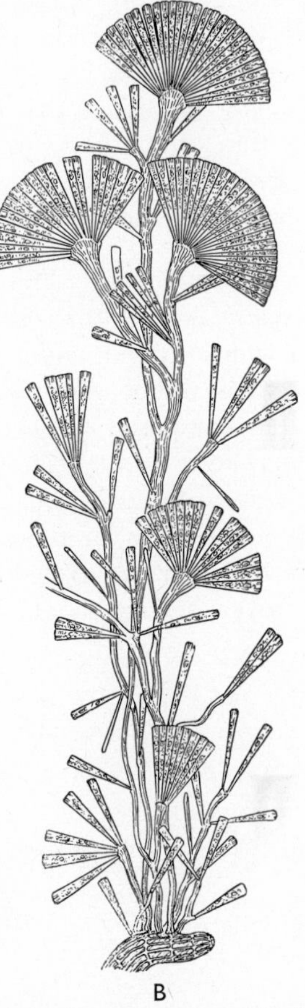


FIG. 6.—Diatoms (Bacillariophyceae). A, various forms (variously magnified); B, a colonial type, *Licmophora flabellata* (× 70).

of the plankton—the more or less passively floating or drifting plant and animal population of seas and lakes—and as such are of vital importance as the ultimate source of food of many fishes and other sea and freshwater animals. They are virtually world-wide in distribution, being found, for example, on and in damp soil and upon as well as under the sea-ice even about the North Pole. When they decompose or are digested by animals, their siliceous valves usually do not decay but sink in considerable quantities to the bottom of the body of water, often forming extensive deposits of 'diatomaceous earth'. This is widely used for scouring, filtering, insulation, and other purposes.

DINOPHYCEAE: These are the Peridinians or Dinoflagellates—usually motile, microscopic unicellular organisms of yellowish or brownish colour and sometimes of marked luminescence. A few are naked but the vast majority have cellulose walls, which are often composed of several sculptured plates. Fig. 7 shows three flagellated, motile examples; but even those types which are non-motile and filamentous reproduce by motile spores (zoospores) that have the form of typical Dinophyceae. These have a particularly characteristic feature—two grooves at right-angles, one of which encircles

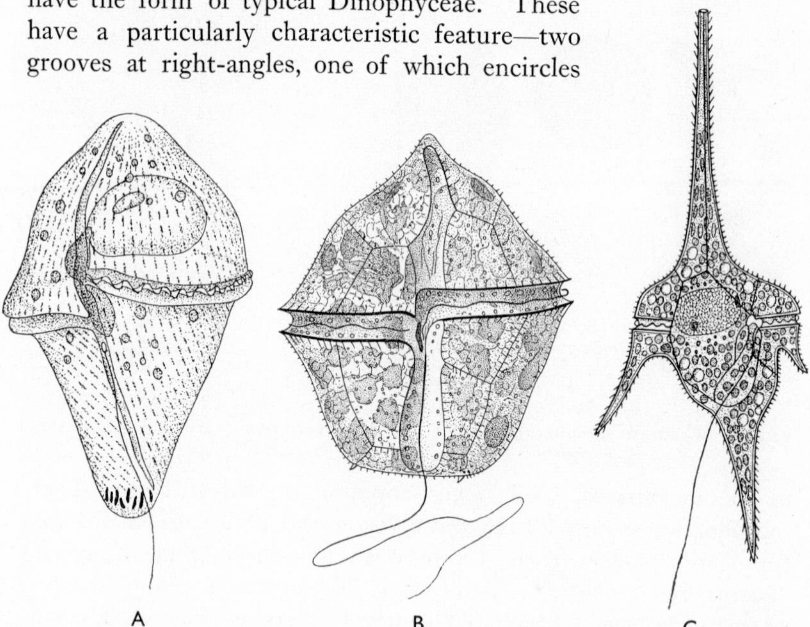


FIG. 7.—Dinophyceae (Dinoflagellates). A, *Gymnodinium*, a type without plates (× about 1560); B, *Goniaulax*, a type armoured with plates (× about 1200); C, *Ceratium*, with plates and form-resistance (× about 300).

the cell transversely while the other runs longitudinally along one side. Two flagella are inserted where the grooves cross each other—an undulating one which lies in the transverse groove and appears to be largely responsible for the rotation of the organism, and a more normal-looking one running down the posterior portion of the longitudinal groove and effecting movement forward.

Nutrition is mainly by photosynthesis, food being stored as either starch or oil. Not only is a reddish eye-spot frequently present, but some types have colourless bodies and are saprophytic, while a few, at least, ingest solid food and so are animal-like in their feeding. As these are among the organisms that are on the border-line between animals and plants, they are liable to be claimed also by zoologists. Reproduction is chiefly effected asexually by the division of an individual into two dissimilar halves (the cells are often markedly asymmetric at first), after which each half regenerates the missing half.

Peridinians are very widely distributed in both fresh and salt waters and may be especially abundant in the ocean. Thus in arctic seas they tend at some times of the year to outnumber even the Diatoms and, temporarily, to form the main constituent of the plankton. Consequently they are an important source of food for marine animals—including, ultimately, Fishes, Seals, and even the greatest Whales.

PHAEOPHYCEAE: This large group, commonly called the Brown Algae or Brown Seaweeds, are characterized by their brown or olive-green colour which is due to the chloroplasts containing a special brown pigment in addition to chlorophyll. They are practically all marine, being among the most abundant and familiar seaweeds of temperate and more austral (southern) as well as boreal (northern) coasts. The thallus is multicellular and usually attached, but shows a very wide range of different forms, some examples of which are shown in Fig. 8. Though sometimes slender and filamentous, the thallus is more often complex. Frequently it is relatively massive, being differentiated into a disk- or root-like organ of attachment to tidal rocks or sea-bed objects, and a stem-like part of varying length and thickness bearing a ribbon- or leaf-like portion. This last may be branched or unbranched and is usually elongated and flexible, streaming easily with the current or, in shallow water, often floating. Such buoyancy is commonly aided by the inclusion of air bladders, which are usually conspicuous and large enough to ‘pop’ when trodden upon—as in the familiar Bladder Wrack (*Fucus*

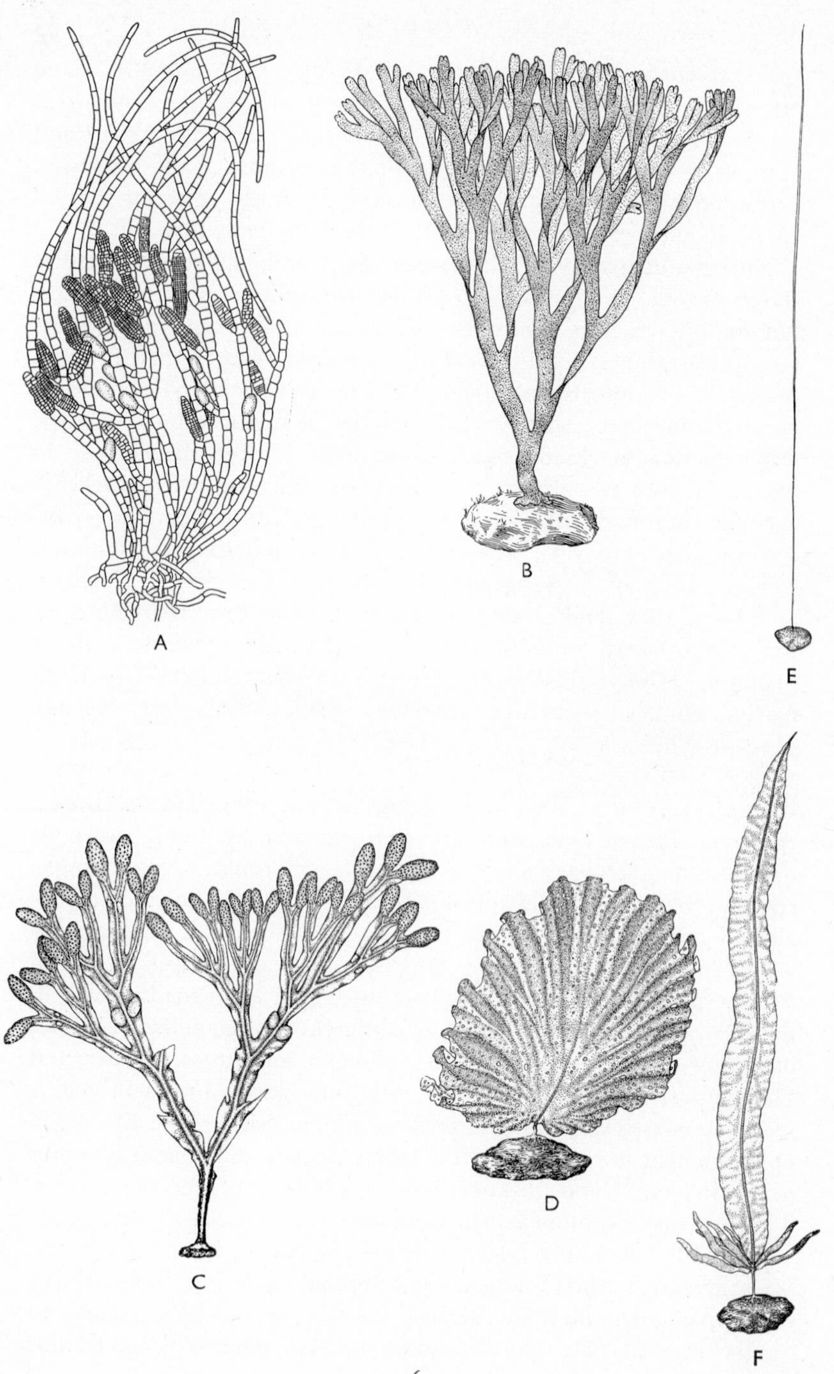
A
B
E
C
D
F

FIG. 8.—Some Brown Algae (Phaeophyceae). A, *Ectocarpus*, a filamentous type (× 45); B, *Dictyota* (× $\frac{1}{2}$); C, *Fucus* (× $\frac{1}{4}$); D, *Agarum* (× $\frac{1}{12}$); E, *Chorda* (× $\frac{1}{4}$); F, *Alaria* (× $\frac{1}{20}$); G, *Ulopteryx* (× $\frac{1}{10}$); H, *Sargassum* (× $\frac{3}{4}$).

*vesiculosus*). Types of Brown Algae living between tide-marks, as many do, are usually whippy and tough enough to remain uninjured by the waves. In some of the giant Kelps the 'fronds' have a relatively complex internal structure and may be around 200 feet in length. (Reports of much greater lengths do not appear to have been authentic.)

The Brown Algae obtain their food for body-building, growth, and energy by means of photosynthesis, the raw materials for this, carbon dioxide and water, being absorbed over the entire surface, as are also the needed salts, etc., in solution. Reproduction is effected asexually by fragmentation of the thallus or by liberation of motile spores (zoospores), or, sexually, by the fusion either of two similar motile gametes or of dissimilar gametes. When there are dissimilar gametes one, the male, is motile and small while the other, the female, is non-motile and relatively large. Thus sexuality may here be comparable in several ways with that of most animals. Many types of Brown Algae have an alternation of sexual and asexual generations—usually of strikingly different sizes and forms, as in the case of Pteridophytes (*see* pp. 55 *et seq.*).

Although a few simple types occur in fresh water, the vast majority of Brown Algae live in salt seas or in brackish lagoons and estuaries. They are abundant in the tropics, but tend to be still more prominent in colder waters, even persisting to the northernmost arctic shores. Being often of considerable size, they are commonly the most conspicuous features of many northern rocky shores between tide-marks and for some distance below, forming extensive and often almost pure 'beds'. These may cover and obscure the rocks or boulders, to which the plants are attached by holdfasts so tough that they are normally detached only during severe storms. Thereafter they may be cast up in large piles upon the beach, or float until they die and ultimately disintegrate. A few special kinds of Brown Algae, however, seem able to live indefinitely in a detached floating state, forming extensive masses; of these masses the largest and most notable characterizes the Sargasso Sea in the western Atlantic Ocean.

The distribution of the Brown Algae seems to be world-wide wherever suitable sea-shores are found. Nor is their economic significance negligible. Thus some are extensively harvested for human food or animal fodder, particularly in eastern Asia, while their use as manure after being cast up during storms is widespread. The ash obtained by burning certain Kelps and Wracks, particularly, is still in some places an important source of iodine and potassium. Finally, owing to their peculiar food-storing and other biochemical activities, Brown Algae are nowadays an important source of often unique organic chemicals. An example of these is 'algin', the production of which runs into about a thousand tons annually in the United States alone.

RHODOPHYCEAE: These are the Red Algae, or Red Seaweeds, which tend to be more prolific in different species but are generally less bulky and abundant as individuals than the Brown Algae. This is especially the case in the seas of temperate and boreal regions, where Red Algae may be little in evidence. They are characteristically red or purplish owing to the presence in the chloroplasts of special pigments besides chlorophyll, although some may be greenish, bluish, olive, or brown. The thallus is again very various in form in the different genera or even species, ranging from filamentous (very rarely unicellular) to densely branched and coral-like (owing to encrustation with 'lime'), and from a flat blackish disk to a ribbon-shaped or widely expanded 'frond'. Attachment to the substratum is by disk-like holdfasts or special filaments; or the whole plant body may form a close investment. Many Red Algae are very intricate and beautiful in form: a range of examples is shown in Fig. 9. The internal structure is peculiar and relatively complex, though none of the Red Algae approaches in size the larger Brown Algae.

The nutrition of the Red Algae is much like that of the Phaeophyceae, except that many of the chemical products of photosynthesis and subsequent metabolism are different; these include the food-storage materials, of which a unique starch-like substance is the chief. The reproduction is remarkable in lacking any self-propelled, flagellate stage. Sexual reproduction is effected by fertilization *in situ* of a large and fixed female cell by a small male one or its discharged contents—in either case carried along, aimlessly as it were, by an impinging water current. Instead of resulting in the formation of a new, 'daughter' plant, fertilization leads to further development which results in the formation of special asexual spores called carpospores. These in the simpler Red Algae germinate to produce sexual plants; but in the vast majority of types they give rise instead to asexual plants producing another kind of asexual spores, called tetraspores, which in their turn germinate to produce sexual plants. In such cases there is a regular alternation of a sexual generation with two asexual ones of which the second is on a separate plant.

The Red Algae are very widespread. Not only do they occur in fair numbers in the habitats occupied by Brown Algae—with which they are commonly interspersed even to the extent of frequently growing superficially on their bodies, as epiphytes—but there are also a number and range of forms inhabiting cool streams and other freshwater habitats. Many of the marine types tend to grow in deeper water than the Brown or Green Algae, being supposedly adapted through their special pigments to photosynthesize far under the surface of the water by absorbing the shorter wave-lengths of light which penetrate to relatively great depths. Red Algae also tend to be more numerous in warm than in cold seas, although not a few occur well north in the Arctic. At their best they may dominate the deeper layers, especially, of marine coastal vegetation. Of the Red Algae, again, the carbohydrates and carbohydrate derivatives

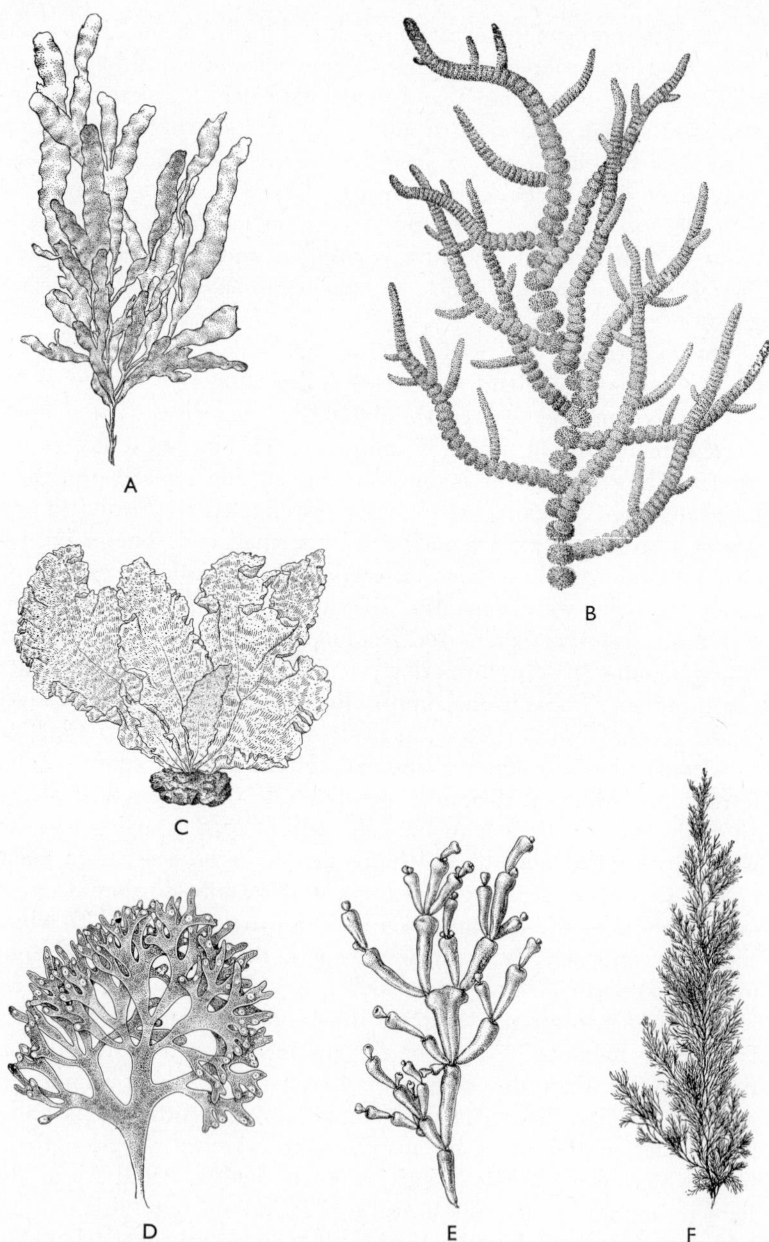


FIG. 9.—Various forms of Red Algae (Rhodophyceae). A, *Phyllophora* (× about $\frac{1}{3}$); B, *Batrachospermum* (× 5); C, *Grinnellia* (× about $\frac{1}{3}$); D, *Chondrus* (× about $\frac{1}{2}$); E, *Corallopsis* (× about $\frac{1}{2}$); F, *Polysiphonia* (× about $\frac{1}{2}$).

are used commercially in the production of colloidal substances that are widely employed for food and in industry. Instances are 'Carrageen' or 'Irish-moss', used for food, and agar, which is of great importance in bacteriological and allied work, though it is even more extensively used in other connections.

MYXOMYCETES: These are the Slime-moulds, or Mycetozoa, which, as the latter name implies, exhibit animal as well as plant characteristics, being indeed near the border-line of the two kingdoms, though widely considered as Thallophyta. They are simple organisms which in the vegetative condition (i.e., when not reproducing) consist of naked, multinucleate masses of protoplasm termed 'plasmodia'. These show the animal characteristics of slowly creeping movement and ingestion of food, and the plant characteristics of reproduction by spores (which in some genera have cellulose walls) formed in a special spore-producing organ (sporangium). The vegetative plasmodium tends to shun the light and to be shapeless and often several inches in diameter, growing as long as food is available, though when food is scarce it may form a mere starved network of living strands. Its outer layer is less liquid than the inner portion and is usually devoid of nuclei; the commonly slimy appearance has led to the name of Slime-moulds. Although chlorophyll is lacking, the plasmodium may be variously and often brightly coloured—most frequently yellow or brown, but sometimes orange, red, black, or even greenish.

Nutrition of Slime-moulds is primarily saprophytic, the plasmodium living upon a variety of organic materials such as rotting wood and dead leaves, apparently ingesting tiny particles of these and breaking down the complicated carbohydrates in them to simple sugars which are used as food. Frequently, living bodies such as Bacteria and fungal spores are ingested; indeed, Slime-moulds can be grown experimentally on an exclusive diet of appropriate Bacteria. Fruiting bodies (sporangia) may be made when food becomes scarce; these are very various in form in different types, as indicated in Fig. 10. Often they are gracefully stalked, with rounded or elongated sporangia consisting of an outer membrane enclosing a mass of very small uninucleate spores and, frequently, a system of ramifying tubes. Sometimes almost the whole mass of protoplasm becomes a single, large, spore-producing structure. The spores are eventually released by rupture of the outer membrane and are scattered by the wind. They germinate in water, each spore producing one to a few flagellated swarm-cells. These, following a period of swimming and often of division, become *Amoeba*-like, and after feeding and further division behave as gametes, fusing in pairs to form zygotes. The zygotes may grow each into a single plasmodium, or numerous zygotes or plasmodia may fuse together, or one plasmodium may divide into two or more.

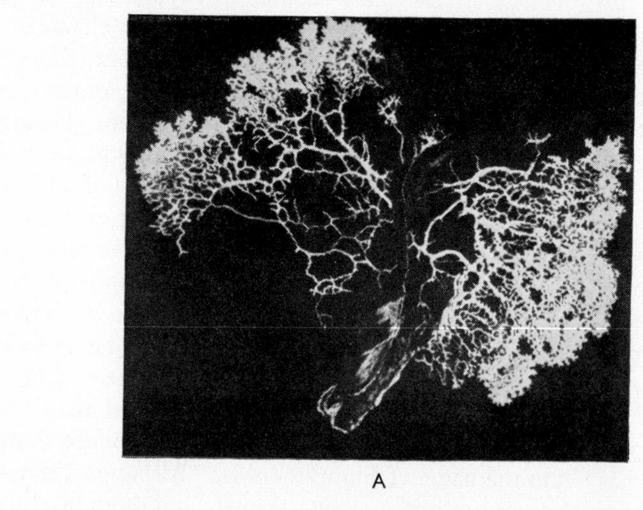


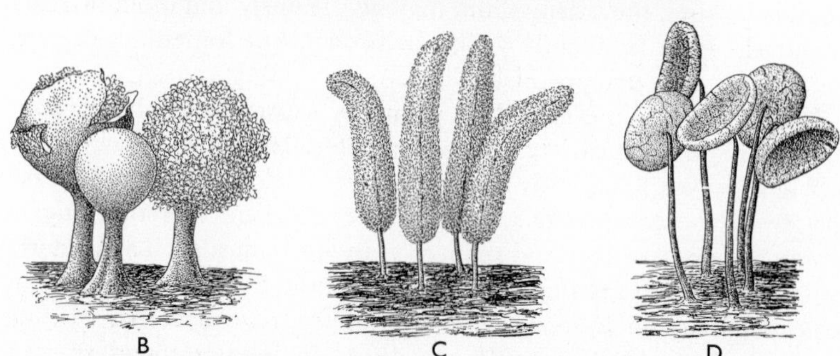


FIG. 10.—Slime-moulds (Myxomycetes). A, Plasmodium of *Didymium* (× 1); B, Sporangia of *Hemitrichia* (× 15); C, *Comatricha* (× 20); D, *Trichamphora* (× 10).

Whereas for spore-formation the plasmodium will usually creep to a light and airy place, in general Slime-moulds are found on decaying vegetable matter in moist and shady situations. Thus they are very widespread in damp woods and thickets, though scarcely ever forming any appreciable feature of local vegetation. If the group be taken in the wide sense as including also those organisms which cause such diseases as club-root of Cabbages and allied plants and wasting disease of Eel-grass, it has a considerable economic nuisance-value. Otherwise its members, however interesting, can hardly be regarded as doing more than a very minor amount of scavenging.

FUNGI: These are the Mushrooms, Toadstools, Moulds, Rusts, Smuts, Yeasts, etc., and comprise, with the Bacteria, the main ultimate scavengers of the organic world, besides causing many of the worst plant diseases. The Fungi are a large and diverse group of relatively simply organized plants. They are usually composed of branching tubular filaments (' hyphae ', collectively forming the so-called ' mycelium ') and always lack chlorophyll, though occasionally they may be green in colour. Some are unicellular, and many others are microscopic though filamentous; commonly, however, the filaments are sufficiently numerous or massed to be evident to the naked eye—usually as a soft whitish investment. They contain numerous tiny nuclei and may be divided internally by cross-walls (septa), or, alternatively, be non-septate. When reproduction is taking place Fungi may be variously, even very brightly, coloured; this is especially the case with some of the larger and often highly characteristic fruiting-bodies, such as (those of) Toadstools and Puffballs, which can reach a considerable size. Fig. 11 shows some of these fruiting-bodies and other reproductive structures of Fungi, which exhibit a great diversity of form. In these fruiting-bodies the masses of filaments, instead of being soft and cobwebby as in the Moulds, are so closely interwoven as to form a solid or even hard structure of definite organization.

As they lack photosynthetic pigments and are not, alternatively, chemosynthetic, Fungi have to obtain their food for energy and body-building by living either parasitically (on or in other living organisms) or saprophytically (by the breakdown of dead organic materials). As parasites they are the cause of numerous and often devastating diseases, especially of plants, and as saprophytes they cause widespread decay and effect a large proportion of the breaking down of elaborated materials such as leaf-mould. Without such breakdown and return of the raw materials into circulation, life on earth would be brought ultimately to a virtual standstill, or even cease altogether—hence the vital significance of Fungi and Bacteria as scavengers. Animal characteristics exhibited by Fungi include

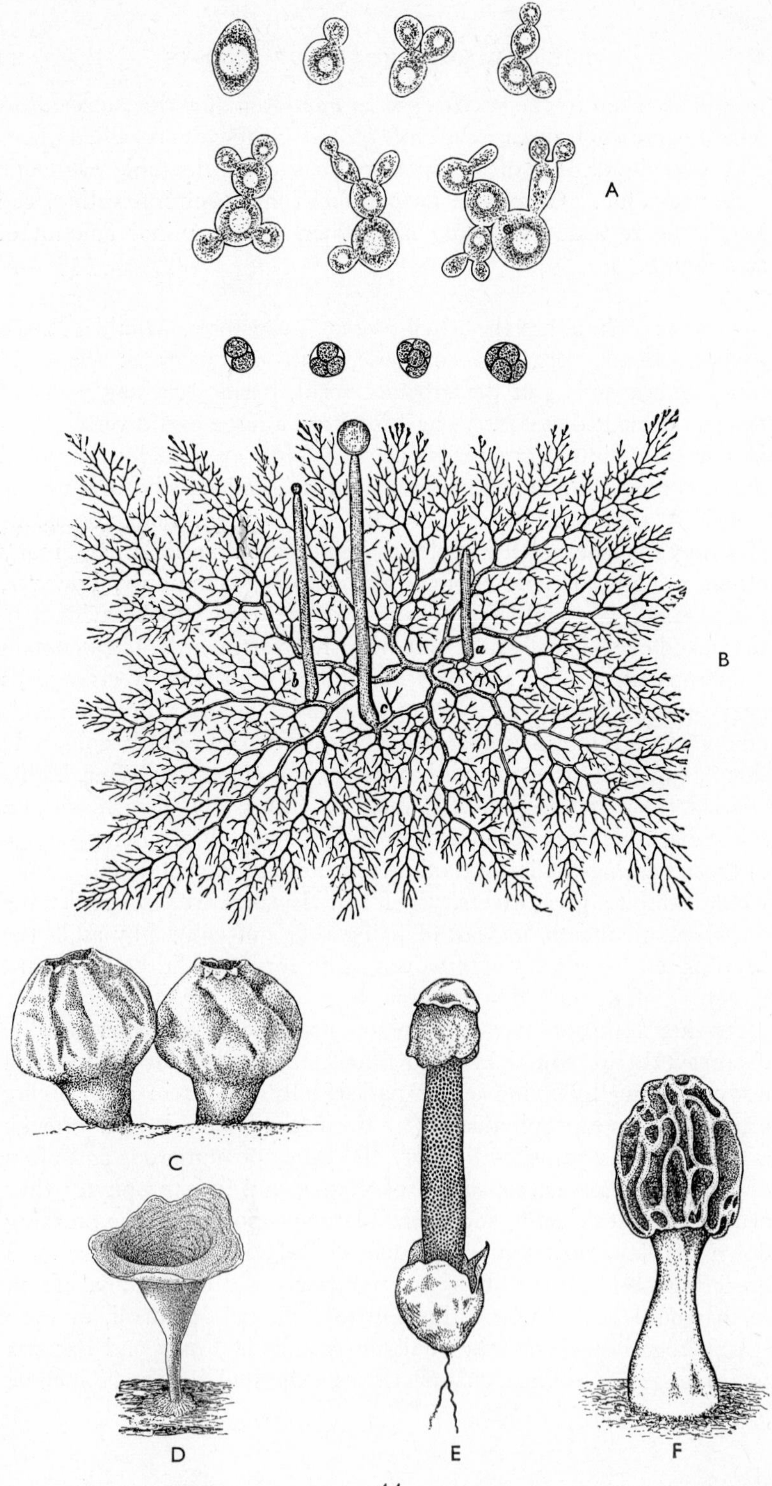
A
B
a
b
c
C
D
E
F

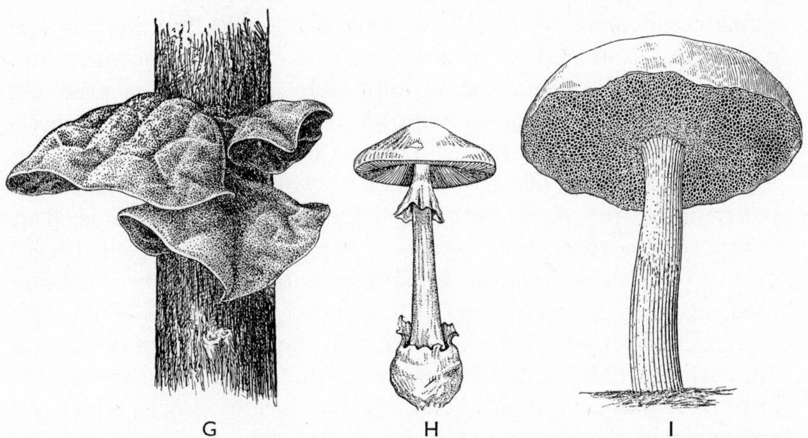


FIG. 11.—Some Fungi. A, cells of Yeast (*Saccharomyces*) budding actively ($\times$ 960); B, Diagram of *Mucor mucedo*, a common Mould, showing the mycelium growing symmetrically from a central spore, and developing sporangia, successive stages of which are marked *a*, *b*, *c*, ($\times$ about 20); C, Puffballs (*Lycoperdon* sp.) which have opened at the top ($\times \frac{3}{10}$); D, *Stereum affine* ($\times 1\frac{1}{2}$); E, a Stinkhorn, *Ithyphallus* ($\times \frac{1}{2}$); F, Morel (*Morchella*) ($\times \frac{2}{3}$); G, *Auricularia* ($\times$ 1); H, the Deadly Amanita (*Amanita phalloides*), a Gill Fungus ($\times \frac{1}{4}$); I, *Boletus*, a stalked Pore Fungus ($\times \frac{1}{2}$).

the commonly chitinous cell-walls and the storage of food mainly as glycogen. Their reproduction may be effected vegetatively by separation and subsequent development of part of the mass of filaments, and asexually by spores which are usually of very small size and produced in enormous numbers (sometimes millions of millions by a single fruiting-body). In some of the simpler Fungi these asexual spores are swimming zoospores; usually, however, they are non-motile and are enclosed in a more or less resistant wall. Various sexual processes occur, usually involving the fusion of unlike gametes, gametangia, or hyphae, and resulting in the production of resting or airborne spores. The 'budding' practised by Yeasts is another effective mode of vegetative propagation (*see* Fig. 11, A, above; the formation of spores internally is seen below).

Fungi find habitats for existence almost everywhere there are either living organisms to parasitize or dead and decaying organic materials to attack. Many are aquatic, including marine, and some grow actively even in the absence of free oxygen. The other familiar habitats are soils, dung, and various foods, fabrics, and wooden or other structures, which Fungi frequently cause to rot. Thus they occur throughout the world wherever life is possible and they can find materials upon (or in) which to grow. Yet as actual components of vegetation their role is usually minor, unless it be very locally and temporarily when food supplies are plentiful. However, in economic connections their importance is vast and multifarious : the frequency with which they cause diseases, especially of plants, has already been referred to. Such diseases result in many hundreds of millions of dollars' worth of damage to crops yearly in North America alone. Also explained above is their significance as scavengers, returning the products of organic breakdown to the air and soil in simple forms that can be absorbed and used again by green plants. Many other saprophytic Fungi are outstanding nuisances to Man in causing spoilage of food and destruction of fabrics, timber, and so forth. Yet others are valuable in positive ways, examples being the activities of Yeasts, which are employed in the making of wines, beer, and bread, and the use of Mushrooms and Toadstools as human food. There are also the 'industrial' Fungi that provide valuable sources of certain food proteins and vitamins, and the 'medicinal' ones that provide such antibiotics as penicillin. Finally, Fungi play a significant role in the nutrition of many higher plants—including forest trees, in or upon whose roots they live and form mycorrhizas.[1]

The above nine groups, which we have treated as classes, are considered by many authorities to be subdivisions (subphyla) or, especially in some instance, full divisions (phyla). The same is true of a few other, smaller groups which are of very little importance phytogeographically, or as components of vegetation, and which we are accordingly ignoring.

LICHENES : These are the Lichens—peculiar dual organisms produced by the intimate association of two plants, a Fungus and an Alga or a Schizophyte, and accordingly belonging to different groups. They seem best treated as a separate class or subdivision of the Thallophyta. Such a 'living together' for mutual benefit is termed a symbiosis, and of this Lichens afford *the* great example, though mycorrhizas (*see* above) are another. In the formation of Lichens the Fungus usually forms a tough, often leathery, investment, the algal or schizophyte cells or filaments being interspersed or grouped within, most typically forming a layer near the upper surface. Lichens are often luxuriant and may live for centuries, the symbiosis being evidently a mutually beneficial relationship in that

[1] For an up-to-date account of this intriguing subject, *see* Dr. J. L. Harley's *The Biology of Mycorrhiza* (Leonard Hill, London, pp. xiv + 233, 1959).

the ' algal ' element is enabled, by the protection afforded by the fungal envelope, to live in dry and exposed situations where otherwise it could not exist, while the Fungus derives food which results from the photosynthetic activity of its partner in places where otherwise none would be available.

The ' algal ' elements in Lichens may be members of either the Chlorophyceae or the Cyanophyceae and, like the Fungi concerned, are usually definitely identifiable. With the varying combinations involved, as well as differing heritages, habitats, and growth tendencies, a vast array of different forms of Lichens result, though their growth tends to be very slow. In size, Lichens vary from minute to some which are whole metres in diameter. In colour they may be of almost every conceivable shade, being often of brilliant hue ; on the other hand a great many are a dull greenish-grey, as a result of combination of the colours of the components. The main groups of forms are (1) ' crustose ' (crustaceous), forming a thin crust over (or sometimes mainly beneath the surface of) the rock or other material on which they grow, (2) ' foliose ', being more or less prostrate and flat, with leaf-like lobes, and (3) ' fruticose ', being upgrowing, branched, and often bush-like, or pendulous from the branches of trees. A range of types is shown in Fig. 12.

The nutrition of Lichens is primarily by the photosynthesis of their ' algal ' components, in which connection the fungal element may in a sense be considered parasitic. Vegetative reproduction is by fragmentation of the plant body, especially when this becomes old and decrepit and liable to break down, or by special structures termed soredia, which are groups of fungal filaments interspersed with ' algal ' cells. These soredia become separated from the parent, being often produced in large numbers, and blow about easily. Sexual reproduction is confined to the fungous partner and follows its particular pattern, usually involving the formation of spores in a special structure, following a fusion of gametes. On germination of these spores, new lichen plants are formed only if some fragment of the appropriate Alga or Schizophyte is present.

Lichens occur plentifully in a great variety of habitats, usually of dryish nature. Thus they favour the trunks and branches of trees, exposed rocks, and bare ground provided the surface is stable. In these and other situations they are to be found practically everywhere on land, though shunning large cities owing to their sensitivity to fumes. Although particularly characteristic of high mountain peaks and of arctic and antarctic regions, where they may dominate or virtually constitute the vegetation over considerable areas of the drier habitats, they are also found as minor—but sometimes conspicuous—constituents of the vegetation in temperate and even tropical regions. They are especially significant as pioneer colonists on bare areas, and in boreal regions where they afford much of the winter food of wild Reindeer and Caribou. Economically they are important chiefly in the feeding of domesticated Reindeer, on which

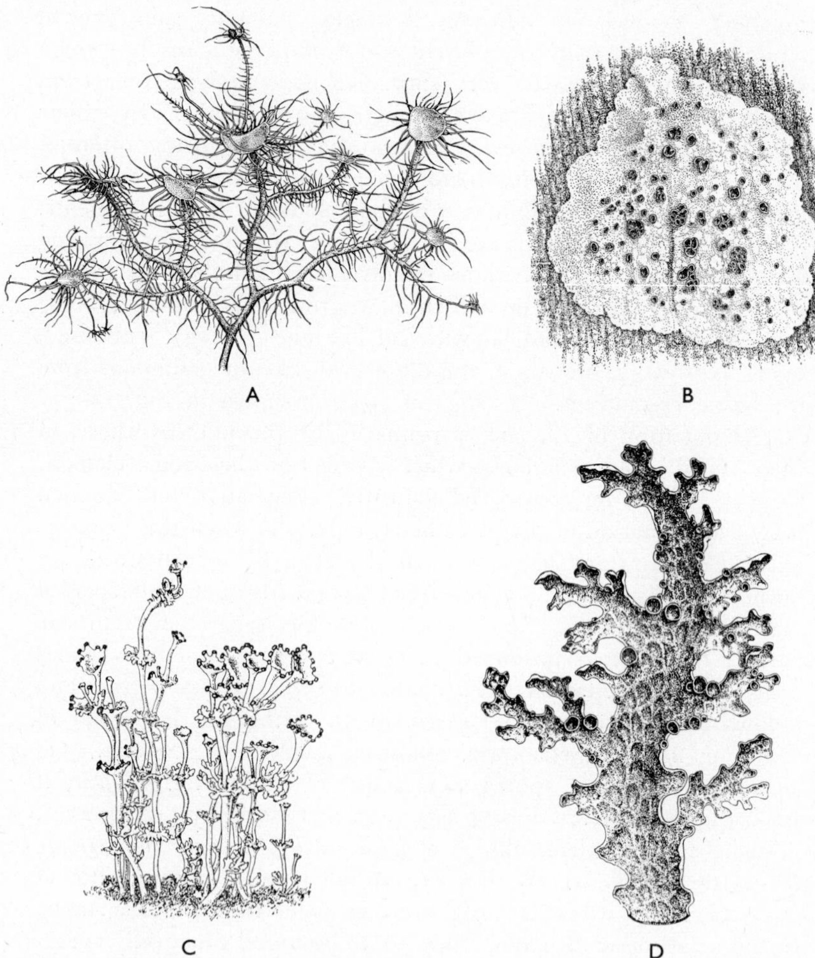


FIG. 12.—Various forms of Lichens (Lichenes). A, *Usnea barbata*, a branched epiphytic type (× 1); B, *Haematomma puniceum*, a crustaceous type (× 1); C, *Cladonia verticillata*, a terrestrial fruticose type (× ½); D, *Lobaria pulmonaria*, a foliose type (× ⅘).

whole tribes of northern peoples depend for the wherewithal of life. Their plentiful storage of a starch-like carbohydrate also makes some of them, such as 'Iceland-moss', useful for human food, though most are highly unpalatable. The use of certain Lichens as sources of attractive dyes has greatly diminished with the chemical advances of recent years, but some dyes, such as litmus, are still widely obtained from them.

## Bryophyta

Hepaticae: These, the Liverworts, are a smallish class of usually green photosynthetic plants of relatively small size, though always multicellular and visible to the unaided eye. There are two main forms: the thalloid, having a thin and more or less flat, prostrate plant body which tends to branch frequently and equally, and the 'leafy', consisting of a creeping central axis up to a few inches long, provided with delicate leaf-like expansions. These last are only one cell thick and lack a midrib; they are usually arranged in two rows, lying on either side of the often prostrate axis, with commonly a third row of smaller lobes lying along the under surface. Noticeable on the lower surface, especially of the thalloid types, are numerous thin root-like 'rhizoids', primarily serving the purpose of attachment to the ground or other material on which the plant grows. Often there are air-chambers or other special features on the upper surface. The main photosynthesizing plants are the gametophytes, so termed because they produce the gametes; they comprise the gametophytic generation which alternates regularly with the spore-producing (sporophytic) one to complete the life-cycle.

The gametes are formed in minute male and female organs, the male spermatozoids swimming freely to fertilize the passive and well-protected female 'eggs', from which, after fertilization, the sporophytes develop. In most types these last consist of an absorbing foot, a more or less elongated stalk, and a roundish capsule (sporangium) in which the microscopic spores are produced in considerable numbers. The foot is embedded in the tissue of the gametophyte, from which it absorbs nourishment. This is passed on to the rest of the sporophyte, which in most types lacks chlorophyll and is thus parasitic on the gametophyte. In some simple forms there is no foot or stalk, the sporangium being embedded in the gametophyte, and in one group the sporophyte is photosynthetic and grows continuously from near the base. But in any case there is a regular alternation of gametophytic and sporophytic generations, such as we shall see later in all normal higher plants. Though the gametophyte tends to be more evident and 'dominant', these generations in the Liverworts have no independent existence, and consequently their dual significance is somewhat difficult to grasp. Both generations are depicted in each of the different types of Liverworts shown in Fig. 13.

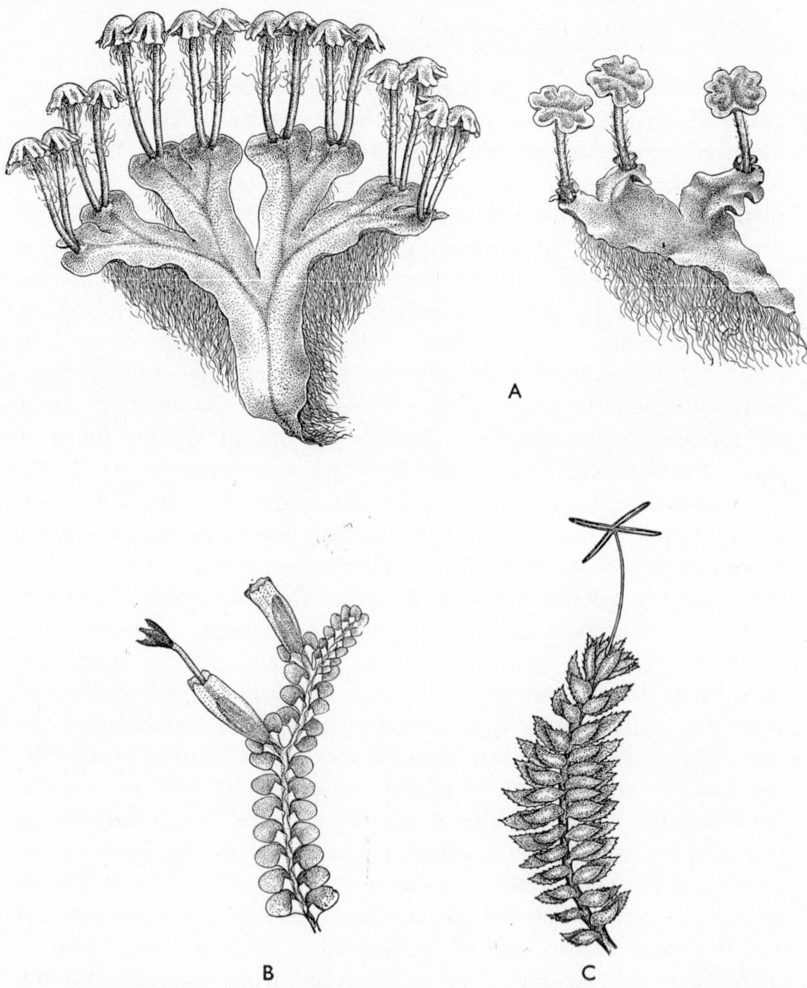


FIG. 13.—Types of Liverworts (Hepaticae). A, *Marchantia*, a thalloid type, showing female plant on left and male on right (× 1½); B, C, leafy Liverworts (B, × 4; C, × 1).

The spores, given suitable conditions after liberation, can germinate to form fresh gametophytes, so completing the life-cycle. They usually afford the main means of multiplication, although vegetative methods, such as fragmentation of the gametophyte or formation by it of special bud-like bodies called gemmae, may also be effective in some cases. Liverworts chiefly inhabit damp places, such as stream-banks, sheltered nooks, and the boles of trees and decaying fallen branches in shady forests. They also grow on moist soil and in tufts of Mosses, etc., and are practically world-wide in distribution on land. Many grow on the leaves of other plants in the tropics, and some in freshwater habitats. With the exception of a very few which are saprophytic, the nutrition of the gametophyte is primarily by photosynthesis ; on this the sporophyte is, as we have seen, in most instances parasitically dependent. Although they are sometimes important as pioneers on bare ground and may even form more or less ' pure ' patches some yards in extent, Liverworts in general play only a minor role as ' fillers ' in higher vegetation. Nor have they any particular value for Man, except sometimes as aids in the binding and consolidation of eroding surfaces.

MUSCI : These are the Mosses, which, in accordance with their near relationship, are in many ways closely comparable with Liverworts. The Mosses are all rather small plants in which the gametophyte, during the greater part (but by no means all) of its life, consists of a more or less upright stem bearing small leaves. These leaves, unlike their counterparts in leafy Liverworts, usually have midribs and are spirally arranged on the stem, which may vary from a fraction of an inch to perhaps a foot in length. The midribs contain elongated cells, and a central strand in the stem usually contains similar elongated cells which are supposed to conduct water and nutrients. True roots are absent, but the base of the stem in most types is plentifully supplied with anchoring rhizoids. In one characteristic and important group, known as Bog-mosses or Peat-mosses, the leaf is not only peculiar in lacking a midrib but unique in consisting of a network of small living cells separating large dead ones which are transparent and perforated, soaking up and holding water with extraordinary efficiency—hence the water-retaining capacity of many bogs which are largely formed by such plants.

On the gametophyte are borne the minute male and female organs, commonly in groups that are made evident by the modification of the surrounding leaves, and either on the same (hermaphrodite) plant or, more often, on separate (male and female) individuals. Fertilization is again by a motile spermatozoid which, when water is present, swims to the passive and protected egg. The body formed by this sexual fusion develops into the sporophyte which, when mature, consists of an absorptive foot, a usually long stalk, and a more or less complicated and characteristic capsule. Fig. 14 shows both the gametophyte and sporophyte of different types of Mosses, for here again the two generations are unseparated, forming one continuous plant body, the sporophyte being at first parasitic on the gametophyte but later becoming at least partly self-supporting through its possession of chlorophyll.

The spores, formed in the capsule and liberated often by some complicated mechanism that works only in dry air (which is more beneficial than moist air for their further dispersal), are again the main mode of multiplication. But instead of growing directly into a typical new gametophyte as in the Liverworts, they develop in the Mosses, on germination, into an extra stage known as a 'protonema'. This is an independent, cellular plant containing chlorophyll and manufacturing its own food. It is filamentous and branched in most types but in some it is thalloid, like the gametophyte of many Liverworts. On the protonema develop lateral buds which grow

FIG. 14.—Some Mosses (Musci). A, gametophyte of a Moss, showing a group of male and female organs at the top (× 7); B, a typical species of *Sphagnum*, the Bog-mosses (× about 4); C, *Atrichum* (*Catharinea*), showing at the base the masses of rhizoids and protonemal filaments from which grow the leafy gametophtyes bearing, above, the sporophytes (× 2).

into the main, leafy gametophytes ; thus is the life-cycle completed. Mosses can also propagate by gemmae and multiply by fragmentation, and they are remarkable for their power to remain alive after long periods of desiccation. Their nutrition is again primarily by photosynthesis, starch being stored, although some appear to be partially saprophytic.

Mosses grow on a wide variety of exposed surfaces—particularly, but by no means entirely, in damp situations. Thus they occur plentifully on the ground, on tree-trunks in moist woodlands, on decaying wood, on old brick and stone structures, on rocks and boulders, and in both still and running fresh water. They are also common as subsidiary forms in higher vegetation. Mosses are more numerous in species and individuals than Liverworts, and tend to cover considerably larger areas and to be far more conspicuous—especially in arctic and boreal regions, and high up on mountains. They are relatively important as components of natural vegetation and frequently dominate substantial areas especially of bogs, whose water-level they often raise. In so doing they may even destroy tracts of forest and make terrain difficult to traverse, thus affecting the economy of Man. On the positive side they are important as producers of peat, which often consists largely of the remains of Bog-mosses, and as stabilizers of sand-dunes and other erosive systems whose surfaces they help to bind. Peat is used extensively as fuel and in the improvement of soils. Owing to their insulating properties when dry, Bog-mosses are also used in construction work and packaging, and, owing to their absorptive and water-retaining powers, for surgical dressings and the transport of living plants.

The above groups all belong to the non-vascular cryptogams and lead up to the vascular plants (*Vasculares*, or Tracheophytes), to which all the remaining groups belong. The vascular plants are those possessing a vascular system, and include all the most advanced, or evolutionarily 'higher', types; these are generally the largest and most dominant on land. A vascular system consists mainly of special tracts (bundles) of elongated wood (xylem) and 'bast' (phloem) cells forming a continuous system linking all the main parts of the plant. Its chief manifestations are such bundles in the stem and veins in the leaf. The primary purpose of such a vascular system is the conduction of water, mineral salts, and elaborated food materials to portions of the plant where they are needed, so that it is partly comparable with the blood and lymphatic systems of higher animals. Its secondary function is to give mechanical support, especially in the 'secondarily thickened' older stems of perennial plants which consist largely of vascular tissues and have the whole crown to support. An account of the general make-up of a vascular plant was given in Chapter I, with some indication of how 'The Ideal Plant' lives and grows (pp. 12–14).

## Pteridophyta

Equisetineae: These are the Horsetails, of which the living examples are mere depauperated relics of a group which was much more important in earlier geological ages, when it included larger tree-like forms. Those remaining belong to a single genus of perennial, herbaceous plants consisting of an underground stem (rhizome) beset with fibrous roots, and sending up usually erect and

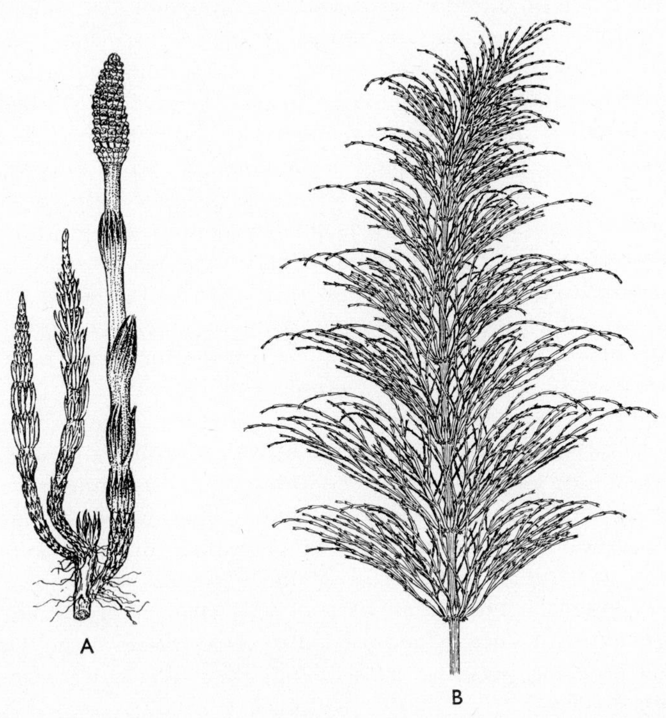


Fig. 15.—Field Horsetail (*Equisetum arvense* agg.). A, sporophyte with fertile branch (on right) and two young sterile branches ($\times \frac{3}{5}$); B, mature sterile branch ($\times \frac{2}{5}$).

stiff, grooved aerial stems that are generally slender but hollow and bear at the nodes (parts of the stem where leaves arise) close whorls of rudimentary scale-leaves. The stem is commonly green and photosynthetic, rarely more than a few feet high, and either unbranched or, more often, bears whorls of slender branches (which may themselves be much-branched) in the axils of the scale-leaves. Fig. 15 shows a characteristic modern Horsetail. Such plants practise the mode of nutrition of normal vascular types, namely, photosynthesis together with absorption of the necessary elements (usually in simple compounds) from the air and soil, or, when the plants are aquatic, in solution with the water in which they live. In common with almost all of the plants remaining to be described, the main food-storage substance is starch.

These relatively large plants are the sporophytes, which comprise the main, dominant generation in this and all the remaining groups. The spores are produced in special organs (sporangia) developed on short outgrowths which are compacted into distinct, cone-like 'strobili' that are commonly developed at the tops of the stems. The spores are all alike but unique in having attached to them at one point four slender processes that bend or straighten rapidly with changes in atmospheric humidity, consequently often causing the spores to move. On germination the spores produce a gametophytic body called a prothallus. This is small and possessed of rhizoids, irregularly branched, green and photosynthetic, and usually each one produces organs of only a single sex. After fertilization by the peculiar spiral, multiflagellate swimming spermatozoid, the egg develops *in situ* into a young sporophyte plant which soon becomes independent, so completing the life-cycle.

In spite of the limited number and variational range of living forms, Horsetails occupy a considerable array of land and freshwater habitats and are geographically very widespread, extending from the tropics to the highest latitudes of land. They especially favour marshes, lakesides, and damp sand or silt, which they may colonize aggressively; but as components of more mature vegetation they are very minor. The outer part of the stem is often heavily impregnated with silica, which has led to some species being widely used for scouring pots and pans—hence their alternative name of Scouring-rushes.

LYCOPODINEAE: These include the living Club-mosses (Ground-pines), Spike-mosses, and Quillworts, as well as numerous huge trees of earlier geological ages that are now known only as fossils. The present-day representatives are lowly, herbaceous, and differentiated into stem, roots, and leaves, the last being numerous and usually small as well as simple. The stems are rarely more than a matter of inches in height or feet in length. Most species are evergreen, overwintering without the aerial parts dying back. The stems are trailing or upright and usually branched, or, in the Quillworts, unbranched and extremely short; these last, peculiar types, also have relatively large, elongated leaves. In them and some other members, the leaf has a characteristic tongue-like appendage (ligule) near its base. Fig. 16, showing examples of some types from this group, indicates the range of existing forms. These are the main, sporophytic plants, and they produce spores in sporangia borne singly in the axils of special and usually modified leaves (sporophylls) that either occur in groups at intervals along the stem or, more often, form terminal cones. In some types the spores are all of one kind, but, in others, different sporangia produce numerous small 'microspores' or relatively few (occasionally one) large 'megaspores'.

On germination the spores produce prothalli, representing the gametophyte generation. These are always small and relatively obscure bodies. However, they vary in different types from lobed photosynthetic ones or underground non-green tuberous ones living saprophytically with the aid of mycorrhizas (in either case usually producing both male and female organs on the same prothallus), to limited growths largely enclosed within the old spore-wall in those instances where spores of two different sizes occur. In such instances the megaspores each produce a few female organs and the tiny microspores only a single male organ, the 'prothalli' being dependent upon the food stored earlier in the spore by the sporophyte. Following fertilization by the spirally-shaped, swimming spermatozoid, the egg develops *in situ* into a new sporophyte plant which is photosynthetic and independent from an early stage, so reversing the situation met in Bryophyta. Some Club-mosses produce bulbils or gemmae which are effective in multiplying the sporophyte. Moreover, vegetative propagation following fragmentation of large old plants often occurs, at least among the longer trailing types.

The Lycopodineae are fairly numerous in species and wide in their habitat tolerance. Though most characteristic of shady woods from tropical to boreal regions, or, in the case of Quillworts, of the beds of freshwater lakes, they also occur in more exposed heaths and marshes and, in such situations, range far north in the Arctic. Nevertheless, as components of vegetation—except very locally and then usually far beneath the dominants, or occasionally in deserts where little else grows—they are so very minor as to be almost negligible. Very different was the position of some of their fossil relatives, which, as we shall see in Chapter V, apparently dominated whole forests in much earlier geological ages, and greatly contributed

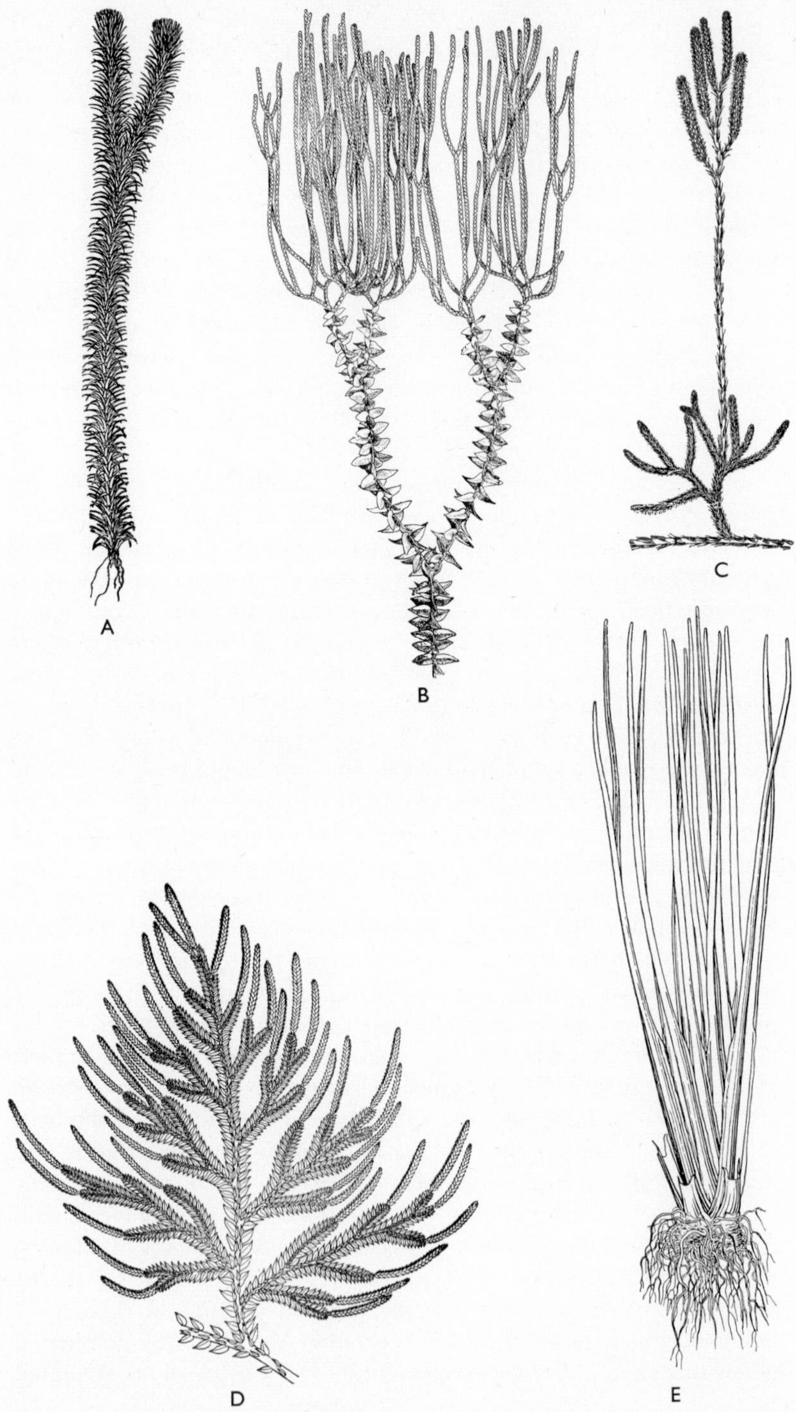


FIG. 16.—Types of living Lycopodineae. A (× ½), B (× about ¼), C (× about ⅓), all Club-mosses (*Lycopodium* species); D (× 1), a Spike-moss (*Selaginella*); E (× about ½), a Quillwort (*Isoetes*).

to the formation of coal. Otherwise their economic significance is very limited: some warmth-loving species are used as pot-plants, and trailing Club-mosses are made into Christmas-wreaths (hence another name, 'Christmas-greens'), while the minute spores of members of the same genus are so highly inflammable owing to stored oil that they can be used to produce 'stage lightning'. They are still employed in dusting operations where a fine powder is required, and for demonstrating sound-waves in physics.

FILICINEAE: These are the Ferns, and include the majority of living Pteridophyta as well as some extinct forms. They are perennial plants, sometimes small and moss-like but usually of ar least substantial size. The stems range from creeping and slendet to erect and stout, and from subterranean to aerial or occasionally aquatic; in Tree-ferns, the often massive, erect aerial stems may be several yards high. There are usually plentiful fibrous roots below, and, above, leaves (fronds) that characteristically are large and compound, composed of more or less numerous segments. Occasionally, however, the leaves are small and simple; indeed the Ferns are very varied in form, as may be seen from Fig. 17, which shows a range of different types. These, of course, are all sporophytes, the gametophytes being always small and insignificant.

The spores are formed in sporangia which are commonly borne in groups upon or partly within the lower surface of the ordinary leaves, though in many cases the spore-producing leaves, or parts of leaves, are modified—sometimes so drastically that they are scarcely recognizable as leaf members. In most types the spores are all of one kind and produce on germination a filamentous, or more often a flat, green prothallus rather like a small unbranched thalloid Liverwort, anchored to the ground by rhizoids and bearing both male and female organs, though a few types have a subterranean and saprophytic prothallus. However, in the small and usually aquatic group known as Water-ferns, which have slender stems and small and sometimes very simple leaves, separate microspores and megaspores are formed, which produce male and female organs, respectively, on germination. Following fertilization by the swimming, corkscrew-like spermatozoid, the egg develops into a fresh sporophyte plant which soon becomes photosynthetic and independent. This is its primary mode of nutrition. Thus the life-cycle, involving as usual in these vascular land-plants an alternation of sexual and asexual generations, is completed. The sporophytes

A

B

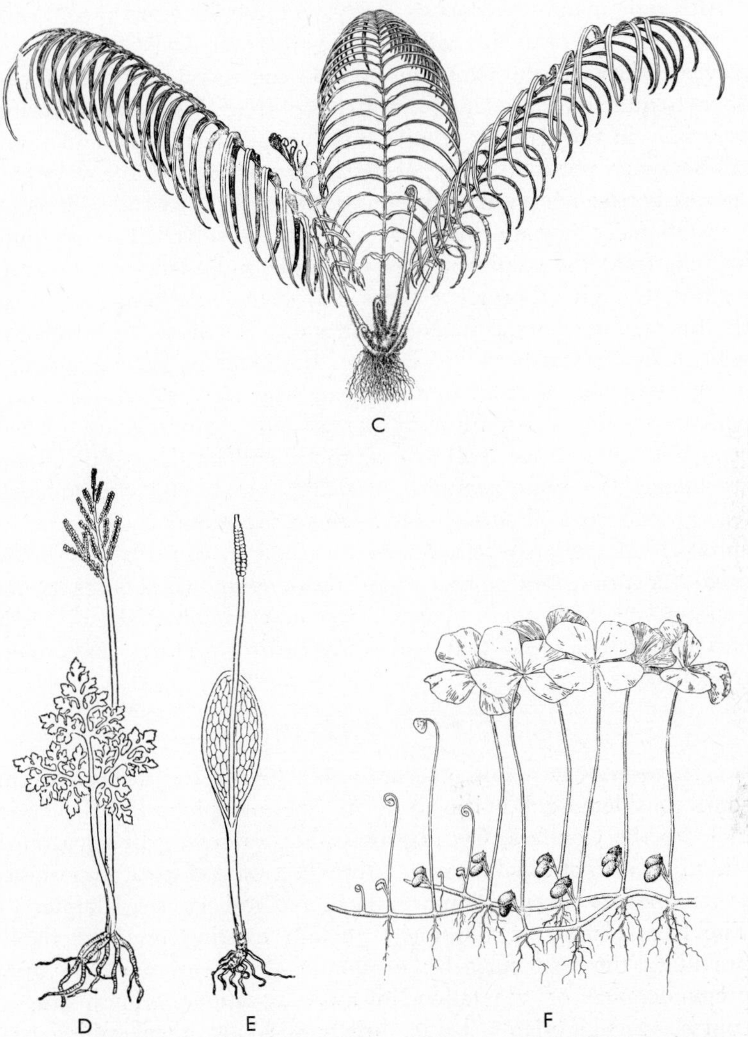


FIG. 17.—Various types of Ferns (Filicineae). A, Shield-fern (*Dryopteris*) (× $\frac{1}{5}$); B, a group of Tree-ferns, *Cyathea* (scale indicated by man in foreground); C, *Pteris longifolia* (× $\frac{1}{10}$); D, Moonwort (*Botrychium*) (× about $\frac{1}{3}$); E, Common Adder's-tongue (*Ophioglossum vulgatum*) (× about $\frac{1}{2}$); F, a Water-fern (*Marsilea*) (× about $\frac{1}{2}$).

of many Ferns also propagate vegetatively—for example, when the old parts of types with branching rootstocks die off and fragmentation results, or through the growth, after detachment, of special bulbils or plantlets that develop on the leaves of some species.

Although mainly favouring shady and humid situations, Ferns occupy a wide array of habitats ranging from dryish heaths and crevices of rocks to wet mud and open fresh water, and from forest floors to quite lofty branches or crutches of trees. They are plentiful especially in the damper tropical and temperate regions and reach the southern portion of the Arctic in fair array, while a very few species persist northwards to almost the highest latitudes of land. Vegetationally they are chiefly of importance as subsidiaries in humid habitats from the tropics northwards and southwards to temperate regions, though arborescent types may contribute substantially to the forest, for example in New Zealand. North of the temperate regions in the northern hemisphere they tend to become scarcer, being often absent from dry areas and almost negligible as components of vegetation in most boreal and arctic regions. Their economic significance is chiefly aesthetic and horticultural; many are among the most beautiful of living things, and consequently fern-growing is a popular hobby. Some are minor constituents of animal fodder or may be employed as food by humans or cut and dried for litter, but probably far outweighing these uses is the nuisance-value of others—particularly the common Bracken, which is a pestilential weed that widely overgrows pastures and young tree plantations.

## Spermatophyta

Gymnospermae: This, the more primitive of the two classes (by some considered subdivisions) of the Spermatophyta (Seed-plants), includes the Conifers, Cycads, and Gnetales among living groups, and many extinct fossil representatives that were of great importance as components of vegetation in earlier geological ages (*see* Chapter V). The Seed-plants are the main phylum existing on land today, providing the vast majority of dominant species and the great preponderance of vegetation in most situations. They are, of course, vascular plants, being, briefly speaking, those which bear seeds. A seed is an organ peculiar to this 'highest' division of the plant kingdom and is the product of a fertilized ovule, consisting of an embryo that is often embedded in a nutritive tissue and is normally enclosed by one or two protective seed-coats. The large, complicated visible plant is always the sporophyte generation, the usually microscopic female gametophyte being embedded within it and never having a separate existence, while the male gametophyte is even more reduced.

of lateral shoots or branches and their separate growth on segregation from, or death of, the parent.

Among the Gymnosperms, the usually stocky and unbranched Cycads, with their palm-like crown of huge compound leaves, are chiefly characteristic of the drier areas of the tropics and subtropics, as are the much-branched, bushy Ephedras, though their broad-leafed relatives, the Gnetums, favour moist tropical habitats. Far more numerous, important, and widespread, however, are the Conifers, different members of which occupy almost the complete range of land habitats from swamps to dry sands. They dominate vast areas of temperate and boreal forests, many of which they virtually compose, and constitute the northern limit of arborescent growth practically around the top of the globe, as well as, often,

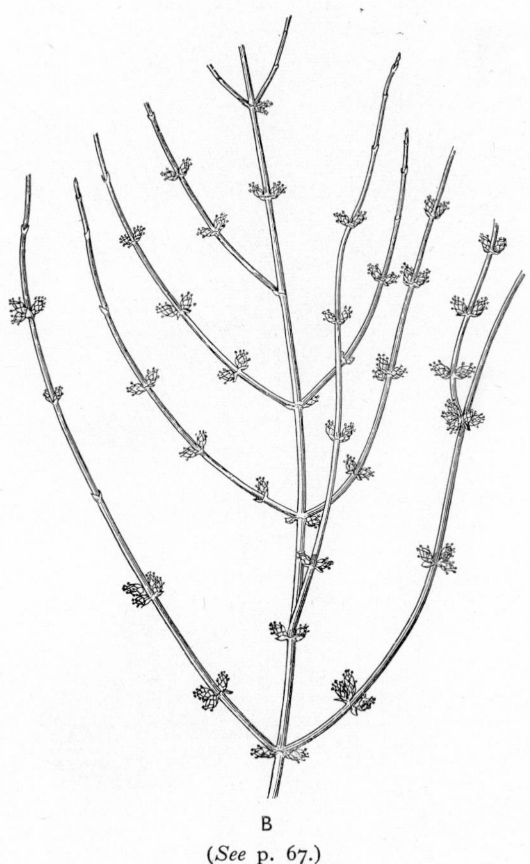

B

(*See* p. 67.)

the altitudinal limit on mountains. Altogether they probably play a role in constituting higher vegetation on land, which is second only to that of the other, last remaining group which we shall discuss next. Moreover, their economic importance is in keeping with such a position, for besides affording shelter and greatly affecting Man's environment, they provide him with a large proportion of his timber, pulpwood, turpentine, firewood, and numerous other commodities, besides minor foods and other items of everyday or local life too numerous to mention.

C

(*See* p. 67.)

D

FIG. 18.—Some examples of Gymnosperms (Gymnospermae). A, a Cycad (*Cycas rumphii*) ($\times \frac{1}{26}$); B, male twig of *Ephedra* ($\times \frac{5}{8}$), a member of the Gnetales; C, twig of typical Conifer (*Pinus insularis*), showing female cones of the three latest years ($\times \frac{1}{3}$); D, Coastal Redwood (*Sequoia sempervirens*), another Conifer (scale indicated by standing man). (Phot. W. S. Cooper.)

ANGIOSPERMAE: These, the flowering plants, are evolutionarily the highest, and vegetationally and economically the most important, of all groups in the world today. They are seed-plants, but distinguished from Gymnosperms by having their seeds enclosed in an ovary—a variously shaped, but commonly roundish, vessel formed by the enclosing 'carpel' (or 'fused' group of two or more carpels) which produces the seed or seeds internally. After fertilization, the ovary becomes the fruit. The Angiosperms are also generally to be distinguished from the Gymnosperms by their internal structure and by their possession of flowers, which are specialized short reproductive shoots bearing typically four different sets of organs in close proximity. These are (1) on the outside the sepals, which are usually leaf-like and protective in the bud stage, and inside of which come (2) the petals, which are commonly attractive in colour, form, and odour ; then (3) the stamens, producing the pollen grains (microspores), and finally (4) the one or more carpels lying in the centre and producing the ovule or ovules.

Various types of Angiosperms are so entirely familiar to us all that it would be superfluous to illustrate them here. Instead, Fig. 19 (pp. 70–71) shows a diagrammatic representation of a dicotyledonous (*see* p. 73) Angiosperm flower, and, in addition, sections of stems of monocotyledonous (*see* p. 73) and dicotyledonous plants to indicate the disposition and something of the appearance of the vascular bundles when magnified. Many examples of Angiosperms will be found illustrated in the chapters on vegetation (especially Chapters XII–XIV), and of their fruits and seeds there are accounts in Chapter IV, whilst the two main groups of them, Monocotyledons and Dicotyledons, are distinguished in the last paragraph of the present chapter. Familiar Angiosperms include all of our common agricultural and garden crops, all Grasses and other flowering herbs whether annual or perennial, and almost all broad-leafed trees and shrubs such as Oaks, Elms, Beeches, Maples, Birches, Poplars, and Willows. There is consequently no need to emphasize that each consists primarily of roots, stem or stems, and leaves, nor to describe the form of these organs.

Sexual reproduction is the object of the flowers and with it the stamens and carpels are particularly concerned. Frequently the stamens and carpels are in different flowers or even on different plants, in which event the individuals are unisexual. In any case the function of the stamens is to produce the pollen grains, usually in large numbers, for transference (by such agencies as wind, animals, or water) to the stigma, which is the receptive part of the carpel. Within this last the ovules are formed, each containing a female gamete. The pollen grains germinate on the stigma, sending out pollen tubes which come to contain the male gametes and usually grow through the underlying tissue, deriving nourishment as they go. This growth of pollen tubes normally goes on until the tip of one reaches the immediate proximity of the female gamete in the ovule, there discharging the male gametes, one of which effects sexual fusion. From the fertilized ovule the seed develops, contained in the ovary which commonly becomes the fruit. Seeds and fruits, though often alike in appearance, are technically very different and should always be distinguished. Many fruits are attractive to animals, or are winged or plumed to be caught in the wind, or buoyant to float on water, being dispersed by these agents with the seed inside. However, in those fruits which contain more than one seed, it is more effective to liberate the seeds and have these individually attractive or appendaged for separate transportation. In any case the embryo within, if still alive and given the right conditions, germinates to form a new sporophyte plant which soon becomes independent of any stored food-reserve and so completes the life-cycle. Such is the general story—though there are all manner of variations and even exceptions—in which it should be noted that the gametophytes, both male and female, are microscopic, vestigial, and entirely dependent on the sporophyte for food, the female being so embedded therein that to all appearances there is only the one, sporophyte generation.

Asexual reproduction is extremely common and widespread in Angiosperms. Not only are there numerous species which are habitually parthenogenetic, the ovules developing successfully without fertilization, but there is a wide array of vegetative means of propagation in nature quite apart from those commonly practised by Man. Familiar examples are the underground stems (rhizomes and rootstocks) as well as suckers and overground runners and stolons of many plants which, rooting at the nodes, constitute daughter individuals on severance from or death of the parent. Also familiar is the fragmentation of many water or colonial plants, as well as separation of bulbs and tubers, while the production of bulbils or young plantlets in place of flowers in many species, or in the axils or even on the margins of leaves in others, affords further ready means of vegetative propagation. Indeed, so common and effective are these or other asexual methods, that many plants resort to them habitually, and frequently are enabled by employing them to reproduce and live indefinitely in regions where climatic or other conditions prevent the ripening of fruit or even successful flowering.

The mode of nutrition of most flowering plants is primarily by their own photosynthetic activity, which takes place mainly in their green leaves. Here, with the aid of chlorophyll in the light, they

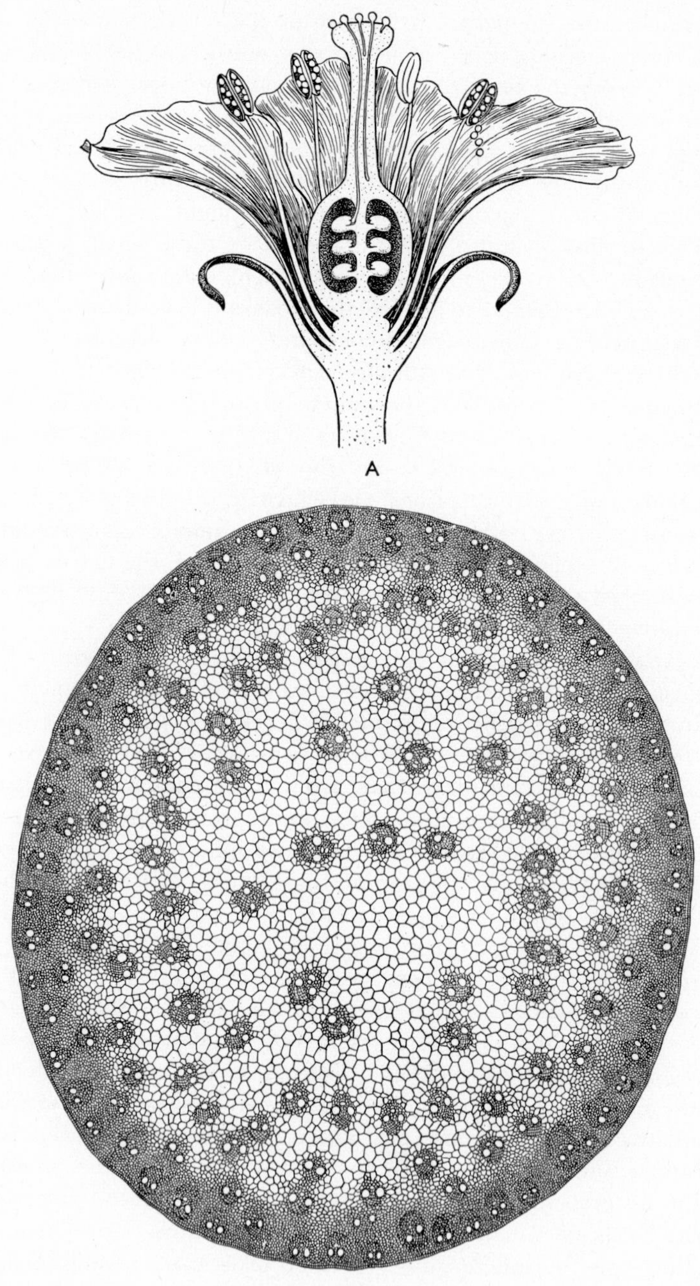
A
B

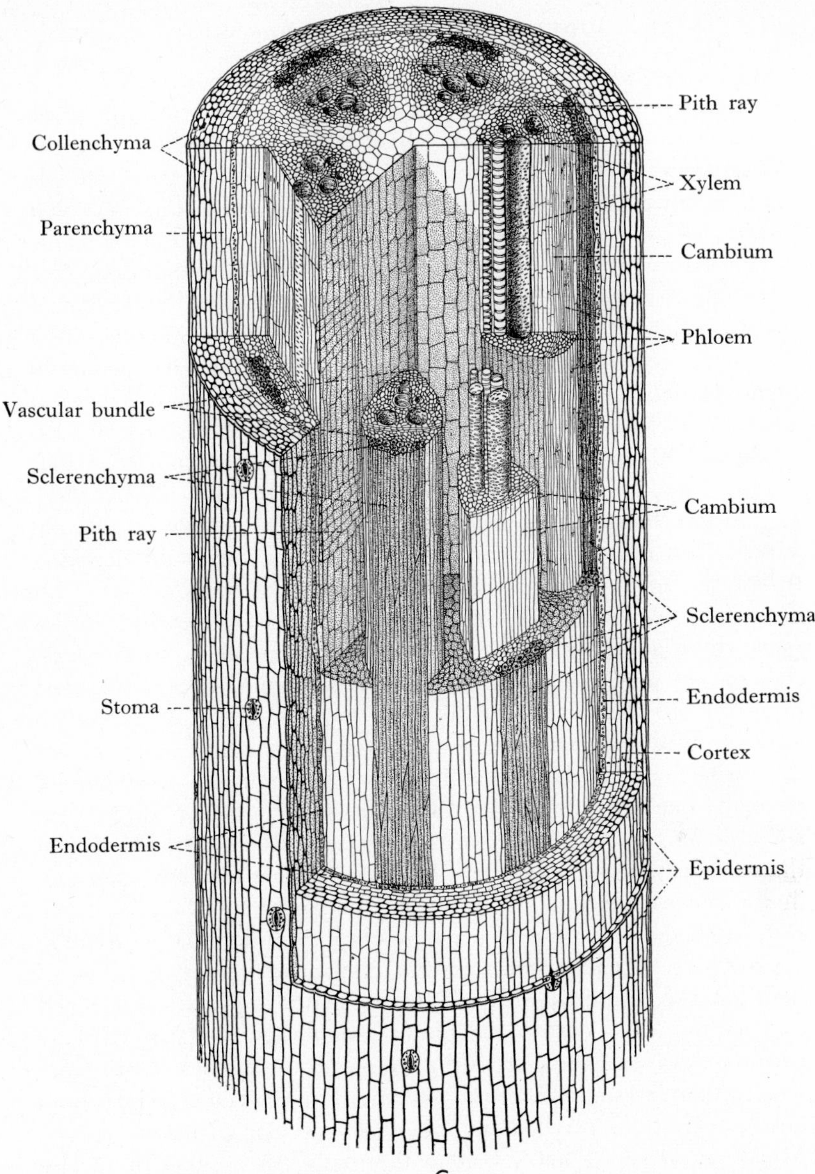


FIG. 19.—Features of Angiosperms. A, diagram of section of flower at time of fertilization, showing pollen grains (greatly magnified) germinating on the stigma and pollen tubes growing down towards ovules (seen in centre). Ranged around are the stamens, the large attractive petals, and the sepals which protected them when in bud. B, cross section of stem of a monocotyledonous Angiosperm (*Zea mays*) (× about 30); the dark oval areas are sections of vascular bundles which are characteristically scattered (instead of being disposed in a more or less peripheral ring, as in most Dicotyledons). C, diagram of portion of stem of a dicotyledonous Angiosperm dissected in cross, radial, and tangential sections to show the various tissues of which it is composed (× about 80, but not all parts to precisely same scale).

build up simple raw materials to complex carbohydrates. But besides carbon dioxide and water they also require, like the lower plants, certain mineral elements which are usually obtained from the soil or water in which they grow ; alternatively, some other materials may be objectionable or even poisonous to them. The likes and dislikes, as well as requirements and inabilities, of different plants in the matter of water or soil constituents, often complicate their distribution patterns, and constitute, as we shall see later, one of the many sets of factors determining their actual or potential areas on earth. Not a few of the Angiosperms which are primarily photosynthetic appear to be aided in their nutrition by mycorrhizal associations with Fungi in their roots—examples being the Heaths, Orchids, and many forest trees. It has even been suggested that the majority of vascular plants may be so aided. In addition there are entire groups of Angiosperms that are either wholly or partially parasitic on other plants, or saprophytic on a variety of decaying substrata—again largely with the aid of mycorrhizas.

As for their habitats, Angiosperms tend to be plentiful almost everywhere anything can grow on land or in shallow fresh water, though they may be scarce in, or even absent from, some of the most inhospitable situations such as rock faces, deserts, or mountain summits where nevertheless some lower plants may exist. Except in warm regions where free-floating types flourish, they do not normally occur in deep open water ; nor do they grow directly on snow or ice, as some lower organisms can. Relatively few live in the sea, and these appear to be limited to rather shallow water and in no instance to extend northwards beyond the low-arctic zone. But, in general, Angiosperms are practically ubiquitous in anything approaching orthodox situations for plant growth, and a recital of their habitats would be practically that of plants in general as outlined in Chapter XI. Within the limits stated they are also virtually cosmopolitan, extending from the tropics to the farthest north land, which many attain, and also to the Antarctic Continent, which does not appear to be reached by any other vascular plants nowadays. Moreover, it seems likely that in the matter of number of species they may be the largest of all plant groups, the order of 250,000 being currently suggested, though of course a great deal depends on what precisely is understood by a species.

Finally, in the matter of vegetational and economic significance, Angiosperms are of paramount importance in the world today, affording the main dominants of most plant communities on land

and of many in the water, and comprising almost all agricultural and horticultural crops as well as the majority of forestral products. To one or other of these aspects the remainder of this book will bear such abundant testimony that it would be superfluous to give details here, though the reader may be referred especially to Chapters XII–XVI for vegetational aspects and to Chapter IX for economic ones. It is by the distribution and growth potentialities of angiospermic plants, more than any other group, that human migrations have been affected in the past, and civilizations have been caused to wax and wane.

In view of their general importance it seems desirable here to point out the two main groups (subclasses if the Angiosperms be considered a class) into which the latter are usually divided (though the individual criteria are not infallible). These are the Monocotyledones (Monocotyledons), characterized by having a single seed-leaf (cotyledon), and the more numerous Dicotyledones (Dicotyledons), characterized by having two seed-leaves. In addition, the Monocotyledons usually have (*a*) narrow leaves with parallel veins, and (*b*) the vascular bundles in the stem loosely scattered and unable to extend ; also (*c*) rarely any woody development, and (*d*) the flower-parts most often in whorls of three. The Dicotyledons, on the other hand, usually have (*a*) broad foliage leaves with net-like veins, and (*b*) the vascular bundles disposed in a ring in the stem and commonly able to extend indefinitely ; also (*c*) often extensive woody development to form shrubs or trees, and (*d*) the flower-parts most commonly in fours or fives. Examples of Monocotyledons are the Grasses, Sedges, Aroids, Orchids, Palms, and Lilies ; of the Dicotyledons, most forest trees (other than Conifers, Palms, etc.), members of the Pea family, and such crops as Beets, Cabbages, Tomatoes, and Cucumbers, in addition to the majority of broad-leafed herbs and shrubs.

## Further Consideration

Many more details and illustrations of each of the main systematic groups of plants may be found in almost any modern textbook of general botany, such as R. D. Gibbs's *Botany ; an Evolutionary Approach* (Blakiston, Philadelphia & Toronto, pp. xiii + 554, 1950), or R. C. McLean & W. R. Ivimey-Cook's *Textbook of Theoretical Botany*, vol. I (Longmans, London etc., pp. xv + 1069, 1951)—or, for the predominant Angiosperms, vol. II (ibid., pp. xiii + 1071–2201, 1956). It should, however, be remembered that authors rarely agree as to the status and disposition, or even the limits, of every group.

An attempt to cover all the groups is made in A. Engler & K. Prantl's *Die natürlichen Pflanzenfamilien*, second edition (Engelmann, Leipzig, or latterly Duncker & Humblot, Berlin, numerous volumes from 1924), and, in greater detail, in A. Engler's very incomplete *Das Pflanzenreich* (formerly published by Engelmann, Leipzig). Also primarily under Engler's name are published from time to time revised editions of the handy *Syllabus der Pflanzenfamilien* (Borntraeger, Berlin), giving an outline of the entire plant kingdom.

For further details the following treatments of the various groups should be consulted:

C. E. Clifton. *Introduction to the Bacteria*, second edition (McGraw-Hill, New York etc., pp. xiv + 558, 1958).

K. V. Thimann. *The Life of Bacteria : their Growth, Metabolism, and Relationships* (Macmillan, New York, pp. xviii + 775, 1955).

F. E. Fritsch. *The Structure and Reproduction of the Algae* (Cambridge University Press, Cambridge, Eng., vol. I, pp. xvii + 791, 1935, and vol. II, pp. xiv + 939 and 2 additional maps, 1945).

G. M. Smith (ed.). *Manual of Phycology* (Chronica Botanica, Waltham, Mass., pp. xii + 375, 1951); also Algae.

E. A. Gäumann & F. L. Wynd. *The Fungi* (Hafner, New York & London, pp. 1–420, 1952).

C. J. Alexopoulos. *Introductory Mycology* (Wiley, New York, pp. xiii + 482, 1952); also Fungi.

A. L. Smith. *Lichens* (Cambridge University Press, Cambridge, Eng., pp. xxviii + 464, 1921).

F. Verdoorn (ed.). *Manual of Bryology* (Nijhoff, The Hague, pp. ix + 486, 1932); Bryophytes.

F. Verdoorn (ed.). *Manual of Pteridology* (Nijhoff, The Hague, pp. xx + 640, 1938); Pteridophytes.

G. M. Smith. *Cryptogamic Botany*, vol. II, *Bryophytes and Pteridophytes*, second edition (McGraw-Hill, London etc., pp. vii + 399, 1955).

C. J. Chamberlain. *Gymnosperms : Structure and Evolution* (University of Chicago Press, Chicago, Ill., pp. xi + 484, 1935).

G. H. M. Lawrence. *Taxonomy of Vascular Plants* (Macmillan, New York, pp. xiii+823, 1951); Angiosperms, etc.

# Chapter III

# PHYSIOLOGICAL REACTIONS, 'ADAPTATIONS', AND LIFE-FORMS

Plants can grow only where the conditions are reasonably suitable for them, and different species have often entirely different needs. It follows that local conditions are a primary factor in limiting the distribution of any particular kind of plant. Tropical plants cannot survive in arctic conditions, nor aquatic plants in a desert. The same holds good to varying degrees in less obvious instances, down to examples where the balance is so fine that the difference between success and failure, or actual life and death, is struck by some barely perceptible difference in local conditions. Very often a complex of interacting factors will be found operating, whose differences may be extremely small but nevertheless sufficient to determine whether or not a particular plant can grow successfully in a given situation.

What actually determines the reactions of a plant to the conditions making up the environment in which it finds itself ? Fundamentally it is the general physiological make-up of the *kind* of plant involved, although the state of development of the *individual* and its degree of adaptation to local conditions may also come into play. Plant physiology deals primarily with the internal workings of plants, whether biological, chemical, or physical. The main physiological characteristics that are found in a particular species are usually inherited and, taken together, largely determine the conditions under which it can grow and the places where it can survive.

## Physiological Make-up

Later in this chapter we shall give an account of special features which enable plants to offset or at least limit the effects of unfavourable conditions. Such so-called ' adaptations ' include physiological acclimatization, and are commonly responses to external conditions. When not inherited they seem best considered as mere temporary modifications in make-up. Their real value to the plant can be seen from such obvious examples as the tall stems of forest plants which reach for light, or the long roots of desert plants which seek out water.

Before considering these adaptive modifications, we must deal with those physiological attributes which are most significant in affecting plant distribution, for they are fundamental to plant geography.

Water is essential for the life and growth of plants, being a constituent of their bodies and necessary for many of their life-processes. Consequently its availability is among the most important factors of a plant's environment. Where there is no water, plants cannot long persist in an active state ; although seeds may survive bone-dry for many years, they need water to germinate as the plants do to grow. Between a desertic lack and an aquatic superabundance of water, which are extremes that only suitably adapted plants can withstand, there are various degrees of water availability to which particular species are accustomed and often limited. The need for water largely determines the distribution of plants on the face of the earth, as we may see when passing from any lastingly dry area to a wet one, when the flora and vegetation will change drastically.

The actual effect of available water may be complicated by conditions, such as temperature and atmospheric humidity, that affect its utilization within the plant—for example through controlling absorption by the roots, movement in the stem, or loss from the leaves, etc. Particularly susceptible to atmospheric changes are the microscopic pores (stomata) through which most water-vapour and other gaseous exchange takes place between the internal tissues of higher plants and the atmosphere at large. Consequently the all-important water economy of the plant is affected by conditions in the surrounding air as well as by the availability of water in the soil.

Temperature is another of the most important factors of the plant's environment. Particular plants require particular temperature-ranges for their life-processes and normal development, and, different temperatures being characteristic of different climates, such requirements widely limit the geographical distribution of plants. And along with plants, of course, go the vegetation-types which they make up.

Under otherwise constant conditions each plant has an optimum temperature at which it does best, and, on either side of this, a range extending to maximum and minimum temperatures beyond which it cannot grow normally and may even be killed. However, for most plants, in the words of one specialist correspondent, 'temperature requirements depend on illumination; in low light [intensities] the optimum is cooler than in high light'. In nature, temperatures fluctuate more or less markedly and affect different life-processes differently, so that the optimum must take into consideration such natural fluctuations on one hand and the optima for different life-processes on the other. Even the maxima and minima, outside of which death may result, often vary with other physical factors and with the recent experience as well as evolutionary history of the plant in question. They may also vary with the time of exposure as well as with the state of the plant structure or its stage of development. Thus resting seeds and other reproductive bodies are, in general, far more resistant to extremes than are adult plants or, particularly, tender young parts: whereas the killing of young shoots and blossoms by even the slightest frosts is an all-too-common experience in temperate regions, more mature parts of the selfsame plants often survive. Indeed there are numerous known instances, involving all the main groups of plants, of such resistant bodies as spores and seeds surviving much lower temperatures in laboratories than are ever found in nature—including those of liquid hydrogen or even of liquid helium near absolute zero.

Far from all vital activity ceasing at the freezing point of water (32° F. = 0° C.), there are known instances of such physiological functions as photosynthesis and respiration proceeding at temperatures below this point in higher plants, while some Bacteria and Fungi are capable of growth at temperatures as low as 16° F. (− 8·89° C.). It has even been claimed, in Russia, that flagellate Algae have been observed swimming in drops of brine cooled artificially to − 15° C. On the other hand, whereas most plant bodies are killed by heat at much lower temperatures than the boiling point of water at sea-level (100° C.), some bacterial spores are merely stimulated to germinate by being so boiled (though of course the actual germination only takes place subsequently, at lower temperatures).

The responses of plants to night temperatures have recently been demonstrated to have considerable significance in connection with their geographical distribution. Thus the Big Bluegrass (*Poa ampla*) of western North America flowers equally well at day temperatures of 20, 23, and 30° C.—but only when the night temperature is below 14° C., for at 17° C. night temperature it does not flower at all, even though vegetative development is good. Again, the English Daisy (*Bellis perennis*) dies when grown continuously in a warm greenhouse: with a day-temperature of 26° C. the plants survive only at night temperatures below 10° C., and flower abundantly only at still lower night temperatures. Accordingly such plants are unable to reproduce normally in consistently warm climates. In other instances, closely related strains may differ markedly in their night-temperature requirements for flowering; these requirements may be decisive in determining which strains, if any, can flourish in a particular area. This is true of Tomatoes, where fruit-set is dependent upon a very narrow range of temperatures—a phenomenon which is reflected in very large differences in yield in varying circumstances and with different strains having even slight deviations in optimal requirements. Numerous instances are now known in which, for these or other reasons, slight differences in the temperature-response of plants will exert a controlling influence on their local survival and consequently on their distribution.

In the many parts of the world that have markedly varying seasons, one of the main concerns of their plants is to tide over unfavourable periods—usually of cold or drought. To this end is expended a good deal of what might be called evolutionary ingenuity, and also much physiological effort—for example, in storing food for the adverse period and for subsequent development. Among the most successful methods employed is the annual habit, in which the adverse period is evaded by being passed over in the form of a resistant seed or fruit, the parent having meanwhile died. Numerous common weeds, such as Chickweeds (*Stellaria* spp.) and Shepherd's-purse (*Capsella bursa-pastoris*), practise this method, as do many of the diminutive 'ephemerals' which blossom so pleasingly after rain in the less extreme deserts. In the Arctic and some other rigorous regions, however, the growing-season, though fairly regular, is too short and cool to allow full development—from seed through seedling and adult to flower and seed again—in a single season. Accordingly almost all the plants there are perennial, passing the adverse winter period in a more or less resistant and dormant state—often after dying down (in the case of herbs) or losing their leaves (in the case of deciduous shrubs and trees). Most Mosses and some other plants have the fortunate capacity to endure drought by drying up almost entirely without ill effect, resuming normal life again when moistened. All these, as well as any growth-responses they involve, are physiological activities (or inactivities) and, in a sense, adaptations to environmental conditions. On a plant's capacity for them may depend its geographical range.

The production of reproductive bodies involves various physiological activities that are closely correlated and indeed wonderfully integrated, yet may be affected by environmental conditions in a unique way. Although some trees may live for more than 2,000 years, there is no known instance of life being really permanent in any individual. So in order to persist a plant must reproduce, and any condition which prevents it from doing so in a particular area will preclude that area from its normal range (that is, in the absence of persistent immigration). Many conditions—climatic, nutritional, or otherwise—can and frequently do prevent the normal reproduction of certain plants, so limiting the geographical areas they occupy. Some plants circumvent this either by separating off parts of their bodies for 'vegetative' reproduction or by the development of special organs for the same purpose, thereby enabling themselves to persist in areas where seed etc. cannot be produced. This is true of many plants living under extreme conditions, for example in the Arctic.

Although on land there is almost everywhere sufficient light to enable plants to grow, the effect of light-climate on their reproductive processes affords another instance of range-limitation. For many plants require a day-length within particular limits before they can flower successfully, and, in latitudes where the length of day during their flowering period is outside these limits, are unable to reproduce sexually. This appears to be one reason why many southern species fail to flower in the north, and *vice versa*. However, such reactions are by no means immutable, but tend to vary with other conditions, and may also be changed by treatment with certain chemicals.

The ranges of particular species may be limited by chemical 'antagonism' (*i.e.* active opposition to growth, etc.), nutritional conditions, and other factors bound up with the soil. Familiar instances are afforded by some plants which require much 'lime' (actually, calcium carbonate) in the soil, and others which avoid it. Examples of the former category are Yellow Mountain Saxifrage (*Saxifraga aizoides* agg.) and Salad Burnet (*Poterium sanguisorba*), and, of the latter, most Heaths (Ericaceae). Often the merest trace of a particular compound or element, such as boron, can have a profound effect in encouraging or precluding particular species. Deficiency diseases, due to lack or insufficiency of particular substances, are common. These diseases, with the ones produced by attacks of various Fungi, Bacteria, Viruses, and Nematode Worms, and the browsing of lower animals such as Locusts and of higher ones such as Goats, may drastically limit plant distributions. Often the very presence of a plant species in a spot is dependent upon the absence there of serious pests and predators.

The areas of parasites and saprophytes are naturally limited to ones where suitable hosts or elaborated materials, respectively, are available for attack. Thus, for example, the devastating Late-blight of Potatoes and Tomatoes, caused by the Fungus *Phytophthora infestans*, is limited to the areas of those crops and of some other members of the family (Solanaceae) to which they belong. Again, the deadly White Pine Blister-rust, *Cronartium ribicola*, is virtually limited to areas supporting both of the hosts that are necessary for the completion of its life-cycle, namely, five-needled Pines and species of *Ribes* (Currants and Gooseberries).

As regards physiological antagonisms due to poisonous residues and excretions, it seems that these may be important in some circumstances, such as ' fairy rings ' and the avoidance by some plants of the shade of certain trees. Thus the roots of Black Walnut (*Juglans nigra*) have long been known to excrete a toxic substance, juglone, that inhibits the growth of many other plants and can even kill Apple trees. There are also the cases of the western North American members of the Daisy family (Compositae), *Parthenium argentatum* and *Encelia farinosa*, which are known to poison other plants by minute amounts of chemical excretions, thereby reducing competition. Is it possible that this may be one of the factors lying behind the notorious success of this family as colonists ? We do not know, and indeed our information in such fields of study is still only fragmentary. Also undetermined but pregnant with possibilities for research, is the extent to which antibiotic substances may be effective in nature.

## Ecological Limitation

The realms of physiology range imperceptibly into those of ecology, which in part may be looked upon as the application of physiology to ' field ' conditions. The ecological requirements of different plants are widely various and, as we have seen, commonly limit their geographical areas. This limitation is actually to those regions where appropriate ' habitats ' (*i.e.* living places) exhibiting suitable conditions are found, and, within such regions, naturally to those habitats themselves. Consequently plants in nature are limited not only to areas of particular climate but more precisely to special habitats within these areas, the final limitation being ecological. In such cases as oases in a desert or islands in an ocean, this limitation may be extreme.

The subject of modification by, or adaptation to, various conditions is dealt with in the next section. Here we should mention the manner in which, quite apart from any special antagonism, sheer physical competition among plants for the requisites of life may limit the habitat and actual range of a particular species or even strain. Especially may root-competition for water and aerial competition for light prove veritable struggles for existence in which the weaker individuals succumb. Generally speaking, the closer any two types are in their ecological requirements, the keener will be the competition between them : in such even contests the slightest advantage to one competitor can swing the balance in its favour.

As most plants living on land need soil in which to root and some well-lit space in which to grow, it is particularly in ' open ' areas not yet covered with higher vegetation that competition is least and plants can enter and establish themselves successfully. Most such areas tend to be colonized by successive waves of plants that usually start with primitive or other lowly types but in favourable regions normally lead up to forest. This progressive colonization is called ' succession ', and is described in Chapter XI. The farther it proceeds, the less space there is left for new colonists and the more tendency there is for former colonists to be ousted by coarser competitors. Meanwhile animals, including Man, are continually opening up new habitats and abandoning old ones—often after destroying the natural vegetation, and rarely without disturbing it considerably. For these and other reasons the geographical areas of plants and plant communities are rarely if ever static.

## Structural ' Adaptations ' of Vegetative Parts

Numerous features help plants to offset the effects of unfavourable conditions and consequently widen their potential ranges. Having noted already such functional modifications as acclimatization of various sorts, and physiological ' adaptations ' such as the ability of many plants to evade unfavourable periods of cold or drought, we shall deal here with changes of *form* that appear to be developed in relation to the needs of plants to combat adverse conditions. Through such structural changes they may be enabled to maintain their geographical areas and even to extend them. Those modifications of reproductive bodies that are helpful in dispersal will be dealt with in the next chapter, the present section being concerned primarily with the ' vegetative ' parts—comprising, in higher plants, the stems, roots, and leaves.

The water relationships of plants often involve strikingly ' adaptive ' features—particularly ones that are helpful in tiding over periods of water deficiency, for example by increasing absorption or decreasing loss, or by storage against times of need. Instances are seen in the deep roots of many plants of deserts or semi-deserts, allowing the tapping of underground reserves, and in the matted turf of the Grasses of semi-arid regions, which aids retention of such water as becomes available from atmospheric sources. Actually, as pointed out by Professor Kenneth V. Thimann (*in litt.*), ' roots elongate when aerated ; hence in dry soils (which are therefore full of air) they grow longer. . . . I should call [this] a simple response to external conditions. Low nitrogen also favors elongation of roots, with obvious ecological advantages in nitrogen-poor soil.'

The aerial parts of a wide range of plants are modified to reduce water-loss, often to the slightest proportions in times of shortage. This may be done, for example, by protection of the stomata in grooves or among a mass of hairs, by general reduction of the ' evaporating surface ', and by covering with wax or hairs, etc., even those areas that remain. Often the leaves are reduced to spines or scales, their normal functions being taken over by green stems. In addition many plants, such as the more massive succulents of the Cactus, Spurge, and some other families, store water extensively in special stem or other structures which are modified into reservoirs. There may also be one or more layers of large water-storing cells in leaves and other green parts. The development of some of these features, such as the tall stems of many trees in dense forests, may depend upon the conditions under which an individual grows, whereas in other cases the features may develop regularly, irrespective of local conditions, as part of the normal form of the plant. But in either instance the ' ability ' has to be present, else the plant could not develop the desirable adaptation and benefit accordingly. Fig. 20 shows some examples of features that help land plants to conserve or obtain water ; conversely, many water plants have special tissues or growths that enable them to float or otherwise improve their

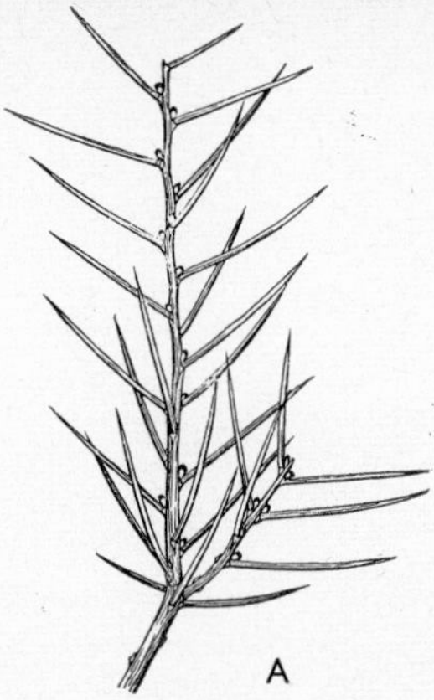

A

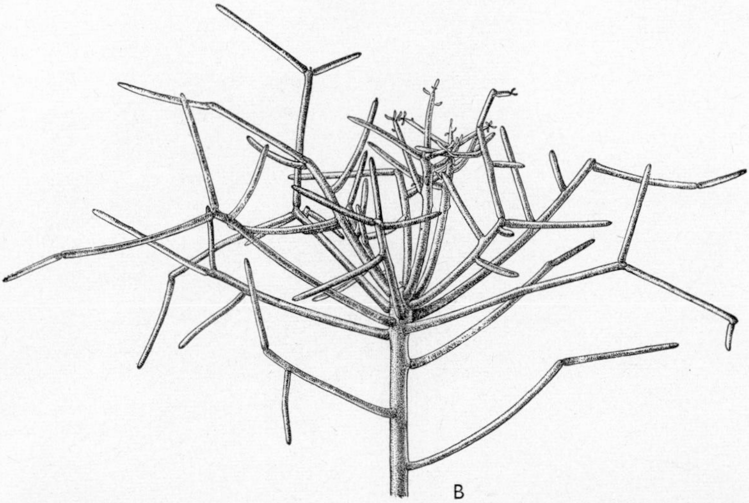

B

C

(*See* p. 85.)

D

(*See* p. 85.)

E

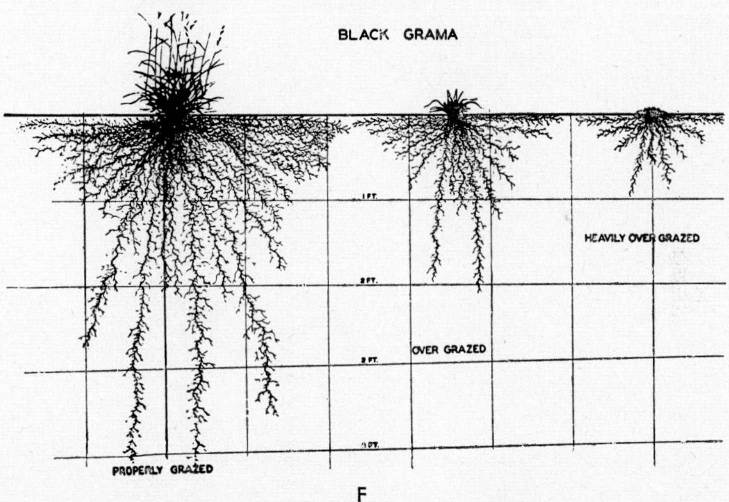


F

FIG. 20.—Features aiding water conservation or absorption. A, branch of a desert plant, *Hakea*, with the leaves modified as spines (× $\frac{1}{2}$); B, stems of *Euphorbia tirucalli*, specialized for photosynthesis and water storage (× about $\frac{1}{3}$); C, Arizona desert with large Cacti (phot. F. Shreve); D, cut bank on Jornada Experimental Range, New Mexico, showing deep rooting of low desert plants—in particular a Mesquite bush about 12 inches (30 cm.) in diameter and only 6 inches high but with roots about 8 feet (nearly $2\frac{1}{2}$ metres) deep (phot. U.S. Forest Service); E, 'bisect' diagram of above- and below-ground parts of forbs and Grasses in the Palouse prairie grassland association of western central Idaho, U.S.A. (courtesy of U.S. Soil Conservation Service); F, Black Grama Grass (*Bouteloua eriopoda*) grown under three degrees of grazing, showing effect on root system (courtesy of U.S. Soil Conservation Service).

aeration, three examples being shown in Fig. 21. Among these last the Water-hyacinth affords an example of how floating may aid in dispersal without involving special reproductive bodies, for individuals may be transported considerable distances by water cur-

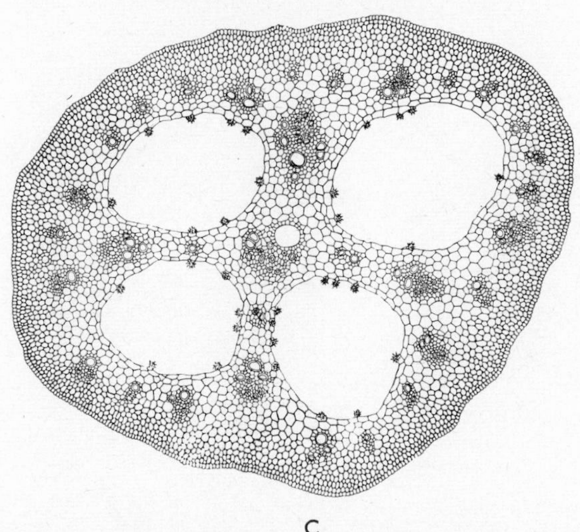


FIG. 21.—Features promoting aeration. A, *Jussiaea repens*, a rooting or floating aquatic with numerous inflated roots which project upwards into the air and contain a great development of air spaces through which air can pass to submerged organs (× $\frac{1}{4}$); B, Water-hyacinth (*Eichhornia crassipes*), with leaf-stalks modified for buoyancy, the whole plant floating freely (× $\frac{1}{3}$); C, cross section of leaf-stalk of a Water-lily (*Nymphaea stellata*), showing large air-passages (× 30).

rents, and, having so migrated, often multiply to cover large areas of water.

Also significant in enabling plants to grow in many situations where otherwise they could not exist, are modifications for climbing, twining, scrambling, and running. Examples are shown in Fig. 22. Further modifications apparently playing a similar role in plant geography include those for catching insects to supplement the food supply, and those for storing food to tide over the adverse period of winter. Examples of carnivorous plants and of food-storage in special underground organs are shown in Fig. 23 ; included in the latter category are Potatoes and many bulbs and other structures that are, besides, reproductive in function.

The giving off of water-vapour from the aerial parts of plants helps to keep them cool, and many are further protected from intense sunlight by their structure or covering, so that 'scalding' and other injury may be averted even in very hot and sunny deserts. The structural changes which restrict or accelerate the rate of water loss are in general either hereditary and consequently characteristic of the race, or are acquired by an individual plant or part of a plant

A
B
C

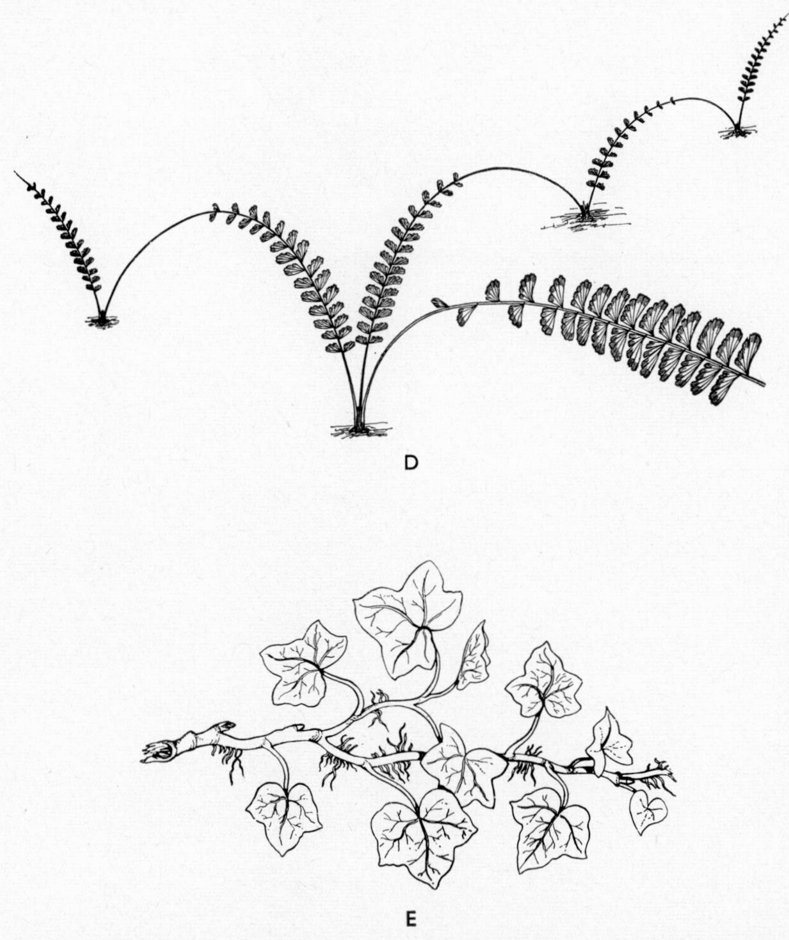


FIG. 22.—Various adaptations for climbing, twining, scrambling, and running. A (× ⅓), leaf-tendrils of Common Pea (*Pisum sativum*, left) and Clematis (*Clematis* sp., right); B, branches of *Bougainvillaea* modified as spines used in scrambling (× ⅖); C, Dodder (*Cuscuta*), a parasitic twiner that sends haustoria into the host-plant (× 1); D, a 'Walking' Fern (*Adiantum caudatum*) (× ⅓); E, Ivy (*Hedera*), showing climbing roots (× ⅓).

in response to the particular conditions under which it has grown. Thus in the latter instance we may even get large but thin 'shade' leaves and small but thick 'sun' leaves on the selfsame branch of a tree, whereas no matter under what conditions most compact desert plants are grown they will not become tall and lax, the characteristic of compactness being in such instances usually hereditary

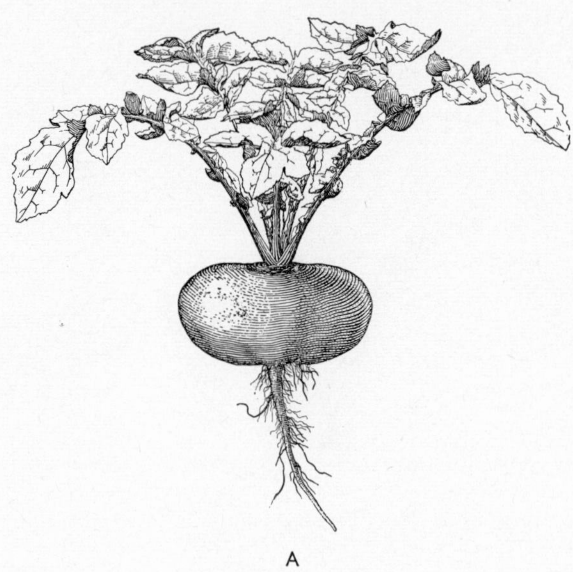

A

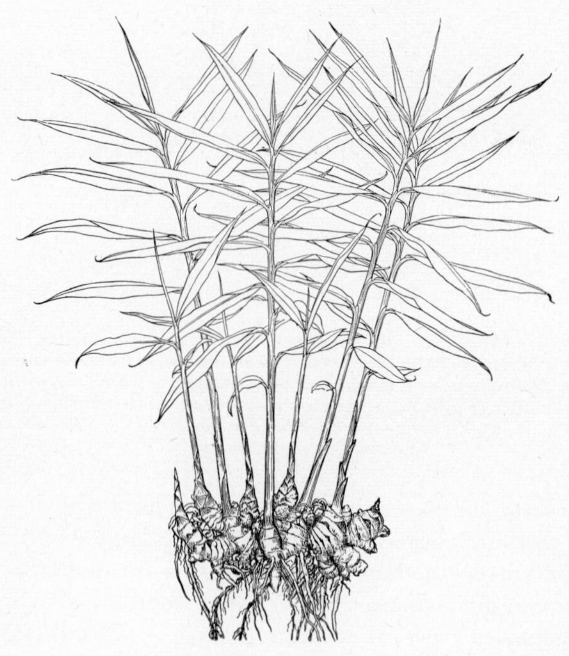

B

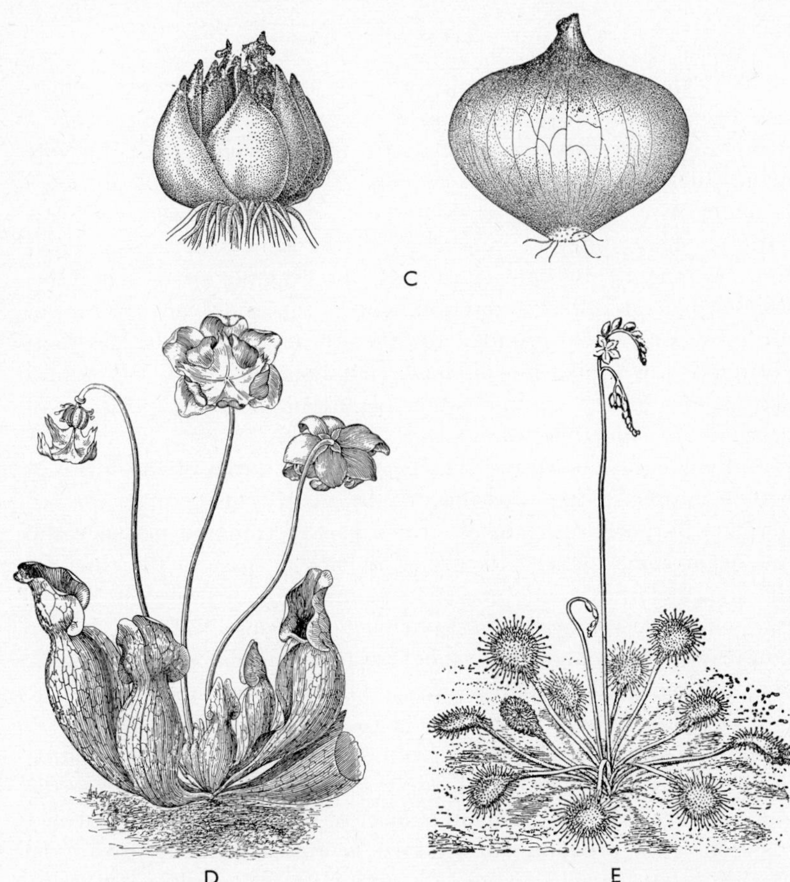


Fig. 23.—Modifications for storing food or catching insects. A, expanded storage-root of Turnip (*Brassica campestris*) ($\times \frac{1}{3}$); B, Ginger (*Zingiber*) plant with enlarged storage rhizomes ($\times \frac{1}{6}$); C, bulbs of Lily (*Lilium* sp., left) and Onion (*Allium cepa*, right) ($\times \frac{3}{4}$); D, *Sarracenia*, a Pitcher-plant, showing flowers and pitcher leaves ($\times \frac{1}{4}$); E, Sundew (*Drosera*), a carnivorous plant ($\times \frac{1}{2}$).

and ‘ fixed ’ through long evolutionary history.[1] Of such a deep-seated and lasting nature are most of the vegetative and reproductive features which go to make up a plant species, giving it its special form or morphology. By this we classify it as part of a systematic hierarchy in the manner explained at the beginning of Chapter II.

[1] Often the same character-manifestation is hereditary in one group of plants and due to direct environmental impress in another—an example of the latter being the compact form of many alpine plants as opposed to those characteristic of deserts. In such instances special cultivation may be necessary to determine to which category a feature belongs.

## Classification by Life-forms

The 'life-form' or 'growth-form' of a plant is the form which its vegetative body produces as a result of all the life-processes, including those that are affected by the environment within the plant's life-time and are not heritable. Although a plant's life-form is among its most striking characteristics, it may be of a rather fickle nature. Thus different individuals of the same species can sometimes belong to different life-forms, for example when they have been grown in different environments; for under any particular life-form are merely grouped together those plants which, in their entirety, show similar morphological adjustments. Life-forms may accordingly give a fair indication of environmental impress, or at least tell us something about local conditions.

Although the description of vegetation in terms of life-forms is widely imprecise, and classification by them is inadequate for our ultimate purpose, nevertheless it is a part of common parlance and can be of some value. Its use goes back at least to the times of the ancient Greeks, who classified plants into trees, shrubs, herbs, etc., which are among the most obviously differing life-forms. Even nowadays to the general geographer or other non-biologist the species, etc., making up plant communities are often less significant than the prevalent life-forms. These last may yet be of importance in two allied biological fields, namely, plant sociology, where consideration of life-forms may help in the description of the structure of the communities that are the main subject of study, and ecology, where mention of the predominant life-form is often sufficient to give some idea of the local environment.

In spite of the limitations mentioned above, there is one particular system of life-forms which as plant geographers we may find useful, although it suffers from rather difficult Greek terminology. As originally elaborated by the late Professor C. Raunkiaer of Denmark and usefully modified by, among others, Dr. J. Braun-Blanquet of Montpellier, this system lays stress primarily on the adjustment of the plant to the unfavourable season, and particularly employs the position of the perennating[1] buds relative to the soil surface in attempting to classify together plants of similar habit. The result is a series of life-forms that is especially interesting to the more statistically minded among us, the main categories of which are as follows:

[1] Perennation is the act of tiding over an unfavourable period, such as a cold winter or a dry summer.

(*a*) *Phanerophytes* (tall aerial plants). Perennials, mostly trees or shrubs, with their renewal buds on shoots at least 25 cm. (about 10 inches) above the surface of the ground, and hence exposed to unfavourable weather. Phanerophytes are especially numerous in moist areas of the tropics and subtropics, where they tend to predominate in the matter of numbers of species as well as individuals. Elsewhere the species are usually few, even if the numbers of individuals are great and their dominance is overwhelming.

(*b*) *Chamaephytes* (surface plants). Perennial herbs and some undershrubs with renewal buds between ground-level and a height of 25 cm.—hence usually enjoying only such protection as may be afforded by the plant itself or by snow, and consequently plentiful in boreal and alpine regions.

(*c*) *Hemicryptophytes* (half-earth plants). These have perennial shoots and buds at ground-level or within the surface layer of soil, etc., and hence protected by the habitat. Such plants are particularly preponderant in high alpine and arctic regions but are also plentiful in the temperate zone.

(*d*) *Geophytes* (earth plants). These have the perennating organs (such as bulbs, tubers, or rhizomes) well buried in the soil and therefore not exposed in unfavourable seasons. They tend to be commonest in temperate regions but also persist in fair numbers farther north and south.

(*e*) *Hydrophytes* (water plants). These include all water plants, whether anchored or not, apart from microscopic free-floating or swimming types which form the main basis of the separate category known as ' plankton '. This group of hydrophytes tends to cut across the other main ones and so is often omitted from ' spectra ' (*see* pp. 94–5).

(*f*) *Therophytes* (annuals). Plants which complete their life-cycle, from germination to ripe seed, within a single limited vegetative period, surviving the unfavourable times as seeds, spores, or other special (usually resistant) reproductive bodies. They are especially abundant in deserts where the unfavourable period may be particularly severe and prolonged, but are largely lacking in arctic regions where the growing-season is too short or the warmth is insufficient to allow them to complete development before winter comes again.

Examples of (*b*), (*c*), (*d*) and (*f*) are illustrated in Fig. 24. Almost all trees and tall shrubs belong to (*a*), while examples of (*e*) were illustrated in Fig. 21.

Further categories may, if desired, be added to the above system —such as *epiphytes* growing on trees etc. Moreover, refinements may be used such as the subdivision of phanerophytes into *nanophanerophytes* (shrubs) in which the renewal buds lie less than 2 metres above ground, *microphanerophytes* (small trees) in which they lie at a height of from 2 to 8 metres, the taller *mesophanerophytes* (8–30 metres), and the still taller *megaphanerophytes* (above 30 metres); also *phanerophyta scandentia* (lianes), which are woody climbing plants whose renewal buds pass the unfavourable season high above the ground.

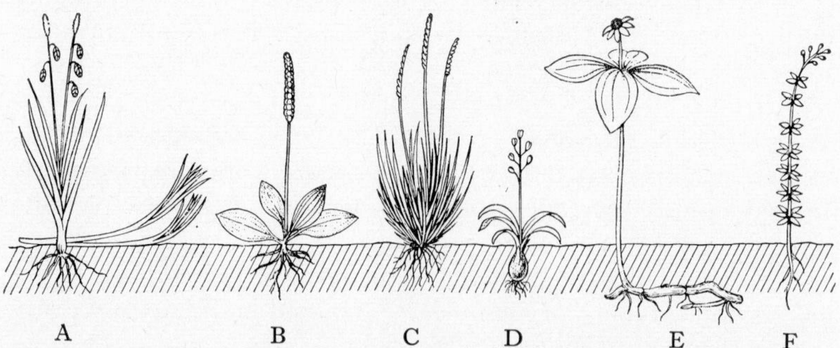


FIG. 24.—Diagrams illustrating some Raunkiaer life-forms. A, a creeping chamaephyte; B, a rosette hemicryptophyte; C, a tufted hemicryptophyte; D, a bulb geophyte; E, a rhizome geophyte; F, a therophyte. (After Braun-Blanquet.)

The values of this system are relative, its applications limited. Being based on wide life-form categories, it certainly cannot take the place of detailed description of vegetation including naming of the main species concerned, which alone will indicate to the qualified reader the precise nature of each named species and, through these, reveal much concerning the community itself. Its use is, moreover, limited in arctic and alpine regions where the success of a particular plant in life is apt to depend not so much on its adaptation to a rigorous winter as on its adjustment to the very short and cool summer. Nevertheless, in the hands of the student who is statistically but perhaps not taxonomically minded and trained, not wanting or able to name specifically the plants concerned, this system is useful in giving a fair analysis of the components of a community or flora in terms of the representation of each life-form.

Such an analysis is usually expressed as a ' biological spectrum ', indicating the percentage of the total flora belonging to each of the life-forms involved. Considering only vascular plants and excluding hydrophytes, examples from areas in the main climatic belts whose land-vegetation is described in Chapters XII–XIV are as follows, in round figures:

(i) *Temperate*—phanerophytes 15, chamaephytes 2, hemicryptophytes 49, geophytes 22, therophytes 12;

(ii) *Arctic*—phanerophytes 1, chamaephytes 22, hemicryptophytes 61, geophytes 15, therophytes 1;

(iii) *Tropical* (moist)—phanerophytes 61, chamaephytes 6, hemicryptophytes 12, geophytes 5, therophytes 16;

(iv) *Tropical* (arid)—phanerophytes 9, chamaephytes 14, hemicryptophytes 19, geophytes 8, therophytes 50.

With the above it is interesting to compare the 'normal' spectrum for the world as a whole, which is claimed to be: phanerophytes 46, chamaephytes 9, hemicryptophytes 26, geophytes 6, therophytes 13.

Altogether it may be concluded that such life-form spectra can give a useful if generalized impression of the biological effects of climatic features and hence help characterize the various phytogeographical regions. But dealing as they do with wide categories, and with flora rather than vegetation (that is, with the different *kinds* of plants inhabiting an area, regardless of their abundance and relative importance), they are no adequate substitute for more thorough description with structural details, precise naming, and, wherever possible, good illustration. Thus, for example, a small group of species or even a single species may dominate and largely characterize a plant community or sometimes a whole region, and yet scarcely 'tell' in the spectrum. This, however, is an objection to the spectrum method of counting species rather than to the life-form classification itself.

## Further Consideration

The principles of plant physiology can readily be acquired from W. O. James's *An Introduction to Plant Physiology*, fifth edition (Clarendon Press, Oxford, viii + 303, 1955) or, in more detail, from such a text as B. S. Meyer & D. B. Anderson's *Plant Physiology*, second edition (Van Nostrand, New York etc., pp. viii + 784, 1952).

More details and examples of structural 'adaptations' that apparently enable plants to maintain or extend their geographical ranges, may be gained from almost any good modern work on structural botany, or from G. Haberlandt's classic *Physiological Plant Anatomy*, translated by M. Drummond (Macmillan, London, pp. xv + 777, 1914, reprinted 1928).

The system of life-forms outlined above is clearly elaborated in Chapter XII of J. Braun-Blanquet's *Plant Sociology* (McGraw-Hill, New York & London, pp. xviii + 439, 1932); there are some refinements in the second German edition, *Pflanzensoziologie: Grundzüge der Vegetationskunde* (Springer, Wien, pp. xi + 631, 1951). However, for a detailed account of the development and application of this system, the interested student should refer to the volume of collected papers of the late C. Raunkiaer, entitled *The Life Forms of Plants and Statistical Plant Geography* (Clarendon Press, Oxford, pp. xvi + 632, 1934). A briefer account is given in the same author's *Plant Life Forms*, translated by H. Gilbert-Carter (Clarendon Press, Oxford, pp. vii + 104, 1937).

Any walk in the country, or even in a garden or public park, with due contemplation of the seemingly endless variety of plants encountered—the Lichens or green powdery algal cells on the bark of many trees are just as truly plants as the giants on which they grow—should convince even the most sceptical layman of the need for classification. The more intelligent and interested will almost inevitably find themselves comparing similar plants and mentally putting them into groups, which may be either systematic or life-form ones. It may be noted in the course of such observations that the life-forms chiefly give some indication of the physiognomy of the vegetation. This is largely dependent on local environmental conditions and may look alike even where quite different kinds of plants are involved. On the other hand, systematic relationships (*e.g.* following the lines indicated in Chapter II) depend also considerably on past and present geographical connections and barriers, so that only an account including floristic determinations and details of frequency etc. can give the more complete picture for which we strive.

## Chapter IV

# DISPERSAL AND MIGRATION: AIDS AND BARRIERS

Having stated our objectives and familiarized ourselves with the main groups of plants, we must consider the methods by which different plants increase their areas, at least potentially, by special 'adaptations' of the reproductive bodies and by seizing such opportunities for their transport as may be offered. These adaptations are of the nature of beneficial structural modifications (*see* Chapter III). The areas attained are the mainstay of our plant geographical studies, and although they are liable to be profoundly affected by past history (as we shall see in the next two chapters) and are further greatly limited by the physiology of the plants themselves (as we have already seen in Chapter III), these areas must to a large extent be a function of the plants' own aptitudes. In the final analysis, areal spreading is often limited by the ecological reactions of the plant to a new environment which may, for example, be too cold or too dry for its successful establishment. Such reactions are primarily physiological, and, though their outcome is often capable of modification, as we have already seen, they commonly determine the potential or ultimate area which a species can occupy when there is fully effective dispersal. The actual areas within the physiologically circumscribed potential ones are largely determined by barriers to successful migration.

It should be noted that dispersal and migration, although closely connected, are different activities. Dispersal merely involves dissemination from the parent and distribution (in the dynamic sense) to a new spot, whereas migration implies also successful growth and establishment (ecesis). Thus dispersal is a necessary forerunner of migration, which is actually accomplished only on establishment in a new place. In nature only a small proportion of the plant bodies which become dispersed, and which may conveniently be termed disseminules (diaspores), actually become established and effect migration. Not only do many of them die prematurely or fall on 'barren ground', or come to rest where they cannot even start a new life, or fail to survive the struggle with stronger competitors, but the ecological conditions and physiological reactions have to lie within often narrow limits for ultimate success. In any case, therefore, the vast majority of disseminules are doomed.

These disseminules, the actual bodies moved, are most often reproductive structures such as spores, seeds, or fruits. In numerous instances, however, they are special structures of a vegetative nature, or unmodified parts of plants, whole plants, or even groups of plants—though in the last instance usually effective only by chance. An example of a whole plant being transported was the Water-hyacinth mentioned in the last chapter and shown in Fig. 21, B.

Often the same plant species or individual will produce more than one type of disseminule, thereby increasing its chances of effective migration. Thus, whereas the majority of our familiar north-temperate forest trees, such as Oaks and Spruces, normally reproduce by seed, they may also do so by means of suckering, layering, or other vegetative activity. Moreover, many of the plants that are most successful in colonizing vast areas, resort to more than one means of dispersal. Thus the Common Reed (*Phragmites communis* agg.), which is often claimed to be the most widely distributed vascular plant species in the world, has the multiple advantages of wind-dispersed, plumed fruits, water-dispersed, buoyant rhizomes, and long runners—besides considerable variability in form, and an ability to occupy a wide range of moist to aquatic habitats. These it colonizes so aggressively and holds so strongly that its 'beds' form a formidable barrier against immigration by other plants. On the other hand, one of the numerous unsolved problems of plant geography is that of why many plants with seemingly excellent advantages in dispersal are not widely distributed. Yet another major question is posed by the number of groups and even species that are widespread without seeming to have any adequate means of dispersal. That precisely the same type of plant should have evolved separately in several different places is almost unthinkable to most students, and so it is widely assumed that the areas currently occupied by particular plants are due to dispersal and effective migration. Now that we have explained the distinction between these terms, they need not henceforth be separated. Rather will we refer to dispersal when the question of establishment can be ignored, and to migration when such establishment is to be emphasized.

## Wind Dispersal

A walk in the woods and fields of a north-temperate region on a boisterous autumn day should convince any sceptic that air currents of one kind or another are important in the dispersal of many different plants. Not only do winds blow leaves, and sometimes small branches, about—and with them adhering parasites or saprophytes, for example—but they obviously transport some seeds and fruits for considerable distances. The more efficiently adapted of these, whose bodies are so light or whose ‘ form-resistance ’ is such that they sink only slowly in still air and float almost indefinitely in a light breeze, may be transported far from the parent. This undoubtedly happens with such plumed seeds as those of Milkweeds (*Asclepias* spp.) and Fireweed (*Epilobium angustifolium* agg.), or with such ‘ parachute ’ fruits as those of Dandelions (*Taraxacum* spp.) and many other members of the Daisy family (Compositae).

Even more effective is the dispersal by air currents—including upward eddies that carry them into the upper atmosphere—of microscopic spores, especially of Fungi and Bacteria. Such dispersal may take place over distances that in numerous instances have been proved to run into many hundreds of miles. The present writer has studied this subject for years and is convinced that these smaller ‘ botanical particles ’ or ‘ spora ’ can be (and often are) carried thousands of miles in the atmosphere, frequently without losing their power to resume active life on regaining suitable conditions. Thus he has trapped some spora in the immediate vicinity of the North Pole under both winter and summer conditions, as well as elsewhere at vast distances from their nearest conceivable point of origin.

Quite apart from disseminules which are specially modified for transportation by winds, and others which are so minute that they need not be so modified to be transported, there are many recorded instances of large and heavy bodies being blown for considerable distances by hurricanes, etc., on special occasions. After the devastating tornado in and around Worcester, Massachusetts, in June, 1953, abundant shingles and often bulkier roofing materials and sizeable living branches of trees were to be seen littering the ground fully 20 miles nearer the coast than the closest point at which the ‘ twister ’ had struck. There are also records of windfalls of uprooted plants scattered over wide areas. It need scarcely be remarked that, as successful transportation and growth of a single plant or disseminule is sufficient for its establishment in a new region, even extremely rare occurrences may be important and involve quite unexpected species and circumstances. Instances in point include exceptional winds in various regions, and the blowing of seeds, fruits, or whole plants over the ice or compacted snow in arctic regions in winter. Not only may such blowing over ice be effective from time to time, in the case of higher plants, but, more often as they tend to remain longer alive, it may also result in the dispersal of parasitic or saprophytic Fungi, etc., growing upon or within the bodies of these higher plants. When we recall that, not very many thousands of years ago, ice covered vast tracts of what are now among the most populous parts of the northern hemisphere, as well as, doubtless, the adjacent seas, we can imagine that such dispersal may have been of great importance in the migrational history of plants in areas far south of the present-day Arctic.

It is instructive to consider briefly the main organs or methods of wind-dispersal, and particularly those plant bodies which are especially modified for the purpose. For this, there should be recalled the distinction between seeds and fruits which was explained on page 69, and the very different origin and nature of spores in different cases.

(*a*) Spores. These, as we saw in Chapter II, are the main disseminules of most of the groups of plants up to and including the Ferns, and are often produced in fantastically great numbers. Thus a single specimen of the Pasture Mushroom (*Agaricus* (*Psalliota*) *campestris*) has been estimated to produce 1,800,000,000 spores, while a large specimen of the Shaggy-mane Mushroom (*Coprinus comatus*) may produce 5,240,000,000 spores, and some Puffballs many times that number! Although extremely variable in size and form, spores are commonly minute and easily blown about by the wind—being frequently borne by upward air-eddies rising from warm plains and carried into the upper atmosphere where they may be transported vast distances. Indeed, like volcanic dust, they are probably sometimes blown around the world without settling to earth. Bacterial and some other minute cells may belong to the same category as spores in the matter of size and aerial buoyancy. The spores are often extremely resistant to low temperatures and desiccation which in fact appear to prolong their life, so that many caught in the most remote situations are alive, able to germinate when given suitable conditions, and, as we say, 'viable'. They may live for many years and, apparently, often withstand the radiation effects of high altitudes. According to Ridley, whose monumental work on plant dispersal is cited at the end of this chapter, 'There is no part of the world where some are not present, and there appears to be a constant rain of the more minute kinds falling everywhere.' With little doubt this easy wind-dispersal of many of the Bacteria, Fungi, and other so-called spore-plants is the primary reason for their extremely widespread distribution; a secondary reason is their often wide tolerance of conditions and modest requirements for life.

(*b*) Dust seeds (and minute fruits). The seeds of many plants, such as the members of the Orchid family (Orchidaceae), and the one-seeded fruits (for example) of some of the mainly tropical parasitic family Balanophoraceae, are also minute and extremely light, as well as sometimes winged, and so tend to be blown away and about in much the same manner as spores.

(*c*) Plumed seeds. These usually bear a light tuft of silky hairs at one end and are liberated from a capsular fruit which, on splitting, only releases them gradually, often one by one. The plants involved are usually herbs or climbers, good examples being species of Willow-herb (*Epilobium*) and Milkweed (*Asclepias*), and they generally occur in open situations, in or from which they can travel for hundreds of miles.

(*d*) Plumed fruits. These include the familiar 'parachutes' of Dandelions (*Taraxacum* spp.), the long feathery fruits of species of Avens (*Geum*), and the silky-haired ones of Cotton-grasses (*Eriophorum* spp.). Their appendages cause them to be detached by the wind and floated away, often for very considerable distances. The plants concerned are usually herbaceous, and include many Grasses. An extreme case is that of some disseminules of Grasses which have been trapped in the air several thousands of feet above the ground, and in view of the highly fortuitous nature of such observation it would seem likely that they may reach the upper air currents quite frequently.

(*e*) Winged seeds. In these it is usually a thin portion of the seed-coat which forms a wing that catches in the wind when they are liberated, often in considerable numbers, *e.g.* by splitting of the containing fruit-wall. They chiefly occur on trees, shrubs, and lianes (woody climbers), and so are liberated some distance above the ground—which is just as well, for their dispersal mechanism tends to be much less efficient than those of the categories mentioned above. Good examples are afforded by members of the *Bignonia* family (Bignoniaceae), and by Pines and Spruces and many other Conifers.

(*f*) Winged fruits. Again chiefly occurring on trees and shrubs, these are so modified as to cause the fruit, on detachment by the wind, to be borne at least out of the immediate sphere of influence of the parent plant, or to trundle along as is the case with many bladder-fruits. Often the flight is a spinning one and, though spectacular, not very efficient in terms of distance. Each fruit (as in the Birches, *Betula* spp.), or half of a separating fruit (as in most Maples, *Acer* spp.), is usually one-seeded—functionally, at least.

(*g*) Long-haired seeds and fruits. These are sufficiently alike to be considered together, while also approaching (*c*) and (*d*), their main feature being that the surface is covered with long silky or woolly hairs. Such disseminules tend to be less efficient than plumed ones but are nevertheless capable of travelling for some miles. The plants, as in categories (*e*) and (*f*), are most commonly trees or shrubs. Examples of seeds of this nature are those of Cotton (*Gossypium*), Willows (*Salix* spp.), and Poplars (*Populus* spp.); and of fruits, those of some Anemones (*Anemone* spp.). That this mode of dispersal is abundantly effective, at least so far as transport of the seeds is concerned, has been frequently and strikingly demonstrated to the writer when he has looked out from his laboratory windows in the ancient Botanic Garden at Oxford and thought a snow-storm was raging, the 'flakes' being masses of hairy seeds blown from pollarded Willows mostly hundreds of yards away.

(*h*) Tumble-weeds. Such plants, or detached portions bearing the seeds, tend to roll before the wind or be blown across open country, usually scattering their seeds or fruits as they go. They are commonly short-lived herbs that branch densely and stiffly from a central stem and have a rounded form. Normally they break off easily near ground-level and have the seeds or fruits so loose that they are lost as the aerial part trundles along. Tumble-weeds occur chiefly in deserts or arid prairies or steppes. Examples include the so-called Russian-thistle (*Salsola pestifer*) in North America and *Eryngium* sp. on the northern border of the Sahara in Egypt (R. W. Haines *voce*). In less ideally displayed form, all manner of plants or parts of plants can, in special circumstances, act fortuitously as tumble-weeds—including the so-called Rose of Jericho (*Anastatica hierochuntina*), and some Lichens and Mosses in the Arctic.

(*i*) Other organs or methods. These include pieces of such

epiphytes (plants growing on other plants) as Spanish-moss (*Tillandsia usneoides*) which get blown to new situations on the trees on which they grow, often abundantly ; seeds which fortuitously stick to or get curled up in dead leaves and are transported with them for considerable distances ; small seeds or fruits which adhere to sticky stalks (for example of Catch-flies, *Lychnis* spp.) that are blown about after detachment ; and soredia of Lichens as well as bulbils, for example of such Grasses as *Poa alpina*, that may be usefully scattered by the wind.

(*j*) Jactitation. This is the slinging of seeds out of fruits such as the capsules of Poppies (*Papaver* spp.) or Mulleins (*Verbascum* spp.), which are held aloft on long stalks that are liable to be bent before the wind or jolted by passing animals—often springing back subsequently to jerk out some more of the contents in the opposite direction. Such a ' censer mechanism ' is commonly feeble, barely (or even not at all) removing the seed from the immediate sphere of influence of the parent ; but given the good fortune of a strong wind to carry the seed farther, or a favourable slope down which it can bounce and roll, jactitation may occasionally be quite effective.

Fig. 25 shows a wide range of wind-dispersed disseminules.

Here it seems reasonable to suggest that the primary objective of a disseminule, so far as transportation is concerned, is to get away from the immediate parental influence and possible competition of seedlings developing from its brothers, which for many small plants is effected by displacement of merely a matter of centimetres. Most dispersal is probably of this relatively minor nature, the long-distance ' saltatory ' dispersal (that may drastically extend the area and ultimately increase the importance of a race) being supposedly much rarer.

Before proceeding to the next main topic we should give some consideration to the barriers and deterrents to wind dispersal, remembering that it often includes blowing about on the surface of water whose currents may, moreover, carry originally airborne disseminules much farther. Wind dispersal operates chiefly on free, air-buoyant spores etc. in open places—so that it is not unexpected to find that in treeless, high-alpine and arctic regions an unusually large proportion of the native plants have wind-borne disseminules, whereas in dense forests and other sheltered areas wind is little effective. A great deal of wind dispersal, at least of the larger fruits and seeds, is discontinuous, bodies being blown up by a gust of wind and soon alighting to await another gust, the process in some

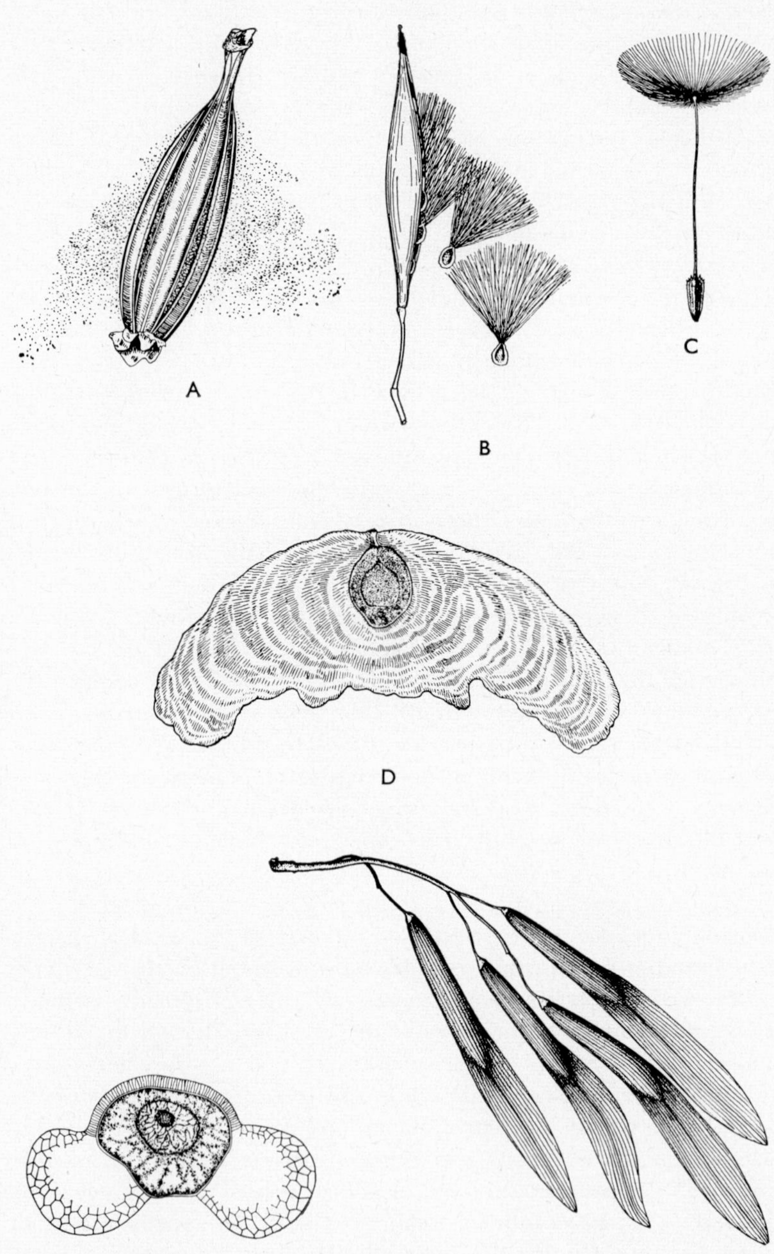
A
B
C
D
E
F

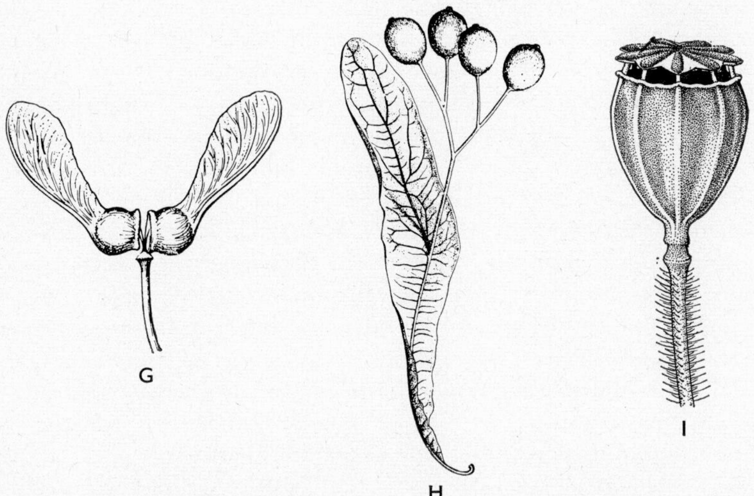


FIG. 25.—Wind-dispersal mechanisms and disseminules. A, capsule of an Orchid (*Cymbidium*), open, with minute seeds being scattered by the wind (× ½); B, fruit of Milkweed (*Asclepias*), showing liberation of the effectively plumed seeds (× ½); C, ‘ parachute ’ fruit of Dandelion (*Taraxacum*) (× 2); D, flattened seed of *Macrozanonia* with large papery wing (× $\frac{5}{12}$); E, pollen grain of a Pine (*Pinus*), with inflated, bladder-like ‘ wings ’ making it buoyant in air (× 390); F, flattened fruits of an Ash (*Fraxinus*) (× 1⅙); G, fruit of Maple (*Acer*) with flattened wings (× 1); H, fruit of Linden (Lime-tree, *Tilia*), adapted for wind dispersal by being attached to a specialized leaf (bract) (× ⅔); I, capsule of Poppy (*Papaver*), from which the seeds are liberated only on violent shaking (× 2½).

instances being repeated again and again. When such bodies alight on even small tracts of water, these are apt to constitute insuperable barriers to disseminules which cannot float for a protracted period. Thus it has been observed that plants depending on winged seeds or fruits for their dispersal are rare on oceanic islands. Dense forests may have an effect similar to oceans, though of a less finite nature. However, the fact that many disseminules await a particularly strong gust of wind before becoming detached from the parent, is obviously advantageous in that such stronger winds are the more likely to carry them afar.

Mountain ranges also prove a barrier in many instances—though the lighter disseminules are easily blown up and over them—as, to a lesser degree, do cliffs, walls, and fences. This is evidenced by the fact that beneath such obstacles a wide range of wind-borne seeds and fruits are often to be found germinating, having been stopped in their flight and fallen down. Pits and other depressions have much the same effect in providing a barrier against the heavier disseminules. The lightest and most effective of these bodies, on the other hand, come to grief chiefly through the action of moisture which clogs their 'flying apparatus', or condenses on them and weighs them down. In this connection rain is extraordinarily effective in removing, often during a single shower, practically all of even the lightest spores, pollen grains, etc., from the atmosphere through which it falls. For this reason, and because the strongest and most lasting winds are chiefly at high altitudes, it is mainly those botanical particles which reach the upper air which travel really great distances. The fact that many do so appears to be primarily due to the upward air currents resultant on the warming of dark land-surfaces by radiant energy absorbed from sunlight. Finally, for effective migration the plant has to become established, and to that requisite any lack of suitable climatic or edaphic or other conditions constitutes an insuperable barrier.

## Dispersal by Water and Ice

The earliest forms of plant life were probably aquatic and water-dispersed, and water still plays a very important part in the dispersal of plants—particularly of those that live in or near it. But although modifications that appear to be for water dispersal are found in a wide variety of land plants, they are not so striking, or so widely necessary, as those for wind dispersal. For practically any light disseminule may be effectively dispersed by water up to the limit of its ability to float and retain the power of germination—that is, until it becomes waterlogged and sinks or decays, or until it is killed, or, having begun to germinate, has failed to reach a suitable habitat. Hence the main requirements for water dispersal are sufficient buoyancy and impermeability, their degree of development in a particular disseminule being often the most important factor determining its success.

Among Algae and many higher plants (such as the Canadian Water-weed, *Elodea canadensis*) which normally live submerged in water, there is no need for impermeability: the plant or special disseminule merely drifts with any water current, sometimes attached to floating logs, etc. Such drifting appears to be the main mode of distribution of most seaweeds. Free-floating plants such as Duckweeds (*Lemna* spp.) or Water Crowfoots are widely dispersed as they float on the surface of the water, though they may sink to the bottom to perennate. A fine tropical example is the Water-hyacinth (*Eichhornia crassipes*), whose dilated leaf-stalks act as floats, as illustrated in Fig. 21, B. It is not, however, by any means necessary to float on or drift in the body of water to be water-dispersed. Thus some seeds or fruits sink at first but rise to the surface on germination, to drift until they become stranded—perhaps under conditions ideal for further growth—while many are carried short distances by rainwash or sudden rushes of water over the ground or frozen surface, for example during snow-melt in alpine and arctic regions. Severe floods may dislodge and transport whole trees, as well as innumerable seeds and fruits that are deposited on the wet flood-plain when the water ultimately recedes. Also apt to transport living materials are islands of drifting branches etc., icebergs, drifting ice-floes, and the still larger and more lasting ice-islands. These are largely fortuitous and probably capable of involving almost any category of plant from time to time, whereas the regularly water-dispersed plants normally live in or near the water and are modified accordingly.

The main modes of water dispersal may now be considered:

(*a*) Sea currents. These can cause very effective long-distance dispersal of suitably modified disseminules, in some known cases for over 1,000 miles. For this the body must normally be able to float for a long time without becoming waterlogged and must also belong to a littoral species that can establish itself under saline conditions on a sandy, muddy, or other sea-shore. Coconuts are so dispersed, even if there is some doubt as to whether actual migration is thereby effected; and among familiar plants of north-temperate and boreal shores that evidently migrate in this manner may be mentioned the Oysterleaf (*Mertensia maritima* agg.) and Sea-beach Sandwort (*Arenaria* (*Honckenya*) *peploides* agg.). Excellent tropical examples are afforded by the characteristic dominants of mangrove swamps, such as species of *Rhizophora* and *Avicennia*, the seedlings of which float widely. Also normally dispersed by sea currents in the manner of seaweeds are further herbaceous maritime Angiosperms—most often as whole plants, parts of plants, or asexual propagules. On the other hand, the vast numbers of seeds and fruits of freshwater and normal land plants, and of course individuals themselves, that are blown into the sea or carried thereto by rivers, in general perish.

(*b*) Rivers and streams. These commonly transport fruits, seeds, and other parts of plants—sometimes as far as from their sources right down to the sea. In other cases they may help with the seeding of inundated areas. Such dispersal is, however, virtually limited to the direction of the current and to the particular land-mass concerned, the disseminules of other than marine and strand plants rarely surviving protracted flotation in the ocean. Thus all manner of seeds, fruits, and living fragments of aquatic or river-bank plants are to be seen among the ' flotsam ' of debris floating downstream, often to be left stranded in situations suitable for growth and establishment, while in tidal estuaries migration is often away from the mouth of a river, aided by tides which run upstream as well as down. The ebb of a high tide where the water is brimming widely is particularly effective in the deposition of floating materials. Examples of flowering plants regularly dispersed by freshwater streams are many of the Pondweeds (*Potamogeton* spp.), whose small fruits in some instances can float for months on end, and the Yellow Water-lily (*Nuphar lutea*), the pulpy fruit of which floats for a few days before disintegrating and releasing the seeds, which sink and later germinate. An example of a species whose seeds, as such, are commonly distributed by water, is the Summer Snowflake (*Leucojum aestivum*). Casually, almost any plant or its disseminules may be transported downstream by flotation, striking examples being the alpine species that are often to be found in open streamside habitats in the lowlands. Familiar instances in the boreal regions are such ' open-soil ' types as Mountain Sorrel (*Oxyria digyna*), Moss Campion (*Silene acaulis* agg.), and various Saxifrages.

(*c*) Rainwash, floods, and lakes. Rain not only splashes out the seeds or spores from open organs but, when forming a wash, may carry them much farther than other agencies commonly do—especially when it develops into a flush or extensive run-off, perhaps in time to form a rivulet or even to join a major stream. A considerable run-off may be noted in boreal regions when the snow melts in spring but the ground remains frozen and impervious. Often it is not necessary that disseminules, in order to be washed away, should be able to float, though to reap the benefit of wider dispersal by ordinary floods they should do so, as of course they must normally do to be blown about on lakes. Almost any plant or part of a plant may in certain circumstances be dispersed by drastic floods, involving as they do the uprooting of trees and the carriage of all manner of debris, sometimes for considerable distances—perhaps to be deposited in a silty flood-plain well suited to the establishment of migrant plants. In lakes the methods and plants involved are in general similar to those in streams, but there is more limitation of effective dispersal to aquatic and semi-aquatic types, and the distances of dispersal are usually small. Most often, partially corky or other air-containing tissues cause the body involved to float, or buoyant vegetative parts are detached by feeding Mammals or wildfowl.

Fig. 26 shows a range of water-dispersed bodies.

(*d*) Icebergs, ice-floes, etc. The ' rafting ' of all manner of material, including living plants and their disseminules, after blowing, falling, or spring-time washing on to fast-ice near the shore or on to glaciers which later ' calve ' to form icebergs, has been widely recognized in arctic and subarctic regions. There can be no doubt that by this means much material is transported out to sea and often far away before the ice melts and releases it, though it seems unlikely that the disseminules of land plants find their way back to suitable habitats at all frequently. Probably more important, and certainly more frequent, is the dispersal of Diatoms, particularly, which grow upon the ice-floes and may in time travel hundreds or even thousands of miles with them, or of such strand-plants as Creeping Alkali-grass (*Puccinellia phryganodes* agg.) which are ' picked up ' after being frozen solid in ice that forms about the shores on which they grow. It may be presumed that these occurrences were more widespread during the Ice Ages, though there are instances occurring even well south nowadays—*e.g.* in the estuaries of the Atlantic seaboard of the United States. Ice floating down rivers or blown about lakes may also be of significance in carrying disseminules that do not float. The present writer has investigated the plant materials collected on a large ice-island in the vicinity of the North Pole, that had drifted many hundreds of miles from the point where they were washed or blown down from the land on which they grew. Almost all of these materials were dead, but those collected when the ice-island had drifted at the very least 3,000 miles, and quite possibly several times that distance, included an extensive though thin tussock of the Moss *Hygrohypnum polare* which was found to be still alive.

Charles Darwin, in *The Origin of Species* (6th edn., 1873, p. 326), after noting that the natives of the coral islands in the Pacific procure stones for their tools solely from the roots of drifted trees, remarked that these roots also frequently enclose small parcels of earth ' so perfectly that not a particle could be washed away during the longest transport : out of one small portion of earth thus *completely* enclosed by the roots of an oak about 50 years old, three dicotyledonous plants

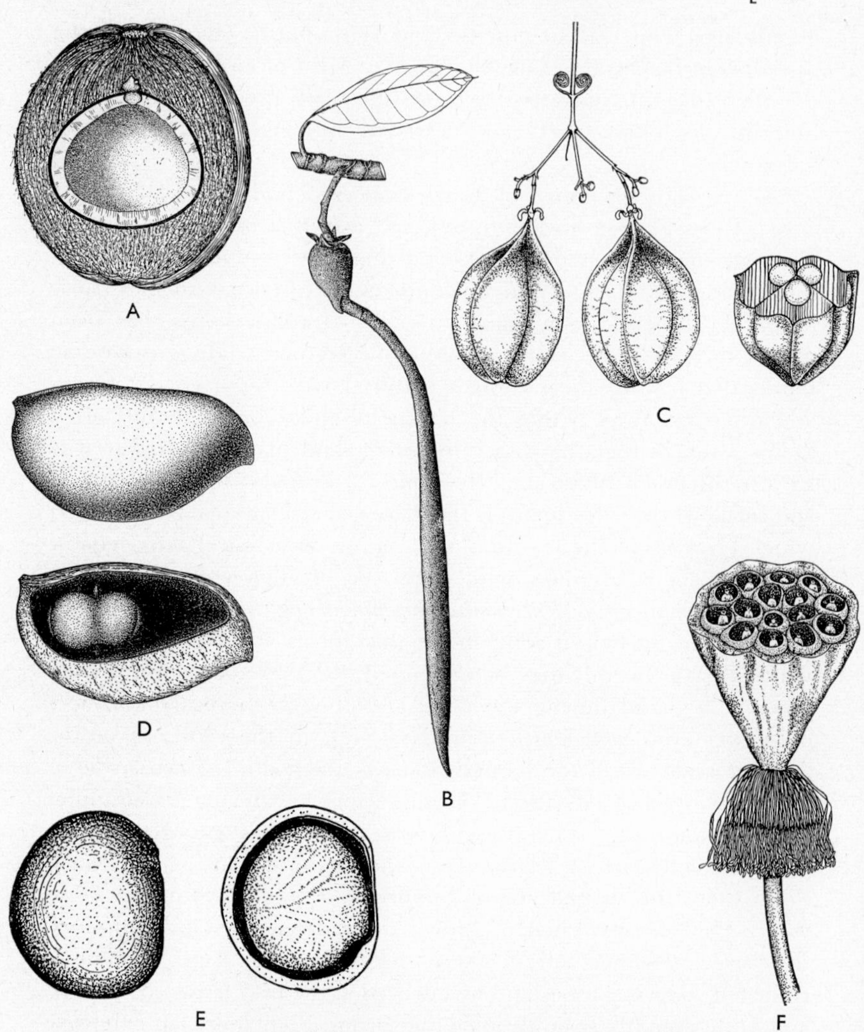


Fig. 26.—Water-dispersed fruits and other bodies. A, sectional view of fruit of Coconut (*Cocos nucifera*) showing the thick fibrous outer husk which encloses much air and enables it to float protractedly ($\times \frac{2}{15}$); B, germinating seedling of a Mangrove (*Rhizophora*) projecting from a fruit that is still attached to the tree (many such seedlings on detachment can float in the sea for weeks on end) ($\times \frac{1}{3}$); C, inflated capsules of *Cardiospermum*, the one on the right having been cut through to show the contained seeds (such fruits may be blown about as well as float) ($\times \frac{2}{3}$); D, fruit of *Heritiera littoralis*, adapted for water dispersal by its thick fibrous husk enclosing an air-cavity (seen in the half-specimen below) ($\times \frac{1}{2}$); E, seeds of *Macuna gigantea*, adapted for water dispersal by having an impervious coat and contained air-cavity surrounding the embryo (seen in the half-specimen on right) ($\times$ 1); F, fruits of Lotus (*Nelumbo nucifera*), embedded in top of enlarged receptacle (both fruits and receptacle are buoyant) ($\times \frac{1}{2}$).

germinated : I am certain of the accuracy of this observation. Again, I can show that the carcases of birds, when floating on the sea, sometimes escape being immediately devoured : and many kinds of seeds in the crops of floating birds long retain their vitality : peas and vetches, for instance, are killed by even a few days' immersion in sea-water ; but some taken out of the crop of a pigeon, which had floated on artificial sea-water for 30 days, to my surprise nearly all germinated.' Darwin had already made a conservative estimate that the seeds of about one in every ten ' plants of a flora, after having been dried, could be floated across a space of sea 900 miles in width, and would then germinate '. Although in the light of modern knowledge this would seem a rather optimistic guess, at least so far as practical opportunities are concerned, there is no reason to doubt that odd instances of such off-chance, accidental long-distance dispersal do occur from time to time.

As for the barriers and deterrents to water- and ice-dispersal or effective migration, these obviously include any absence of water, any obstacle to its movement, or, temporarily, any freezing ' solid ' to the bottom. There also seems to be extremely little effective interchange between salt and fresh water, while a wide ocean or even lake may constitute a barrier to disseminules which cannot float and live long enough to cross it ; so may, in addition, a different climate which proves unsuitable for the establishment of a transported plant.

## Dispersal by Animals (Apart from Man)

With their obvious mobility and life among plants on which they are largely dependent for food and in other ways, many animals are important agents of dispersal. Although there are numerous refinements in the method of carriage of the disseminules, there are two main categories—those that are carried externally, by adhesion to the surface of the animal's body (the so-called ' ectozoic ' or ' epizoic ' form of transportation), and those that are carried internally, after swallowing (' endozoic ' transportation). For this latter type of dispersal the seed, fruit, or other disseminule (or container of disseminules) is commonly modified by being attractive in appearance and particularly as food, for example by its bright colour and palatable flesh. This should commonly be sweet and juicy when ripe, as in Peaches, Figs, Raspberries, and Plums. In addition, the embryo or other vital part should be protected from digestion by a resistant covering, in which case germination is often hastened by passage through an animal. For ectozoic dispersal the disseminule is adhesive sometimes by means of a sticky surface or, more often, by its possession of hooks or other devices by which it catches on to the fur, etc. Anyone who has tried to extract the fruits of Burdocks (*Arctium* spp.) or Beggar-ticks (*Bidens* spp.) from woolly garments will be aware of the effectiveness of such adhesion.

Some examples of disseminules modified for dispersal by animals are shown in Fig. 27.

In addition to such ' official ' types of dispersal there is the frequent ' pecking apart ' by birds : for example, of the seeds or fruitlets contained in Apples and Rose-hips. There is also the transport of materials for nest-building, and the still more fortuitous adhesion of disseminules to the feet, etc., of animals in mud and clay or by freezing to their fur or feathers. Thus, for example, Darwin (*op. cit.*, p. 328) mentions removing a considerable amount of clayey earth from the feet of Partridges, reporting that in one instance around the wounded leg and foot there was ' a ball of hard earth adhering . . . weighing six and a half ounces . . . but when . . . broken, watered and placed under a bell glass, no less than 82 plants sprung from it. . . . With such facts before us, can we doubt that the many birds which are annually blown by gales across great spaces of ocean, and which annually migrate—for instance, the millions of quails across the Mediterranean—must occasionally transport a few seeds embedded in dirt adhering to their feet or beaks ? ' Quite apart from this, Rabbits, etc., will often drag twigs for some distance when these are attached to their fur, and Water-fowl have frequently been observed carrying sizeable pieces of Pondweeds (*Potamogeton* spp.) on their backs or around their necks —even when in flight.

(*a*) Birds. On account of their abundance almost everywhere in the world, of the very great distances which many regularly fly, and of their consequent power to cross wide expanses of water, Birds tend to be the most important group of animals from the point of view of plant dispersal. Although it has been contended by some authors that Birds ' fly clean ' on migration, this does not seem to be always the case ; indeed, according to Ridley (*op. cit.* p. 444), it is ' strongly negatived by much evidence '. Moreover, they are apt to ' neglect their toilet ' when unwell, and similarly can have materials sticking or frozen to their beaks, feet, or feathers when flushed or

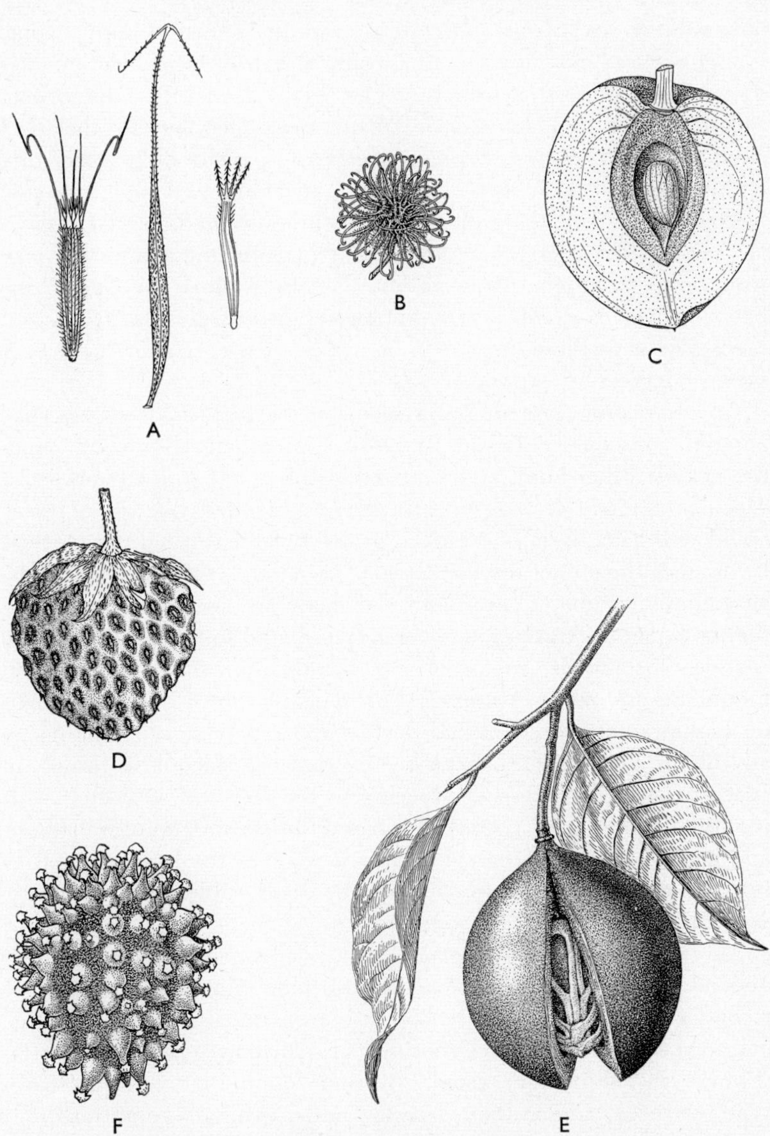


Fig. 27.—Adaptations for dispersal by animals. A, fruits (× $2\frac{1}{5}$) of *Elephantopus* (left), *Cosmos* (centre), and Beggar-ticks (*Bidens*, right), which catch on to animals; B, fruit of *Triumfetta* (× 1), with hooks causing adhesion; C, sectional view of fruit of Peach (*Prunus persica*) (× $\frac{1}{2}$), showing attractive flesh, protective 'stone', and central seed; D, fruit of Strawberry (*Fragaria*) (× 1), showing superficial resistant 'pips' enclosing embryos; E, ripe fruit of Nutmeg (*Myristica*), splitting to show seed adorned with attractive coloured 'aril' (× $\frac{1}{2}$); F, fruit of Chinese Forget-me-not (*Cynoglossum amabile*) (× 4), bearing sticky, hook-like appendages.

blown out to sea in a gale—or during repeated shorter ' hops ' which sooner or later may amount to considerable traverses. Ridley cites numerous instances of aquatics, etc., being evidently dispersed to isolated ponds and marshes by Water-fowl. Kerner (*see* the work cited at the end of this chapter), like Darwin, secured ' a sufficiently striking result ' with fertile seeds in ' the mud obtained from the beaks, feet, and feathers of swallows, snipe, wagtails, and jackdaws . . . and when it is remembered that pigeons and cranes traverse from 60 to 70 kilometres in an hour, whilst swallows and peregrine falcons cover as much as 180 kilometres, it is clear that fruits and seeds affixed to these birds may be carried in a very short time over several degrees of latitude '.

An interesting case in point seems to be furnished by the subantarctic Macquarie Island, situated approximately 650 km. from the nearest other land, and supporting thirty-five known species of vascular plants. It has recently been contended that all of these could well have been, and indeed probably were, brought in by Sea-birds since the end of the Pleistocene glaciation. Of these Sea-birds, vast numbers inhabit the island and many are known to make long flights to South America, to New Zealand, and to other subantarctic islands. Moreover, many of the habitats on the island, as on mountains and in the Arctic, are conveniently ' open ' for the growth of immigrants. Unidentified seeds, apparently not belonging to any of the local species, have been found on Macquarie Island on Black-browed Albatrosses, adhering to the feet and so coated with regurgitate that they ' could be carried almost indefinitely in flight and could withstand immersion in sea water if the bird alighted to rest, yet on landing the seeds would be easily rubbed off ' (*Ecology*, vol. 35, p. 570, October 1954).

As for endozoic transportation, the effectiveness of this will depend not only on resistance to digestion but also on times of retention within the Bird's body. Sometimes, especially after gorging, seeds may be regurgitated at a distance, without passing through the alimentary canal. Kerner found that whereas many types of Birds have in their excreta ' under ordinary conditions ' no seed capable of germination, some others may void unharmed up to 88 per cent. of the small and smooth seeds or fruits eaten, though retention in such cases is commonly for only some two or three hours. But Ridley quotes a report of Pigeons being shot at Albany, N.Y., ' with green rice in their crops, which it is thought must have been growing, a very few hours before, at a distance of 700 or 800 miles'; he also gives this distance as the one up to which he believes frugivorous Birds have visited very many islands, carrying germinable seeds in their viscera and consequently stocking these islands with plants.

Earlier, Darwin had similarly remarked (*op. cit.*, pp. 326–7):

> 'after a bird has found and devoured a large supply of food, it is positively asserted that all the grains do not pass into the gizzard for twelve or even eighteen hours. A bird in this interval might easily be blown to the distance of 500 miles, and hawks are known to look out for tired birds, and the contents of their torn crops might thus readily get scattered. Some hawks and owls bolt their prey whole, and, after an interval of from twelve to twenty hours, disgorge pellets, which, as I know from experiments made in the Zoological Gardens, include seeds capable of germination. Some seeds of the oat, wheat, millet, canary, hemp, clover, and beet germinated after having been from twelve to twenty-one hours in the stomachs of different birds of prey; and two seeds of beet grew after having been thus retained for two days and fourteen hours.'

What a distance they could have gone in a migrating Peregrine Falcon!

(*b*) Mammals. These, among animals, stand next in importance to Birds as disseminaters of plants. Except in the case of Fruit-bats, which can transport seeds, etc., over stretches of sea much as Birds do, their disseminative powers are confined to individual land-masses —apart, of course, from traversable shallow or very narrow waters or sea-ice in arctic regions (there are no land mammals in Antarctica). The Mammals are important dispersal agents of many herbaceous plants with small seeds, which they swallow with the foliage, etc., of the plants they consume, and are also the main transporters of plants with adhesive disseminules. Even though many herbivorous Mammals effect such thorough digestion that the vast majority of seeds and fruits which they take into their bodies are incapable of germination after voiding, there are nevertheless plentiful instances of disseminules being excreted unharmed, and we should always remember the odd animal that dies suddenly, or is killed and eaten by a predator. Ridley (*op. cit.*, p. 336) remarks that, in the case of stone-fruits, 'almost invariably the seeds pass through the intestines of the animal, not only unharmed, but much benefited by the treatment. Seeds so passed are known to germinate more quickly and produce stronger plants than those which have not been swallowed by bird or animal and acted on by the gastric or intestinal fluids.'

Fruits destined to have their contained seeds disseminated by Mammals tend to be less conspicuous than those primarily intended to attract Birds, *e.g.* when flying. And even as Birds will devour the attractive part of a fruit and scatter the seeds without ingestion, so will many Mammals do to large fruits. Arboreal Mammals, such as Monkeys, commonly do not eat fruits when they gather them, but quietly remove them to a distance—apparently to avoid being robbed. If they drop a fruit they do not pick it up, but go on to another. Moreover, such types as Squirrels make large winter caches that may involve extensive transportation and frequently are not eaten in the end. These and many other activities of Mammals can help plant dispersal within continental confines.

Because of their frequently furry coats, Mammals tend to be more commonly effective than Birds in the ectozoic transportation of adhesive fruits, such as those with hooks or other devices for attachment. Many fur-coated Mammals wander extensively, or travel far on migration, some even crossing wide tracts of sea-ice in the Arctic. Apart from being furnished with obviously effective hooks or spines, some seeds and fruits adhere to animals by viscid glands, gummy exudations, or owing to their wholly sticky nature, while the spikelets of many Grasses do so by jagged parts or minutely toothed awns. Many other seeds and fruits which are normally wind-dispersed, will adhere to animals by entanglement or sticking of their hairs or plumes especially when wet. There is, indeed, no lack of means or instances of such dispersal, as inspection of one's clothes at the end of an autumn walk in a temperate woodland will show. Moreover, it should be remembered that animals, like plants, are selective of habitat, and tend to keep, as Birds tend to alight, within a single habitat-range—so increasing the chances a disseminule would have of coming to rest in a place suitable for germination and successful establishment. For instance, the rocky ridges and ravines in boreal regions that are inhabited by such birds as Snow Buntings and Ptarmigan, which commonly ingest seeds and migrate from one to another such area, afford numerous habitats for open-soil Saxifrages and Sandworts which may be lacking in intermediate areas.

(*c*) Lower animals. Although most of the Reptiles of the present era are carnivorous, some feed on fruits and may disseminate them. More important in this respect are freshwater Fishes, many of which are vegetable feeders that swallow the seeds of aquatics and semi-aquatics, and some of which can migrate overland, usually through wet Grass. Of a wide range of seeds or fruits of aquatic plants, such as Bog-bean (*Menyanthes trifoliata*) and Pondweeds, that have been fed to Perch and Roach, nearly all germinated after being retained in the viscera for one to three days before being passed naturally. These fish are liable to be eaten by such predators as Fishing Eagles, Herons, and Pelicans, which, after an interval of many hours, either reject any contained seeds in pellets or pass them in excreta—often still in a viable condition, as was shown by Darwin. The same doubtless happens to many Algae, aquatic Fungi, etc. By the time such plant material is ejected, the carrying bird may have flown many miles. Some of the larger aquatic Crustacea and Mollusca as well as, of course, Reptilia, obviously play a part in the dispersal of Algae which grow epizoically upon them or their shells ; while on land, Snails and Slugs disperse seeds and spores that adhere to their bodies or have been swallowed. Indeed, it is said that the spores of some Fungi will only germinate after passing through a Slug ; and when the latter is eaten by a Toad, Bird, or other predator, the possibility occurs of far more extensive dispersal.

Insects are probably the most important of the groups of lower animals in the matter of plant dispersal, especially of very small bodies such as fungal spores. Transport is commonly by swallowing and ' passing ' in the excreta, by carrying to their nests for food, and by adhesion. Locusts are said to afford examples of the first method, sometimes over considerable distances, and ants frequently transport seeds with edible appendages, while flies and many other insects often carry spores of cryptogams adhering to their bodies—especially when the latter are densely hairy. Further instances are the well-known transmission of Fungi- and Bacteria-engendered diseases by insects, as well as important viruses (such as those of Potatoes) having aphid vectors.

It seems desirable here to treat briefly the subject of pollen. As we saw in Chapter II, pollen is composed of vast numbers of microscopic ' grains '. These, though capable of producing on germination only a tiny particle of plant, and hence scarcely to be considered as true disseminules, nevertheless carry the potential male gametes and, in them, the genes introducing hereditary characters. As it is now known that transport of pollen can in some circumstances take place naturally over many hundreds of miles, and that given suitable conditions some detached pollens can live for many months, it seems conceivable that by this means heritable characters may be transported vast distances. To be sure, the grain has to find its way to a receptive female stigma to have any chance of effective survival. But when it is recalled that pollen grains are formed each year in trillions of trillions, and that a single pollen 'bullet' finding its stigmatic billet in a millennium might suffice to carry thither the genes of any subspecific characters it may possess, the possibility can scarcely be denied of what has facetiously been termed 'absent-treatment hybridization'. Wind and insects are the chief transmitting agents of pollen, though carriage is also effected by some other animals (especially small Birds) and by water. Most of the strikingly beautiful features of flowers, as well as their possession of nectar and scent, are adaptations to attract insects to gather pollen for the purpose of cross-fertilization, and so it is to be expected that this is very commonly effected, though chiefly over rather short distances.

### Dispersal by Human Agency

There can scarcely be any question that Man is the most active agent of vegetational change—including plant dispersal—of modern times. He is the greatest despoiler of forests and causer of erosion, dispersing weeds as well as growing crops. As he travels about the world in greater and greater numbers and with ever-increasing speed and ease, he is always transporting the disseminules (or sometimes transplanting whole individuals or groups) of plants either intentionally or unwittingly. Also of vast importance is his indirect effect, through the pasturing of his domestic animals or his disturbance of natural communities of herbivorous animals. As a result, there are few parts of the world where the vegetation and its component flora do not bear the stamp of Man's interference, and quite a few areas, for example in Hawaii and Ceylon, where the native plants have been largely ousted by alien ones. In general, however, unless there is some drastic disturbance of the natural vegetation, recently introduced plants fail to compete successfully with the native dominants and, consequently, take only a minor part in the constitution of most plant communities. Often these aliens are limited almost entirely to burned-over or otherwise cleared areas—such as waysides and abandoned fields, which characteristically support hosts of weeds.

Between the extremes of those plants, such as many horticultural strains, which are restricted to gardens and need constant tending, and those which, following introduction, have so thoroughly established themselves by natural agency that they are distinguishable from the indigenous flora only by their known history, we see all manner of degrees of success in establishment. Some aliens flourish for a time and then disappear, while others, after many years of restriction to one locality, suddenly burst forth all over a countryside. A notable example of the latter category is the Oxford Ragwort (*Senecio squalidus*), which was introduced into the Oxford Botanic Garden late in the seventeenth century but scarcely spread at all until late in the nineteenth century, when it started migrating along the railways. Thereafter, migration proceeded so extensively that by the nineteen-twenties it became known from the vicinity of railways in other counties, and when, in the nineteen-thirties and -forties, the present writer was in charge of the botanical collections at Oxford, it was apt to be sent in from quite remote districts of Great Britain as a curiosity or for identification.

It will be sufficient—without going into detailed examples which could fill whole chapters—to indicate here some of the main methods by which Man introduces plants to new areas and, often, new countries and even continents (for it is said that the majority of alien plants in Australia and New Zealand come from Europe). In addition to intentional transport of desirable plants for agricultural, horticultural, forestral, medicinal, or other purposes, weeds are often dispersed unwittingly with the seeds of vegetables, cereals, and garden flowers, as well as with pot plants and in making transplants. All manner of disseminules and whole plants are dispersed accidentally (but quite commonly) by land or water traffic, garbage removal, and in baggage and soil transportation, while admixture in animal fodder, litter, and manure are other extensive means of transport. Dispersal used to be widely effected in ships' ballast and still is in many packaging materials, often to the far corners of the earth, as it is also in bird-seed and building material, or as algal growth attached to ships' hulls. Other sources of dispersed disseminules are timber and drug and spice materials—such as Caraway seeds imported by the Danes to Greenland for flavouring bread, with the result that the plant, *Carum carvi*, is now common around many of the settlements. Indeed, very many kinds of commercial export–import traffic must involve the carriage of disseminules, some of which evidently lead to fresh introductions; the same is true of personal travel, for people often carry a considerable range of seeds and fruits about their clothing, and, doubtless, greater numbers of microscopic spores.

In this connection air travel may be particularly effective, for one steps on to an aircraft in one continent and off it in another, often with little movement meanwhile to brush off adhering seeds and fruits. Much the same may be true of transported animals, which are always apt to carry seeds and fruits in their wool and fur, or otherwise about or in their bodies, and evidently account for many plant introductions. Moreover, there is practically no limit to the number and diversity of seeds and fruits that adhere to men and women when they fall or merely walk in mud and clay, to be brushed or picked off later, or are transported by them for food or as curios—often to be discarded at a distance. And to the abilities of some seeds to pass through the human digestive tract unharmed, the 'spontaneous' growth of Tomato plants in sewage farms bears ample testimony. Finally, with their hosts are frequently carried parasitic (and also saprophytic) species. That such spread of plant diseases can be very serious is indicated by the rigid restrictive measures adopted by many governments against the importation of living plants.

The great differences often observed in the actual migration of thus 'artificially' introduced plants are, however, probably due more to the adaptability of the species to local environments than to the dissemination itself, essential though this is. As we shall see in Chapter VI and elsewhere, plants tend to be adaptable when they are variable—in habitat requirements as well as in form. Accordingly, some familiar European weeds, such as Shepherd's-purse (*Capsella bursa-pastoris*), Common Chickweed (*Stellaria media* agg.), and the little grass *Poa annua*, have become practically world-wide without having any special adaptations for long-distance dispersal, whereas other plants the disseminules of which are doubtless more commonly, and sometimes more widely, carried, are still relatively restricted in their geographical area. Often the climatic, soil, or other local conditions are unsuitable; or the competition of native plants is so severe that 'open' habitats have to be found—especially by weeds. Such open habitats are commonly due to Man's activities, soon becoming closed over with vegetation when abandoned, so that the colonizing aliens become restricted or often ousted. In time the signs of human interference may virtually disappear, though, as has already been emphasized, such interference is nowadays so widespread and drastic in various ways as to constitute the most active agent of vegetational change in the world. Moreover, as compared with earlier times, the barriers to dispersal by human agency are greatly diminished now that men can (and frequently do) travel to almost all parts of the world in a matter of days, and traverse vast distances in a very few hours.

## MECHANICAL DISPERSAL

Although it is usually effective over only short distances, mechanical propulsion or even extensive growth can be of distinct advantage in migration. Thus plants which shoot out their disseminules can thereby launch them into a goodly wind or on to a passing animal that will carry them for miles. And often it is agitation by wind or an animal which sets off the explosive mechanism. Furthermore, the aggressive growth of overground runners (Fig. 28, B) and underground stems (rhizomes, *see* Fig. 28, A) often gives plants a distinct advantage in competition over their neighbours, so that when, as is often the case, the peripheral growth is detached as a separate plant, for example by the death of the parent, it may be established at an appreciable distance ; and such distances mount up usefully through the generations. As examples, Ground-ivy (*Glechoma hederacea*) can trail a distance of 20 feet (about 6 metres) along the ground, and Elms can reproduce by suckers from underground roots at fully 50 yards (about 46 metres) from the parent tree. Even such growth as that of the Walking Fern shown in Fig. 22 leads, in due course, to a worthwhile amount of dispersal.

Particularly effective are the explosive spore-discharging mechanisms of some Fungi, which, usually on sudden rupture to relieve stresses, may shoot their spores or spore-producing organs in some instances as much as 15 feet. However, in the case of spores, a tiny distance to take them into the free air is often sufficient to launch them in atmospheric currents that may carry them practically anywhere. Also capable of being shot out for distances of as much as 3 feet are the bulbils of some Club-mosses (*Lycopodium* spp.). Better known, however, are the explosive mechanisms of some fruits, of which examples are shown in Fig. 28 and more may be cited. The ' records ' seem to be held by species of a genus of small parasitic Mistletoes (*Arceuthobium*), followed by tropical American trees of the Spurge family (Euphorbiaceae), particularly the Sand-box Tree (*Hura crepitans*), which can throw its seeds more than forty feet, and Para Rubber (*Hevea brasiliensis*), whose performance is nearly as good. The explosion of a *Hura* fruit is spoken of as a ' regular detonation '. In a similar manner, on drying of the fruits, even small herbaceous members of the Spurge family often shoot out their seeds for a distance of a dozen or more feet. In the case of

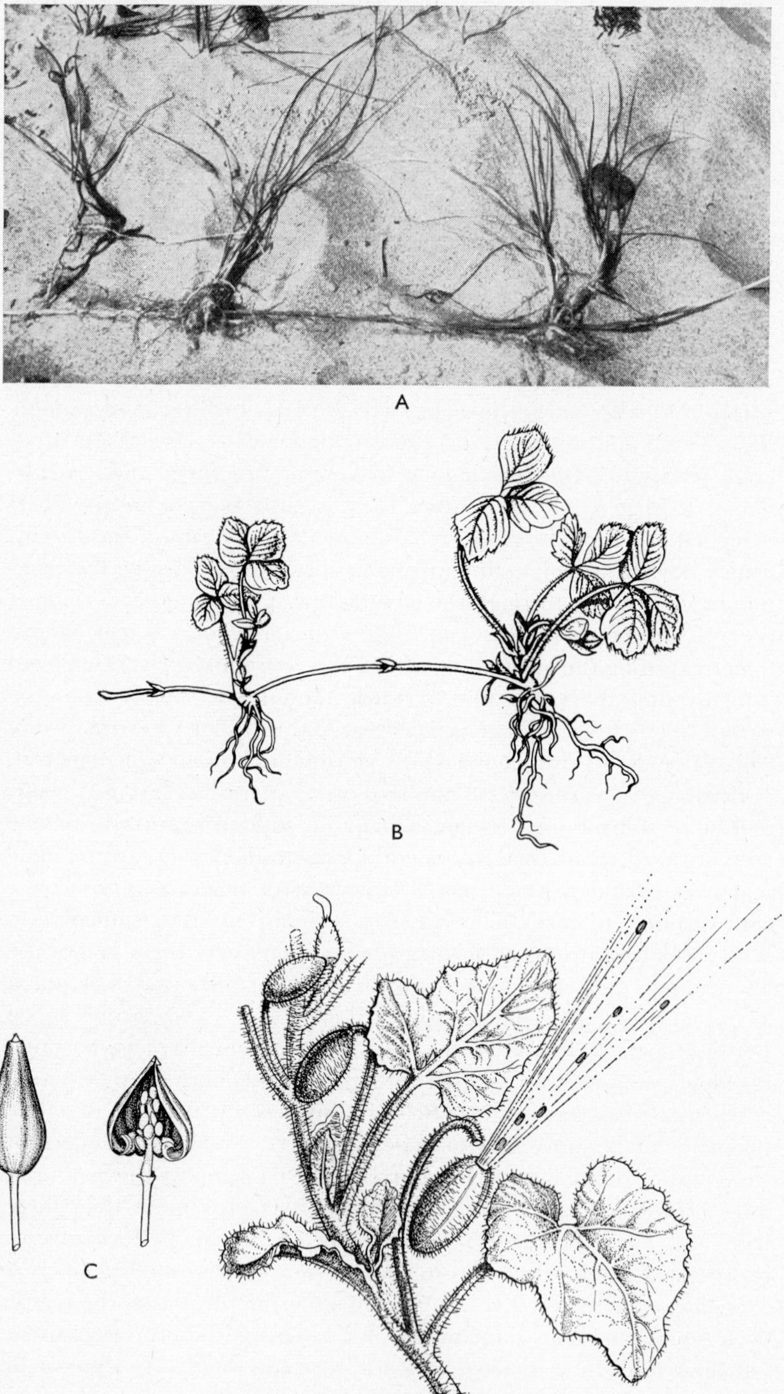

A

B

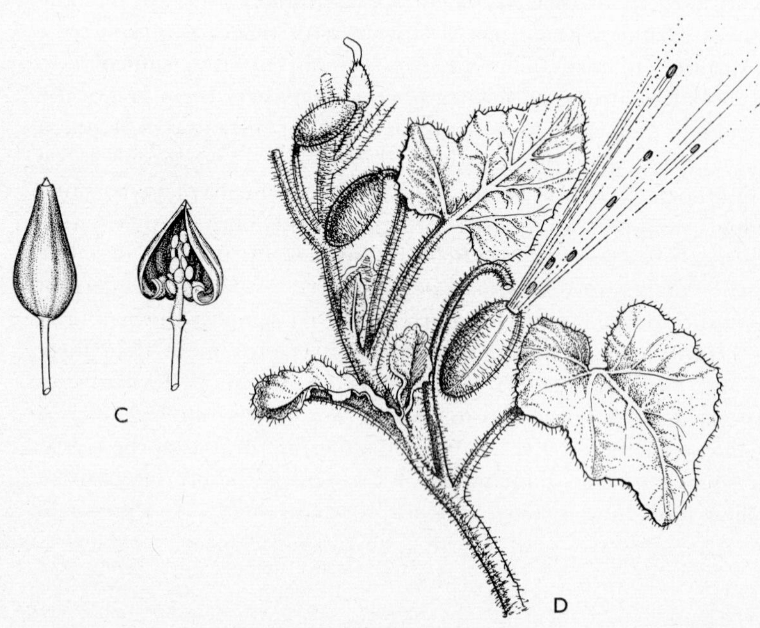

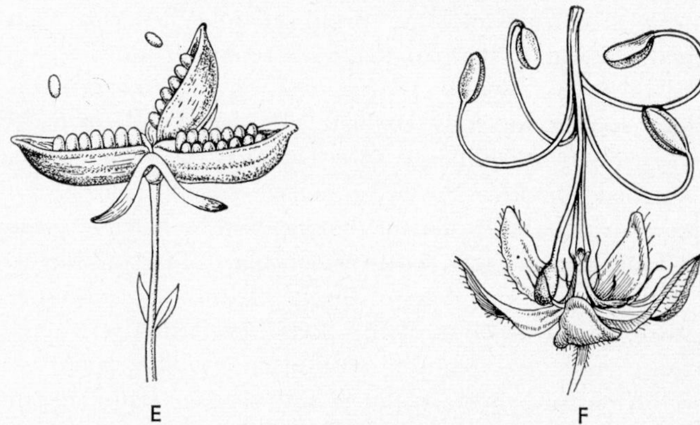


FIG. 28.—Dispersal by extension of growth or by mechanical propulsion, etc. A, horizontal rhizome of a Grass (the sand-binding Marram Grass, *Ammophila arenaria*) (× about ⅓); B, Strawberry (*Fragaria*) runner establishing daughter plant (× ½); C, fruit of a Balsam (*Impatiens balsamina*), which explodes and scatters the seeds (× 1); D, seed dispersal in the Squirting Cucumber (*Ecballium elaterium*) (× about ½); E, ripe fruit of Pansy (*Viola* sp.), showing seeds ready to be, and being, shot out (× 2); F, over-ripe fruit of Geranium (*Geranium* sp.), showing slings which have thrown out the seeds (× about 2½).

one species of *Arceuthobium* the tiny bullet-shaped seeds have been reported to travel over 66 feet (about 20 metres) from a point 8 feet above the ground, and in one instance large numbers were collected from the roof of a cabin one-quarter of a mile (about 402 metres) from the point of liberation—presumably after transportation by wind, though the seeds are also viscous and apt to be carried by birds.

Such a combination of explosion and adhesion is utilized also by the Squirting Cucumber (*Ecballium elaterium*), shown in Fig. 28, D. When the fruit is ripe, it breaks from the stalk, and through the hole thus left the internal pressure is relieved by the seeds being ejected with an abundance of mucilage and with such force that they commonly fly for several feet through the air. A slight touch will send off the ripe fruit, so that a passing animal is liable to receive a broadside—and, incidentally, carry the adhering seeds much farther. There are many varieties of this type of turgor-engendered explosion, another being exhibited by certain Cresses (*Cardamine* spp.) that have explosive pods of which the narrow valves, on being touched when ripe, suddenly curl outwards with some violence, shooting out the seeds—sometimes for more than 2 feet. In the case of such diminutive plants, this is ample to take the seeds away from the parental sphere of influence. Notable among the rather many and diverse plants which do this sort of thing are the Balsams (*Impatiens* spp.), in which the wall of the fruit is made of three layers of which the innermost consists of large turgid cells. When ripe, especially if touched, the wall of the fruit suddenly separates into five segments that curl inwards violently (*cf.* Fig. 28, C), shooting out the seeds —in some species for fully 20 feet. In the Wood-sorrels (*Oxalis* spp.) the ripe fruit suddenly splits lengthwise or by lateral slits when touched, shooting out the mucilage-covered seeds.

In many fruits the explosion that leads to a forcible ejection of seeds is caused by stresses set up on drying. The audible cracking of the pods of some members of the Pea family (Leguminosae) is of this nature, the two valves of the pods (for example, when drying in the sun) suddenly separating with often a violent spiral twisting, and forcibly ejecting the hard and smooth seeds. Familiar European examples of this are furnished by the Gorses (*Ulex* spp.). The action is due to a hard layer of strongly thickened, elongate cells lying transversely, and to which the softer tissues offer little resistance. The distances to which seeds are shot by these means vary greatly, but in some instances are said to exceed 40 feet and at least rival the ejections of *Hura* and *Hevea*. Thus the turgor- and drying-induced methods may be about equally effective.

Many species of the familiar genus *Viola*, including some wild Violets, in which the fruit splits into three boat-shaped valves (Fig. 28, E), shoot out their seeds for up to 15 feet as a result of unequal drying of the layers of the fruit wall. This drying causes a curving of the sides of the valves and the consequent pressing of the glossy seeds together—until they ' pip out ', one after another, being often further dispersed by rainwash. Also dispersed on explosion of the hard ripe fruit are the seeds of almost all members of the family Acanthaceae—sometimes to nearly 30 feet from the parent—and those of *Claytonia*, *Montia*, some Phloxes, and the Witch-hazels (*Hamamelis* spp.). In the last instance the drying fruits may exert such pressure on the seeds that these are discharged, like miniature bullets, to distances of up to 40 feet—again rivalling *Hura* and *Hevea*.

In many members of the Geranium and Stork's-bill family (Geraniaceae) the fruit suddenly splits into strips which curl up and act as slings (Fig. 28, F) to throw out the seeds, which may travel as much as 20 feet. Some fruits are also effectively dispersed by mechanical propulsion, including those of Flat-figs (*Dorstenia* spp.) which are embedded in the large fleshy receptacle that shrinks on drying, setting up pressures which lead to the tiny fruits being forcibly ejected. The spores of many Ferns are well known to be discharged forcibly into the air by the springing backwards of part of the capsule when it has dehisced and attained a certain degree of desiccation, while the movements of teeth of Mosses are hygroscopic, curving backwards to open the capsule and disseminate the spores. These actions take place chiefly in dry weather when conditions are best for dispersal. Also able to move as a result of hygroscopic changes are many awned fruits, etc. Finally, it should be recalled that the spores or even the whole bodies of many of the lower cryptogams are actively mobile, swimming by means of flagella being particularly common among them.

## Barriers

When we reflect that in many species of flowering plants, such as Flixweed (*Sisymbrium sophia*) and Pigweed (*Amaranthus retroflexus*),[1] a single individual may produce a million or more seeds in one summer, and that some cryptogams, such as the Giant Puffball (*Lycoperdon* (*Calvatia*) *giganteum*), may produce as many as several million million spores, and yet none overruns the world,[2] it is obvious that only an infinitesimally small proportion of the plant disseminules produced ever attain their real biological *raison d'être*. To realize its full potentiality, a propagule must develop into an adult which in turn reproduces. This stupendous mortality is due to the action of various types of barriers—either to dispersal or to actual survival—of some of which we have already seen examples as applied to particular agents of dispersal. They are of four main types:

(1) *Physiographic*, due to features of the earth's surface. The most obvious of these for terrestrial plants are expanses of water, and, for aquatic plants, bodies of land. Another physiographic barrier is afforded by mountains—both directly by constituting a mechanical impediment, and indirectly by changing climatic and allied conditions such as air temperatures and currents. Many local winds are caused by a combination of physiographic and climatic factors, and constitute virtual barriers to dispersal in one direction even as they may aid it in another.

[1] An individual of this annual species has been known to produce an estimated 2,350,000 seeds.

[2] It is said that an individual Giant Puffball can produce 7,000,000,000,000 spores, and it was calculated by the late Professor A. H. R. Buller (*Researches on Fungi*, vol. III, 1924) 'that, if every spore of this puff-ball had germinated and given rise to a puff-ball like its parent, and if every spore of the second-generation puff-balls had likewise germinated and given rise to a puff-ball like its parent, then, at the end of these two filial generations only, there would have come into existence a mass of puff-ball matter equal to 800 globes the size of the planet on which we live!'

(2) *Climatic*, involving different temperature, humidity, light, and other conditions. Owing to the close dependence of plants on climatic conditions, zones of vegetation and climate tend to correspond with one another, the climate commonly determining the general limits of a plant's distribution. A change of climate, such as a migrating plant is apt to find in a new land, often constitutes a very real or insuperable barrier—not only as a whole but, very often, as to one or other of the climate's component factors, which may react in a particular way on the plant's physiological make-up or a vital part thereof. Moreover any condition, including lapse of time, which proves lethal to disseminules may constitute a major barrier, lack of viability being an important factor militating against migration.

(3) *Edaphic*, due to features of the soil. These are again various, involving physical structure, chemical composition, moisture content, temperature conditions, or even content of living organisms, any one of which alone can prevent a disseminule from establishing a plant in a new area, even if it germinates quite successfully. Either in combination or separately, edaphic conditions tend to limit the distribution of plants (and, of course, vegetation) rather drastically within the main climatic belts—commonly to particular habitats, which may be narrowly prescribed in their type and of very limited extent. Absence of the suitable habitat, or at least of the required conditions, is apt to constitute an insuperable barrier to successful migration.

(4) *Biotic*, due to living organisms, including other plants. The competition for space, light, water, etc., of other plants already established in an area and growing in reasonable equilibrium with local conditions, is apt to constitute an insuperable barrier to the successful establishment of newcomers, as is grazing or other disturbance by animals (including Man). Consequently widespread immigration is largely limited to more or less ' open ' areas, such as cliffs, sands, and disturbed ground—where other sets of barriers come into play. If they did not, virtually every scrap of soil or ray of light would probably be utilized ; for the struggle for existence is a very real and desperate one, taking place chiefly between organisms where the general conditions for life are good, and predominantly with the physical factors of the environment where conditions are bad.

The magnificent perseverence and virtual ubiquity of plant life are vividly exemplified to the author by the myriad Diatoms which may so impressively if variously colour ice-floes on arctic seas. During long flights over the North Polar Basin and elsewhere he has observed such ' dirty ' floes in many places up to almost the highest latitudes (the ice immediately around the North Pole appears to be ' clean '). From the air, some of the browns and yellows of these floes seem not far removed in colour-effect from some barren arctic limestones—as the author and his pilot had occasion to remark once in 1946 when flying over Foxe Basin and sighting an unexpected island of limestone which turned out to be some 90 miles long and nearly as wide. It was officially ' discovered ' two years later by the Royal Canadian Air Force and added to the world's map as ' Prince Charles Island ', being, with its neighbours which were also noted on that 1946 occasion, evidently the last major land discovery or confirmation to be made in the world. Subsequent exploration failed to reveal any unexpected features of plant life. Until the advent of general air travel not so long ago, many areas even in comparatively low latitudes were difficult or at least tedious to visit. But now in superb antithesis we are looking to other planets for explorational opportunities, and the prospects of space travel are advancing so rapidly that the author is prompted to guard himself by remarking that the present volum is concerned purely with vital phenomena as we know them on theEarth and in its immediately surrounding atmosphere—regardless of any possibilities elsewhere.

## Further Consideration

H. N. Ridley. *The Dispersal of Plants throughout the World* (Reeve, Ashford, Kent, pp. xx + 744, 1930). A monument of usually authoritative information on the methods and effectiveness of plant dispersal, covering almost all aspects of the subject. Its author died recently at well over 100 years of age, maintaining that such studies, of which there are still not nearly enough, are fine preservers of life.

Charles Darwin. *The Origin of Species by means of Natural Selection*, sixth edition, with additions and corrections (Murray, London, pp. xxi + 458, 1873).

H. B. Guppy. *Plants, Seeds, and Currents in the West Indies and Azores* (Williams & Norgate, London, pp. xi + 531, 1917). A work of wider implication than its title suggests.

A. Kerner (von Marilaun), & F. W. Oliver. *The Natural History of Plants*, vol. II, pp. 790 *et seq.* (Blackie, London, 1895).

Sir E. J. Salisbury. *The Reproductive Capacity of Plants* (Bell, London, pp. xi + 244, 1942).

L. V. Barton. *Seed Preservation and Longevity* (Leonard Hill, London —in press).

C. T. Ingold. *Dispersal in Fungi* (Clarendon Press, Oxford, pp. viii + 197, 1953).

## CHAPTER V

# EVOLUTIONARY DEVELOPMENT AND PAST HISTORY

In Chapter II we gave a brief general account of each of the main classes of the plant kingdom now living, mentioning that the sequence used was probably indicative of evolutionary history at least in broad outline. The classes treated were usually those most important as components of vegetation at the present time, regardless of their significance in the past. Those omitted even included some that had been vastly important in earlier ages but had subsequently become extinct or nearly so.

Evolution is a continuous process, that started with the earliest forms of life and still goes on abundantly today. And even as the numerical representation and importance of a particular group of organisms may go down as well as up, so may evolution manifest itself in simplification or decline as well as advance. This is particularly evident in many parasitic forms of both plants and animals. Nevertheless the general trend is towards advancement in complexity if not always in size, economy in the use of material being also important ; with these tendencies and the need for adaptation to the environment and other circumstances constantly in mind, we can place the forms known to us in a sequence that seems most likely to be the actual one of their own evolution. This will be done briefly below for those groups that are important as fossils, regardless of the significance of relatives living today, but with close reference to these in order to link relationships in the mind's eye.

It is necessary here to give an outline account of the geological time-sequence. In this, four major eras are defined, the last three of which are divided into several periods or epochs each. It is now believed that the earth had its beginnings about 4,500,000,000 years ago. The latest measurements indicate the age of the oldest known rocks to be about 3,300,000,000 years, and the era from that time to about 550,000,000 years ago constitutes the pre-Cambrian. This era has often been divided into two—the 'older' Archaeozoic (of metamorphic and igneous rocks) and the 'younger' Proterozoic (of sedimentary rocks). At least in the latter time, relatively simple Algae and Sponges and apparently also Fungi and Bacteria were widespread. The pre-Cambrian was followed by the Palaeozoic era, of invertebrates and Fishes and large Pteridophytes. This extended for about 370,000,000 years from the Cambrian period through the Ordovician, Silurian, Devonian, and Carboniferous (Mississippian and Pennsylvanian) periods to the Permian period, which ended about 180,000,000 years ago. Next came the Mesozoic era, which extended for some 130,000,000 years through the Triassic, Jurassic, and Cretaceous periods and was the great era of Reptiles and Gymnosperms. Finally, extending over the last 60,000,000 or so years, has been the Cainozoic (Cenozoic) era, of Angiosperms and Mammals. This is commonly considered to consist of two periods, the Tertiary (made up of the Paleocene, Eocene, Oligocene, Miocene, and Pliocene epochs) and the Quaternary. In the higher latitudes and altitudes this last period consisted of alternating glacial and interglacial times and may be referred to as the Pleistocene epoch, the ' recent ' being the time since the last ice recession took place, although some consider this a mere interglacial. The Quaternary period has extended over perhaps the last 1,000,000 or so years[1] and has seen the advent and ascendancy of Man. A chart showing the eras and main periods etc. is given in Fig. 37 (p. 145).

## Groups of Fossil Lower Plants

We can only guess at the form of the first living organisms, which were probably not distinct as either plants or animals, but must have possessed the powers of deriving energy from outside sources and of sustaining themselves. Presumably they were microscopic bits of naked protoplasm far simpler than any organisms of which fossils are known. From such a source sprang the ' tree of life ', near the bottom of which the Bacteria appear to remain. These organisms play such essential roles as agents of decomposition that it is difficult to conceive of the balance of nature being maintained without them, and indeed there is evidence that they were in existence in very

[1] According to F. E. Zeuner's *Dating the Past : an Introduction to Geochronology*, third edition (Methuen, London, pp. xx + 495 and 24 additional plates, 1952). Other modern estimates range from one-half to double this total, a difficulty being to decide at what point in time the Quaternary began. Very recently, Professor Zeuner has suggested (*in litt.* 1957) that ' an estimate of 600,000 years for the period from the First [Pleistocene] Glaciation onwards is a reasonable one '.

early geological times. Thus in rocks far back in the pre-Cambrian[1] are found supposed signs of Bacteria in the form of filamentous chains and minute spherical bodies, often associated with slender branching filaments and other remains believed to be of Blue-green Algae (*cf.* Fig. 29, C). What appear to be the oldest known structurally preserved organisms that clearly exhibit cellular differentiation and original carbon complexes are in pre-Cambrian sediments of southern Ontario and represent Blue-green Algae and simple forms of Fungi or possibly Algae (*see* Fig. 29, D). It seems probable that their age exceeds 1,000,000,000 years, and it may quite likely be nearer to 2,000,000,000 years. From later on, and at least beginning with the Devonian around the middle of the Palaeozoic era,[1] there are plentiful indications that Bacteria were practically ubiquitous, as indeed they are today. Nor is there evidence of major evolutionary change in their structure through those many millions of years.

Algae, which among living plants probably rank next in importance to vascular ones in the formation of contemporary vegetation, are also significant for the roles they appear to have played in the formation of petroleum and limestone. As a result of Algae obtaining carbon dioxide for photosynthesis from (soluble) calcium bicarbonate, the relatively insoluble calcium carbonate was left as a

[1] *See* previous page and Fig. 37 concerning the geological eras, etc., with their dominant forms of life and supposed ages. Fig. 37 also indicates the approximate relative development of the main plant groups at different times. It is now thought that the earth may be of the order of 4,500,000,000 years old, and that life may have begun on it about half-way along the time to the present.

A

B

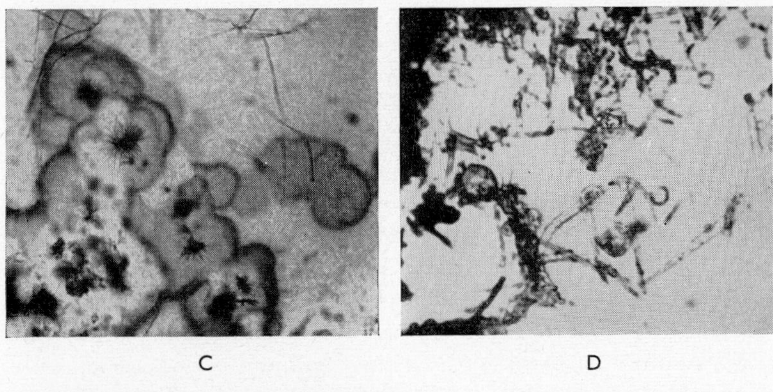

FIG. 29.—Some primitive plant fossils. A, *Collenia undosa*, a Proterozoic fossil believed to have been formed by the action of one or more Blue-green Algae (after Walcott) (× $\frac{1}{2}$); B, *Newlandia concentrica*, a Proterozoic fossil apparently formed by the action of a Blue-green Alga (after Walcott) (× $\frac{3}{4}$); C, a Proterozoic fossil, apparently a colonial Blue-green Alga consisting of aggregations of filaments in globose sheaths (courtesy of E. S. Barghoorn and *Science*) (× about 200); D, a Proterozoic fossil of fungal or possibly algal type, showing spores and non-septate hyphae (courtesy of E. S. Barghoorn and *Science*) (× about 400); E, a Cambrian Alga, *Dalyia racemata* (after Walcott) (× about 3); F, a Cambrian Alga, *Marpolia aequalis* (after Walcott) (× about 2).

residue and became deposited as limestone. Limestones believed to have been formed in this manner by Algae occur in extremely early rock formations, and apparently such deposition of calcium carbonate as a result of algal activity has been going on ever since. However, owing to such features as their generally soft bodies, Algae often leave no traces of their original cellular structure, and so as fossils they are difficult to recognize with certainty. In any case there seems no doubt that, well before the end of the Cambrian period, not only an abundance of Blue-green but also large numbers of Green and some Red and probably Brown Algae had evolved. Certainly all of the first three groups were plentiful in the Ordovician. Two examples of fossil Algae of the Cambrian period are shown in Fig. 29, E and F. Although Desmids and even Stoneworts are now known to go back into the Palaeozoic, being present in the Devonian period, the Diatoms appear to be of more recent origin, none being known before the Jurassic period in the middle of the Mesozoic era. It may well be that many groups of Algae have remained evolutionarily static throughout the time since their remote ancestors laid down some of the earliest fossils of which we have knowledge.

It was indicated above that the Fungi as a group are also very old, and there is no reason to doubt that they have acted as scavengers throughout their long geological past, even as they act today. Indeed it appears that fossils were chiefly formed when deposition of plant material took place under conditions unfavourable to fungal growth, so that the usual destructive activity of Fungi was evaded. Well-preserved fungal mycelia and spores have been found in the tissues of vascular plants as far back as the Devonian, and Fungi apparently occur in sedimentary deposits of much earlier date (*see* p. 130). Such discoveries have not, however, shed any clear light on the origin of the Fungi, which have long been believed to have evolved from Algae through the loss of chlorophyll. However, some authorities now hold that Fungi were derived from a distinct group of primitive organisms, the similarities with Algae being due to parallel evolution, and it may well be that, unlike the various members of most other groups, Fungi had no common starting-point but originated at different times and in various groups. Fossils of higher Fungi do not appear with certainty until the Cretaceous, and no indubitable early fossils of Lichens are known.

The Nematophytales comprise an extinct group of spore-producing Silurian and Devonian plants of uncertain relationship, in which the plant body was composed of a system of interlacing tubes. It may be that their affinity is with the Algae, and it even seems conceivable that they may represent the long-sought link between that group and the lowest land-plants. A further link may be forged by certain cellular forms producing firm-walled spores, which forms, like some Nematophytales, have a covering cuticle resembling that of land-plants, but which seem to belong to a relatively advanced group without actually being typical land-plants in other respects.

Fossil remains of Bryophyta are not common, probably owing to the fragile nature of the plant body. Some Liverworts are known from as early as the Carboniferous towards the close of the Palaeozoic era ; traces of Mosses have also been found in rocks laid down before the end of the Carboniferous. From the Triassic period onwards, fossil Bryophytes tend to become less rare, so that a considerable number are known from the Pleistocene. It now seems that fossil Bryophytes throw little if any light on the problem of the origin of vascular plants, and that there is no justification for thinking them ever to have served as intermediate stages in the evolution of higher plants. Instead, these presumably evolved from Algae, as also with little doubt did the Bryophytes—but in this latter instance without going much ahead. Consequently they are little changed to this day, although they are now numerous and often ecologically successful within the limits prescribed by their relative diminutiveness.

By the close of the Silurian period there were undoubted land-plants, the primitive aquatic or semi-aquatic Algae (perhaps through more advanced types such as the Nematophytales or others of which we have no knowledge) having apparently come out on land and given rise to vascular forms. As we saw in Chapter II, these last are characterized by the possession of a conducting system composed essentially of wood and bast elements ; nor is it by any means impossible that such a system was developed among marine Thallophytes, the more adaptable of which may gradually have become transformed to withstand permanent life on land. At the same time their holdfasts could have developed into rhizome-like structures bearing rhizoids. For such are the earliest known land-plants, and so may the great ‘ subaerial transmigration ’ have taken place.

The earliest known plants that were clearly adapted to life on land belong to the class Psilophytineae, which was probably more primitive than any of the other Pteridophytes, and of which some reconstructed examples are shown in Fig. 30, A and B. They range from the middle Silurian to the upper Devonian periods of the Palaeozoic era,

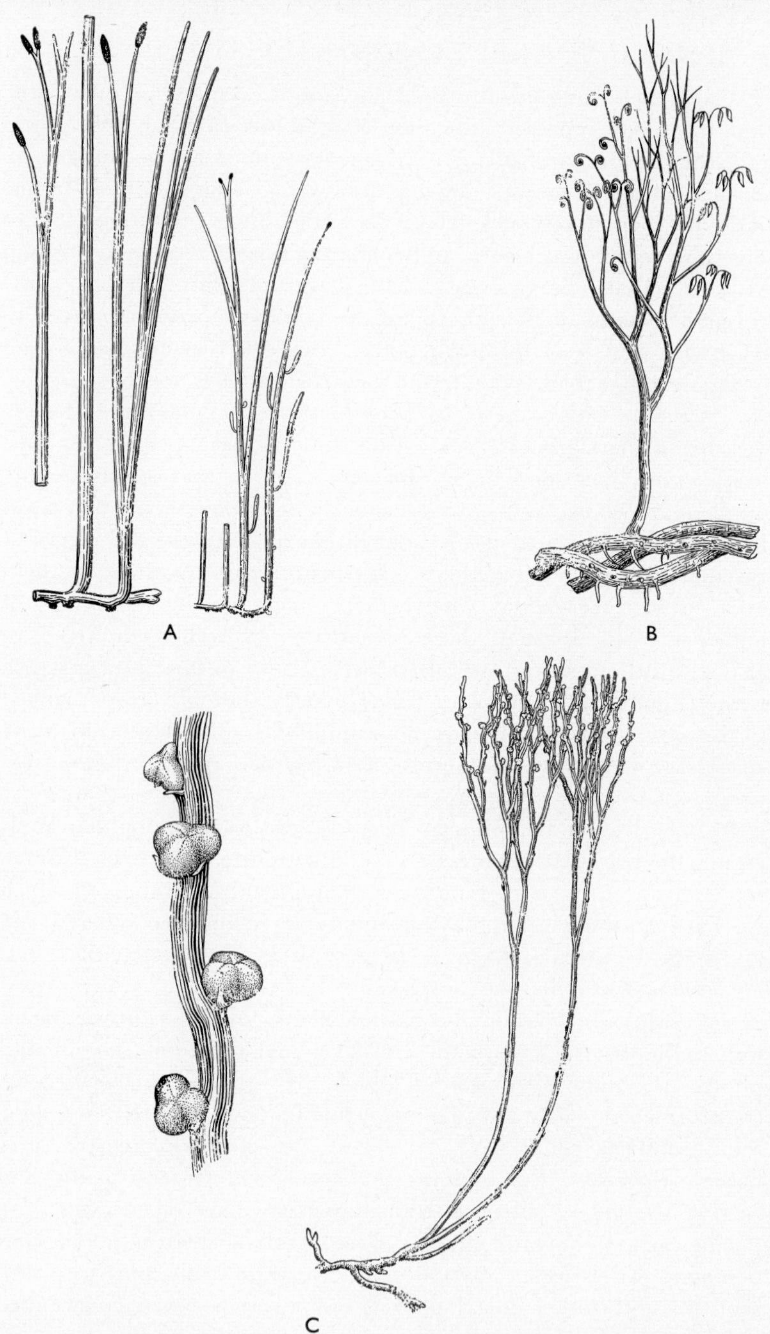


FIG. 30.—Some Psilophytineae. A, two species of *Rhynia*, showing the sporangia at the ends of the branches (after Kidston & Lang) (× $\frac{1}{3}$); B, *Psilophyton princeps*, showing rhizomes below and, above, young branches uncurling at left and branches bearing sporangia at right (after Dawson) (× probably about $\frac{1}{10}$); C, *Psilotum triquetrum*, showing the habit (× $\frac{1}{2}$) and, enlarged, on left, part of a branch with sporangia. A and B are reconstructed fossils, C is drawn from life.

and appear to be represented by a very few allies living today. Of these the best known is *Psilotum* (Fig. 30, C), which is widespread in warm regions. Both extinct and living members are branched, with naked or spiny stems having cuticle and stomata on the surface, and sometimes small simple leaves. They form spores of one size, produced in characteristic sporangia. Further details regarding the Psilophytineae and also some other groups of ancient vascular plants of often obscure relationship, may be obtained from such works on fossil botany as are cited at the end of this chapter, though comparisons will show how difficult it sometimes is for authorities to agree. Thus the present group are sometimes given the status of a division, as the Psilophyta (or Psilopsida).

The Equisetineae (Horsetails) have also a very ancient history, the present-day representatives, already dealt with in Chapter II, being mere depauperated relics of a once large and important group that flourished at least as far back as the Devonian. With their extinct fossil representatives they are sometimes given the rank of a division, under the name of Arthrophyta (or Sphenopsida). They show plentiful adventitious roots and small whorled leaves, and sometimes secondary thickening. Of this major group there are five subsidiary groups or orders, of which the most important are: (1) the lowly Sphenophyllales, which had slender reclining stems and expanded, wedge-shaped or lacerate leaves usually less than 2 cm. in length; (2) the Calamitales, which were like giant Horsetails, attaining heights of some tens of feet and with their jointed, hollow stems sometimes exceeding 20 cm. in diameter; and (3) the Equisetales, which were characterized by their slender, jointed stems and were altogether very like the representatives living today. Although the Equisetales appeared only in the Carboniferous, they were and are closely allied to the earlier Calamitales, and consequently *Equisetum* may be regarded as the oldest living type of vascular plant; indeed some authorities maintain the Calamites and Equiseta in the same order. Probably both groups arose from some common source, the Equisetales lingering on to the present day without major changes and representing the end of a once virile line whose ecological aggressiveness still saves it from extinction. It should be noted that in some Calamitales there was differentiation into large megaspores and small microspores. A living *Equisetum* is shown in Fig. 15, and in Fig. 31 may be seen fossils of typical members of the other two main groups.

Living representatives of the Lycopodineae (Club-mosses and

their allies) are described in Chapter II and illustrated in Fig. 16. They, too, have a long fossil history, both as the small herbaceous types which we know today and as huge trees that flourished chiefly in the Carboniferous period, when they evidently composed a large part of the vegetation, at least in coal-forming swamps. Subsequently, near the beginning of the Mesozoic era, the tree types appear to have become extinct, much as in the case of the giant

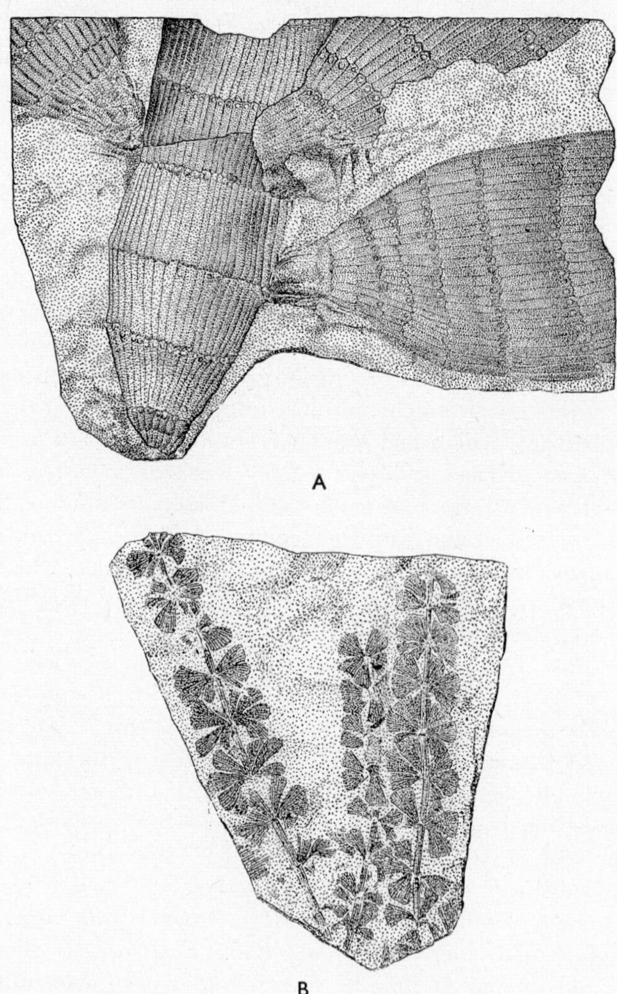


FIG. 31.—Fossil Equisetineae. A, a Calamite, *Calamites suckowi* (× about ½); B, a Sphenophyll, *Sphenophyllum emarginatum* (× about 1). (Both after Zeiller.)

Horsetails. Outstanding examples are *Lepidodendron* and *Sigillaria*, shown in Fig. 32, which were characterized by extensive rooting systems of a unique kind, spores of two sizes, and usually tall and straight, woody trunks covered with the scars left by the spirally-arranged leaves. These last were narrow and grass-like but ligulate,

FIG. 32.—Fossil Lycopodineae. A, *Lepidodendron*, two figures on the left, and *Sigillaria*, five figures on the right, showing also the characteristic rooting sytsem (after Grand'Eury) (the tallest is about 16 metres in height); B, *Lepidodendron lycopodioides*, showing the small leaves and leaf scars (after Zeiller) (× about $\frac{2}{3}$).

and in *Sigillaria* are said occasionally to have exceeded 50 cm. in length. Some of the earlier groups quite likely go back to Silurian times, and probably evolved from the psilophytinean complex; later ones became highly specialized trees, sometimes with seed-like organs. But, having become structurally modified for life in swamps, with extensive tissues for gaseous exchange and very little for water conduction, they were apparently unable to adapt themselves to the more adverse climates following the Carboniferous. Meanwhile the small herbaceous types survived and gave rise to those persisting at the present time, even though they apparently represent another evolutionary end-line. Like the Psilophytineae and Equisetineae, this group is sometimes given the rank of a division, as the Lycopsida ; for it is now realized that these groups of so-called 'fern-allies' represent separate lines of development as far back as it is possible to trace them.

Of Filicineae, the Ferns, characterized by large complicated leaves and gaps in the vascular cylinder, there are plentiful fossils—which go well back into the Devonian in the case of the long-extinct Coenopteridales. The earliest of these 'Primofilices' were only partly distinct from their presumable psilophytinean forebears, but others soon became characteristic and prominent elements of the flora. Further groups arose towards the end of the Palaeozoic era and persist to the present day—in the case of the relatively primitive ones such as the Marattiales apparently in decreasing numbers, but in the case of the more orthodox and modern Filicales still plentifully. Many even in early times were much like those, living nowadays, that are described in Chapter II and illustrated in Fig. 17.

## Fossil Seed-Plants

Probably more important than true Ferns in the Carboniferous, and certainly accounting for a large proportion of the fern-like foliage of that and the following periods up to the mid-Jurassic, were the Pteridosperms or Seed-ferns, also called Cycadofilicales. As their names imply, these were fern-like (often tree-fern-like, but with secondary thickening) in some respects. But they bore seeds, as may be seen from Fig. 33, which shows a reconstructed plant and part of a frond of different types. The seeds were more or less naked, this group belonging to the Gymnosperms ; but although there are abundant differences, there remain sufficient deep-seated similarities to suggest that they may have given rise to the groups dealt with in the next paragraph, even as they themselves probably arose in pre-Carboniferous times from Ferns or fern-like stock that had not advanced far beyond the psilophytinean stage. Apparently allied or belonging to this group are the Caytoniales, which in some respects suggest primitive Angiosperms. The Gnetales may perhaps have sprung from the same stock ; but such fossils of them as are known are relatively modern, and so the origin and relationships of this group remain obscure (in Fig. 37 it is left near the Angiosperms).

The Mesozoic has often been called the era of Cycads, owing to the presence in its deposits of some Cycads and of many more

FIG. 33.—Pteridosperms (reconstructed). A, *Lyginopteris oldhamia* (after Berry) (× about $\frac{1}{10}$); B, *Sphenopteris tenuis*, portion of leaf with seeds (after Halle) (× $\frac{3}{4}$).

Cycad-like Gymnosperms (Cycadeoidales) which between them comprise the Cycadophytes. The living Cycads (an example is illustrated in Fig. 18, A) are apparently the relics of a once more important and widespread group, whereas the Cycadeoidales have long been extinct. By many authors the Cycadeoidales are kept as a separate group, also called the Bennettitales, on account of their remarkable reproductive structures that were apt to look more like flowers than cones (a reconstructed example is shown in Fig. 34, A) ; others were slender and branching but probably never very big. The Cycadophytes presumably arose from pteridospermous ancestors during the late Palaeozoic, the living Cycads supposedly representing the end of a line that in most respects has changed little since the early

A
B

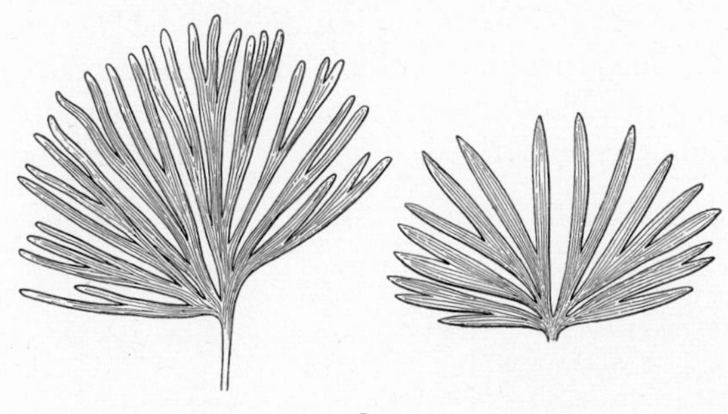


FIG. 34.—A reconstructed Cycadeoid and parts of living and fossil Ginkgoales. A, *Cycadeoidea*, showing the flower-like strobili on the squat stem (× about $\frac{1}{10}$); B, branch of *Ginkgo* with seeds (× $\frac{3}{4}$); C, leaves of two species of *Baiera*, Mesozoic Ginkgoales (× about $\frac{2}{3}$).

Mesozoic, when its members were far more (probably very) widespread.

Of comparable antiquity, extensive development in the Mesozoic, and bare persistence to the present day are the Ginkgoales, represented among living types by only the Maidenhair-tree, *Ginkgo biloba*. This is very restricted in anything like a wild state, but is widely familiar in cultivation ; a female sprig is shown in Fig. 34, B, as also are leaves of relatives which were almost world-wide in the Mesozoic. Like the Cycads, *Ginkgo* has motile sperms ; its obviously primitive characters have led to its being called a ' living fossil '.

An earlier, long-extinct and apparently quite distinct group of Gymnosperms, the Cordaitales, flourished chiefly in the later part of the Palaeozoic, constituting with the Pteridosperms the bulk of the seed-plants of the Carboniferous coal-forests. Their origin is obscure, the earliest known members apparently being already far advanced. The Cordaitales were mostly large trees with sizeable flattened leaves and bearing their pollen and seeds in slender strobili as indicated in Fig. 35.

The other major group of fossil Gymnosperms is the Conifers, whose surviving representatives afford the vast majority of living Gymnosperms. Examples of Conifers are illustrated in Fig. 18, their general features being described in Chapter II. They bear some resemblance to Cordaitales, and as fossils went back at least to the upper Carboniferous, an example from that time being shown in Fig. 36, A. Subsequently they appeared to reach their developmental climax in the Mesozoic, when several were similar in external form to those surviving today. Before the end of that era they began to tail off, some groups becoming less diverse and more restricted in geographical range, though as a whole they remained fairly numerous as well as various and ecologically important. It is widely supposed that the Coniferales derived originally from cordaitalean stock,

FIG. 35.—Cordaitales (reconstructed). A, various Cordaitales (about 20 metres in height); B, end of a branch of *Cordaites* with strobili and a young branch (middle, right) (× about ½). (Both after Grand'Eury.)

though we cannot yet be certain of this. And in spite of the aggressive nature of some familiar types—such as the Pines and Spruces which still dominate huge tracts, especially of the colder lands—it seems that many others are eking out a rather precarious existence.

Thus the group as a whole appears to be retreating before the angiospermic onslaught, from which it has suffered since before the dawn of the Cainozoic era. Much as in the case of the so-called Pteridophytes, it may be that the Gymnosperms represent several largely separate stocks as far back as we have yet any knowledge of them.

The Angiosperms, as we saw in Chapter II, are the most highly evolved and successful group of plants at the present time, affording most of the dominant species on land. After an apparently slow start at least as early as the Jurassic, they gave rise before the end of

A

B

Fig. 36.—Fossil parts of Conifer and Angiosperm. A, branch of *Lebachia* (*Walchia*) *frondosa*, one of the Palaeozoic Coniferales (after Renault) (× about ½); B, leaves of a dicotyledonous Angiosperm (× about ½).

the Cretaceous to a vast assemblage of forms that between them rapidly came to cover practically the whole surface of the earth, comprising most of the land-vegetation we know today, and a good deal of that developed in water. A considerable proportion of the genera and even species which are familiar to us nowadays as common shrubs or trees, particularly, seem to have persisted throughout the Cainozoic—often with little if any apparent change, and sometimes doubtless as dominants. Of the two main groups of Angiosperms, the Monocotyledons are much less numerous as fossils, and especially as early fossils, than the Dicotyledons. An example of these last is shown in Fig. 36, B.

Altogether the Angiosperms seem to be still in their early stages of expansion, with their fossils not yet expressing clear developmental trends. As to their future evolution we can only conjecture, and in regard to knowledge of their origin we are scarcely better off; for each and every one of the gymnospermous groups, and in addition the Ferns, have been suggested by different authorities as having been their precursors. The outcome has been to stress our ignorance and leave the question unanswered, as we know of no series of fossil forms connecting the flowering plants with more primitive groups. Yet it does seem probable that they evolved from some primitive unspecialized group rather than from any modern and familiar one. At present it appears that if precursors of the Angiosperms are ever to be found, it will most likely be in the early Mesozoic or just possibly the late Palaeozoic, and that the Pteridosperms afford the most likely source of such stock as, conceivably, may in due course have evolved into the Angiosperms we know. This speculation arises from the facts that the Pteridosperms do not seem to constitute such a 'dead end' as the other groups of Gymnosperms, whether living or extinct, and that some of their members or allies (the Caytoniales) have their seeds largely enclosed in a recurved cupule which is suggestive of the arrangement in the angiospermous fruit. As pointed out by Dr. H. Hamshaw Thomas (*in litt.*), the possible connection of the Angiosperms with the Pteridosperms is further suggested by the similarities of structure in (*a*) wood anatomy (homologous types), (*b*) leaf form, for example in *Glossopteris* and *Gigantopteris*, (*c*) male flowers, and (*d*) seeds, especially as regards Angiosperms with integumentary bundles.

## Past Ages and Their Plant Life

Fig. 37 aims to show the distribution of the main plant groups in geological time, with some suggestion of their relative abundance as far as this is known and can be indicated by varying the thickness of the figures representing the respective groups. It also indicates the geological eras and main periods, etc., mentions in sequence the dominant forms of life, and gives a series of supposed ages (*cf.* pp. 128–9).

We will now proceed to a brief review of the main floras of the past, having familiarized ourselves with the sequence of geological time and with the chief groups of plants concerned.

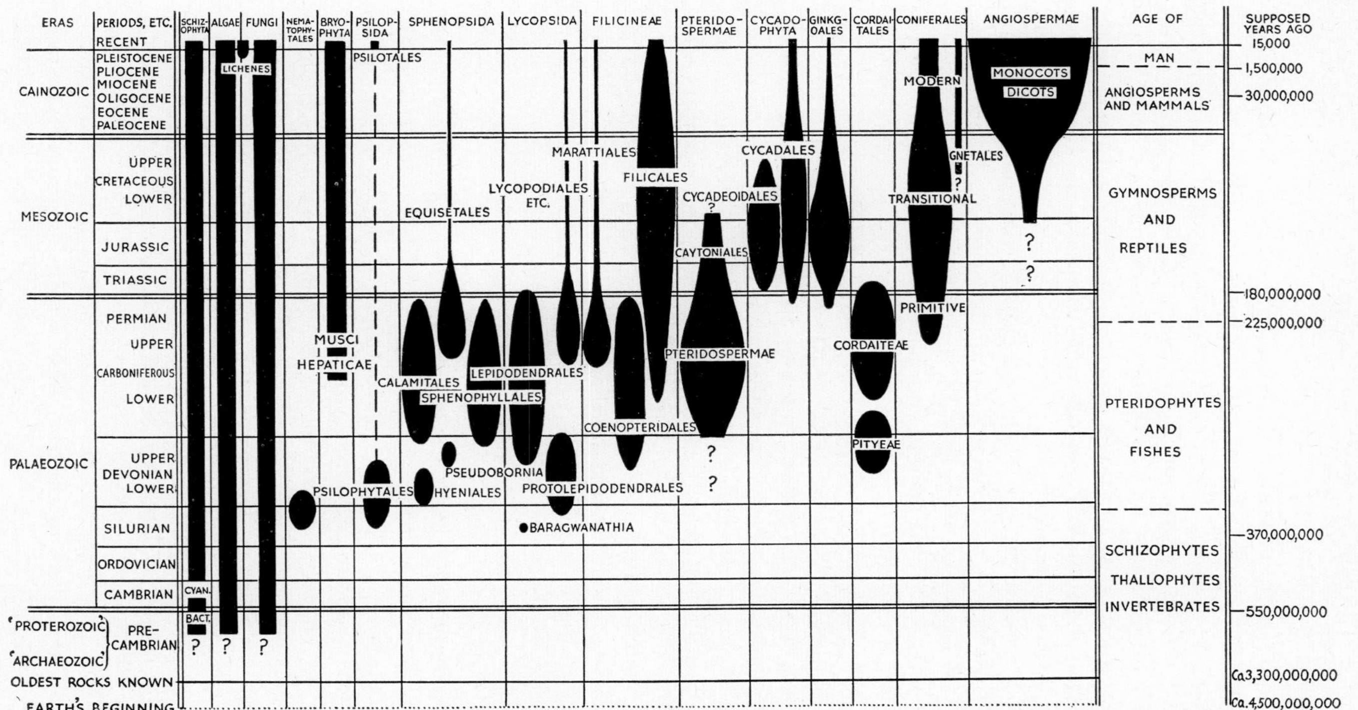


FIG. 37.—Distribution of plant groups in geological time as far as known (after Arnold, modified and extended).

The pre-Cambrian and early Palaeozoic preceding the Devonian together represent probably more than nine-tenths of known geologic time and constituted the age of Schizophytes, Thallophytes, and invertebrate animals. Bacteria, Blue-green Algae, Fungi, and true Algae of various groups appear to have been the main plants living through most of this time, although towards the end of it, in the Silurian, there seem to have been added the first land-plants in the form of some primitive Psilopsida and Lycopsida, and the still more problematical Nematophytales.

The Devonian and Carboniferous periods constitute the real age of Pteridophytes and Fishes, even if these groups had an earlier origin. Thus in the Devonian the primitive groups already mentioned apparently continued to flourish, as have Bacteria, Fungi, and Algae to the present day, while there were added various Sphenopsida, etc. Apparently none of these early Pteridophytes has survived, at least at the generic or lower level, any more than have the primitive Ferns which first appeared in that period, or possibly the Gymnosperms which were well established before the end of the Carboniferous. Although the early Devonian is often spoken of as primarily psilophytinean, there appear to have been plentiful other Pteridophytes living at the time. These evidently became more diverse and numerous in the upper Devonian, when the Psilophytales seem to have died out, and by then to have included some of tree dimensions. These may show what appear to be annual rings and indicate marked seasonal changes. An attempted reconstruction of a late Devonian forest is shown in Fig. 38.

The Carboniferous period was the culmination of the age of Pteridophytes, including many of large tree form as indicated in the diagrammatic reconstruction (Fig. 39). To these the Lycopsida, Sphenopsida, and Filicineae all contributed, and, in addition, the early gymnospermous Pteridosperms and Cordaitales. The Bryophytes first appeared at this time, at least so far as known indubitable fossils are concerned, as did several of the modern groups—including the true Club-mosses, Horsetails, and some Ferns—while before its end there existed some primitive Conifers. The upper Carboniferous or Pennsylvanian was the great Palaeozoic coal age, and evidently a time of damp and widely favourable 'even' climate in both northern and southern hemispheres. The vegetation which gave rise to the immense coal deposits of the northern hemisphere seems to have been one of the most widely luxuriant of all time, though the coals of the southern hemisphere appear to have been

FIG. 38.—Reconstruction of a late Devonian forest of New York. The trees are *Protolepidodendron primaevum*, a Lycopsid, and the supposed Seed-fern is *Euspermatopteris textilis*, of which actual fossil stumps are seen in the foreground (phot. J. A. Glenn, courtesy of the New York State Museum).

formed from the remains of a flora which was relatively poor in species and almost certainly belonged to a later age.

Of late Carboniferous time the early Permian was essentially a continuation, though, later, arid conditions became widespread, the

FIG. 39.—Generalized reconstruction of a Carboniferous forest. The tall, much-branched trees on the left are *Lepidodendron*. Below these are *Sigillaria* and leaves of *Lyginopteris*. In the centre foreground is a slender type of Calamite and in the background are much-branched tree types. To the right of the water in the foreground are more Sigillarias and a Tree-fern. On the extreme right are lofty Cordaitales, and, in the undergrowth, several Pteriodosperms, among which is seen a *Sphenophyllum*.

big Pteridophytes and the Pteridosperms tending to decline and become replaced by other groups—including the drought-resisting Cycadophytes and more Conifers. At the same time the characteristic if limited *Glossopteris* flora existed under the relatively cold conditions of the south, in the areas of India, Africa, South America, Australasia and Antarctica that were supposedly occupied by the ancient ‘ Gondwanaland ’. For the Permian was a period of active mountain building and rearrangement of large areas of land and sea, with severe glaciation at least in the South. It may be considered as starting the real age of higher Gymnosperms, which held sway throughout the Mesozoic era. In contrast with the generally uniform growth of trees in the coal age, those which grew during and immediately following the Permian glaciation show strongly developed 'annual' rings.

The early part of the Triassic period, at the beginning of the Mesozoic, tended to have an arid and generally unfavourable climate in the northern hemisphere, the fossil record being, moreover, fragmentary. Pteridosperms, Cycadophytes, Ginkgoales and Conifers appear to have been plentiful, as well as numerous Ferns and a lesser number of Lycopods and Horsetails. In Argentina, South Africa, and much of southeastern Asia, the climate was humid at that time, and supported a rich flora. It became drier and probably arid in these regions towards the close of the Triassic, when to the north conditions became much as in the Jurassic. Nevertheless the wide occurrence of similar floras indicated that comparable conditions extended over an extremely wide area. Fig. 40 shows an attempted reconstruction of a Triassic landscape, with plentiful Cycadophytes, etc., and some large Horsetails.

Jurassic floras were apparently developed under warm and moist conditions as indicated by fossil deposits, and were widely distributed. Indeed, their composition appears to have been fairly uniform all over the world, involving (with relatively minor variations) such far-flung lands as continental Europe, Spitsbergen, Greenland, temperate North America, Mexico, India, Japan, Australia and New Zealand. They included numerous Cycadophytes, Ginkgoales, and Conifers, besides representatives of most of the modern groups of Pteridophytes, though the giant Lycopods and Horsetails had long since disappeared, as had the Cordaitales. During this period the Pteridosperms declined and, according to some authorities, the first indubitable Angiosperms appeared.

The Cretaceous period witnessed the latest transformation of the plant world, in which the Angiosperms really came into their own. Conversely, most of the other groups of vascular plants were on the decline. It is interesting to note, however, that the lower cryptogams had meanwhile often held their own, as many do to this day—presumably because they do not normally compete with Angiosperms, though actually they have not been widely dominant on land since early Palaeozoic times. Thus, of the widespread upper Cretaceous 'Dakota flora' of North America, more than 90 per cent. of the species were Angiosperms, most of them belonging to familiar woody genera of Dicotyledons, although the presence of a few Palms indicated a fairly warm climate. Cycads were reduced to 2 per cent. and the Conifers were only slightly better represented. Whereas apparently still more warmth-loving floras appeared during the Cretaceous even in the continental United States, the existence at that time in Greenland and other arctic regions of floras of temperate or warmer type suggests that the climate was widely genial, and again probably of comparable nature over most of the world.

FIG. 40.—Reconstructed Triassic landscape (after Heer).

In the early part of the Cainozoic, individual species of plants tended to be more widely distributed than they are today. Of the first five parts of the era, making up the Tertiary, the second,[1] or Eocene (by many considered the first that is really distinguishable), affords widely distributed floras indicating still favourable conditions.

[1] The Paleocene is nowadays frequently distinguished as the first, especially in America.

Thus in North America and across Eurasia, conditions were substantially more favourable than at the present time, with Palms extending plentifully into Canada and England. Already the flora had a largely modern aspect, though herbaceous species in general and Monocotyledons in particular appear to have been far less abundant relatively to woody types than at present.

There may have been some deterioration of climate in the northern hemisphere in the next age, the Oligocene, but it appears to have been slight, with plentiful large trees prevailing well north. In any case in the southern hemisphere the climate seems to have remained more comparable with that of today than it did in the northern hemisphere.

The Miocene was a time of widespread volcanic activity in North America, when uplifting of the Cascade Range deprived the area to the east of much of its accustomed rainfall, so that increasing aridity prevailed—and probably lower temperatures, although the climate was still warm over wide areas. Fig. 41 shows a reconstructed scene in Miocene times, with Palms and Cycads growing in what is now a cool-temperate region.

By the Pliocene, conditions in America east of the Cascade Range had become generally unfavourable for the growth of dense forests and for the preservation of their remains, trees apparently occurring chiefly along the streams. As a result of the general cooling in the North, the vegetation became more like that of today, and actually in North America and eastern Asia the Pliocene deposits contain a large proportion of the species still found living in the same regions. On the other hand, many of the wide-ranging species then occurring in Europe have since disappeared therefrom.

In spite of all these changes in various parts of the Cainozoic, the same major plant groups appear to have persisted through it to the present day, even if the species and often higher taxa have changed; particularly striking is the dwindling importance of some of the Conifers.

The Pleistocene and Recent together make up the Quaternary and are now estimated to involve only the last million or fewer years (*cf.* p. 129), of which the Recent or post-Pleistocene occupies perhaps one-hundredth part. Remains of Pleistocene vegetation are preserved chiefly in unconsolidated lake and stream deposits, in peat bogs, or in a frozen condition, while postglacial peat deposits are still accumulating. In general only modern species are represented, most of these being still living and familiar; but in Pleistocene deposits they often extend far (and in post-Pleistocene ones sometimes considerably) beyond their present limits, suggesting substantial changes in climate since they were laid down. Indeed, such changes we know to have taken place in the northern parts of Eurasia and

Fig. 41.—A reconstructed scene in Switzerland during Miocene times (after Heer).

America, where several periods of advancing and declining glaciation widely affected the climate, and where further changes are indicated by such evidence as that afforded by sub-fossil pollens and other remains of contemporary plants preserved in bogs. These remains, when identified with plants of known climatic requirements, afford a valuable indication of local conditions. And as a further instance of the significance of climatic change, we shall see in the next chapter how the great diversity of woody plants in North America and eastern Asia is attributable to the fact that in these regions such plants were able to migrate far south before the extending ice and return north after its margin had receded, whereas in Europe they were supposedly forced against the southern mountains or sea and exterminated. For such reasons we must examine in the next chapter the historical bases of modern geographical ranges, before we can deal in an understanding way with the distributions we actually find.

## Further Consideration

The facts and theories advanced in this chapter, as in the case of most others, have usually been gleaned from various specialist and often highly technical sources which the general reader will scarcely wish to consult even if they are available to him. However, further details (and sometimes other opinions) may readily be obtained from one or more of the following generalized or introductory books in English:

Sir A. C. Seward. *Plant Life Through the Ages* (Cambridge University Press, Cambridge, Eng., pp. xxi + 601, 1931).

C. A. Arnold. *An Introduction to Paleobotany* (McGraw-Hill, New York & London, pp. xi + 433, 1947).

H. N. Andrews. *Ancient Plants and the World They Lived in* (Comstock, Ithaca, N.Y., pp. ix + 279, 1947).

John Walton. *An Introduction to the Study of Fossil Plants*, second edition (Black, London, pp. x + 201, 1953).

## Chapter VI

# FOUNDATIONS OF MODERN DISTRIBUTIONS

The distribution of each kind of plant making up a modern (and presumably any other) flora is apt to depend upon (1) the history of the plant in geological and recent times, (2) what may be called its migrational ability, and (3) its adaptability in physiological and other ways to the conditions of such new environments as it may reach. To a considerable extent migrational ability depends upon the efficiency of dispersal (as described in Chapter IV), and adaptability on plasticity of form or function (as treated in Chapter III). This leaves the 'fossil history' and recent vicissitudes to be dealt with next, at least in such aspects as are best known or most pertinent.

Whereas we have seen that, apart from such periods of local or regional change as occurred most notably in the Permian, the flora and vegetation of the aerial parts of the globe tended to be widely comparable in different regions during the earlier geological ages up to and including the Mesozoic, this relative uniformity was not maintained through the Cainozoic. There is plentiful evidence to show that still later than the end of the Mesozoic, during early Tertiary times, the forests tended to be more widespread and more uniform than at present—practically throughout the land of the northern hemisphere, including what are now high-arctic regions. And although climatic belts doubtless existed during these and earlier times, they can scarcely have been as marked in favourable periods as those we know nowadays ; for, with luxuriant vegetation flourishing within a few degrees of both the North and South Poles, the tropics would have been too hot for normal life—at least if the land of the world had at all the conformity it has today. But particularly from the Miocene onwards there were marked local changes in conditions, and so these latest fossil and sub-fossil floras are of great significance to us when considering the problem of the origin of the flora existing today.

## Some Effects of Relatively Recent Climatic Changes

At the close of the Tertiary or beginning of the Quaternary, although the vegetation of the tropical and adjacent zones continued in considerable luxuriance, there was a marked lowering of temperature in most other regions, that led to the covering of some by glaciers and to complete changes in the floras of others. Climate being the primary controller of vegetation, the flora in favourable warm areas probably continued, as it does to the present day, much as it had done at least through the middle Tertiary. But in the less favoured belts to the north and south, a lowering of temperature and decrease in precipitation—for instance in much of the Mediterranean Basin, in eastern Europe, and in northern and central Asia—led to the widespread replacement of the warmth-loving floras by hardier types. It may be presumed that there was at the same time a reduction in numbers of species and individuals, and in the general luxuriance of the vegetation. And whereas in the boreal regions, and even in the Arctic, there had formerly flourished (and according to some authorities evolved) a vast array of warmth-loving or at least mesothermic (*i.e.* liking moderate temperatures) types, these were in time pushed far south or, in some cases, doubtless exterminated.

Although evolution in general is a gradual process, it seems to be accelerated by sudden changes in habitat conditions. Thus the violent upheavals of the earth's crust or direct changes of climate appear to have induced sudden inherent and hereditary changes involving the abrupt creation of new races and, in time, of new species. Contemporaneously and for similar reasons, floras have been caused to migrate. These variations of conditions over long periods of time have probably led to a far more intricately adjusted and highly evolved general flora and vegetation than would have obtained if conditions had remained as they were, for example, in the Carboniferous. Indeed, some authorities have pictured a world of gigantic Reptiles instead of Mammals, and of giant Club-mosses and Horsetails instead of Angiosperms, as continuing today if the Carboniferous climatic and other conditions had persisted.

Besides direct climatic changes and others depending on such geological revolutions as the thrusting up of mountain ranges, there have evidently been changes in the conformation of land and sea—even, according to some authorities, in the positions of the continents with regard to one another and in relation to the geographical poles. All such changes would inevitably lead to alterations in the distributions of plants and of the animals that are dependent upon them, profoundly affecting also their evolutionary development. Thus, whereas in the northern hemisphere the distribution of the climatic zones favoured the development of relatively luxuriant vegetation over wide areas up to nearly the end of the Tertiary, in the southern hemisphere conditions appear to have been much more disturbed. Particularly did the great Permian glaciation, whose principal centre of development apparently lay in South Africa, play havoc with the flora and fauna; to it is attributed in some degree the poverty to this day of the flora of tropical Africa as compared with the floras of South America and Asia. It is supposed that relatively arid conditions prevailed subsequently over much of the southern hemisphere, which may have been further diversified by the separation of the continents beginning as far back as the Mesozoic. Thus tropical Africa is supposed to have been cut off from the rich vegetation of Eurasia by a wide sea occupying the position of the Sahara during the Cretaceous, and, in later times, by the Sahara Desert as we know it today—both sea and sand being effective in barring the migration, it has been suggested, of the majority of species from the North.

The climatic deterioration that began well back in the Tertiary led ultimately to widespread glaciation in the northern hemisphere. Thus, early in the Quaternary, vast areas of North America and northern Eurasia became enveloped in ice which may be compared, in extent and continuity if not in thickness, with that covering most of Greenland and Antarctica today. This Pleistocene ice reached a maximum extent and receded probably four times, the limits reached in each extension being different. The intervening, 'interglacial' periods were protracted and relatively favourable to plant life, being apparently for long periods at least as warm as the present day. The ice largely ousted the previously rich floras of the North, the plants being forced to migrate before its advance or, if they could not do so successfully, being exterminated—apart perhaps from some which persisted on mountains or other ice-free refugia, a subject to be discussed in the next section.

The poverty of the present western and central European flora is commonly ascribed to the fact that the Tertiary components were largely destroyed shortly before or during the Ice Age, by being driven into the sea or against high mountains. For post-Pleistocene restocking across the Mediterranean, over the Alps or Pyrenees, or from the floristically poor regions lying immediately to the east, was problematical to say the least, and from the west was wellnigh impossible as the Atlantic was now indubitably in existence. On the other hand, in North America and eastern Asia the warmth-loving plants among others were free—and evidently often able—to migrate far south in the lowlands or along mountain ranges, subsequently to return when the ice retreated and suitable conditions were reinstated in the North. Much the same appears to have happened in the Balkan region. To such considerations is attributed the presence of many living woody plants, such as members of the Magnolia family (Magnoliaceae), in eastern North America and

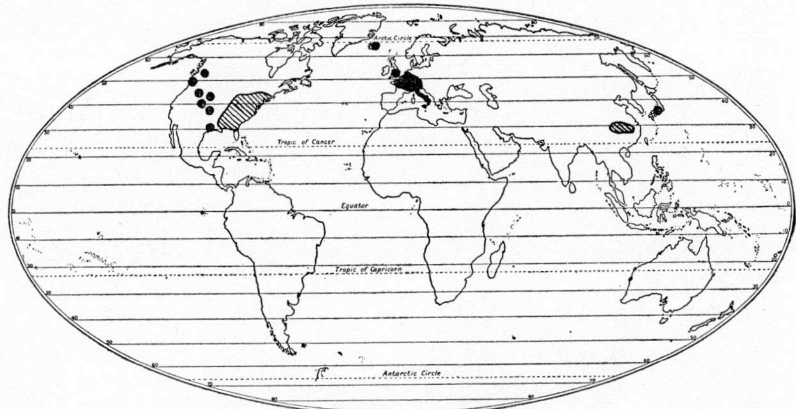


FIG. 42.—Known distribution of species of *Liriodendron* in Tertiary times (black) and nowadays (hatched). (After Good).

southeastern Asia but, on the other hand, their absence from Europe, though their remains in fossil deposits indicate that they were once widely distributed and locally plentiful in all three of these continents. Fig. 42 shows the known distribution of Tulip-trees (*Liriodendron* spp., Magnoliaceae) in Tertiary times (black) and living today (hatched), and Fig. 43 shows the even more drastic restriction of the giant Redwoods. Fig. 44 indicates the periods during which the various parts of North America are supposed to have been free from major ice-sheets. Even in the last of the interglacial periods, many plants persisted much farther north than they grow today—most notably in Europe—and it has been suggested that we have still not emerged permanently from the Ice Age.

Whereas it is thought that considerable expanses of territory in northern Asia and smaller ones in northern continental North America, as well as the northernmost insular tracts, were free from major ice-sheets throughout the Pleistocene, owing for example to their 'continental' climate and especially low precipitation, it is believed that ice at one or more stages of the Pleistocene engulfed

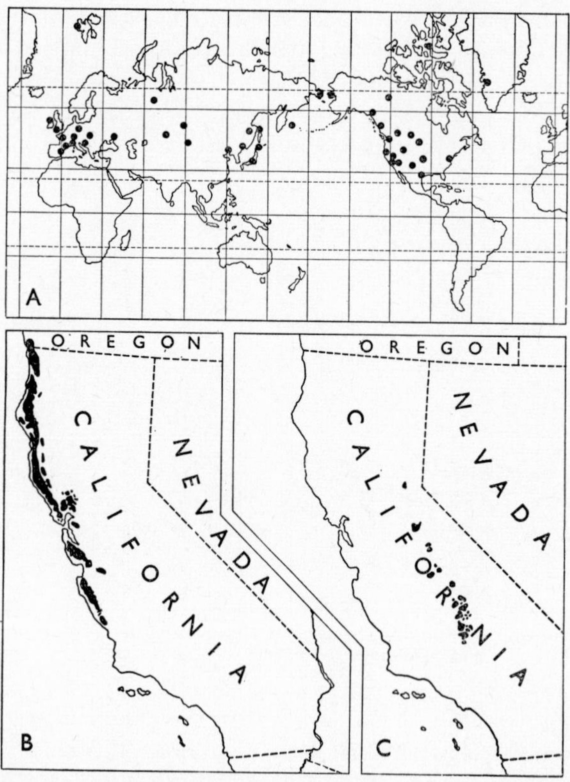


FIG. 43.—Past and present distributions of Redwoods. Above, known localities of fossil Redwoods (after Chaney); below, modern (relic) areas of Coastal Redwood (*Sequoia sempervirens*) on left and of Sierra Redwood or Big-tree (*Sequoiadendron giganteum*) on right. (Modified from Cain: *Foundations of Plant Geography*, copyright 1944, Harper & Brothers.)

much of northern North America (*see* Fig. 44) and virtually the whole of western and central Europe as far south as the Thames Valley in the west and the Carpathians in the east. Nor could such extensive glaciation of northern territories obtain without being reflected in a lowering of temperatures to the south and even in the tropics, where some mountains became glaciated, and where

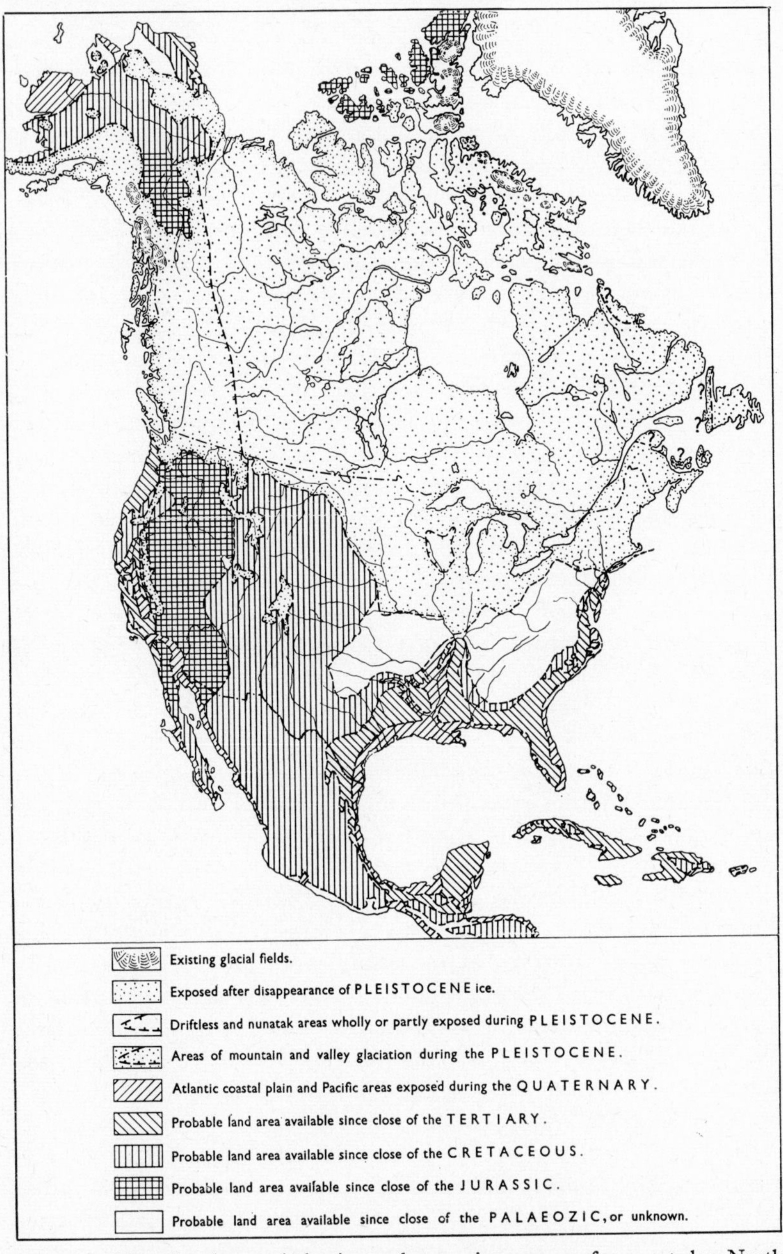


FIG. 44.—Map showing periods since when various areas of present-day North American land have supposedly been free from major ice-sheets, etc. (Harvard University handout, modified after Flint and others.)

warm lowlands (at least in the southern hemisphere) experienced 'pluvial' periods of increased precipitation. Simultaneously there was more extensive glaciation in some regions of the South, notably the uplands of South America and southern Australasia. All these and allied changes were gradual, the advance and retreat of the ice each time occupying many thousands of years, and allowing plants to migrate before its face in accordance with climatic changes.

Numerous living genera, especially of woody plants, are known once to have been far more widely distributed than they are today (striking examples are shown in Figs. 42 and 43). Many of our species and even vegetational associations are of similar nature to, but geographically more restricted than, those developed as far back as the Miocene. It seems that by this time most of the major land-masses of today had been formed, at least in outline, and that thereafter the deterioration in climate was marked, leading to a considerable reduction of the areas of many species of plants and animals—quite apart from the restriction effected by or through the Pleistocene glaciation. Already in the Pliocene the floras had tended to be markedly impoverished as compared with those of the Miocene, considerably less than 1,000 species of plants being known from the Pliocene in contrast with over 6,000 from the Miocene. The analogy of animals would suggest that over 80 per cent. of Pliocene plant species are still living today—some of them, *e.g.* the Bog-cypress (*Taxodium distichum*) and Black Oak (*Quercus nigra*) in Alabama, in the selfsame region. In other instances they are not now known to live in a wild state within thousands of miles of their old haunts—as in the case of the Water-chestnut (*Trapa*), fruits of which are widespread in deposits in North America up to the Pliocene, though it appears to be no longer a native of the New World. An interesting set of examples is afforded by a middle Pliocene flora of western Europe whose closest agreement is to be found with some areas of southeastern Asia; on the other hand, the flora yielded by the overlying late Pliocene beds finds its closest relationship with the existing flora of central Europe and indicates an already much cooler climate.

It is supposed that the Miocene and early Pliocene floras were practically circumpolar in distribution and also widespread latitudinally. Then the increasingly colder conditions in the North, often accentuated locally by the uprising of mountain ranges which furthermore caused aridity in their rain-shadows, forced the plants to migrate southward. It has been suggested that in this pre-

Pleistocene southward migration there were three principal avenues of escape, determined primarily by the prevailing direction of the mountain systems: (1) along the lowlands of eastern Asia, (2) along the mountain ranges of North America, and (3) down the Scandinavian Peninsula and adjacent areas into western and central Europe. The first route may have led to intermixture of northern species with the original native flora and so may largely explain the richness of the existing flora of China. The second route may have had much the same effect in America and would, moreover, explain the similarity between the floras of eastern North America and eastern Asia. In the third instance, however, the great European mountain ranges with axes lying east and west would have prevented further southward migration, with resulting impoverishment both currently and as regards possible recolonizing elements even after the final Pleistocene recession, as we have already seen. However, there has been some opposition to this hypothesis, and serious doubts expressed, for example, as to whether southwestern France was cold enough at this time to cause the postulated extermination, though this might still have been effected by the persistence there of closed communities, which are among the toughest barriers for a migrant to cross. Nor is it known whether the great extinction of plants and animals in Europe took place before the end of the Pliocene or during the Pleistocene. Probably it was a gradual process, each advance of rigorous conditions leading to the loss by the flora of some of its less hardy elements, so that potential waves of recolonizing vegetation became successively more impoverished.

## Pleistocene Persistence *versus* Subsequent Immigration

The Pleistocene itself, as we have seen, was a climatically unsettled period of cold spells with extensive glaciations, which were separated by relatively long warm intervals (interglacials). In general the plants living during the Pleistocene were specifically identical with those of the present time, the chief differences exhibited by them being in spatial distribution. During some at least of the interglacials the climate appears to have been similar to that of the present day—which indeed has led to the suggestion that we may nowadays be merely in another interglacial. Thus more than 70 per cent. of the species whose remains have been identified from an interglacial deposit in Germany live in the same district at present, and so do most of those in a deposit near Toronto in southern

Canada grow close by, though a few are now restricted to areas slightly farther south.

The climate near the margin of the ice during the glacial stages was probably rather like that of southern Greenland today, where arborescent growth is to be found within a few miles of the terminal face of the ice-cap; even more striking is the situation in New Zealand, where subtropical Tree-ferns may be seen growing a bare mile from the end of a glacier. Thus the Pleistocene tundra (treeless plain) in North America probably formed only a narrow belt around the margin of the ice-sheet, with conditions becoming rapidly more equable away from it. In Europe the ice-free zone appears to have been relatively wide, at least during the later glacial maxima. In central Eurasia the tundra was apparently bordered by steppes, while in North America extensive deposits of loess (wind-transported sediment) suggest a drier climate than now prevails. To the south of the tundra and steppe belts lay more or less broken forest, although it seems likely that in some places the advancing ice impinged directly on the forests. When precipitation decreased or the climate became warmer, the ice retreated and the whole series of vegetation zones followed its margin northwards—only to be pushed south again when conditions deteriorated and the ice advanced once more.

It is often supposed that in Alaska and eastern Asia the glaciation was chiefly of the local, mountain type, considerable areas being left free or at least not covered by extensive ice-sheets. It also seems that, because the precipitation was locally insufficient for extensive accumulation of ice, the northernmost parts of Greenland and the Canadian Arctic Archipelago remained largely unglaciated. There is no reason to doubt that many plants persisted in these unglaciated areas—in some cases probably throughout the whole of the Pleistocene, in others at least through its latest glacial maximum (which was by no means everywhere the greatest in extent as compared with its predecessors).

But whereas it is an observation of today, and a supposition for similar phenomena of the past, that many plants can and do grow on ice-free areas even when these are surrounded by ice, it is another matter to explain apparent anomalies of modern distribution in terms of such survival throughout long periods of intense glaciation. Yet this has been so widely assumed that it seems necessary to point out the seemingly overwhelming counter-arguments to this 'nunatak' hypothesis—so called from the Eskimo word for a mountain sticking out of an ice-cap, for on such mountains much perglacial persistence is supposed by some students to have taken place.

To begin with, much of the supposed evidence brought forward for survival, such as the 'relict' nature of particular plants in particular areas, has proved to be either capable of other interpretation or actually erroneous. Thus, geologists have insisted that several of the areas claimed by the advocates of persistence to have been 'refugia' during the Pleistocene, were in fact glaciated. Moreover, latterly there have been numerous instances of plants of supposed isolation or disrupted distribution (which were claimed to indicate such refugia) being found in intermediate positions—sometimes even on islands that have only recently risen out of the sea. Nor does endemism (restriction to particular geographical areas) necessarily indicate isolation and persistence; it sometimes actually suggests the opposite, as in some cases of hybrid origin!

It is noticeable that many of the isolated or restricted (endemic) species, which are made so much of by advocates of the nunatak hypothesis, are characteristic of, or sometimes restricted to, calcareous soils. It has been strongly counter-claimed that their spotty or localized occurrence can best be correlated with soil characteristics, the presence or absence of signs of recent glaciation being of little or no consequence. And when we remember that many of these are far-northern plants which favour 'open' soils where competition is lacking, and that in boreal regions calcareous areas are notable for their poor vegetation but diversified flora, other possibilities spring to mind and the nunatak hypothesis becomes less and less attractive.

There are also objections to the nunatak hypothesis on the ground of far easier and wider dispersal than its adherents will admit—for example by Birds, and as regards characters of higher plants transported in pollen, and through airborne disseminules of lower plants. Thus in the manner of plants, Birds also have their habitat preferences, often traversing great distances from one to another similar spot. Although normally they are supposed to 'fly clean' when on migration, they must surely (as already mentioned in Chapter IV) sometimes carry materials frozen or otherwise stuck to their plumage, etc.—especially if flushed unexpectedly or unwell, when they are apt to 'neglect their toilet'. Pungent instances seem to be afforded by the seeds, coated in protective regurgitate, that have been found adhering to migrant Birds on the subantarctic Macquarie Island, but apparently do not belong to any of the local species, as noted already on p. 114. And in the final analysis it must be remembered that a single disseminule in many millennia may be sufficient to 'plant' a species.

But whereas the idea of certain plants persisting in tiny areas for hundreds of thousands of years, unchanged and unaffected by the coming and going of ice-ages and hordes of other migrants, is scarcely in accordance with our saner biological reflection, some persistence on ice-free tracts, for example through the last glacial maximum, may well have taken place. And restocking may indeed have been helped by plants surviving on temporary sheltered 'islands' surrounded by ice, or on ice-free coastal strips—thence to recolonize surrounding areas on release from the bondage of glaciation. On the other hand, the plants surviving on mountain nunataks would be mainly arctic or high-alpine ones accustomed to rigorous conditions and unlikely to recolonize lastingly the surrounding plains on recession of the ice and marked amelioration of conditions. Thus, as was pointed out by Professor G. E. Du Rietz (*in litt.*), 'Scandinavian botanists have believed more in glacial survival in coastal areas than on nunataks', and such an 'hypothesis of glacial survival' would seem more reasonable; nor are the criticisms of the nunatak hypothesis which apply to North America necessarily valid in northern Europe where conditions tend to be different. Many persisting plants, however, appear to become depleted in biotypes and, owing to a consequent narrowness of ecological amplitude, rather passive; some become reactivated by cross-breeding following release from glaciation, aggressively recolonizing surrounding areas from their vegetated 'islands'. Thus, although the nunatak hypothesis in its strictest form seems unsound and indeed unnecessary, some residue of it may well be valid and still found useful, in spite of the fact that the recolonization of deglaciated areas appears in general to have taken place by immigration of plants that tided over the inimical period in distant (usually southern) areas. Thence the plants subsequently migrated, for the most part by gradual stages.

Persistence through the Pleistocene, or at least through its latest phases, may also help to explain the existence of 'arctic' plants on mountains far to the south, although in some cases migrating birds are probably responsible. In other instances, the similarity to arctic conditions evidently enabled properly acclimatized plants to retreat to the mountain tops, even as they were able to persist near the margin of the ice and follow it north. For in both these situations the plants were able to get away from the competition of ranker (but often less hardy) types.

Altogether it seems most reasonable to consider the post-Pleistocene flora of those territories of the northern hemisphere which were freed from the last major glaciation as being made up of: (1) some elements which had with little doubt persisted in at least recent unglaciated ' refugia ', particularly in sheltered coastal areas, (2) elements spreading from sheltered refuges afforded particularly by mountain systems where the Ice Age did not have such catastrophic consequences as to destroy the characteristic Tertiary flora even if it did cause impoverishment, (3) probably numerous elements which migrated northwards from the territories bordering the southern extremity of the ice after it retreated, and (4) recent immigrants from afar (or at least from regions not drastically affected by the Pleistocene), whose establishment has been favoured, in areas recently freed from glaciation, by the local lack of competition from already closed (*i.e.* continuous) vegetation. These recent migrants were aided by natural means—wind, water, or animals—or by Man, through intentional or accidental importation, and many such migrations are still going on plentifully all the time. Examples are afforded by the considerable numbers of weeds that have recently become established in ' open ' areas, including inhabited parts of West Greenland, and the westward advance of Asian species into Europe.

## Continental Drift, Shifting Poles, Land-Bridges, etc.

The present distribution of any given plant species is in part a reflection of the geological revolutions and climatic changes that have occurred in the world during the period of its existence as a species. In former sections of this chapter we considered the effects of climatic change in the past and particularly the significance of the Pleistocene Ice Age. It is now time to examine some other leading theories that have been advanced in an attempt to explain the current distribution of particular plants.

Perhaps the most promising and plausible (though still highly controversial) theory in this connection is that of ' continental drift ', which is often identified with the name of its principal proponent of recent times, the late Dr. Alfred Wegener. This ' displacement hypothesis ' is based on the assumption that the present-day continents once formed part of a single land-mass (Pangaea), or, according to a recent modification, two land-masses, whose continents started breaking and drifting apart during the Mesozoic era and went on doing so until they came to reach the positions they now occupy. According to some advocates of the theory, this drifting is still proceeding and actually demonstrable in the case of Greenland. Such recent drifting might conceivably have left Europe and North America in contact with one another until the early Quaternary, and likewise Antarctica and South America may be presumed to have remained long in contact. The theory also accounts for considerable rearrangement of the climatic zones on land, as the drifting of the continents was supposed to involve changes in their several positions relative to the North and South Poles. This in turn would allow marked changes in the distributions of living organisms, and bring plants and even entire floras to regions whose present climates are barely adequate for their growth. Still more spectacularly, it would allow fossil remains to drift with their enclosing land-masses to distant parts of the globe—and hence into entirely different climatic belts—and this could explain, for example, the presence of fossils of warmth-loving plants in the Far North.

Although it is rejected by some geologists and, especially, geophysicists, the theory of continental drift has won the ardent support of others—even if only for earlier geological times than those which allow most help to the biogeographer in theorizing about the anomalies he finds. To many of the botanists among these biogeographers, it seems to constitute the most plausible working hypothesis upon which they can base their suppositions as to the history of plant ranges. In one connection or another, the controversy rages back and forth and probably will continue to do so for a long time to come, though it may be noted meanwhile that the maps produced by proponents of the theory are extraordinarily suggestive, and would, one imagines, if analyzed statistically, indicate a very high degree of probability (*cf.* Fig. 45, A). However, geologists and geophysicists are prone to put back the time of possible rift and major displacement of continents well before the beginning of the Mesozoic, when it would be of little if any help to plant geographers in their search for explanations of striking similarities of flora in certain areas that are now widely separated by oceans. For it is obvious that, as differences between species commonly involve the establishment of various genetically independent mutations (sudden changes), the chances that two isolated populations will evolve in exactly the same way are incalculably low, while convergence in every respect of previously dissimilar types is even more improbable. Accordingly, similarities across wide stretches of water are more popularly explained by suppositions of previous proximity or even contiguity, though, as we have already suggested, dispersal may be more effective than is commonly supposed, and, conceivably, responsible for some at least of the apparent anomalies of distribution.

If it were accepted for Mesozoic and later times, the hypothesis of continental separation and drift would make unnecessary, or at all events less necessary, several of the following and other theories that are of interest in plant geographical considerations—though it may be confidently assumed that it will not be so accepted without far more conclusive evidence than has yet been presented. Meanwhile it should be noted that this theory is supported by, or is in accordance with, a great many data on the migrations and inter-relations of different floras and plant groups in past geological ages, besides explaining many anomalies of plant distribution of the present day. On the other hand it offers no explanation of the similarities of the floras of eastern Asia and North America, or of the floras of islands in the Pacific which suggest trans-Pacific connections—or at least migrations. Indeed, according to Professor G. E. Du Rietz (*voce*), who yet believes it possible that the same taxonomic entity may have arisen independently in more than one area, the flora of New Zealand is contrary to the hypothesis of continental drift, bearing similar relationships to both its east and its west.

The theory of polar oscillations or ' shifting of poles ', sometimes called the ' pendulum theory ', also aims at explaining, on the basis of incidental earlier climatic changes, some phenomena of plant distribution that are far out of line with climatic zones as they now exist. It is presumed that changes in climatic zones, as indicated *inter alia* by the distributions of fossil plants, were caused by changed location of the continents in relation to the sun's orientation, and this theory of polar oscillations attempts to explain these phenomena by assuming that periodic changes have occurred, owing to the position of the geographical poles oscillating back and forth like a pendulum, or at least ' wandering ' quite widely. This must not be confused with the now well-known movement of the North Magnetic Pole. It should be noted that continental drift and (geographical) polar wandering are considered to have quite possibly taken place together, in view of the plasticity implied by the former, and that proponents of the latter are prone to put an earlier position

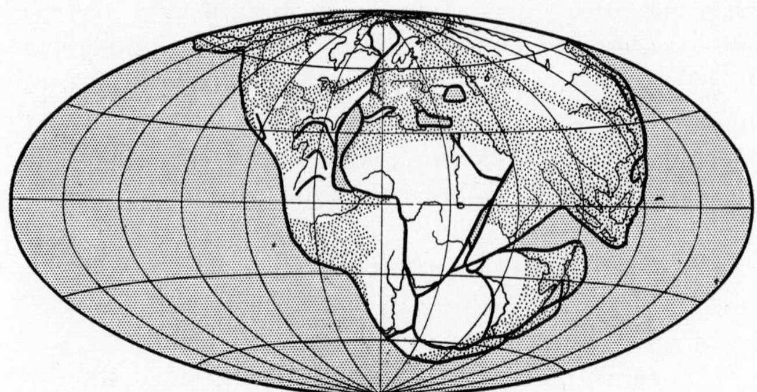

Upper Carboniferous

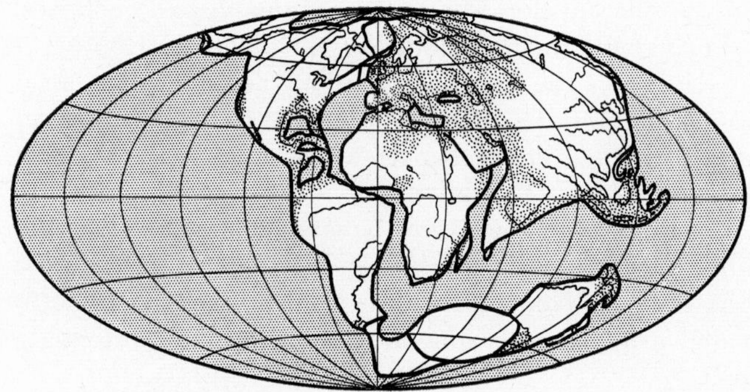

Eocene

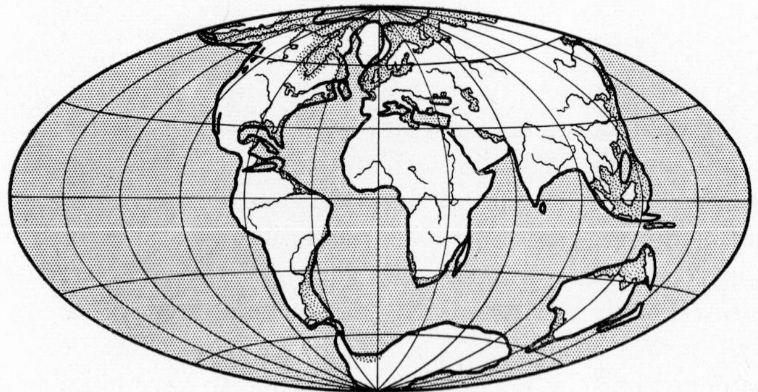

Old Quaternary

A

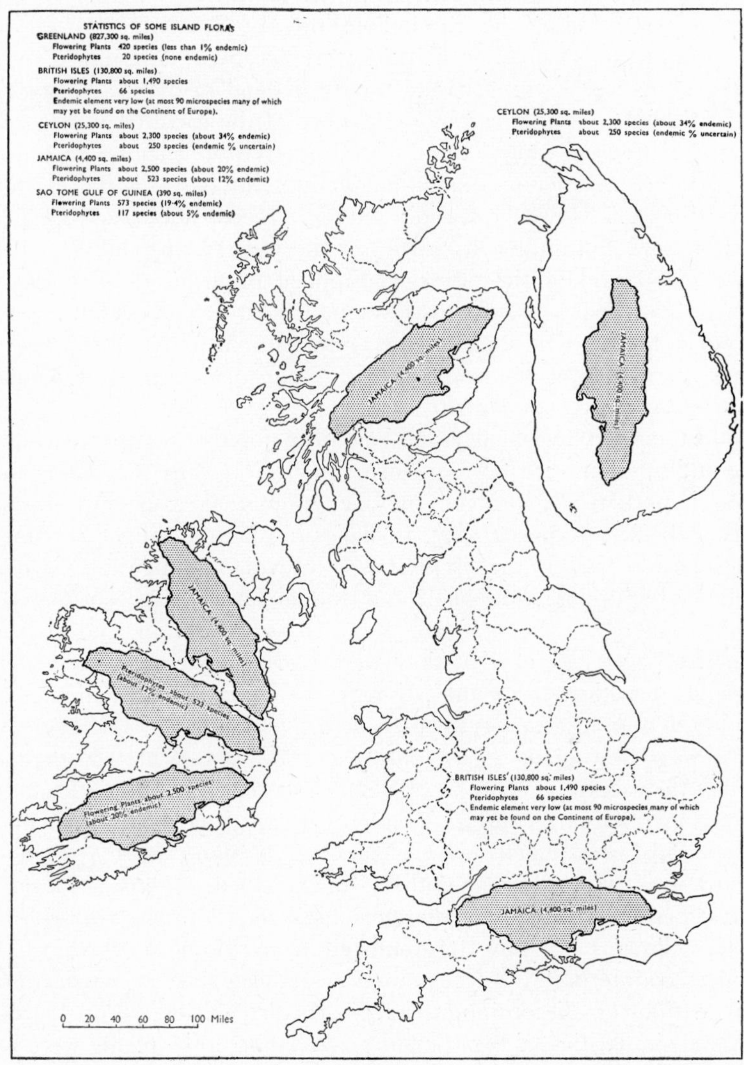


FIG. 45.—Maps illustrating 'continental drift' and the proximity of land-masses as apparently affecting floristic richness. A, reconstructions of the map of the world at three stages according to the theory of continental drift, the thinly stippled areas being shallow seas, while present-day rivers, etc., are shown merely for purposes of orientation (after Wegener); B, comparison of areas and floras of islands in relation to the proximity of major land-masses and their floristic richness (prepared by W. T. Stearn).

of the North Pole in the North Pacific, the implied change in the earth's axis bringing the South Pole into the South Pacific.

If the theory of polar oscillations were accepted, it would in turn make unnecessary any separate theory of land-bridges, as changes in level of the sea induced by oscillations of the earth (that are presupposed to have caused those of the poles) would suffice to cause the joining together or separation of different parts of the earth's land surface. However, in spite of some recent attempts at resurrection, and continuing discussion of the possible instability of the earth's axis and of the phytogeographical implications this might have,[1] this theory of polar oscillations is said to possess little geophysical foundation or geological support. Moreover, if it were made to explain some anomalies of plant distribution, it would apparently merely precipitate others!

The theory of land-bridges has long been popular in some quarters, and indeed there are few seas or even deep oceans that have not been hypothetically bridged by one or another over-enthusiastic author to explain present-day anomalies in plant or animal distribution. And certainly the simplest way to explain similarities (sometimes only supposed) of plant and animal life between such areas as Europe and eastern North America, or Australia and South America, is to assume that they were once connected by a bridge of land or a 'lost continent', though the bridging and hence possibility of migration across the present-day ocean need not necessarily have been continuous at any one time. But altogether the theory strikes the sceptic as being too artificial and 'convenient' for reality, and again there are contrary geophysical and geological arguments. It was advanced chiefly as a concession to some aspects of biogeography, while leaving others unexplained. Thus it leaves unclarified why plants in former geological ages flourished in regions whose climates are now far removed from those to which their modern counterparts are accustomed, and it also gives no satisfactory explanation of discontinuous areas of distribution. For if the floristic similarities of two distant areas having alike plants were to be explained by their having once been joined by a 'bridge', it would be necessary to assume that the entire extent of that bridge offered similar ecological conditions suitable for the migration of these plants. This requires more imagination than to visualize recent dispersal by the means discussed in Chapter IV, or, perhaps,

[1] *See*, for example, *Nature*, vol. 175, p. 526, 1955, vol. 176, p. 349, 1955, and vol. 176, p. 422, 1955.

continental drift involving the ' like ' areas being once together but subsequently separated!

It seems, however, that the theory of land-bridges is justified to the extent that such phenomena come and go nowadays on a small scale—for example with the emergence and submergence of isthmuses with changes in the relative level of water, and with the throwing up or destruction of beaches by the sea. Also, there can be little doubt that such ' bridges ' have existed on a bigger scale in the past, at least to the extent of once linking together some present-day islands with their adjacent mainland over an area of continental shelf, and joining in continuity such close land-masses as Alaska and easternmost Siberia. Nor, according to some authorities, can certain distribution-patterns in the southern hemisphere well be explained without the supposition of an Antarctic land-bridge. This may have joined South America to Australasia, to which two regions such restricted genera as *Nothofagus* (Southern Beeches) and *Fitzroya* are common, while also occurring as fossils on the Antarctic Continent (*cf.* Fig. 58, p. 195).

The theory of permanence of oceans and continents, which grew out of objections to, and largely opposes, those of land-bridges and continental drift, presupposes the land-masses to have occupied their present positions from pre-Cambrian times. However, it still leaves unexplained many biogeographical phenomena—particularly those that suggest the continents to have been connected at some period—and is unable to cope with the high-arctic flourishing of luxuriant vegetation in earlier ages. For although it has been suggested, and may yet be maintained, that plants might have changed their climatic requirements in the past, they can scarcely have done this sufficiently to account for such extreme cases.

This brings us to the theory of the polar origin of floras, which in one or another form has some eminent advocates to this day. When it was believed that climatic conditions were uniform throughout the world in early geological ages, with differentiation into climatic zones not taking place until the end of the Cretaceous or beginning of the Tertiary, it was widely thought that the floras of the world spread rapidly from a single centre lying in the north polar region—through Europe into Africa, through eastern Asia into Malaysia and Australia, and through North America into South America. This was the arctic or monoboreal theory of the origin of floras. Subsequently such discoveries as that of fossil floras in Antarctica indicated that a similarly drastic reduction in temperature has taken place there, and suggested that the lands of the Far South had once been connected with one another by way of the Antarctic Continent. This provided a basis for the presumption that there had probably been a centre of species-formation there too, and that life originated in the lands encircling both geographical poles. However, neither theory can well be accepted, for it is now recognized that climatic zones have existed as long as there has been life on earth, and that ice-ages occurred previously to the Pleistocene and in parts of the world other than the present polar areas. Moreover, other centres of plant development have been strongly advocated —particularly in the tropics.

An interesting example of the importance of historical and other factors in the diversity and constitution of present-day island floras is illustrated in Fig. 45, B, kindly contributed by Mr. W. T. Stearn, of the British Museum (Natural History). This shows that whereas the flora of Jamaica is large and diverse although its area is small, the flora of Ceylon is smaller although its area is larger than that of Jamaica, while the flora of the many times larger British Isles is smaller still. Each island having a comparable degree of topographic variation, and the climates of Jamaica and Ceylon being similarly favourable and that of the British Isles not unfavourable, it seems reasonable to presume that the greater floristic diversity of Jamaica is due to its proximity to the Central American region of continuous evolution from early geological times. Ceylon, on the other hand, although also tropical and humid and likely to be capable of supporting a large flora, is near the geologically much younger and floristically poorer southern portions of India, and consequently has had a less diverse flora to draw upon. In the British Isles, the flora and proportion and also degree of endemism are all smaller than in Jamaica and Ceylon, owing in part to relatively recent glaciation, in part to the prevailingly less favourable climate, and in part to the proximity of (and only recent separation from) the mainland of Europe. Greenland, most of whose still greater area is covered by ice, has an even smaller flora, owing, it seems clear, to the widely inimical climate and severe Pleistocene glaciation. Its about 475 species of vascular plants (including well-established introductions and 31 Pteridophytes) show an extremely low proportion and degree of endemism, with none at all among the Pteridophytes. (These are the latest statistics which have become available since the preparation of Fig. 45, B.)

## Postglacial[1] Changes

Climatic change has affected plant distribution right up to the present time, and indeed such changes and their effects on plant life are still going on and presumably will always continue. The postglacial sequence of changes is best known and perhaps most marked in temperate Europe, where the sequence has been briefly as follows:

(1) the earliest deposits following the last glacial recession show evidence of an arctic–subarctic–arctic sequence of vegetation-types characterized by Dwarf Birch (*Betula nana* agg.), shrubby Willows (*Salix* spp.), and Mountain Avens (*Dryas octopetala* s.l.),[2] developed under probably rather dry as well as cold conditions except around the middle of the period, which persisted for example in the British Isles until about 11,000 years ago. This 'Subarctic' period was followed about a millennium later by

(2) a 'Pre-Boreal' period of variable but milder climate, characterized by Scots Pine (*Pinus sylvestris*), Birch (*Betula pubescens* s.l.), and Elm (*Ulmus*), with Spruce (*Picea*) dominant in some eastern regions. This was in turn followed by

(3) a 'Boreal' period of relatively warm and dry 'continental' climate which towards its end supported mixed hardwood forest—particularly of Oak (*Quercus*) with abundant associated Hazel (*Corylus*) in the temperate belt, and persisting there until probably seven or eight thousand years ago. Thereafter followed

(4) a still warmer but wet 'Atlantic' period characterized by mixed Oak and Lime (*Tilia*) forest, constituting the so-called 'climatic optimum' (*i.e.* for northwestern Europe) that lasted until 5,000 or fewer years ago. This was in turn followed by

(5) the more continental, drier 'Sub-Boreal', which lasted until about 2,500 years ago, and in which there occurred a reduction of bog growth but an increase of Conifers and the entry of Beech

[1] It is said that we are still not out of the Pleistocene epoch and that, consequently, we should not speak of the Present or Recent or post-Pleistocene; from our point of view, and although because of variability in different places it cannot be satisfactorily defined, the time since the last great glacial recession is all postglacial, and seems best so termed (informally, with a small 'p'). While suggesting this course, Professor R. F. Flint confirms (*voce*) that the terms Recent and Holocene, which are often used for postglacial time, have also not been properly defined.

[2] Also, Professor Gunnar Erdtman informs me (*voce*), by such 'pioneer' plants as species of *Artemisia*, *Helianthemum*, members of the Chenopodiaceae, and even *Ephedra*.

(*Fagus*) and Hornbeam (*Carpinus*). In early historical times the climate tended to be cool and moist, yielding

(6) the 'Sub-Atlantic' period, which was characterized by considerable bog formation. This appears to have given way during the last millennium, and particularly in recent decades, to a warmer and drier period. Meanwhile the forests have been gradually destroyed by Man.

So far as has been determined, and indeed as might be expected, details of the above changes have varied considerably in different areas, so that in some more, but in others fewer, phases have been recognized. Nor, according to Dr. H. Godwin (*in litt.*), were the periods as certain and defined as is commonly believed. In general, the tendency has been to find less favourable temperatures to the north, and especially in the Arctic, where at best conditions approximating those of the present-day Subarctic have prevailed. Moreover, different workers have placed different interpretations on the 'sub-fossil' and other evidence available, only the simplest generalization being applicable to the majority of the drastically affected parts of the world. However, there has clearly been a climatic succession consisting of three main phases, viz. (1) increasing temperature, (2) culmination in warmth-loving trees, and (3) decrease of warmth-loving trees and appearance of those predominating today. Thus in temperate America there are scarcely any profiles known to yield such tundra plants as occurred in the Subarctic of Europe, but the other periods are closely comparable with the European, comprising a cool Pre-Boreal (Spruce–Fir), a warm and dry Boreal (Pine), a warm and moist Atlantic (Oak–Hemlock–Beech, etc.), a warm and dry Sub-Boreal (Oak–Hickory), and a cool and moist Sub-Atlantic (Spruce–Hemlock, Oak–Beech, etc.). Age-checks by such methods as 'carbon-14' have recently indicated that these climatic changes on the two sides of the Atlantic approximately coincided in time.

This hypothesis of climatic change suggests that, of the plants which may be segregated into groups because of their preponderance during one or another of these periods, the Atlantic and Sub-Atlantic species favour regions having an oceanic climate and the plants of the earliest or Subarctic period do not avoid coastal regions nowadays, whereas the Boreal and Sub-Boreal ones favour inland areas of continental climate that tend to be drier and warmer though often given to extremes. Sometimes the species of one category will be so grouped together in an area as to suggest a particular postglacial history or origin, such considerations again being important as a basis of present-day distribution. So here again we see instances of the significance of historical causes for an understanding of the present distribution of species and of their groupings in vegetation.

## The Genetical Heritage

The remaining aspect to be considered as part of the historical background of plant distributions is the genetico-evolutionary one, an outstanding example being afforded by polyploids, treated in the next section. It seems reasonable to suppose that the physiological tendencies and habitat preferences of particular plant entities have long been much as they are today, as have, doubtless, many of the habitats themselves, and that morphological (that is, of general form) and anatomical (of internal structure) indications of ecological relationships that hold nowadays are also largely applicable to plants which lived in earlier ages. Indeed such assumptions are behind many of our contentions regarding climatic and other changes in bygone ages. Nevertheless, evolution has doubtless proceeded at various speeds and with varying results throughout the period in which there have been advanced forms of life on earth, and among the characters affected have surely been such ones as migrational abilities, acclimatization potentialities, and habitat preferences. Consequently, we should consider in broad outline the evolutionary tendencies that manifest themselves in these characters, and some facts and fallacies of resultant areal indication, before proceeding with the more practical parts of this treatise.

Just as most obvious manifestations of form are inherited by each generation from the last, and this process is repeated virtually *ad infinitum*, so are different functions, different physiological attributes, usually so inherited—including those which control the migrational abilities, acclimatization potentialities, and habitat preferences of different plants. Indeed these last three groups of factors are best considered as one, being in any case all dependent on inherent tendencies that can scarcely be separated. An outcome of this inheritance, generation after generation, in particular lines or strains of plants, is the obvious suitability of certain plants for certain areas, the converse holding often more strongly—namely, that certain other plants are unfitted for growth in these areas. Just as evolution of form results from the action and often interaction of one or more processes such as mutation (including chromosomal multiplication or other change), hybridization (producing new combinations of genic materials), isolation, and natural selection, so does evolution regardless of form result in particular physiological make-up. Here are included those physiological factors on which depend the suitabilities of particular plants to grow in particular areas.

By such means is delimited the potential area of a species, outside of which it cannot grow naturally. The ultimate limits are accordingly genetically controlled, being restricted primarily to areas of a particular climatic range and secondarily, within these, to areas of particular sorts of soils, etc. And even though acclimatization allows some latitude, this can only be within genetically fixed limits —unless, of course, there is some fundamental evolutionary change in the race. This sometimes happens, for example through mutation or hybridization. Also effective in this direction is some change in the population, such as can take place through isolation and selection of the forms best adapted to withstand particular local conditions. The latter type of instance is not so much genetically controlled as genetically allowed, for, as we have already seen, a population even of a single species or lower entity usually consists of more or less numerous biotypes differing slightly in their inheritance. Owing to different groupings of biotypes occurring in different local populations, or at all events to varying selection, different geographical races of a species often appear that have different habitat preferences and, consequently, ranges. And geographical isolation promotes evolutionary divergence—not merely because of differing selection-pressures and variational tendencies, but also because mutations appearing subsequently cannot be shared around by interbreeding ; in time, new species may result.

In spite of this relative ease and speed of evolution in some instances, it appears to be extremely slow in others. Thus it is supposed that most at least of the woody species of temperate regions date well back into the Tertiary, having existed for five million or more years. That, as we have seen, was a time when equable climates extended much farther towards the poles than they do nowadays, and woody species of temperate regions tended to be much more widespread. One of the most active principles tending to blur the immediate effects of evolution is introgression, which is the gradual infiltration of the germ-plasm (and hence inculcation of facets of the character) of one species into that of another as a result of hybridization and repeated back-crossing with the original parental lines. Disturbance of the habitat is known to favour hybridization, and when such disturbance is so common and widespread as in the Arctic, with the frequent frost-heaving of open habitats where there is little competition, we may expect ready gene-flow—hence perhaps in part the notorious ' plasticity ' of arctic plants. For related populations can be lastingly sympatric (that is, coexist in the same territory) only if they are reproductively isolated. Length of life may be an important factor controlling hybridization and introgression—especially where uniformity is maintained by a preponderance of vegetative propagation, with consequent restriction of gene-flow and limitation of genetical recombination. In such circumstances, the ill-adapted offspring tend to be easily eliminated by competition. On the other hand, with free gene-flow and a fair amount of mutation in rapidly succeeding generations, much new ' raw material ' is provided for natural selection to work upon, and evolution may be expected to proceed with some dispatch.

The distribution patterns of organisms, like the external appearance and genetic constitution of the component individuals themselves, are the end result of the interaction of evolutionary processes and climatic, pedological, and other changes over long periods of time. Now similarity of distribution patterns suggests similarity of general background including evolutionary history, and this may give some possibility of divining the history of an organism well represented in the fossil record but unknown genetically—provided we have others of comparable distribution that are well known in this last respect. Such elucidations, and indeed the broader ones of plant geography, must, however, be indulged in only on the basis of all known facts, and then only with the utmost caution.

In the light of modern knowledge, some old assumptions should be discarded or at least greatly modified—for example, that the diversity of a group is dependent upon its age, which may be determined, at all events relatively, by counting the number of members now living; and that the age of a species or other taxon is directly related to the size of its area of distribution. Such are the main tenets of the hypothesis of ' Age and Area', discussed further on pp. 182–3, 209. And although ideally there may be some basic truth in these assumptions, some aggregate responsible effect in that diversity may come with time and increase colonization potentialities, even as time itself may increase the chances of dispersal, in actual fact evolution and migration have proceeded at very different rates in different groups and at different periods, both because of inherent differences and of being rarely unimpeded.

Again, such generalizations as those which seek to give directions for determining the place of origin of a particular plant group are apt to be dangerous, as for example the supposition that the original home of a group is the place in which the largest number of its representatives exist. Thus old groups have frequently survived great alterations of climate and have died out in major regions where they formerly flourished—sometimes, with little doubt, including those in which they originated—and have apparently found secondary centres of diversity in favourable areas where, it may be expected, conditions for evolution are different. And it should be noted that for genera and higher taxa of Mammals, where the fossil record is far more nearly complete than with plants, the evidence is largely contradictory to this hypothesis of diversity indicating the centre of origin. Nor is the newer generalization, that the centre of origin is the area in which the most advanced species are found, any less dangerous—especially with its stated corollary that the most primitive species will be those remote from this centre. Indeed, in many groups of plants, the more advanced members differ from the primitive ones in being more effectively specialized for dispersal and more genetically ' open ' for migration, so that they may be expected to overtake their ancestors in colonizing the earth.

Finally, even the common assumptions of a single (polar or tropical) region of origin and differentiation of the groups of higher plants, and of a simple basis for their migration from one continent to another, are presumptuous in view of the present meagre state of our knowledge and the assertion that the main centres of mammalian differentiation have been at middle latitudes in the interiors of the large land-masses. For, as we have seen, evolutionary change and migration are fundamental activities that seem to go on practically all the time everywhere, though at very different rates in different instances and places.

## Polyploids and Their Areas

The plant geographical implications of polyploids (organisms whose body-cell nuclei contain more than two haploid or single chromosome sets) have been so much discussed in recent years that, although most conclusions still remain tentative, the subject needs to be mentioned here. Polyploids are found in most of the major groups of plants and, in the Angiosperms, are particularly plentiful among perennial herbs. They are often more vigorous than their diploid (that is, with body-cells having double the number of chromosomes basic to the species or group and characteristic of the reproductive cells) relatives even of the same species, and, in addition to anatomical differences such as larger cells and pollen grains, may show morphological deviations such as usually larger flowers and coarser stems. Nevertheless it is customary, unless these differences of form are striking, to keep related diploids and polyploids in the same (major) species. Polyploids also exhibit a greater tendency to adopt vegetative or asexual means of reproduction than related diploids. Even more important from our point of view is the fact that they may show very different ecological preferences and geographical distributions from diploids, though no definite rules can safely be formulated to govern their behaviour in this respect.

It has been widely contended that polyploids are more hardy and consequently more northerly (in the northern hemisphere) and high-alpine in distribution than the diploids from which they have been derived. About this there is, however, no unanimity of opinion—largely because there are numerous exceptions to what still appears to be a distinct tendency. Suggestions that polyploids are unusually prevalent in hot and dry regions and that they favour coastal rather than inland areas, seem to be based on less factual evidence and, indeed, to be without adequate foundation when the situation is viewed on a sufficiently broad basis. There does, however, appear to be some tendency for polyploids, especially when they have arisen through hybridization (allopolyploids), to have a wider geographical range than diploids: thus of 100 examples assembled by Professor G. L. Stebbins as recounted by him in his book *Variation and Evolution in Plants*, 60 polyploids were more widely and 33 less widely distributed than their diploid relatives. It is thought that the proportions of polyploids showing wider distributions would be higher if the examples were limited to closely related pairs of entities, such as polyploids and their more immediately ancestral diploid progenitors. There are also indications that polyploids may be more prevalent in regions that were glaciated in the Pleistocene than in those which were not, and in the peripheral areas or near the ecological boundaries rather than towards the centres of distribution of particular plant groups. This tendency evidently goes hand in hand with variation, and results from the fact that polyploids have changed reaction norms. As Professor

S. A. Cain writes in his *Foundations of Plant Geography*: 'Ecological advantages may arise from the competitive ability of the polyploids that allows them to associate favorably with or even to replace their progenitors, or from the capacity of the polyploids to occupy new climatic or edaphic situations, and hence areas in which they are not confronted with competition from their close relatives.'

Altogether it seems that the phenomenon of polyploidy may have considerable significance in ecological and geographical connections. Thus some of the changes which are apt to accompany polyploidy, such as alterations in plant stature and leaf-size, in the frequency and size of stomata, and in hairiness, may affect transpiration and hence the water economy of the plant. Although some of these characteristics are evidently beneficial to polyploids, others, such as their commonly-observed retarded rate of development and lateness of flowering, may militate against their own good, weakening their competitive ability. Various physiological changes have also been observed to be associated with polyploidy, including changed cold- and perhaps drought-resistance which may have great survival and hence phytogeographical significance. The outcome, however, apparently varies with circumstances and with the particular case under consideration. The same is true of life-form changes, perennials being often polyploid in contrast with their annual relatives. These and other features affect the adaptability and competitive power of the plant and hence its ecological amplitude and, consequently, geographical distribution. Moreover, any tendency it may have to dominate is thereby affected, and, where dominance is concerned, so is the habitat and, ultimately, the distribution of other species. In view of the ease with which polyploidy may now be induced in plants by various laboratory practices, it may be that this tendency will become of even greater importance in the future than it is today—for example in the production of larger and better crop plants. On the other hand, it should be recalled that some species which lack the benefit of chromosomal races 'do' just as well as those with polyploids, showing great ecological and geographical amplitude owing probably to a richness in biotypes or larger genetic entities.

## Further Consideration

E. V. Wulff. *An Introduction to Historical Plant Geography* (Chronica Botanica, Waltham, Mass., pp. xv + 223, 1943); for various palaeobotanical and allied aspects.

W. C. Darrah. *Principles of Paleobotany* (Chronica Botanica, Leiden, Holland, pp. [vi +] 239, 1939).

R. F. Flint. *Glacial Geology and the Pleistocene Epoch* (Wiley, New York, pp. xviii + 589 & maps, 1947).

R. F. Flint. *Glacial and Pleistocene Geology* (Wiley, New York, pp. xiii + 553 and 5 additional maps, 1957).

S. A. Cain. *Foundations of Plant Geography* (Harper, New York & London, pp. xiv + 556, 1944); for a philosophical discussion of the origin and history of plant types and areas.

G. L. Stebbins. *Variation and Evolution in Plants* (Columbia University Press, New York, pp. xx + 643, 1950).

Nicholas Polunin. *Arctic Botany, vol. I: Exploration, Taxonomy, Phytogeography* (Oxford University Press, London etc., in press); for application to the far-northern regions of the world.

H. Godwin. *The History of the British Flora* (Cambridge University Press, Cambridge, Eng., pp. viii + 384 and additional table, 1956); for application of recent stages to a more limited area.

An interesting instance of protracted persistence after introduction was noted by the present writer in 1936 in southwestern Greenland, where he discovered living descendants of plants which had evidently been introduced *from North America* by the Norsemen whose Greenland settlements are known to have died out several centuries ago. As certain of these plants are of known but restricted (in two instances barely overlapping) distribution on the eastern North American seaboard, they give a clear indication of where their ancestors probably came from, and where, accordingly, Viking relics should be sought which would prove once and for all that North America was known to Europeans long before the birth of Columbus.

In connection with the wide acceptance of sub-fossil pollen grains as evidence of former climates, the author cannot forget that through much of the summer of 1950 he found the most plentiful pollen in the air near the ground in West Spitsbergen to be that of *Pinus sylvestris*, the nearest trees of which were growing on the Scandinavian mainland several hundreds of miles away to the south. This indicates the need for caution in interpretation—including the desirability of statistical comparisons and, above all, avoidance of any tacit assumption that a small deposit or reasonable amount of an airborne pollen was necessarily produced locally.

## CHAPTER VII

# TYPES AND AREAS OF NATURAL DISTRIBUTIONS

In the last chapter we considered what lies behind the geographical distributions of plants as we see them today. We must now concern ourselves with those distributions that appear to be *natural*, leaving until the next chapter the 'artificial' ones which have obviously been made or modified by introduction or other interference by Man.

Each different kind of plant has its own particular distribution or range, which is dependent, as we have seen, on its history, migrational ability, and adaptability. Indeed, it is doubtful whether any two of the hundreds of thousands of different kinds of plants known to science have precisely the same distribution; and in any case distributions are changing all the time. It is consequently impracticable, and wellnigh impossible, to consider such matters in detail; yet when a broad view is taken many interesting facts stand out, and generalization may be valuable. For whereas any hard and fast system of classifying ranges would be artificial, because it would not reflect the natural diversity observed, some useful categories can, and for practical purposes should, be widely recognized.

The term *area* (or range) in plant geography is applied to the entire region of occurrence of a particular taxonomic entity (taxon, *plural* taxa) or vegetational unit (econ, *plural* eca). Within this range it is often necessary to consider the local distribution, sometimes called 'topography', which at best is no more nearly continuous than are possible habitats for the entity or unit in question. For whereas climatic limits usually constitute the chief boundaries of plants, local topographic, edaphic, and biotic factors are all apt to have their effect—as will be explained and illustrated further in Chapter X. This, albeit secondary, effect is usually considerable, often drastically limiting the areas of plants, within the bounds prescribed by climate, to those offering otherwise favourable conditions.

Mention should be made here of the hypothesis of 'Age and

Area', which claims that the area occupied by a species is proportionate to its age (*i.e.* the time it has existed). In spite of what has just been said, this is often true and is indeed somewhat axiomatic, as reconsideration of dispersal and migrational 'mechanics' would lead us to expect. For if two or more species with identical capacities in these respects begin their migrations at different times, the earliest starter will be found, at any particular time, to have extended the farthest. Yet actually there are so many superimposed factors causing complications, and such numerous and often striking exceptions, that the hypothesis is of very doubtful value, and at best may be considered a mere generalized working one—*cf.* p. 209.

Before proceeding to the main topics to be considered in this chapter, we should explain the additional taxonomic concepts of ecads, ecotypes, and clines. An *ecad* as understood in this work is a plant type or form produced within the life-time of the individual in response to a particular habitat factor. An *ecotype* is a distinct race resulting from the impress or selective action of a particular environment. A *cline* is a geographical or ecological gradient in phenotypic characters (*i.e.* physical make-up). These entities are below or outside the usual specific bounds but should be borne in mind as exhibiting much the same geographical characteristics as do the usually higher taxa which we are more prone to consider.

## 'Continuous' Intercontinental Ranges

Except perhaps if it is very limited, the area of a taxon or of a vegetational feature is never really continuous; in reality all manner of interruptions occur, resulting in some characteristic topography (using this term as implying local distribution-pattern). Nevertheless we tend to refer to those distributions which involve spreading over a whole territory as 'continuous', at least provided the various stations are not more widely separated than the normal dispersal-capacity of the plants concerned.

Among the most frequent causes of interruption is the lack of suitable habitats, which indeed may themselves be widely separated or sparsely distributed. In such circumstances it is a matter of proportion, and consequently of opinion, as to whether a particular range should be considered continuous or otherwise. Thus whereas the Sea-beach Sandwort (*Arenaria peploides* agg.) is found on almost all sea-shores of temperate and boreal regions, where its distribution may in the wide sense be considered virtually continuous, it is usually absent inland, and accordingly in the floras of many individual regions it is either lacking or actually of disjunct distribution. Again, a 'continuous' area may have ribbon-like prolongations extending beyond its main boundaries and even lack continuity in these prolongations—especially when they are narrow, as for example along river valleys which are interrupted by narrow gorges.

Of continuous intercontinental ranges we may consider four main types: the cosmopolitan, the circumpolar, the circumboreal (or, alternatively, circumaustral), and the pantropic.

(1) *Cosmopolitan*—distributed all over the globe. In reality no species is truly so, or, probably, found in all edaphically similar and hence potentially suitable habitats. Thus even without the fundamental effect of climate and the common interference of other living organisms, it seems unlikely that any one kind of plant can be really cosmopolitan. Those which most closely approach being so are the ones which are least exacting in their habitat requirements, tending to be ubiquitous. These wide-ranging plants which tend to be indifferent to environmental conditions are called 'cosmopolites' or 'pan-endemics'; in view of the merely relative nature of the condition, the newer term 'semi-cosmopolite' seems more accurately descriptive of them. They should at least occur in all of the six widely inhabited continents. Actually, outside of weeds of cultivation that have followed Man, they seem to be confined to the lower groups of cryptogams.

(2) *Circumpolar*—distributed around the North or South Pole. This term, again, has been used far too commonly and loosely. It seems desirable to apply it only to plants which reach the arctic or antarctic 'polar' regions, wherever else they may occur, and preferable, at least in the present writer's opinion, to accept as 'arctic circumpolar' only those plants which occur at least in all of the ten sectors into which he has divided the Arctic for such purposes.[1] For these plants are truly ranged around the North Pole. Whether such criteria can be used in the case of the Antarctic has not yet become clear. Even if the limits of the Arctic are rather narrowly set, so as to exclude for example the whole of continental Scandinavia and Iceland, there are rather numerous arctic circumpolar species already known among the higher plants, and many more among the lower cryptogams which tend to be relatively easily dispersed and less exacting in their habitat requirements. Still others will, clearly,

[1] *Cf. Circumpolar Arctic Flora* (Clarendon Press, Oxford, pp. xxviii + 514, 1959).

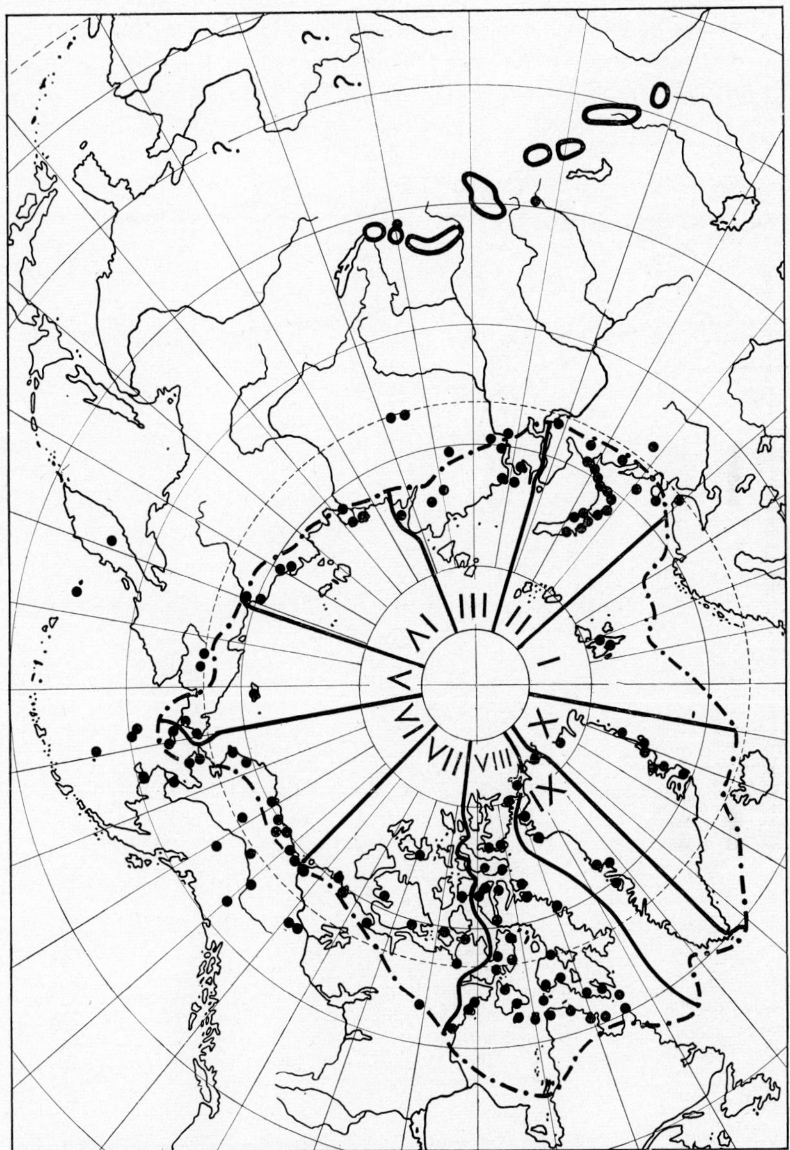


FIG. 46.—Map showing arctic circumpolar distribution as exemplified by Edwards's Eutrema (*Eutrema edwardsii*). (From data kindly supplied by E. Hultén.) The broken line indicates the southern boundary of the Arctic as proposed by the present author, and the 10 sectors (given Roman numerals I–X) into which the region is divided are those he employs in phytogeographical citations.

be added with further exploration; meanwhile familiar examples of flowering plants belonging to this category are the Purple Saxifrage (*Saxifraga oppositifolia* agg.) and Edwards's Eutrema (*Eutrema edwardsii* (*see* Fig. 46).

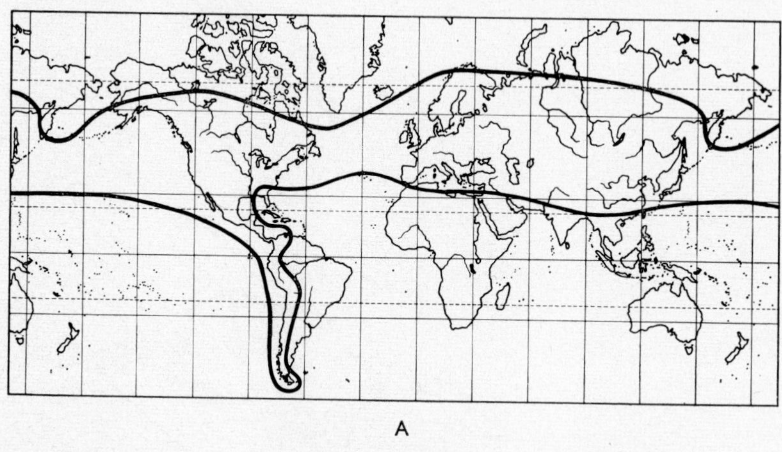

A

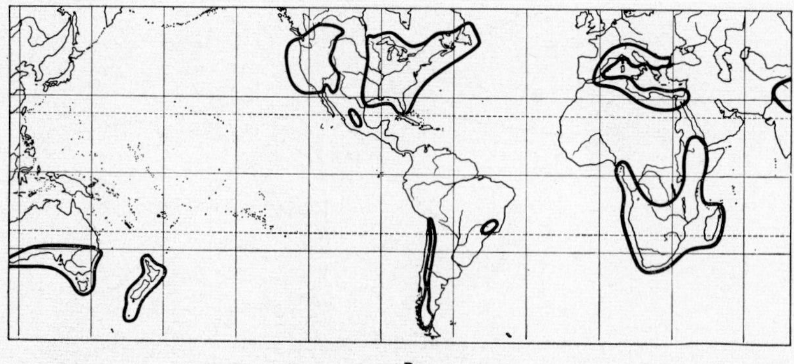

B

FIG. 47.—Maps showing circumboreal and circumaustral distributions. A, *Ribes* spp. (Currants and Gooseberries), circumboreal (after Hutchinson), but omitting some arctic stations; B, southern species of *Danthonia* (Poverty-grasses and Wild Oat-grasses), circumaustral (after Fernald); also northern range, but omitting a station in southwestern Greenland.

(3) *Circumboreal* (or *circumaustral*)—distributed around the top (or bottom) of the world in the boreal (or austral[1]) zone. It seems desirable to separate this category from the circumpolar, though clearly a plant can belong to both, as in the case of the Purple

[1] Beware confusion with the other uses of this word in biogeography.

Saxifrage, which is also alpine (*cf.* Fig. 49). Indeed, most circumpolar plants are at the same time circumboreal, though the converse is by no means true. The boreal and austral zones lie next to the arctic and antarctic ones, and seem best considered as extending to the border of the subtropics. Examples of groups having such distributions are shown in Fig. 47, the circumboreal being the genus *Ribes* (Currants and Gooseberries) and the circumaustral the southern species of *Danthonia* (Poverty-grasses and Wild Oat-grasses).

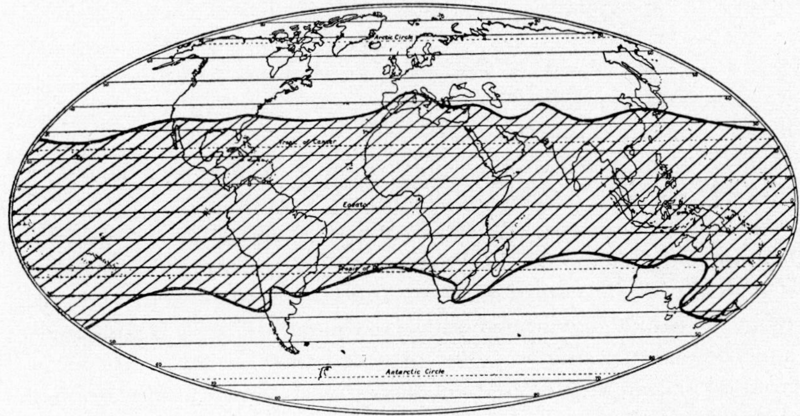


Fig. 48.—Map showing pantropic distribution of the Palm family (Palmae). (After Good.)

(4) *Pantropic*—extending practically throughout the tropics and subtropics, or at least widespread in the tropical regions of Asia, Africa, and America. A fine example is the Palm family (Palmae), as indicated in Fig. 48. Most, but by no means all, pantropic species appear to have been introduced by Man through much of their range.

It may be noted in the above that when a very wide view is maintained, mere outliers can be overlooked and even oceans practically ignored, distributions across them being considered continuous. Moreover, as we proceed from the poles to the tropics and the distances involved expand, there is a tendency for fewer and fewer minor taxa to be circumglobal. Indeed, in the tropics, subtropics, and adjacent warm-temperate regions, it is not uncommon for whole genera and even larger groups to be limited to closely adjacent or even single land-masses.

## Discontinuous Ranges

In discontinuous or disjunct ranges the plants are separated by wider gaps than the dispersal capacity of their propagules would normally bridge. Sometimes the distinction from the so-called continuous ranges is doubtful, in being a mere matter of degree, but often a taxon will inhabit two or more widely separated areas whose elucidation may be a difficult matter. In many cases, however, areas once thought to be entirely distinct have been found to be otherwise on exploration of intervening tracts, in which the plant or plants in question have appeared, and consequently supposed gaps have been closed (*cf.* Fig. 62). In yet other cases, ranges may if desired be considered continuous provided there is an absence of any suitable habitat between the colonized areas, though here again a discreet sense of proportion must be exercised and such major barriers as oceans and ice-caps often recognized.

The above discussion affords instances emphasizing the need for caution in describing the distribution of a particular plant—especially if it is of a small or insignificant nature, or is adapted to a limited range of habitat conditions and consequently has a ' fragmented ' and complex topography. But provided these warnings are borne in mind and no inflated body of theorizing is based on unwarranted supposition, the concept of discontinuity of area is a very real one and has greatly stimulated research and philosophical speculation in plant geographical and allied fields.

As for the main causes of discontinuity (apart from the controversial extremes of sudden long-distance dispersal or ' historical ' wiping out in intermediate areas, both of which have obviously taken place in the past), they are usually environmental in being due to particular topographic, climatic, edaphic, or biotic characteristics which lead to areas being separated from each other by tracts of different character. This sets aside for the time being the possibility of polytopic origin (*see* pp. 206 *et seq.*).

We should mention some of the general types of discontinuity, regardless of cause. An area is described as (1) *diffuse* when it is broken up into small, more or less numerous and equal parts ; (2) *bipartite* when it is composed of only two separate parts in the same hemisphere, one of which is extensive and forms the main part, and the other of which is subordinate ; (3) *bipolar* when it is composed of two parts widely separated in the northern and southern hemispheres ; (4) *altitudinal* when it is composed of one part

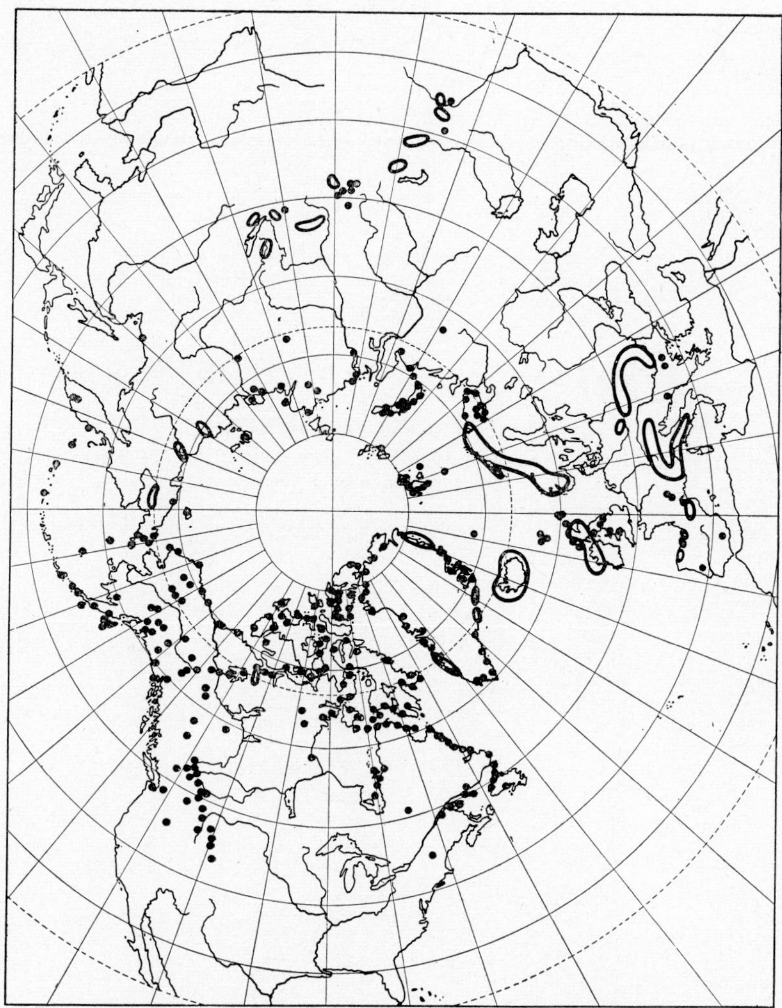

FIG. 49.—Map showing arctic-alpine distribution as exemplified by *Saxifraga oppositifolia* agg. (from data kindly supplied by E. Hultén).

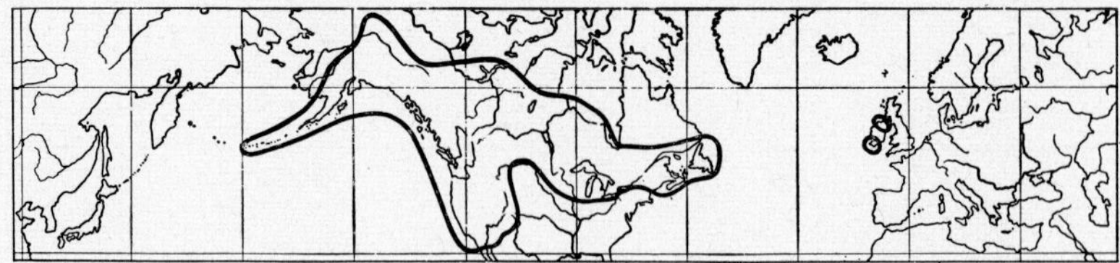

Fig. 50.—Map showing range of Drooping Ladies'-tresses (*Spiranthes romanzoffiana*) (North Atlantic, etc., distribution). (After Fernald, amended according to directions given by E. Hultén.)

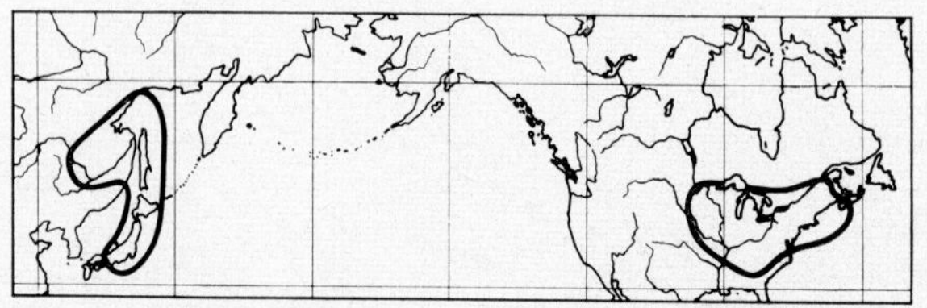

Fig. 51.—Map showing range of Skunk-cabbage (*Symplocarpus foetidus*) (North Pacific distribution). (After Fernald.)

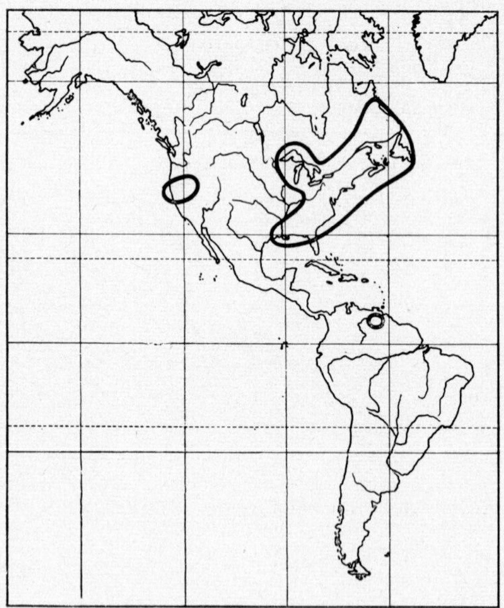

Fig. 52.—Map showing North-South American distribution of Pitcher-plant family (Sarraceniaceae). (After Hutchinson, amended.)

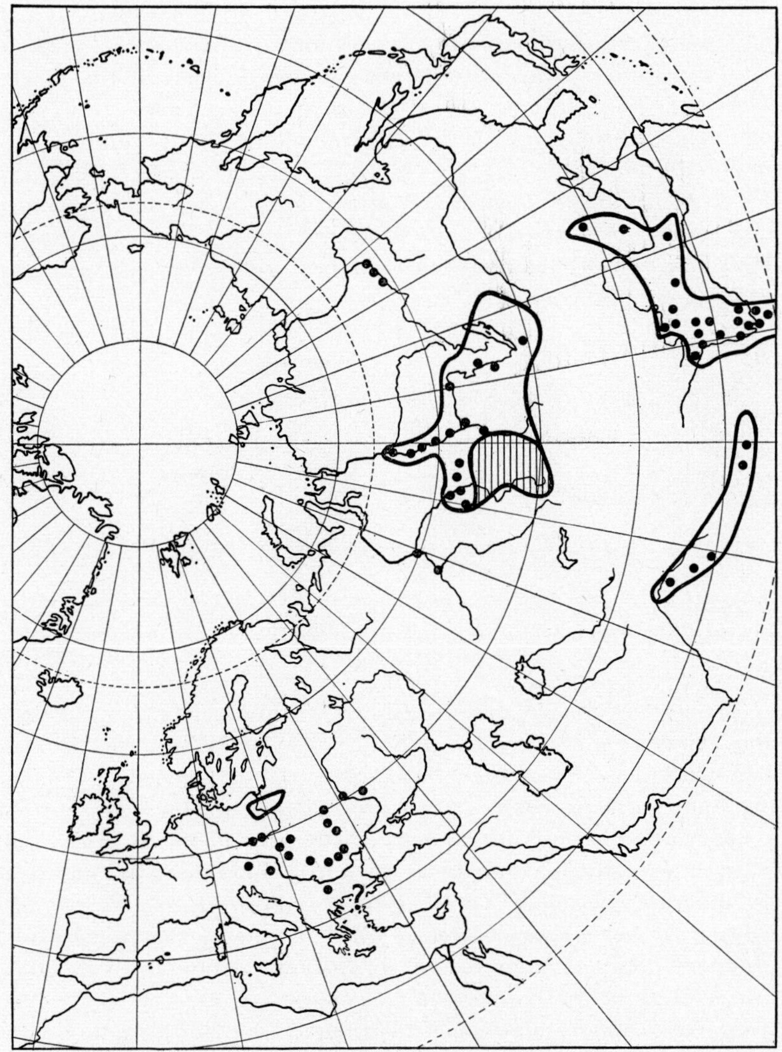

FIG. 53.—Map showing range of *Cimicifuga foetida* (Europe-Asian distribution). (Contributed by E. Hultén.)

situated in one altitudinal zone, and another in another zone not directly adjoining; and (5) when diffuse, bipartite, or otherwise, and populated by identical forms, it is said to be *homogeneous*—as opposed to the *heterogeneous* discontinuity that involves related or vicarious forms occupying different component parts of the range.

As for more specific types of discontinuous ranges, we may mention the following as being among the most familiar and important:

(1) *Arctic-Alpine*—distributed in the arctic region and in mountain systems of temperate or even warmer zones; examples are the Herb-like Willow (*Salix herbacea*) and the Purple Saxifrage (*Saxifraga oppositifolia* agg.), *see* Fig. 49.

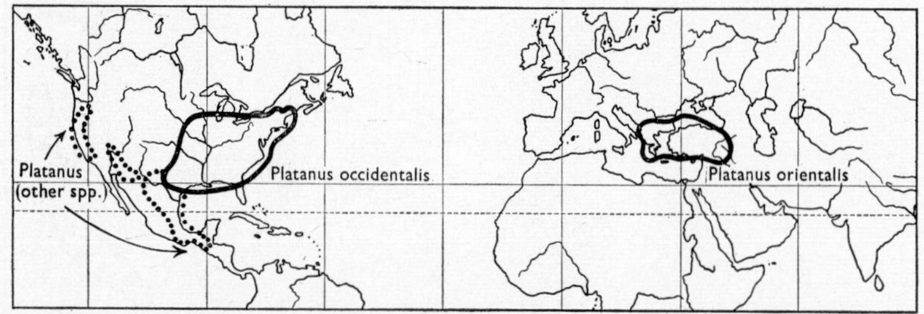


FIG. 54.—Map showing range of species of *Platanus* (Plane-trees, or Buttonwoods). (After Fernald, amended.)

(2) *North Atlantic*—distributed in North America and Europe, and sometimes also locally in Asia; examples are the familiar Bog Club-moss (*Lycopodium inundatum*) and the Hooded or Drooping Ladies'-tresses (*Spiranthes romanzoffiana*), *see* Fig. 50.

(3) *North Pacific*—distributed chiefly in North America and Eastern Asia, though sometimes elsewhere; examples are afforded by different species of Torrey Pine (*Torreya*) and by the Skunk-cabbage (*Symplocarpus foetidus*), which is one of that remarkable group of species common to eastern Asia and eastern North America but wanting in the regions lying between—*see* Fig. 51.

(4) *North-South American*—distributed in North and South America but lacking continuity between; an example is afforded by the members of the Pitcher-plant family (Sarraceniaceae), *see* Fig. 52.

(5) *Europe-Asian*—distributed in Europe and Asia but lacking continuity between; examples are *Leontice altaica* and *Cimicifuga foetida*, *see* Fig. 53.

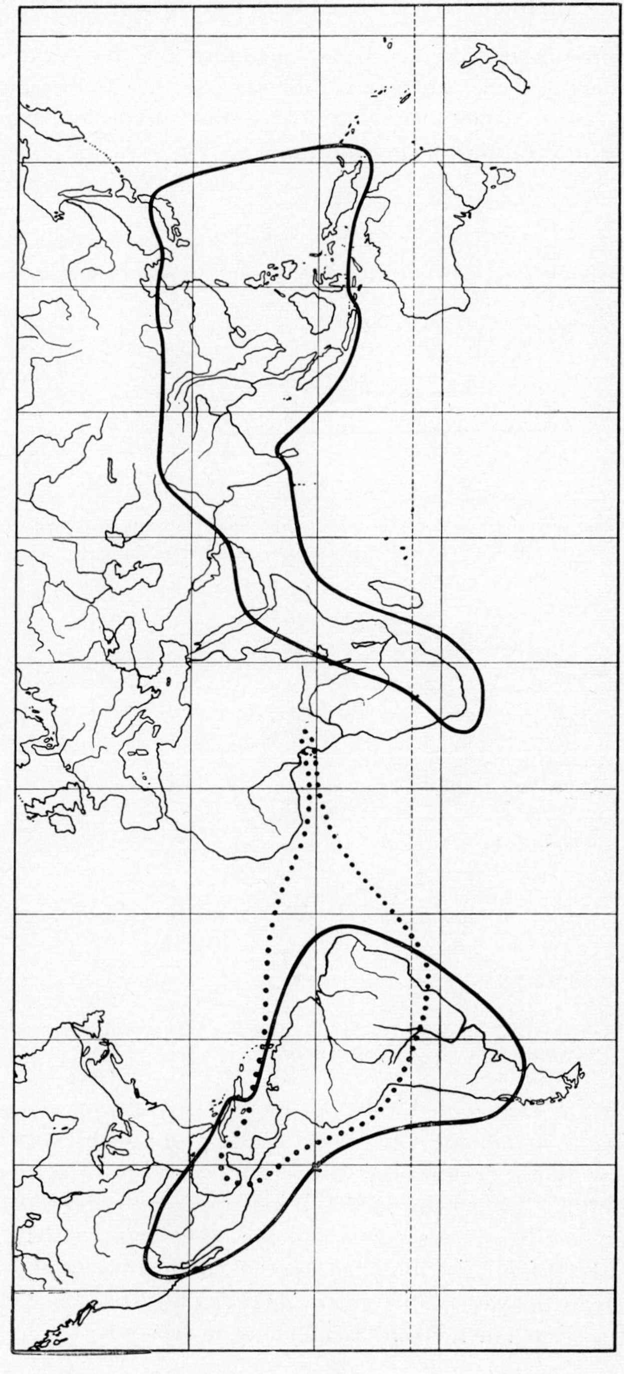

FIG. 55.—Map showing pantropical discontinuous range of the genus *Buddleia* (Loganiaceae) (solid line) and the mainly neotropical range of the family Vochysiaceae (broken line). (After Hutchinson.)

(6) *Mediterranean*—various types including the European and African shores of the Mediterranean Sea, or the Mediterranean basin and some distant continent—as in the species of *Platanus* (Plane-trees, or Buttonwoods), indicated in Fig. 54.

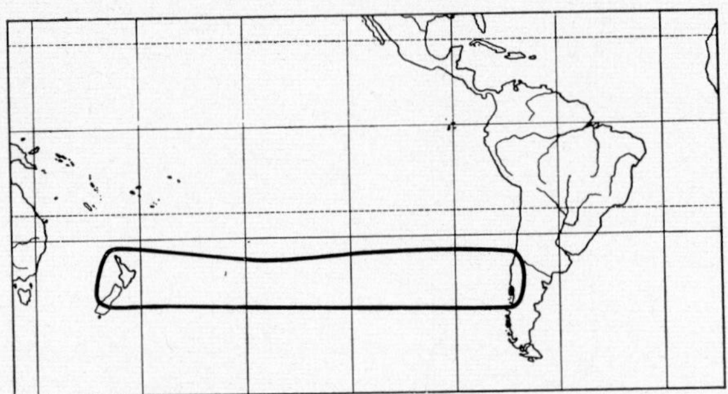

FIG. 56.—Map showing range of the genus *Jovellana* (Scrophulariaceae) (South Pacific distribution). (After Hutchinson.)

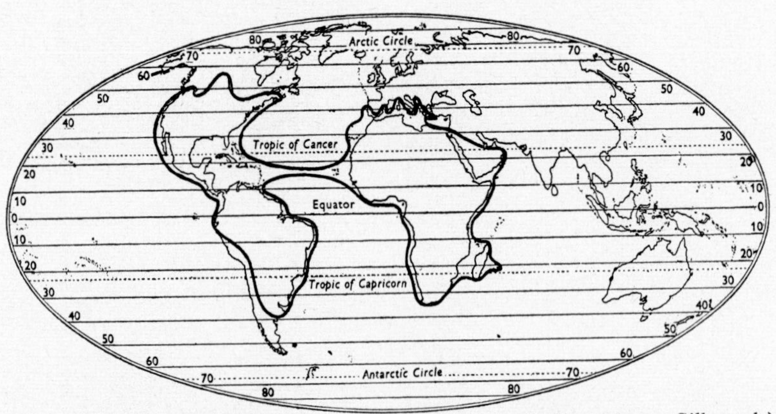


FIG. 57.—Map showing range of the genus *Asclepias* (Milkweeds, or Silkweeds) (South Atlantic, etc., distribution). (After Good.)

(7) *Tropical*—distributed in two or more separate tropical regions such as occur within the Old World (palaeotropical discontinuity) or the New World (neotropical discontinuity) or both (pantropical discontinuity). Among the various minor types, two are illustrated in Fig. 55, one being of a genus and the other of a family.

(8) *South Pacific*—distributed at least in South America and New Zealand, as in the case of the genus *Jovellana* illustrated in Fig. 56, and often also in other Pacific islands and in Australia.

FIG. 58.—Map showing (Antarctic) range of the genus *Nothofagus* (Southern Beeches). (Contributed by E. Hultén.) (There are also fossil records of both wood and leaves from the sector of Antarctica lying opposite South America.)

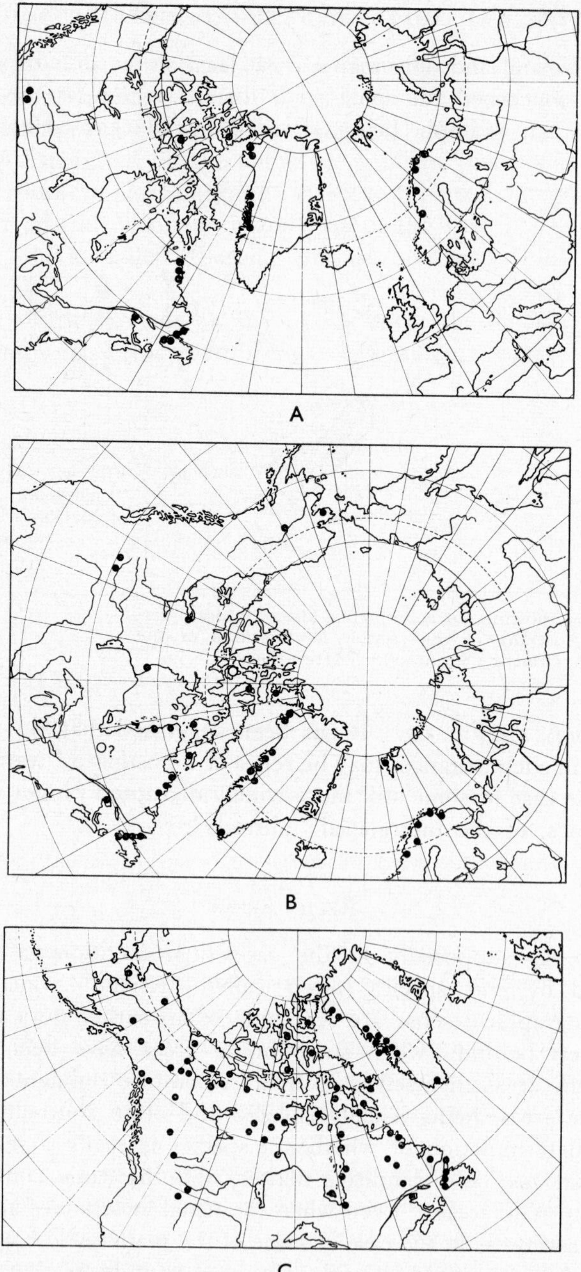


FIG. 62.—Maps showing known localities of Low Sandwort (*Arenaria humifusa*). A, as published by Nordhagen (1935); B, as published by Polunin (1943); C, as published by Porsild (1957) for the New World only, including areas that have been heavily glaciated and islands that have only recently emerged from the sea. Still further localities are now known.

plants were found there too, the ranges being in fact almost as nearly continuous as habitat suitability allowed. Fig. 62 illustrates this point. Ideally the finding of fossil remains of the plant in question, in surrounding areas where it does not now grow, will demonstrate its relic nature and indicate from what period of time its local

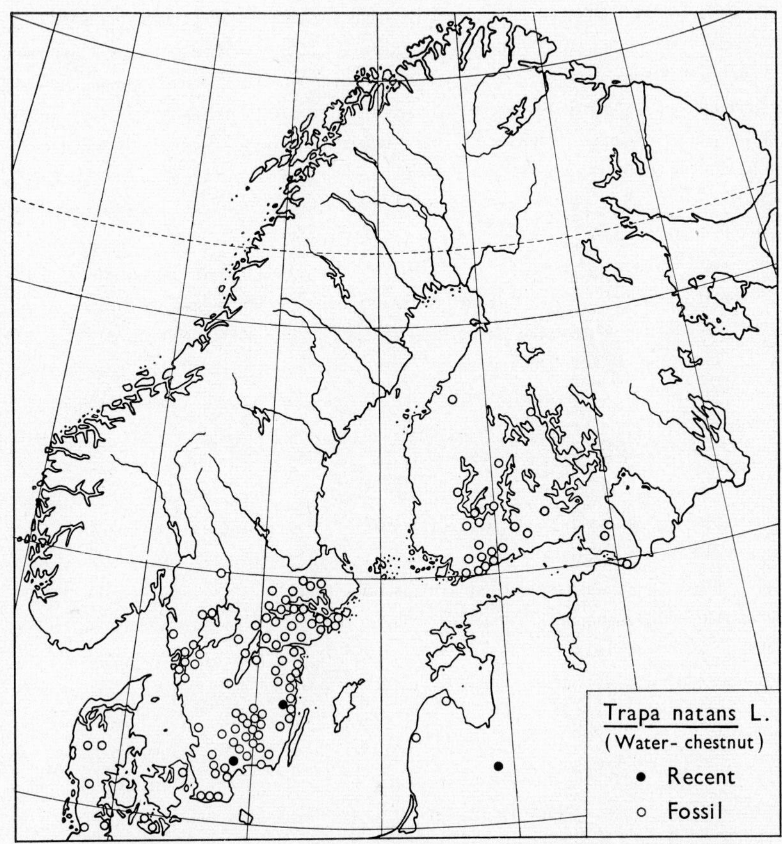


FIG. 63.—Map showing recent (dots) and 'fossil' (circles) stations of the Water-chestnut (*Trapa natans*) in Scandinavia. (After Hultén.)

occupation dates. This is illustrated by the present-day and 'fossil' stations of the Water-chestnut (*Trapa natans*) in Scandinavia (shown in Fig. 63) and of the giant Redwoods in the northern hemisphere in general (indicated in Fig. 43). In this connection it is interesting to note that whereas *Trapa* is now known in North America only as an introduced weed that is apt to be aggressive, there is much fossil evidence that it was formerly widespread there in the wild state (*cf.* p. 160).

In general the main, non-relic part of an area either occupies its original territory, any outlying parts having become separated owing to habitat changes, or results from secondary dispersal, in which case the relic part may actually lie within the main area. An example of this latter type is afforded by the Scots Pine (*Pinus sylvestris*), which has relic portions of its area in the mountains of Europe, whereas its extensive occupation of surrounding sandy lowlands is the result of secondary colonization. Such colonization may even take place *from* a relic area, for example when climatic conditions, whose deterioration in surrounding areas had led to isolation, subsequently improve so that suitable plants can recolonize around the isolated area. Much the same often occurs with the removal of heavy grazing which had caused the restriction of some plants to limited areas (that in a sense were then relic ones), whence they spread again when the animals moved off or died.

A species which occupies a relic area throughout its range may be termed an 'absolute relic', while one of which only an isolated part of the area is relic is known as a 'local relic'. An 'endemic relic' is one that is restricted to a single region. Those relics which achieve a secondary distribution by the occupation of suitable habitats are known as 'migrant relics', the more recently occupied habitats being termed 'pseudo-relic' and the plants 'pseudo-relics' (or '-relicts'), though these terms may also be applied in cases where a plant acquires the apparent character of a relic without actually being one. Most of these principles may be applied equally to single species or other taxa, groups of species (as in relic colonies), or entire floras.

Many relics, having long been in partial disharmony with present-day habitat conditions, have become depauperated in biotypes; the consequent loss of the capacity for variation and adaptation has led to their being considered conservative. Such plants have often been called 'senescent'. Being commonly restricted to narrowly specific environmental conditions, they may fail to retain even their limited area, in extreme cases becoming extinct. However, if favourable conditions should reappear and, for example, allow the approach of formerly segregated variants so that hybridization can take place and new forms thereby arise, the species may take on its former vigour or even exceed it and become aggressive.

Leaving aside the so-called 'anthropogenic relics' whose areas have become drastically reduced through the activities of Man, and the ‘ cultivated relics ’ whose sown area, owing to their low economic value, has been reduced to small compass and few localities, we may usefully distinguish three main classes of relics on the basis of the type of natural habitat-change which has isolated them.

(1) *Formation relics* that occupy limited areas within the boundaries of major plant communities (formations) which have undergone considerable changes in composition. Striking examples are the residual wooded tracts that are sometimes found in some extensive grasslands.

(2) *Geomorphological relics* that are connected in their habitat preferences with particular ecological conditions but that, owing to edaphic or allied changes, are no longer provided with the conditions of growth to which they are accustomed. Familiar examples include marine plants inhabiting freshwater lakes, and shore plants growing along the edges of dried-up gulfs.

(3) *Climatic relics* that give evidence of having originated and formerly flourished under other climatic conditions than those in which they now grow. Examples are the mesothermic plants to be found in some boreal areas that have cooled at least since the ‘ postglacial optimum ’ when such plants presumably migrated to these areas.

While it is scarcely possible to distinguish further classes of ‘ biotic relics ’ resultant on grazing, etc., as distinct from those engendered by Man or his animals, or on plant competition with our present limited knowledge thereof, there is another basis on which relics may be classified, namely, their age and origin, the main such classes being : (1) pre-Tertiary, (2) Tertiary, (3) glacial, (4) interglacial, and (5) postglacial relics.

## Vicarious Areas

These are areas belonging to closely-related taxa (vicariads) derived from the same common ancestor and tending to be mutually exclusive of one another in naturally (*i.e.* without human interference) occupying separate areas. Sometimes, and especially when their ecological requirements differ only very slightly, vicariads may be mutually exclusive through being closely competitive. This is the case with many subspecies and closely-related species ; on the other hand, with higher groupings—and even families and whole communities may in a sense be vicarious—there is less reason to suppose that their mutual exclusiveness is due to competition. From their very nature, ecotypes often tend to be vicarious, as do the extreme 'ends' of clines. In any event, the process of genesis of geographical races seems to be the main basis of the formation of 'vicarious areas', at least among the lower taxa, and this and any subsequent segregation tends to take place towards the periphery of the range of the 'parent' species, where the latter is in general least happily adapted to the environmental conditions.

Examples of vicariads are to be found in almost any modern taxonomic monograph in which the series of closely-related entities inhabiting independent geographical areas are commonly recognized as subspecies or even species. These tend to be mutually exclusive, although sometimes their areas may show some overlapping; and it is often a matter of opinion (as well as, of course, the degree of difference they exhibit) whether they should be termed subspecies or raised to the rank of species. This is one of the most persistent sources of controversy between the 'lumpers' and the 'splitters' (of species). Numerous instances are afforded by major species that are represented by different minor species or varieties (which most often seem best considered as subspecies) on the two sides of the North Atlantic—as, for example, the European Royal Fern, *Osmunda regalis*, and its North American subsp. *spectabilis* (*see* Fig. 64). Polyploids, dealt with towards the end of the preceding chapter, are often vicariads (*see* also p. 204).

Here it may be well to quote Jordan's 'Law of Geminate Species': 'Given any species in any region, the nearest related species is not likely to be found in the same region, nor in a remote region, but in a neighbouring district separated from the first by a barrier of some sort or at least by a belt of country the breadth of which gives the effect of a barrier.' Such pairs of twin or 'geminate' species (or subspecies) actually constitute vicariads, differing in only minor characteristics that are of later origin than their common characters.

True vicariads (which have arisen from a common stock) should be distinguished from false ones which have not this close genetic relationship. Frequently these last are members of different sections of a genus that have developed similar life-forms through 'convergent evolution'. True vicariads (and consequently the areas they demarcate) may be classified according to the manner of their separation from one another into (1) horizontal (geographical), (2) altitudinal (physiographic), (3) habitat (ecological), and (4)

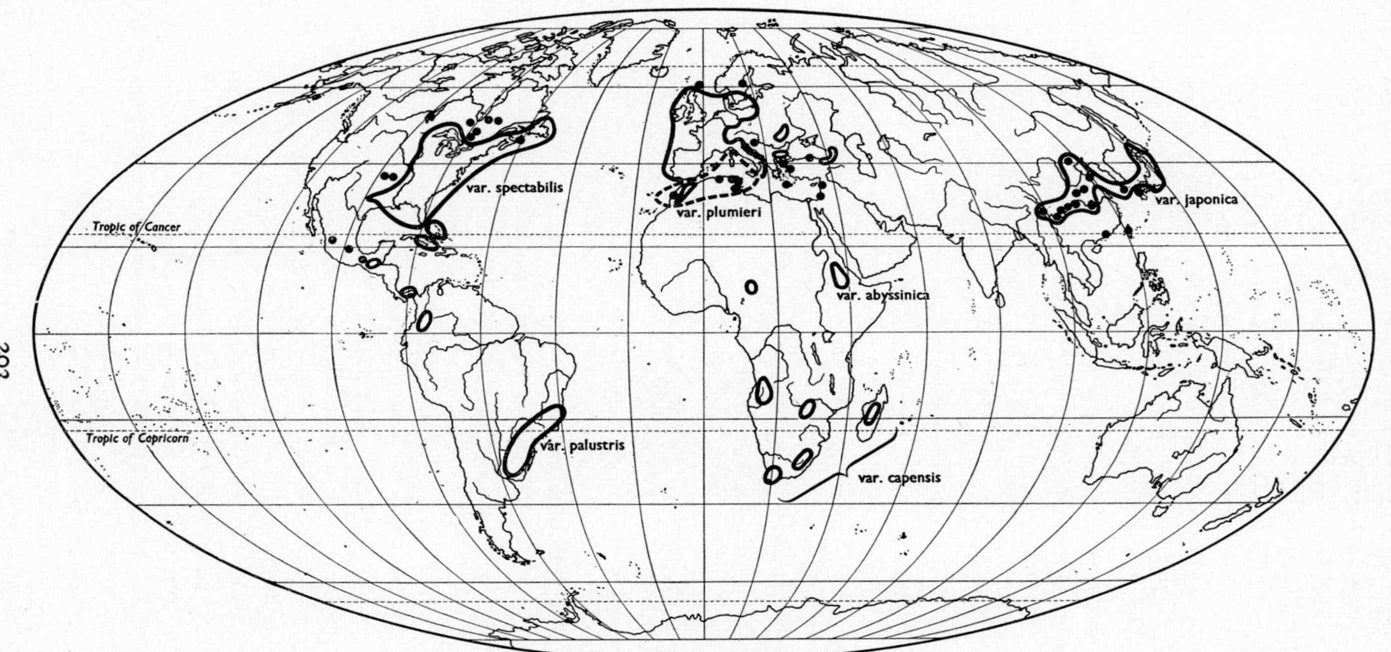


FIG. 64.—Transatlantic vicariads. Map showing ranges of the European Royal Fern, *Osmunda regalis*, and its North American subsp. ('var.') *spectabilis* and other 'varieties'. (From data kindly supplied by E. Hultén.)

seasonal (exhibiting seasonal dimorphism, as in the case of closely related forms differing in their times of development).

Most ' systematic ' vicariads, consisting of pairs or sets of the higher taxa which are vicarious, belong to the first or geographical category, a good example being afforded by the various races of Bracken (*Pteridium aquilinum* agg.) inhabiting different parts of the world. There are also plentiful examples of physiographic vicariads inhabiting lower and higher altitudes, respectively—for example the Wood and Alpine Forget-me-nots (*Myosotis sylvatica* and *M. alpestris* agg.), and the Common and Alpine Timothys (*Phleum pratense* and *P. alpinum* s.l.). As examples of ecological vicariads growing in different habitats and characterizing different communities, we may cite : in fresh and mainly salt marshes, respectively, the Bulrush and Glaucous Bulrush (*Scirpus lacustris* and *S. tabernaemontanii*) ; in soils with high and low available water, respectively, the Water and Wood Avens (*Geum rivale* and *G. urbanum*) ; and in calcium-rich and calcium-poor soils, respectively, the Yellow Mountain and Brook Saxifrages (*Saxifraga aizoides* agg. and *S. rivularis* agg.). Such vicariads are commonly intraregional, not infrequently growing as closely together as their habitat requirements permit, whereas the geographical ones tend to be more widely regional.

We have already indicated that vicariads, at least of the lower taxonomic orders, tend to evolve chiefly about the periphery of a migrating ' parent ' taxon. Here new characters are particularly prone to arise by mutation or other chromosomal change, and help the better-adapted offspring to survive under conditions which are less favourable to the parent. Thus autopolyploidy, the phenomenon of multiplication of a plant's own chromosome set, may result from extreme habitat conditions and be accompanied by evident changes in the plants involved, autopolyploids often having very definite geographical ranges differing from those of their ancestors which possessed the normal (diploid) number of chromosomes. When the changes accompanying polyploidy are very marked, a new species may be constituted, which is often a vicarious one. Vicariads may also arise as a result of hybridization, which is frequently accompanied by a multiplication of chromosomes (allopolyploidy) ; or they may be a consequence of mere local differentiation resultant on changes in climatic or other habitat conditions in some part or parts of a plant's range. As a result, the initial species may ' break up ' into a number of vicarious ones, or of subspecies with distinct geographical ranges.

## Endemic Areas

In contrast with the plants exhibiting various types of discontinuous range, and which may be widely scattered or at all events *polyendemic* (polytopic—*see* next section), are those whose range in each case is confined to a single restricted area, not extending beyond some one region, island, or other circumscribed tract. Such plants are called *endemics*, although this term again is largely relative. An *endemic area* is the area of a species or other taxon that, in its distribution, is limited to some single natural region or habitat, the history or conditions of which mark it off from others. Islands and mountain massifs are particularly pertinent in this connection.

Of endemics there are two main types. There are the old ones whose range was once far more extensive than it is today, and which, being remnants or survivors of former floras, may be called *relic endemics* or *epibiotics*. These may make up a large proportion of the species of ancient islands or mountain massifs, being said to involve 72 per cent. of the thousand or so native vascular species of New Zealand and 85 per cent. of those of St. Helena. A good example of this type of endemism is furnished by the giant Redwoods of the western United States, which used to be extremely widespread in the northern hemisphere (*cf.* Fig. 43). Their drastic contraction in range seems the more remarkable when we recall that they include what are probably the oldest individual living organisms today, some being reported to exceed 3,000 years in age. The other main type of endemic is made up of the relatively young taxa, usually below the rank of species, and then usefully termed *micro-endemics*, which are characteristic of newer portions of the earth's surface. Thus, when ecological conditions change within the limits of some natural region, there is a tendency for new forms to evolve, and these may be closely bound to the region owing to its special habitat conditions or because they are physically unable to spread beyond its confines. Such plants may be called *neo-endemics*.

The determination of the proportion of these main types of endemism in a particular flora is an important factor in its analysis, capable of telling us much about its age and history. Relic endemics are particularly useful in indicating antiquity, isolation, and diversification of habitats, for these factors all tend to produce additional endemics and help in their survival, as probably do also suitable conditions for the development of vegetation. Such endemics tend to be deficient in biotypes and are usually recognized by their relic character and geographical isolation, their small amplitude of variation and narrow restriction to particular ecological conditions, their relatively small chromosome number, and their generally retrogressive nature. On the other hand, neo-endemics, being secondarily derived types, commonly have larger chromosome numbers ; they also tend often to be relatively aggressive. This is especially the case when they are rich in biotypes, for example owing to hybridization.

Apart from the so-called 'pseudo-endemics' that have been encountered only in one place and appear to be mutants, etc., and unlikely to persist, there are the *ecological endemics* which have arisen in relation to particular habitat conditions.

Some endemics are confined to very limited areas, such as a single small island or mountain peak, and may be called *local endemics.* Such restriction is usually due (1) to their recent origin (so that dispersal has only just begun), or (2) to their antiquity (so that the area is a contracted one or even a 'last remnant'), or (3) to their high specificity with regard to habitat conditions (which prevail only at a given spot within the area that can be reached by viable disseminules), or (4) to the impossibility of expansion (owing to physico-geographical obstacles).

It has been mentioned that isolated islands are often particularly rich in endemics ; this is especially the case with those which are at least some hundreds of miles from the nearest major land-mass, and which may accordingly be termed *oceanic.* Although the distinction is far from definite, it is sometimes useful to think of other islands, whose flora bears a closer relation to an adjacent land-mass, and which are usually within at most a few hundred miles' distance from it, as *continental.* These islands are phytogeographically like fragments of continents or larger islands and are usually inhabited by larger numbers of species than are comparable oceanic islands, containing as they do both plants and animals for which transoceanic transport seems virtually impossible. Some remote islands, such as those surrounding Antarctica, are apt to be considered relics of a formerly more extensive continent and hence scarcely oceanic.

## Polytopy and the Incidence of Areas

Polytopy is the occurrence of a species or other taxon in two or more separate areas, such species being termed *polytopic* or *polyendemic.* The discontinuous ranges involving disjunct areas which we dealt with earlier in this chapter are examples of polytopy, which we must now consider briefly from the point of view of the origin of the areas involved.

Excluding the old conception of special creation, it is yet believed by some that polytopic approximate forms may have had an independent origin in their existing plurality of areas whose populations are similar because of parallel descent from a common ancestor. This would explain discontinuity on the basis of the species concerned having evolved independently in two or more separate areas. But whereas this seems possible where a common near-ancestry and minor taxa are concerned (for example, through natural selection acting on a similar set of mutants), it scarcely seems conceivable for members of major species whose common ancestry was remote and whose distinctive characters are numerous. Largely separate is the contention of the differentiation hypothesis that different species of the same genus may have 'crystallized out' from an ancestral complex in two or more areas independently. Some students even hold that the polytopic populations in different areas have had an independent origin from taxonomically different ancestors and have arrived at their present similarity through convergent evolution. However, in the words of Cain (in the work cited at the end of the last chapter) such *polyphylesis* 'for most students of evolution, genetics, and taxonomy, represents only the result of inadequate knowledge, or the forming of groups (genera, families) for practical convenience, except in cases of hybrid descent . . .'

More widely accepted is the hypothesis that polytopic forms are immediately related, the intervening tracts having been 'bridged' in the past either by a continuous series of populations or by long-distance dispersal. However, as in other biological instances, it seems likely that different explanations apply in different cases. Thus concerning dispersal, it has been calculated that even if the probability that some member of a population will cross a barrier in any one year is virtually nil, during the course of a million years the event will be probable, and in ten million years almost certain. With regard to the disruption of areas that were previously continuous, though not necessarily at one and the same time, we have already discussed, especially in the last chapter, such possible causes as continental drift, land-bridges, and climatic and other change. We have also seen how isolated centres of survival may become *centres of dispersal*, upon the return of more favourable conditions

—at east if the biotype depauperization of the relic community has not been too extreme.

The *centre of origin* of an area of other than a lower taxon, at least in the absence of extensive palaeobotanical data, is apt to be so difficult and hazardous of determination that little will be said about it here. For its indication about a dozen criteria are commonly employed, though sometimes a fair one may be given by *isoflors*, which are lines delimiting regions supporting equal numbers of species, *e.g.* belonging to a single genus. From the generic centre outwards the number of species may be expected to decrease regularly, and to assume a pattern which suggests the tracts of past migration, which conversely may be followed backwards and found to converge upon the generic centre. Even here, palaeobotanical confirmation is wellnigh essential. Groups also have their single or multiple centres of variation, where there are concentrated the greatest diversity and wealth of forms (also called the *mass centre*), and their centres of frequency, where there are accumulated the greatest numbers of individuals or stations.

With single species or lower taxa the situation may be far simpler. Thus the tendency to decrease in the number of individuals of a species towards the periphery of its area, is closely connected with adaptability to definite habitat conditions. For whereas in the centre of its area the habitat conditions most nearly approximate to the optimum—so that the species can grow under fairly diverse conditions, as it often does on different types of soil—nearer the periphery of its area anything approaching this optimum is of increasingly rare occurrence, and there is often lacking even the minimum of conditions required for its normal existence. Thus the European Beech (*Fagus sylvatica*), which ordinarily is capable of growing on a variety of soils, is largely confined near the western (moist) periphery of its range to the drier calcareous ones.

As regards an area itself, its shape is best indicated on maps by connecting all the peripheral points of its distribution. The shape generally depends primarily on the physico-geographical conditions of the country, and secondarily on the biological peculiarities of the taxon involved. In the frigid and temperate zones the diameter of most specific areas is much greater from west to east than it is from north to south, whereas in the torrid zone species tend to have a relatively larger latitudinal amplitude than elsewhere.

An area of a species or subspecies usually comes into being largely through migration and the operation of barriers thereto, the parent species during its dispersal often running into climatic and/or edaphic habitat conditions to which it is unaccustomed and which in time may lead to modification of the incipient area. From some such beginnings further migration usually leads to the current area. However, sometimes drastic change may lead to evolution *in situ*. Especially in the cases of young species and of those that have had their ranges reduced by relatively recent catastrophes, the area at present occupied is only a part, and often only a very small part, of what it might be. For, as we shall see in the next chapter, each species tends to have, besides its actual area, a *potential area* which may be demonstrated by artificial introduction and is often of great practical importance in the regional allocation of crops. It can also be of significance with regard to the nuisance caused by weeds. Indeed, it seems probable that the majority of present-day ranges are by no means complete so far as the occupation of areas of suitable climate and soil conditions are concerned. Sometimes this incompleteness is due, as implied above, either to an insufficient lapse of time since the entity evolved, or to the basic inefficiency of its dispersal—or a combination of youth and inefficiency. But probably it is more often due to historical changes such as glaciation, or to the operation of boundaries set by physical barriers such as seas or mountains or deserts, by ecological conditions, or by competition with other species.

Although there is a natural tendency for the areas occupied by many plants to increase with age, which can be an important factor in biogeographical considerations, the relationship of area to age is by no means as direct as has sometimes been supposed. To be sure, with some genera and species, especially in certain tropical regions, the area of spread is roughly proportional to the age (as was suggested by the now unpopular hypothesis of ' Age and Area ' —*see* pp. 182–3), but in others this is so far from being the case that the area at present occupied gives little or no indication of age. This is true, for example, where ancient fossils indicate a much wider distribution than now obtains, as in the case of the giant Redwoods (*cf*. Fig. 43). For actually, at least outside of some favoured regions, there have been so many, often drastic disturbances that the general situation appears to be that the size of an area occupied by a species depends less on the age of the species than on other factors. These include its adaptability and competition-rigour, the circumstances of its genesis, and whether or not ecological conditions and any dispersal mechanism or mechanisms have favoured successful migration.

## INTRANEOUS, EXTRANEOUS, AND OTHER ELEMENTS

It is sometimes useful to classify the forms growing in a particular territory according to whether in each case the occurrence is well within the area of the form (*intraneous*) or near its periphery (*extraneous*). For instance, the disjunct arctic species occurring in the White Mountains of New Hampshire are extraneous there but intraneous in their characteristic region of habitation, namely, the Arctic.

The components of such groupings form special *elements*, which are severally recognizable in most floras. Thus we may have intraneous and extraneous elements in a flora, a preponderance of either characterizing certain areas. This leads us naturally to consideration of specific phytogeographic or *floral elements*, which are closely related to migration. Ideally each such element is the floristic expression of a territory of limited extent, in that it involves the taxa and phytogeographic groupings characteristic of a given phytogeographic area—such as the Mediterranean region, giving rise to a ' Mediterranean element '. Often, however, it seems preferable to extend this concept of floral elements to include other and much wider applications.

Before a flora can be divided into its main general elements we must eliminate all aliens and ' wides ' (also called ' polychores ', *i.e.* species having such an extensive range that they embrace several phytogeographic regions). Then the endemics should be studied and, as far as possible, assigned to their various categories. Thereafter the remaining species may be divided into groups according to the geographical character of their areas, with the object of determining the regions whence these groups originated, and so perhaps establishing the genesis of the flora. For this grouping, five main principles should be followed and elements sought (apart from those already accounted for):

(1) *Geographical elements*—grouped according to the types of their total areas, their altitudinal ranges, or their distributions within the region concerned. This is, however, often insufficient to determine the origin of a flora that is not a migration one, for relic and endemic elements so grouped do not reflect the genesis of a flora. Even with a marked arctic-alpine element it is often doubtful which way the components have spread—whether they are arctic types which have migrated southward into the mountainous regions offering somewhat comparable conditions, or *vice versa*. All that can be

done is to divide the species into apparently arctic and apparently alpine groups; and much the same applies to the subarctic or, as it is sometimes called, subarctic-mountain element. Other geographical elements are fortunately apt to be less vague, examples being the Mediterranean and the Atlantic ones. The broader types of ecological groupings may also be included here when they characterize geographical regions—as, for example, certain life-zones and formations (or, better, *biomes*, which are climax formations of plants and animals considered together, such as the characteristic Spruce-Moose biome of most of the continental regions of Canada). Often it is possible to decide on the geographical element to which a species most likely belongs by locating its 'mass centre' (of maximum variation), for that is the part of its area which is most likely to be basic.

(2) *Genetic elements*—grouped according to their region of origin and accordingly reflecting the genesis of the flora. For this, detailed monographic study of the groups involved is necessary, and so at best it is usually possible to classify in this manner only a few chosen species. These first two types of general element are considered by some students to be the most important bases for floristic analysis.

(3) *Migration elements*—grouped according to the routes by which they migrated to the region concerned. Examples of migration routes are particular mountain passes, river valleys, and suitable coasts. Unfortunately, species are apt to reach the domain of a given flora by more than one route, so that the establishment of particular migration elements is difficult or futile—though often well worth attempting, as such elements may provide valuable clues to the history of a flora.

(4) *Historical elements*—grouped according to the time (such as the postglacial climatic optimum period) when they became a part of the flora concerned. Further examples are the so-called arctic-Tertiary element of evergreen and deciduous trees, and the boreal-Tertiary one which included such southerly members as Palms; these examples represent the inhabitants of the arctic and boreal, respectively, regions in Tertiary times, while to their south, stretching from southern England to Japan in those far-off days, lay the tropical region of megatherms, *i.e.* plants adapted to high temperatures.

(5) *Ecological elements*—grouped according to their immediate habitat preferences. Most significant are the *oceanic* and *continental* elements, embracing, respectively, those species which are adapted

to a humid maritime climate and those which prefer an arid continental one of marked temperature extremes. The oceanic elements are generally considered to be the more ancient, the initial land flora having been evolved from an aquatic one and further evolution having been along lines of emancipation from dependence on water and, accordingly, adaptation to more continental habitats. Such ecological elements can be of great significance in elucidating the history of a particular flora and any major vagaries of climate to which it may have been subjected. It should be remembered, however, that within the limits of a country or natural region there may be found tracts, such as mountain massifs, in which particular conditions predominate and which accordingly give refuge to ' alien ' plants. These may be termed *inclusions*, in contradistinction to the *basic element* of types properly belonging to the floral region, and the more general *penetrants* from outside.

## Major Regions

These will be considered here only in the broadest outline, as several subsequent chapters are devoted to them. Vegetational regions, being based on life-form rather than on taxonomic proximity, may cut across the ranges of systematic units and also differ greatly from zoogeographical realms characterized by particular animal communities. Fig. 65 indicates the main vegetational-climatic regions of the world in highly generalized form, and shows the basis of the division followed in Chapters XII *et seq.* It may be noted that the western Old World desert region, which is sometimes separated as a special one, is here included in the tropical region, as the Mediterranean is in the temperate region. This gives us a central tropical belt and, to both the north and the south, two others. These are the temperate (in the wide sense) and polar belts, the former ranging approximately from the polar tree-lines and including the subarctic and warm-temperate zones, while the tropical belt conveniently includes the subtropics. Each of these broadest of regions is itself complex, tending to show latitudinal gradation—so much so that accurate detailed maps are scarcely conceivable, at least in our present state of frequent ignorance of local features.

## Further Consideration

Most of the subjects dealt with in this chapter are further discussed by Wulff and Cain in their works cited at the end of the preceding chapter.

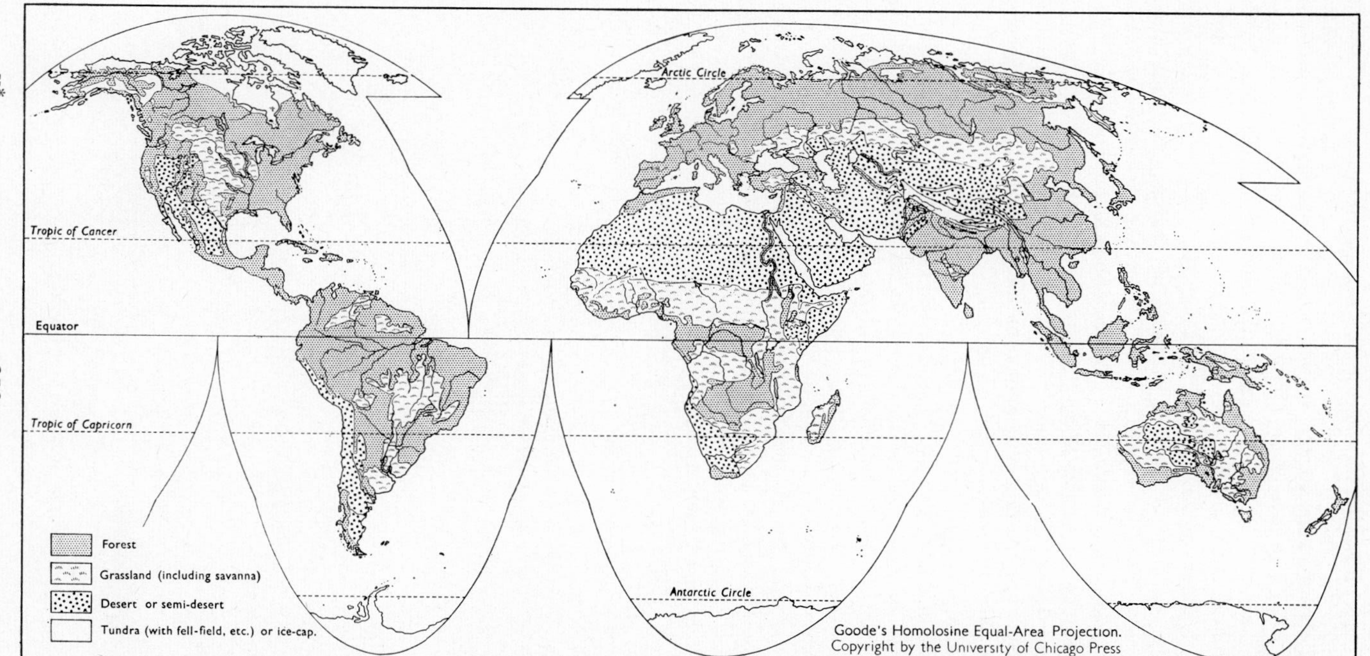


FIG. 65.—Map showing main vegetational-climatic regions of the world in highly generalized form. The four primary divisions of land vegetation are forest, grassland (including savanna), desert or semi-desert, and tundra (with fell-field, etc.). To reach this present-day situation, Man's interference tended to increase the areas of the last three categories at the expense particularly of the first—*cf.* p. 556

For useful examples in several instances, reference may be made to R. Good's *The Geography of the Flowering Plants*, second edition (Longmans, London etc., pp. xiv + 452, 1953), and, for a comparison with zoogeographical areas, to M. I. Newbigin's *Plant and Animal Geography* (Methuen, London, pp. xv + 298, 1936).

A valuable example of detailed mapping of the ranges of individual species in a well-known region (northwestern Europe) is E. Hultén's *Atlas över Växternas Utbredning i Norden* (Stockholm, pp. 119 + 512, 1950). A somewhat similar project is afoot for the British Isles, and it is to be hoped that, in time, more and more regions will be covered in this manner. For the ranges as known to date of many different species and larger groups, see *Die Pflanzenareale* (Fischer, Jena, vols. I–V, 1926–40).

The floras of different areas are dealt with in numerous works to which S. F. Blake & A. C. Atwood's *Geographical Guide to Floras of the World* affords the most comprehensive introduction and selective bibliography. Part I, covering 'Africa, Australia, North America, South America, and islands of the Atlantic, Pacific, and Indian Oceans', was published in 1942 by the United States Government Printing Office, Washington, D.C. (U.S. Dept. Agric. Misc. Publ. No. 401, pp. 1–336), while Part II, treating western Europe, is to be published by the same agency. It is contemplated that a third part will cover the rest of the world.

## Chapter VIII

# MODIFICATION AND DISTRIBUTIONS OF CROPS (AND WEEDS)

It is now time to deal with the so-called 'artificial' changes wrought by Man, whether intentionally or accidentally, in the distributions of plants. In this connection Man seems during recent centuries to have been the most potent factor in the world; and as his activity increases and more and more barriers are broken down by transport, his effectiveness as a distributor grows ever greater. This transportation is quite apart from the changes Man brings about incidentally in the course of his ever-extending activities of husbandry or desecration.

From what was said in the last chapter it should be clear that, whereas plants have their own distribution patterns, and particular taxa have particular areas which they are capable of occupying, it is rarely if ever that a vascular plant taxon will occupy anything like the whole of the geographical area or areas where the climate is suitable for it. Usually, numerous unsuitable habitats will intervene, and even then there are commonly left areas of suitable habitat which the plant in question has failed to reach, or in which, if it has arrived, it has failed to establish itself and survive. In other words, the present areas occupied by particular plants tend to fall far short of the maxima which they are capable of occupying: artificial introduction of a plant outside its present *natural area* will frequently demonstrate its ability to grow in a wider range of situations both geographically and ecologically. Thus, besides its own natural area of distribution, each species has, at least in most instances, a wider *potential area* which, if we include places where it can be grown in cultivation or otherwise in the virtual absence of competition, is often very much more extensive. This principle is of great significance in connection with the introduction and production of crops on which Man largely depends.

The dispersal of plants by Man was considered in a special section of Chapter IV. Here we must deal with the results of such transport so far as the all-important crops of field and forest and the recognized weeds of cultivation are concerned, not forgetting the more devastating diseases of those crops. We must also consider the effects of cultivation—and of the removal of Man's protection, whether such protection had been intentional, for crops, or unintentional, for weeds.

## Effects of Cultivation

It is a common experience of farmers and gardeners that cultivated plants and the weeds infesting them or their ground tend to lack the ability to spread independently of Man and, in many cases, even to maintain themselves unaided. This inability to hold their own in the face of natural forces—including, in particular, competition from other plants—may even be observed within the natural region and habitat range of the more immediate ancestors of the cultivated plant or weed. The reason is that Man's influence on a plant under cultivation is apt so to change its genetical make-up, structure, and physiological capabilities that it is deprived of 'key' advantages in the general struggle for existence. These advantages will have been acquired, often by the rigours of natural selection, in preceding periods of the plant's evolutionary history, but may be lost overnight, as it were, by artificial selection or, more gradually, by the 'protection' afforded by numerous generations of cultivation.

We may here note a 'round dozen' of the many and diverse types of changes wrought by Man in the make-up and structure of cultivated (and infesting) plants.

(1) *Genetical changes*—involving the loss of characters that are obviously beneficial and often needed for the plants' survival in natural conditions. Besides the examples indicated among the following categories, and plentiful others resulting from such activities as artificial hybridization and the induction of polyploidy, there are the numerous instances of physiological or otherwise less structurally obvious but fundamental hereditary changes.

(2) *Physiological changes*—which are commonly hereditary and hence included in the above category, but which in other instances manifest themselves in the life of a single generation and cause it to 'pay the price'. Thus, for example, plants that have not been suitably hardened may succumb on transplantation to a less favourable habitat than the one in which they originally developed and to which they had become accustomed.

(3) *Structural changes*—often bound up with physiological ones,

and, although commonly hereditary, nevertheless often the result of environmental impress during the life of the individual. Seedlings rendered weak by competition with their fellows under otherwise favourable conditions of cultivation may not so much as survive on transplantation ; or again, thin and delicate ' shade leaves ' of some trees are liable to shrivel on exposure. Though drastic, these are examples of mere ontogenetic change during a single plant's life-time.

(4) *Loss of adaptations for dispersal*—or even for the initial act of dissemination. The fruits of cultivated Flax and of the Opium Poppy do not dehisce when ripe, whereas those of their wild relatives do. Again, among weeds, the inflorescences of some noxious Brome-grasses break up less effectively than those of their wild counterparts, which also tend to have longer awns.

(5) *Loss of protective coverings and sturdiness*—for example in cereals whose fruits are deprived of the usual outer husks, and in the pods of many cultivated members of the Pea family (Leguminosae) which lack the fibrous lining characteristic of their wild relatives. Presence of the fibrous lining also causes the valves to curl up and thus helps dissemination of the seeds. The commonly lesser development of fibrous tissue in crop plants is apparently connected with their growth in close stands—often protected from winds and under conditions of favourable humidity, nutrition, and shading, which all tend to promote rapid growth. Similarly, in a dense forest the trees usually have tall and slender trunks and weakly developed crowns, so that individuals left isolated on removal of their neighbours are liable to be blown down, whereas in the open the same species tend to be far more sturdy.

(6) *Increase in size of seeds and fruits*—usually accompanied by a decrease in their number. This tends to reduce their chances of dispersal while at the same time reducing the plants' opportunities for propagation. Moreover, the production of unnecessarily large seeds and fruits is wasteful so far as the plants' economy is concerned. How much more economical are the fruits of Fireweeds than of Pumpkins, and how much more successful as colonists are the former plants !

(7) *Improvement of flavour*—of seeds and fruits, which is a common objective of cultivation, tends to cause animals to eat them more voraciously and completely, and so militates against effective dispersal.

(8) *Conversion of perennials into annuals*—is common in the

domestication of plants, as for example among the cereals. This is advantageous from Man's point of view in speeding up crop-production, and may favour the plants' own chances of survival in 'open' habitats such as those prepared for cultivation; but it places them at a great disadvantage in competition with natural vegetation, which in most undisturbed land habitats is dominated by perennials.

(9) *Absence of successful fruiting*—for example due to atrophy of the sexual organs, to absence of pollinators far from the plants' native habitat, or to the desecrations of Man—results in such plants being incapable of self-perpetuation by the usual means.

(10) *Seedless fruits*—which are often an objective of plant breeders for cultivation, likewise render a plant incapable of independent existence unless it has some effective means of vegetative propagation, in which case it will still lose the benefits of sexual reproduction (such as hybrid vigour and the exchange of genic material).

(11) *Double flowers*—involving for example the 'conversion' of stamens into petals—again render the plant incapable of self-perpetuation by the normal means.

(12) *Loss of defensive adaptations*—such as spines, thorns, hairiness, and hardness—renders the plant defenceless against animal grazing and, often, more susceptible to injury from excessive loss of moisture.

The above features may occur already among wild plants as abnormalities, but in cultivated strains they tend to become intensified by Man's conscious or unconscious selection and, often, perpetuated through his propagation and protection. When no longer cultivated, or, in the case of weeds, enjoying the benefits of cultivation, such horticultural or agricultural strains tend to disappear. Having been modified by Man in ways most likely to suit his needs (but at the same time harmful to the chances of persistence of the plant as an independent organism), they are no longer able to help even in maintaining the area of the species to which they belong, at least in many cases in the absence of Man's influence.

The weeds most notably modified through cultivation are those that constantly accompany particular crops, thanks to which they have long been involuntarily cultivated by Man. Some of them—such as, apparently, the cultivated Rye—have become so transformed as to be now themselves objects of cultivation. For in weeds, just as in intentionally cultivated plants, there tend to be such changes as increase in size of seeds at the expense of their number, and loss by fruits of their protective coverings and abilities to disseminate.

A good example of weeds closely associated with particular crops is afforded by the so-called ' linicolous ' plants that accompany Flax (*Linum*). These appear to lack the normal adaptations for accommodating their development to seasonal changes, and may even be dependent for the completion of their life-cycle upon being gathered with the Flax crop when their seeds are ripe, kept in a storehouse through the winter, and sown on open soil the following spring. In extreme instances the plant has become so modified through long association with the crop that its wild progenitors are unknown, as is the case also with some crop plants. Examples of such weeds of uncertain ancestry infesting cultivated Flax (as indeed their specific epithets indicate) are a Campion, *Silene linicola*, and a Dodder, *Cuscuta epilinum*. There is thus not merely a very close association but also a tendency to parallel variation between many crops and some of their more commonly accompanying weeds, *e.g.* through their disseminules being difficult, or mechanically impossible, to separate from those of the crop itself.

## Naturalization and Acclimatization

Although, in general, weeds tend to be hardy and to have a very wide range of tolerance to differing environmental conditions, so that they can spread far and rapidly, at least in ' disturbed ' areas, crops are often fastidious in their habitat requirements. Both have accompanied Man in his migrations over the world, however, and from time to time have given rise to ' escapes ' or, more rarely, have become established as naturalized aliens. But it is one thing to escape from cultivation or a cultivated area into adjoining terrain, perhaps repeatedly and under the beneficial influence of Man, and quite a different problem to become sufficiently acclimatized to hold sway in a fully wild state in undisturbed habitats among the local natives. This latter is a relatively rare feat, as we shall see. Indeed for the most part not only crops but also weeds are limited to areas that are, or recently have been, in some way disturbed by Man.

It is sometimes useful when dealing with plants transported out of their normal areas to distinguish between *naturalization*, in which they grow under natural conditions that are similar to those to which they have been accustomed, and *acclimatization*, in which they are adapted to new environmental conditions differing markedly from those of their native habitat or habitats. Although instances of at least some degree of the former are common and widespread, there are relatively few of the latter unless it be among weeds. For acclimatization, except in unusually hardy and tolerant plants, involves adaptation to different habitat conditions which is so very gradual that the time-span required would be likely to exceed that during which Man has been a potent factor in plant distribution. It may be expected to involve the natural selection of suitable biotypes or more extreme mutants, towards which naturalization is no more than a step.

That such naturalization, at least, is going on widely in the world today, is a further indication, if any were needed, that the various regions of the globe do not support by any means all of the species which could thrive there—at least in the absence of competition. However, special studies indicate that, quite apart from the effects of competition, plants transferred to regions of seemingly comparable habitat may have serious obstacles to overcome before they can be considered fully naturalized. These obstacles may be introduced by climatic or other environmental conditions which, although they appeared similar, are actually significantly different from those of the plants' original habitats (as in minor variations of soil composition), or are not commonly recognized as important (as in the case of some light and temperature effects). This frequent difficulty of naturalization is one reason for the rather small percentage of alien species that actually enter into the composition of most wild floras in undisturbed tracts. Even of the numbers that may be able to propagate successfully and remain year after year in one spot, or sometimes increase their area by aggressive extension, few are known definitely to be permanent and able to persist in the absence of Man. Most lengthening of the floristic lists by aliens is probably only temporary.

This brings us to the other main reason, namely the need for Man's continued protection, behind the rarity of fully naturalized alien plants even relatively to the number of aspirants. A plant which has escaped from cultivation or a cultivated area on to some adjoining rubbish dump or otherwise disturbed tract, even if it manages to perpetuate itself there for years as many do, is far from attaining the status of full naturalization. In between mere escape and complete naturalization lie the various stages of success—including capabilities of spread, colonization, and possibly even the attainment of a dominant position. This last is often accomplished locally or sometimes extensively by plants which are effectively dispersed and rank in growth, as in the case of Fireweed (*Epilobium angustifolium* agg.). But that is merely on territory where the native vegetation has been disturbed or destroyed: if such vegetation is then left alone to develop naturally, the aliens, however rank and aggressive they may once have been, will in most instances disappear within a very few years. Likewise have the plants which used to be transported in ships' ballast largely disappeared, since the discontinuation of the dumping of such ballast, from the stations in which they formerly grew as aliens. The discontinuation of a road or railway-line is apt to have a similar effect, and even those aliens which have managed to spread from the immediate vicinity of the travelled track usually disappear when Man's influence is removed and the surrounding vegetation comes back into its own.

All this does not mean that Man's influence in changing the distribution of plants is other than enormous, but rather that it is in many instances merely temporary, as the plants involved have become only incompletely naturalized and certainly not lastingly acclimatized. It should also be remembered that, with Man's increasing mobility, for every disappearance of a plant from an area there is probably on the average at least one new introduction elsewhere, though in this connection particular plants tend to have their ups and downs. Even in those parts of the world, such as New Zealand and Hawaii, where the native plants have been largely ousted over considerable tracts by adventive aliens, this has happened only following disturbance of the native plant communities as well as importation of the aliens by Man or his domestic animals. There it is widely contended that removal of Man's influence would lead to a reversal of the situation through return of the natives whose stronger competition would ultimately oust the alien colonists. This matter of strength of competition is one of the most important in the life of organisms, and is often the key to the present-day distribution of plants as well as to their potential ranges. Crop plants, sheltered and pampered as they are (and have usually long been accustomed to being), are notoriously weak in competition, and consequently rarely to be found in a truly naturalized state.

The adaptations of plants to particular habitat conditions are varied and sometimes so precise as to remain unnoticed, yet sufficient to prevent the leading of an independent life. Often a mere slight change in environmental conditions will threaten the very existence of a species. For example, a Mexican species of Birthwort (*Aristolochia*) when transplanted to Java flowered abundantly but failed to bear fruit—not because of any lack of pollinators but because the climate there was too humid for its normal biological development, the pistillate stage of each flower being over by the time it opened. As has been pointed out by Wulff in the work cited at the end of this chapter, if to such precise needs 'we add the unceasing struggle for existence and the competition with the indigenous vegetation, we should not be surprised at the relatively small number of those species introduced by man for cultivation or accompanying him in his migrations that became fully naturalized components of the local flora'. As an outstanding example it may be mentioned that, of the nearly one thousand alien species in the flora of Madagascar, it is claimed that only one, which is particularly easily dispersed, has gained a foothold in plant communities undisturbed by Man. Only such territory may be considered as ecologically fully occupied.

For cultivation, land has in general to be cleared of native vegetation and otherwise specially prepared. Such ousting of the native flora gives the adventives a chance to spread; so does less complete destruction of the vegetation, for example by domesticated animals. But once the cultivation or other disturbance is discontinued, there ensues a struggle between the alien and native plants which usually ends in victory for the latter and return to approximately the original condition. This is particularly noticeable and rapidly effected in the more favourable forested regions, whereas in some others, such as the drier grasslands, the breaking of the sod or other disturbance may so upset the ecological balance as to make its return extremely slow or even problematical. Another interesting example of this appears to be afforded in some of the most favourable situations in southwestern Greenland. Here the clumps of Willows in many valleys are nowadays separated by grassy tracts (*cf.* Fig. 116) much as they presumably were at the time of the extinction of the Viking colonies and their pasturing Sheep several centuries ago: at least, the present writer has been unable, during hundreds of miles of wandering in those now uninhabited regions, to think of any other explanation of a remarkable phenomenon. Nor have the tree Birches returned at all widely, either in those parts of Greenland or in Iceland, since the 'forests' were decimated in the early centuries of the present millennium.

The majority of really widespread weeds, such as those which qualify as semi-cosmopolites, tend to be collective species (such as the Common Dandelion, *Taraxacum officinale* s.l.) or to consist of numerous races (as in the Couch-grass, *Agropyron repens*) adapted to diverse habitat conditions. The distinction between these two categories is largely a matter of degree and hence of opinion, the important feature from our point of view being that such ' polymorphs ' are able to occupy a wide range of situations and hence, often, of regions. This is, however, chiefly where Man has disturbed the native vegetation. At the other extreme we have the highly specialized ' monomorphs ', such as most cultivated strains, which for successful growth have to be given conditions within a very narrow range of amplitude. In such circumstances they may grow well enough year after year and seemingly indefinitely. But once Man's influence is removed and the coarser local indigenes are allowed to return to the area which is their normal heritage, such pampered cultivates will disappear with surprising rapidity and even aggressive weeds will usually fail within a very few years. Thus in the famous Broadbalk Wilderness of Rothamsted Experimental Station in southern England, according to Sir William Ogg (*in litt. et incl.*), ' The Wheat plants on the strip . . . which was allowed to run wild survived for only four years ', being by then reduced to ' a few stunted plants . . . barely recognizable as cultivated Wheat '. Subsequently ' a dense growth of bushes and young trees ' developed, which soon ceased to include even the hardier wheat-field weeds.

## Some Herbaceous Crops and Their Areas

Most of the important plant products on which Man's sustenance depends come from field or other herbaceous crops of short duration. The plants involved are usually special domesticated strains that have been so highly selected and long cultivated that they are unable to compete with natural vegetation—perhaps anywhere in the world—but, with Man's aid, they fortunately flourish sufficiently to enable him to maintain his position of supremacy. Human civilizations have largely developed in relation to the availability of suitable crops, in particular cereals, and there is altogether widespread interdependence between crops and Man. Communities living outside the cereal belts are often backward to this day.

Whereas each of the various crops commonly had a single region of origin—as indicated, for example, in the works of DeCandolle and Vavilov cited at the end of this chapter—the main ones have usually become important through having their areas spread by Man into other regions. It has even been said that ' no world crop originated in the area of its modern commercial importance '. Not only are these regions, the present-day areas of particular crop plants, often virtually as extensive as climatic possibilities allow, but by special breeding and cultivation techniques Man is always endeavouring to extend the potential areas into new regions. This is notably true in the case of Wheat, the northern limit of which has been pushed farther and farther towards the Arctic in recent decades. It is chiefly with the currently attained areas of the most important herbaceous crops (as opposed to ' woody ' ones, treated afterwards) that the present section will be concerned. And whereas the major vegetational belts and hence natural plant distributions may to some extent have conditioned human migration in the past, it is largely the crop-growing potentialities of different regions that determine the density of human population today. This we shall see in the next chapter, though with the modern ease and efficiency of transport, particularly, this general conclusion tends to become less and less applicable in some areas of intense industrial or mining productivity.

We will now indicate briefly on a world-wide basis the significance and chief areas of cultivation of some of the more important and familiar herbaceous crops ; ornamental ' flowers ' are apt to be even more widespread owing to the special care, often including development under greenhouse or other highly artificial conditions, that is lavished upon them. The chosen examples of herbaceous crops will be treated under eight main headings.

(1) *Grains*—The principal grains occupy about one-half of the world's croplands and of them Rice (*Oryza sativa*) is probably the most generally important, being ' an indispensable food of over half the population of the world '. It replaces the other cereals as the staff of life in many tropical and subtropical countries, and in several of the most densely populated of these its cultivation is the chief agricultural industry. Although 95 per cent. of the Rice cultivation of the world is in the Orient, where the crop presumably had its origin far back in antiquity, Rice is now cultivated practically wherever in the tropics its usual needs of abundant moisture can be economically satisfied, its distribution affording a good example of that of a warm-climate crop (*see* Fig. 66). For the many types of lowland Rice, which have to be flooded during part of their development, are the ones grown almost exclusively ; relatively unimportant is ' upland ' or ' hill ' Rice, which can be cultivated in drier situations much like those favoured by other cereals.

Wheats (*Triticum vulgare* and other species) constitute the chief cereals of temperate regions and the ones most important to the

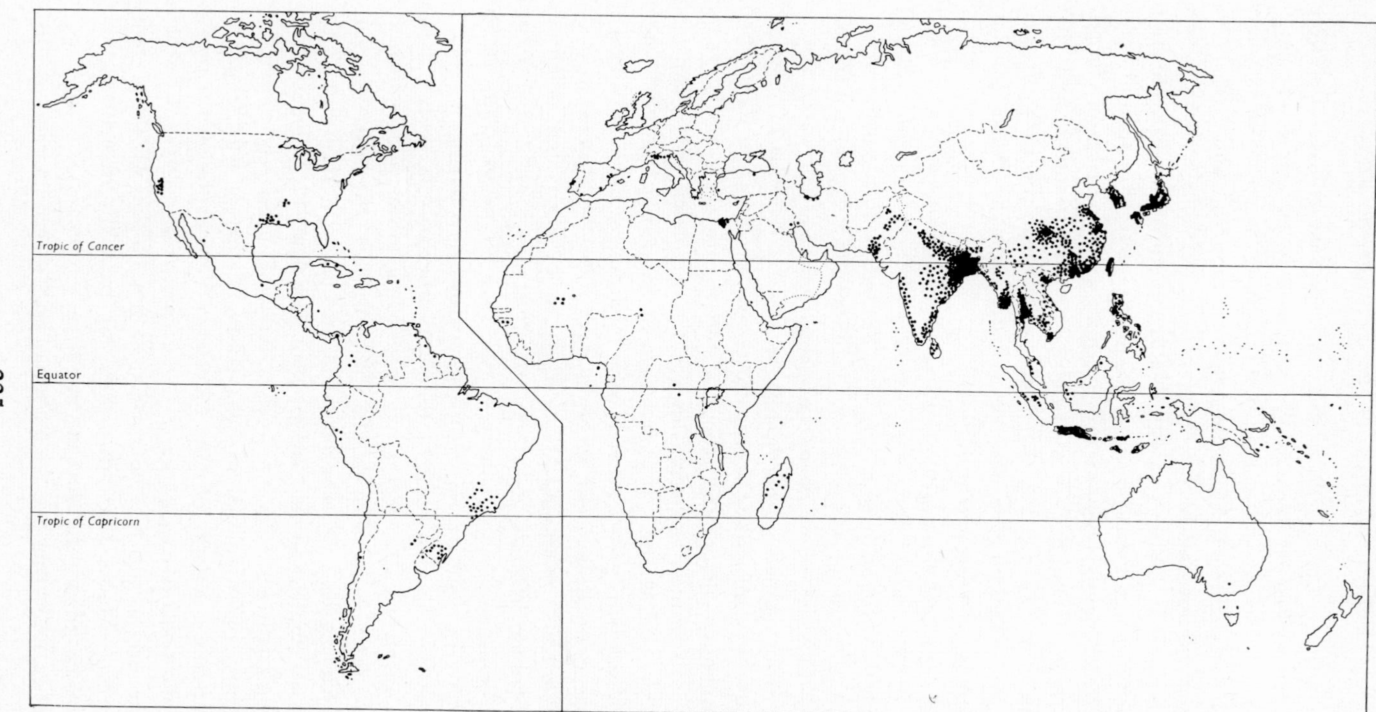


FIG. 66.—Geographical distribution of world Rice production. Annual average for 1953–55, each dot representing 100,000 metric tons. Data from U.N. Yearbook.

white race nowadays. Their areas of origin are doubtful but were evidently diverse as regards the different forms, some of which appear to have been cultivated for at least 6,000 years. Nevertheless the predominance of Wheats is relatively modern, other cereals, or mixtures comprising maslin, having been previously more widely used for bread. Wheats were probably developed by selection from weedy types and hybridization with other Grasses, but are still being improved today. They are grown under a wide variety of climatic conditions, including some tropical ones (in winter), and, like polymorphic weeds, are the more widespread because of their diversity. Nevertheless the general distribution of Wheats is mainly temperate, as indicated in Fig. 67.

Less widespread and important are Barley (*Hordeum vulgare* s.l.), Oats (*Avena sativa* and other species), and Rye (*Secale cereale*), though the first of these is probably the oldest of our major cereals and possibly of all currently cultivated plants. It was widespread already in Neolithic times and was used for bread even before Wheat. Oats probably had a long history as a weed in fields of primitive Wheat before becoming a crop in its own right, while Rye, which was unknown before the Iron Age but is now the world's second most important bread crop, apparently originated as a grain-field weed in Asia Minor. It can be grown on poorer soils than other cereals. Owing to its greater winter hardiness and ability also to mature grain under less generally favourable conditions than the other cereals mentioned, Rye tends to be cultivated chiefly in mountainous regions and about the northern limit of the Wheat belt, being important chiefly in the cool-temperate parts of the northern hemisphere—*cf.* Fig. 68. However, Barley is able to mature in a shorter summer than the other cereals, and so is the only one which the writer has seen being grown successfully for grain north of the 70th parallel of latitude in Norway.

Maize (*Zea mays*) is the largest of the cereals. According to that foremost student of its history, Professor Paul C. Mangelsdorf of Harvard University (*in litt.* 1957), 'No wild ancestor is known with certainty, but fossil pollen believed to be that of wild Maize has been found at a depth of more than seventy meters below the present site of Mexico City. Other evidence points to cultivated forms of Maize originating on the eastern slopes of the Andes in South America. Maize cultivation goes far back in prehistoric times. Grains found in burial sites in Peru already represent several different varieties, indicating that the plant had been grown for many centuries

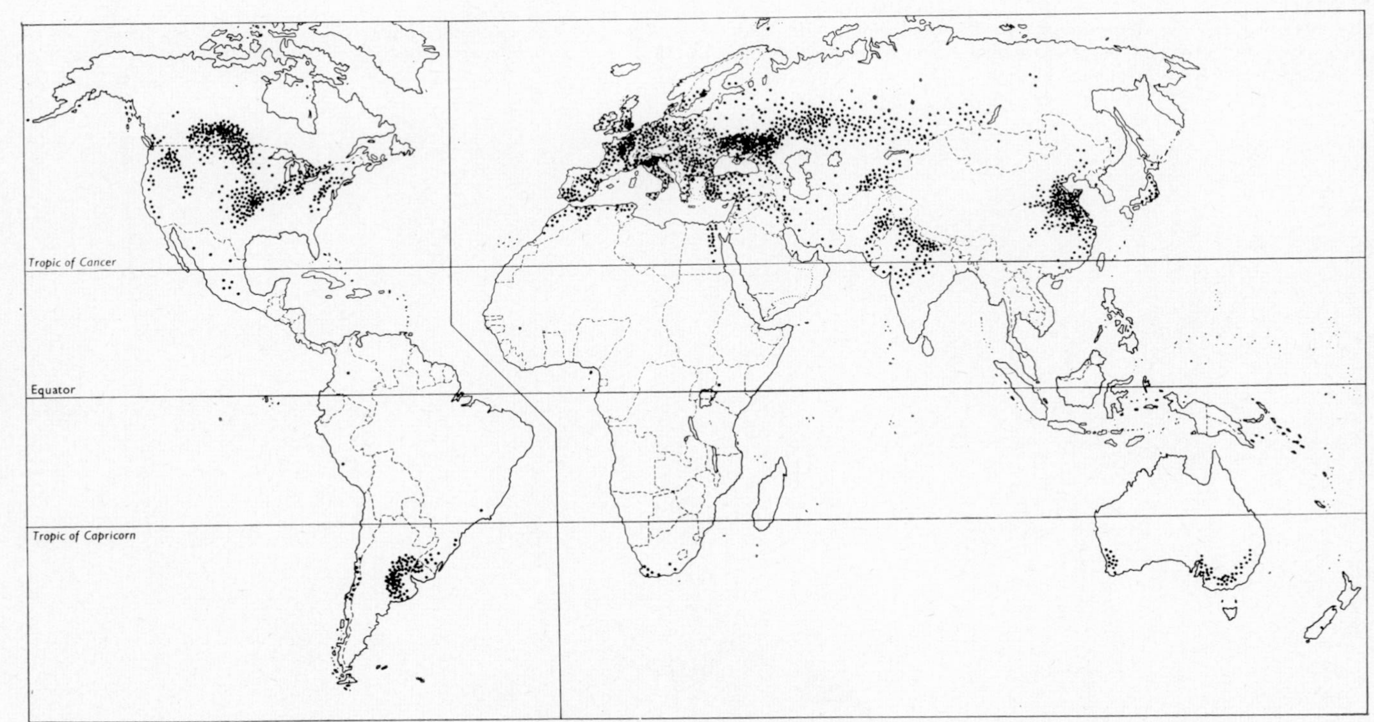


FIG. 67.—World Wheat production. Annual average mostly for 1953–55, each dot representing 100,000 metric tons. (Data from U.N. Yearbook, except for U.S.S.R. and some satellites which are 1948–50 average and taken from Oxford Economic Atlas.)

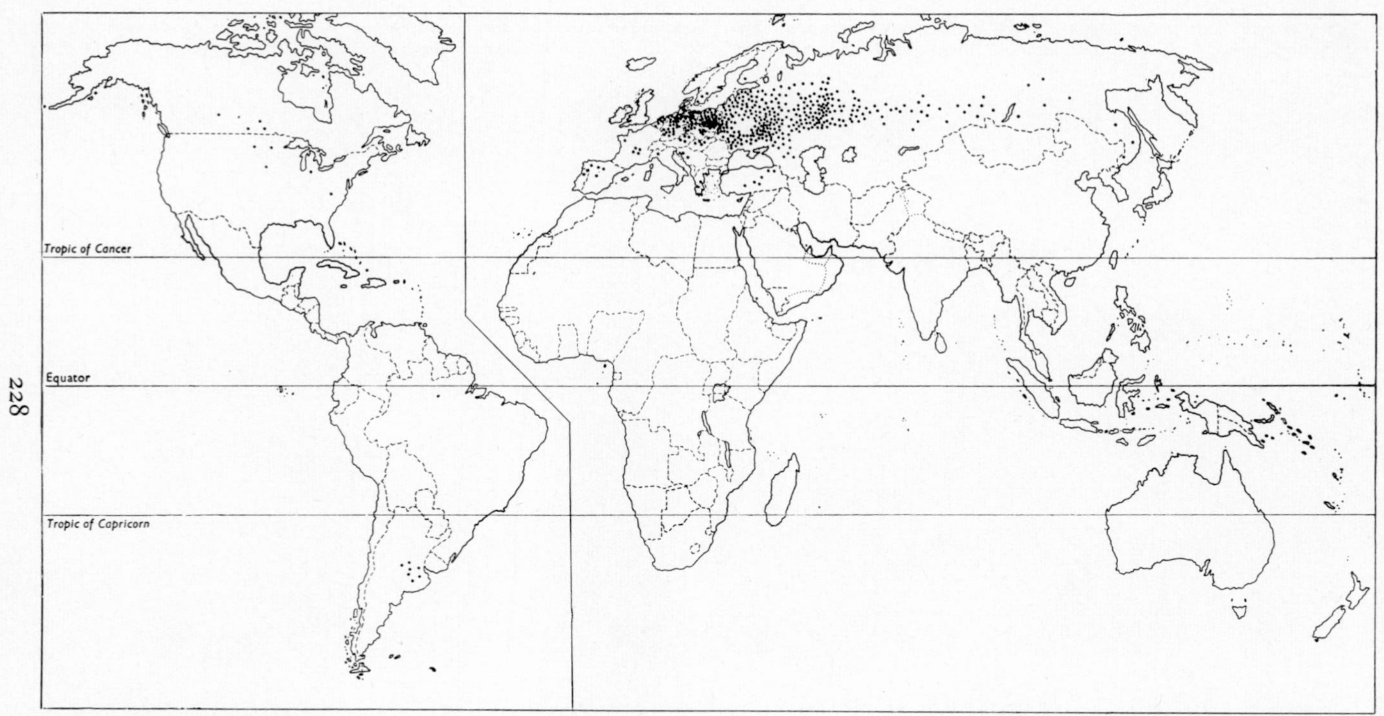


Fig. 68.—World Rye production. Annual average mostly for 1953–55, each dot representing 100,000 metric tons. (Data from U.N. Yearbook, except for U.S.S.R. and Czechoslovakia which are 1948–50 average and taken from Oxford Economic Atlas, and Romania and Bulgaria which are omitted but were both producers.)

before the period of the Inca civilization. Radiocarbon determinations of primitive cobs found in Bat Cave in New Mexico, indicate that this material was between 5,000 and 5,600 years old.' In spite of its numerous forms, Maize is a crop mainly of rather exacting requirements of considerable summer moisture in warm countries. It does not ripen far north; indeed not many regions have the right combination of environmental conditions for the raising of Maize on a large scale. Most notable is the eastern half of the United States, which produces about half the world's crop, although there are other considerable centres of production in South America, southern Europe, and eastern Asia, as indicated in Fig. 69. Maize is used principally for feeding Hogs and other domesticated animals, but is also favoured as a vegetable.

The various types of Millets, belonging to several different genera of Grasses, and the Sorghums, belonging to the genus *Sorghum*, should also be mentioned as widely grown for forage, grain, and many other purposes. The Sorghums have been cultivated in Asia and Africa since very early times, constituting a staple food for millions of native peoples. Latterly they have come to be grown in other tropical and warm-temperate regions, being particularly useful because of their ability to grow under dry conditions and actually withstand droughts.

(2) '*Root*' *Crops*—Of these the Irish or White Potato (*Solanum tuberosum*) is the most widely important, having no rival as an efficient producer of food, especially in relatively moist and cool countries. Although the Potato's origin lay in the mountainous portions of South America, over 90 per cent. of world production is now in Europe, whose population has increased substantially as a result of its cultivation. In comparison with the other leading food-crops, the average annual world production during 1934–38,[1] expressed in millions of metric tons, has been estimated as approximately 233 for Potatoes, 167 for Wheat, 152 for Rice, 115 for Maize, 65 for Oats, 52 for Barley, and 47 for Rye. Actually these figures, although interesting, are only fragmentary for some crops,[2] and are moreover misleading in that Potatoes contain at least 78 per cent. of water, against an average of only about 13 per cent. for cereals. Consequently, the official dry-weight food production of Potatoes in that period was only about 51 million tons, whereas for Wheat it was approximately 145 million tons, and for Rice and Maize also

[1] The last period for which the F.A.O. Yearbook (vol. IX, part 1, 1955) gives pertinent statistics for the U.S.S.R.

[2] *E.g.* Potatoes underestimated owing to gardens?

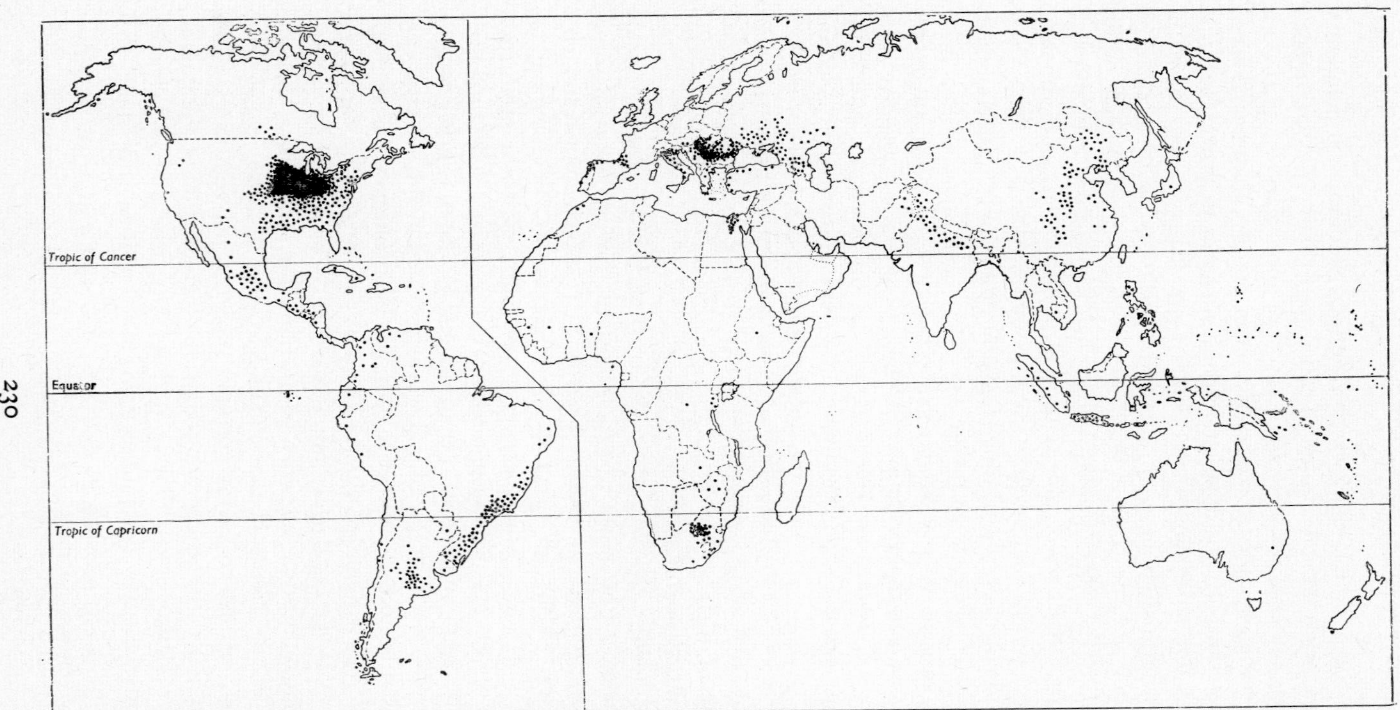


FIG. 69.—World Maize production. Annual average mostly for 1953–55, each dot representing 100,000 metric tons. (Data from U.N. Yearbook, except that U.S.S.R., China, Romania and Bulgaria are 1948–50 average and taken from Oxford Economic Atlas.)

greatly in excess of that of the White Potato. Yet under suitable conditions of moist climate and rich but light soil, the Potato is able to supply considerably more human food per unit area than any of the cereals, the world crop during 1934–38 being produced by about 22 million hectares as opposed to an estimated 168 million hectares under Wheat. Relatively to the following two so-called ' root ' crops, the Potato is hardy, especially in some of its numerous forms, Fig. 70, A, indicating most of its cultivated range in the world. In addition the present writer has eaten quite large home-grown Potatoes in central Alaska and far down the Mackenzie Valley, and small ones in southern Greenland and in northernmost Scandinavia near 71° N. lat. He has even eaten tiny ones much farther north in Spitsbergen, grown on the pyre of a burned-out hut. In the White Potato the storage tuber is really an underground stem structure bearing buds (the so-called ' eyes ').

The Sweet Potato (*Ipomoea batatas*), an ancient crop of tropical America, is now widely cultivated in the warm parts of the world, being in fact a standard article of food in practically all tropical and subtropical regions. It requires a sandy soil and a moist climate for successful growth. Another very important tropical food plant of this nature (though actually shrubby) is the Cassava (*Manihot esculenta*), which originated in South America in prehistoric times. It can be cultivated in hot, seasonally arid climates where cereals, etc., will not grow. Its many varieties now furnish the basic food for millions of people, particularly in Central and South America, and also supply the world with tapioca.

Other important ' root ' crops which are widely used as vegetables include various types of Yams (*Dioscorea* spp.) in warm regions, and Turnips and Rutabagas (Swedes), which are used also for animal feed, particularly in temperate regions. There are also Beets (*Beta vulgaris*) and Carrots (*Daucus carota*), which both succeed under a wide range of climatic and soil conditions. Beets were domesticated first as a leaf vegetable, then as root crops, and finally as a source of sugar (*cf.* upper part of Fig. 75); they are probably derived from one variable species that is native in the Mediterranean region. Carrots are likewise of ancient origin, various form, and now very widespread cultivation.

(3) *Other Vegetables*—This somewhat vague category includes some structures (such as Tomatoes and the pods of Beans) which technically are fruits. Examples are the Broad Bean (*Vicia faba*), which is one of the world's commonest and most important beans

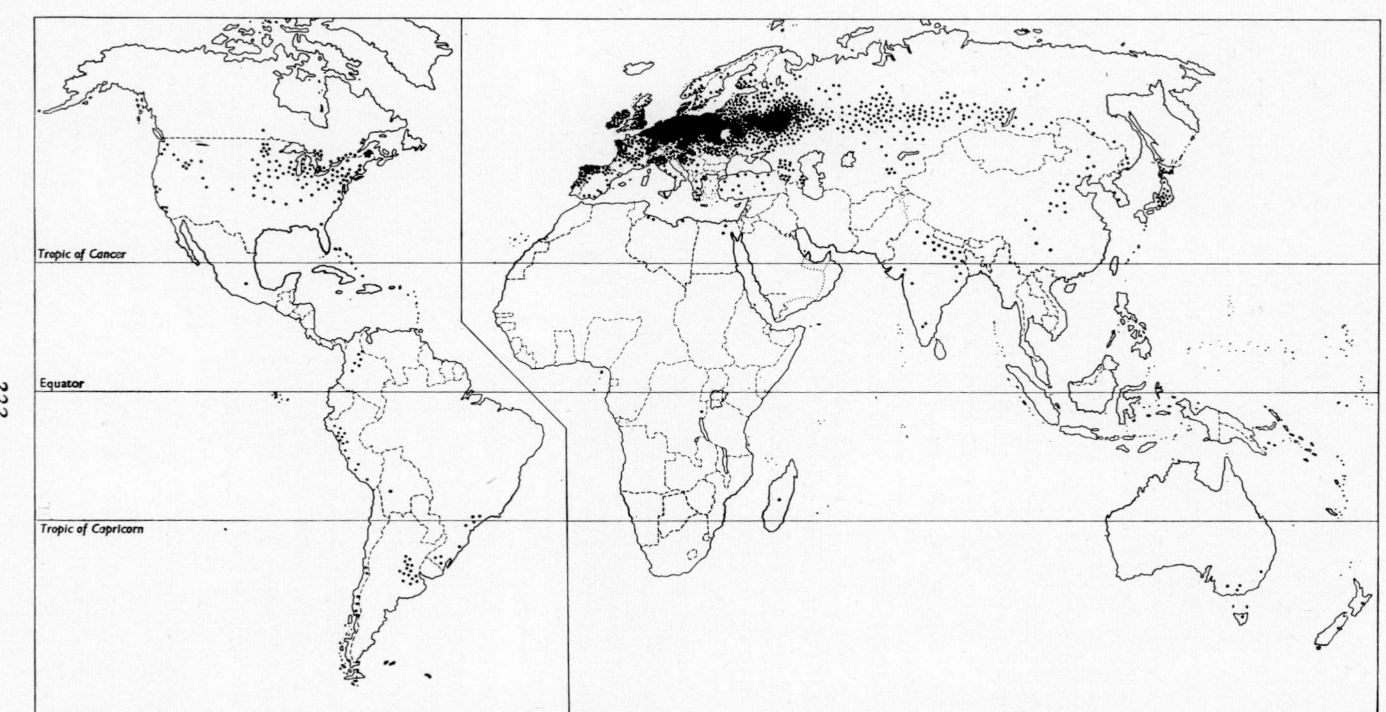


FIG. 70, A.—World production of main Potato countries, annual average for 1953–55, each dot representing 100,000 metric tons. (Data from U.N. Yearbook, except that U.S.S.R., Czechoslovakia, China, Portugal and Switzerland are 1948–50 average based on Oxford Economic Atlas, and data on Romania are based on pre-war figures.)

FIG. 70, B.—Bed of young Kale, with, behind, tall Rhubarb, in Lichtenau Fiord, southwestern Greenland. The native family are standing on a raised path in front of the old mission house from which the garden slopes downwards.

and was the only edible one known in Europe before the time of Columbus; the Common or Garden or Kidney Bean (*Phaseolus vulgaris*), which has long been cultivated in the New World where it probably originated; and the Soybean (*Glycine max*), which is of great antiquity in the Orient, where over one thousand varieties are grown. Soybean, particularly, has a very wide range of uses, the seed, containing about 20 per cent. of oil and 30–45 per cent. of protein, being the richest natural vegetable-food known. The climatic and soil requirements ideally are much like those for Maize, and the crop is becoming more and more extensively cultivated in temperate regions—including the United States, where it is grown chiefly as a source of oil and stock feed.

Other important legumes are the Common Pea (*Pisum sativum*), which is now very extensively cultivated, and the Chick Pea (*Cicer arietinum*), which is an important food plant—particularly in India and other parts of Asia, in Africa, and in Central America. Both these plants appear to be natives of southern Europe or adjacent regions, where they have been grown from early days and are still extensively cultivated, and neither is known in the wild state. The

Common Pea needs plentiful moisture but thrives in cool regions, whereas the Chick Pea is well adapted to dry conditions. Another widespread and important crop plant of this general affinity is the Lentil (*Lens esculenta*), which has been cultivated since Neolithic times and is thought to have originated in southwestern Asia.

Mustards are extensively cultivated for their oil and use as greens in Asia, as are the related Cabbages and Kales and their allies (*Brassica oleracea*) in Europe and elsewhere for human and domestic animal consumption (though originally for their oily seeds). The Cabbages, etc., were evidently developed far back in antiquity from a variable Mediterranean species exhibiting numerous local races; now they are grown practically around the world, occupying a wide variety of soils and climates ranging from the low-Arctic to the sub-tropics. Fig. 70, B, shows a fine bed of young Kale growing in southern Greenland, with, behind, tall Rhubarb.

Finally we should mention a few 'fruit vegetables' such as the Squashes and Cucumbers and their allies, many of which have been extensively cultivated from early times, and the widely important Tomato (*Lycopersicum esculentum*), which springs from a group of small-berried weedy natives of Peru. Most of these types do best in warm and moist regions, to which some are practically confined.

(4) *Forage Plants*—While several of the above-mentioned crops may be used in part for forage, there are some more specific forage plants to be mentioned primarily in this connection. Foremost among these are various Grasses, of which the Bluegrass or Meadow-grass (*Poa pratensis* s.l.) is an outstanding example. Cytotaxonomically it is one of the most complex mixtures of polyploid hybrids-*cum*-apomicts known, appearing in numerous forms whose origin is often obscure. Geographically it is widespread, particularly in the cooler regions of the world. Ecologically it is unexacting and aggressive, frequently forming a major constituent of pastures whether or not it has been sown. Another important and widely-cultivated forage plant is Alfalfa or Lucerne (*Medicago sativa*), which was probably the earliest forage crop to be developed—apparently in southwestern Asia. Alfalfa prefers a deep, well-drained soil but is grown under a wide range of moisture as well as temperature conditions. It belongs to the Pea family as do also the Clovers and Vetches, which are themselves of considerable significance in pasturage and hay.

(5) *Fibre and Oil Plants*—In this extensive category the Cottons (various species of *Gossypium*), Flax (*Linum usitatissimum*), Hemp (*Cannabis sativa*), Jute (species of *Corchorus*), and Peanut or Ground-

nut (*Arachis hypogaea*), are outstanding in importance and widely cultivated. The first three are used chiefly for fibre and oil, Jute for fibre, and Peanuts for oil and food. All are plants primarily of warm regions, Flax alone being successful far to the north (*cf.* Fig. 71). Cotton as a whole is often claimed as the world's greatest industrial crop and chief source of fibre; its multiple origin is shrouded in the mists of time. The world distribution of Cotton production is indicated in Fig. 72. The others, too, are of ancient and often uncertain origin—mostly in the Old World, but the Peanut very likely in South America, though it is now extremely widespread (*see* Fig. 73).

Other important vegetable fibres are Ramie or China-grass (*Boehmeria nivea*, widely cultivated in Asia), Sunn-hemp (the Asiatic *Crotalaria juncea*), the chiefly Philippine Abaca or Manila-hemp (*Musa* spp.), Sisal and other *Agave* types, cultivated in Africa and North and Central America, and filling fibres such as Kapok (the floss from the seeds of the now widespread tropical tree *Ceiba pentandra*). Of oils there are the essential or volatile types used particularly in perfumery, and the fatty or fixed types which include the drying (*e.g.* Tung, from species of *Aleurites*, native to China), semi-drying (*e.g.* the Asian Sesame), and non-drying (*e.g.* Olive) categories. Olives are cultivated chiefly in the Mediterranean lands but to some extent also in the United States, South Africa, and Australia. In addition there are the vegetable fats such as palm oil (obtained from the African Oil Palm, *Elaeis guineensis*) and coconut oil (obtained from the Coconut—*see* pp. 242, 266). Of the sources mentioned above, cottonseed oil, obtained from Cotton, is the most important semi-drying oil, linseed oil, obtained from Flax, is an important drying oil, and hempseed oil, obtained from Hemp, is another, while peanut oil is a non-drying oil.

(6) *Fruits*—Whereas, technically, many of the above-mentioned products are fruits or derived from fruits, the term is used here in the popular sense. Most of our main fruits are borne by trees or shrubs and will be dealt with in the next major section. The Pineapple (*Ananas comosus*) and Melon (*Cucumis melo*), and, for all its appearance, the Banana (*Musa paradisiaca* s.l.), are, however, strictly herbaceous, as are Strawberries and some other favourites. The cultivated Strawberry (*Fragaria grandiflora*) is, according to Professor Edgar Anderson, 'the one crop of world importance to have originated in modern times'—actually in the eighteenth century as a true-breeding polyploid hyhrid from artificial crosses between wild

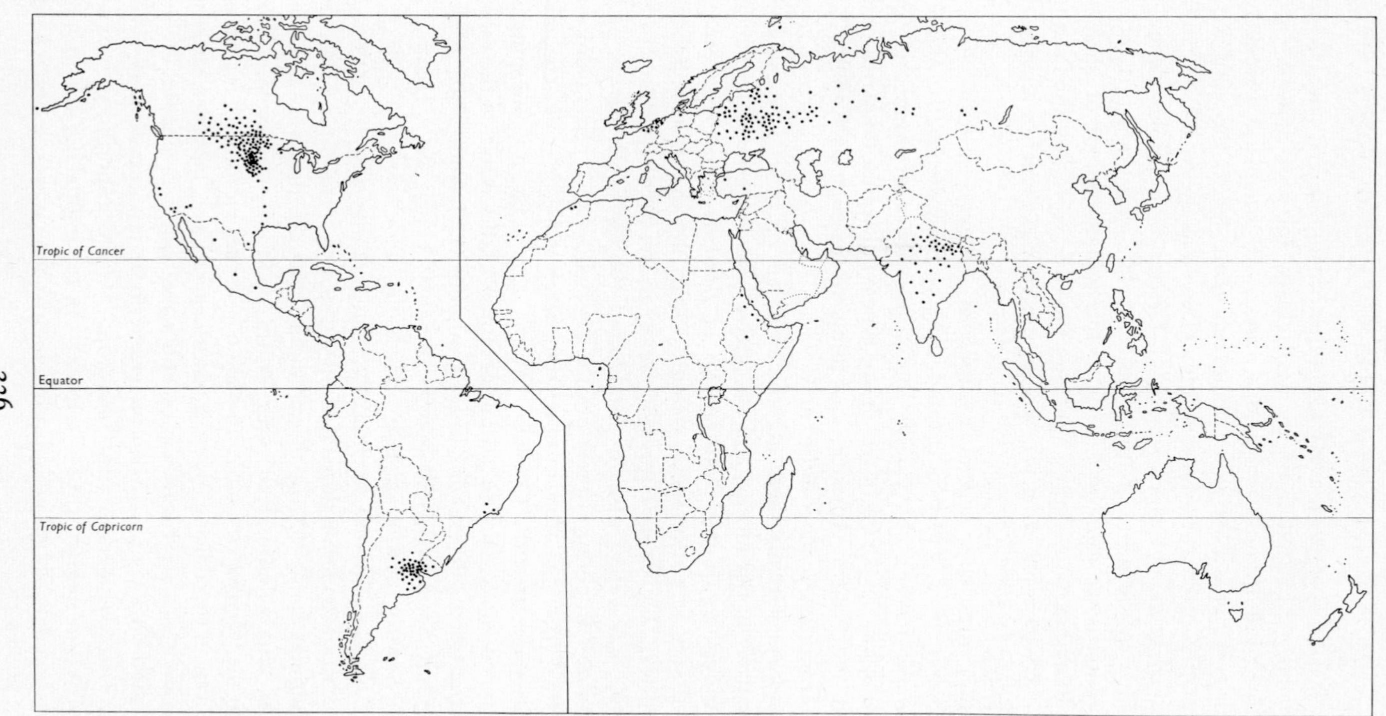


FIG. 71.—World Flax-seed production. Annual average mostly for 1953–55, each dot representing 10,000 metric tons. (Data from U.N. Yearbook, except that U.S.S.R. is 1948–50 average and taken from Oxford Economic Atlas.)

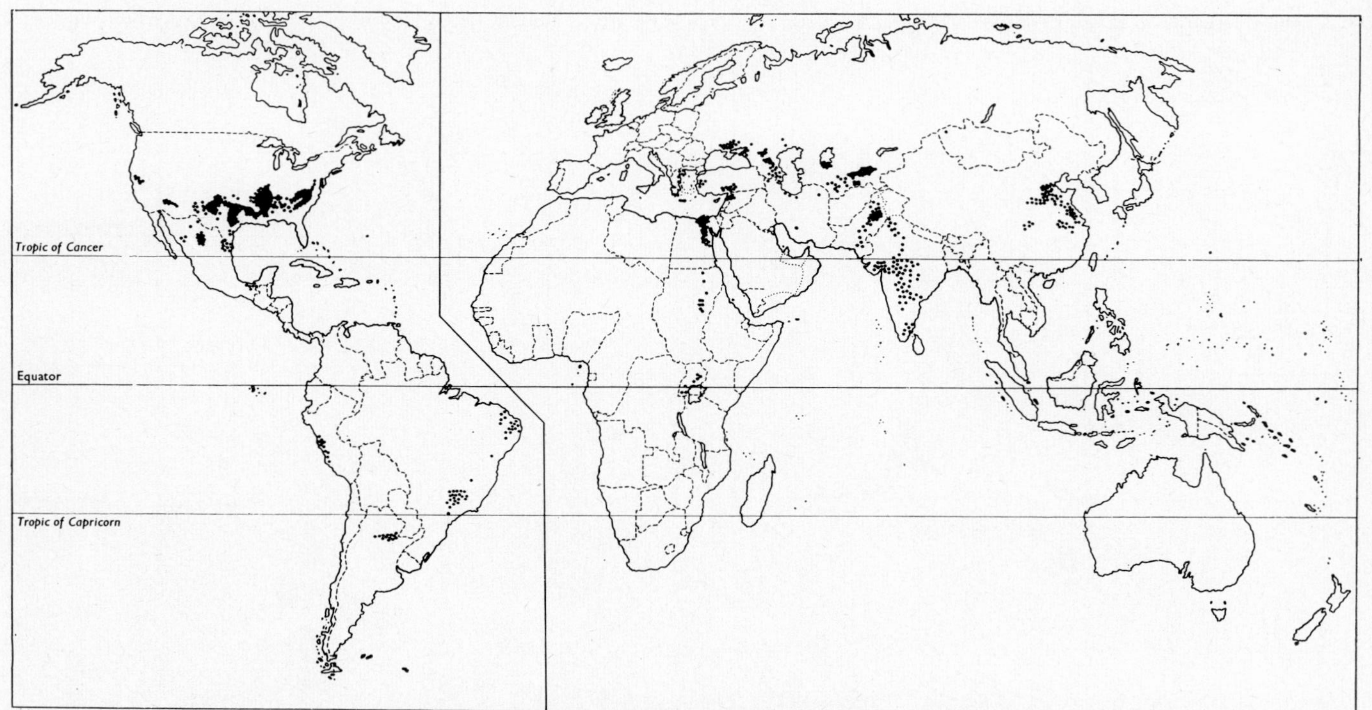


FIG. 72.—World Cotton production. Annual average ginned for 1953–55, each dot representing 10,000 metric tons. (Data from U.N. Yearbook.)

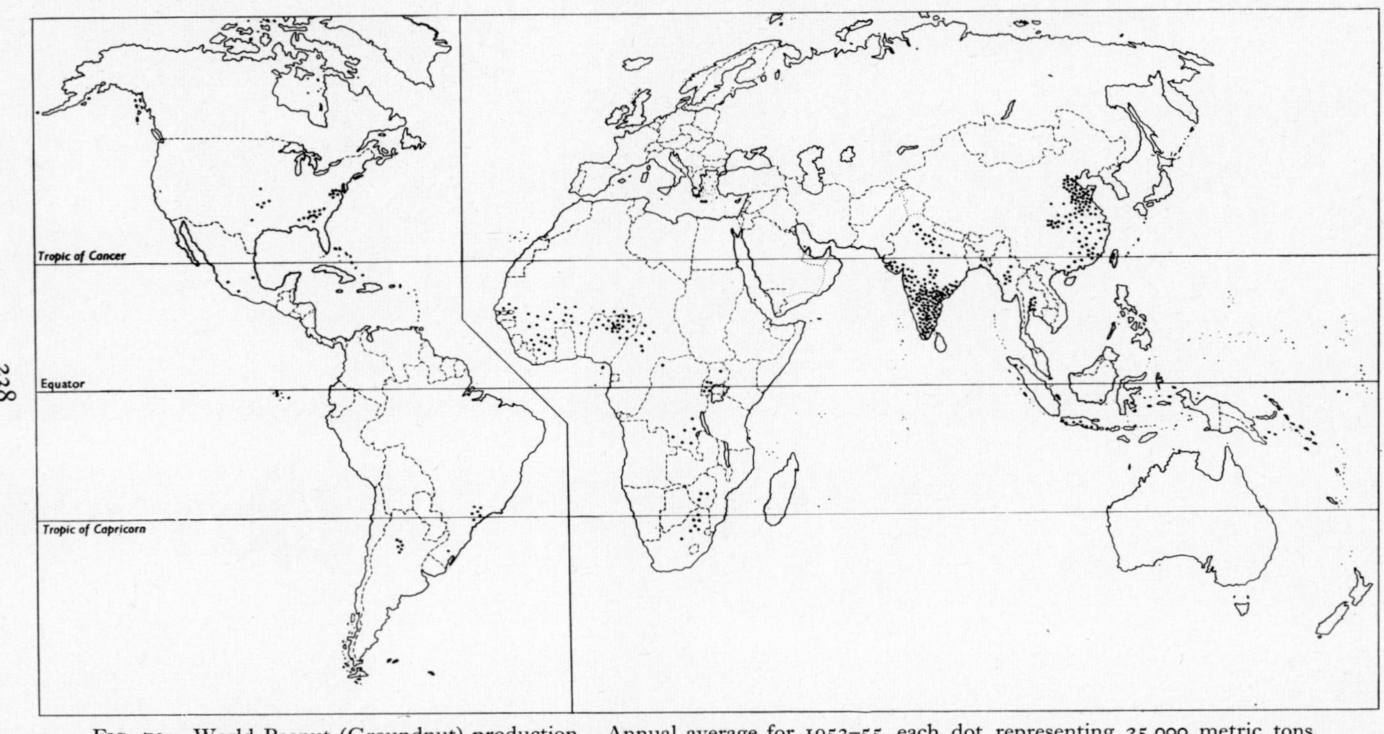


FIG. 73.—World Peanut (Groundnut) production. Annual average for 1953–55, each dot representing 25,000 metric tons. (Data from U.N. Yearbook.)

North and South American types. Other Strawberries have long been grown elsewhere, the fruit as a whole being a favourite in all temperate countries. In contrast, Pineapples, Bananas, and Melons are mainly tropical types of ancient origin. The Malay Peninsula appears to have been the chief centre of origin of cultivated Bananas, whereas South America gave us the Pineapple, and Africa or southern Asia various Melons ; but all three types are now grown practically around the globe.

(7) *Other Crops*—Especially important among these are Tobacco (*Nicotiana tabacum*) and Sugar Cane (*Saccharum officinarum*), while the Hop (*Humulus lupulus*) and various Buckwheats (*Fagopyrum* spp.) are of no mean significance in some areas. Tobacco is apparently a true-breeding polyploid hybrid between two weedy inhabitants of South America, where it probably arose in cultivation in early pre-Columbian times. Now it is grown extensively in various of the sufficiently summer-warm regions around the globe, as indicated in Fig. 74, and is an important commodity throughout the inhabited world. Sugar Cane, a vigorous-growing perennial Grass, is the chief source of sugar at present, although at times in the past it has been rivalled by Sugar Beets. Sugar Cane probably originated in southeastern Asia and comprises an assemblage of forms that are unknown in the wild state but are now cultivated in practically all moist tropical and subtropical regions, the main areas of production of sugar from it and from Sugar Beets being indicated in Fig. 75. Cane sugar probably constitutes the greatest export crop of the tropics.

(8) *Raw Materials for Industry*—A large proportion of these are afforded by plants in limitless supply. This category largely cuts across the others, which in most instances contribute familiar examples to it, and so we need scarcely add details. Suffice it to say that industrially important raw materials include not only the examples already mentioned, such as various grains, roots, fibres, oils, carbohydrates, and their derivatives, but also a wide range of forest products including rubber and pulp. The field-crops involved are grown in the main crop-producing parts of the world and the forest products are obtained mostly in major forested regions. Further information about the sources of these all-important raw materials supplied by plants will be found in the books cited at the ends of this chapter and the succeeding one which stresses further their vital economic significance.

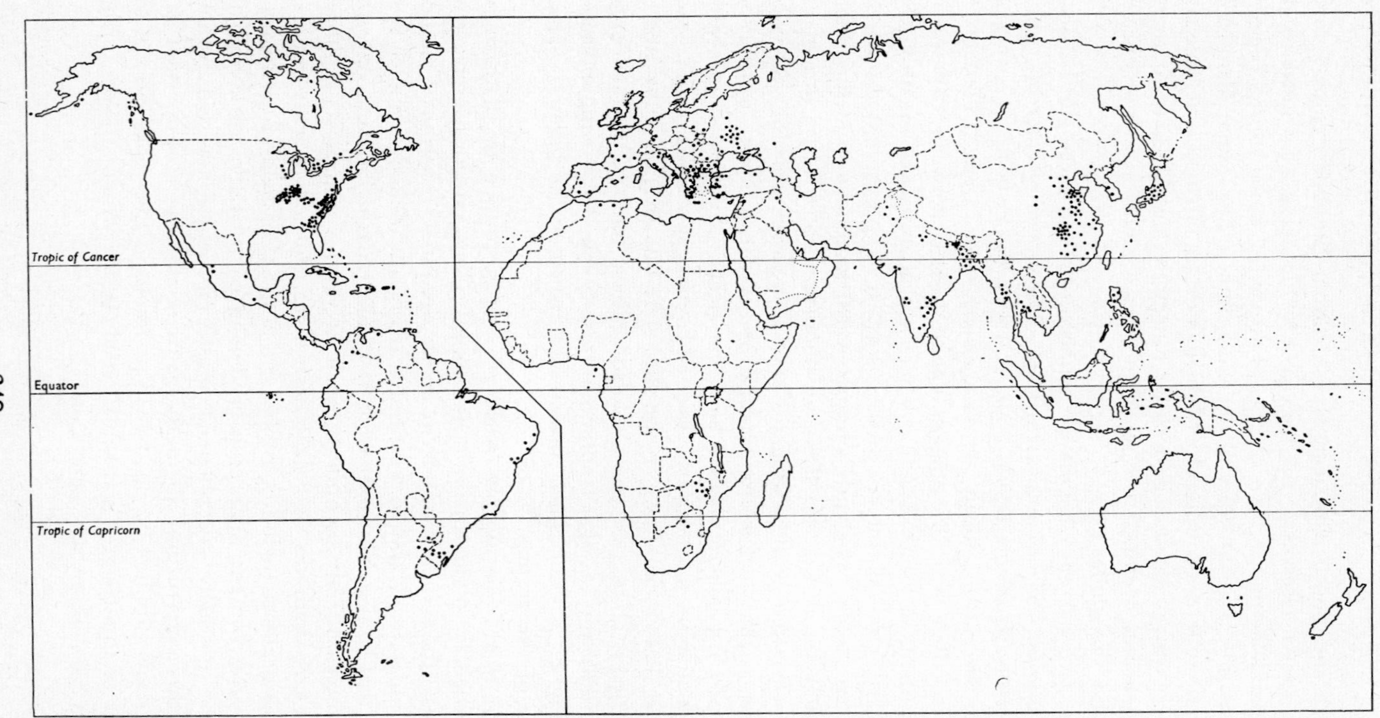


FIG. 74.—World Tobacco production. Annual average mostly for 1953–55, each dot representing 10,000 metric tons. (Data from U.N. Yearbook, except that U.S.S.R. is 1948–50 average and taken from Oxford Economic Atlas.)

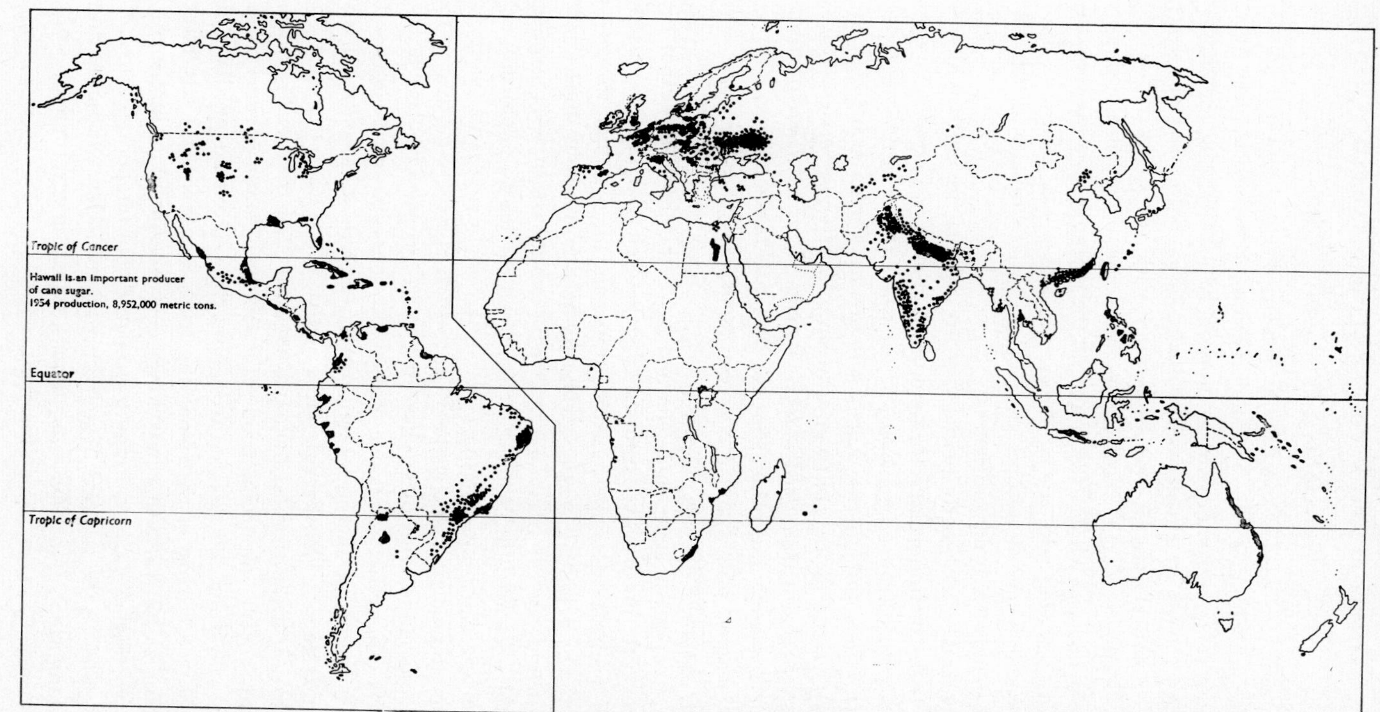
Tropic of Cancer
Hawaii is an important producer
of cane sugar.
1954 production, 8,952,000 metric tons.
Equator
Tropic of Capricorn

FIG. 75.—World distribution of annual Cane and Beet sugar production. Each dot represents 10,000 metric tons. (Data from F.A.O. Yearbook, 1956.)

## Forestry and Other Woody 'Crops'

The practices of forestry, being largely directed towards more effective utilization of the forested regions of the world, are to a large degree concerned with cropping. Especially when artificial planting of trees or shrubs is involved—often with marked effect on their natural ranges, and sometimes with the maintenance of special strains—do the results demand some consideration here. Woody plants as a whole greatly extend the category of fruits (No. 6) introduced above, add one of beverages, and above all contribute their own vast one of timbers and cognate products with which we can deal only in brief outline.

Trees and other woody plants that are extensively cultivated for edible fruits of importance to mankind include the Coconut (*Cocos nucifera*), Breadfruit (*Artocarpus altilis*), Olive (*Olea europaea*), Date Palm (*Phoenix dactylifera*), Fig (*Ficus carica*), Citrus fruits (*Citrus* species), Grape (*Vitis vinifera*), Currants and Gooseberries (*Ribes* species), Mango (*Mangifera indica*), Papaya (*Carica papaya*), Plum (*Prunus domestica* and other species), Peach (*Prunus persica*), Apple (*Pyrus malus*), and Pear (*Pyrus communis*). The first three are scarcely fruits in the lay sense.

The Coconut is sometimes claimed to be the most important or at all events thoroughly exploited of cultivated plants, being used also as a source of timber, thatch, fibre, and many other things—especially by primitive peoples, who may be almost wholly dependent upon it and use all parts. A native of southeastern Asia, where the wild trees are still cropped, it has been carried to practically all tropical and subtropical shores (Fig. 160), being extensively planted. Another important Palm is the Date, which is widely cultivated in the tropics and subtropics where it can be grown with less water than any other crop. It is one of the oldest of crops and is supposed to have originated in southwestern Asia, though it is unknown in the wild state. The Breadfruit, a native of Malaya that is now widespread in the tropics, having been cultivated from early times, is another very important food fruit (in the botanical sense). A Man is said to be able to live throughout the year on the products of a single tree. Most of the remaining fruits mentioned are attractive and familiar cultivates that have long been widespread in the climatic belts which they favour, ranging from the cool-temperate Currants and Apples to the tropical Mango and Papaya. Here we might add the Mangosteen (*Garcinia mangostana*), which is regarded by some as the world's most delectable fruit.

Important beverages obtained from woody plants include Cacao (*Theobroma cacao*), the source of cocoa and chocolate, Coffee (various species of *Coffea*), and Tea (*Camellia sinensis*). The Cacao tree is a native of tropical America; the others originated in the warm parts of the Old World. All are now extensively cultivated in the tropics, and, in the case of Tea, in other warm regions. Fig. 76 indicates the main centres of production of Cocoa beans and exemplifies a tropical crop of restricted origin that is now widespread. Fig. 77 gives similar indications for Coffee, about half of which still comes from Brazil, whose economy is bound up with this single crop to an economically unhealthy degree.

Passing over further categories such as nut-bearing, rubber, and drug plants, whose important products are often obtained from wild sources, we come to the last great one of timbers and cognate forest products. For details of these, reference may be made to such works as that of Zon & Sparhawk or, for the New World, of Record & Hess, both of which are cited at the end of this chapter.

Besides the timbers employed almost all over the world for construction, fuel, and other purposes, important forest products include tanning and dyeing materials and a great assortment of useful gums, resins, oils, preservatives, cork, and latex products—to name only a few. Many of these are taken with fair regularity as a kind of crop, sometimes from planted trees. And whereas in the tropics the vast array of generally mixed timber trees are usually of rather restricted distribution, the relatively few types occurring in temperate and boreal regions are often widely transported and cultivated. Good examples are found among the Conifers that are successfully planted in Europe, which is deficient in native trees for reasons that were discussed in Chapter VI. Such Conifers have often been transported from North America (as in the case of the Douglas Fir, *Pseudotsuga taxifolia*) or Asia (whence come especially numerous ornamental types, though admittedly these scarcely constitute crops), but do quite well at least as long as Man's influence prevails. Apart from such artificial introduction, there are very few large woody species common to both sides of the Atlantic—in contrast to the situation with numerous herbaceous species especially in the boreal and arctic regions. The tree *genera*, however, are commonly the same in Europe and the temperate parts of North America and eastern Asia, though some have disappeared from Europe in recent geological ages.

Forests occupy about one-quarter of the total land-area of the

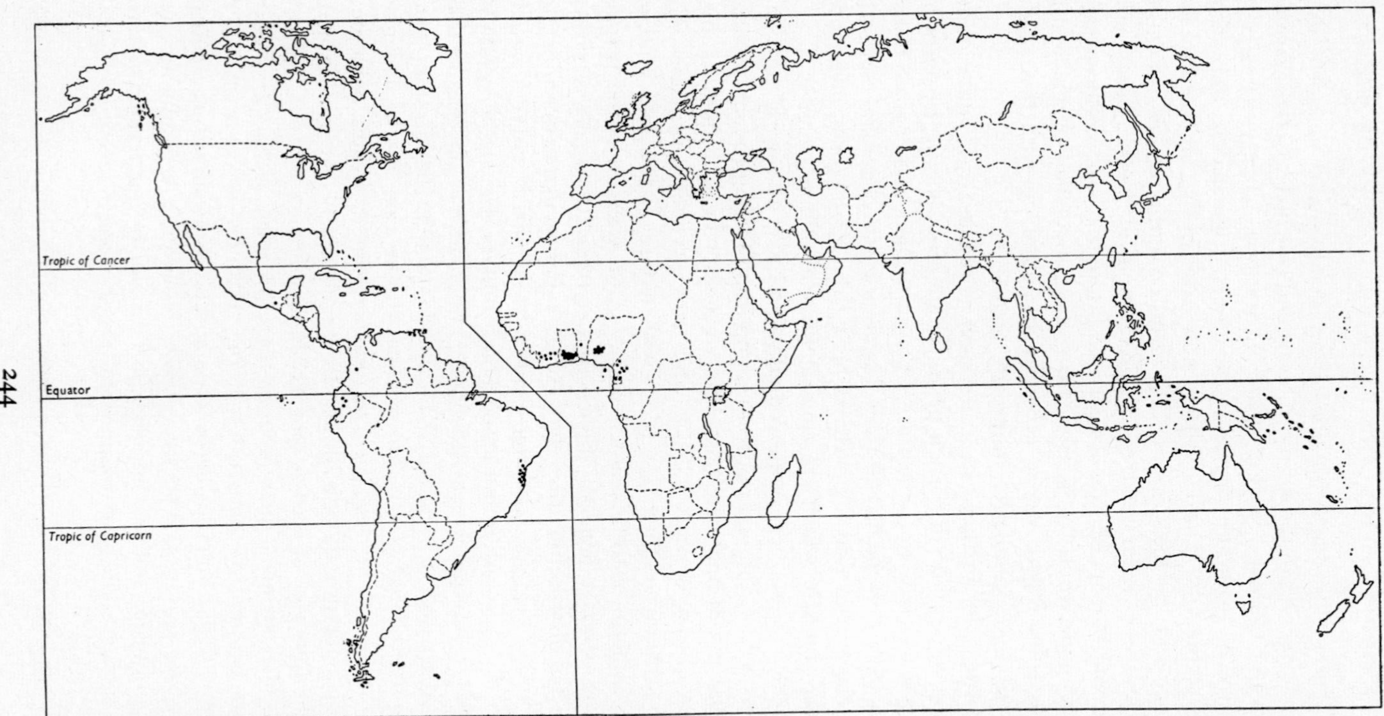


FIG. 76.—World production of Cocoa beans. Annual average for 1953–55, each dot representing 10,000 metric tons. (Data from U.N. Yearbook.)

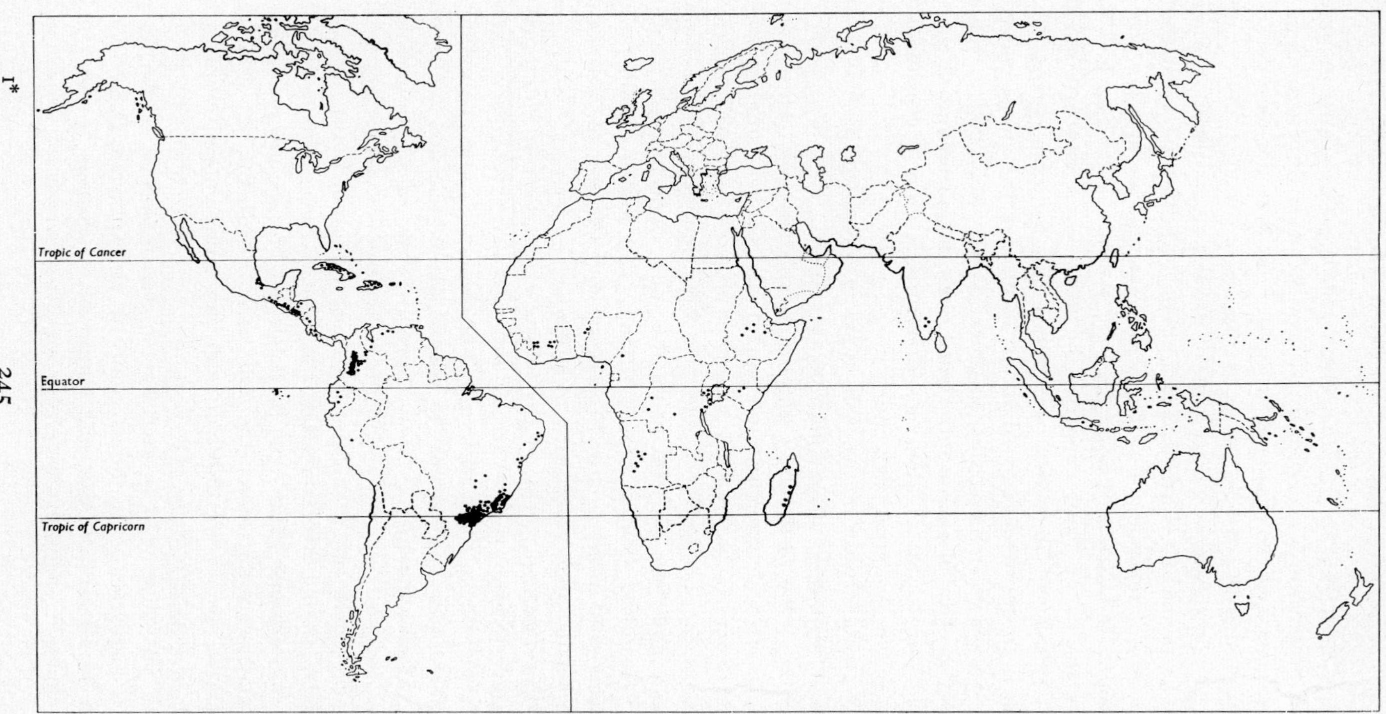


FIG. 77.—World Coffee production. Annual average for 1953–55, each dot representing 10,000 metric tons. (Data from U.N. Yearbook.)

world, as indicated in Fig. 65, which also suggests that a roughly similar proportion is occupied by each of the other three main types of landscape, namely, grassland (with savanna), desert or semi-desert, and tundra (with fell-field, etc.). It has been estimated that South America now has about 44 per cent. of its land area forested, Europe about 31 per cent., North America about 27 per cent., Asia about 22 per cent., Africa about 11 per cent., Australia about 6 per cent. (although New Guinea has 80 per cent.), while Antarctica has no forests at all. In many countries the forests were formerly much more widespread than they are today, the reduction being due primarily to interference by Man, but in some of the more civilized lands extensive reforestation is now being undertaken. This planting is often of exotics introduced from distant regions of comparable climate, the plantations representing a kind of crop whose range is thereby greatly extended.

The characteristics of the main types of forest will be described below in the appropriate chapters on vegetation. Here it will suffice to mention a few of the more important timber trees which in most instances are widely planted and tended (and to that extent, as well as in their regular use by Man, qualify as crops). In North America nowadays the Yellow Pines, Douglas Fir, Hemlocks, White Pine, Cypress, and Spruces tend to be the most important softwoods, with Oaks, Red Gum, Maples, Birches, and Poplars leading the hardwoods, of which the area occupied and the annual 'cut' are much smaller than in the case of softwoods.

In Europe, 74 per cent. of the forests are classed as coniferous, and such forests, as in America and Asia, are particularly characteristic of the northern portions. The principal European Conifers, which are frequently grown in special plantations, are the Scots Pine (*Pinus sylvestris*), Norway Spruce (*Picea abies*), and Larch (*Larix decidua*), though the American Douglas Fir and certain other Pines are extensively planted. The most important European hardwoods tend to be certain Oaks, but Beech (*Fagus sylvatica*), Ash (*Fraxinus excelsior*), and some Birches and Elms are also prominent. The genera are thus much the same as in North America although the native species are different, and this situation continues over much of northern Asia. Here, in the west, European species are found, but these tend to give way to Asiatic species of the same genera farther east. Conifers comprise an estimated 42 per cent. of the forest area of Asia, and temperate hardwoods 27 per cent., the remainder being made up of tropical hardwoods which in many countries south of the Himalayas comprise nearly 100 per cent. of the trees. The species of tropical hardwoods in an area are often very numerous, India, for example, being estimated to have fully 2,000. The dominance tends to be intricately mixed, although Teak (*Tectona grandis*) and various members of the Dipterocarp and Pea families are often prominent. Important commercially, if not always ecologically, are Ebony (various plants including *Diospyros ebenum*), Satinwood (*Chloroxylon swietenia*), and Burmese Rosewood (*Pterocarpus indicus*).

South America, as we have seen, bears a greater proportion of forested area than remains on any other continent. Nearly 90 per cent. of its forest is tropical hardwood—mainly dense rain forest which characterizes the great river basins and tends to be very luxuriant and intricately mixed (there are said to be over 2,500 different tree species in the Amazonian forests alone). In some drier areas an open deciduous type of tropical forest occurs, and on the high mountains are mixed forests of Conifers and temperate hardwoods. Important woods of tropical America include Balsa (*Ochroma lagopus* s.l., the lightest of commercial timbers), Spanish-cedar (*Cedrela odorata* s.l., forms of which are native in some areas but introduced in others), Greenheart (*Ocotea rodioei*), Lignum-vitae (species of *Guaiacum*), Locust (*Hymenaea courbaril*), and Mahogany (chiefly *Swietenia macrophylla* and *S. mahagoni*, of which the latter has been widely introduced).

In Africa, contrary to popular conception, forests cover only about 11 per cent. of the land area. Tropical hardwoods predominate, comprising some 97 per cent. of the forests. Here again there are two main types, of which the dense and much-mixed rain forest is the more extensive but is replaced by an open, park-like type where the rainfall amounts to only 30–40 inches per annum. Of the woods that have so far been exploited, an outstanding example is the African Mahogany (*Khaya senegalensis*), which is widely exported.

Although in Australia forests cover only a very small proportion of the land area, in New Zealand the percentage is about 26 and in Oceania 71. In Australia tropical hardwoods predominate—particularly species of *Eucalyptus* and *Acacia*—and in Oceania they make up the entire forest. On the other hand in New Zealand 68 per cent. of the forests are coniferous and the remainder temperate hardwoods, though the genera tend to be different from those predominating on other continents.

## Significance and Distribution of Weeds and Plant Diseases

Although there are many tens of thousands of species of higher plants in the world, only a few dozens of these are really troublesome weeds which are able to reproduce and thrive in the presence of cultivation and other interfering human activities. More numerous by far are the weedy plants and 'escapes', both herbaceous and woody, which for the present purpose may be considered with the more noxious weeds, and which link the latter with the categories of cultivated plants. Yet the annual loss due to weeds is enormous, often amounting to millions of dollars in a relatively small area.

Weeds are injurious to agriculture, *e.g.* by robbing crops of needed water and nutrients, by crowding them out through root-competition or overgrowing, by choking and pulling them down in the case of (sometimes parasitic) climbers, by having seeds or fruits so similar to those of the crop that they are difficult to separate and so adulterate it and reduce its value, by harbouring undesirable insects or plant diseases, by being poisonous or injurious to stock, by tainting milk, and so on. The nuisances caused by Bindweeds and Couch-grass are all too familiar to almost every gardener as well as farmer in the temperate belt; the Prickly-pears (species of *Opuntia*) which were introduced into South Africa and Australia as a stock feed now usurp the ground; Barberries and Currants harbour (as alternative 'hosts') the devastating Wheat Stem-rust and White Pine Blister-rust, respectively (*see* pp. 251–2).

Regardless of the common 'effects of cultivation' listed near the beginning of this chapter, annual weeds often produce numerous seeds whose germination may be distributed over many years—for example, after being buried for decades.[1] Moreover, the seeds or fruits of many weeds, such as Thistles and Dandelions, are provided with efficient means of dispersal. Otherwise their wide distribution seems to be largely due to Man's transportation activities—such as, for example, the shipment of commercial seeds and grain. These are often of much the same size and shape as the disseminules of

[1] The longevity of seeds and fruits comprises an interesting study for which more and more *authentic* data are needed. Discounting claims of longer periods of burying in marshes etc. which are not fully authenticated, and stories of 'mummy Wheats' which are clearly bogus, the record seems to be held by a 'seed' reputedly of *Nelumbo nucifera* (syn. *Nelumbium speciosum*, the Sacred or Indian Lotus) which was germinated in the British Museum (Natural History), South Kensington, London, during the bombing of 1940, apparently about 250 years after it had been collected.

the weeds which adulterate them, and which are apt all too easily to be shipped and sown with them. It is apparently largely in this manner—though further means were listed in Chapter IV—that, among others, the following pernicious European weeds have become dispersed to temperate America, South Africa, New Zealand, and temperate Australia: Couch-grass (*Agropyron repens*), Crab-grasses (species of *Digitaria*), Russian-thistle (*Salsola kali* var. *tenuifolia*), Bindweeds (species of *Convolvulus*), Sheep Sorrel (*Rumex acetosella* agg.), Dodders (species of *Cuscuta*), Plantains (species of *Plantago*), Wild Carrot (*Daucus carota*), Prickly Lettuce (*Lactuca scariola*), and Sow-thistles (species of *Sonchus*). Europe is not, however, by any means the only source of weeds: although it has contributed some 500 to North America alone—including all present-day American representatives of *Lamium*, *Melilotus*, *Medicago*, *Malva*, and some other familiar genera—many weeds have been dispersed in the opposite direction. Some have even gone much farther afield than across the North Atlantic—*e.g.* Canadian Fleabane (*Erigeron canadensis*) and Gallant Soldier (*Galinsoga parviflora*, a native of South America).

These and others among the most widespread of weeds are the 'semi-cosmopolites' mentioned in the last chapter, and it is noticeable that some of them lack special means of dispersal—commerce having gradually distributed them to all the major regions where they can thrive. This is notably the case with such other types as Shepherd's-purse, Common Chickweed, Annual Meadow-grass, and Lamb's-quarters (*Chenopodium album* s.l.), which are among the most widespread of all flowering plants because, primarily, of Man's unwitting transport and, secondarily, of their variability which enables them to grow in a wide range of different habitats. However, as we have already seen, this is usually manifest only so long as Man continues to interfere by clearing areas or at least keeping the native vegetation at bay; competition tends to be too much for weeds which lack Man's help. This help often extends to breaking up underground parts from which vigorous regeneration can take place—for example in the case of the rhizomes of Couch-grass and Bracken, and the roots of Dandelions. Such weeds are particularly difficult to eradicate.

Although the semi-cosmopolitan weeds tend to have such a wide tolerance to environmental conditions that they are capable of invading almost any agricultural or otherwise disturbed area, at least within their normal climatic limits, other weeds are far more exacting and restricted. Consequently some regions have a characteristic weed-flora of their own, to which many of the component species are largely limited. Thus whereas many weeds have nowadays the type of distribution exhibited by some crops, that is, practically world-wide within climatically limited bounds, others are restricted by special conditions to particular areas for which they are suitable. In the former case peripheral portions of the distribution are often very temporary besides being artificial, Man having extended the area far beyond its natural bounds. Moreover, as we might expect from examination of the ranges of wild plants, weeds in areas outside those of their climatic optimum tend to be restricted to particular habitats where such factors as soil type or microclimate compensate for unfavourable climatic conditions. Here even vigorous weeds may be only sporadic in appearance, easy to control, and liable to disappear quickly in the absence of human interference. Nevertheless, many of the weeds which follow particular crops are almost as widespread as the crops they accompany.

Modern plant pathology, the scientific study of plant diseases, is a large and important subject in its own right—as may be gathered for example by perusal of such works as those of Butler & Jones, Walker, and Boyce, cited at the end of this chapter. Only a few selected distributional and allied items can be touched upon here, for almost any abnormal state of plants, such as may depress the yield of a crop, is liable to be considered as a disease.

Plant diseases may conveniently be classified into three primary groups: (1) non-parasitic, incited primarily by such physical or chemical factors as low or high temperatures, unfavourable oxygen or soil-moisture relations, atmospheric impurities, lightning, and mineral or other excesses or deficiencies; (2) parasitic, incited by Bacteria, various groups of Fungi and their allies, Angiosperms, and animals such as insects and Nematode worms; and (3) virus diseases. Examples of most types can be lethal—sometimes to all the plants belonging to a particular species throughout a tract of country. They are therefore of great importance to plant distribution; for they are apt in some cases to attack any part of the area of a particular species or even wider taxon, and consequently to be of the utmost significance to mankind whose crops they so frequently affect adversely or ruin or even basically destroy.

Whereas very numerous and often serious diseases of wild plants are known throughout the world, it is chiefly among cultivated types that the worst ravages are caused or at all events noted. Here epidemics are of frequent occurrence and sometimes vast proportions. For by growing crops in close plantations, Man offers to parasites a great opportunity for rapid growth and reproduction, while non-parasitic diseases which affect a particular crop plant may be strikingly evident owing to the absence of other species which might mask the effect.

Although Bacteria and viruses cause many serious plant diseases, by far the most important group in this connection are the Fungi. They may range from very local to very widespread in distribution, sometimes covering virtually the whole area occupied by the plant attacked (commonly called the ' host '). Indeed it seems quite likely that particular diseases have been responsible for the complete extermination of some plants in the past, even as they can nowadays cause the disappearance of particular plants from considerable areas. This can obviously be of vast significance in plant geography. As an example we may cite the notorious Chestnut Blight which in recent decades has almost exterminated Sweet Chestnut trees from the United States, where formerly they were of major importance both ecologically and economically. Another example of an important plant disease is Late-blight of Potato, which led to the great Irish famine of the eighteen-forties that resulted in the deaths of hundreds of thousands of people and started the wholesale Irish peasant migration to the United States. Yet another is Wheat Stem-rust that has caused an estimated loss in western Canada alone of as much as $200,000,000 in a single year. In the tropics, another Rust Fungus caused the disappearance from Ceylon of the Coffee industry which had long been the mainstay of its prosperity, and further instances could be cited of such epidemic plant diseases, often introduced from afar, profoundly influencing the economic development of a country, or causing enormous loss or acute distress over considerable areas.

The examples mentioned are all of airborne pathogens, dispersed, in part at least, as minute spores which are blown by the wind often for considerable distances. Accordingly such diseases as the cereal Rusts and similarly airborne Smuts are present in all cereal-producing countries. The chief means of combating them is by the breeding and cultivation of resistant or immune strains, or, in the case of the more intensive crops, by poisonous sprays, etc., which are lethal to the infecting organism. In other instances suitable treatment of contaminated soil or seed, or eradication of infected plants, will destroy the parasite. Or again, the imposition of strict quarantine barriers can be effective, while with some virus and other diseases which are spread by insects, the killing of these vectors, or growth of the crop in areas where they do not occur, should suffice for successful control. Some plant pathogens have an alternative host in which part of the life-cycle is spent. In such cases eradication of this alternative host is effective, an example being afforded by the White Pine Blister-rust, which threatens the life of all five-needled Pines in North America, and whose alternative host is the genus *Ribes* (Currants and Gooseberries). It should be noted, however, that such systematic eradication may not merely affect the distribution of the species concerned but also the local ecological balance, which may be seriously upset. Similarly, DDT spraying against harmful insects may at the same time kill off all the bees which are necessary for pollination!

## Further Consideration

E. V. Wulff. *An Introduction to Historical Plant Geography* (Chronica Botanica, Waltham, Mass., pp. xv + 223, 1943); for further details about many of the topics discussed in the early part of this chapter.

Origins of Crops:

Alphonse DeCandolle. *Origin of Cultivated Plants* (Kegan Paul & Trench, London, pp. ix + 468, 1884); still useful.

N. I. Vavilov. *The Origin, Variation, Immunity and Breeding o Cultivated Plants*, translated by K. S. Chester (Chronica Botanica, Waltham, Mass., vol. 13, Nos. 1–6, pp. xviii + 364, 1951); *see also* below.

Edgar Anderson. *Plants, Man and Life* (Little, Brown, Boston, Mass., pp. [vii] + 245, 1952); stimulating.

E. D. Merrill. *The Botany of Cook's Voyages* (Chronica Botanica, Waltham, Mass., vol. 14, Nos. 5–6, pp. i–iv + 161–384, 1954); for additional information, with a master's pungent criticisms of some previous contentions.

For Details about Herbaceous Crops:

E. E. Stanford. *Economic Plants* (Appleton-Century-Crofts, New York, pp. xxiii + 571, 1934).

K. H. W. Klages. *Ecological Crop Geography* (Macmillan, New York, pp. xviii + 615, 1942).

A. F. Hill. *Economic Botany*, second edition (McGraw-Hill, New York etc., pp. xii + 560, 1952).

L. H. Bailey *et al.* *Manual of Cultivated Plants*, revised edition (Macmillan, New York, pp. 1–1116, 1949).

For Details about Forest Products:

R. W. Schery. *Plants for Man* (Prentice-Hall, New York, pp. viii + 564, 1952).

R. Zon & W. N. Sparhawk. *Forest Resources of the World* (McGraw-Hill, New York & London, 2 vols., pp. xiv + 1–493 and vii + 495–997, 1923).

S. J. Record & R. W. Hess. *Timbers of the New World* (Yale University Press, New Haven, Conn., pp. xv + 640, 1943).

S. Haden-Guest, J. K. Wright, & E. M. Teclaff (eds.). *A World Geography of Forest Resources* (Ronald Press, New York, pp. xviii + 736, 1956).

Weeds and their Control:

L. J. King. *World Encyclopaedia of Weeds and their Control* (Leonard Hill, London—in press).

W. C. Muenscher. *Weeds*, second edition (Macmillan, New York, pp. xvi + 560, 1955); mainly northern United States and southern Canada.

W. W. Robbins, A. S. Crafts, & R. N. Raynor. *Weed Control*, second edition (McGraw-Hill, New York etc., pp. xi + 503, 1952).

Plant Diseases:

Sir E. J. Butler & S. G. Jones. *Plant Pathology* (Macmillan, London pp. xii + 979, 1949).

J. C. Walker. *Plant Pathology*, second edition (McGraw-Hill, New York etc., pp. xi + 707, 1957).

J. S. Boyce. *Forest Pathology*, second edition (McGraw-Hill, New York etc., pp. xi + 550, 1948).

In conclusion it may be interesting to speculate as to the main centres of origin of our crop plants. It has long been thought that the cultivation of plants by Man began independently in each of the three main centres of ancient civilization, viz., the eastern Mediterranean, the Oriental of southeastern Asia, and the American of southwestern North America and at least the northwestern portions of South America. Nowadays there is a tendency to extend or multiply these to include other areas of supposed early cultivation. Vavilov (*op. cit.*) visualized eight major centres, which he found to be those of greatest diversity of cultivated plants, as follows: (i) Chinese, (ii) Indian (with a suggested separate Indo-Malayan area), (iii) central Asiatic, (iv) near-Eastern, (v) Mediterranean, (vi) Abyssinian, (vii) south Mexican and Central American, and

(viii) South American (Peruvian-Ecuadorian-Bolivian and two minor areas). Much further extensive as well as intensive investigation should, however, be carried out before (if ever) broad generalizations may be indulged in where so many intangibles are involved ; definite information is still largely lacking. This is why such a fascinating and potentially important subject does not receive more consideration in this book. But it does seem that cultivated plants mostly originated in warm regions, if often in their upland areas.

As this book is in the press, there comes news of the discovery in Jericho of a Neolithic culture considerably older than any formerly known. All possibility of observing signs of the ancient cultivation which must have existed around the site has been destroyed by modern agriculture. But the large extent of the area of sedentary occupation constitutes reasonably certain proof that agriculture of some sort must have been prosecuted at that time, which on the evidence of carbon-14 dating was around 7000 B.C. (K. M. Kenyon *voce*). Among other plants, *Linum* appears to have been cultivated in the plains of Iraq as early as around 5000 B.C. (H. Helbaek *voce*).

## Chapter IX

# VITAL IMPORTANCE TO MANKIND

Early in this work we indicated that the green plant is the only satisfactory mechanism for transforming the energy of the sun into organic compounds on which, as an animal, Man is dependent for food and other requisites of life. In the last chapter we mentioned some instances of such dependence, chiefly in connection with the distribution of leading crops. It is the object of the present chapter to give a systematic account, with chosen examples, of the multifarious and often vital ways in which plants and plant products are important to mankind. For Man is unable to synthesize, at all events economically and in useful bulk, most of the materials which he needs in such great quantities—often for his very existence. Even though he can, for example, convert starch into alcohol and the latter in turn into all manner of useful products, he needs the Wheat or some other plant to make the starch for him. In such food materials is locked radiant energy from sunlight, which can then be liberated by the process of respiration that goes on in all living bodies and is rapid in warm-blooded animals. This process usually requires oxygen in large quantities and consequently is again dependent upon green plants as, during photosynthesis, they liberate this vital gas and return it to the air, so purifying and maintaining the atmosphere.

Not only, as we shall see, do plants afford for mankind, either directly or indirectly, his food and many other requisites of life, but they largely condition his environment. Thus, for example, forests are very different to live in from grassy plains, and deserts and areas of arctic tundra are again widely different. Many present-day grasslands and treeless cultivated areas are, however, due to Man's clearance of forests, and although he shows a natural tendency to avoid desert and tundra areas, the correlation of forest or grassland (*see* Fig. 65) with dense human population (Fig. 78) is not always close. Rather has Man wandered and settled where he most conveniently could, having in mind his need for subsistence, which meant in large measure the finding or growing of plants—or of

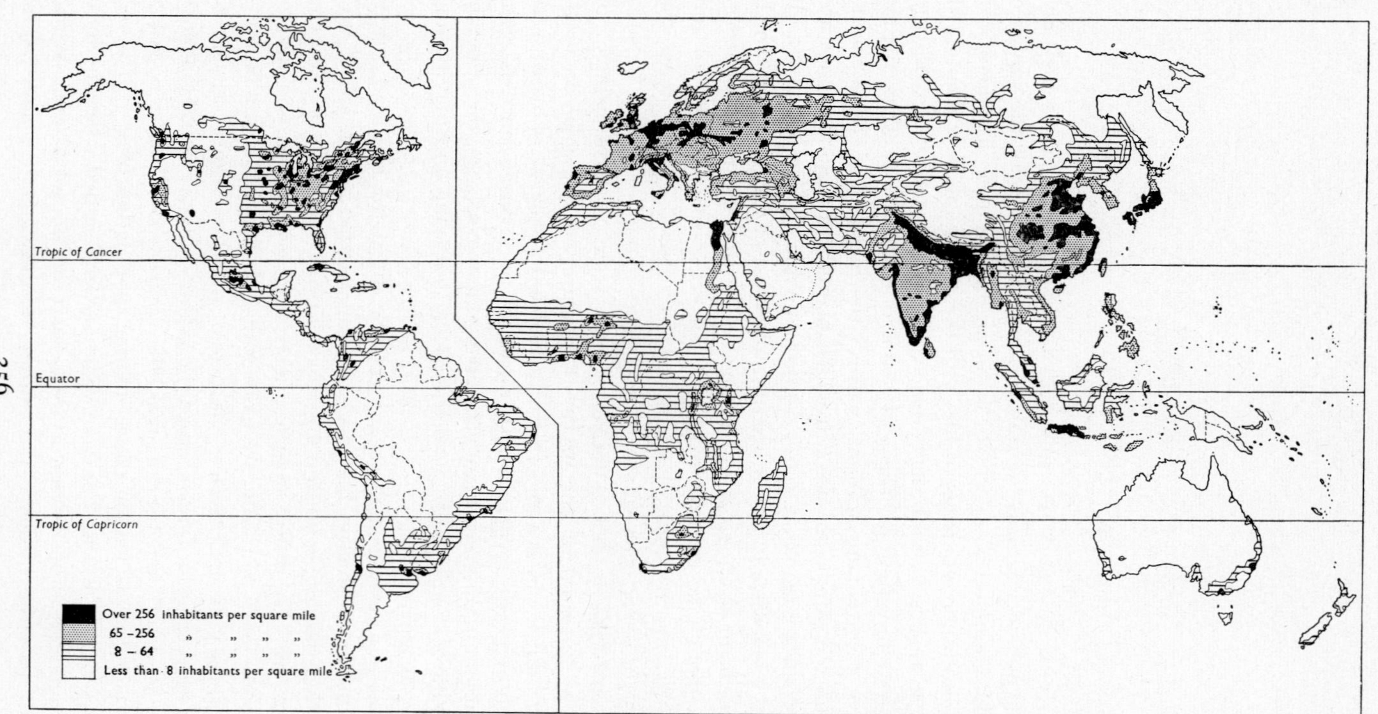


FIG. 78.—Distribution of the world's human population.

animals which are dependent upon them. Thus the migrations of Man have been dependent in considerable degree on plant distribution, even as his present population-density is conditioned by the crop-growing potentialities of different areas.

From the point of view of what they are used (or, occasionally, to be avoided) for, plants and plant products may be classified into seventeen main (or often multiple) categories whose consideration will occupy the remainder of this chapter. As each is apt to be a large subject, the accounts will be brief or in mere outline ; it should also be noted that the categories are neither hard and fast nor mutually exclusive. Indeed a good deal of repetition is inevitable. Many of the more important plants are dealt with elsewhere in this work, though usually in other connections, and some are mentioned in more than one category—though without cross-referencing, as this can be done through the index. Nor, in this primarily ' economic ' chapter, will technical botanical usages and names be maintained in the manner in which they usually are elsewhere in this book, and practically have to be for the use of scientists.

## Foods

Though whole volumes can be—and have been—written about food plants and Man's dependence upon them, this theme is too obvious to require detailed treatment here. It has latterly been extended to include vitamins, of which plants are the main primary source. Suffice it to say that practically every item of food of all animals comes from plants. For even if one animal eats another, and it in turn consumes yet another, when we follow back the food-chain we come, sooner or later, to a point of dependence upon green plants, as these alone are able economically to build up complex food substances from simple inorganic materials. This is true not only on land but also in fresh and salt waters, where the ' producer ' plants are often microscopic, larger and larger ' consumer ' animals succeeding one another to constitute the later stages in the food-chain. Any exceptions are insufficient in scale to have serious effect.

The most important plants used directly for food by Man (as opposed to those used indirectly through pasturage of his domestic animals) are those affording abundant carbohydrates and other energy-producing materials. Outstanding are the cereal and other ' grains ' (such as Wheat, Rice, Maize, Barley, Rye, Oats, Sorghums, Millets, Quinoa, and Buckwheat) and ' roots ' (such as Potatoes,

Sweet Potatoes, Yams, and Cassava), on one or other of which practically the whole human population of the world is primarily dependent. Useful additional 'vegetables' include Beets and Chard, Salsify, Carrots, Parsnips, Radishes, Swedes, Turnips, Jerusalem Artichokes, Taros, Dasheens, Onions and their allies, Artichokes, Asparagus, Cabbages and Kales and their allies, Celery, Chicory, Endive, Lettuces, Rhubarb, Spinach, Dandelions, Water-cress, Avocado, Breadfruit, Jack-fruit, Cucumber, Pumpkins and Squashes and their allies, Yautias, Chayote, Egg-plant, Okra, Tomato, etc. There is no need to point out that the staples among the above constitute the mainstay of human life on earth, different ones in different regions affording the chief (and often almost sole) food of teeming millions.

Other important groups of foods are legumes (the fruits of members of the Pea family, Leguminosae) and nuts (the term being used in the layman's sense). The former category includes Peas of various kinds, Chick Peas, Pigeon Peas, Cowpeas, Beans of various kinds (produced by several different genera), Soybeans, Peanuts, Lentils, Lablab, Algaroba and other Mesquites, Carob and other Locusts. The nuts include some with a high carbohydrate content, such as Chestnuts and Acorns, others with a high protein content, such as Almonds, Beechnuts, and Pistachio-nuts, and many more with a high fat content, such as Coconuts, Brazil-nuts, Cashew-nuts, Hazel-nuts, Macademia-nuts, Hickory-nuts and Pecans, Walnuts and their allies, Pili-nuts, and Pine-nuts.

Fruits used regularly by Man for food, and commonly cultivated, are very numerous as well as various in their botanical significance. Those produced mainly in temperate regions include such 'stone' fruits as Plums and Prunes, Cherries, Peaches, and Apricots, such 'pome' fruits as Apples, Pears, and Quinces, such 'gourd' fruits as Melons and Watermelons, and such 'berries' as the various kinds of Grapes, Blackberries and Raspberries, Blueberries and Huckleberries, Cranberries, Currants and Gooseberries, Strawberries, and Mulberries. The fruits produced in warm regions or often only in the tropics include the diverse types of Citrus fruits such as various Oranges, Lemon, Grapefruit, Lime, Citron, Tangerine, Kumquat, and products of their hybridization, Bananas of various kinds, Custard-apples and their allies, Dates, Durian, Figs of various kinds, Guavas and their allies, Granadillas of various kinds, Jujube, Litchi, Loquat, Mamey, Mangoes and their allies, Mangosteen, Olive, Papaya, various Persimmons, Pineapple, Pomegranate, Sapodilla and its allies, Tamarind, and many more. Jams and other preserves are chiefly made from fruits and sugar, often with the addition of some flavouring, preservative, and/or stiffening principle.

The above outline, which serves to indicate the range and variety as well as importance of plant foods for Man, is exclusive of beverages and such adjuncts as spices and other flavourings, which will be dealt with in the next section. The dependence, on green plants, of practically all other forms of life either directly or indirectly for food, goes of course for the animals which are used extensively by Man for his own sustenance, and so we should here recall this further dependence of Man on the natural vegetation or cropping-possibilities of each region. Many of the above-mentioned cereal Grasses, food Legumes, and 'vegetables' such as Kales and Turnips, are grown partly for domestic animal fodder, as are, in addition, numerous Grasses such as Timothy, Sudan-grass, Johnson-grass, Orchard-grass, Redtop, Bluegrass, etc. Furthermore there is an important class of non-grassy forage crops which, like some of the above-mentioned cereal and other plants when green, are often used for silage. These include Mangel-wurzels and such leguminous plants as Alfalfa, various Clovers and Vetches, Kudzu, and Lespedezas, in addition to Peanut, Soybean, Cowpea, and others among those already mentioned in different connections. These and other Legumes, together with various Grasses, largely make up hay. From the utilitarian point of view, forage plants may be looked upon as a means of turning plant carbohydrate and protein into meat and dairy products.

A number of usually minor foods are afforded by the lower plants. Thus the use of Mushrooms, Truffles, Morels and other Fungi, is ancient and familiar, Mushrooms in particular being widely cultivated. Food Yeast is another important fungal product. Although the use of Lichens for human food has largely died out except in times of severe shortage in northern regions, they are still important in the feeding of the Reindeer on which whole cultures of boreal peoples are largely centred. More widely used for human food nowadays are marine Algae, which in the Orient and some Pacific Islands constitute a major article of diet, many being cultivated, especially in Japan. In Europe and North America the only Algae that are at all extensively used in food are Carrageen or Irish-moss, Dulse, Murlins, those that give agar and some other products, and various Lavers. But extensive research is in progress on the possibility of using cultures of freshwater Algae, such as *Chlorella*, for food.

### Beverages and Flavours

The major non-alcoholic beverages, although not as vitally essential as the major foods, are yet so familiar that their significance is in no need of explanation. They are tea, which is used by fully one-half of the population of the world, coffee, which is used by almost as many people, and cocoa—the 'beans' affording this last also yield chocolate and cocoa butter. Other beverages include maté or Paraguay-tea, obtained from the leaves of various species of Holly; guarana, from the seeds of an Amazonian climber; cola, obtained by powdering *Cola* seeds; khat, a tea-like drink of northeastern Africa, and cassine, a rather similar beverage of North America; also yoco, which is made from the bark of a South American tree. All these beverages contain some caffeine and consequently have a stimulatory and refreshing effect; and numerous others are, or once were, widely prepared from parts of various plants.

Other non-alcoholic beverages are the so-called 'soft drinks', which include a vast array of preparations that tend to rise and fall in popularity—more, perhaps, with the amount of advertising lavished by their producers than with their inherent value, though most contain a fair amount of sugar and so are a source of energy. Many contain plant flavourings, etc., such as ginger, sarsaparilla, malted Barley, wintergreen, cola, or fruit juices—the last constituting many popular and valuable drinks.

Of alcoholic beverages there are two main groups: the *fermented* ones in which the alcohol is formed by the fermentation of sugar, and the *distilled* ones obtained by distillation of some alcoholic liquor. The sugar is either present naturally, as in most fruit juices, or is formed by transformation of starch—for example in cereals or potatoes. Wines, of which there are almost endless types of varying delectability and to suit different palates and pockets, are the oldest and most important of the fermented beverages. They are mostly formed by fermentation of sugar in the juice of grapes through the activity of wild Yeasts present on the skins of the fruit, though a wide range of other plants and their products may be similarly employed. The agreeable aroma and flavour are due to the presence of various aromatic substances, though the characteristic 'bouquet' develops only after some years or even decades of ageing.

Beer, ale, and the like make up the other most important group of fermented beverages. In their production, cereal starch (usually in Barley) is transformed into sugar in the process of malting, and this sugar in turn is dissolved out and the resulting product flavoured by boiling with Hops, after which Yeast is added to bring about alcoholic fermentation in the main process of brewing. In addition there are numerous relatively minor fermented alcoholic beverages including cider, made from the juice of Apples ; perry, from Pear juice ; mead, from honey and water ; sake, from Rice ; Palm wine, from the juice of Palm inflorescences ; chicha, from Maize ; and various so-called beers made from infusions of various roots and barks, with the addition of sugar and yeast. Furthermore, acetic acid fermentation by Bacteria leads to the formation of vinegar, another widely-used product.

The chief distilled alcoholic beverages (' spirits ') are made by successive distillations of fermented mashes or wines. Thus whisky is obtained from malted or unmalted cereals or potatoes and, after distillation, has to be aged to eradicate unpalatable principles. Vodka on the other hand is bottled directly after distillation. Brandy is distilled from wine, or, in the case of fruit brandies, from fermented fruit juices. Good gins are obtained from a mixed mash of barley-malt and rye, the flavour being due to added oil of juniper or other aromatic essential oils. The numerous liqueurs and cordials consist mainly of sugar and alcohol or spirits flavoured with various essential oils, being often blended according to some secret formula.

Spices, condiments, and other food adjuncts are almost innumerable, so only the most important can be mentioned here. Man's craving for spices has done much to change the course of history and affect international and inter-racial relations. The value of spices and condiments lies in their ability to increase the attractiveness of food, etc., usually owing to the presence of essential oils. Besides their use as food adjuncts, spices are employed in various industries, including perfumery, drug and soap manufacture, dyeing, and in the arts. The vast majority are still obtained from the tropics, chiefly from Asia.

Most of these flavouring materials originate in seeds and fruits. They include allspice or pimento, obtained from a small tree of tropical America ; capsicum or red pepper (including chilis, paprikas, and sweet peppers), from several plants now widely cultivated ; black and white and some other peppers, from weak climbing or trailing shrubs that are widely cultivated in the tropics ; cardamon and grains of paradise ; the various mustards (black, white, and Indian), from allies of the Cabbages growing often in cool climates ; nutmeg and mace, from the Nutmeg tree which is now cultivated principally in the East and West Indies ; anise and star anise, caraway, coriander, dill, fennel, vanilla and its substitute tonka beans, and many others.

Spices obtained from flowers or flower-buds include cloves, capers, and saffron, while from leaves are obtained such familiar ones as peppermint, balm, basil, marjoram, sage, the savouries, spearmint or mint, bay, thyme, lemon thyme, parsley, wintergreen, tansy, and tarragon, most of which can be (and commonly are) grown in gardens in temperate regions. Spices or flavourings obtained from barks include cinnamon and cassia, from various species of Cinnamon trees grown chiefly in southeastern Asia, and sassafras, from the familiar North American tree of that name. Important spices obtained from roots and rhizomes are angelica (other parts of the Angelica plant are also used), now cultivated chiefly in Germany ; ginger, from the Ginger plant which is widely cultivated in the tropics ; horse-radish, widely grown in temperate regions ; sarsaparilla, from several tropical Catbriars ; and turmeric, cultivated in various tropical regions and employed to colour as well as flavour curries, etc.

## Medicinals and Drugs

The history of the medicinal use of plants is long and intricate, being largely bound up with the beliefs of primitive peoples—for example, that disease was due to the presence of evil spirits in the body, which could be driven out by the use of unpleasant substances. After the Dark Ages came the herbalists with their compilations of what was known or supposed about the medicinal value and folklore of plants, and the ' doctrine of signatures ' according to which plants were supposed to possess some sign indicating the use for which they were intended. Thus the Maidenhair Fern, so called from the black hair-like ' stalks ' of the leaflets, was considered a specific for baldness, and plants with heart-shaped leaves were believed to be valuable for use against heart ailments. Plants were believed to have been placed in the world for Man's use, and to have clear indications of their particular usefulness provided by the Almighty.

From such crude beginnings developed modern pharmacognosy, which is concerned with the knowledge and commerce of crude drugs and their sources, and pharmacology, the study of the action of drugs. The medicinal value of drugs is due to the presence in them of special substances having a particular physiological action on the human body : commonly such substances are alkaloids, some of which are powerful poisons if administered unwisely, while others are dangerously habit-forming. Yet in small quantities skilfully administered, even the most poisonous or dangerous drugs can be of value to human health and well-being.

Throughout the world there are used for medicinal purposes some thousands of different plants or plant products—many of them only locally by savage peoples. The use of others has been rendered obsolete by synthesis of their active principles. Some are widely cultivated, but many more are gathered chiefly or entirely in the wild state and are still important commercially. A few of the most significant, classified according to the part of the plant from which they come, are the following:

Obtained from fruits and seeds : chaulmoogra oil, from a south-east Asian tree, containing principles effective in the treatment of leprosy ; colocynth, from a widespread perennial vine now cultivated in the Mediterranean region, serving as a powerful purgative, as does also croton oil, obtained from a shrub or small tree of south-eastern Asia ; nux vomica, obtained from a tree ranging from India to Australia, used as a stimulant in small quantities as it contains strychnine ; strychnine itself, obtained from the same and allied plants ; opium, obtained as an exudation from the injured fruits of the widely cultivated Opium Poppy, employed to relieve pain but flagrantly misused as a narcotic in the Orient ; psyllium, from Plantains, used chiefly as a laxative ; strophanthus, from two African lianes, used as a heart stimulant ; and wormseed, a native of the warm parts of the New World, used in the treatment of hookworm infections.

From flowers are obtained chamomile, which is rather widely cultivated and used for a variety of purposes ; hops, extensively cultivated in temperate regions and used for their sedative and tonic properties as well as in brewing ; and santonin, one of the best remedies for intestinal worms.

The vegetative parts of plants contribute numerous drugs. From leaves are derived, for example, aloe, from African and American Aloes, used as purgatives ; belladonna, from the Deadly Nightshade of Europe, etc., but now extensively cultivated, used for the local relief of pain and for a variety of other commendable purposes ; cocaine, from the leaves of the South American Coca shrub that is now extensively cultivated in the tropics, used chiefly as a local anaesthetic ; digitalin, from the leaves of the European Foxglove, almost indispensable in the treatment of heart ailments ; eucalyptus, from various Blue Gum-trees of Australia but now widely cultivated elsewhere, extensively used in medicine, for example in the treatment of nose and throat disorders ; hamamelis, from the North American Witch-hazel, used as an astringent ; henbane, from the widespread weedy herb of that name, used as a sedative and hypnotic ; stramonium, from the widespread and weedy Thorn-apple, used as a narcotic and in the treatment of asthma ; and many others.

From stems, etc., come ephedrine, from Asiatic Ephedras, used in medical treatment *e.g.* of colds and hay-fever ; guaiacum, used as a stimulant and laxative ; and quassia, used as a tonic and in the treatment of malaria. From barks are obtained cascara, from the American Western Buckthorn, used as a tonic and laxative ; curare, from a variety of South American plants, a very powerful poison used also in medicine and surgery ; slippery elm, made from the familiar North American tree, useful for its soothing effect ; and, above all, quinine, the great anti-malarial drug, obtained from several allied trees native to South America and now cultivated especially in southern Asia.

From roots and other underground parts come an important series of drugs including aconite, from the Eurasian Monkshood, used particularly to relieve pain ; colchicum, from the Meadow Saffron, whose active principle is colchicine, used in the treatment of rheumatism and gout and also important in the plant sciences as it produces doubling of chromosomes ; goldenseal, from the North American plant of that name, used as a tonic and in the treatment of catarrh ; ipecac, from forest-floor plants of tropical America, almost indispensable in the treatment of amoebic dysentery and pyorrhoea ; liquorice, from the Liquorice plant now much cultivated in Eurasia, used as a flavouring, etc. ; squills and senega, used as expectorants and stimulants ; ginseng, considered a virtual cure-all in the Orient ; and valerian, from Garden Valerian, used to relieve nervous afflictions.

From various parts particularly of the Camphor Tree come camphor and safrole, which have a wide variety of industrial and medicinal uses. Among Pteridophytes, the tiny spores of some Club-mosses are variously used for covering pills as well as in industry and even warfare, while aspidium, obtained from certain Ferns of the north-temperate regions, has long been employed to expel Tapeworms.

The lower plants come notably into their own as sources of drugs: penicillin, streptomycin, aureomycin, chloromycetin, terramycin, and others recently developed from Fungi and their allies are being found extremely valuable in the treatment of some of the most severe diseases. Ergot, produced from the common fungal disease of cereals bearing the same name, has long been known and is used in the treatment of haemorrhages. Agar, widely obtained from a number of Red Algae, is employed medicinally to prevent constipation, as well as industrially in food, paper, and cosmetic manufacture, and as a culture medium for Fungi and Bacteria. Algin, a product of the larger Kelps, is used in a variety of cosmetics, foods, drugs, and as a sizing for paper; these Brown Algae are also important as sources of iodine and potash.

## Fatty Oils and Waxes

Fatty or fixed oils are those which, unlike the essential oils (*see* pp. 274–5), do not easily evaporate, and so cannot be distilled without becoming decomposed. Those which are liquid 'oils' at ordinary temperatures become solid 'fats' on cooling, even as fats become oils on sufficient warming. Like animal fats, they consist of glycerin in combination with a fatty acid, and form soaps when boiled with alkalis. Fatty oils (as they may in general be termed) are produced in considerable quantities by many different plants, often being stored in seeds for use in germination. Of them four main classes may be recognized, as follows:

1. *Drying oils*, which on exposure dry into thin elastic films and are of great importance in the paint and varnish industries. Examples include linseed oil, obtained from Flax, and its substitute tung oil, obtained from two Chinese trees; soybean oil, which is widely used in human foods as well as industry, etc.; and such oils as perilla, walnut, Niger seed, hempseed, poppy, and safflower.

2. *Semi-drying oils*, which form a soft film only after long exposure, examples being cottonseed oil, obtained from Cotton, and used for human food, animal fodder, fuel, and in a variety of industries; sunflower oil, obtained from the common Sunflower, used for the same purposes as cottonseed oil and also in the paint, varnish, and soap industries; and such oils as corn, rape, and camelina.

3. *Non-drying oils*, which remain liquid at ordinary temperatures. These include olive oil, obtained from the Olive and used principally for food and in medicine (though inferior grades are employed in soap-making and as lubricants); its widely-used substitute, peanut

oil, obtained from the Peanut ; and castor oil, obtained from the Castor-oil plant and formerly used chiefly in medicine but now much more widely in industry.

4. *Vegetable fats or tallows*, which are more or less solid at ordinary temperatures. These include coconut oil, obtained from the ' meat ' of the Coconut, and widely used for making margarines, candy-bars and other sweets, soaps, cosmetics, stock-feed, and as an illuminant ; palm oil, obtained from the African Oil Palm and used for some of the same purposes as coconut oil ; palm-kernel oil, the Brazilian palm oils, cocoa butter, and many others.

Waxes are chemically allied to fats but tend to be harder. They usually occur as coverings of leaves, etc., and help to prevent too great a loss of water by transpiration. Among those of value to mankind are carnauba wax, obtained from a South American Palm, widely used in the manufacture of candles, soaps, paints, varnishes, ointments, and many other products ; cauassu wax, which can be used for much the same purposes ; and the American candelilla, myrtle, and jojoba waxes.

Lather-forming products of the cultivated Soapwort, of the South American Soapbark tree, of the Soapberry, and of California Soaproot, are used commercially as soap substitutes—as are many others more locally.

## Smoking and Chewing Materials

Of these ' fumitories and masticatories ' the most universally employed is tobacco, obtained principally from a tropical American species that is now very widely cultivated, but to some extent also from a North American species which was extensively grown by the Indians before the time of Columbus. Important chewing materials are betel, obtained from the widely cultivated Betelnut Palm and said to be used by over 400,000,000 people ; cola nuts, from the West African Cola tree which has now been widely introduced elsewhere, whose use results in slight stimulation and temporary increase in physical capacity ; and, in addition, chewing gum and spruce gum.

In contrast to the above more or less harmless principles, the true narcotics contain powerful alkaloids that make them gravely detrimental to human health if used habitually, although they are valuable in medicine in exceedingly small amounts. Among the chief are opium and cocaine, obtained as already mentioned above under drugs, and constituting important relievers of pain. The eating or smoking of opium, which at first produces alluring dreams and pleasurable visions, may become an uncontrollable addiction leading to delirium and death. The chewing of the leaves of the Coca shrub, containing cocaine, gives resistance to fatigue and hunger and at the same time a feeling of exaltation; but if habitual, it may in time lead to severe physical deterioration and even death.

Other important narcotics are cannabis, obtained from the Hemp plant and widely used in medicine to relieve pain as well as in the treatment of nervous disorders; fly agaric, obtained from the poisonous Fungus of that name, which when chewed or added to beverages has an intoxicating effect involving hallucinations and finally unconsciousness; peyote (mescal buttons), from an American Cactus, mostly chewed for the feeling it produces of well-being accompanied by hypnotic trances; products from Thorn-apples and Henbane, which when smoked or eaten produce excitations, illusions, and sometimes fanatical acts; and the Oceanian kavakava, whose use as a beverage has a sedative and soporific action, bringing about pleasant sensations. Cannabis consumption as hashish, marijuana, etc., causes states of ecstasy and stupefaction and may have serious results, as when it leads to fanatical acts by addicts.

### Structural and Sheltering Materials

It can scarcely be questioned that wood is nowadays, and from before the dawn of history has been, the most generally important of all structural materials. Its uses in the construction of human habitations and shelters, furniture and utensils, vehicles and boats, tools and all manner of fittings and fencings, etc., are too universally familiar to require detailed enumeration. If we reflect that until a century ago ships were made almost entirely of wood, without which the exploration and colonization and general development of most of the world would accordingly have been impossible, we have one impressive indication of its immense significance in human affairs; and to this day wood is the most widely used commodity, apart from foodstuffs and, perhaps, clothing materials. It is also highly versatile as a raw material (and one of the few that can perpetually be renewed) for conversion into products as varied as paper and textiles, soap and lubricants, stock-feed and motor fuel, plastics and disinfectants, explosives and preservatives (to mention only a few).

Quite apart from questions introduced by their local availability, different woods vary markedly in mechanical and allied properties and, consequently, in usages. Important features are general strength, hardness, stiffness, toughness, fineness of grain, cleavability, density, moisture content, the commonness of defects, and susceptibility to insect damage and to decay. Expression of many of these depends upon the age of the tree from which the wood was cut and the treatment it has received since cutting, and all of them naturally vary with the kind of tree involved. It is said that the annual consumption of wood in the world amounts to some sixty thousand million cubic feet, of which nearly half is used in North America.

The two main types of timber are softwood, obtained from coniferous trees such as Spruces, Pines, and Larches, and hardwood, from Angiospermous trees such as Oaks, Maples, and Mahoganies. Besides its use as a popular fuel and employment as a raw material for conversion into diverse products whose origin is often unrecognizable, wood is used, as such, in the form of structural timber for buildings and bridges, as boarding and flooring, girders and rafters, pit-props and railway ' sleepers ', poles and posts, piling and cooperage, veneers and plywood, shingles and woodenware, parts or the whole of ships and boats, furniture and vehicles, boxes and crates, fences and hoardings, and for innumerable other purposes of which some have already been mentioned.

Among specific sheltering materials other than wood, the leaves of such woody plants as Palms, and herbaceous materials such as straw, are widely used for shelters and thatches in different parts of the world. Also extensively employed are various soft or comminuted plant products for insulating and packaging, familiar examples being Bog-mosses and hay for insulation, and sawdust and shavings for packaging.

## Industrial Uses and Extractives

Many of the items discussed under other captions, such as fuels, fats, and fibres, might be included here, but the chief classes to be considered in this section are those whose chemurgical treatment or processing makes them important sources of industrial derivatives —namely, sugars, starches, cellulose, and some distillation products. To take this last item first, the destructive distillation of woodwaste produces such valuable materials as charcoal, tar, oil, turpentine, wood alcohol, acetic acid, and wood gas.

Sugar, as we have already seen, is obtained principally from the Sugar Cane and the Sugar Beet, and though primarily used as food it has also become an extremely important industrial chemical, with thousands of different derivatives. About 35,000,000 tons are produced annually. When speaking of sugar we normally mean sucrose, which is by far the most important and the one usually stored, though other sugars have their places and uses. Further important sources of sucrose are Maize, Sugar Maple, Sorghum, certain Palms, and honey.

Starches constitute the chief type of food-reserve for most green plants, being stored in the cells in the form of minute grains. Starches are chemically complex but, being easily convertible into sugars, are vastly important as human foods, the chief sources being potatoes, various cereals, arrowroot, cassava, and sago. They are also widely used in industry, for example in laundry and textile work, in sizing, and as sources of glucose, dextrin, industrial alcohol, and explosives.

Still more complex is cellulose, the chief constituent of the cell-walls of most plants, which yields numerous textile fibres both natural and artificial. The chief sources nowadays are cotton, which is almost pure cellulose, and wood, which by chemical and mechanical treatment is made to yield pure cellulose. This may be made into fibres or plastics, or transformed into wood sugar, which in turn may be made to nourish Yeast or yield alcohol and thus become available for food or industrial use. In addition there is hemi-cellulose, which forms the so-called 'vegetable ivory'—obtained from certain tropical Palms and useful as a substitute for ivory in the manufacture of buttons and other small, hard objects.

While paper can be made from most fibrous materials, the chief commercial sources are wood fibres, cotton, and linen. The last two, formerly the main source of paper, still yield the finest grades, but wood fibres nowadays make up the vast bulk. They are obtained from a wide range of trees of which various Spruces, Pines, Hemlocks, and Poplars are among the most important, while sawmill waste is increasingly used. Other raw materials for paper-making include papyrus, esparto, straw, mulberry, and various textile fibres. By special processes the wood or other raw material is pulped, after which a series of operations, including the addition of rosin or other 'sizing' of plant origin, lead to its manufacture into one or another of the almost innumerable types and grades of paper. The coarser materials are often made into cardboard.

Cellulose is soluble in various solvents such as concentrated nitric acid, and this has led to the development from it of ' plastics ' and unbreakable glasses and many other important products including guncotton, cordite, collodion, celluloid, cellulose acetate, viscoses such as Cellophane, and various varnishes and fabrics including cloth and leather substitutes. Photographic film is made chiefly from cellulose nitrate or acetate coated with gelatin, while further breaking down of cellulose yields various sugars which in turn yield alcohol and, with appropriate treatment, Torula Yeast or other foods. Altogether cellulose products are countless in number and of great value and usefulness ; moreover, being formed often from forest waste, they seem endlessly replaceable.

### Clothing Materials and Other Fibres

Clothes, one of Man's primary requisites, are made largely from plant fibres or materials obtained from animals which are dependent on plants for food. In addition, fibres and fabrics are used by Man in innumerable other ways. Indeed, fibre-yielding plants are probably second only to food plants in their influence on civilization and their general usefulness to Man. But although there are many hundreds of fibre-yielding plants known, only a few are of commercial importance.

From the point of view of their utilization, fibres produced by plants or from plant materials may conveniently be classified into seven groups : (1) Paper-making fibres, which were discussed in the last section dealt with above. (2) Artificial fibres, whose production is nowadays a great and expanding industry. The main raw materials are (*a*) cellulose, derived from wood pulp or cotton linters, whence are made the various so-called ' rayons ', and (*b*) soft coal, whence are produced the various nylons and related materials which between them have now some hundreds of important uses. (3) Textile fibres, used as fabrics, netting, and cordage. These include cotton of various kinds, flax, hemp, jute, ramie, Manila hemp, sisal, coir, and many others. (4) Brush fibres, which are tough and stiff, the chief being the piassavas and their allies, obtained from certain Palms, and Grasses such as Broomcorn, Broomroot, and Spartina. (5) Plaiting and tough-weaving fibres, employed for making straw hats, baskets, chair-seats, matting, wickerwork, etc., for which the stems of various Palms, Grasses, and grass-like Sedges and Rushes are used. (6) Filling fibres, used for upholstery, stiffening, packaging, and caulking, the outstanding example being kapok (*see* p. 235) and its various substitutes, which include the silky hairs on the seeds of the familiar Milkweeds. There is also Spanish-moss, an excellent substitute for horsehair. (7) Natural fabrics, etc., consisting of tough interlacing fibres that can be extracted from bark in layers or sheets and used as a substitute for cloth. Examples include the Polynesian and Oriental tapa cloth and the Jamaican lace-bark, as well as such fibrous products as the so-called vegetable sponges or luffas which are used for making hats, for scouring, for filtering, and as substitutes for bath sponges and body scrapers.

## Fuels (including Fossil, etc.)

Fuel, as a source particularly of heat, light, and power, is one of the greatest necessities of human life, and in general consists of plants or plant products whether modern or belonging to earlier epochs. A few of the main groups of plant materials that are widely used as fuels may be outlined : (1) wood, probably still used more for fuel than for any other purpose, certain hardwoods being in general better than other types, but almost all woods making useful fuels when dry ; (2) vegetable oils, used principally in this connection for illumination and for powering Diesel engines ; (3) peat, consisting of compacted deposits of partially decomposed vegetable matter, which is widely used for heating and cooking in northern lands especially where wood is scarce ; (4) manure, which is the almost universal fuel of hundreds of millions of people in southern Asia ; (5) coal, the compressed and fossilized remains of plants that lived in much earlier geological epochs and are now largely decomposed and converted into carbon, being a valuable and widely-used source of fuel and power and also of gases which are employed particularly for heating and illuminating ; (6) coke, which is left when coal-gas is driven off from coal, and is nearly pure carbon, forming an excellent fuel which burns without appreciable smoke or flame ; (7) charcoal, which bears a similar relationship to wood, and is the chief domestic fuel in many tropical countries ; (8) sawdust, etc., used principally in the form of briquettes ; and (9) petroleum, whose familiar products of distillation include the all-important gasoline (petrol) as a source of power, and paraffin and kerosene as sources particularly of heat and light. Although no trace of plant structure remains in petroleum, it is generally supposed to have had its origin in minute primitive forms of plant life that flourished in much earlier geological times.

## Latexes and Exudates

Of the products obtained from the milky juice (latex) of various plants, rubber is by far the most important. In spite of the considerable employment of synthetic forms, over a million tons of natural rubber are used annually, most being produced in south-eastern Asia. Over three-quarters of the crude rubber consumed goes into tyres and inner tubes, while other important uses are in footwear, packaging, waterproof clothing, road construction, tubing and belting, electrical insulation, etc. Rubber is produced principally from various tropical woody plants of the Spurge, Mulberry, and Periwinkle families, some of which are now cultivated. Besides wild and plantation rubbers produced from the Para (Hevea) Rubber tree, which is by far the most important source of rubber, there are such other natural types, produced from different sources, as Assam, castilla, ceara, guayule, and even dandelion rubbers, the last being cultivable in the cool-temperate belt.

Other latex products include the non-elastic gutta-percha and balata, obtained from tropical trees and used for insulation, piping, golf-balls, telephone receivers, and many other purposes, and chicle, obtained from the tropical American Sapodilla tree, which is the basis of the chewing-gum industry.

The gums which exude from plant stems either naturally or in response to wounding, and the resins which are usually secreted in definite cavities or passages, may conveniently be classed together as exudates. Gums are used principally as adhesives, as sizing for paper, in medicine and polishing, in cosmetics and ice-cream, in printing and finishing textiles, as a glazing for paintings, and in the confectionery and paint industries. The chief commercial varieties are gum arabic, obtained from certain Acacias of arid northern Africa, gum tragacanth, from certain Milk-vetches of arid south-western Eurasia, and its substitute karaya, obtained from a tree in India whence several million pounds are exported annually. The related pectins are widely used to make foods jell, in pharmaceuticals and cosmetics, in sizing and adhesives, fibres, films, and other preparations. They come chiefly from citrous and apple wastes, but many other fruits, etc., afford potential sources.

Resins are more various and tend to be still more important than gums, though usually tapping is necessary to obtain them in commercial quantities, or they may be collected in the fossil state. For the most part they are forest products. Some of the more valuable, with their uses, are (1) the various copals, utilized as varnishes and in making paints and linoleum; (2) amber, a fossil resin particularly from an extinct species of Pine, which is used for beads, ornamental carvings, and mouth-pieces of pipes, etc.; (3) damars, used principally in varnishes; (4) lacquer, a natural varnish which hardens on exposure to air and affords remarkable protection even against acids and alkalis; (5) shellac, excreted by a particular insect on twigs of certain trees on which it feeds, widely used in insulation and decoration and for making varnishes, sealing-wax, size, drawing inks, gramophone records, and many other products ; and (6) turpentines, chiefly obtained by tapping coniferous trees and yielding on distillation oil of turpentine and rosin. Oil of turpentine is of major importance in the paint and varnish industry as a solvent and thinning agent, and in chemical manufacture, while rosin is the chief sizing material for paper and is also used in many manufactures as well as in greases and lubricants.

Other noteworthy products in this general category include Canada balsam, used in mounting microscope slides and as a cement for lenses ; spruce gum, used as a masticatory ; Venetian turpentine, used in varnishes and veterinary work ; and various balsams, used in medicine, adhesives, soaps, lotions, and cosmetics, as well as for the flavouring of foods and as fixatives in the perfume industry. There are also such products as ammoniacum, used in medicine and perfumery ; asafoetida, widely used in medical treatment ; copaiba, used for making varnishes and lacquers, as a fixative of perfumes in soap, and in photography and medicine ; elemi, used in various artistic, cosmetic, and medical operations; frankincense, used in incense, cosmetics, and fumigation ; and myrrh, used for cosmetic and medicinal purposes as well as in incense and embalming.

## Tanning and Dyeing Materials

Tanning involves the reaction of strongly astringent tannins with such proteins as are present in animal skins, thus forming the strong and resistant, flexible commodity we know as leather. Although tannins are very widespread in plants, relatively few species are known to contain a sufficient proportion to be of commercial importance, and these are in great demand. The sources occur mostly in the wild state and include the woods of Quebracho and Sweet Chestnut, the leaves of Sumac and Gambier, such fruit products as myrobalan, tara, and valonia (from the Turkish Oak), root materials from Tanner's Dock and Palmetto, and barks of Hemlock, various Oaks, Mangroves, Eucalypts, Wattles (Acacias), Larches, Spruces, Birches, and Willows. However, the tannin content in the last four instances is too low to warrant their general use. Tannin-inks are the most important inks at the present time, their tannin being derived largely from the insect galls formed in great abundance on the twigs of the Aleppo Oak ; to these galls or an extract made from them are added an iron salt, an agglutinant such as gum arabic, and a colouring matter such as logwood (*see* below). Other inks, too, are made substantially from plant products.

Of natural dyes and stains obtainable from plants there is a vast array involving almost all colours, though latterly most have been supplanted at least in part by the synthetic or aniline dyes obtained from coal-tar products. Such ' artificial ' dyes tend to be brighter, cheaper, and more lasting, and with them only a few vegetable dyes compete nowadays. These vegetable dyes are especially useful in dyeing fabrics, but are also employed to colour a wide range of other familiar products. Some of the more important of these natural colouring matters, grouped according to the plant part from which they come, are: from seeds and fruits—annatto, Persian berries, and sap green ; from flowers—safflower and saffron ; from barks—quercitron, lokao, and gamboge (an exuded gum resin) ; from leaves—indigo, henna, woad, and chlorophyll (which is harmless and consequently used in foods and toothpastes) ; from woods—logwood or haematoxylin (of which many thousands of tons are used annually to give colours ranging from reds to purples and black), fustic, cutch, osage orange, sappanwood, and brazilwood ; and from roots and tubers—alkanna, madder, and turmeric. Lichens yield some fine dyes, among which archil and litmus still find extensive use.

## Essential Oils and Scents (Perfumes)

Very different from the fatty oils already considered are the so-called essential oils which have a pleasant taste and strong aromatic odour, easily volatilizing in air. They are complex in chemical nature but tend to be readily removed—by distillation, expression, or solvent-action—from the many and various plants that produce them. Their main uses are for scenting, flavouring, or medicinal purposes—for example in the manufacture of perfumes, soaps, and other toilet preparations, in cooking and the production of all manner of foods and beverages, and for therapeutic, antiseptic, and bactericidal purposes. Other uses are as clearing agents and solvents, as insecticides and deodorants, and in such diverse products as printer's ink and toothpaste, library adhesives and chewing-gum, shoe-polish and tobacco.

We have already dealt with the flavouring and medicinal sides, and noted the industrial uses, of various essential oils, and shall be concerned with insecticides, etc., in the next section; here we must mention some of the more important 'essentials' used in perfumes (or scents, as they are called in Britain). These often highly-priced products commonly consist of blends of the essential oil or oils in alcohol, usually with a less volatile fixative. Examples are rose oil or otto (attar) of roses, obtained principally from flowers of the Damask Rose which are distilled without delay after being picked in the early morning just as they are opening; orange blossom oil (neroli), formerly obtained from citrous plants grown for the purpose but nowadays often synthesized and used in cosmetics, etc.; lemon-grass oil, from the leaves of a particular Grass and used in cosmetics and medicine; oil of citronella, from another member of the same genus and used in cheap perfumes and as a deodorant and insect repellent; geranium, distilled from the leaves of various species of 'Pot Geraniums' (Pelargoniums) and widely used in making perfumes and soaps; ylang-ylang, from the flowers of an Asiatic tree and now said to be present in almost every perfume; cassie, from one of the Acacias; cedarwood oil, from the Eastern Red Cedar; bergamot, from a type of Orange; bay rum, from a West Indian tree; calamus, from the Sweet-flag; camphor (in spite of its solid form); lavender and rosemary which are used extensively in eau-de-cologne and soaps; and very many others. Although numerous synthetic products are now available, most of the best perfumes are still of botanical origin and in increasing demand, the annual gathering of flowers for this purpose alone being said to exceed 10,000,000,000 lb. (over 4½ thousand million kilos).

## Insecticides and Herbicides

Although more than twelve hundred species of plants have been reported to have some insecticidal or at least insect-repellent properties, the vast majority are of little importance and even the best tend to be overshadowed nowadays by such synthetic insecticides as DDT. Nevertheless some plant products continue to be used very extensively and even increasingly to combat insects and other vermin, and accordingly to be of great service to Man. The three most important are: (1) nicotine, extracted from leaves of Tobacco plants and used as a spray that is lethal to some of the worst insect pests; (2) rotenone, obtained from the roots of various tropical trees or shrubs belonging to the Pea family, and long used as a fish-poison as well as, latterly, in powdered form or spray to kill various insect pests of crops and livestock; and (3) pyrethrum or insect flowers—likewise used as dusts or sprays that quickly paralyse insects including pests afflicting Man, and obtained from the flower-heads of certain members of the Daisy family that are widely cultivated for the purpose.

There are also such repellents, etc., as camphor, which is obtained principally from the Camphor tree but is also synthesized, cedarwood oil, the Mexican ' Cockroach plant ', and the Chinese ' Thunder-god vine '. Most botanical insecticides are harmless to human beings and other warm-blooded animals. However, red squill, obtained from the bulbs of a small herb of the Mediterranean region, is an important ' raticide ', having little effect on animals other than Rats and Mice.

Whereas the old-fashioned herbicides are usually more or less caustic chemical compounds (' weed-killers ') that kill off vegetation indiscriminately, investigation of plant growth hormones in recent decades has led to the discovery and use of ' hormonal ' herbicides that are highly selective in their action in killing some plants while leaving others, and animals, unharmed. Outstanding in this respect is 2,4-D, which at suitable concentrations kills most dicotyledonous plants without affecting most monocotyledonous ones. Thus it forms an effective lawn or wheat-field spray, killing most of the (dicotyledonous) weeds without injuring the Grass or grain crop. Plant growth substances are now synthesized in quantity and are used in various horticultural practices such as the promotion of rooting in cuttings.

## Environmental and Ecological

In spite of the increasing ease and effectiveness of transport in the modern world, the availability of this or that plant product in a particular place depends to a considerable extent on whether the plant from which it comes can be cultivated locally—especially if it is bulky and needed in large quantities or in a fresh state, as so many foods, etc., are. And quite apart from this direct dependence of mankind on the crop and other plant productivity of different areas, we get very different environments created by different types of vegetation—as was already pointed out in the second paragraph of this chapter. Among many other things, trees give shade and shelter, and when they are widely aggregated into forests, these may regulate climate to a considerable extent, ' damping down ' temperature and humidity fluctuations in their shade. In some ways, in spite of their transpiration, trees may also help to conserve water, for example by preventing run-off and floods, meanwhile checking erosion. Forests moreover afford shelter and range for livestock and wild animals, and recreation for human beings.

The widespread use of such ecological devices as sand-binding Grasses or other plants and wind-breaking trees and shrubs, is further testimony to the value of plant life to mankind. Particularly are various surface-binding plants of importance in combating erosion, which is one of the world's worst scourges, as is further indicated in our concluding two chapters.

Finally it should be noted here as well as in the next section that, in the local environments which Man makes for himself, the importance of gardens of one sort or another is enormous practically the world over. And the supply and use of agricultural, forestral, and horticultural implements such as harvesters, saws, and lawnmowers, and the general tending of plants, involves vast industries almost everywhere.

## Aesthetic and Ornamental

In most landscape views, plants form the chief embellishment, and landscapes would suffer greatly without them. Apart from the vital needs they satisfy and the material benefits they bestow, plants greatly enhance Man's aesthetic appreciation of the world in which he lives—both in their natural growth as vegetation, whether arborescent or otherwise, and through their cultivation for ornamental purposes. Almost everywhere Man lives, gardens are cultivated for recreational and other reasons, and the dustiest city streets and drabbest homes are enlivened by greenery and pot or cut flowers.

Floriculture, the branch of horticulture concerned with the commercial production of flowers, is really a huge industry that is important on an almost world-wide scale, but especially in the temperate zone. The actual growing is often scientifically regulated in many ways, as in greenhouses, and the organization for transport and selling is complex and vast. Lawn-growing and landscaping are also of considerable importance in urban areas and elsewhere, for recreational and ornamental purposes; their primary function, however, is the growing of plants. All this, moreover, involves extensive trading in seeds, bulbs, etc., and sometimes in apparatus for plant growth—for example in hydroponics, their cultivation without soil.

## Microorganisms and Miscellaneous

We have already mentioned the importance of some microorganisms in affording drugs (such as penicillin) and foods (such as Food Yeast), and, towards the end of the last chapter, in causing plant diseases. Others are of vast importance in bringing about desirable changes—for example the Yeasts in causing fermentation of sugars to alcohols, and various Bacteria in effecting further fermentation to vinegar as well as in the 'curing' of tobaccos and 'ripening' of cheeses. On the positive side, further valuable fermentation, fibre-retting, organic acid and vitamin production, hide-dehairing, nitrogen-fixing, sewage-disposal, purification and preservation, cooking and silage and all manner of other operations, are carried out only by or with the aid of microorganisms. On the negative side, there are the numerous human and other animal diseases which they cause, as well as loss by rotting, putrefaction, and general decay. These last activities involve the breakdown of complex carbohydrate and other materials to simpler ones and ultimately to the raw materials whence they came. Such 'degradation' is essential to keep the world going, for without it the vital raw materials such as carbon dioxide would all be used up sooner or later and life would come to a standstill. Consequently non-green microorganisms, which are almost entirely responsible for the breakdown and return of the essentials to general circulation, are the world's great scavengers, and, as such, are of fundamental importance to all life.

Nor, among microorganisms, must we overlook the smaller Algae, which possess chlorophyll and so are able to build up complex foods from simple beginnings. For they afford the ultimate source of sustenance for most of our Fishes, Crustaceans, and other ' sea food ', help form Food Yeast, and give us such useful products as limestones and the diatomaceous earth (*see* Chapter II) which is widely employed in toothpastes, abrasives, filters, and so forth. On the negative side, Algae may be a nuisance in clogging and scumming and even poisoning fresh waters.

Among miscellaneous items introduced largely by higher plants are the various animal litters and ' farmyard ' manures that form such an important part of the farmer's microcosm ; there are also the ' green ' manures used, for example, in crop rotation, and the organic mulches, etc., that are employed to conserve soil moisture and improve soil texture.

Yet another important product of higher plants is cork, obtained principally from the Cork Oak, a tree native to the Mediterranean region. Commercial cork consists of the outer bark of the tree and can be removed every few years without injury to the tree as it grows. Being exceedingly light, compressible but resilient, a low conductor of heat and sound, and above all resistant to the passage of moisture, it has numerous uses in industry, either in its natural form or after being moulded as ' composition ' cork. Among the more familiar of these uses are : as stoppers, corkboard, tips of cigarettes, and handles of various kinds, in mooring-buoys, lifebelts and life-jackets, footwear, tropical helmets, and various sporting equipment, and in linoleum and linotiles.

It should also be recalled that, as implied earlier, green plants enable us to breathe by returning oxygen to the air during photosynthesis. They are also the primary source of most vitamins, without which we would expire from a combination of deficiency diseases. And all the time these same plants afford valuable research materials on which many of the greatest scientific discoveries have been made and important studies continue practically throughout the world.

## Some Nuisances.

The significance of various lower plants, particularly, in causing diseases of animals and other plants has already been referred to. Thus, such human diseases as tuberculosis, brucellosis, tetanus, typhoid and some other fevers, plague, cholera, diphtheria and many more, are all due to Bacteria, while the Potato and Chestnut Blights and Cereal Rusts and Smuts are due to Fungi, which alone cause many hundreds of different plant diseases, often of devastating effect and vast importance. Other plant maladies may spoil amenities, an example being the Dutch Elm disease which threatens the various Elms that form such an important feature of the landscapes in temperate regions on both sides of the North Atlantic. Some higher plants and Fungi, particularly, are dangerously poisonous; but although large doses may be lethal, small ones are often beneficial (as we saw when discussing drugs). Consequently such plants are not unmitigated curses; and indeed, provided they are known and understood, they may be of real benefit. On the other hand, some of the selective herbicides may, like disease-provoking organisms, yet be turned to destructive use in biological warfare.

The saprophytic Fungi and Bacteria that cause harmful decay, putrefaction, and often loss of food and fabrics, etc., have also been mentioned above; in many circumstances there would be no organic breakdown without them. At all events the beneficial ' scavenging ' which these organisms accomplish is so essential as immeasurably to outweight such nuisances as they perpetrate, considerable though the latter may be—especially with the deterioration and spoilage that are so rapid and marked in the tropics.

Weeds are often defined as ' plants growing where they are not wanted '—which is a broader conception than we had in dealing with them in the last chapter. However, the same plant that is useful in one place may be obnoxious in another, in which its necessary control or eradication becomes a laborious and costly procedure; in short, it has become a weed. Modern methods of weed control include chemical spraying with such herbicides as 2,4-D or chlorates, mulching, and the biological use of ' smother crops ' which combat the nuisances by competition. Other methods include the introduction of diseases of the pests involved, as well as such time-honoured activities as weeding, hoeing, harrowing, and the like. Also effective is prevention of the growth of weeds by the use of ' clean ' seed, sterilization of the bed by heat or chemicals, and removal of near-by sources of infection.

Besides being nuisances in the ways mentioned in the last chapter, some weeds, such as the Ragweeds and many Grasses, have airborne pollen to which people suffering from hay-fever are particularly sensitive. Such plants as Poison-ivy are also a great nuisance to some individuals. And finally, not only field and garden crops but also forests and even waters have their weeds—in forests the often valueless but fast-growing and strangling Birches and Cottonwoods, and, in water, the Algae which foul ships' bottoms and reservoirs, clog irrigation ditches and navigation channels, and are troublesome in many other ways.

## Further Consideration

If it is felt that the résumé of economic botany given in this chapter is scarcely appropriate to a work on plant geography, however wide and introductory this may be, it should be recalled that the essence of our subject is *distribution*, and that not only the origin and supply but also the availability where it is needed of a plant product (and hence its geography) is of importance to Man and pertinent to our study. For Man often 'shapes' plants and their distribution even as they, in turn, largely qualify his life and so limit the whereabouts and size of his populations.

The importance of plants to mankind is stressed in the following works:

F. O. Bower. *Plants and Man* (Macmillan, London, pp. xii + 365, 1925).

R. Good. *Plants and Human Economics* (Cambridge University Press, Cambridge, Eng., pp. xii + 202 and additional maps, 1933).

W. W. Robbins & F. Ramaley. *Plants Useful to Man*, second edition (Blakiston, Philadelphia, pp. ix + 422, 1937).

C. J. Hylander & O. B. Stanley. *Plants and Man* (Blakiston, Philadelphia, pp. x + 518, 1941).

J. Hutchinson & R. Melville. *The Story of Plants and their Uses to Man* (Gawthorn, London, pp. xv + 334, 1948).

For further information about most economically important plants:

A. F. Hill. *Economic Botany*, second edition (McGraw-Hill, New York etc., pp. xii + 560, 1952).

R. W. Schery. *Plants for Man* (Prentice-Hall, New York, pp. viii + 564, 1952).

E. E. Stanford. *Economic Plants* (Appleton-Century-Crofts, New York, pp. xxiii + 571, 1934).

K. H. W. Klages. *Ecological Crop Geography* (Macmillan, New York, pp. xviii + 615, 1942).

R. Zon & W. N. Sparhawk. *Forest Resources of the World* (McGraw-Hill, New York & London, 2 vols., pp. xiv + 1–493 and vii + 495–997, 1923).

W. W. Robbins. *The Botany of Crop Plants*, third edition (Blakiston, Philadelphia, pp. x + 639, 1931).

United States Department of Agriculture 1950–51 Yearbook. *Crops in Peace and War* (U.S. Government Printing Office, Washington, D.C., pp. [xviii +] 942, 1951). A veritable mine of information *inter alia* on chemurgical uses and future possibilities.

Poisonous plants are commonly treated on a local basis :

L. H. PAMMEL. *A Manual of Poisonous Plants : chiefly of eastern North America...* (Torch Press, Cedar Rapids, Iowa, Pt. I, pp. viii + 150, and Pt. II, pp. 153–977, 1911).

J. W. HARSHBERGER. *Textbook of Pastoral and Agricultural Botany* (Blakiston, Philadelphia, pp. xiii + 294, 1920). Gives some idea of the magnitude of the subject on a wider basis.

As well as the above more general works, there are various books which are devoted to particular crops or closely-allied groups of crops. Along these lines, apart from individual works, there are three special series in English of which (1) the Economic Crops series of Interscience Publishers, New York, has so far published books on Apples, Bananas, Cherries, Cocoa, and Sweet Corn, while in (2) Longmans Green & Company's Tropical Agriculture series there have appeared books on Cocoa, Rice, Tea, and Bananas ; in preparation are Coconuts, Rubber, Oil Seeds, Sorghum, Oil Palms, Cotton, and Spices. Also extensive and uniform will be (3) the World Crops Books series of Leonard Hill Limited, London, in which the volumes so far in press or arranged include separate ones on Alfalfa, Barley, Brassicas, Coffee, Cucurbits, Eucalyptus, Flax and Linseed, Hops, Jute, Mangoes, Mushrooms and Truffles, Oats, Onions and their allies, Peanuts, Pineapple, Rubber, Rye, Sugar Cane, Taros and their allies, Tomatoes, Tropical Cash Crops, Vegetable Fibres, and Wheat. Each of these World Crops Books deals with the botany, cultivation, and utilization throughout the world of the crop or group of crops concerned, and each is profusely illustrated and fully documented. An allied series, entitled Plant Science Monographs, also published by Leonard Hill Limited, deals especially with research advances involving *inter alia* many of these and other important crops.

## Chapter X

# ENVIRONMENTAL FACTORS

We have now dealt sufficiently with special kinds and systematic groups of plants and their distributions, and must proceed to consider the results of their natural aggregation, namely, vegetation. As a basis for this we must deal in the present chapter with ecological factors and, in the next chapter, with the main habitats these factors constitute. In addition there will be considered in Chapter XI certain fundamental tendencies and attributes of vegetation whose recognition is essential to the full understanding of vegetational changes and types.

Ecology is the study of the mutual relations among organisms and between them and their environment—environment being the aggregate of all external conditions and influences affecting life and development at a given spot. Ecological or environmental factors are many and diverse, and often intricately mixed and interdependent. Either singly or in combination, the various ecological factors may affect the presence or absence, vigour or weakness, and relative success or failure, of various plant communities through their component taxa. Although the subject is enormously complex, the immediate vehicles of influence are very few, being chiefly food, light, temperature, water, and dissolved substances; these are affected by variations in the ecological factors which characterize different habitats and consequently lead to the differentiation of vegetational types.

The four main classes of ecological factors with which we shall deal below—namely, climatic, physiographic (of topography, etc.), edaphic (of soil), and biotic (due to living organisms)—are themselves commonly interrelated and intricately mixed. Often they work through one another, acting and reacting together, as in the case of physiographic changes which bring about local climates that in turn may affect the soils and competition-impress. Accordingly this classification, like so many other biological ones, is to some extent artificial. Yet all categories affect the plant either directly or indirectly through modification of its reactions, bringing about functional responses or differences in growth or structure, although different plants vary widely, of course, in the nature and degree of such response.

## Climatic

The climatic factors comprise the general features of regional climate, often being rhythmic—exhibiting, for example, diurnal, seasonal, or long-term cyclic fluctuations. They may also vary locally, to give local climates, and even do so in extremely restricted confines, to give *microclimates*. Examples of local climates are found on steep northern or southern hill-slopes, and of microclimates on the leeside of boulders which protect the immediately neighbouring plants and animals from wind and insolation. In general the factors classed as climatic have a dominating influence. Nevertheless, so far as plants are concerned, these factors are often but poorly expressed by meteorological records which, for example, are usually taken at some standard height above the ground (rarely the height of the plant) and fail to observe the often rapid fluctuations which can be so important to a sensitive organism. There are five main climatic factors which we must now consider in turn: it is their different combinations which largely prescribe vegetation-types, and so they cannot well be placed in order of relative importance.

(1) *Light*. This, as we have seen, is essential for photosynthesis, though fortunately sufficient illumination for this purpose is present almost everywhere on land and in surface waters; it may also be important for some reproductive processes. Fig. 79 shows the Moss Campion (*Silene acaulis* agg.) flowering only on the top and south-facing side of its domed tussocks in high-arctic Spitsbergen, where it can constitute a reliable compass; the effect is *thought* to result from differing light intensities.

The light-climate at a spot depends on the duration, time-distribution, intensity, and quality of the insolation there obtaining, though so far as the plant is concerned the effective period may be modified by cold or drought. Moreover, for successful flowering many plants require a relatively long (or, alternatively, short) day, apparently regardless of the intensity or quality of the light, and consequently such plants are largely limited to high (or low) latitudes, respectively. The effect of light on photosynthesis depends largely on intensity, which also influences growth. In the open, elongation is checked and lateral organs enlarge, whereas with congested conditions, for example in forests, the form tends to be more elongated and narrow. In temperate forests, too, the seasonal aspects are apt to be important—in particular the prevernal (*i.e.* before spring) one of herbs which flower before the shading tree-leaves expand. Thereafter different levels or layers in the forest usually have different light-climates.

The measurement of light tends to be unsatisfactory, for no instrument indicates precisely the quality as well as intensity, much less the total quantity; usually only the intensity at a particular point

FIG. 79.—Moss Campion (*Silene acaulis* agg.) flowering only on the south-facing sides and tops of its domed tussocks near 80° N. in Spitsbergen. The surrounding terrain is a mixed 'half-barren'.

in time and space is measured, and that is done only as far as the measuring device employed is sensitive to the component wavelengths encountered. The particular rays of the spectrum which are most effective in the diverse plant-functions affected by light, also tend to be different. Nevertheless photoelectric cells and actinometers of sensitized paper are useful, especially for purposes of comparison, and both are widely employed by ecologists in the field.

(2) *Temperature.* This factor is vitally important as it conditions the speed of the chemical actions and activities comprising life. The great world vegetational zones, like altitudinal ones, depend primarily on temperature, and we find it convenient to distinguish between *megatherms* (plants favouring warm habitats), *microtherms* (plants favouring cold habitats), and the intermediate *mesotherms.*

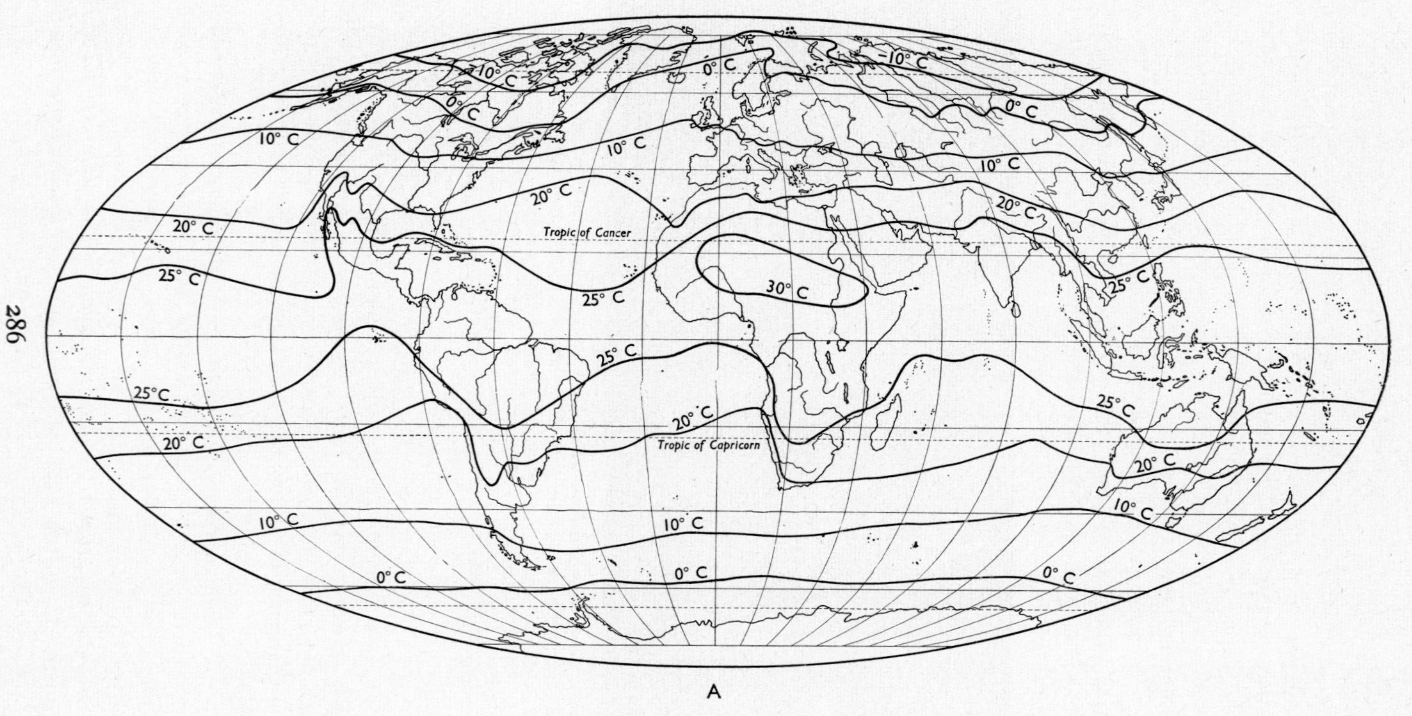

-10° C
-10° C
0° C
0° C
0° C
10° C
10° C
10° C
20° C
20° C
20° C
Tropic of Cancer
25° C
25° C
30° C
25° C
25° C
25°C
25° C
20° C
20° C
Tropic of Capricorn
20° C
10° C
10° C
10° C
0° C
0° C
0° C


A

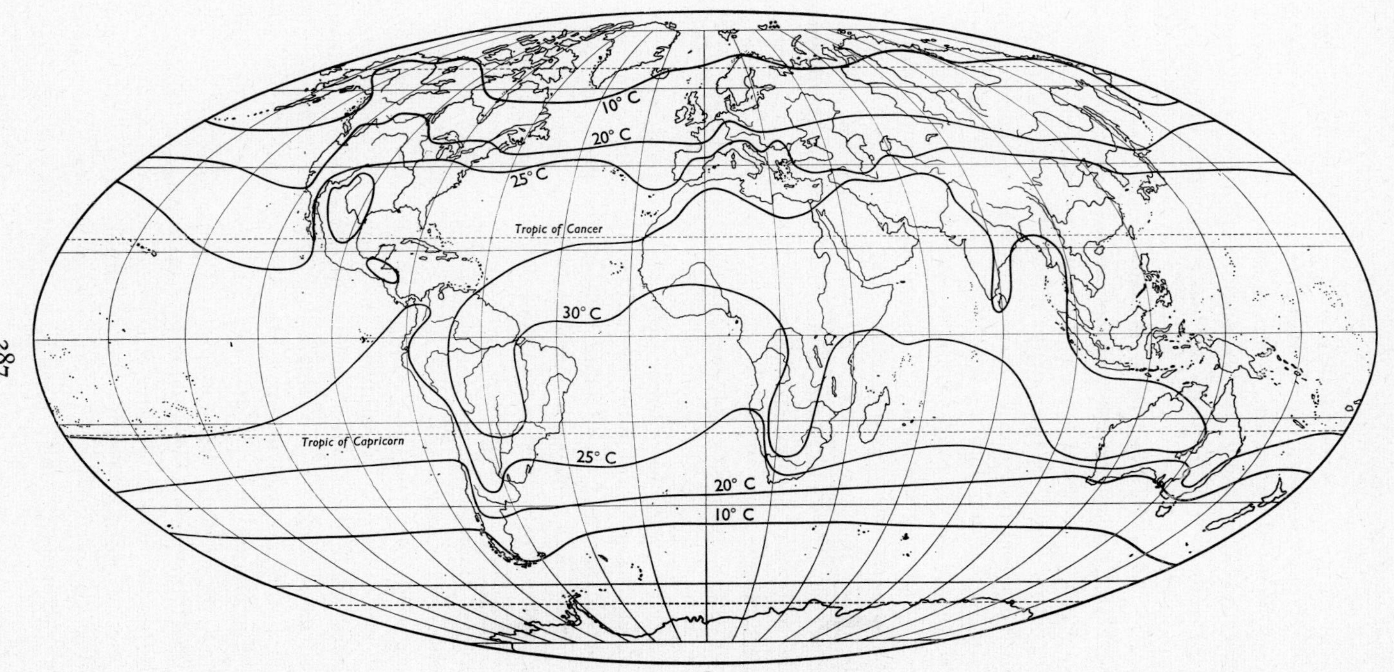


FIG. 80.—Annual mean, and mean temperature of the warmest month, in different parts of the world (in °C.). A annual mean temperature; B, mean temperature of the warmest month of the year.

Different plants are variously adapted as to the minimum, optimum, and maximum temperatures for their life as a whole as well as for its component physiological functions, even though these actual temperatures may change with variations in other conditions and with the state of the plant (as well as, of course, differently with different plants).

Winter is normally a resting period when activity is at a minimum in temperate regions, though many plants are active at much lower temperatures in the polar lands and waters—some even below 0° C. On the other hand, temperatures above the freezing point may already be lethal to tropical plants; so may temperatures above 45° C. if evaporation does not cool and save them. However, there can be few places that are naturally too hot or too cold for *any* plants. Important indirectly are clouds and other influences reducing the amount of direct insolation, and relative humidity which greatly affects the loss of water by evaporation. The soil also has a marked local effect, dry and dark types warming up much more quickly than heavy waterlogged ones.

Temperatures vary markedly at different levels as well as at different times, and meteorological means (*i.e.* averages) are therefore of little value to the ecologist. An annual mean well below freezing point is found in some continental regions where forests abound, and although monthly means, and especially monthly mean maxima and minima, are of more value to the plant scientist than annual means, a thermograph tracing showing the continuous change on the spot is most desirable for ecological purposes. To give anything like a complete picture of the temperature-climate as it strikes the plants, tracings should be obtained synchronously at each different level or layer of vegetation and root-infested soil. In intricate work involving, for example, the surfaces or the internal tissues of leaves, thermocouples are employed instead of thermometers, while for determining the approximate temperatures of hard surfaces, etc., thin shavings of paraffins of different known melting points are convenient. Fig. 80 indicates (A) the annual mean temperature, and (B) the mean temperature of the warmest month of the year, in different parts of the world.

(3) *Precipitation.* The amount of rain, especially, falling in an area during the year constitutes a factor of outstanding importance, as it often mainly determines the availability of water for growth and other vital processes. To this availability the local vegetation largely corresponds; and although the year's total is apt to be the

feature most important for trees, the season in which it falls may matter a great deal to herbaceous plants and grasslands. These last are especially favoured by spring rainfall in regions of cold winters. With hot and dry summers but winters warm enough for growth, there may be a preponderance of sclerophyllous shrubs (*i.e.* having rather small, leathery leaves). With less and less rainfall there tend to be still more xeromorphic plants (*i.e.* with features aiding them to conserve water, as illustrated in Fig. 20, *xerophytes* being in general plants which grow in dry places). At the other extreme are *hydrophytes*, living more or less submerged in water (Fig. 21), and *hygrophytes*, or moisture-loving plants, while between xerophytes and hydrophytes lie the so-called *mesophytes*, living in habitats that usually show neither an excess nor a deficiency of water.

Rain is caused by the cooling of moisture-laden air. Rainfall is usually reported in the form of monthly means, which are the amounts falling in the various calendar months but averaged over a period of years, though the number of rainy days in each month gives a better indication of its distribution. Moreover, sudden heavy rain is apt to be largely lost as run-off, and may cause bad erosion. Because of the often marked local differences with physiographic changes, it is desirable for an ecologist to have his own automatic rain-gauge which, like his thermograph, needs tending only once a week.

Other forms of precipitation are snow (which may lie on the ground to form a valuable protective blanket and also a reservoir of water, but is apt to limit the growing-season by its late melting), hail (which may cause serious injury especially to young crops), sleet, and dew (which is important in some deserts where it provides much of the surface water on which the ephemeral plants depend). Fig. 81 indicates the average annual precipitation in different parts of the world.

(4) *Evaporating power*. The evaporating power of the air is a factor of the utmost importance to the life of plants, as it directly affects their transpiration. It is indicated approximately by the relative humidity (the ratio of the water-vapour present in the atmosphere to that necessary for saturation at a particular temperature), or, more accurately, by the 'saturation-deficit', which takes account also of temperature, and determines the 'pull' exerted by the atmosphere on the water-economy of plants.

The relative humidity is commonly measured by means of a 'wet and dry bulb' hygrometer (psychrometer), the difference in

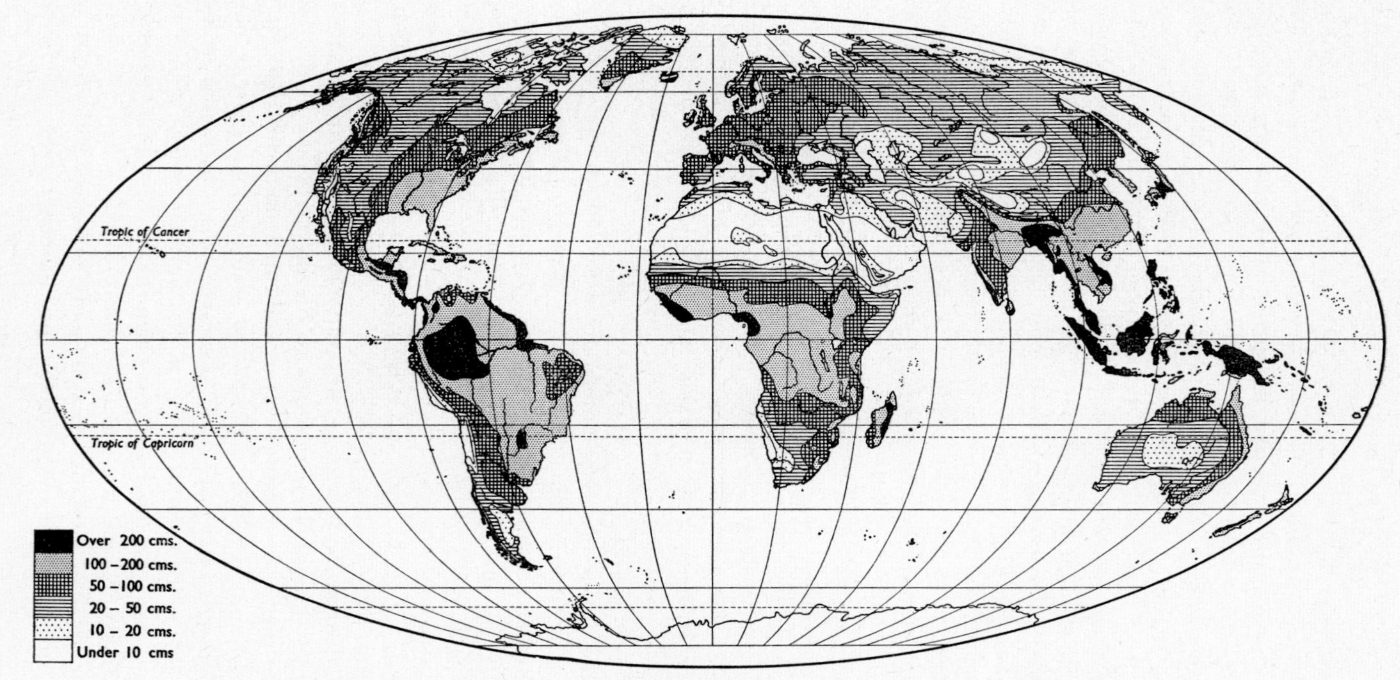


FIG. 81.—Average annual precipitation in different parts of the world (in centimetres)

temperature of the wet and dry thermometer bulbs giving a measure of the deficiency of water-vapour below saturation point in the air tested, while the saturation-deficit can be calculated directly from these different readings. Although this instrument is customarily swung through the air to simulate wind and replace any saturated layers that may form around the wet bulb, from our point of view it is best kept stationary as plants are. Even the hygrometer gives readings only at a particular time ; often it is more important to know the effect over a given period, and this may be measured by using an ' atmometer ' (evaporimeter), which indicates the water-loss by evaporation from a given area of porous pot. This integrates the water-vapour content of the air with temperature, wind, and the time-factor, and may be compared with a plant which it is placed beside. Or, for continuous recording, a tracing may be made by an automatic hygrograph, such as those using strands of human hair which is highly sensitive to changes in atmospheric humidity. Batteries of such instruments will often show marked differences in different strata of a forest, for example—indicating local variation which may be of great importance in varying the ' pull ' exerted on different plants, on the same plant at different times, or even on different parts of the same plant at a particular time.

(5) *Wind.* Owing to the friction of the soil surface, rocks, buildings, and above all major physiographic features and masses of vegetation, winds tend to increase in velocity with height above the ground. Wind commonly affects other ecological factors in a given spot—for example, water content and temperature, through its effect on evaporation—but can also have a direct influence on vegetation, especially by uprooting trees or by breaking off branches or other portions. It has a similar, usually drying, effect upon the soil, or may occasionally act in the opposite direction by bringing up moister air which reduces transpiration and evaporation, and may actually lead to deposition or precipitation. Most widely important to plants, however, is the manner in which wind increases water-loss, by constantly bringing unsaturated air into contact with leaves and young shoots. Mechanically, wind can also cause erosion of soil and abrasion of vegetation through carriage of particles, and physiologically it can decrease growth by replacing damp by dry air, and consequently increasing the transpiration and reducing the turgor of organs on which it impinges. This explains the frequent growth of trees and shrubs chiefly away from the direction of the prevailing wind in exposed situations (*cf.* Fig. 82, A),

and their restriction to tangled dwarfs in sheltered depressions (Fig. 82, B). In strong dry winds young parts of plants may even become shrivelled and killed in a few hours, and surface soil may become dried out. Such effects may be observed in the warm foehn

A

B

FIG. 82.—Effect of wind on trees. A, deformed outliers of Black Spruce (*Picea mariana*) near Churchill, Hudson Bay. The prevailing winds are from the left. Note in foreground the luxuriant prairie-like tundra of the arctic–subarctic ecotone. The lower branches of such Spruces tend to form a dense layered mat that is well protected by drifted snow from desiccation in winter, the farthest outliers (on left) often being limited to such growths. Upper branches (on right) 'trail away' to leeward. B, deciduous broad-leafed and evergreen coniferous tree species forming a dwarfed tangle in sheltered depressions on exposed hill-side on coast near North Berwick, Scotland. The Grasses and other herbs reach the height of the gnarled 'trees' which scarcely anywhere exceed the level of the surrounding terrain.

or chinook winds that, sweeping down from mountains, can raise the temperature of the air locally by as much as 30° C. in a very short time. For such reasons a good deal can be inferred about the wind-climate of a habitat by direct observation of the vegetation, etc. Wind velocity is measured by an anemometer, but its effect is included in observations obtained from stationary hygrometers and atmometers.

As we saw in Chapter IV, wind is an important agent of dispersal. It may also be of significance phytogeographically in determining the local distribution of species or communities of plants, some types being markedly more wind-resistant than others, and many being unable to flourish or even exist in exposed situations. Thus the tree-limit on the sides of mountains is apt to be due largely to winds, as may be seen by the frequent persistence higher up of groups of trees in sheltered pockets; such trees further reduce exposure very locally and enable tender herbs to grow in their company.

Ocean currents, such as the warm Gulf Stream or the cold East Greenland Current, may have a considerable effect on temperature both locally and on land at a distance—especially when the winds are predominantly on-shore. By bringing in fresh materials, such currents may also alter the conditions with regard to nutrient salts, etc. Moreover, as we saw in Chapter IV, water currents can be an important aid in plant dispersal.

### Physiographic

The physiographic factors are those introduced by the structure, conformity, and behaviour of the earth's surface—*e.g.* by topographic features such as elevation and slope, by geodynamic processes such as silting and erosion, and consequently by local geology. Other causes of physiographic change from place to place include the blowing of sand or dust which in time or special circumstances can assume vast proportions. It is in such connections that the various landforms described in Chapter XVII tend to be most significant to students of plant geography and ecology.

Physiographic factors act on local vegetation largely through climatic or edaphic features which they engender. They are consequently sometimes classed with these other groups. Yet, ecological factors being so widely interdependent in any case, it seems more conducive to clear understanding to consider the physiographic ones separately—especially as they are well marked in their effect on vegetation in regions of drastic topography and harsh climate. Strong topographical relief tends to produce marked local climates, summits for example being very different in these respects from sides of mountains, and narrow valleys from open plains. Quite apart from the tendency to greater windiness and exposure at higher altitudes, the air and soil temperatures tend to get lower and the relative humidity greater as we ascend, with atmospheric pressure decreasing and heat-radiation increasing in intensity. Altogether, climatic variation becomes more and more extreme and rapid with increasing altitude.

As an example of physiographic effects in arid regions, we may rise from unproductive plains to fertile slopes and forests on mountain sides, and at very high altitudes reach again an unproductive zone of low absolute humidity and rigorous exposure. The changes are due largely to local climate but would not take place if it were not for the physiography. Moreover, major topographic features often affect the climate at a considerable distance—as, for example, mountain ranges which may cause rainfall locally and decrease it in their lee—while in Chapter IV we saw how such features, and wide expanses of water, can act as barriers to plant migration.

Another important physiographic effect is aspect : in the northern hemisphere, north-facing slopes tend to be more hygrophilous (adjusted to moist conditions) than south-facing ones at similar altitudes (Fig. 83, A). This is owing to the effect of insolation on air and soil temperatures, and consequently on relative humidity and evaporation and, through them, on the local water situation (even when precipitation is the same). For vegetational differences due to topography are most often correlated with moisture, and naturally tend to be marked chiefly where water is deficient and consequently is a critical factor. Sometimes for this reason there may be entirely different vegetations and even floras on the two sides of a deep valley or steep mountain (Fig. 83, B), as in the dry Mediterranean region, while if similar zones are developed they tend to be at higher altitudes on the south- than on the north-facing slope. The western slopes of mountains may be noticeably warmer and drier than the eastern ones, owing to the sun's afternoon warmth. Quite drastic effects may often be seen already on a microclimatic scale, for example in the shelter of rocks or even stones on exposed sea-cliffs and mountain summits. Here we may refer again to Fig. 79, which shows a striking aspect effect in the Arctic.

A

B

FIG. 83.—Aspect effects in Colorado and Nepal. A, Colorado, U.S.A.: the relatively damp and cool, north-facing slope (on left) is covered by a stabilized forest of Douglas Fir, whereas the south-facing slope supports mainly dry Oak scrub and scattered Poncerosa Pines. (Phot. G. E. Nichols. By permission from *Plant Ecology*, by Weaver & Clement s, copyright date 1938, McGraw-Hill Book Co.) B, Jumla, West Nepal, c. 3048metres (10,000 feet) in the Himalayas: the north-facing slope (on left) is forested with *Abies spectabilis* and *Betula utilis*, and, lower down, some *Pinus wallichiana*, whereas the dry and sunny south-facing slope supports chiefly herbs and Grasses, with some scattered low *Juniperus* bushes. (Phot. O. Polunin.)

Important in itself is the steepness of a slope, for it largely determines the stability of the surface and retention of water, and also the effect of aspect or exposure—especially in the higher latitudes. Thus in the northern hemisphere a steep south-facing slope will receive the strong midday sun's rays more or less perpendicularly, while a steep north-facing slope may receive only oblique and weak morning and evening rays, or perhaps none at all. These differences often have a marked effect, especially on the water and temperature conditions in the two places, and consequently on the vegetation. For besides the intensity, the duration, quality, and quantity of incident light are at the same time affected.

Slope can also greatly affect the character as well as the amount of soil which accumulates. This, like the nature of the underlying rock, is often reckoned as an edaphic factor ; but in so far as either determines or results in topographic change, it is to be considered as physiographic. Different textures and types of rocks will produce different topographies which bring about local climatic differences that are physiographically engendered. Such differences may also affect the water conditions, including the level below which the ground is waterlogged or frozen, and so again drastically affect the habitat.

Geodynamic agencies are particularly active in mountain districts and about coasts, causing all manner of changes in topography—sometimes almost from day to day. Steep slopes and river banks are constantly being eroded, the material sliding down as talus, etc., or being washed down and deposited elsewhere. Such activities often cause the formation of new ' open ' habitats, both in the places whence the eroded material came and in the areas in which it comes to rest. Frosts may help disintegration through their heaving, splitting, and other erosive tendencies, while avalanches often clear off the surface materials from considerable areas. And even as mountain slopes change their surfaces, and river-beds alter their outlines and vary courses, so do sea-coasts and cliffs vary in their conformation, erosion being widely at work. In other places there are silting salt-marshes or gradually moving sand-dunes or shingle-banks—to mention only a few of the geodynamic sources of physiographic change.

### Edaphic

The edaphic factors are those which are dependent on the soil as such—on its constitution, water and air content, inhabiting organisms, and so forth. We have seen how climatic factors, such as temperature and precipitation, are of supreme importance in determining the general character of the vegetation over wide areas ; here and in the next section we shall deal with the edaphic and biotic factors, respectively, which are apt locally to modify the conditions and vegetations of these major climatic belts. Especially has it long been recognized, and utilized in agricultural, horticultural, and forestral practice, that differences in the soil are often largely responsible for differences in vegetation within the same climatic region : consequently they are of great significance in plant geography.

Soil may be considered as the unconsolidated superficial material of the earth's crust, lying below any aerial vegetation and undecomposed litter, and extending down to the limits to which it affects the plants growing about its surface. Beneath the soil lies the subsoil or unaltered rock. Though usually composed primarily of material derived from the parent rock, the soil has come into being largely through interaction of this ' substratum ' with climate and living organisms. Thus its texture may be dependent largely on water- and frost-action and other ' weathering ' tendencies, while its content of humus (partially decomposed organic matter) results from the contributions and activities of inhabiting plants and animals. For soil is a veritable ' microcosm ' or little world—with its own physical structure, chemical composition, atmosphere, flora, and fauna. And characteristically it exhibits a perpetual series of actions and reactions between organisms and environment. In it about one-third (by volume) of the bodies of higher plants spend their lives—influencing, and being influenced by, the particular conditions obtaining in the soil. These conditions, through the subterranean organs of plants, in turn influence their living aerial parts.

Soils that are undisturbed by agriculture and other factors commonly become stratified into layers or ' horizons ' at different depths, which often have very different compositions as well as natures. Such ' profiles ' are, however, largely destroyed by cultivation. Normally, three main horizons or groups of horizons are exhibited, namely, the upper or ' A ' zone of extraction of soluble salts and fine-grained materials, the middle or ' B ' zone of their concentration, and, below, the ' C ' zone where neither extraction nor accumulation has occurred at all extensively. The characteristic profiles so formed are to a considerable extent climatically engendered, and so mature soils can be classified broadly into climatic types or 'world groups', such as *podzols* (developed chiefly in cool regions of high precipitation relatively to evaporation), *brown earths* (with generally lower rainfall and higher temperatures), *chernozems* (with low rainfall in continental regions), *prairie soils* (with higher rainfall), *chestnut-brown soils* (in warmer and drier places), *laterites* (with high rainfall in the tropics), *red loams* (with lower rainfall in warm-temperate regions), *tundra soils* (of polar regions where the subsoil remains frozen and organic decomposition is retarded), and so on. Fig. 84 shows three characteristic soil profiles and Fig. 85 indicates the distribution of the primary soil groups of the world.

As we shall see towards the end of the next chapter when dealing with plant succession, soil development and vegetational development are intimately connected, both being largely controlled by climate. Meanwhile the essential constituents of most soils may conveniently be treated in five categories :

(1) *Mineral fragments* of various sizes resulting from the disintegration of rocky materials by physical and chemical weathering ; the parent material may be either local or otherwise, as may be the weathering. These mineral constituents form the inorganic framework and differ widely according to the physical and chemical nature of the parent material. They affect plants particularly by bringing about variations in soil water and aeration, as water retention is much affected by mechanical composition (the relative proportions of different-sized mineral particles present). The mineral constituents may also affect the composition of the soil water in important ways (*see* below).

Soils are mechanically analyzed by separating into 'fractions' the particles whose sizes lie within definite arbitrary limits, ranging from larger stones and gravel (more than 2 mm. in diameter) down through various sizes of sand and silt to clay (less than ·002 mm. in diameter). The majority of mature soils consist largely of silica and silicates which are relatively insoluble and form a more or less permanent basis, any calcareous material tending to become dissolved ('leached') out of the surface layers and many of the finer insoluble particles being carried down mechanically to lower levels (this process is termed 'eluviation'). Particularly important in leaching and chemical weathering is the acid-forming carbon dioxide dissolved in soil water. The particles forming the soil's inorganic framework tend to be coated with colloidal material of very fine clay or of organic origin, which may help cement them into compound particles or grains and increase the 'crumb structure' of the

FIG. 84.—Three soil profiles of comparable depth. On left is a podzol with a thick covering of forest duff and top-soil underlain by a whitish $A_2$ horizon. In centre is a prairie soil of less striking stratification, and, on the right, a chernozem which is characteristically dark above. (Left and centre phot. C. E. Kellogg; right phot. Roy W. Simonson.)

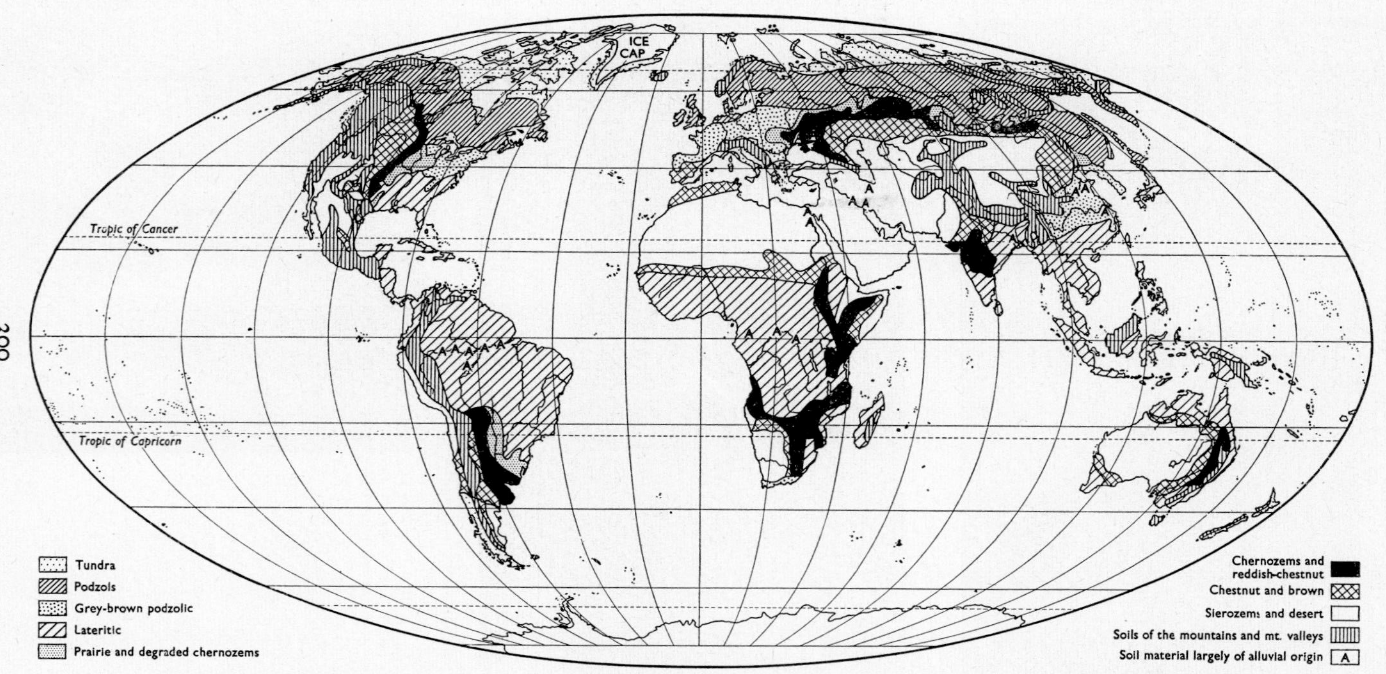


FIG. 85.—Distribution of primary soil groups of the world. (U.S. Department of Agriculture Yearbook.)

soil and its ability to hold water and salts. Sandy soils are porous, 'light' to work, easily penetrated by roots, and they dry readily; in contrast, clayey soils are retentive of water, heavy, poorly aerated and sticky when wet, and hard when dry. For most working and plant-growing purposes, mixed 'loams' are best.

(2) *Soil water* containing dissolved substances is also of fundamental importance, being commonly the chief source of water for plants. Water is of course essential to plants as usually their main constituent by weight, as the medium for physical and chemical changes, and because large quantities must be absorbed to cover the continual loss by transpiration from their surfaces. Except in extremely dry soils and below the level of permanent ground-water, the soil water mainly forms films around the component particles of the soil. The amount of such water and thickness of the film depends on such factors as the soil's mechanical constitution, on the recency of precipitation and tendency to run-off, on subsequent weather conditions, on humus content, on the covering of vegetation and litter, etc., and on the effect of this covering on water loss by transpiration and evaporation. Especially does water percolate through and evaporate from coarse gravelly or sandy soils, and remain suspended in fine clayey and humous ones with their high capillary action and immense aggregate surface of microscopic or colloidal particles. However, in such retentive soils much of the water may be so strongly held that it cannot be abstracted and used by the plants, so that it is often necessary to distinguish between water which is available to plants (the so-called *chresard*, above the point of permanent wilting, though this may vary somewhat with different species) and that which is so strongly held as to be unavailable (*echard*). The entire water content of the soil may conveniently be termed the 'holard'. Water tends to promote the stratification of soils, and the soil's content of available water is often the chief factor underlying local differences between plant communities.

Another important factor affecting vegetation is the soil water's content of dissolved inorganic salts, etc., which are derived from the mineral matter present and from organic breakdown. Certain of these salts' constituent elements are essential to the plants' continued well-being and even to their life, while others are apt to be obnoxious or actually poisonous. Outstanding are the extremely saline soils which are inhabited only by specially adapted plants (halophytes). In these connections the various needs and abilities of different plants lead to correlations with the chemical content of the soil water, which frequently constitutes a determining factor in plant geography. Examples occur in the cases of plants which seem to require ' lime ' (*calcicoles* or *calciphytes*) and those which appear to avoid it (*calcifuges* or *oxylophytes*), though frequently such preferences are bound up rather with questions of basicity or acidity, respectively. For the soil ' reaction ' (hydrogen-ion concentration) also can determine the presence or absence of particular species locally.

Thus can the varying tolerances of many plant species, etc., to different environmental factors come into play as particularly important phytogeographically, though it should be remembered that away from their optimum sphere plants tend to be more and more susceptible to competition and other influences, and hence to show less and less ability to persist. Consequently it is especially towards the limits of their ranges that they are liable to be most narrowly restricted to special habitats involving particular environmental conditions.

(3) *Soil atmosphere* mainly occupies the interstices between the soil particles or crumbs, with their covering films of water. It tends to contain a slightly lower proportion of oxygen and a much higher one of carbon dioxide than ordinary air, and to be normally saturated with water-vapour. This may not be the case in the surface layers of very dry soils, while at the other extreme waterlogged ones are liable to be deficient in oxygen, their lack of aeration making them unsuitable for most forms of plant and animal life. Normally, plentiful oxygen in the soil is necessary for the life of most of the microorganisms and other inhabitants and for the respiration of the underground parts of higher plants growing in it, the differences in composition from the free air being reflective of the gaseous exchanges involved, namely, absorption of oxygen and giving out of carbon dioxide. However, interchange with the free air by diffusion and other agencies appears to be fairly rapid.

(4) *Organic matter*, arising from the death of plants or parts of plants, or of animals or added as manure, forms another highly important constituent of most soils. Included are roots that decompose *in situ*. Indeed all soils which bear vegetation (and according to some authorities all true soils) contain dead organic matter, usually more or less broken down to humus, though the amount may vary from very little in fresh ' new ' soils to virtually 100 per cent. of dry-weight in peat and leaf-mould. In the dissemination

and breakdown of the dead plant and other remains, Earthworms may be important in dragging down and partly digesting the material. After this, soil Fungi and Bacteria cause further disintegration and ultimately decomposition into more or less simple salts (such as ones containing nitrogen and phosphorus which are essential to plants), carbon dioxide, and water. These are the fundamental plant foods, and the organic matter is the chief seat of the activities of the microorganisms liberating (and sometimes producing) them. Such decomposition and disappearance takes place relatively rapidly in warm, moist, and well-aerated soils, these conditions being favourable to the activity of the 'scavenging' organisms. On the other hand, in cold and wet soils that are poor in salts and acidic in reaction, the debris may long remain on the surface as scarcely decomposed 'raw humus' (*mor*).

Ordinary humus, having become structurally unrecognizable and largely colloidal, improves both heavy clay and light sandy soils, lightening the former and giving consistency and water-holding capacity to the latter, as well as adding plant food in each case. The 'reaction' of a soil—its degree of acidity or basicity—is also important to many plants and may affect their distribution, as particular species are apt to show a distinct preference for soils whose reaction lies within certain limits. This reaction again is largely bound up with humus content, humus being the main source of acidity in soils.

(5) *Living organisms*, together with the roots and other underground parts of aerial plants, comprise the other widely essential constituent of the soil. They include, as we have already seen, the mainly microscopic soil flora and fauna whose life is usually centred on the soil's humus content and which are often very sensitive to changes in the conditions of their limited environment. They also include the main mixing and 'scavenging' animals and above all saprophytic Fungi and Bacteria, etc., which are so vitally important in the maintenance of ecological balance and indeed of life in the world. For higher plants, as we have already noted, these organisms make available various essential food substances, including nitrogen in usable form.

In highly acid soils, Fungi largely replace the decomposing and other useful Bacteria—such replacement in itself involving significant phytogeographical changes. Indeed these soil communities and their component organisms have their distributions and other geographical implications in much the same manner as higher types.

Besides various essential or beneficial substances including growth-stimulating ones, harmful toxins may be produced in the soil by living organisms or parts of organisms—with corresponding effects on plant distribution. And then there are various mycorrhizal associations, Algae, and other units in the microcosm, all of which may have their importance to the vegetation and to plant geography, though quite how is often not well understood. Nor should we forget the importance of soil temperature, which can act in so many and various ways—as, for example, through the soil's living content.

## Biotic

The biotic factors in the wide sense are those due to living organisms, whether animal or plant—ranging, as it were, from Man and the great herbivores and trees down to the lowly but often vitally important soil microorganisms with which we have just dealt. It is useful to visualize the total components of an immediate environment or recognizable habitat as forming a self-contained *ecosystem*, composed on one hand of the inorganic and dead parts and, on the other, of the various organisms which live together in it as a sociological unit and comprise the *biota*. A large, primary biotic community in which the climax vegetation (*see* next chapter) is more or less uniform is termed a *biome*. Our interest is primarily in the living components, the inert ones being from our point of view mere factors conditioning the existence, structure, and development of the biome—chiefly through their effect on one or more of its component organisms. These are the individual species or other taxa, divisible approximately into animals and plants. The latter form the plant community, which may be loosely defined as an entire population of plants growing together and maintaining as a whole a corporate individuality that is not the same as the sum total of the separate manifestations and effects of its components.

The component plants of a community have many immediate internal (' autogenic ') effects upon one another and upon their own habitat, as for example in competition and the deposition of humus, and by producing various changes in the soil ; they even have ' allogenic ' effects in sheltering other plants and in dispersing themselves outside the immediate community. It is convenient, however, to treat these plant-engendered repercussions under succession (*see* next chapter) and to regard separately as introducing the (collective) biotic factor chiefly those animals which have a marked effect upon the community or any part thereof. These are largely external in origin. For practical purposes such factors manifest themselves in the totality of direct and indirect effects of animals on plants. It is, however, also convenient to include with the animals such plants as the lowly scavengers and agents of chemical change, and, in addition, those which are damagingly parasitic. Also mentionable here are ' insectivorous ' (carnivorous) plants, climbers, epiphytes, and mycorrhizas—which last, like Lichens and other symbioses, are concerned with the existence of more than one species at a point.

Apart from changes engendered by the main or subsidiary component plants themselves, organisms of many other sorts may affect a plant community in numerous and diverse ways. There are the soil Bacteria, causing all manner of important chemical changes; the Protozoa, which devour the Bacteria; the Earthworms which help disintegrate organic matter and aerate the soil; the Fungi which carry this breakdown further; the Snails which eat plants; and the browsing Mammals which may have the most profound effect—for example in turning forest into treeless pasture. Other important effects may be produced by Man and his domestic animals and fires, by the Beavers which fell trees and turn valleys into lakes, by the caterpillars and Locusts which may devastate whole areas, by the Insects and Birds which pollinate flowers and carry diseases, by the various animals which are so important in dispersing seeds and other disseminules, and by the parasitic Fungi, etc., which in extreme cases may even kill the dominant plant and change the whole aspect locally.

Parasitic lower plants (or sometimes invertebrate animals or vascular plants) are, as we have already seen, very important to crops whose mode of growth often encourages them or their ' carrying ' insects. Less known is their effect on ' natural ' vegetation; seemingly it tends to be less drastic as equilibria are approached, though we still do not know what organisms may be kept out by potential predators, or perhaps so weakened in competition as to fail to become established. Certainly the death-rate of seedlings tends to be very high. If we had not plentiful records and even recollections of the Sweet Chestnut forests of eastern North America, how could we know that they had been devastated by blight and that their absence nowadays is not due to some inimical climatic or other factor ? And is it not possible that some other plants, whose remains tell us that they once flourished in areas where they do not now grow, were ousted by parasites or other biotic impress rather than by the climatic vagaries which are indubitably the usual cause of such major distributional change or extinction ? The fan-shaped and 'feathery' Elms of New and Old England, respectively, which are such an important feature of the landscape of those two delightful parts of the world, are threatened by the so-called Dutch Elm disease which has already considerably changed the local environment in many areas. The White Pine Blister-rust is apt to kill the dominant species of some of the most widespread and important forests of North America. These are but a very few instances of devastating parasitic attacks on natural or semi-natural vegetation.

The small herbivores include Snails, Slugs, Locusts, and the larval stages of Insects such as caterpillars (the larvae of Butterflies and Moths). These often cause considerable local damage and even devastation—particularly to individual crops but sometimes to native species or whole tracts of vegetation.[1] But their exclusion even for experimental purposes is often difficult, taxing the ingenuity of the investigator. The effects of the smaller vertebrate animals, such as Voles and Mice, tend to be most conspicuous where Man has upset the balance of nature by destroying their enemies, such as Hawks and Foxes. Rabbits may be especially troublesome, often converting heaths or even forest into grassland by their gnawing and prevention of regeneration of such dominant trees as Beech on chalk in England. This is easily demonstrated experimentally by effectively wiring off areas (the bottom of the netting must be sunk in the ground) which soon come to exhibit the early stages of forest regeneration, whereas the pastured surrounding tracts remain close-cropped and grassy. Care must be taken also to exclude small Rodents and Birds which can destroy tree seedlings, for example, by nipping off the tender young shoots. It will be interesting in due course to observe the effect on the local vegetation of the virtual (if only temporary ?) extermination of Rabbits by myxomatosis in several European countries.

Of large browsing Mammals such as Buffaloes, which used to inhabit the great grassy plains, the natural populations are now widely destroyed. They were probably important in the maintenance of the grasslands, at least in the damper areas where trees are able to grow, but are nowadays largely replaced by domestic herds,

[1] It has even been suggested that a plague of caterpillars may have been a leading cause of the dying out of the ancient Norse settlements in West Greenland —by devouring the vegetation and hence starving the Sheep on which the Norsemen were largely dependent.

which have a similar effect upon the vegetation. Thus the forest generally tends to advance on the grassland with the removal of the heavy pasturing which ordinarily keeps it in check. Commonly, browsing cattle kill all the young trees, so preventing forest regeneration, and by their trampling, grazing, and other activities lead to the replacement of the characteristic forest-floor litter and vegetation by Grasses (Fig. 86). For the Grasses are hemicryptophytes, having their buds protected within (or at least lying at) the surface of the soil, and far from being killed by grazing, may actually be stimulated by it. Certainly they are encouraged by the removal of their broad-leafed and woody competitors, so that they will normally extend their area if the factor or factors suppressing these competitors are increased in intensity. Overgrazing may, however, lead to replacement of the Grasses by unpalatable herbs such as the weeds of open soils—perhaps followed by erosion if the rainfall is heavy, so that a barren waste may result (Fig. 87).

These last biotic effects are commonly regulated by Man but tend to be destructive, often getting far out of hand, as in bad cases of erosion. However, animals are still often helpful to vegetation—for example in distributing seeds, fruits, and spores, etc., in effecting pollination, in loosening or compacting soil as well as in manuring it, in trampling seeds into the soil (for example, of range Grasses) and favouring regeneration, in keeping down injurious Rodents etc. (in the case of carnivorous Mammals and predatory Birds), and, in the instance of Man, in such activities as irrigation, the construction of wind-breaks, soil-improvement and cultivation of many sorts, and the transplantation of useful plants and even the creation of new ones.

Human activity is, indeed, the outstanding biotic factor in the world today, at least if we include consideration of Man's domestic animals. Especially is Man the enemy of forests, whether he realizes it or not. His 'shifting cultivation' in the tropics is particularly damaging to vegetation, trees being girdled and the forest burnt, after which the accumulated fertility of the soil is exhausted in a very few years by cultivation; thereupon a move is made, similarly to cultivate and desecrate a fresh area. Consequently some secondary and usually inferior type of forest now replaces the original one over vast areas. In other cases still more devastating erosion may result from forest clearance as indicated above, from over-pasturing, or from 'exsiccation' leading to extension of desert areas. In such instances of penetrating and serious

A

B

Fig. 86.—Some important effects of grazing. A, Sugar Maple–Beech forest in central Indiana, showing plentiful regeneration and litter; B, similar forest type in same region but subjected to heavy grazing by cattle. In the latter instance Grasses and a few unpalatable herbs have taken the place of the usual plants and litter of the forest floor, while tree regeneration has been eliminated so that the forest's life is jeopardized. (Reprinted with permission from R. F. Daubenmire, *Plants and Environment*, copyright date 1947, John Wiley & Sons, Inc.)

disturbance, return to anything like the original vegetation is problematical. Appropriate measures following proper study are, however, nowadays leading to more and more effective conservation —for example of vegetation with the object of maintaining water supplies, of ranges against erosion, and of forests against fire. Elsewhere by irrigation or drainage, damming, building, persistent mowing, road and railway construction, mining and all manner of other enterprises, Man alters the water and other conditions over

FIG. 87.—Devastating results of overgrazing. Rill, gully, and sheet erosion on overgrazed slope in San Joaquin Valley, California. (Courtesy of U.S. Forest Service.)

vast areas—as he sometimes does the biological balance by the introduction or extermination of various animals and weeds or other plants.

In many regions fire is an important factor which, because it is nowadays usually caused and controlled by Man, seems best considered here. The effect is rather like grazing or cutting in that material is removed and if only small areas are affected they generally return to something like the former state—especially if the fire is a surface one that does not kill the larger thick-barked trees. However, big and severe ' crown ' fires may destroy the humus and disseminules as well as most or all plants, and result in a community of colonists followed by a distinct ' burn succession ' of vegetation.

Repeated burnings usually change the dominants and entire communities to ones which can regenerate after fires and, so to speak, withstand them. A few species, for example among the Grasses, seem actually to be stimulated by exposure to fire, while some Conifers, besides possessing thick and resistant bark, have cones which are opened by fire to liberate the ripe seeds earlier than would otherwise be the case.

Although it may leave survivors open to fungous and other attack through unhealed burn-scars, fire tends to favour the more resistant species by removing their less resistant competitors; it also alters many factors of the environment that favour some species rather than others. These principles apply to most types of vegetation, including forests, heaths, and grasslands. And whereas the general tendency of fire is towards vegetational degradation, the result is of course influenced by climate and human agency quite apart from the frequency and intensity of the burning. Indeed there are some circumstances in which firing will benefit desirable species and consequently may be intentionally practised by Man, as in pastures in many parts of the world where the old growth is burned off regularly.

In conclusion we should outline the principles of cultivation, through which Man now largely controls the plant life of much of the land surface of the world and of some shallow waters. Cultivation consists basically in preparing the surfaces of suitable substrata for the reception of seed (using this term in the widest sense), normally after the area has been cleared of any natural vegetation. Accordingly the early stages of growth of the crop are favoured by a minimum of competition, although this may in time develop with weeds or between the plants of the crop. Consequently effective cultivation will include proper control of weeds and also sowing at such intervals of space as will reduce the ill-effect of competition to a minimum. Effort may also have to be given to maintaining other conditions favouring the growth of the crop.

In order to continue satisfactory cropping year after year in the same area, it is commonly necessary to repeat for each crop such a 'tillage' operation as digging or ploughing, which turns over the soil and helps to maintain it in a suitable state. Lime or peat or clay may also be added to some soils to improve their texture. Often there has to be also some form of manuring, from animal or mineral or chemical sources, to maintain the fertility of the soil by replacing the necessary substances which are removed in cropping.

Moreover, in such arid lands as Mesopotamia, whence western civilization apparently sprang, successful cultivation also involves the artificial supply of water by irrigation. Conversely in many excessively humid or waterlogged areas, drainage is necessary before most crops can be sown.

As a particular crop will remove more and more of the same (often necessary) substances from the soil, and perhaps add more and more of the same undesirable ones, it is common either to leave land fallow (*i.e.* cropless) for one year out of every two to four, or else to practise a ' rotation ' of different crops grown successively on an area. In such cases more or different weeds will be fostered, with obvious plant-geographical implications. Indeed the practices of and incidental to cultivation, such as removing natural or semi-natural vegetation, establishment (however temporarily) of artificial vegetation in the form of crops, the introduction of weeds and diseases whether they are controlled or not, and the opening up of fresh areas for plant colonization and succession, have a continuous and very widespread effect on the distribution and luxuriance of flora and vegetation in the world, and, accordingly, on local landscape and amenities. With Man's predominant position in modern times, his biotic or, more precisely, ' anthropic ' influence has become widely overwhelming.

## Further Consideration

Three small introductory books, treating *inter alia* the factors of the environment, are :

Sir A. G. Tansley. *Introduction to Plant Ecology* (Allen & Unwin, London, pp. 1–260, 1947).

William Leach. *Plant Ecology*, fourth edition (Methuen, London, pp. vii + 106, 1956).

H. Drabble. *Plant Ecology* (Arnold, London, pp. 1–142, 1937).

Further useful treatments, which are mostly more detailed but by no means uniform in their groupings and terminology, include :

A. G. Tansley & T. F. Chipp. *Aims and Methods in the Study of Vegetation* (Crown Agents for the Colonies, London, pp. xvi + 383, 1926).

J. Braun-Blanquet. *Plant Sociology* (McGraw-Hill, New York & London, translated, etc., pp. xviii + 439, 1932).

J. E. Weaver & F. E. Clements. *Plant Ecology*, second edition (McGraw-Hill, New York & London, pp. xxii + 601, 1938).

R. F. Daubenmire. *Plants and Environment*, second edition (Wiley, New York, pp. xi + 422, 1959).

H. J. Oosting. *The Study of Plant Communities*, second edition (Freeman, San Francisco, Calif., pp. viii + 440, 1956).

W. B. McDougall. *Plant Ecology*, fourth edition (Kimpton, London, pp. 1–234, 1949).

Most of the above books give references to appropriate specialist ones, *e.g.* on soils.

The following may be found pertinent in particular connections

V. J. Chapman. *An Introduction to the Study of Algae* (Cambridge University Press, Cambridge, Eng., pp. x + 387, 1941). Deals *inter alia* with the conditions in fresh and salt waters—*see* also our Chapters XV and XVI.

V. J. Chapman. *Salt Marshes and Salt Deserts of the World* (Leonard Hill, London, pp. xvi + 392, 1960). Describes the often peculiar conditions introduced by excessive salinity.

H. U. Sverdrup, M. W. Johnson, & R. H. Fleming. *The Oceans: their Physics, Chemistry, and General Biology* (Prentice-Hall, New York, pp. x + 1087, 1946).

Useful recent works on the general ecology of plants and animals considered together include:

E. P. Odum. *Fundamentals of Ecology*, second edition (Saunders, Philadelphia & London, pp. xvii + 546, 1959).

George L. Clarke. *Elements of Ecology* (Wiley, New York, pp. xiv + 534, 1954).

A. M. Woodbury. *Principles of General Ecology* (Blakiston, New York & Toronto, pp. viii + 503, 1954).

## Chapter XI

# MAIN HABITATS, SUCCESSIONS, AND CLIMAXES

Whereas originally the term ' habitat ' referred simply to the place (locality or station) in which an organism or community lived, ecologists nowadays take it to mean rather the *kind of place*, involving the sum of effective conditions (operative influences) characterizing a particular type of area or inhabited by a particular species or community. Thus as a scientific term it involves all the conditions affecting an individual or community that are incidental to the place in which that individual or community lives, and we have to distinguish between the general habitat of a community and the partial habitats of its component species, etc. These partial habitats may vary greatly within the orbit of a single example of a single general habitat. Thus with a Beech forest growing on a calcareous soil under certain climatic conditions, there may be rather similar general factors of soil and climate under which the dominant trees flourish in different spots within the same area or even in different areas in the same region. Very different may be, for example, the ' microhabitats ' of Mosses or Algae growing on their boles or branches, and of herbs upon the forest floor. In the present treatment of the main different types of plant habitats that are discernible, we shall have to confine ourselves largely to general terms in showing how the factors of the environment dealt with in the last chapter constitute the habitats of the various types of vegetation to be treated in the next five chapters.

The habitat is thus made up of the many and various environmental factors having any kind of influence upon life within it, and themselves interacting complicatedly. The sum of effective ecological conditions has many widely different manifestations which range for instance from dry land to open water : and indeed water conditions seem to provide the best criterion for the primary subdivision of habitats. But even as most biological pigeon-holing is notoriously imprecise, involving many an arbitrary cut-off across a more or less complete line of gradation, so is it with any of the main types of habitat that seem recognizable as entities. Within each of these categories are almost endless variations : for practically any change of one or more of the various ecological factors dealt with in the last chapter can cause marked variation in the habitat—leading in turn to differences in the vegetation and, incidentally, often adding to the vast assemblage of habitats on the face of the earth or in salt or fresh waters. The significance of landforms is dealt with in Ch. xvii.

Perhaps the usual identity of vegetation with habitat, and the ease with which the former is classified at least into such broad categories as forest, scrub, grassland, etc., is in itself a reason why no satisfactory over-all classification or even inventory of habitats is available. For our present purposes, however, we must attempt some general enumeration of the main types of habitat. But owing to the diversity and variability of the factors involved, their numerous possible combinations, and the frequent overlapping, a clear and unequivocal delimitation of habitats according to operative factors is scarcely attainable. Except for broad outlines, such as those given next below, we have to go to the plant communities and their component species to obtain satisfactory criteria, and then find ourselves dealing with vegetation rather than with the habitats which support it.

## Terrestrial Habitats

Even as these are separated from the other main category, aquatic habitats, by water conditions, so are their main subdivisions often dependent upon the relative availability of water locally. Leaving aside as largely aquatic the sea- and lake-marginal ones whose inhabitants all spend at least a substantial part of their time more than half submerged, we nevertheless have the marginal habitats of the sea-shore that are characterized by salt spray or occasional inundation, and of lakesides and streams where the bed is so shallow and sheltered that ' reed-swamp ' types can grow up in such a manner that most of their bodies are aerial. In addition there are the various tropical swamps and mangroves. Also abundantly supplied with water (but in these cases not normally covered by it) are silty marshes (whether salt or otherwise), base-rich fens, acidic bogs, and the gently sloping and usually mossy ' mires ' through which water percolates.

Of less aqueous land habitats there are many, often of very various types. Beginning with the ones which are reasonably moist and flat or nearly so, we may mention those of a wide range of soils in regions favourable for cultivation, and which still comprise habitats even when they are prepared for, and further altered by, various forms of husbandry. Here all manner of changes in climatic and edaphic conditions from place to place give rise to a great variety of different habitats—usually supporting different types of forest if undisturbed, or of arable or pasture land if used for agriculture. Moreover, in these agriculturally favourable regions more than most others, Man is constantly changing old habitats or opening up new ones. There is no need to dwell upon examples, which are familiar in almost all areas ranging from the Subarctic to the tropics. With drastic reduction in rainfall, the resulting habitats favour diverse forms of 'parkland', scrub, heath, or grassland vegetation.

In truly arctic regions various types of treeless 'tundra' and 'barrens' take the place of forests, etc., in most of the flatter areas, with a tendency for less and less of the vegetation to be continuous over the surface (*i.e.* 'closed') as we go farther north. The growing-season is greatly reduced and frost-heaving and allied influences are active and, frequently, disruptive. These conditions are partly, but by no means wholly, simulated on mountains elsewhere—in general, at higher and higher levels as we travel towards the Equator—so that even in the tropics we may get, at very high altitudes, whole series of habitats and attendant communities reminiscent of those of the Arctic (*cf.* Fig. 137, B, and Fig. 138).

Concavities and convexities in the general surface of the earth may lead to all manner of local variations—including marked changes in water conditions—resulting in what amounts to a wide range of different habitats. So may local cliffs and talus or gravel slides or wave-washed banks, blow-out or wash-out or other erosion effects, and many other types of surface phenomena, profoundly affect conditions locally. In arctic and alpine regions, features leading to deep drifting of snow in winter (*see* Chapter XIII) are also very important in changing local conditions and resulting in whole series of special habitats. Here the dynamic or other inimical forces of nature may prevent vegetation from taking a hold and changing the habitat and whole aspect as it usually does elsewhere. In general, however, vegetation rings many changes before coming to a state of relative equilibrium with the environment, by which time various factors of the habitat have usually become altered quite drastically. The connection with landscapes is treated in Chapter XVII. Change in habitat conditions through the activity of vegetation is particularly marked in forested areas; but it may also be considerable where the vegetation is less prolific, and even where this is entirely dwarfed. It tends to be least where the vegetation forms least of a 'show', and especially where plants fail to stabilize the surface, as in the case of many dunes and coastal or desert or high-arctic areas. Plants are again relatively impotent in places of drastic topography and consequently strong geodynamic influences and recurrent catastrophe, for here the physical forces of nature usually rule, rather than the vegetation, and our recognition tends to be of habitats rather than of their inhabitants.

Deserts are areas where the water conditions are too unfavourable (in the sense that the drought is lastingly too severe) to allow the support of any extensive continuous development even of short Grasses or scrub. They cover wide areas of flattish or other topography and in a sense are simulated on a small scale by areas of porous sand, gravel, shingle, or rock, where arid conditions may prevail even in regions of plentiful precipitation. The so-called cold deserts are the high-polar and high-alpine regions where frozen conditions make water unavailable to plants during most of the year. Even where the precipitation is extremely small in these rigorous regions, as in some high-arctic areas, there is, however, usually plentiful water available from melting snow for fair plant growth in favourable situations, at least early in the growing-season; moreover there is normally frozen ground-water not far below the surface, so the regional appellation of 'desert' seems inappropriate.

In passing, mention should also be made of the so-called 'aeroplankton', consisting of spores, etc., which float freely and unharmed in the air (although they can scarcely be considered as normally living thus), of the microscopic 'cryoplankton', which really live in and on the surface layers of snow or ice (*see* Chapter XV), and of the 'edaphon', the flora and fauna of the soil, which actually forms a special habitat for numerous recognized soil organisms.

## Aquatic Habitats

Even when we divide these into the two main groups of saline and freshwater habitats, there are left intermediate 'brackish' ones which seem best considered with salt waters. The degree of salinity can, and frequently does, greatly affect the habitat and attendant community. Freshwater habitats, apart from the marginal ones already considered, comprise those of lakes, tarns, and ponds where the waters are relatively static, and those of rivers and streams where they are more or less dynamic. But streams can be reduced to chains of pools in dry weather, and lakes can have considerable convection and wind-engendered currents as well as run-off streams, so that here again any distinction is not wholly valid. Major variations in salinity found in different seas, estuaries, salt-lakes, etc., and the light, temperature, tranquillity or shelter from disturbance, size and depth of the body of water, possibility of attachment, and content of dissolved substances, are all important factors leading to the existence of whole series of different aquatic habitats. Further variable factors may be the ' reaction ' (acidity, neutrality, or basicity), aeration, and seasonal or tidal or other changes in the level of the surface.

Let us briefly consider examples of these and some other factors as they may affect aquatic habitats : further details are given in Chapters XV and XVI. Light, being essential for photosynthesis, severely limits (to those depths to which a sufficiency penetrates) the possibilities for normal plant development, while towards the lower limit at which photosynthesis is possible, this vital function is insufficiently active to sustain life—unless it be of specially adapted organisms. Some Red Algae seem to be so adapted, for they can grow at depths of nearly 200 metres in exceptionally clear seas, while some phytoplanktonic organisms have been dredged from, and can apparently live at, fully 200 metres. The larger Brown Algae, on the other hand, do not seem to be able to grow at any such depths, while vascular plants in fresh water usually extend no deeper than 10 metres even in the clearest lakes, and in shallower water form zones correlated with their light requirements. However, in the Mediterranean Sea one flowering plant, *Posidonia*, is reported to extend down to depths of 80 or even 100 metres.

Of the other factors, temperature differences frequently have much the same effect in aquatic as in aerial habitats, although major bodies of water will act as reservoirs militating against rapid changes in temperature. Consequently, conditions in water tend to remain more ' even ' than in the air, with the result that aquatic organisms and communities are often surprisingly widespread. Shelter from wave or ice action, and tranquillity from currents and tides, is another important factor profoundly affecting the habitat and attendant vegetation, macroscopic (*i.e.* visible to the naked eye, as opposed to microscopic) plants often being limited to sheltered bays, etc. This is often bound up with the size and depth of the body of water, on which convection and wind-engendered or other currents frequently depend, as does the degree (if any) of freezing. But such matters of size, depth, and shelter also introduce factors of their own, including light and temperature variations and the question of whether rooted or otherwise attached plants can grow up sufficiently to perform all their vital functions. This also depends upon the possibility of rooting or other attachment, which is usually dependent upon a suitable ' bed ' that of course varies for different types of plants.

As regards the content of dissolved substances, this can range from ' ocean ' or even more extreme salinity down to varying degrees

FIG. 88.—Margin of tropical oligotrophic lake, with steep rocky sides and rapidly deepening water, supporting few larger plants. The hill-top vegetation is a semi-arid savanna with prominent Acacias. Lake Tanganyika, E. Africa. (Phot. R. Ross.)

in ' fresh ' water. Often in bodies of fresh water the acidity and especially the nutritive salt content are of key significance for the development of planktonic communities—at least, within particular temperature ranges. In this connection it is often useful to distinguish three types of such bodies, of which the first may give rise to the others : (1) *oligotrophic*, of waters poor in dissolved minerals, typically with Desmids abundant but supporting at most a narrow zone of rooted higher plants because of a hard rocky bottom and rapidly deepening water (Fig. 88) ; (2) *dystrophic*, with waters also poor in nutrients but rich in humus and acidic in reaction, often coloured, containing Desmids and Bog-mosses ; and (3) *eutrophic*, distinguished quantitatively from the oligotrophic type in being usually poorer in the numbers of species but richer in individuals and poor in humus though commonly silted and shallow. The eutrophic type is also relatively rich in combined nitrogen, phosphorus, and often calcium, typically contains plentiful Blue-green Algae, and has a broad zone of rooted Pondweeds, etc., and a surrounding one of luxuriant reed-swamp (*cf.* Fig. 89).

FIG. 89.—Lake of eutrophic type near Prout's Neck, Maine. It is silted and shallow, with floating-leaf plants outside the broad marginal reed-swamp dominated by tall Cattails.

In addition, the reaction (or ' pH level ', whether acidic or basic, of a body of water is commonly important to many organisms) while lack of oxygen may be a limiting factor deep down in sheltered situations. Also often limiting are seasonal and other changes of level in shallow places. Any substantial tidal activities are especially significant, as may be the speed and flow of currents and the presence and particular powers of various living organisms.

Even as the zoned vegetation of sea-shores indicates the existence of different habitats at different levels, *e.g.* above and below normal low-tide mark, so do zones exist at different depths around the margins of deep lakes. Moreover, seas (such as the Sargasso) and especially lakes of warm regions, may bear extensive macroscopic floating vegetation. Yet, in major bodies of water, far more extensively occupied plant habitats are usually provided by the surface waters where sufficient light penetrates for photosynthesis. Here develop various planktonic communities of free-floating or swimming organisms, the vast majority of which are microscopic. The habitat, and consequently the community, may vary greatly with climatic factors and the presence of solutes and suspensions in the water, the whole being often subject to marked seasonal fluctuations including exhaustion of nutrients when the population is around its ' peak '. In the deeper layers of water and on deep ocean or lake floors where light does not penetrate, there are still habitats—especially for saprophytic plants living on the ' rain ' of sinking bodies. Indeed it is here that Bacteria are often especially numerous.

## Microhabitats

We have seen that the environmental and internal factors of living organisms have intricate and highly complex interrelationships, belonging as they do to a plethora of variables and potentialities that may be set in motion by all manner of ' master ' forces. Yet it is only the ' thin shell ' of environment directly impinging on, or immediately adjacent to, the organism that is of primary causal significance to it. So we get what in effect are ' partial habitats ' (microhabitats), for example in areas of drastic relief or uneven ground, or in different situations in a forest or other gross and complex community. Consequently it is rare for the measurements recorded by meteorological instruments to be actually those of the conditions of the microhabitat affecting the growing plant or, more precisely, the growing *part* of the plant.

Microclimates are really the ultimate multiple expression of the local climatic effect which is so commonly and variously engendered by physiographic change, and microhabitats are their environmental result, though they may often be based on edaphic or other variations. Very commonly one factor will compensate for another so far as some plants are concerned, but not in a manner satisfactory to the requirements of other plants—so leading to a jumbling of local communities—and this effect may be extended to microhabitats. Moreover, an alteration in one factor may initiate whole series of adjustments in others, often having far-reaching consequences. Especially are such effects apt to be complex when concerned with groups of factors that are closely related to one another—such as light, heat, and moisture relations, which vary simultaneously with every change in the intensity of insolation.

In such circumstances it is difficult or sometimes impossible to segregate individual factors experimentally. Instead of physical apparatus we may use ' phytometers ', which are standard plants or clumps of vegetation that have the advantage of integrating all effective factors of the environment and expressing the result in their own responses. They react only to changes that matter to the plant or plants, whose protoplasm has the power of making adjustments. But much as species are usually composed of more or less numerous biotypes, so may general habitats or even single examples of them be made up of *biotopes*, which are the ultimate expression of environmental variation, being defined as the smallest natural area of space that is characterized by a particular environment. The biotope (or ' ecological niche ' of some authors) is thus the primary ' topographic ' unit used in habitat classification. The community of forms inhabiting it is termed a *biocoenosis*, and the biotopes having similar characters are united into larger divisions called *biochores*. Many of these are apt to be represented in any small area, so whole series of phytometers, covering at least the different microclimates, may be necessary to determine the impress of even a single example of a general habitat ; moreover they should be accompanied by batteries of instruments adequate for the establishment of quantitative relationships between stimulus and response.

In addition, matters can change rapidly with time. Thus even under a canopy of vegetation, such items as the movement of leaves by the wind, the changing angle of the sun, and various effects of weather and season, cause variations in the movement of shadows and sun-flecks across the ground. This in turn causes drastic changes in the amount of light-energy received at a given point—on which, as we have already seen, much else may depend. Altogether it is not surprising that experimental ecology has become an exacting (though scarcely exact) science. A saving grace is the fact that, apart from the grosser direct effects of animals and drastic physical agents, the actual effects of environmental factors upon plants are resolvable into a few physical and chemical processes. Examples are those which underlie the influence of light on photosynthesis and growth, the effect of temperature on chemical changes in the plant body, the evaporating power of the air on the water in the plant, and the effect of the soil solution on the absorbing organs and other parts of the plant.

Drastic microhabitat development may take place at different levels or other situations in a forest, or on different sides of a hillock or even pebble. Thus the conditions under which an Alga or Moss lives on the bole of a tree are substantially different from those of an epiphyte in a crutch or on a branch high up in the crown, or of course from those of a herb on the sheltered forest floor. And again, the shelter from wind and sun given by even a minor projection from the ground, may enable a delicate plant or small community to grow there which could not exist in the exposed surrounding areas. The effect may even extend to the soils and their biota, and affect the plant habitat through them. Especially striking are the differences of temperature (and consequently of important dependent factors) on the north- and south-facing sides of tussocks at high latitudes in summer, which may vary by more than 20° C. within a few centimetres, and allow active growth to take place in one spot when adjacent areas are frozen solid. Such effects may be the key not only to the micro-distributions of plants but also to their ranges over wide areas. Consequently it is important that we recognize the concept of microhabitat, for it is a very real and indeed fundamental one.

Finally it should be recalled that not only different (phylogenetic) strains and even differently treated individuals may respond differently to microhabitat or other vagaries, but that different stages in the (ontogenetic) development of an individual may have critically different reactions, young seedlings being in general relatively feeble. Similarly, the tender young parts of older plants often differ greatly, in their resistance, from the remaining portions of the same plants—hence the familiar ' killing back ' of shoots by frosts in temperate regions, the rest of the plant being commonly unharmed.

## Main Successions

When dealing in the last chapter with environmental factors, we referred briefly to the competitive and other ' internal ' ones engendered by the plants themselves. Thus weeds compete for space and nutrients, some of those introduced to inhabited regions creating major nuisances by choking waterways, destroying the habitats of wildlife, or colonizing and rendering practically useless whole areas of agricultural land. The shade cast by dominant species, and the shelter they give, affect all the plants within the community ; also affected are the local atmospheric humidity and, often, soil structure and development as well as composition.

It is a commonplace that units of vegetation, left to themselves, tend to change in a particular direction—usually from less complex communities of small plants to more complex ones dominated by larger plants of higher life-form (or, at all events, greater competition-impress). The change is continuous, recognizable ' stages ' being mere nodes of vegetational expression. Such is *succession*, the developmental series of communities constituting a *sere* and leading up to a state of relative stability and permanence known as the *climax*. It should, however, here be admitted that not all ecologists accept the idea that vegetation can be widely interpreted in terms of development and equilibrium, while some, such as Professor Hugh M. Raup (*in litt.*), seem to doubt the validity of some of the basic assumptions involved—at least for those parts of the world in which they have themselves worked. Certainly, many of the beliefs involved are mere presumptions, or true only in some degree : thus successions may proceed only in relation to preceding and following stages, and climaxes are only *relatively* stable. This is often expressed by saying they are in ' dynamic equilibrium '. Nor is it for us to write into Nature's book meanings which she does not intend, or to attempt to inculcate for our own convenience an orderliness of pattern which does not exist. But if we deny the existence of seres and climaxes, we do away with two of the most stimulating concepts and useful tools of our trade, and so with this reservation it seems best to proceed to use them. In doing so we ought also to bear in mind that many of the principles with which we are concerned have emerged from work carried out in temperate regions, and that in the Arctic (for example owing to frost action) and in the tropics (where there is often no clear dominance) things may be very different.

We shall deal a little later with the typical stages of some characteristic seres, and, in the next section, with the main types of climax. With the reservations expressed in the last paragraph, some understanding of these and allied concepts seems essential for an appreciation of the mosaic which is vegetation, and whose study, at least in terms of distribution, is the mainstay of modern plant geography. But first we should outline the component (often more or less continuous) actions of a sere, which normally may be considered as follows : (1) *nudation* (the production of a bare area) is the initial prerequisite, whether it be by emergence or submergence, glacial recession, erosion, deposit, climatic change, or biotic agency. Thereafter follow (2) *plant immigration* (including initial colonization) ; (3) *ecesis* (successful establishment) ; (4) *aggregation of germules* to form families (of a single species) or colonies (of two or more species); (5) *competition* (virtually the struggle for existence) among the colonists, particularly for space, light, water, and nutrients; (6) *invasion* by other plants, usually from adjacent areas; (7) *reaction*, which essentially comprises the changes wrought in habitat conditions by the plants themselves (*e.g.* in soil formation); (8) *coaction*, the influence of organisms upon each other; (9) *stabilization*, which of course is only relative, change being inevitable in all living organisms and aggregates thereof; and (10) *attainment of a climax*, by which time competition has generally become so intense that further invasion is problematical unless the community is drastically disturbed.

The complete sere just indicated is a *primary sere* (prisere), beginning on a bare substratum without organic material. The chief types of primary seres are those initiated (1) in fresh water (hydroseres), from which may be distinquished 'haloseres' beginning in saline water; (2) on damp aerial surfaces such as alluvial mud (mesoseres); and (3) on dry materials (xeroseres), of which outstanding examples are those starting on bare rock (lithoseres) and on dry sand (psammoseres). *Secondary seres* (subseres) are merely partial, beginning after the succession has been stopped, and thus not going back to a purely inorganic substratum unaffected by plants. They are distinguished as 'hydrarch', 'mesarch', or 'xerarch', according to whether their initiation is under damp, median, or dry conditions, respectively.

The broad tendency of succession is from simplicity to complexity of organization, and from dominance by lower to higher life-forms which make more and more exacting demands on the habitat. Yet sometimes we see 'retrogression' to dominance by a lower life-form, for example when the habitat undergoes a change to less favourable water conditions. An incidental change in normal successions is from open to closed conditions, involving also an increase in the intensity of competition and marked alteration of local climatic and edaphic factors such as atmospheric humidity, wind, and the humous content of the soil. Such 'reactions' are reciprocal, the plants affecting the habitat, which in turn affects the plants; indeed, many of the higher life-forms only enter when the ground has been suitably 'prepared' for them by the dominants of earlier stages, which in turn they ruthlessly overshadow and frequently oust.

We will now outline examples of the main types of priseres as postulated for temperate forested regions; although the tendencies are generally similar, the outcome is apt to be different in polar and tropical regions, seres in the former being often much mixed and disturbed, and, in the latter, commonly retarded by lack of humus accumulation. These items are explained in the appropriate chapters.

In temperate regions the typical hydrosere, after various non-essential (proseral) stages of plankton, etc., starts in bodies of fresh water whose beds where suitable are colonized by attached or other benthic (*i.e.* bottom) aquatic vascular plants and Mosses besides Algae as deep down as light conditions allow. These plants often form dense mats that collect silt and humus, there being frequently insufficient oxygen for rapid decay. The bed is thus built up gradually until, at a depth of some 1 to 3 metres, it can be invaded by floating-leaf types such as Water-lilies (*Nymphaea* spp.) or certain Pondweeds (*Potamogeton* spp.), which tend to shade out the submerged plants. The long stalks of these floating-leaf plants trap silt and their coarse bodies after death become deposited as, ultimately, humus—so that the bed is built up with relative rapidity until the water is shallow enough for swamp plants to enter the community. These typically form a reed-swamp whose dominants are only partly submerged, building up the beds quickly and ousting the previous types. As the level continues to rise owing to the deposition of humus, etc., fully terrestrial invaders enter to characterize the sedge-meadow stage, the reed-swamp plants disappearing in due course as conditions are rendered unsuitable for them. With further rising in level of the soil surface and relative depression of the water-table, shrubs and ultimately trees enter and in time give rise to a hygrophytic woodland. The Alders, Poplars, Willows, etc., which commonly constitute this, will, in their turn, shade out the lower types and prepare for the climax forest which requires drier and more favourable soil conditions. Fig. 90 gives a diagrammatic representation of the stages of a hydrosere in section, a typical example, extending from the floating-leaf stage, having been shown in Fig. 89,[1] while Fig. 91 continues this to the sedge-meadow and early timbered stages. A more detailed account of the early stages of some hydroseres is given in Chapter XV.

As a characteristic xerosere we will take a lithosere initiated on bare rock. Such surfaces are apt to be extremely difficult to colonize

[1] This was of eutrophic (' good foods ') type, an example of the oligotropic (' few foods ', geologically young) type, which may be expected in time to develop into a eutrophic lake, being shown in Fig. 88.

and consequently may long remain uninvaded unless it be by pro-seral colonies of Bacteria, Blue-green Algae, etc. In time, however, the extreme exposure and general lack of water and nutrients are usually overcome by crustaceous Lichens or other hardy cryptogams as the first essential stage. They spread over the surface, helping the weathering forces of nature by corrosively or otherwise ' eating into ' the rock and adding plant material to form something of a *nidus* (nest) for ecesis of foliose Lichens, etc. These, attached at

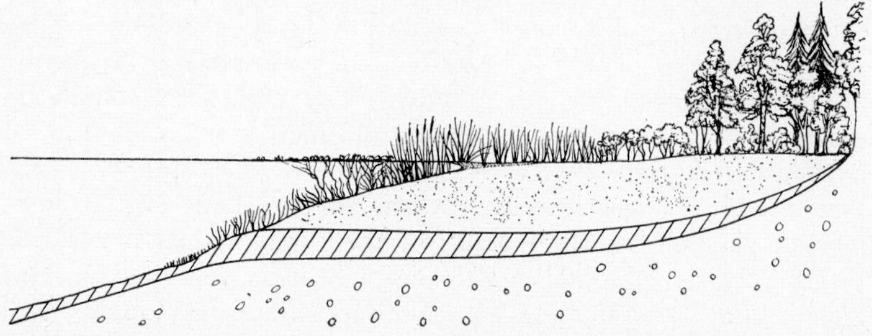

FIG. 90.—Diagram illustrating stages of hydrosere with deposition of peat. The usual stages are discernible on the gently-sloping shore, being, from left to right, submerged benthic, floating-leaf, reed-swamp, sedge-meadow (fen), hygrophytic scrub, hygrophytic forest, and finally climax forest.

FIG. 91.—Sedge-meadow stage of hydrosere colonized by some hygrophytic shrubs and, on right, trees, near Prout's Neck, Maine. An extensive reed-swamp is visible in the middle-distance, surrounding the lake shown in Fig. 89.

a single point, overshadow the crustaceous types, holding water and fragments more effectively than their predecessors, and preparing the way for the moss stage whose components usually start entering as soon as soil particles accumulate in crevices and depressions. Such hardy Mosses are able to withstand prolonged desiccation and sometimes pioneer on uncolonized rock surfaces, making the Lichens unnecessary and 'proseral'. The Mosses usually enter as spores, and, among their closely aggregated axes and often densely matted rhizoids, young soil accumulates rapidly. Sometimes in the larger cushions this accumulation becomes quite thick (Fig. 92), forming

FIG. 92.—Telescoped stages of xerosere in Norwegian Lapland. Gnarled specimens of the dominant Scots Pine have managed to grow in crevices of the rock whose surface is often still colonized by crustaceous Lichens, although in other places cushions of Mosses or ground-shrubs have accumulated some soil.

fine nests for the colonization and establishment of herbs—especially annuals of xerophytic tendency. These contribute further to the humus accumulation and soil-building, and are typically followed by more exacting biennials and herbaceous perennials, which in their turn replace members of former stages while accelerating the further processes of succession. Often more important than colonization of the open rock surfaces is extension from crevices, at which Mosses and ground-shrubs are particularly adept. In time taller woody plants enter, constituting a less enduring stage that tends to overtop and oust the herbs but meanwhile to improve the soil and often conserve moisture, so that, in due course, forest and ultimately some kind of climax can develop (*see* below).

The psammosere usually proceeds much more quickly than the lithosere, the initial problem being the ' binding ' of the surface sand. This is often accomplished by coarse Grasses or other ' advanced ' types (Fig. 93), while on gravel slides and talus slopes the pioneers may be coarse herbs or even woody plants, and succession still more rapid provided a reasonable degree of stability can be attained. Often, and especially on damp substrata that are immediately suitable

FIG. 93.—Psammosere at Prout's Neck, Maine, showing Marram Grass (*Ammophila arenaria*) binding sand above high-tide mark. Some stabilized dunes and coniferous forest are seen behind.

for colonization by advanced types, the phases of succession may be telescoped more or less completely ; but still the general tendency is evident.

It may be noted that in these seres there is a general convergence of water conditions, the hydrosere becoming progressively drier and the xerosere progressively moister—until a mean is reached that in any given climatic region is approximately the same in the two cases. Typically this mean is inhabited by mesophytes and is said to be ' mesic ', though relatively xeric (dry) and hydric (damp) exceptions exist. It has been suggested that ultimately this mean should be the same under particular climatic conditions whatever the initial situation, but although this idea may be theoretically attractive it is evident that, at least in the present state of the world, different areas in the same climatic belt can support widely different climaxes.

## Main Climaxes

Although competition is the chief key to succession, the final outcome of this latter lies in the population best fitted (among those naturally attainable locally) to take advantage of the relatively mesic conditions brought about by past reactions. This population is the ' climax ' (often more cautiously termed ' climax type ', and compare the reservation on page 323) and, being in close harmony with an essentially stable environment, is more or less permanent. Though by no means invariable in time and space, it shows a regularity of physiognomy and floristic composition that is usually lacking in successional stages. Thus in over-all form it persists as long as the climate remains unchanged—provided no new dominant enters or retrogressive change sets in, *e.g.* through impoverishment of the soil or accumulation of toxic substances. Dominance is due primarily to control of some ' key ' factor or factors of the environment, the dominant or co-dominants making of all plants present the greatest demands on the habitat, and normally when the climax is reached excluding invasion by any serious rival. Fluctuations in the community thereafter tend to be minor in the absence of any forceful change.

The climax is thus an equilibrated state of community composition and productivity, that is adapted to maximum utilization of local resources by plants and, normally, animals. This maximum utilization is sustained, the climax being self-maintaining, and its efficiency is determined by the particular habitat as well as by the average climax population, which in turn is determined by migrational possibilities on one hand and, on the other, by all the factors that make up the mature ecosystem. It is evident, however, that, with changes in the environment, plant populations change from one type of area to the next, the vegetation varying largely according to local habitat. That was already indicated above. Consequently, climax and allied vegetation forms a pattern of communities varying with, and largely corresponding to, the pattern of environmental differences and gradients.

In a general way climate determines the dominants and associates that can be present, and their life-form in turn characterizes the climax. This is really the mature stage of vegetation living in a state of more or less dynamic equilibrium with the local environment, though minor adjustments go on all the time. For life, as we have seen, can never be static, and the climax is only relatively so when compared with other stages of the succession. So besides the obvious differences in space, which are often attributable to diversification of the habitat, the climax inevitably shows some variation with time, its state remaining dynamic to that extent. This variation may be no more than that which results from the death and decay of individuals especially of the dominant species—the disappearance of a big tree, for example, leaving a gaping hole in the forest canopy—followed by replenishment. If, on the other hand, there is a progressive change, then we will have a continuing succession.

The climax must at least be sufficiently stable and lasting to outlive the life-span of the dominant species. It commonly consists of patches or phases of different but related composition. However, these are normally at most representative of cyclic changes comprising upgrade and downgrade parts that nevertheless return to much the same climax type. If they do not do so, then a succession or retrogression must be involved, examples of the latter being the colonization of eroded heaths by Lichens and of coniferous forests by Bog-mosses. It is supposed by some that even these changes represent parts of a long-term cycle, but for such generalization the evidence seems inconclusive. We cannot wait long enough to see the true situation, which might take millennia to emerge!

In nature we expect to see some kind of 'regional' or 'prevailing' climax developed in local-climatically suitable situations at least on undisturbed tracts of the better soils of a region. But besides the complications already mentioned, there may be more important local variations of soil, biota, treatment, and so forth, causing the sere to be arrested, after being deflected, at some stage before the climax, and so constituting a *subclimax*. This is an imperfect stage in which the dominants are of lower life-form or competition-impress than those of the climax, the vegetation being 'held back' by artificial or natural causes other than the climate. For the immediate site or ecological peculiarity may largely determine the actual growth. Examples are the subclimaxes due to such treatments as persistent burning or grazing (often called *disclimaxes*, being due to disturbance, or *plagioclimaxes*, owing to the deflection involved), or to marked differences in the rocky or other substratum. This last instance may if desired be termed an 'edaphic climax' by those who doubt whether it will ever attain (or even if there is such a thing as) a 'regional climatic climax'. Similarly the biotically engendered disclimaxes may be termed 'biotic climaxes', and those due to topographic features 'physiographic climaxes'. However, with removal of such a 'master factor' as burning or grazing, the succession usually returns gradually to the autogenic main sere—at all events approximately. And then there are instances in which an apparent climax constitutes in reality a *preclimax* in that its dominant or co-dominants are replaceable by one stage of others more advanced in life-form or competition-impress. This is really only a final type of *sereclimax*, or community arrested and held at some relatively early stage, and comprising the other form of subclimax with seral relationships simpler than the disclimax. Again by some authorities the term preclimax is used for one type of what we have here called subclimax, namely that developing under locally unfavourable conditions. Finally there is the *postclimax*, of vegetation more advanced than that of surrounding climax tracts, due to locally more favourable conditions obtaining in its limited area. This should be distinguished from the *relict* community or fragment of a community that has survived some important change, whether this was towards the improvement or detriment of the general environment.

Whether or not we believe in the 'monoclimax' hypothesis of a full regional climatic climax as not only the highest type which can exist in a given climate but also as the one which will ultimately develop more or less throughout the land area of that climate, the concept has its attractions and adherents. It appears, however, that soil (including water) and other conditions often prevent locally such 'regional' development more or less permanently, and certainly no observer can wait to the end of the geological age and consequent termination of such an 'experiment'. Even if a general regional climatic climax were developed, who is to say that, for example, subsequent leaching or other effects might not lead to differential retrogression. Consequently it seems best to admit the likelihood, in any one region, of several different climax communities as representing what may then be termed a 'polyclimax'. Even examples of the components of such a regional mosaic themselves frequently vary from spot to spot as well as with time, for example as individuals in the dominant layer come and go and all manner of very local fragmentary seres are engendered; indeed such variations can be so endless and perplexing that some ecologists, as has already been stated, doubt the validity of the very concept of climax, let alone its regional expression.

What may well be the true situation is expressed by Professor H. J. Oosting, in the work cited at the end of the last chapter, as follows:

> 'The Clementsian interpretation postulates that a climatic region has but one potential climax; the most mesophytic community that the climate can support. It will be found on sites with average or intermediate environmental conditions, particularly regarding moisture relations . . . Given sufficient time, with accompanying stability of climate and land surfaces, succession will have proceeded to such terminal, relatively mesophytic communities over much of the area. The stands will not be identical, yet they will have such a high degree of similarity that they are obviously related . . . The concept of a regional or climatically controlled climax necessarily includes recognition of the convergence of successional trends toward a similar end. In its simplest statement, it implies that any habitat in a region, given enough time, could ultimately support a community representative of the formation. From this statement it might be inferred that a region of fairly uniform climate would eventually have a continuous and equally uniform vegetational cover throughout. Actually, this is never true . . . Locally, there are always edaphic or physiographic situations whose complex of environmental factors differ to such a marked degree from those of the general climate that they cannot support the regional vegetation type and probably never will . . . Monoclimax theory does not ignore these extreme situations but rather emphasizes that they are to be expected.'

In any case the main, apparently climax, vegetational types of the world are regional and climatic to the extent that they tend to recur on favourable soils more or less throughout a region of particular climate; they are also apt to have their counterparts in regions of different climate. These main types of vegetation are characterized by the life-form of the dominant or co-dominants and include: (1) tropical rain forests, the most luxuriant vegetation of all; (2) tropical forest with a seasonal rhythm, due for example to monsoons; (3) sclerophyllous forest, developed where there is a hot dry season and a cooler moist one, often merging into various parklands and savannas, which appear to belong rather with grasslands; (4) warm-temperate rain forests, of evergreens, where there are few if any frosts; (5) deciduous summer forest, with dominants losing their leaves in winter; (6) northern coniferous forests, dominated mostly by evergreens; (7) heath, dominated by members of the Heath family or heath-like plants such as Crowberry; (8) tundra, the very variable but more or less continuous, treeless vegetation typical of many arctic and alpine regions ; (9) discontinuous 'fell-fields' and sparser 'barrens', etc., characterizing still more frigid regions ; (10) grassland, of various types dominated by Grasses and grass-like plants such as Sedges, often with scattered trees or shrubs forming a savanna ; (11) semi-desert scrub ; (12) desert, with scanty but characteristic vegetation ; (13) mangrove ; (14) salt-marsh, which like some mangrove seems capable of persisting in the absence of disturbance ; (15) benthos, of submerged bottom aquatics ; (16) plankton of free-floating Algae, etc., including those of snow and ice ; and (17) the edaphon or soil communities including numerous Algae, Fungi, and Bacteria. Most of these are major, climatically determined vegetation-types (*formations*) of each of which various different 'aspects' exist. Several are, however, apt to be seral in some instances—as are, of course, the many recognized stages in successions, such as the moss stage in the lithosere and the reed-swamp and bog or fen stages in the hydrosere. But strictly speaking a formation should represent the local climax. Examples of most of the above types and of some other (usually seral) ones, such as various swamps, marshes, cultivated fields, and tracts of weeds etc., are described (and often illustrated) in the next five chapters, which deal with the outstanding vegetational features of the world.

Before describing the vegetational types of different regions and media, we must outline, in descending order of ecological status, the main classificatory units (eca) of vegetation which it seems practicable to recognize :

(1) *Formations.* These are the great climatic units or regional climaxes such as desert, semi-desert scrub, tundra, deciduous forest, coniferous forest, broad-leafed evergreen forest, and some others, such as many heaths and grasslands which are determined particularly by edaphic or biotic conditions but are so distinctive as to rank as formations. Each formation usually covers a wide area involving various conditions and so consists of more or less numerous

(2) *Associations.* These are climax units dominated by normally more than one species having the life-form characterizing the formation to which their association belongs. An association exists under broadly uniform habitat conditions and is uniform in type so far as the general characters of the dominants and main associates are concerned. Such units become aggregated regionally to constitute formations. Examples of associations include various of the mixed deciduous forests of Old and New England, such as an Oak–Beech association. The developmental counterpart of the

association is called an *associes*. It is a more or less advanced seral community dominated by more than one species, and is usually on its way to becoming an association. Commonly each association, having more than one dominant, is composed of two or more

(3) *Faciations* (or else Consociations—*see* below). A faciation is a climax community with two or more, but less than the total number of, associational dominants. The seral counterpart of the faciation is the *facies*. Another local variant of the association is the *lociation*, which varies particularly in the composition of the important subdominants and influents. When there is only one dominant to each climax community we usually have

(4) *Consociations*. These are smaller unit communities whose single dominant still has the life-form characterizing the formation. Such eca commonly occur on different soils, examples being the separate Oak and Beech consociations which make up the European Oak–Beech association. They may conveniently be named by adding -etum to the stem of the Latin name of the genus of the dominant, *e.g.* Quercetum (a consociation dominated by an Oak, *Quercus*) or Fagetum (dominated by a Beech, *Fagus*). The seral counterpart of a consociation, such as a reed-swamp dominated by a single species, is the *consocies*. Commonly recognized within a consociation or association are

(5) *Societies*. These are minor (but still often apparently climax) communities that are commonly recognized within major eca, and usually owe their existence to local variations of habitat. They are dominated by one or more species other than the association dominants, and commonly of lower life-form than these, being frequently subdominants of the higher econ, as in aspect (seasonal) and layer (stratal) societies. Thus a society represents a dominance within a dominance, whose dominant species is (or are) subordinate when we consider the association or consociation as a whole. Examples are the local and often very limited edaphic societies in many woodlands of temperate regions. The seral counterpart of the society is the *socies*, which, if it consists merely of two or more invading species without evident associates, may be called a *colony*. Within societies, etc., there may be

(6) *Clans*. These represent the lowest climax unit, consisting each of a small aggregation of a single very locally but overwhelmingly dominant species. The seral equivalent is the *family*, derived from the multiplication and gregarious growth of a single immigrant.

## Further Consideration

Most of the subjects treated in this chapter will be found discussed —though often in a different light—in each of the books of Tansley, Leach, Drabble, Weaver & Clements, Oosting, and McDougall, cited at the end of the preceding chapter.

More specialized works dealing with the aspects indicated by their titles are :

F. E. Clements. *Plant Succession : an Analysis of the Development of Vegetation* (Carnegie Institution of Washington, Publ. No. 242, pp. xiii + 512, 1916).

F. E. Clements, J. E. Weaver, & H. C. Hanson. *Plant Competition : an Analysis of Community Functions* (Carnegie Institution of Washington, Publ. No 398, pp. xvi + 340, 1929).

Sir E. J. Russell. *Soil Conditions and Plant Growth*, eighth edition edited by E. W. Russell (Longmans, London etc., pp. xvi + 635, 1950).

P. J. Kramer. *Plant and Soil Water Relationships* (McGraw-Hill, New York etc., pp. xiii + 347, 1949).

R. Geiger. *The Climate Near the Ground*, translated by M. N. Stewart and others (Harvard University Press, Cambridge, Mass., pp. xxi + 482, 1950).

It may be noted that whereas ecologists are notoriously prone to make and use technical terms (so that humorists say they will even call a spade a ' geotome '), of which not a few have been introduced in the above chapter, these latter were in most cases selected either for their precision-giving value or because they would be needed elsewhere in this work, and particularly in the following chapters dealing with the main vegetation-types of the world. Many of these terms occur again and again, though in other cases such non-committal words as community (for any grouping of plants, or *econ*) or ' ecotone ' (denoting the transition zone between two communities) are employed. Several ecological terms, such as association and subclimax, are unfortunately liable to be used in entirely different senses by members of different schools of ecological thought ; for the present work the most widespread or generally appropriate use has been chosen, others being commonly ignored in the interests of simplicity. A definition or other indication of the sense employed has usually been given on introduction of each technical term in this book, and may be found through the index.

## Chapter XII

# VEGETATIONAL TYPES OF TEMPERATE AND ADJACENT LANDS

We now come to what in some respects is our main objective—the study and interpretation of the vegetation and its component communities inhabiting different areas of the world. It should, however, be remembered throughout the following treatment that the various types of vegetation described are merely those which we recognize, almost all being apt to intergrade with little or no distinction or even characterization. These intergradings and also the *relative* positions of the main vegetational types will of necessity be largely ignored in the following brief treatment, although the geographical situation and main neighbouring types in each instance can be noted in a general way from the map facing page 1 of the text, which is a highly generalized vegetation map of the world.

We have seen that the systematic relationships of the flora of a region depend to a considerable extent upon its geographical connections or barriers, whether past or present ; on the other hand the physical characteristics of the vegetation are largely conditioned by local environmental factors. Thus when two areas have been separated since far back in geological time by such barriers as wide seas which cannot ordinarily be crossed by plants, their floras (of component species, etc.) will often be very different, whereas if their environmental conditions are similar their vegetation in closely comparable habitats is likely to have the same general appearance. This is because similar external conditions which make up particular habitats tend to produce communities (and life-forms as regards component plants) whose external physical features are much alike —however dissimilar may be their more fundamental reproductive and allied structures by which we usually classify them. For this reason we expect—and generally find—in hot arid habitats succulent plants belonging to very various families, in moist temperate regions deciduous trees, and on high mountains dwarf shrubs and perennial herbs of tussocky growth. Nor does it matter in this connection whether or not the areas concerned are separated from one another by thousands of miles, or, within reason, wherever in the world they may be. For whereas a single factor of the environment may result in a characteristic vegetational feature, it usually takes the entire habitat complex to stamp the community fully. Consequently, to the extent that distant habitats may be comparable in supporting similar vegetation-types, we may deal with them on a world basis. In this the first division is climatic, followed by local differentiation caused by edaphic or other differences: and as the vegetational types of temperate and adjacent lands are the most familiar to the greatest number of us, we may conveniently start with them.

## Deciduous Summer Forests

Summer-green forests, dominated by broad-leafed trees which lose their leaves for the unfavourable period of winter, constitute the main climax formation over much of temperate Europe, eastern Asia, and North America, reappearing in some comparable regions of the southern hemisphere. From the physiological point of view the cold winter tends to be a dry period, owing to the fact that low temperatures often hinder absorption of water by the roots: this is counterbalanced by the leafless condition during winter, for it is chiefly from the leaves that loss of water takes place, and it is mainly such loss which has to be made good by absorption from the soil. If active transpiration continued when the resultant water-deficiency could not be made good by absorption, owing for example to warm weather when the soil remained frozen, serious injury and even death might result. As it is, these deciduous broad-leafed forests typify many of the most populous regions of the world, and although in such areas we may now see around us only patches of anything approaching a climax, this situation is largely due to human disturbance—to clearance for agricultural or other purposes, or to the depredations of Man's domestic animals. For the conditions that have favoured the growth of such forests have also favoured the development of the most prosperous agriculture and grazing, including widespread cultivation of cereals, and consequently of some of the highest stages of human civilization. Owing to the deciduous habit of the main dominants and the characteristic dying down of many of the associated plants, these forests look entirely different in winter (Fig. 94) and summer (Fig. 95).

Deciduous summer forests have their main development (1) in eastern North America in the temperate belt northwards to the

Great Lakes and the upper reaches of the Gulf of St. Lawrence and westwards beyond the Mississippi ; (2) in temperate western Europe whence they extend eastwards to the Urals as a wedge between the northern coniferous forests and the southern steppes, reappearing in the Caucasus region ; (3) in northern Japan and adjacent parts of eastern continental Asia ; and (4) in the southern

FIG. 94.—Leafless condition of mixed deciduous summer forest in northeastern United States—in winter.

hemisphere in limited parts of Patagonia, southern Chile, and Tierra del Fuego. In all these regions there is a cool to severe winter but otherwise temperate and moist climate, with some precipitation all the year round, and a total of from 70 to 151 or more cm. (approximately 28 to 60 inches) annually.

In contrast to the situation in most tropical forests, the trees in deciduous summer forests form only a single main stratum or storey, though there may be tall shrubs or some smaller (often young or unsuccessful) trees forming a partial second stratum below. Such a lower stratum is especially to be seen when the main tree storey is not well developed, for when the latter is dense there is normally but scanty development of tall plants below it, and not much even of under-shrubs and herbs. There are also few climbers in most deciduous summer forests, while any epiphytes consist usually of lowly cryptogams. Consequently such temperate forests tend to

FIG. 95.—Mixed deciduous forest in northeastern United States—similar to that shown in Fig. 94, but in summer. (Phot. G. E. Nichols.)

be far less luxuriant than most tropical ones, as may be seen on comparing Figs. 94 and 95 with Figs. 143 and 144. Often there is far less undergrowth in the temperate forests than is shown in these photographs, so that the contrast with tropical rain forests is still more striking.

In deciduous summer forests the winter buds burst forth and the leaves of the dominants expand quickly, soon after the growing-season starts with the advent of suitable temperatures. The foliage is thus fully developed quite early in the season, so that little time is lost. Flowering also tends to be completed early, giving ample time for the development and ripening of the fruit ; indeed in many types the flowers open before the leaves expand, this ‘ spring flowering habit ’ allowing freer access of wind and the early insects for pollination. Also often taking advantage of the brief period before the leaves of the dominants or other tall plants expand and cut off most of the sunlight, are the small perennial herbs with persistent underground portions that send up flowering shoots and leaves very early in spring, so constituting the ‘ prevernal aspect ’. They flower and fruit rapidly and often die down soon afterwards, as in the case of the Lesser Celandine (*Ficaria verna*) and Virginian Spring-beauty (*Claytonia virginiana*). Somewhat later are the plants of the ‘ vernal aspect ’, such as the Wood-sorrel (*Oxalis acetosella*) and Yellow Archangel (*Galeobdolon luteum*), which flower during the bursting of the buds and expansion of the leaves of the overtopping types. Thus not only are the winter and summer aspects of such forests strikingly different, but also often the spring and autumn ones—for in this last season the brilliant galaxy of falling leaves, including the reds of Maples, the yellows of Birches, and the oranges of various others, makes it in the opinion of many enthusiasts the most beautiful of all.

Although they naturally often intergrade as well as vary complicatedly, some five main types of deciduous summer forests may be recognized in various temperate parts of the world, as follows.

1. Oakwoods of western and central Europe, which tend to be relatively open and light. The dominants are the Pedunculate Oak (*Quercus robur*) and/or the Sessile Oak (*Q. petraea* = *Q. sessiliflora*), the most important associated trees including Ash (*Fraxinus excelsior*), Poplars (*Populus* spp.), Birches (*Betula* spp.), Elms (*Ulmus* spp.), Alder (*Alnus glutinosa*), and Wild Cherry (*Prunus avium*). These change largely according to the nature of the ground. Smaller trees and tall shrubs flourishing in the comparatively light shade include Hazel (*Corylus avellana*), Holly (*Ilex aquifolium*), Hawthorn (*Crataegus monogyna*), Field Maple (*Acer campestre*), Crab Apple (*Pyrus malus*), Mountain-ash (*Sorbus aucuparia*), and Yew (*Taxus baccata*). In a still lower layer are found a great variety of undershrubs and coarse herbs and Grasses, while cryptogamic epiphytes may flourish on the bark of the trees. In areas of prevailingly high atmospheric humidity, some vascular plants may grow as more than fortuitous epiphytes. Ivy (*Hedera helix*) and Honeysuckle (*Lonicera periclymenum*) are common woody climbers in European oakwoods.

2. The more varied and luxuriant mixed forests of eastern North

America, eastern Asia, and southeastern Europe, which differ much from the above in systematic composition, but nevertheless tend to be roughly comparable with them in physical form. Thus various different Oaks (*Quercus* spp.), Beeches (*Fagus* spp.), Birches (*Betula* spp.), Hickories (*Carya* spp.), Walnuts (*Juglans* spp.), Maples (*Acer* spp.), Basswoods (*Tilia* spp.), Elms (*Ulmus* spp.), Ashes (*Fraxinus* spp.), Tulip-trees (*Liriodendron* sp. or spp.), Sweet Chestnuts (*Castanea* spp.), Hornbeams (*Carpinus* spp.), and many others, here may vie with Conifers such as Pines and Spruces and their allies —often doubtless as a result of disturbance. The undergrowth is commonly luxuriant and various, as is the herb layer especialily where light penetrates, while climbers are relatively plentiful. The range and variety, not only between the different regions but even within the main individual ones, is far too great for us to do justice to here, much less to describe the types in any detail. Those of eastern North America are well treated by Braun in the book cited at the end of this chapter, and those of eastern Asia are described by Wang Chi-wu in a work which it is hoped may soon be published by the successors of Chronica Botanica. Examples from eastern North America are shown in winter and summer aspects in Figs. 94 and 95, respectively. Here the main pertinent types to be recognized include: (*a*) the mixed mesophytic type of moist but well-drained, unglaciated plateaux, *e.g.* of the Appalachians, in which dominance is shared by a number of species of trees, particularly American Beech (*Fagus grandifolia*), Tulip-tree (*Liriodendron tulipifera*), several kinds of Basswood (*Tilia* spp.), Sugar Maple (*Acer saccharum*), Red and White Oaks (*Quercus rubra* s.l. and *Q. alba*), and Hemlock (*Tsuga canadensis*); (*b*) the mixed Oak–Hickory type of southern mid-western uplands, extending northwards on to 'glaciated' territory and southwards with the admixture of abundant Pines; (*c*) the Oak–Chestnut type extending eastwards on to the coastal plain from northern Virginia northwards and, now that the Chestnut has largely disappeared as a tree owing to fungal ravage, dominated chiefly by White Oak, Red Oak, Chestnut Oak (*Quercus montana*), and Tulip-tree; (*d*) the Beech–Maple type lying in the glaciated territory to the north of the mixed mesophytic type, and dominated chiefly by Beech and Sugar Maple, though many areas are youthful and still seral; and (*e*) the Maple–Basswood type centred on the driftless area of Wisconsin, in which Sugar Maple and Basswood (*Tilia americana*) are the dominants of the climax, which usually contains much associated Red Oak. In Japan and adjacent China, etc., much the same genera (apart from Hickory) but different species are usually involved in the deciduous forests, examples among the Ashes being *Fraxinus mandshurica* and among the Birches *Betula ermanii*, while the Beech *Fagus crenata* characterizes fine 'Buna' forests.

3. The Beech forests which, especially in Europe, where *Fagus sylvatica* is the species involved, form an almost uniform closed canopy, intercepting the sunlight so effectively that few shrubs and herbs can grow below. The trunks are tall and slender, particularly when the trees grow closely together, and few competitors of the dominant Beeches are able to enter their preserve. A thick brown mat of fallen leaves and leaf-mould covers the ground. It is chiefly in early spring before the Beech leaves expand that small perennial herbs such as Bluebell (*Endymion* (*Scilla*) *non-scriptus*) and Wood Anemone (*Anemone nemorosa*) tend to flourish as a prevernal aspect, often growing gregariously to form attractive carpets. Otherwise herbs are characteristically few, sometimes being largely limited to non-green saprophytes, while the lower shrubs may consist of no more than scraggy Brambles (*Rubus* spp.) in the more open areas. Occasional Ash, Wild Cherry, White-beam (*Sorbus aria* s.l.), or other trees may reach the height of the canopy, or Hollies or Yews form a scraggy subordinate layer. The commonest tall shrubs are Elder (*Sambucus nigra*) and Field Maple, with Spindle-tree (*Euonymus europaeus*), Dogwood (*Cornus sanguinea*), and Wayfaring Tree (*Viburnum lantana*) occurring chiefly in openings.

4. Southern Beech (especially *Nothofagus antarctica*) forests, usually with associated evergreens such as *Drimys winteri*, of southern South America. The trees are closely crowded, shrubs again being relatively few. Ferns and Bryophytes, on the other hand, are numerous and often extremely luxuriant, the latter sometimes forming an almost continuous carpet over the ground and fallen logs, etc., and extending well up the standing trunks.

5. The damper aspect of deciduous woodland developed especially on marshy ground subject to inundation, and dominated by various Alders (*Alnus* spp.), Willows (*Salix* spp.), Poplars, Birches, and the like, with often a tangle of hygrophytic shrubs. Climbers and epiphytes may be plentiful, and on the moist ground often flourish coarse herbs and tussocks of tall Grasses, Sedges, and Ferns such as the Royal Fern (*Osmunda regalis* agg.). These marshy thickets are plentiful in temperate regions on both sides of the North Atlantic, and appear to represent late stages in the hydrosere.

In addition, the Sweet Chestnut forests of various parts of southern and eastern Europe are sometimes described as a further type, and the drier, park-like woodland on limestone hills of central Europe as yet another. Deciduous ' parklands ' also occur in the northern prairies of North America, and though dominated by groups of Aspen and other Poplars (*Populus* spp.) in a manner reminiscent of seral stages, appear in Alberta and Saskatchewan to constitute ' a forest type in its own right ' (H.M. Raup *in litt.*). Also characteristic, if limited, are the deciduous forests of the Pacific coastal regions of the northern United States, and the very luxuriant ones of the western Caucasus where various kinds of Oaks, Beeches, Maples, Horse-chestnuts (*Aesculus* spp.), Cherries, and Cherry-laurel (*Prunus laurocerasus*) are commonly mixed with Conifers and a wealth of shrubs and climbers. On the other hand, the open Birch forests of northernmost Scandinavia, etc., in spite of their broad-leafed deciduous nature, belong to the next group.

## Northern Coniferous Forests

These are also known as ' boreal forests ', ' subarctic forests ', or ' taiga ', although it seems preferable to reserve the last term for their open, park-like northern tracts (*see* pp. 346–8).

The main dominants of these forests, instead of having broad leaves which they shed in winter, typically solve the problem of perennation through that unfavourable period by having narrow or small, needle-like or sometimes scale-like leaves. Besides their size and shape, these leaves usually have other xeromorphic characteristics that help to reduce transpiration to very modest rates. Consequently they can be retained in winter, most such trees being evergreen and having the advantages over deciduous types of being able to photosynthesize whenever conditions allow, and meanwhile of saving the wastage involved in complete annual leaf-fall. However, it is as though at their northernmost extremity such trees were unable to support winter transpiration, for the Larches (*Larix* spp.) among these needle-leafed types are regularly deciduous, losing their leaves every autumn, and in places persisting farther north than the evergreen trees. Thus it is the Dahurian Larch (*Larix dahurica*) that alone forms the farthest north ' forest ' in the world (at about 72° 50′ N. and 105° E. in Siberia).

Although the main dominants of these hardiest of forests are needle-leafed Spruces, Pines, Firs, and other Conifers, they often have associated broad-leafed deciduous Birches, Poplars, and the like—indeed Birches actually form the northernmost (albeit scrubby and open, *see* Fig. 96) 'forests' of much of Europe, and supply the only native arborescent growth in Iceland and Greenland. The groves of Aspen and Balsam Poplars (all *Populus* spp.) are usually (but apparently not always—*see* p. 343) secondary, replacing coniferous stands after felling or fires, while those of Alders (*Alnus* spp.) are normally merely seral.

The undergrowth and ground-flora in well-developed examples of these coniferous, etc., forests tend to be less dense and diverse

Fig. 96.—Open scrubby Birch 'forest' in Finmark, northern Norway ('Norwegian Lapland'). Dark ground-shrubs and Lichens cover the ground, the former being here locally predominant.

than in most broad-leafed deciduous ones. The reasons are apparently (*a*) that there is no season during which the lower layers are not shaded by the leaves of the dominants, (*b*) that the thick and dry carpet of slowly-decaying resinous leaves hinders the establishment of seedlings, and (*c*) that the generally less favourable regions offer fewer potentialities for growth. Nevertheless there may be a fair shrub layer, especially in the damper situations where the ground is commonly moss-covered; on the other hand, in drier areas and in the northernmost sparse forests, luxuriant Lichens often form a continuous ground-investment over vast areas.

One or another type of northern coniferous forest (or, occasionally, its broad-leafed consociations of Birch or consocies of Aspen) occupies most of the northernmost belt of forested terrain around the cool-temperate and boreal shoulder of the globe. Not only do they form the northern, but in many places also the altitudinal, limits of tree growth, extending southwards through often some 15–20 degrees of latitude from this northern limit, with outliers or tongues still farther south—for example in the eastern and western United States of America. There are also important outliers in the mountains of central and southern Europe and Asia (*cf.* Fig. 83, B). In addition, the Pines are highly developed in area as well as species in Mexico and throughout much of the Caribbean region, and, with other genera of Conifers, are important far south in Central America and the Mediterranean region, though these vegetation-types scarcely belong to the above series. For in general the most characteristic and extensive needle-leafed coniferous forests are developed chiefly between the 45th and 70th parallels of north latitude. Nor, in view of the very limited persistence of ice-free land at corresponding latitudes in the southern hemisphere, is it surprising that such forests are not paralleled there, the austral Conifers, although evergreen, being commonly broader-leafed and more warmth-loving (or at least far less cold-resistant).

Except when deciduous trees or shrubs are plentiful, there is relatively little difference in the appearance of the northern coniferous forest at different seasons—apart, of course, from lying snow which characterizes much of this belt more or less throughout the winter. The climate is cool, with the winter extremely cold in the continental regions ; indeed most of the lowest temperatures ever recorded have been within this belt in the interior of the great northern continents. In view of this frigidity, the absolute humidity need not be high for the climate to remain relatively moist, with fairly regular precipitation throughout the year. The soil is generally poor and of glacial origin. Ignoring most of the southern outliers, the following five main types of northern coniferous and allied forests may be recognized.

1. The usually mixed coniferous forests occupying most of the boreal forested parts of Eurasia and North America, dominated by various assortments (or occasionally a single species) of Spruce, Fir (*Abies* spp.), Pine, and Larch. The precipitation is usually between 25 and 100 cm. (approximately 10 and 40 inches) per annum and the mean temperature of the warmest month above 10° C. (50° F.), though the summer is relatively short. In eastern North America

and westwards to the Rocky Mountains the local dominants in the northern or ' Hudsonian ' belt are usually one or more of the following: White Spruce (*Picea glauca* agg.), Black Spruce (*P. mariana*), Tamarack (*Larix laricina*), Balsam Fir (*Abies balsamea*), Jack Pine (*Pinus banksiana*), with or without associated broad-leafed Poplars, Birches, or American Aspen (*Populus tremuloides*). Farther south, other dominants enter and in time there is a grading into the deciduous summer forest. Tall shrubs such as Willows (*Salix* spp.), Scrub-birches, and species of Dogwood (*Cornus*) and Pimbina etc. (*Viburnum*) may be plentiful, especially in damp situations where Mosses form a characteristic carpet. Herbs are, however, usually little in evidence, the normal ground-flora being heathy, including various species of Blueberry etc. (*Vaccinium* spp.), Labrador-tea (*Ledum* spp.), Pale-laurel (*Kalmia* spp.), and the Crowberry (*Empetrum nigrum* s.l.), typically alternating with or growing out of a lichen-rich carpet in the drier situations. In the damper situations the ground layer is contrastingly mossy. Farther west the Balsam Fir and Jack Pine are replaced by other species, particularly by Alpine Fir (*Abies lasiocarpa*) and Lodgepole Pine (*Pinus contorta* var. *latifolia*), while in Eurasia the dominant species are different again. Thus in northern Europe the Scots Pine (*Pinus sylvestris*) is often the sole dominant in the west, with Norway Spruce (*Picea abies*) entering to the south and east, and, farther east still, Siberian Spruce (*Picea obovata*), Siberian Larch (*Larix sibirica* s.l.), Siberian Fir (*Abies sibirica*), and, ultimately, Siberian Stone-pine (*Pinus sibirica*). Except for Norway Spruce these all persist at least well into Siberia proper, or are confined thereto. In the centre and east of Siberia, however, the Siberian Larch is replaced by the Dahurian Larch (*Larix dahurica*) and the Siberian Stone-pine by the Siberian Dwarf-pine (*Pinus pumila*). Apart from this last, which is shrubby, most of these Conifers (including the Lapponian form of Scots Pine) are short-branched, at least above, to give a conical shape. Moreover they tend to be shallow-rooting, and consequently able to grow in open canopy in areas where the subsoil is permanently frozen. Examples are seen in Figs. 97 and 98, the ground-flora almost everywhere being of the characteristic heathy type.

2. The open park-like ' taiga ' occurring towards the northern limit of arborescent growth. This is really only the product of depauperation of the various faciations of northern coniferous forest just described, but it is so striking in appearance as to warrant separate mention. It is characterized by the rather sparsely and

FIG. 97.—Boreal coniferous forest surrounding lake-side bog in sheltered valley in Troms, far north of the Arctic Circle in Norway. The dominant is Scots Pine of the conical Lapponian form. The ground-vegetation is heathy, but in drier situations is apt to consist largely of light-coloured Lichens as in Fig. 98.

FIG. 98.—Outside the taiga in northern Ungava, Canada. The scattered dominants of the taiga, seen in the middle-distance, are Black Spruce (*Picea mariana*) and Tamarack (*Larix laricina*), the ground between, as in the foreground, being largely occupied by swarded Lichens, though many lichen-covered boulders and dark patches of Crowberry (*Empetrum*) and Mosses are visible. In centre is seen a typical Spruce outlier consisting mainly of a lower deck that is protected by snow in winter (*cf.* Fig. 82, A), but with some puny stems straggling above.

often evenly spaced dominants, poverty in associated vascular plants (apart from xeromorphic ' heaths', such as Crowberry and species of *Vaccinium*, in the shelter of the dominants), and richness of the lichen carpet at least in dry places (Fig. 98). The Lichens are usually intricately mixed and inclusive of so-called Reindeer-mosses (*Cladonia* spp.) and Iceland-mosses (*Cetraria* spp.), being typically aggregated into a pale but dense sward several centimetres thick. In damp depressions and especially along the courses of rivers, there occur faciations approaching the ordinary northern coniferous forest of the region. These may project as timbered tongues containing well-grown trees, or even form outliers in the tundra—so constituting the so-called ' forest-tundra '. Such better growth often seems to be correlated with better aeration of the roots where there is active drainage of water (as confirmed by Professor Harold J. Lutz, *voce*). In general, however, the dominants of the open ' taiga ' are of poor development, often gnarled and only a few feet high though ancient,[1] conditions for growth being here largely unfavourable. These dominants are usually the one or more hardiest tree types of the forest lying to the south—for example, White or Black Spruce and/or Tamarack across most of northern Canada, Dahurian Larch in much of Siberia, and a scrubby Birch (*Betula odorata*) in northernmost Scandinavia (Fig. 96).

3. The Pacific ' coast forest ' of western North America, developed chiefly from southern British Columbia to northern California, but with some of the main dominants extending much farther northwards as well as southwards. The region is one of equable climate with high rainfall and atmospheric humidity, and supports the densest coniferous forest of the world as well as some of the biggest and tallest of all trees—e.g. Coastal Redwood (*Sequoia sempervirens*), Big-tree (*Sequoiadendron giganteum*), and Douglas Fir (*Pseudotsuga taxifolia*). These may reach heights of around 100 metres, or, in the case of the first-named, 110 metres, with trunk girths often over 20 metres in the first two cases. A forest of Coastal Redwood is shown in Fig. 18, D. Various further Conifers belonging to several different genera constitute the other main dominants, etc. Although Ferns, including the common Bracken (*Pteridium aquilinum* agg.) and Hard Fern (*Blechnum spicant*), are widespread, herbs in general are little in evidence. However, many characteristic shrubs occur,

[1] Near the northern limit of forest in the Northwest Territories of Canada, the author has counted more than 100 growth-rings in Black Spruces with trunks barely three inches in diameter at the base and five feet high.

including kinds of Spicy-wintergreen (*Gaultheria*), Barberry (*Berberis*), Currants etc. (*Ribes*), *Rhododendron*, Elder (*Sambucus*), and Blueberries etc.

4. The so-called 'lake-forest' of the eastern half of North America, lying between the general northern Hudsonian belt and the deciduous summer forest to the south, and centred on the northern portions of the Great Lakes. The region is one of moderate precipitation (60 to 115 cm.) and considerable temperature extremes, and the forest consists of a single association or associes dominated

FIG. 99.—'Lake-forest' of southeastern Canada, dominated by White Pine (*Pinus strobus*) and Hemlock (*Tsuga canadensis*), in summer. The undergrowth is mixed and relatively sparse.

by White Pine (*Pinus strobus*), Red or Norway Pine (*P. resinosa*), and Hemlock (*Tsuga canadensis*). Associated are various broad-leafed deciduous trees of various ecological affinities, making this forest all the more difficult to delimit; indeed it is now often questioned whether it ought to continue to be recognized as a type. For whether or not it is climax, it is in many respects transitional between the boreal coniferous and southern deciduous forests, from whose migrational buffetings and competition it has suffered. This is reflected in the undergrowth, which tends to be poorly developed owing to the dense canopy but includes many Pteridophytes, saprophytes, and under-shrubs. Fig. 99 shows an example of this type in summer, and Fig. 100 shows the selfsame area in winter.

5. Besides the above we should mention some other Conifer-dominated types such as the montane and subalpine forests of western North America which, as their names imply, are due in part to local physiographic factors ; also the various ' Pine-barrens '

FIG. 100.—The same area of ' lake-forest ' as that shown in Fig. 99, but under winter conditions, with snow covering the ground.

and other characteristic communities of eastern North America, which are due in part at least to fire or other disturbance, and consequently are of seral or subclimax nature. Somewhat comparable (but apparently still more often edaphically engendered) types exist in various parts of Eurasia south of the boreal forest belt, or as outliers for example in the Mediterranean region.

## WARM-TEMPERATE RAIN FORESTS

In warm-temperate as in subtropical regions where rainfall is plentiful and well-distributed through the year, evergreen forests are developed. The total precipitation is usually between 150 and 300 cm. per annum and frosts are no more than occasional and slight. Towards the tropics these hygrophilous (*i.e.* moisture-loving) forests merge into the subtropical and finally the tropical types described in Chapter XIV, but in cooler regions they partake more of the characteristics of the deciduous summer forests described above. In spite of the relative abundance of climbers and epiphytes, even the human inhabitant of cool regions can scarcely consider many of these warm-temperate rain forests as anything like tropical, and so it seems desirable to treat them here and correspondingly reduce the width and complexity of our tropical, etc., belt. At best these temperate rain forests tend to be considerably less luxuriant as well as usually lower than the tropical ones, and to have fewer climbers, epiphytes, and other ' forest furnishings '. Nor are plank-buttresses (*see* Fig. 145) normally found in them. Moreover, they often show a fairly sharp distinction between winter and summer aspects, for example through admixture of deciduous trees. Although the co-dominants are often numerous and inclusive of Conifers, the local dominance is usually less mixed than in the tropics. Also the leaves tend to be smaller and more leathery, and the main canopy less dense, so that in different places Tree-ferns, smallish Palms, Bamboos, small trees, tall shrubs, etc., form a lower tier. Often the undergrowth is very dense and intertwined with herbaceous climbers, the ground and tree-trunks being covered with a mat of cryptogams and small herbs, making the whole quite difficult to traverse.

Warm-temperate rain forests are developed sporadically in the southern portions of the United States bordering on the north shore of the Caribbean, and more extensively in southern Japan and adjacent Korea as well as westwards deep into China, in south-western South America, in the extreme south of Africa, and in New Zealand and some adjacent parts of Australia. Types approaching them are also found in uplands in the tropics, for example of southern Asia. In some places they merge into the sclerophyllous types that are commonly developed in the less summer-humid of the warm-temperate regions and will be considered under the next general heading. Many different faciations characterize different regions, particularly, and could be distinguished for example on the basis of different dominants. They may also be marked by characteristic associates, as in the case of those of Australasia with their Tree-ferns and those of the southeastern United States with their festoons of Spanish-moss (*Tillandsia usneoides*—*see* Fig. 101). Four examples from different quarters of the globe may be briefly described.

1. The rain forest of southern Japan which, where undisturbed, is largely dominated by several species of lofty evergreen Oaks.

Associated are other trees, including members of the Laurel and Magnolia families, and numerous shrubs forming a dense undergrowth. Woody climbers (lianes) are plentiful, as are epiphytic Ferns and some Orchids.

2. The temperate evergreen forest of the southeastern United States (but not southern Florida which is subtropical) where again more or less evergreen Oaks may predominate—especially Live Oak (*Quercus virginiana*) in the so-called ' hammocks '. Here the Evergreen Magnolia (*Magnolia grandiflora*) is often prominent.

FIG. 101.—Warm-temperate rain forest in southeastern United States. Live Oak (*Quercus virginiana*) and other trees are festooned with Spanish-moss (*Tillandsia usneoides*). Aquatic vegetation inhabits a sluggish stream in the foreground.

There are a few lianes and temperate Palms in the rich shrubby undergrowth, and on the trees may be a fair range of herbaceous epiphytes among which the so-called Spanish-moss frequently dominates the landscape (Fig. 101). However, the true broad-leafed forest is rather little represented because of edaphic and biotic and especially fire influences. These lead to subclimax areas occupied respectively by Bald-cypress (*Taxodium distichum*—*see* Fig. 102) or other summer-green swamps or, on dry sands, by evergreen Pine forest or savanna. Prominent Pines in this connection are the Loblolly (*Pinus taeda*), Longleaf (*P. palustris*), and Slash (*P. caribaea*).

3. The rain forest in New Zealand, which is almost entirely

temperate in nature, in spite of the prevalence of large Tree-ferns. Stately Conifers such as the Kauri (*Agathis australis*) and various species of *Podocarpus*, and huge dicotyledonous trees with leathery leaves, are among the various and usually mixed dominants, with species of the smallish-leafed Southern Beech (*Nothofagus*) especially in the less luxuriant upland regions of the south. Although bright

FIG. 102.—Bald-cypress (*Taxodium distichum*) swamp in southeastern United States. The dominant trees have ' breathing ' roots growing up into the air. Their branches are heavily festooned with Spanish-moss. In the foreground are floating-leaf and other early stages of the hydroseer.

flowers are largely absent in this forest, the aspect is one of considerable luxuriance owing to the profusion of shrubs, epiphytes, and climbers—as well as of Ferns and lower cryptogams.

4. The temperate rain forest of southern Chile, which may be almost impenetrable owing to the density of the undergrowth. The dominant trees are again various and usually mixed, including some small-leafed evergreen Southern Beeches and other types, and a few Conifers. Bamboos of the genus *Chusquea* are often important in the dense undergrowth, and a considerable variety of climbers and epiphytes are again to be found.

## Sclerophyllous, etc., Woodlands

In warm-temperate regions having a rather hot and dry summer alternating with a cooler moist season, the dominant trees and shrubs tend to be evergreen and to have small and hard, thickish leathery leaves (sclerophylls). This is characteristic of most of the shores and hinterland of the Mediterranean, after which such climates are commonly named, though they occur also in the southwestern portions of Australia and South Africa, in central-southern and southeastern Australia, in the extreme southwest of the United States and adjacent Mexico, and in central Chile. Although they sometimes abut on areas of warm-temperate rain forest, these sclerophyllous forest areas tend to show greater daily and seasonal temperature extremes, with snow and ice not infrequent around midwinter. Moreover the precipitation, besides falling irregularly, is usually much less plentiful than in rain-forest areas, typically ranging from 50 to 100 cm. (approximately 20 to 40 inches) yearly, while the quantity of moisture in the air varies greatly at different times. The plant communities tend to be rather drab through most of the year but attractively decked at flowering time.

Although shaded uplands and areas of sufficient ground-moisture may bear more luxuriant mixed or deciduous forests, the typical dominants of sclerophyllous regions are lowish and gnarled, examples being rounded or flat-crowned evergreen Oaks, Olives (*Olea* spp.), or similar trees, and needle- or scale-leafed Conifers. They usually grow in more or less open, scattered formation, at least after disturbance by Man, and when destroyed are commonly replaced by a fairly dense scrub of mixed deciduous and evergreen bushes—including members of their own undergrowth. Even the associated herbs often have the form of shrub-like perennials, or store water in massive aerial tissues in the cases of Aloes, Agaves, and Cactus-like or other succulents. Particularly characteristic are a host of geophytes with underground food-stores in bulbs, tubers, etc., ready to develop with the rains. The examples mentioned above in five different continents may be considered briefly.

1. The thin sclerophyllous woodlands of the Mediterranean and southern Black Sea regions. The chief dominants include evergreen Oaks such as the Cork Oak (*Quercus suber*) and Holm Oak (*Q. ilex*), and various Pines such as the Aleppo Pine (*Pinus halepensis*) and Stone Pine (*P. pinea*). However, most areas have been so disturbed by felling and grazing that only sparsely scattered, low and gnarled trees remain, the prevailing vegetation being a pale scrub on limestone terrain, known as 'garigue', and a denser and taller one on siliceous soils, known as 'maquis'. This last is often 3 metres or so in height and in various forms and densities covers vast areas, being composed of a bewildering variety of shrubs—including the subdominants of the original woodlands—such as Cistuses (*Cistus* spp.), Olive (*Olea europaea*, extensively cultivated as a tree), Myrtle (*Myrtus communis*), Rosemary (*Rosmarinus officinalis*), Lavender (*Lavandula latifolia*), and tall Heaths (*Erica* spp.). Some Palms and large Cactus-like succulent Euphorbias may also occur. Epiphytes are generally absent and climbers few, but any open ground tends to support numerous bulbous or tuberous Monocotyledons, xerophilous Grasses, dicotyledonous herbs, and short-lived spring annuals in great variety. Fig. 103 shows a rocky area in open sclerophyllous woodland, with patches of subdominant mixed scrub of maquis and garigue sorts. East of the Mediterranean this type thins out with decreasing precipitation, although some semblance of it is still to be seen on the lower slopes of the mountains of northern Iraq, so invoking the interior of Asia.

2. The Cape region of South Africa of which it has been written: 'There seems to be no doubt that [it] once possessed luxuriant forests of the Mediterranean type, and that the same process of destruction which gave origin to the European maquis largely also transformed these forests into mere brushes' (Hardy, *The Geography of Plants*, p. 246). Now there remains chiefly a wealth of sclerophyllous shrubs such as species of *Protea* and *Leucadendron*, with numerous tall Heaths and other bushy perennials belonging to very various families, and bulbous and tuberous subordinates.

3. The sclerophyllous woodland and scrubby 'chaparral' communities of western California and some adjacent regions. Here

FIG. 103.—Rocky area with patches of mixed scrub of 'maquis' type ('garigue' where light-coloured), with herbs in open tracts and sparse sclerophyllous, etc., woodland in background, in the Mediterranean island of Corsica.

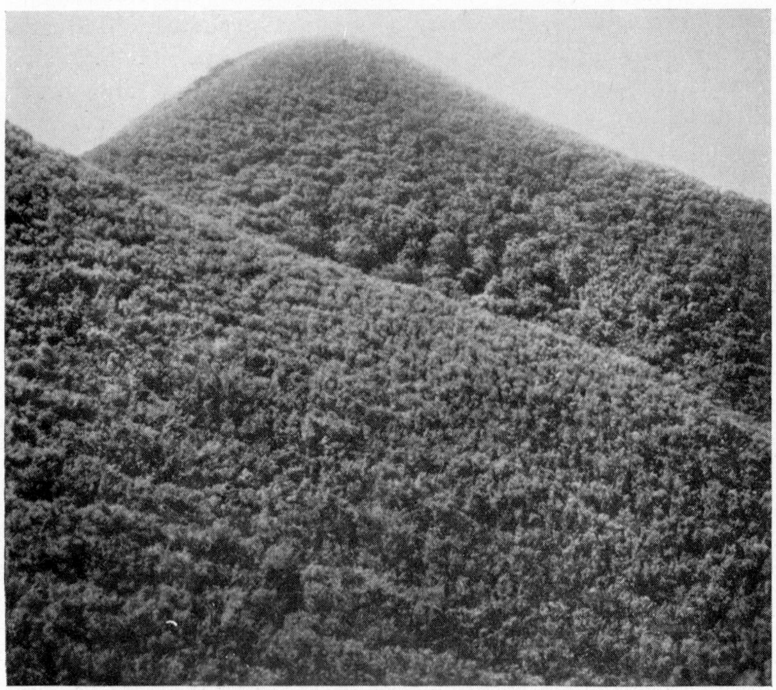

FIG. 104.—Sierran chaparral climax, Santa Barbara, California. (By permission from *Plant Ecology* by Weaver & Clements, copyright date 1938, McGraw-Hill Book Co.)

the dominant trees are often sparse and include Conifers and several species of evergreen Oaks, which in very dry situations are reduced to mere shrubs. The main mass of vegetation is commonly a thick and often tall scrub composed of representatives of very diverse families, with some associated succulents and numerous bulbous and tuberous herbs. Over some considerable areas trees are absent, this being the characteristic chaparral (Fig. 104), while, in others, only occasional isolated gnarled trees rise above the maquis-like scrub. Even where they form a canopy, the trees are typically only 20–40 feet high.

FIG. 105.—Sclerophyllous forest in Australia, dominated by lofty Gum-trees (*Eucalyptus* spp.).

4. Very similar conditions and vegetation-types exist near the coast of central Chile, where maquis-like scrub is widespread and gives way, inland, to slopes of sclerophyllous woodlands often dominated by trees strongly resembling evergreen Oaks. Their systematic allegiance is, however, usually quite distinct, as is that of the associated shrubs. In these woodlands, climbing plants as well as tuberous and bulbous ones may be common.

5. The sclerophyllous woodlands and scrublands of southwestern, central-southern, and southeastern Australia are again in many cases reminiscent of those of the northern hemisphere, though their systematic allegiance is for the most part entirely different, usually involving other genera or even families. The most luxuriant expression of the woodlands is found in the majestic forests of Gum-trees (*Eucalyptus* spp.), with an abundant undergrowth of hard-leafed shrubs often having beautiful flowers, and including Acacias, Mimosas, and Heath-like Epacridaceae. In many places Grasses cover the ground, the trees being scattered or letting through plentiful light owing to their leaves (or leaf-like members in the case of the Acacias) having a tendency to being orientated parallel to the rays of the sun. With less rainfall or more disturbance, the vegetation may be reduced to maquis-like 'mallee' or other monotonous, tangled scrub most often 1–3 metres high. In areas of intermediate water conditions this may be interspersed with stunted Eucalypts, Casuarinas, and various other trees. Fig. 105 shows such a sclerophyllous forest dominated by tall Gum-trees in a region having 75–100 cm. of rainfall annually.

## Heathlands and Grasslands

Areas dominated by characteristic members of the Heath family (Ericaceae), or by narrow-leafed Heath-like shrubs, are common in temperate and adjacent lands, as well as in arctic and alpine regions beyond the limits of arborescent growth. Typically the communities are dense and of the order of 25 cm. in height. In warm lands they may merge into the scrubby types of sclerophyllous vegetation, which often include large Heaths, etc. But their most notable development is in cooler regions with a moist winter—particularly in western and north-central Europe, where the Common Heather or Ling (*Calluna vulgaris*) is often the chief constituent of the vegetation over considerable areas, particularly on acidic soils. Associated may be various Heaths (*Erica* spp.), Bilberries etc.

(*Vaccinium* spp.), and Bearberries (*Arctostaphylos* spp.), with a variety of Grasses and sometimes some taller evergreen shrubs. Especially in the North, the heath-like Crowberry (*Empetrum nigrum* s.l.) is apt to be important and similarly gregarious, as are taller but still low and shrubby deciduous Birches and Willows. On the other hand in the South, the taller shrubs are often evergreen and characteristically have needle-like leaves (*e.g.* Juniper, *Juniperus communis* s.l.) or other photosynthesizing members (*e.g.* Gorse, *Ulex* spp.). The tendency to be gregarious and mycorrhizal is almost general in these plants : most of the chief dominants at least in the North being moreover evergreen, dwarfed, and richly branched chamaephytes, a characteristic dense and dark mat up to a ½-metre in height commonly results.

Whereas most low-lying heathlands in temperate regions are subclimaxes of the disclimax type, being due to intensive grazing or recurrent fires that prevent trees from returning to their once-forested areas, in some coastal tracts especially of northwestern Europe these heathlands are evidently maintained through exposure to winds. In such instances they will be in more delicately balanced equilibrium with the environment and consequently more ' natural '. Much the same delicate balance and relative stability probably obtains in many upland areas, where damper peaty ' moors ' are especially common in cool regions—including the ' highmoors ' (*cf.* Fig. 168) developed on acidic soils inhabited by Bog-mosses (*Sphagnum* spp.), and the ' meadow-moors ' developed on circum-neutral (usually calcareous) soils.

Still more important and widespread are grasslands, which indeed in their various forms constitute one of the main ' world ' types of vegetation. Whereas in tropical and subtropical regions grasslands typically take the form of savannas, with widely-spaced trees and/or tall shrubs as described in Chapter XIV, in temperate lands they are usually without trees or bushes except along watercourses. And although many grasslands are due to interference by Man or his domestic animals, many others, including extensive ones in temperate and allied areas, seem to be entirely ' natural '. Thus if they are due to grazing this is, or at all events originally was, apparently by wild animals.

What seem to be climax grasslands develop in temperate regions chiefly in areas having an average yearly precipitation of between 25 and 75 cm. (approximately 10 and 30 inches), or rather more in warm parts. These grasslands occur especially in the interiors of the great land-masses, the main examples in principally cool regions being the North American 'prairies' and the Russian and adjacent 'steppes', with, in somewhat warmer regions, the South African 'veld', South American 'pampas', and southern Australian and New Zealand grasslands. These last three regional types frequently bear isolated or sometimes aggregated low trees or shrubs and accordingly constitute savannas; indeed much of southern Australasia, particularly, is often indicated as savanna on world vegetation-maps. Nevertheless the real dominants are usually Grasses, so such types seem best classed here. In addition, meadows and other grasslands occur widely in temperate and allied regions as biotic plagioclimaxes.

All grasslands have this in common, that they are dominated over at least most of their often vast area by Grasses—usually by various and often mixed perennial species which are narrow-leafed hemicryptophytes, many of them being gregarious and extremely hardy. Characteristically, the rooting is shallow and the underground parts form a matted turf which holds rainwater when and where it falls, checking penetration to deeper layers and accordingly aiding the grassland plants to prevail in their competition with trees in transitional areas where the rainfall is barely sufficient for arborescent growth. The turf and sod of old dead leaves, etc., may also help to check the successful establishment of tree seedlings. The winter in the so-called climatic grassland areas is often severe and dry, as may be the later summer; but recurrent spring and early summer rains that more than compensate for evaporation will favour the Grasses, which can then vegetate actively.

The main types of grasslands occurring in temperate regions may now be briefly described.

1. The prairies of central and western North America, ranging from well north in Canada southwards into Mexico. The dominant Grasses mostly form clumps (' bunch Grasses ') in the drier regions or more extensive sodded swards in the less arid ones, being interspersed with a large variety of subdominant *forbs* (herbs of other than grass habit). These often give the prairie a distinctive tone locally and fall into mixed societies flourishing for example at different times of the year. In general, however, various greens prevail in the early part of the growing-season, and yellows or greys later on, sometimes followed by darker orange or other autumn tints. Woody plants are usually few and unimportant, except in depressions or as a response to overgrazing, which may also favour Cacti. Yet differences from spot to spot tend to be so marked and unstable

that the whole has been claimed to constitute ' an open system ' in which repeated readjustment to disturbance overrules any tendency to equilibrium. In general correspondence with decreasing rainfall, the Grasses fall into three groups based upon stature and known respectively as ' tall ', ' mid ', and ' short ' Grasses. They range from the height of a Man, or taller, down to a few centimetres in the cases of the most drought- or pasturing-resistant types. Fig. 106, A, shows an area of true prairie in Nebraska, dominated principally by mid Grasses, but with shrubs and even trees in some damp depressions. Fig. 106, B, illustrates an area of short-grass prairie in Colorado, while Fig. 106, C, shows a similar area that has been badly overgrazed. In the prairies there is a long resting stage each year, which is due to low temperatures in the North—the melting of winter snow affording plentiful water in early spring—and to low rainfall in the South and West. The general unity of this grassland climax is evidenced by some of the grass species occurring in nearly all of the component associations, and by the large number of grass genera—such as *Agropyron*, *Bouteloua*, *Elymus*, *Poa*, *Sporobolus*, and *Stipa*—that afford dominants more or less throughout its great range. Nevertheless, differing local conditions lead to preclimax and postclimax communities and different treatments to biotic plagioclimaxes, while near the forest border is an ecotone with trees which elsewhere persist chiefly along watercourses. In such zones of tension, each life-form takes advantage of the slightest variation of edaphic or biotic impress which may be in its favour.

2. The steppes of the U.S.S.R. and adjacent lands, covering vast areas south of the northern forests and north of the central deserts, etc., and ranging from eastern Europe to eastern Asia, with outposts farther west and south. These steppes are similar to the North American prairies in all essential respects, though they differ considerably in the component genera and much more in the species. The Grasses tend to be highly xerophilous and to form dense tufts or cushions composed of the remnants of previous years' growth seated on stools of superficial but much-branched fibrous roots, while the associated forbs are mostly hardy perennials or bulbous geophytes. These associates and any annuals or woody plants are mostly small, few exceeding half-a-metre in height. The growth of trees is almost everywhere prevented by the scarcity of water and by the extremely severe winters, when strong and dry winds blow over the frost-bound soil on which snow may afford protection only for ground-vegetation. Between the northern forests and open

A

B

C

FIG. 106.—The North American Prairie: mid- and short-grass communities. A, Nebraska prairie area dominated principally by 'mid' Grasses, with shrubs and trees in depressions. (By permission from *Plant Ecology*, by Weaver & Clements, copyright date 1938, McGraw-Hill Book Co.) B, short-grass community in Colorado. (Phot. U.S. Forest Service.) C, area similar to (B), but overgrazed and in poor condition, with bad weeds, including Cacti. (Phot. U.S. Forest Service.)

steppes there is often a broad ecotone, rather incongruously known as 'forest steppe', in which the two formations occur intermixed in patches.

3. The Argentinian and other South American pampas and steppes, again developed chiefly on flat or gently undulating plains, and with most of the general characters and range of variation of the above. Quite frequently some low trees or tall shrubs give these grasslands the aspect of savannas.

4. The grasslands and savannas of South Africa and southern Australasia—the grasslands being again closely comparable with the northern steppes and prairies, whereas the savannas have also scattered trees and/or bushes. But although the dominant Grasses tend to be of familiar forms and even genera, the woody plants are very different in different regions, often including unique types (*e.g.* in Australia).

5. The subclimax meadows and other grasslands of various temperate regions that except for biotic disturbance would support vegetation of higher life-form. These probably include considerable areas of present-day steppes and prairies especially towards their forested margins, but are more notably represented by the verdant meadows that form such a prominent feature of the dairy and other pastured lands, for example, on either side of the North Atlantic. Such meadows are typically due to clearance of the forests and more or less long-continued mowing and/or pasturing by domestic animals and wild herbivores such as Rabbits and Hares. This favours the Grasses and other hemicryptophytes that dominate such areas, so that they tend to form a continuous sward with closely-compacted turf which represents a biotic plagioclimax in that it is deflected from the normal succession. However, with removal or reduction of normal grazing, woody plants soon enter the system and the subsere proceeds towards the climax. Much the same Grasses and forbs with buds hidden in the surface layer of soil are protected against fire, which often helps to maintain grasslands, as does the tendency of the turf to retain water. In meadows, the dominant Grasses are usually broader-leafed and less xerophilous than in climatic grasslands, although a wide range of often similar types and even genera are involved. Meadows, moreover, tend to support a wider variety and often greater admixture of forbs. Most of the meadow inhabitants are more or less hygrophilous, lacking marked protective devices reducing transpiration, and, although their flowering-axes die down, many remain uninterruptedly green in

winter. The dominant Grasses are perennial, with axes on the average about half-a-metre high, and typically involve such familiar genera as *Poa*, *Festuca*, *Lolium*, *Agrostis*, *Alopecurus*, *Phleum*, and many others. The associated forbs are also mostly perennial, or, less frequently, biennial, and are often rosette-chamaephytes. Like the Grasses, they may be coarse and 1–2 metres high in favourable circumstances especially in damp situations, but rise scarcely at all above the surface of the soil when intensely grazed; such close cropping cannot, however, be long withstood by most species. Annuals occur chiefly in open patches that are due to overgrazing or drought, while Mosses may form a weak ground-layer especially in the damper situations. Woody plants, like geophytes, if present are usually little in evidence—except where the biotic disturbance is light and there is a tendency towards heath development or reforestation.

## Semi-Deserts and Deserts

Although what amount practically to desert conditions are commonly developed very locally on dry rock and sand or other porous surfaces, these usually show evidence of at least incipient successional change. On the other hand, extensive desert areas tend to be among the most stable vegetationally, owing to the general lack of water for more growth than that of the plants already present. Intermediate in water-relations between true deserts and the drier among the areas whose vegetation has been described earlier in this chapter, and usually intermediate also in geographic position, are various semi- or near-desert areas such as the Sage-brush ones of western North America. These are characterized by the Sage-brush (*Artemisia tridentata*) and other low and often greyish shrubs having herbaceous branches, that dominate a climax in regions having an annual precipitation of 12–25 cm. (approximately 5–10 inches). Such shrubs often belong to predominantly herbaceous families and also thrive in areas of greater rainfall when the competition from Grasses is eliminated. The scrub is low and often broken or of more or less widely-spaced single bushes, the depauperated types merging into the still more xerophytic 'desert-scrub' developed where the rainfall is limited to 7–12 cm. annually. In this latter instance the dominants are bushy shrubs, particularly of Creosote-bush (*Larrea tridentata*), usually ½–2 metres high and spaced on the average 5-15 metres apart through a widely-spreading root system.

In the often comparable ‘ desert steppes ’ of the U.S.S.R., which constitute the transition between the more or less continuously vegetated steppes and the deserts of predominantly bare spaces, other Wormwoods (*Artemisia* spp.) of Sage-brush type tend to be the most characteristic plants. Frequently they are halophytic, the soils being salinized and supporting also such characteristic under-shrubs as Salt-bush (*Atriplex canum*). Often prominent in addition are sod-forming Grasses such as wiry Fescues (*Festuca* spp.) and Feather-grasses (*Stipa* spp.), and dicotyledonous as well as mono-cotyledonous annuals which develop rapidly with spring rains but die down with the advent of hot weather, so leading an ephemeral life. Examples of this last phenomenon are well seen in desert areas of Iraq—*cf.* Fig. 156.

Some Lichens may grow or lie on the surface of the earth, as may Blue-green Algae (including colonies of *Nostoc*), but arborescent growth, for example of Willows and Poplars, is usually limited to occasional damp depressions or the vicinity of watercourses. Such, for example, are the oases of the Gobi Desert. Rather similar conditions and attendant vegetation, with a dry and generally warm climate subject to sharp contrasts of heat and cold, and one or two brief vegetative seasons each of 1–3 months (in spring and/or autumn) characterized by intermittent rainfall and favourable temperatures, are widespread in temperate as well as in warmer countries. Thus they occur on the plateaux of Asia Minor, in belts around the deserts of Central Asia and Australia, in southern South America and South Africa, and flanking the Sahara and Arabian Deserts. Some of these areas support extensive thorny or other scrub and are apt to be so designated on world vegetation maps.

These semi-desert regions of both the Old and the New Worlds are typically made up of vast, flat or undulating expanses of bare soil supporting hoary or dull-grey, often sticky and scented, ‘ heathy ’ or sage-like shrubs $\frac{1}{4}$–2 metres high. Such shrubs may form a continuous but thin or else broken brush, or be ‘ scattered ’ over otherwise naked tracts, though in particularly arid areas the spacing is often more even and apparently due to root-competition. Although there are no green grassy swards there may be bunches of wiry Grasses, and although there are normally no trees there may be tallish Cacti or giant Euphorbias or other large succulents, while saline lagoons, dry most of the year, may be surrounded by fleshy or bushy halophytes. The usually erect or ascending, switchy dominant shrubs often have thickish woody stumps and deep roots.

Their leaves are commonly narrow, leathery and inrolled, less than 3 cm. long and often densely covered with hairs which give them a greyish-white tint. Outside the rainy season, dependence is largely on underground water. Except for those which are deciduous, the dominants frequently show little contrast in appearance at different times of the year—especially as few display at all large and bright flowers. Matters are otherwise with the often plentiful associated ephemerals which burst forth when rain allows, and form quite a display along with such succulents as Cacti, Mesembryanthemums, Aloes, and Agaves, which contain considerable stores of water.

With still more precarious precipitation or other water supply, deserts usually result. But as these usually belong to tropical or subtropical regions, or at least extend well into them, they are treated chiefly in Chapter XIV. Exceptions are afforded by the Transcaspian desert which is an open plain and the Gobi Desert which is a plateau, both lying in temperate parts of Asia. These are mainly areas of prevailing drought and extreme temperature conditions, and consequently are very little vegetated, such plant life as exists being mainly the result of depauperation of the so-called desert steppes described above. Thus dunes may be partly fixed by low and open, shrubby growth, but siliceous and clayey soils, often containing loess, are apt to be virtually barren, as are gravelly and talus-strewn areas over considerable tracts of country. Nor do the frequent saline or ' alkali ' and gypsiferous areas afford much relief to the abiding monotony. Nevertheless one seldom finds at all extensive tracts even in the Gobi that are entirely devoid of some kind of vegetation, and very commonly the transition to steppe or at least desert-steppe is marked by a scattering of poor Grasses ranging from some 25 cm. high in exposed situations to a metre in height in depressions where water collects in the rainy season. Besides Grasses and some Sedges, xeromorphic members of the Daisy (Compositae), Goosefoot (Chenopodiaceae), and Tamarisk (Tamaricaceae) families tend to be prominent in these temperate deserts, as do geophytic monocotyledons such as *Tulipa uniflora*, *Iris sisyrinchium*, and species of *Gagea*. Desert-like ' bad-lands ', often characterized by lowly Cacti or brush-like shrubs, also occur more locally in parts of temperate North America and southern South America.

For examples of desert areas in warm-temperate regions we may go to central Iraq. Fig. 156, A, shows a quadrat in a typically gravelly area in which one small perennial tuft is visible but there

A

B

FIG. 107.—Salt desert and salt-marsh of a warm-temperate region. A, an area of salt desert near Shithatha, in southern central Iraq. Clumps of the co-dominants are up to 2 metres wide and 60 cm. high. Cracking of the surface encrustation is noticeable in slight depressions. The dots at the foot of the distant scarp are grazing Camels. B, saline marshes outside the oasis of Shithatha, Iraq. The vegetation is mostly closed and sedgy-grassy, with some Tamarisks (*Tamarix* spp.).

are numerous tiny seedlings springing up after heavy rain. Fig. 156, B, shows a close-up of a near-by less gravelly area when the ephemerals have developed. Fig. 107, A, shows an area of salt desert near the oasis of Shithatha, in southern central Iraq, where higher vegetation occupied from one-eighth to one-half of the surface, bushy Chenopodiaceae affording the main dominants. Soluble salts totalled 7·5 per cent. of air-dry soil at the surface where tested but decreased markedly below; the pH was 8·3 at the surface and scarcely varied from this below. Some widish and flat, white-encrusted areas tended to be barren, though in places where water could collect in the rainy season and Blue-green Algae grew, loose mud 'medallions' covered the surface.

## Salt-Marshes

Whereas various salts, such as nitrates, sulphates, and phosphates of potassium, calcium, magnesium and iron are essential, at least in the small concentrations that are usually present in soils, for the normal development of land vegetation, excessive salinity (*e.g.* of more than 0·5 per cent.) is harmful to the growth of most plants. Such high salinity, particularly due to sodium chloride, is most commonly found around sea-shores, and is the most constant factor leading to the replacement there of normal land-vegetation by plants which habitually grow in very salty soils (halophytes) or at least *can* grow in such soils (facultative halophytes). Thus in maritime salt-marshes, which are primarily determined by periodic immersion in salt water and mostly lie between the levels reached by the higher neap and ordinary spring tides, the components of the characteristic vegetation are almost all peculiar to the habitat. And whereas, if the tide is effectively excluded and there is adequate drainage, the salt in time is washed out of the soil and non-halophilous species colonize the area, 'There is no good evidence that salt marsh can develop by the mere accumulation of silt or humus, without human assistance, into a non-maritime vegetation' (Tansley, *Introduction to Plant Ecology*, p. 78). Consequently the salt-marshes of temperate and allied regions seem best considered here among subclimax or local climax types.

Salt-marshes are chiefly developed on mud-flats about sheltered tidal estuaries. In them such Green Algae as *Rhizoclonium* and *Enteromorpha*, or such halophilous vascular plants as succulent or shrubby Glassworts or Saltworts (*Salicornia* spp.), are the normal pioneers, followed typically by Alkali-grasses (*Puccinellia* spp.) or other halophytic Grasses. Any such growth tends to impede the flow of water and increase the deposition of silt, helping to raise the level of the bed. Higher up, on the ' flats ' covered by most of the spring tides, a mixed vegetation is usually developed. This is the general salt-marsh community which, for example on both sides of the North Atlantic, characteristically includes such types as Sea Plantain (*Plantago maritima* s.l.), Sea Arrow-grass (*Triglochin maritima*), Sea-blite (*Suaeda maritima*), and Sea-pink (*Armeria maritima* s.l.), with shrubby Chenopodiaceae especially in warm-temperate regions. Various Brown and other Algae, often of peculiar habit and squalid mien, are commonly associated. Still higher up, where the saline flats are covered only by the higher spring tides, a more or less close turf usually develops with the help of grazing, composed of halophilous Grasses with associated forbs. At the uppermost levels reached only by the very highest spring tides or storm-waves, less markedly halophilous types such as Red Fescue (*Festuca rubra* s.l., a facultative halophyte) tend to predominate, with often an admixture of ordinary land species that can tolerate small amounts of sea-salt in the soil. At the higher levels in river estuaries the water is alternately fresh and brackish with the ebb and flow of the tide, so inhabiting plants must be physiologically specialized to withstand rather sudden and extreme changes in the osmotic value of the inundating water.

Whereas such geodynamic factors as tidal action may cause the maintenance of a condition of equilibrium between accretion and erosion, and thus of a lasting type of vegetation in maritime salt-marshes, it seems probable that in some instances at least there is gradual continuation of accumulation and advance towards normal land vegetation—even without human interference—as in the case of sand-dunes and shingle beaches, and in spite of what was quoted above. But at all events the types just described are commonly both long-lasting and distinctive, and consequently had to be treated as special entities.

In many arid regions, for example of interior Asia and western North America, there occur salt lakes or smaller basins or seasonally dry ' alkali pans ' exhibiting a similar range of conditions of varying salinity which is, however, often more extreme than on sea coasts. Inland, these saline areas result from excessive and prolonged evaporation, changes in level and salinity in individual cases being seasonal instead of tidal, though they may vary rapidly with the weather. Still, the sequence of zones is often remarkably definite, and in a general way reflects not only the prevailing degree of salinity but also the poor aeration accompanying the increasing soil-moisture. Here again there is no certainty that succession will ever proceed to any proper climatic climax in the absence of biotic disturbance, especially as the tendency is for the salinity to increase rather than decrease with time. Consequently it seems best to consider the marginal vegetation as forming a zoned series of sub-climaxes so far as the general region is concerned (or edaphically limited climaxes of their own immediate areas). In any case it appears likely that the local allogenic conditions will have more effect upon the future of these inland saline areas than will any autogenic seral tendencies. Fig. 107, B, shows an area of saline marsh outside the oasis of Shithatha, in southern central Iraq. The vegetation is mostly closed and sedgy-grassy, with some shrubby Tamarisks, being dominated by such types as *Scirpus maritimus*, *Cyperus distachyos*, *Aeluropus littoralis*, and *Tamarix pentandra*. The pH was 8·6 where tested and the area was said to remain damp throughout the year, having some shallow pools of open water at least in spring. Open mud ' polygons ' were bound by mixed *Oscillatoria*, *Lyngbya*, and other primitive Algae.

Some hitherto productive cultivated areas in arid regions requiring irrigation have become too saline for the growth of crops—owing to prolonged evaporation leaving the salts of the ' raw ' irrigation water behind when no drainage was provided. In other cases the crops are limited to facultative halophytes such as Date Palms (*Phoenix dactylifera*) or Barley. Much of central and southern Iraq is of this nature, and as Man has not yet become proficient at remedying such soil salinity on a wide scale, the increasing amount of irrigation is worsening the situation.

## Seral Communities

Besides subclimax communities, various other deflected or ' straight ' successional ones have been described or implied above, while many others are of such limited occurrence or importance (as in the cases of salt-sprayed coastal areas or the ' serules ' occurring for example on fallen logs) that we can scarcely even mention them in this brief outline of the main vegetational types of temperate and allied lands. However, to complete our picture there remain a number of (mostly seral) communities that should be cursorily elucidated, some of these being sufficiently widespread to demand more attention.

Notable are the characteristic types afforded by the sand-dune and shingle-beach successions which occur chiefly (but in the former case by no means entirely) near sea coasts. Thus sandy sea-shores that are wetted by the highest tides are commonly inhabited in sufficiently sheltered situations by a characteristic open community of halophytic shore-plants such as Sea-rockets (*Cakile* spp.), Sea-purslane (*Arenaria* (*Honckenya*) *peploides* agg.), and species of Orache (*Atriplex*). These tend to arrest any dry sand that is blown on to them, and, consequently, to form the basis of hillocks through which the shoots grow, the effect being cumulative in that the deeper the sand comes to be piled up, the higher the plants will grow, and *vice versa.* More important in this connection are the major dune-formers—coarse Grasses such as, particularly, Marram Grass (*Ammophila arenaria*) and Lyme-grass (*Elymus arenarius* s.l.) in north-temperate regions. These have similar powers of colonization and sand-accumulation but grow chiefly farther back from the sea and more extensively, binding the sand by the ramifications of their rhizomes and roots. This is illustrated in Fig. 93, which shows Marram Grass doing the binding on the coast of Maine. Meanwhile the motion of the surface particles is checked by the tall and usually tufted aerial parts, and other species, which cannot colonize moving sand, are enabled to establish themselves between the axes of the main pioneers. These secondary colonists typically include Lichens, Mosses, and less coarse Grasses, which finally bind the surface and consolidate the community. Maritime shrubs and in time climax forest typically follow if the land is not severely pastured or turned into golf links (for which old, grass-covered dunes are the traditional sites). Meanwhile there will have been produced some characteristic, though seral, vegetational types whose non-halophytic counterparts may occur far inland, as for example around the Great Lakes of North America.

Shingle-beach vegetation has considerable affinity with that of dunes, especially when sand is admixed and the habitats are thereby rendered similar. Where sand is lacking, various Lichens may colonize the surface of the stones inland of the usual ' storm-crest ', and over them may extend clumps of such maritime flowering plants as the Sea-pea (*Lathyrus maritimus* agg.) and halophytic Grasses. These often persist for a long time, the plants being rooted in the crevices between the pebbles. Ultimately the crevices become filled with sand and plant remains, and gradually the vegetation extends to form a complete covering of the shingle, so that on old shingle beaches away from the direct influence of the sea, inland types of vegetation commonly develop, and in time scrub or even forest.

Except that, usually, only inland plants are involved and the early stages tend to form long downward stabilized strips separated by dynamic tracts, much the same sequence takes place on many talus screes and heaps of detritus. These, when reasonably stable and including a fair amount of comminuted ' soil ', can, with the help of their surface crevices, run the whole gamut of the xerosere with relative speed and ease right up to a forest climax. Otherwise the lithosere is usually very slow in progressing, especially in its early stages. Although these stages may be represented by highly characteristic cryptogamic or herbaceous communities, these normally occupy only very limited areas of rock, such as occur naturally in temperate regions chiefly on cliffs and rocky outcrops.

The hydrosere, also, affords characteristic seral communities such as floating-leaf, reed-swamp, sedge-meadow, and damp scrub ones, which were outlined in the last chapter and may severally cover considerable areas. Although they vary widely in different instances and especially in different regions within the temperate and allied belts, these communities are mostly too familiar and obvious to require description in any detail here. Dominants on both sides of the North Atlantic include Water-lilies (*Nymphaea* spp.) in the floating-leaf stage, Cattails or Reedmaces (*Typha* spp.) in reed-swamp, various Sedges (*Carex* spp.) in the sedge-meadow, and Alders (*Alnus* spp.) in the damp scrub. Examples of most of these features are described and illustrated elsewhere in this chapter or the immediately preceding one (stages of hydroseres being shown especially in Figs. 89, 90, 91, and 102).

Besides the various natural or semi-natural scrublands mentioned above, there are the often characteristic scrubs and thickets belonging to subseres that follow cutting or burning of forests in temperate and allied regions. These unstable types may occupy considerable areas, though usually not without more or less recent human disturbance or intervention. Even the later and taller stages of these secondary growths are frequently dominated by plants—such as ' weedy ' Birches or Poplars—that do not occur in the climax forest.

There remain to be mentioned among types naturally occupying substantial areas in temperate and allied regions the various marshes, fens, bogs, mires, moors, and waterside zones, that commonly represent part of some hydrosere or other. As such, many have been covered above, at least by general implication ; in other instances they seem to form subclimaxes, for example of plagioclimax nature where a continuing ' master factor ' is involved, and, at least when covering considerable areas, appear needful of some treatment. Outstanding are the marshlands, fenlands, and boglands which may be distinguished respectively according to whether the soil is formed mainly of silt, of peat containing considerable quantities of lime or other bases, or of peat very poor in such bases. With marshlands of one sort or another we are already fairly familiar, while further examples are mentioned in the following chapters.

Fenland occupies the alluvial borders of rivers and streams as well as parts of old estuaries and the borders of certain lakes—especially of those into which streams bring ' hard ' water rich in lime. Its most characteristic manifestations represent stages in the hydrosere—particularly reed-swamp, sedge-meadow, and, if the latter is not regularly cut or pastured, damp scrub or woodland ' carr ' dominated by Alders or sometimes Birches, or constituting meadow-moors in exposed situations. The vegetation in these cases is largely calcicolous, whereas in the general run of alluvial marshlands it is less exacting.

Bogs or ' mosses ', on the other hand, develop chiefly where the water is very poor in calcium and other basic salts, and support entirely different communities—for example around the shores of lakes and tarns in areas where the rock is deficient in basic mineral salts and the water is consequently ' soft '. Typically the growth consists largely of Bog-mosses (*Sphagnum* spp.) supporting a number of characteristic higher plants such as Cotton-grasses (*Eriophorum* spp.) and Sedges (*Carex* spp.), and often ' insectivorous ' associates such as Butterworts (*Pinguicula* spp.), Sundews (*Drosera* spp.), and Bladderworts (*Utricularia* spp.). In areas of cool and wet climate where the drainage is poor, such communities may cover considerable flattish tracts and be known as ' blanket bogs '. Owing to the Bog-mosses' remarkable power of holding water in their sponge-like cushions (*see* p. 51), these last can grow in height and enormously in width, extending over marshes and even fens or open water, depositing peat and raising the surface on which they grow. Such ' raised bogs ' tend to be strongly acidic in reaction and reddish-brown in colour.

Although bogs are commonly colonized by Heaths or even larger woody plants, the Mosses seem to control matters as long as they remain fully active. However, with draining or natural drying out of the surface, the succession usually proceeds to the local forest or other climax—such as highmoors or drier heathlands in exposed situations. Lowland- or meadow-moors are usually hydroseral communities occurring on circumneutral peat accumulations resulting from the filling up of lakes and preceding the timbered stages of succession. Here the upper layers above the level of ground-water are often acidic in reaction, and either support heathland communities dominated by Heaths in drier parts, or bog-like ones dominated by Cotton-grasses or Moor-grass (*Molinia coerulea*) in damper parts. Where acid conditions are developed by such humus accumulation above basic rocks, ' flushes ' from springs or superficial drainage may continually bring down fresh supplies of basic salts and lead to ' spring flush ' communities very locally. Especially in regions of marked topographical and geological variation is it common to find whole series of moorland, dry heathland, pastured grassland, and scrub or woodland communities existing side by side within a relatively small area.

Besides the more extensive hinterland communities already mentioned, those of sea and other cliffs, and of river and other banks, may be distinctive, though usually they are very limited in area and too variable for detailed consideration here. Notable, however, is the occurrence of cushion and other alpine plants along the dry margins or beds of watercourses in the lowlands of mountainous temperate countries on both sides of the Equator. Presumably their disseminules are washed down from the uplands and their growth is favoured by the ' open ' conditions and general lack of competition by ranker lowland types, which would prevent their ecesis or rapidly succeed them in most other habitats.

Finally there are the various weed and allied communities that follow anthropic disturbance ; for such activities as cultivation or forest-cutting and their aftermaths are so widespread that in temperate regions there is relatively little truly natural vegetation left. Indeed of the more favourable areas capable of supporting climax forest there can scarcely remain any that are wholly undisturbed by Man or his domestic animals, though there are many which we think of (and study) as practically natural. Even crops may be considered to comprise communities of a sort, however artificial and temporary they may be. Representative crops and some weeds were dealt with earlier in this work ; especially do weeds form many and various if rather ephemeral communities, examples of which are all too familiar to every farmer, gardener, and estate-owner. Moreover, owing to almost universal introduction by Man and to the similar 'openness' of the habitats involved, these colonies of weeds tend to be remarkably alike in similar situations throughout the temperate and allied regions, often involving the selfsame species in both Old and New Worlds, and in both Northern and Southern Hemispheres. But in spite of the common luxuriance of such weed communities, the full abandonment of agricultural or other waste areas usually allows succession to proceed so rapidly towards the local climax that within a very few years the weeds are liable to have disappeared entirely. These areas being usually in tracts that had been cleared of former forests, the weeds are commonly superseded in the first few years by scrub or such weedy trees as Birches or Poplars, before the return of anything like the climax forest. Meanwhile any crop plants have usually long disappeared.

## Some Physiographic Effects

Many physiographic effects, such as differences in exposure and water-conditions due to ridges and depressions, have already been dealt with, and the vegetation of uplands above the limit of arborescent growth is treated in the next chapter. Outstanding, however, are differences due to aspect and particularly altitude below the tree-line, which can lead to marked differences in conditions and local vegetation. This we have already mentioned and illustrated in Figs. 83, A, and 83, B, but must consider further here. Such differences are largely due to differences in local climate as explained in Chapter X. The communities involved usually lie within the orbit of those described elsewhere and so need not be treated in any detail, though a few examples of the effects of (1) aspect and (2) altitude in temperate and allied regions may be given with advantage.

The most widespread and commonly obvious aspect effect is that due to orientation with regard to the sun's rays. For example, in the Mediterranean region some ridges lying east and west may bear almost entirely different vegetation on their north- and south-facing slopes, in extreme instances having not a single ecologically important species in common. Thus the south-facing slopes, exposed to the full glare of the midday sun, tend to be occupied by the highly xerophilous maquis or garigue of more or less sparse shrubs and herbs. The lower parts of any steep north-facing slope, however, will be protected from at least the strongest insolation and may bear at the same altitude deciduous forest with hygrophilous ground-vegetation. On the other hand in moist northern regions the most luxuriant vegetation may be developed on the southern and western slopes which receive the greatest benefit from the sun. The tendency is of course reversed in the southern hemisphere. However, north-and-south-running mountain ranges may show instead another aspect effect, namely, marked differences in rainfall on their two sides. Thus of New Zealand the eastern side, sheltered from the prevailing westerly winds, has in places no more than one-tenth of the rainfall of the forested western side, and supports only poor tussocky grassland over considerable areas.

The general tendency towards cooler and damper conditions as we ascend mountains usually leads to marked attendant changes in the vegetation. These may run the gamut from arid plains or lowland forests, dealt with above, all the way to high-alpine regions of perpetual snow. With the tundra and other communities lying above (as in latitudes beyond) the tree-limit, we shall be concerned in the next chapter. Those communities developed between such extremes and the general run of lowlands in temperate regions usually involve faciations or extensions of one or other of the forest types already described. However, in some instances, as most notably the desert uplands of parts of temperate Asia, there may be instead almost plantless wastes or expanses of moving sands—with salt tracts of various extent, and only occasional oases supporting deciduous trees such as Poplars.

A good example of the usual forested sequence in mountainous districts is seen in western North America, where, above a basal zone of ' improved ' plains vegetation, the ' montane forest ' extends from the arid foothills upwards into the mountains through an altitudinal range of often some 2,000 metres. The main dominants are Ponderosa Pine (*Pinus ponderosa*), White Fir (*Abies concolor*), and Douglas Fir (*Pseudotsuga taxifolia*), though many others occur, the closest relationship being with the Pacific ' coast forest '. Extending above, through an altitudinal belt of commonly some 1,000 metres, comes the ' subalpine forest ', which is related primarily to the boreal forest but also to the coast and montane forests, the main dominants being species of *Picea* and *Abies*—particularly *P. engelmannii* (Engelmann Spruce) and *A. lasiocarpa* (Subalpine Fir), with often some Lodgepole Pine (*Pinus contorta* var. *latifolia*) and allied species. While the multiplicity of dominants makes for varied groupings, there is a tendency towards pure consociations near the timber-line ; at its upper levels the forest also becomes less luxuriant and the canopy lower, until it passes into 'elfin wood' and ultimately 'Krummholz' of stunted and twisted trees (*see* Fig. 108) about where the alpine tundra begins. However, mountain vegetation has no uniform pattern but varies from range to range. Thus in many mountainous regions of the temperate

FIG. 108.—Pine 'Krummholz' at timber-line in the Rocky Mountains. (Phot. W. S. Cooper.)

belt, as for example in central Europe and the White Mountains of New England, there is a tendency for the lower zone of montane forest, like the basal tracts, to be dominated by broad-leafed deciduous trees, and only the higher (subalpine) levels to be predominantly coniferous. Often a fairly wide belt of mixed deciduous and evergreen forest intervenes ; and although there is a general tendency for corresponding zones to decrease in altitude towards the poles, there may be wide variation according to local conditions even on the selfsame line of latitude.

## FURTHER CONSIDERATION

Although this chapter represents in outline the results of considerable reading and personal experience, often in obscure periodicals or remote places, further details about most of the subjects treated may with advantage be obtained from the standard general works dealing with the vegetation of the land-masses of the world. These include:

A. F. W. Schimper. *Plant-geography upon a Physiological Basis*, transl. and revised edition (Clarendon Press, Oxford, pp. xxx + 839 and 4 additional maps, 1903). *See* also the 'third' German edition revised by F. C. von Faber and cited on p. 23.

M. E. Hardy. *A Junior Plant Geography* (Clarendon Press, Oxford, pp. 1–192, 1913).

M. E. Hardy. *The Geography of Plants* (Clarendon Press, Oxford, pp. xii + 327, 1920).

D. H. Campbell. *An Outline of Plant Geography* (Macmillan, London (and New York), pp. ix + 392, 1926).

A. G. Tansley & T. F. Chipp. *Aims and Methods in the Study of Vegetation* (Crown Agents for the Colonies, London, pp. xvi + 383, 1926).

M. I. Newbigin. *Plant and Animal Geography* (Methuen, London, pp. xv + 298, 1936).

Concerning pertinent ecological principles, and for some local examples, *see* the works of Tansley, Leach, Weaver & Clements and Oosting, cited at the end of Chapter X.

Treatment of the vegetation of different regions is extremely 'patchy', even of the most populous of the temperate and allied lands as they were considered in the present chapter. Thus whereas on many areas there is an extensive literature, including numerous accounts prepared by trained and accomplished observers, on others there is very little. The total, however, is vast but scattered. Particularly have many valuable and often well-illustrated accounts appeared in the British *Journal of Ecology*, which has been published continuously since 1913. Others have appeared from time to time in the American journal *Ecology*, which has been published regularly since 1920, in the companion *Ecological Monographs*, of which a volume has appeared each year since its institution in 1931, and in the German *Vegetationsbilder*, of which 26 volumes were published during 1904–44. Further accounts are appearing in the more recently founded international journal *Vegetatio* (Junk, Den Haag, 1948–). Many of the pertinent papers are cited in S. F. Blake & A. C. Atwood's *Geographical Guide to Floras of the World* (*see* p. 214).

A model of the kind of work which is desirable for each and every region is Sir A. G. Tansley's monumental *The British Isles and Their Vegetation* (Cambridge University Press, Cambridge, Eng., pp. xxxviii + 930, 1939), of which a new edition in two handier volumes is now available. Examples of useful books on other, mainly temperate, lands include L. S. Berg's *Natural Regions of the U.S.S.R.* (Macmillan, New

York, transl. edition, pp. xxxi + 436, 1950) and those published in *Die Vegetation der Erde*—such as J. W. Harshberger's *Phytogeographic Survey of North America* (Engelmann, Leipzig, pp. lxiii + 790 and map, 1911) and L. Cockayne's *The Vegetation of New Zealand*, second edition (Engelmann, Leipzig, pp. xxvii + 456 and additional illustrations, 1928). As examples of what may with advantage be done in elucidating a single if generalized type of vegetation in one important region, we may cite E. L. Braun's *Deciduous Forests of Eastern North America* (Blakiston, Philadelphia & Toronto, pp. xiv + 596 and map, 1950) and J. E. Weaver's *North American Prairie* (Johnsen, Lincoln, Nebr., pp. xi + 348, 1954), and, as a study of a particular ecological aspect wherever it may crop up, V. J. Chapman's *Salt Marshes and Salt Deserts of the World* (Leonard Hill, London, pp. xvi + 392, 1960).

Whereas the world's *longest* plants are probably some lianes of the tropical rain forest which are reputed to exceed 656 feet (200 metres, *cf.* p. 431) in length (and hence not to be rivalled by the giant Pacific Kelp *Macrocystis pyrifera*, at least according to recent accounts—cf. p. 535), it is in the temperate regions that there grow what appear to be the world's *tallest* plants—*see* p. 63. For this proud title there is considerable doubt about the validity of claims of the past and some even about contentions of the present, but the oft-quoted and apparently well authenticated 364 feet cited on p. 63 as that of the tallest living Coastal Redwood no longer stands, as the tree has lost its top and is now only 346 feet high. News of this unfortunate loss has arrived as the present volume is in the press, and, at the same time, from Dr. Lincoln Constance, of the University of California at Berkeley, details of another tree of *Sequoia sempervirens*, growing in the Bull Creek Flat area, that is reported to be 368·7 feet high, though he stresses that this measurement has not been finally authenticated. Whereas even this height was apparently exceeded by some Eucalypts growing is southeastern Australia in fairly recent times, where heights of up to 500 feet are widely cited and one of 375 feet for a specimen of *Eucalyptus regnans* seems to be well accepted (cf. A. R. Penfold & J. L. Willis's *Eucalyptus : Botany, Cultivation, and Utilization*, Leonard Hill, London, in press, and J. L. Willis *in litt.*), there do not appear to be among standing trees any very close rivals of the tallest *Sequoia sempervirens.* Moreover, as the tallest known living Eucalypt (growing in Tasmania, and also of the so-called 'Mountain-ash', *E. regnans*) was only 322 feet high in June, 1956, it is likely to be a good many years before the Australians can again rival their American cousins in the possession of the world's tallest living tree.

## Chapter XIII

# VEGETATIONAL TYPES OF POLAR LANDS AND HIGH ALTITUDES

The Arctic and Antarctic make up the ' polar lands ' and are roughly those lying, respectively, north or south of the limit of arborescent growth, even as the high altitudes here considered are those above the timber-line. This ' tree-limit ' approximately coincides with a mean temperature of 10° C. (50° F.) for the warmest month (normally July in the Arctic). Actually, though use of the tree-limit is a great improvement on the astronomically determined but biologically misleading arctic and antarctic circles, satisfactory delimitation of the Arctic and Antarctic can scarcely rest on such a simple basis ; nevertheless for our present purpose it will suffice to tell us approximately what to consider in this chapter, and what to exclude.

Beyond the stunted ' elfin wood ' and twisted ' Krummholz ' that top the upper timbered slopes of mountains in forested regions, or the usually more open ' taiga ' that terminates the poleward limit of forests, is normally a zone of relatively luxuriant ' tundra '. This, by definition, is treeless, though in its most southerly tracts it may contain shrubby examples of the forest dominants as well as, in favourable situations there and elsewhere, bushes of other sorts. The great and extensive examples are afforded by the Arctic, the Antarctic having relatively little ice-free land apart from scattered islands, and the high-alpine tracts being also limited. Consequently most of this chapter is concerned with the Arctic, followed by briefer mention of some antarctic and high-alpine features which are often comparable—without, however, being by any means identical.

If we recognize some modern refinements[1] the Arctic may be generally characterized as treeless, with the winters largely dark and cold and the mean temperature of the warmest month *plus* one-tenth of the mean of the coldest month over a cycle of years not more

[1] As suggested, for example, in the *Journal of Ecology*, vol. 39, pp. 308–315, 1951.

than 9° C., with less than fifty days between spring and fall frosts, with the subsoil in most places permanently frozen, with an annual precipitation normally below 50 cm. (commonly and widely below 25 cm.) and largely in the form of snow which drifts and is packed tightly by the wind, with the soil generally moist in the summer, and with sheltered salt as well as fresh water frozen over during much of the winter. Both arctic and high-alpine regions typically exhibit marked microhabitat effects and consequent variability from spot to spot. Their slopes may also undergo ' solifluction ', which is a slow flowing or creeping downwards of the comminuted surface material over a frozen or other hard substrate, while in flatter areas the sorting in relation to frost action of the surface soil into various kinds of ' polygons ', most often with the finer material in their centres, is extremely widespread especially in the Far North.

In spite of its treelessness and generally dwarfed nature, giving, to the layman, an impression of monotonous sameness, the vegetation of arctic regions varies very markedly from place to place. This variation is often extreme in closely contiguous areas of different habitats or, it sometimes seems, without involving any marked difference in conditions—even suggesting that repeated readjustments to disturbance outweigh any tendency to equilibrium. Indeed one of the most striking features of arctic vegetation is its extreme variability from one small area to the next—in the absence of sufficient growth to control the physical conditions of the environment, which conditions themselves often vary rapidly and even drastically from spot to spot. Thus whereas in a forest, for example, the vegetation largely determines habitat conditions (including the microclimate), in the Arctic the vegetation is relatively impotent. Here the struggle of plants tends to be with the inimical forces of a harsh physical environment rather than with hostile competitors as in more favourable situations, though there is still plentiful competition between plants in the more favourable arctic habitats. Such competition is particularly rife where growth is relatively luxuriant towards the southern limit of the Arctic; similarly in high-alpine regions it is found mainly towards the lower limits, as in the Antarctic towards the northern boundary.

In the arctic regions land is ranged practically around the North Pole, though unlike the situation in the southern hemisphere there is none at the very highest latitudes. In spite of considerable differences in flora, especially at the lowest latitudes of what we recognize as the Arctic, the over-all picture of vegetation is closely similar in the different sectors into which the Arctic may conveniently be divided (*see* Fig. 46). Thus the vegetation developed under similar habitat conditions in any particular climatic belt ranged around the top of the globe tends to look much the same in whatever sector it may lie, and there do not seem to be any major subsidiary regions that can be singled out, such as the Mediterranean or various semi-deserts in the temperate zone.

Under the prevailing cool conditions, water is very widely sufficient in the Arctic for such limited growth as the climate, etc., allows, and the main vegetational differences in any particular belt are rather in accordance with the actual habitats (such as were described in Chapter XI). Thus local edaphic or physiographic variations can ring the most immediate and fundamental changes in the local plant life. On the other hand a progressive and almost regular over-all depauperation of the vegetation is to be observed as we go farther and farther north; and as this tends to be rather closely comparable in the various sectors, it is deemed expedient to separate each sector (and consequently the Arctic as a whole) roughly into three main belts. These are the *low-Arctic*, in which the vegetation is continuous over most areas, the *middle-Arctic*, in which it is still sufficient to be widely evident from a distance, covering most lowlands, and the *high-Arctic*, in which closed vegetation is limited to the most favourable habitats and is rarely at all extensive.[1] The following outline account of the main vegetational types of the Arctic will accordingly have, under each major heading, some consideration of the expression of this type in each of these three belts, ranging from south to north. Examples of low-arctic lands are the southern portions of almost all sectors, of middle-arctic lands Jan Mayen Island and the vicinity of Point Barrow, Alaska, and of high-arctic lands the whole of the Spitsbergen Archipelago, and the Canadian Eastern Arctic north of Lancaster Sound.

## Arctic Tundras

The term ‘ tundra ’, meaning essentially a treeless plain, has been used in so many and often such vague senses that it seems desirable, if we are to retain it at all, to limit its use so that it will have a more precise scientific connotation. In the present work the tundra proper is understood as the usually ‘ grassy ’ formation lying beyond (or in some extra-arctic places forming patches within) the limit of

[1] *See* Frontispiece for a first, tentative attempt to delimit these three arctic belts.

arborescent growth—except where shrubs or undershrubs predominate (in scrub and heathlands), or vegetation covers less than half of the area (in ' fell-fields ' and ' barrens '). Although this still includes such special cases as salt-marshes and manured areas, it is customary to consider these separately, as is done in the present work. On the other hand, it excludes the taiga and at least the forested parts of the mixed ' forest-tundra ' described in the last chapter (p. 348). Generally comparable types occur in antarctic regions where, however, suitable land areas are relatively small. Alpine tundra bears a similar relationship to the timber-line on mountains. Instead of true Grasses which, however, are rarely absent, grass-like plants such as Sedges (*Carex* spp.), Cotton-grasses (*Eriophorum* spp.), Rushes (*Juncus* spp.), and Wood-rushes (*Luzula* spp.), commonly afford most of the ' grassiness ' of the tundra, though various perennial forbs are usually associated, as are often a sprinkling of dwarf woody plants.

Even in this restricted sense the tundra developed in almost any arctic region is usually very variable, different areas supporting widely different types. The variation takes place particularly with differences in exposure and in water and other soil conditions, and, at all events in low- and middle-arctic regions, affords faciations far too numerous even to mention here. We may, however, distinguish and outline, besides a general central type, the tundras of damper depressions on the one hand and of drier exposed areas on the other.

The general run of tundra which covers a large proportion of the lowland plains and some less extensive upland areas of most low-arctic regions is commonly a rather thin ' grassy ' sward dominated by mesophytic Sedges such as the Rigid Sedge (*Carex bigelowii* agg.) and Grasses such as the Arctic Meadow-grass (*Poa arctica* s.l.), with various associated forbs and under-shrubs including dwarf Willows. The whole forms a continuous if often poor sward commonly 15–35 cm. (approximately 6–14 in.) high in which a mixture of various Bryophytes and Lichens usually forms a rather poorly-marked second layer a very few centimetres high.

Commonly the low-arctic tundra is a mosaic made up of faciations having each some lesser number of the total association dominants, and including consociations having only one of these. The areas of the component communities are often small and the variation from spot to spot in the tundra is accordingly usually considerable. In addition there are often local societies dominated by species other than the association dominants. The (sometimes unaccountable) mixing and even intergradation of all these communities is often intricate and may be suggestive of their relative youth, many having apparently failed to come to a state approaching equilibrium with the environment since emergence from glaciation or other extreme disturbance. Actually, it may be questioned whether, in many areas, even relative equilibrium can be attained in the face of the persistent frost-activity, and it has been claimed that the whole system constitutes an 'open' one in which the main tendency is repeated

FIG. 109.—Tundra on Southampton Island, Hudson Bay. The depressions support low bushy Willows.

readjustment to almost perpetual disturbance. Fig. 109 shows an area of low-arctic tundra in eastern Canada.

With the generally poor drainage resulting from the soil being permanently frozen to not far beneath the surface, damper depressions or marshy open tracts tend to be plentiful although often of quite limited extent ; indeed they are rarely absent except in regions of porous substrata and low water-table. In the low-Arctic they are commonly rather luxuriantly vegetated, the sward often being taller than it is in drier areas. They are usually dominated by Cotton-grasses and relatively hygrophytic Sedges such as marshland ecads of the Water Sedge (*Carex aquatilis* agg.), and by Grasses such as the Arctagrostis (*Arctagrostis latifolia* s.l.), with a few hygrophilous Willows or other ground-shrubs and many hygrophilous or ubiquitous forbs. Typical among these last are Viviparous Knotweed (*Polygonum viviparum*) and the bright-flowered Yellow Marsh Saxifrage (*Saxifraga hirculus* agg.). The fairly luxuriant cryptogamic layer is largely composed of Mosses, and helps to consolidate the whole. An example is seen in Fig. 110. Often these marshy areas are beset with small hummocks commonly about 25 cm. high, and introducing drier conditions on their tops, which may then support heathy plants and Lichens. Such hummocky tracts are known as

FIG. 110.—Marshy tundra near the south shore of Hudson Strait, dominated by Cotton-grasses, Sedges, and Grasses, with dwarf Willows creeping among the subdominant Mosses.

'hillock tundra'. In other instances tundras, especially of the damper types, are liable to be much interrupted by various of the geodynamic influences prevalent in cold regions—such as, particularly, solifluction and 'patterned soil' (polygon—*see* p. 381) formation of various kinds.

The drier tundras of raised areas or well-drained surface material in low-arctic regions tend to be much poorer and thinner than the damper types. Typically they are composed of an extremely various array of more or less xerophilous Sedges (such as the Rock Sedge, *Carex rupestris*), Willows (particularly the Arctic Willow, *Salix arctica* s.l.), Grasses (such as Alpine Holy-grass, *Hierochloe alpina*),

Northern Wood-rush (*Luzula confusa* agg.), and various forbs (such as the same Viviparous Knotweed), in addition to Mountain and Arctic Avens (*Dryas* spp.), which are somewhat woody, and which may dominate considerable areas. But although scattered heathy plants occur in them, these areas are scarcely heaths, any more than are the lichen-rich ones dominated by xerophilous Sedges that characterize dry and exposed situations (*see* p. 392). Moreover their vegetation is usually rather poor, often barely covering the

FIG. 111.—Dry tundra on raised area overlooking Hudson Bay, composed principally of an intricate mixture of xerophilous Lichens, Grasses, Sedges, and other herbs. Dwarf woody plants also occur, and the surface is interrupted by projecting lichen-covered boulders.

ground in spite of a plentiful admixture of Lichens and sometimes also of Bryophytes. Fig. 111 shows such an area in which boulders project through the thin and somewhat heathy, lichen-rich vegetation. Especially on limestone or porous sandy substrata is growth often poor and the vegetation relatively sparse, although the component flora particularly in calcareous areas may be very various.

It would accordingly seem that the major variations in the precise type of tundra take place chiefly, but by no means solely, with local water conditions working through exposure or edaphic factors, while very locally the effect of frost action may be paramount. Thus differences in substratum, as between limestone and acid-weathering rock, can introduce vegetational differences due to particular plants' preferences quite apart from water-relations, while, as an example of the entry of another factor, heavy pasturing can lead to increased grassiness as in temperate regions. In addition, polygon-formation and solifluction may cause persistent disturbance. It may be noted that, whereas the dominants are usually at least specifically distinct in different types of low-arctic tundra, some of the less exacting, more tolerant associates may be present in a wide range of habitat types. This again is comparable with the situation in cool-temperate regions and, it often seems, obtains still more forcibly to the north. Thus in the Far North some of the hardier plants, such as Viviparous Knotweed and some of the Saxifrages, grow in an extraordinarily wide variety of habitats, ranging from wet to dry, exposed to sheltered, and open-soil to vegetationally ' closed '.

The middle-arctic belt is characterized by tundras of a generally poorer type, both in the matter of flora and luxuriance of development, than the low-arctic ones. Thus some of the plants which were important in low-arctic tundras are absent, though all of the dominants, etc., mentioned above for low-arctic tundras can, and frequently do, occupy a similar position also in middle-arctic regions. Moreover the range of types is much the same, damp, mesophytic, and drier ones being distinguishable. An example of the second, dominated by mixed Grasses and Sedges, in northernmost Alaska overlooking the Arctic Ocean, is shown in Fig. 112, from which it may be seen that growth tends to be lower and poorer than in low-arctic regions, though this particular area is only just middle-arctic in type.

In high-arctic regions still further depauperation is general, and indeed only limited and relatively few areas are sufficiently vegetated to be designated as tundra. These areas are chiefly marshy ones and may be still dominated by Sedges, Cotton-grasses, and Grasses —often of the same species as in the South, and including similar associated forbs, though woody plants apart from prostrate Willows are usually absent. Mosses commonly consolidate the whole, and in some places appear to dominate. Fig. 113 shows an unusually extensive area of marshy tundra in Spitsbergen, characterized by peaty hummocks up to 25 cm. high, and of a type commonly termed ' hillock tundra '. While the main dominants in such areas are commonly Sedges and Grasses growing on the sides or tops of the

FIG. 112.—Mesophytic Sedge-Grass tundra on the north coast of Alaska near Point Barrow, overlooking the Arctic Ocean. Ice-pups are seen stranded on the shore, and in the distance the margin of the polar pack-ice is visible. The tundra in flat areas is usually closed; but on slopes, where disturbed by geodynamic influences, it is commonly discontinuous.

FIG. 113.—Extensive area of damp 'hillock tundra' on the coast of Spitsbergen. Note the grassiness of the hummocks but frequent puddles of water between.

hummocks, the microhabitat effect is extreme, the microhabitats ranging from depressions occupied by dark boglets or puddles of 'free' water (seen in Fig. 113) to dry hillock tops occupied by Lichens or, in favourably sheltered situations, xeromorphic ground-shrubs.

Tracts of 'grassy' mesophytic tundra of any substantial extent

FIG. 114.—Discontinuous tundra-like tract of mixed Grasses, Northern Wood-rush (*Luzula confusa* agg.), forbs, and Polar Willow (*Salix polaris* agg.), in inland valley, West Spitsbergen, grazed by a pair of wild Reindeer. Beyond is the dry bouldery bed of a melt-water stream that is dry during most of the summer, and, behind, barren scree and other slopes.

are not common in the high-Arctic, though Fig. 114 shows a discontinuous but tundra-like patch of mixed Grasses, Northern Wood-rush (*Luzula confusa* agg.), forbs, and Polar Willow (*Salix polaris* agg.), that is sufficiently developed to attract Reindeer. It is situated in a sheltered valley well inland in Spitsbergen, by the side of a bouldery bed of a snow-water stream that is dry during most of the summer. Still drier types of tundra in these farthest north lands tend to be dominated largely by Lichens and to be much interrupted by rocks or bare patches—especially in exposed situations.

So far as regular ecological successions are concerned, these are especially problematical in the Arctic. It has, however, been suggested that the marshy and dry tundras may be subclimax and the mesophytic ones climax or preclimax, the scrub and heathlands, which are developed in the most favourable situations (*see* below), being either postclimax or, perhaps, indicative of a more general climax to be expected ultimately in sufficiently favourable situations, though at present a mixed ' polyclimax ' is commonly found. The significance of different ' stages ' in the hypothetical successions may, however, vary from place to place. Thus, in the Far North, heathy plants are apt to be so restricted to the most favourable situations as to suggest that without major climatic change they could not become widely dominant in the manner already obtaining in some places in the low-Arctic. Moreover, frost and other disturbance is so widespread, *inter alia* impeding or even preventing the maturation of soils, that it seems as though many areas undergo a kind of perpetual readjustment rather than exhibit the tendency to equilibrium which is implicit in a real climax.

## Arctic Scrub and Heathlands

A shaggy scrub of Willows and/or Birches is commonly developed on the most favourable slopes, in damp depressions, and especially along watercourses and the margins of lakes in low-arctic regions. It is commonly around 60 cm. (about 2 feet) high, as in the example shown in Fig. 115, but tends to become lower and more restricted northwards until, about the centre of the middle-arctic belt, it becomes usually very limited in extent and stature. However, in the most favourable situations in the extreme south the Willows may be luxuriant (*cf.* Fig. 116) and even exceed the height of a Man, and especially in southwestern Greenland the scrub is quite extensively developed, in some places including arborescent Birches. These Greenland Birch ' forests ' are of very limited extent, with the trees scattered and scraggy though sometimes nearly 6 metres in height and 25 cm. in stem diameter. Their areas have been termed subarctic but seem too limited to separate on an over-all, world basis; they are also too fickle, the development of an arborescent habit being evidently dependent on local shelter, etc. Apart from these larger Birches, the main dominants in differernt regions are most often the Dwarf Birch (*Betula nana* agg.) or Scrub Birch (*B. glandulosa* agg.), or such shrubby Willows as the Glaucous

FIG. 115.—Tangled Willow scrub in the low-arctic belt of the Northwest Territories, Canada. The scrub occupies a slight depression whose depth is indicated by a spade resting on the ground (in centre).

FIG. 116.—Patchy scrub of Glaucous Willow (*Salix glauca* s.l.) and Scrub Birch (*Betula glandulosa* agg.), up to nearly 2 metres high, in southwestern Greenland. The scrub is interrupted by grassy tracts of fair turf which appear to result from ancient pasturing (*see* page 222).

Willow (*Salix glauca* s.l.), the Broad-leafed Willow (*S. cordifolia* s.l.), the Feltleaf Willow (*S. alaxensis* agg.), or Richardson's Willow (*S. richardsonii* agg.). Often two or more of these shrubs will dominate a mixed association. In some places bushes of Green Alder (*Alnus crispa* agg.) are present and may be locally dominant.

Such scrub at its best is so thickly tangled and produces so much litter that few associated plants occur, apart from tall Grasses such as Bluejoint (*Calamagrostis canadensis* agg.) and occasional straggling forbs. But where the dominants are less luxuriant, an extensive flora is often found, including a considerable variety of herbs and Mosses, or, in dry situations, subdominant heathy plants such as Crowberry (*Empetrum nigrum* s.l.). Also characteristic of dry scrub are patches of tall Cladonias, Stereocaulons, and other Lichens, with or without Polytricha or other coarse Mosses. To the north such scrub thins out gradually, its most northerly expression about the northern limit of the middle-arctic belt being usually in the form of single or scarcely confluent bushes that rarely exceed 50 cm. in height and are usually much lower, though often quite wide.

Heathlands are more widespread and various in the Arcitc than is scrub, though still commonly occupying only a very small proportion of the total area. They are usually characterized by being dominated by members of the Heath family (Ericaceae) or by heath-like plants such as, particularly, Crowberry. Sometimes, however, broad-leafed plants such as Avens (*Dryas*), or Sedges such as the Nard Sedge (*Carex nardina* s.l.) or Bellard's Kobresia (*Kobresia myosuroides*), may dominate dry and usually exposed, lichen-rich areas that are often classed as heathlands rather than among the drier tundras with which they seem more properly to belong (*see* p. 386). Leaving aside such cases it may be said that heathlands in the Arctic tend to be confined to the more favourable, sheltered situations that are snow-covered in winter—provided they are not too moist in summer. In many regions they characterize coarse-grained rather than clayey soils, as pointed out by Professor Thorvald Sørensen (*in litt.*).

In the low-arctic belt the heathlands are usually covered by a continuous thick sward of mixed woody and herbaceous plants, the main dominants being typically 8–15 cm. high. These commonly include Crowberry, Arctic Blueberry (*Vaccinium uliginosum* subsp. *alpinum*), Mountain Cranberry (*V. vitis-idaea* agg.), Arctic Bell-heather (*Cassiope tetragona*), Narrow-leafed Labrador-tea (*Ledum palustre* agg.), Dwarf Birch, and various diminutive Willows. Often the dominants themselves are much mixed, and usually they are consolidated below by a layer of cryptogams in which Mosses or Lichens commonly subdominate—according to whether the situation is relatively moist or dry, respectively. Fig. 117 shows an area of dense mixed heath on the south shore of Hudson Strait. In the drier situations there may occur frequent gaps in the heath which are actually dominated by Lichens—particularly by 'Caribou-moss' Cladonias that may form a sward 5 or more cm. high. In depressions and behind obstructions where snow drifts deeply in winter,

FIG. 117.—Dense low-arctic heath dominated by Arctic Blueberry (*Vaccinium uliginosum* var. *alpinum*) in northernmost Quebec. Light-coloured Lichens and leaves of dwarf Willows and Sedges are visible. To the left of the sheath-knife is a flowering bushlet of Lapland Rose-bay (*Rhododendron lapponicum*).

a characteristic dark (except when flowering) heath dominated by Arctic Bell-heather usually develops, often with associated Sedges and Mosses at least where the soil is lastingly moist. Such an area is shown in Fig. 118 and, apart from a zone of more mixed heath that may develop outside, usually constitutes the outermost of the zoned series of subclimaxes developed in late-snow areas as described on pages 402–5.

In the middle-arctic belt, heathlands are usually somewhat lower in stature and more restricted in area than to the south, having the appearance of postclimaxes developed in the most favourable situations. Of the cited dominants Mountain Cranberry has usually

FIG. 118.—'Snow-patch' darkened by Arctic Bell-heather (*Cassiope tetragona*), southern Baffin Island.

FIG. 119.—Mixed middle-arctic heath with many light-coloured and other Lichens. Bushlets of Narrow-leafed Labrador-tea (*Ledum palustre* agg.) are seen to the right and left of the pipe, which is 15 cm. long and gives the scale. Northern Baffin Island.

disappeared, and although the taller ones may still exceed 20 cm. in height the sward is usually only 5–10 cm. high. Whereas it may still be fairly dense, more often the ‘ heath ’ is of scattered ground-shrubs with intervening thin patches of Cetrarias, Alectorias, and other Lichens, as seen in Fig. 119.

In the high-arctic belt heathy plants are entirely absent over considerable areas, the tracts that are popularly spoken of as ‘ heaths ’ being usually dominated by Avens, Sedges, or even Lichens. However, Crowberry or Arctic Blueberry plants are to be found in some regions, dominating limited heathy communities in unusually favourable situations, while Arctic Bell-heather is quite widespread, characteristically forming a dark tract where the snow accumulates sufficiently to form a good protective covering in winter (though disappearing early in the growing-season).

## Arctic Fell-Fields and Barrens

These are types in which the evident vegetation occupies less than half of the area ; and whereas the two categories are scarcely to be rigidly distinguished, it is usually those tracts that bear relatively few and scattered plants that are referred to as ‘ barrens ’. Fell-fields typically have a surface of frost-shattered detrital material including much finer ‘ soil ’ and usually support fairly numerous different species forming mixed communities, whereas barrens are apt to be characterized by one prominent size of particle and a single species of plant, such as Mountain Avens or Purple Saxifrage (*cf.* Fig. 128). This is especially the case when they occupy the most exposed situations.

Where sufficient moisture is present these poorly-vegetated areas, like some tundras, are commonly disturbed by all manner of frost-heaving and allied effects—such as solifluction on slopes and polygon-formation on the flatter terrain. The solifluction is generally manifest in streaks extending longitudinally downhill, adjacent streaks being either of different material or accentuated by vegetation which cannot grow on the more dynamic parts. The ‘ polygons ’ are almost endlessly variable but very commonly have the form of polygonal or circular areas ½–2 metres in diameter and composed of finely comminuted soil that is apt to be too dynamic to support any plants at all, separated by narrow intervening tracts containing most of the larger stones and often raised and vegetated or in other cases barren (Fig. 120). Or the polygons may be separated by narrow cracks or troughs that afford shelter for plants which in the Far North often grow better in such microhabitats than in surrounding areas.

On steep slopes and below weathering crags, still more dynamic and often poorly vegetated ' screes ' are common. Also often constituting barrens of one sort or another are ' raised beaches ' near sea-shores ; for although some are well vegetated, many others are the reverse, owing to exposure, recent emergence, or an unfavourable

FIG. 120.—' Polygons ' in northernmost Spitsbergen. The stony intervening tracts are here almost barren, but often in other instances are covered with vegetation.

substratum. Altogether these poorer types of vegetation—or terrain, for often plants are scarcely at all in evidence—are so numerous and variable in the Arctic that only a few examples can be mentioned here.

In low-arctic regions fell-fields, barrens, and the like, are found chiefly in upland districts and in exposed areas near the coast—especially where the substratum is of porous material. Here, owing to lack of stability, to local aridity, or to extreme exposure, such fell-field or ' half-barren ' areas as that shown in Fig. 121 occur, in which Mountain Avens, Nard Sedge, and various tufted Saxifrages and other herbs form irregular patches of vegetation. A fair number of cryptogams are often admixed, though usually they are of poor growth. In the most unfavourable situations of all, this type may thin out to a stony barren supporting little more than diminutive crustaceous Lichens and very occasional depauperated tussocks of Avens or Purple Saxifrage.

Although such poorly-vegetated areas tend to be more numerous and widespread in the middle-arctic zone than farther south, they still do not normally occupy the general run of lowland terrain but are chiefly encountered in exposed situations (as for example in the

FIG. 121.—Fell-field on calcareous soil in exposed situation, northernmost Labrador.

foreground of Fig. 128). An extensive example is shown in Fig. 122, from an altitude of 671 metres (2,200 feet) in central Baffin Island, in which Lichens of poor growth cover much of the surface, vascular plants being virtually absent.

In most high-arctic regions ' open ' and often extremely sparse vegetation is the general rule, and so fell-field and barrens areas are widespread and plentiful. A relatively well-vegetated and extensive area, reminiscent of many observed by the author in far northern Ellesmere Island and Spitsbergen, is seen in Fig. 123, which he took, however, in the vicinity of the North Magnetic Pole on Prince of Wales Island. It shows a monotonous expanse of mixed but scattered and open, diminutive herbs and terricolous (*i.e.* earth-inhabiting) Lichens, with occasional small tufts of Avens (in this case *Dryas integrifolia* agg.). The general aspect is desolate in the extreme

FIG. 122.—Lichen barrens in the uplands of central Baffin Island, looking south. Note the virtual absence of higher plants and the abundance of persistent snow-patches on north-facing slopes.

FIG. 123.—Monotonous tract of prairie-like fell-field in the vicinity of the Magnetic North Pole, Prince of Wales Island, Canadian Arctic Archipelago. The sparse vegetation consists of scattered diminutive herbs, terricolous Lichens, and occasional tufts of Arctic Avens, all growing in open formation.

in most of such exposed high-arctic tracts, with a large proportion of the area typically occupied by barrens supporting little more than occasional tufts of Arctic Poppy (*Papaver radicatum* s.l.) or Purple Saxifrage (*Saxifraga oppositifolia* agg.), although more mixed fell-fields may occur in less unfavourable situations. On well-drained banks there may be Grasses and some hardy but attractive forbs, while very occasionally under the most favourable conditions a limited tract of thin heath may be developed, though often one can trek for days without encountering such a manifestation. The only at all extensive tracts of closed vegetation are mostly of rather thin marshy and often hummocky tundra (Fig. 113), and even here the dominants rarely exceed a height of 30 cm. above the surface from which they grow. Yet most of these vegetation-types and a fair range of vascular plants are to be found right up to the highest latitudes of land, between 83° and 84° N., in marked contrast to the situation in Antarctica (*see* pp. 415 *et seq.*).

## Seaside and Other Local Types

On sandy and fine-shingle maritime beaches in both low- and middle-arctic belts there are usually scattered plants of Sea-purslane (*Arenaria peploides* agg.) and Sea Lungwort (*Mertensia maritima* agg.) on the foreshore and, farther up, stabilizing beds of Lyme-grass (*Elymus arenarius* s.l.) which may be fairly tall and luxuriant (Fig. 124). In the high-arctic belt, Lyme-grass is unknown and the other two are rare, so exposed sandy and shingly shores are liable to be barren around high-tide mark.

In sheltered and less well-drained seaside areas, muddy or sandy 'salt-marshes' are common though usually of very limited extent in the Arctic. Even more than many other types of vegetation, they show close similarity of form all around the southern portions of the Arctic—and also, with natural depauperation, far northwards. Thus in low-arctic areas they typically consist of a dwarfish grassy sward dominated by Alkali-grasses (particularly the Creeping Alkali-grass, *Puccinellia phryganodes* agg.) and Sedges (particularly the Bear Sedge, *Carex ursina*, and phases of the Salt-marsh Sedge, *C. salina* s.l.), with associated Low Chickweed (*Stellaria humifusa*), Scurvy-grass (*Cochlearia officinalis* s.l.), Pacific Silverweed (*Potentilla egedii* agg.), and other halophytes. Fig. 125 shows such a salt-marsh on the south coast of Baffin Island. Except for the usual absence farther north of the Silverweed and the substitution of Salt-marsh

FIG. 124.—Shingly beach bound by swarded Lyme-grass (*Elymus arenarius* s.l.). Farther down, between tide-marks in this sheltered inlet, the shore is darkened by algal growth. Hudson Strait, northeastern Canada.

FIG. 125.—Looking down on a salt-marsh dominated by Pacific Silverweed (*Potentilla egedii* agg.) (flowering) and Creeping Alkali-grass (*Puccinellia phryganodes* agg.) (light-coloured stolons). Pipe gives scale. South coast of Baffin Island.

Sedge by the doubtfully specifically distinct Hoppner Sedge (*Carex subspathacea*), the same plants generally play a similar role in middle- and high-arctic regions, though with increasing depauperation. It seems probable that they are unable to alter their habitat markedly, at least if and when it has reached the approximate level of the highest tides, and consequently that they represent a subclimax which will persist indefinitely.

Another type of local climax is engendered by the perennial manuring that takes place around the 'bird-cliffs' where countless

FIG. 126.—Luxuriant 'patchwork quilt' of mixed and many-coloured Lichens and Mosses developed near top of bird-cliff. Northernmost point of Quebec, overlooking Hudson Strait. Scale indicated by pack on left which is 60 cm. high.

sea-birds nest every summer. Here unoccupied ledges may support coarse Grasses and rank Scurvy-grass, the rock faces being covered by Lichens, often of extraordinary size. The tops of the cliffs typically support near their edges and in damp depressions a rich grassy sward, and, stretching back for 100 metres or so, a luxuriant and dense 'patchwork quilt' of mixed and variously coloured Lichens and Mosses. This is seen in Fig. 126 and is due to manuring effects engendered apparently largely by scavenging Sea-gulls and Birds-of-prey, though in some instances Foxes and Polar Bears are also involved. The situation being usually very exposed, the adjacent unmanured cliffs and hinterland are apt to be practically barren and in striking contrast. More local manuring may also give remarkable effects, such as the grassy or flower-decked swards that develop around human habitations, mammalian burrows, or, particularly, the nesting-grounds of Geese, Eiders, and other gregarious wildfowl (Fig. 127). An instance of a different kind is shown in Fig. 128, in which a dense grassy patch is developed around a boulder in an exposed Purple Saxifrage barren overlooking the sea ; to such prominences Birds and predators repair, manuring the ground in the immediate vicinity and doubtless sometimes

FIG. 127.—Looking down on a luxuriant mossy mat on the manured periphery of a wildfowl nesting-ground in Spitsbergen. The plant flowering on the right, above the matchbox (giving scale), is Yellow Marsh Saxifrage (*Saxifraga hirculus* agg.), the flowers on the left are of Alpine Brook Saxifrage (*S. rivularis* agg.), and the small ones below are of Fringed Sandwort (*Arenaria ciliata* s.l.).

bringing in viable seeds. The result is often a luxuriant if limited sward in an otherwise seemingly sterile situation.

As very little cultivation or other human disturbance has so far taken place in most arctic areas, few tracts bear witness to such change ; on the other hand a common and widespread type of local climax is that engendered by the drifting and late-melting of snow. This tends to take place similarly each year and to lead to characteristic vegetational zonation within the area of the drift. The zones produced are of subclimax nature although the outermost may be considered postclimax—especially in the Far North where the most widespread (and often the sole) heathy plant, Arctic Bell-heather, may be practically confined to such situations. In the low- and middle-arctic belts the outermost zone of such 'snow-patches', which is well protected in winter by snow but does not have its growing-season markedly reduced by late melting, is commonly vegetated by a luxuriant mixed heath (Fig. 129), or, in lastingly damp situations, by a thin Willow scrub. Farther in, where the snow drifts sufficiently deeply for the growing-season to be

FIG. 128.—Purple Saxifrage barren on exposed ridge overlooking the sea in northernmost Baffin Island. The *Saxifraga oppositifolia* agg. forms only scattered tufts and small dark matlets that scarcely show in the photograph; nevertheless, around a prominent boulder that has persistently acted as a perch, there is a luxuriant grassy sward where the ground has been manured.

appreciably shortened, Arctic Bell-heather characteristically forms a dark belt, often being the sole dominant as in Fig. 118. In other instances this belt may be more mixed and only 1–3 metres wide, as in Fig. 129, which shows in the background the more barren inner zones. These are apt to vary considerably in number and vegetation in different places and circumstances. However, they typically include towards the outside a zone of dwarf Willows (particularly Herb-like Willow, *Salix herbacea*, as in Fig. 130), and, farther in where the growing-season is too short for woody plants, a sparsely vegetated zone with a considerable variety of

FIG. 129.—' Late-snow ' patch in the highlands of central Baffin Island, showing in foreground the outer zone of mixed Arctic Blueberry heath, then a narrow belt of dark Arctic Bell-heather interrupted by light-coloured Lichens, and behind, a Herb-like Willow zone (*see* Fig. 130), the centre of the snow-drift area where the snow melts latest being occupied by a herb ' barren.'

FIG. 130.—Looking down on the Herb-like Willow zone of the late-snow area shown in Fig. 129. The rounded leaves are those of the dominant Willow, the ground being characteristically encrusted with cryptogams. Pipe 15 cm. long gives scale.

Bryophytes and open-soil herbs such as the Mountain Sorrel (*Oxyria digyna*).

Many of the smaller snow-patches, of course, disappear well before the end of summer, especially in the South, and consequently show only the outermost zones. On the other hand around the centre of the deeper drifts, which usually form in ravines, depressions, or behind banks or ridges, the snow may melt only towards the very end of summer or in a cool season not at all. Here most herbs are unable to persist and even cryptogams are little in evidence, though some tufts or limited mats of Bryophytes and investments of Algae are usually to be found, together with the diminutive grass *Phippsia algida* agg. (Frigid Phippsia). Towards such centres various plants, including attractive Saxifrages and Buttercups (*Ranunculus* spp.), are often to be found flowering at the very end of summer, sometimes being caught still in bud by the frosts and snow of a new winter. In the Far North the zones are apt to be reduced in number but extended in area, the fell-fields and barrens often representing inner zones where the modest snow-covering melts late under the prevailingly cool conditions. Here, as on mountains farther south, many of the snow-patches are perennial or even eternal, the chief growths near their centres being of Bryophytes and Algae in the run-off below.

## Seral Types

Whereas the apparent arctic counterparts of many southern seral types have already been dealt with, being often seemingly incapable of leading to permanent higher vegetation or best regarded as subclimax (in view either of persistent disturbance or of the extreme slowness of vegetable build-up), other instances of seral stages remain to be mentioned. Outstanding are the marshy and boggy ones of hydroseres (the fully aquatic communities comprising the early stages of which will be dealt with in Chapter XV), various ones of lithoseres, and the ' flower-slopes ' that probably belong to mesoseres.

The hydrosere of arctic lakes and tarns usually has as its first aerial stage a ' reed-swamp ' of aquatic Sedges (particularly the Water Sedge, *Carex aquatilis* agg.) and/or Cotton-grasses (particularly the Tall Cotton-grass, *Eriophorum angustifolium* agg.), though sometimes Common Mare's-tail (*Hippuris vulgaris* s.l.), or such coarse Grasses as the Tawny Arctophila (*Arctophila fulva* agg.), may largely or wholly take their place. Any of these plants may form luxuriant beds where the bottom is soft and not more than about 40 cm. deep. They generally project some 20–40 cm. above the water in the south but usually less in the Far North, where Mare's-tail is normally absent. Commonly such beds are accompanied by aquatic Mosses and, of course, numerous small Algae. Behind there stretches typically a marshy sedge-meadow with the same ' grassy ' dominants and, in addition, Arctagrostis and lowly Willows. This in turn merges into damp tundra. Fig. 131 shows such a sequence in the low-Arctic, though it should be noted that in exposed situations, especially farther north, wave action may prevent reed-swamp formation, a definite ' hard line ' then delimiting terrestrial from

FIG. 131.—Luxuriant lakeside marsh dominated by Water Sedge (*Carex aquatilis* agg.) and Tall Cotton-grass (*Eriophorum angustifolium* agg.), which both extend out into the water. Southampton Island, Hudson Bay.

aquatic communities. On the other hand there may be an ecotone of Willow scrub that, at least on its lower side, probably represents a later stage in the hydrosere.

Boggy areas, typically dominated by Bog-mosses (*Sphagnum* spp.) and rather strongly acidic in reaction, are chiefly developed in the southern portions of the Arctic. Baked-apple (*Rubus chamaemorus*) is a characteristic inhabitant of them. Often they are well developed around pools in peaty tracts and are colonized by heathy plants, with little doubt ultimately turning into heathlands. In the Far North, however, many tarnside areas remain to this day uncolonized by higher plants—as in the right background of Fig. 132, although the foreground is vegetated by a fine bed of Scheuchzer's Cotton-grass (*Eriophorum scheuchzeri*).

Lithosere stages are abundant in the Arctic, where much of the terrain is of more or less bare rock that has, in many cases, been freed from glaciation only in relatively recent times. Nevertheless there is no doubt that succession is proceeding, however slowly—at all events in areas that are not too rigorously exposed or lastingly snow- or ice-covered. Thus rock faces, whether of glacial boulders or of detrital, cliff-face, or some other nature, are apt to be largely invested with crustaceous and foliose Lichens, and to occupy considerable areas. On the other hand, rock crevices or interstices

FIG. 132.—Fine bed of Scheuchzer's Cotton-grass (*Eriophorum scheuchzeri*) beside tarn in northern Spitsbergen, though the waterside behind (on right) is devoid of higher plants.

often support higher life-forms, so that in time a moss-mat or mixed herbaceous community develops, and, ultimately, heathy vegetation in suitable situations.

Screes, if not too active, may also be bound by hardy plants—especially in low-arctic regions, where dark strips stabilized by vegetation often extend down scree slopes. Also commonly stabilized by vegetation are inland sandy areas, though the psammosere may advance little beyond the pioneer stage of sand-binding Mosses (such as *Polytrichum* spp.) and ground-shrubs (such as Crowberry and Alpine Bearberry, *Arctostaphylos alpina* agg.). Consolidation of the ground-shrubs produces already an advanced type of vegetation. On

FIG. 133.—Top of flower-slope below weathering crag in southern Baffin Island. On right is seen flowering Three-toothed Saxifrage (*Saxifraga tricuspidata*), on left Arctic Fireweed (*Epilobium latifolium*) and Alpine Chickweed (*Cerastium alpinum* s.l.). In the centre are two species of Fleabane (*Erigeron*). Knife with handle 12 cm. long gives scale.

FIG. 134.—Spitsbergen flower-slope dominated by Alpine Arnica (*Arnica alpina* s.l.). The background of swarded cryptogams helps to make this high-arctic community look unusually luxuriant.

both rock and sand, a dense mat of the 'silvery' Moss *Rhacomitrium lanuginosum* may cover substantial areas and apparently persist for many years, though in the end it is usually colonized by Lichens and Grasses, etc., to form what is sometimes termed 'Rhacomitrium heath'.

The mesosere is represented by relatively short-lived communities in such favourable situations as alluvial deltas and the beds of receding tarns, and apparently by longer-lived types on the earthy or gravelly 'flower-slopes' that form such a pleasing feature on steep south-facing inclines particularly in low-arctic lands. Fig. 133 shows an example in which Fleabanes (*Erigeron* spp.) and Saxifrages are prominent, although a large variety of other forbs occur—typically much-mixed and in such profusion that the usual dominants are excluded. The writer has even encountered very limited communities of this type near 78° N. in Spitsbergen and at high altitudes in southern Greenland, growing under an unusually favourable combination of conditions of shelter, aspect, water, aeration, and soil—*cf.* Fig. 134.

## High Altitudes

In general, temperatures get lower and lower as we ascend mountains, and higher and higher as we go farther and farther south at a particular altitude (such as sea-level) in the northern hemisphere. Precipitation, windiness, fogginess, and the intensity of radiation also tend to increase with altitude on mountains, though precipitation falls off at the higher altitudes and other conditions often interfere with radiation. Consequently, particular zones of vegetation in general get higher and higher in the mountains as we travel towards the Equator, though something like arctic conditions and attendant vegetation may still be found at very high altitudes in tropical lands. But although a general similarity to high-latitude lands prevails in high mountains even near the Equator, the light and other climatic regimes are by no means identical, while the floras are not necessarily even comparable. Nevertheless the very general (but often only superficial) similarity between polar regions and high altitudes elsewhere, which to some degree may extend to the vegetation, makes it desirable to treat high-altitude plant communities here, though very briefly.

While in high-arctic lands there is the usual general tendency towards limitation of flora and depauperation of vegetation as mountains are ascended, fairly luxuriant if limited patches of more or less closed vegetation are to be seen in some places up to altitudes of at least 700 metres. Around such altitudes extensive grassy tundra can occur in middle-arctic regions, as it can even higher up in low-arctic regions—where, on the other hand, extraordinary barrenness may already prevail lower down. Indeed remarkably drastic variation is apt to be found in arctic uplands, often from spot to spot in closely contiguous areas. Thus while in one place the aspect is as of a plantless desert, in another there are plentiful hardy rosette and other herbs such as Saxifrages and Arctic Poppy (*Papaver radicatum* s.l.), while in favourable situations a more or less continuous tundra may prevail, or even a closed ' heath '. In general, something approaching most lowland communities persists well up into the mountains in the Arctic, while even near glaciers or perennial snow, and at quite high altitudes and latitudes, the climber may be agreeably surprised by a considerable show of vegetation including herb- or moss-mats, and even heaths or flower-slopes in the South. However, at very high altitudes even towards the southern boundary of the Arctic, extreme barrenness is usually encountered, with much snow and *névé* persisting through the summer wherever the local topography allows, and little else save crustaceous and foliose ' Tripe de Roche ' and other Lichens on the exposed rock faces (Fig. 135).

In temperate regions the zone of tundra, etc., just above the timber-line is in many ways comparable with low-arctic regions near sea-level, while higher up in both instances a similar sequence of altitudinal climaxes prevails. Thus tundras of various types roughly comparable with those of the Arctic are found above the elfin wood to the south, with often extensive tracts of scrub (Fig. 136, and *cf.* Fig. 115) where conditions are suitable and pasturing is not too severe. Above this may stretch increasingly limited tracts of ' alpine meadow ' consisting of short and more or less matted Grasses, Sedges, and forbs or under-shrubs (Fig. 137, A); heathlands may develop in particularly favourable situations, and fell-fields or barrens in detrital or exposed ones. Mossy mats are especially characteristic of run-off areas below snow-banks hereabouts.

Still higher up and nearer the Equator there is not merely a rigorous climate to contend with but, also, geodynamic influences which are often powerful, so that conditions and the attendant vegetation may vary considerably from spot to spot. Almost all the vascular plants persisting here are chamaephytes or hemicryptophytes, and

FIG. 135.—High in the mountains near the margin of the ice-sheet in southern Greenland. Valley glaciers are plentiful and patches of snow and *névé* (iced firn) persist through the summer where local topography allows. The macroscopic vegetation is often limited to Lichens on the exposed rocks.

FIG. 136.—Upland scrub of Dwarf Birch and silky-leafed Willows constituting an altitudinal climax above tree-limit in northern Norway.

A

B

FIG. 137.—High-alpine vegetation and flowering. A, a high-alpine 'meadow' in British Columbia, Canada. (Phot. W. S. Cooper.) B, plants flowering at about 5,944 metres (c. 19,500 feet) on Mohala Bhanjyang, West Nepal: visible in the gravelly fell-field are *Lagotis glauca* s.l. (to left of English shilling giving scale), *Potentilla saundersiana* var. *caespitosa*, *Pedicularis* sp., *Arenaria* sp., 2 Leguminosae, and one each of Umbelliferae, Cruciferae, and Gramineae—also several Lichens. (Phot. O. Polunin.)

a large proportion are obviously xeromorphic, being reduced in stature, very hairy, or otherwise modified to conserve water. As compared with those of lowland plants, the leaves tend to be smaller and thicker, with a greater development of protective tissue. Indeed the general aspect is much as in the Arctic, with hardy cushion or rosette plants including bright-flowered Saxifrages often in evidence, and Lichens and Mosses plentiful, any woody plants being excessively dwarfed. However, more and more of the actual species tend to be different as we travel south, until in the tropics very few arctic inhabitants are left, although the general aspect may still be somewhat arctic-like at very high altitudes. Moreover, there are frequently anatomical and other differences between arctic and alpine plants even of very close systematic alliance. Fig. 137, B, shows a wide range of plants flowering at an altitude of about 5,944 metres (*c.* 19,500 feet) on Mohala Bhanjyang, West Nepal, in the Himalayas —higher than flowering plants are commonly supposed to go in any number, and perhaps constituting a record in this respect. The genera are often represented in the Arctic, and at least one arctic species, *Lagotis glauca* s.l., is visible. At lower altitudes in the tropics and especially down near timber-line, the ‘ mountain grassland ’ is often very luxuriant and inclusive of woody associates which do not, however, normally reach a greater height than the herbaceous cover, though in some places a tall scrub may occur between the Krummholz and fell-fields.

In some temperate and tropical regions, especially of an arid nature, and in keeping with the general reduction of precipitation at very high altitudes, dry conditions may prevail above the timberline. Here the effect of aspect is often particularly noticeable. Thus in parts of central Asia, steppe-like vegetation may persist on the southern slopes of mountains, while, on the shadier northern slopes, more luxuriant alpine meadows often occur at similar altitudes. In these meadows may be tall forbs, and on the slopes below are often many trees—in marked contrast to the arid steppe-like communities on the south-facing side (*cf.* Fig. 83, B). Elsewhere, xeric grasslands in which the tussocks of the dominants fail to coalesce may be common on slopes around 3,000–4,000 metres, below the fell-fields, while on plateaux at similar or even higher altitudes, such as the ‘ punas ’ of South America and the ‘ pamirs ’ of Tibet, extremely severe drought and temperature conditions may prevail and the vegetation consist of sparsely scattered tufts of Grasses and hardy cushion-plants (Fig. 138). In the high Andes of Peru, etc., the cushions formed by some species may be so large as to resemble 'recumbent elephants' (C. A. W. Sandeman *in litt.*).

At the very highest altitudes, for example above 6,000 metres (19,685 feet), Lichens are the chief or only macroscopic plants to persist, their growth being usually poor. These very high altitudes also introduce the so-called 'cold deserts' of temperate and even tropical regions which, surrounded by tundra and other high-alpine zones, are developed in the Rocky Mountains of North America and the Andes of South America, in the Himalayas (O. Polunin *voce*), and to some extent in the Norwegian Alps as well as on

FIG. 138.—Alpine puna-like formation near mountain summit in Colombia. Farther south in South America the cushion-plants are often much larger. (Phot. R. E. Schultes.)

mountain ranges elsewhere. They are often snow- or ice-bound, as are of course the ice-sheets of the polar regions, of which the most extensive are the Greenland ice-cap in the northern hemisphere and the Antarctic ice-cap in the southern hemisphere. Even around 21,000 feet there may be occasional flowering plants persisting in the Himalayas, although crustaceous Lichens are more frequent and go higher (O. Polunin *voce*, and *cf.* above).

Whereas in some cases particular zones of vegetation may encircle a mountain at a fairly uniform level and preserving a fairly uniform breadth, frequently they are tilted, being often higher on the equatorial side; or else they may be narrow on one side, or discontinuous, or merely partial. Moreover as they usually merge only gradually into one another, such vegetational zones are often difficult to distinguish unless they are in full development.

## Antarctic Types

The vegetation types of antarctic and adjacent regions have become sufficiently known in recent years for the broad generalization to be made that they are reasonably comparable with those of the Arctic, even if there is a tendency towards more tussock formation and less woody plants in the South. They also tend to be treeless to much lower latitudes; in conformity with our delimitation of the Arctic, these treeless regions and their vegetation will be considered here as more or less antarctic, even though many of the islands lie far from the Antarctic Continent and are commonly referred to as subantarctic. Although the floristic composition is largely different, the antarctic flora being in general very limited and widely peculiar, with often a high degree of endemism, plant communities in low-antarctic regions often look much like those developed in the Arctic under comparable circumstances in similar situations. Furthermore, much the same range of vegetation-types is found in the Antarctic and Subantarctic as in the Arctic, whose plant communities we have described and illustrated sufficiently above. Consequently a very general account of the main antarctic and subantarctic types should suffice. In this it should be recalled that antarctic and subantarctic lands are for the most part widely scattered, often being extremely isolated and having extraordinarily limited floras, which in the case of the ice-free portions of the Antarctic Continent consist almost entirely of lowly cryptogams.

The Antarctic is a very bleak and stormy region possessed of two main climatic areas. The northern one may be described as subantarctic and is maritime, with warmer winters and cooler summers than much of the Arctic, and powerful winds throughout the year. There is heavy precipitation in the form of snow or rain, and little distinction between the seasons. The subantarctic islands have this climate. The other, southern and central region is extremely cold and stormy, having a continental climate without summer warmth. Thus on the entire Antarctic Continent there is scarcely any place having the mean of the warmest month of the year above 0° C.

In contrast to the Arctic, which apart from ice-caps is largely free from snow in summer and widely favourable for plant life, the Antarctic Continent is permanently ice-covered except for very limited areas chiefly about its borders. Here the ice and snow may disappear for a brief period in the most favourable season and allow some depauperated, almost entirely cryptogamic, vegetation to grow. A few 'oases' up to a reputed 300 or so square miles in area have been reported in recent decades to occur at varying distances inland, though mainly near the coast. They are largely free from snow

FIG. 139.—Crustaceous and foliose Lichens on rocks near shore, Goudier Islet, Antarctica. From these rock faces, especially where attacked by Lichens, and from marine and wind-borne debris, there may accumulate in crevices and depressions a fair soil on which fruticose Lichens and Mosses often grow. (Phot. I. M. Lamb, courtesy of Falkland Islands Scientific Bureau.)

in the favourable season and are reported to have lakes green with Algae but to be otherwise devoid of evident life, though apparently they have not been scientifically investigated. Many rock faces even well away from the ice appear entirely barren, at least from a distance, though in some places especially near the shore a fair growth of crustaceous Lichens may be found; here there may be an accumulation of soil, and, growing on it, fruticose Lichens and Mosses (Fig. 139). This poverty of the antarctic vegetation especially on the Continent must be related to the very unfavourable climate—

particularly to the coolness of the ' warm ' season and to the frequency and persistent strength of the winds—and also to the isolated situation which makes immigration extremely difficult. Almost the entire Continent belongs to the zone of ' perpetual frost ', only a few peripheral areas having a ' tundra climate ', though this is enjoyed by most of the subantarctic islands.

Only two species of vascular plants, a Grass and a Caryophyll, are at all well known from the Antarctic Continent (a segregate of the Grass is claimed by some to constitute a third species), but there are fairly numerous Lichens, Mosses, and Algae, many of which are widespread. The microthermic vascular flora of surrounding islands, however, includes a fair number of more or less circumpolar species. Characteristic components of this flora are *Colobanthus crassifolius* and *Lyallia* spp. (the former being known from the Antarctic Continent, and both belonging to the Caryophyllaceae), *Pringlea antiscorbutica* (the Kerguelen Cabbage, belonging to the Cruciferae), *Acaena* spp. (Rosaceae), *Azorella* spp. (Umbelliferae), and the Grass *Deschampsia antarctica* (also found on the Antarctic Continent). Mixed with various hardy cryptogams, these and other vascular plants form a thin tundra which, with increasing luxuriance, extends northwards over the Antarctic Islands and into much lower latitudes—for example in southern South America. Nevertheless this ' subantarctic ' tundra occupies only a tiny area when compared with its arctic counterpart. Like the latter, it includes some shrubby plants, mostly of cushion-form, and often tussocky Grasses, as on South Georgia.

The Antarctic Continent is largely covered by the world's greatest ice-cap and consequently is a vast polar waste. Only here and there, on ice- and snow-free spots of the shore or inland ' oases ', on steep walls of rock or stony slopes, and on mountain-peaks protruding from the ice, are found the Lichens, Mosses, and Algae mentioned above—the vegetation at the best being in general far poorer than is to be found in all but the most barren of arctic habitats. Even Bacteria appear to be relatively few in number. Most of them, and many of the largest known patches of macroscopic vegetation, have been found in the Graham Land sector of western Antarctica below the 68th parallel of S. latitude. Here, in the most suitable situations within areas of favoured climate, may be found the two or three truly antarctic vascular plant species and patches of cryptogamic vegetation that are locally more or less closed—particularly with such Mosses as *Brachythecium antarcticum* and species of *Grimmia* and

*Andreaea*. The most luxuriant vegetation is often found in areas that are manured (but not much trampled) by Penguins, etc. Lichens inhabit the rocks, and include species of *Caloplaca* that introduce bright colours much as in the Arctic, while Mosses may form an almost continuous investment very locally (Fig. 140). But in general the vegetation even around the periphery of the Continent is sparse and only encountered in occasional favoured areas, most tracts being ice-covered and devoid of evident plant growth, though the

FIG. 140.—Luxuriant growth of Mosses, broken chiefly by rocks bearing Lichens, extending up snow-melt gully in area frequented by Penguins, Deception Island, Antarctica. Rarely is more luxuriant vegetation to be seen on or near the Antarctic Continent. Note the small tussocks formed by the chief Moss, and the more typical barrenness of the ground behind. (Phot. I. M. Lamb, courtesy of Falkland Islands Scientific Bureau.)

surface snow when tested has usually proved to contain some viable Bacteria and often also spores of Moulds and Yeasts which had presumably been carried thither by air currents.

Further south, in the perpetually frozen zone, only a few sheer walls of rock or peaks or other situations that become bare of snow in the brief ' summer ' carry a sparse vegetation consisting entirely of hardy cryptogams. However, some Mosses and Algae and fairly numerous Lichens persist to at least 78° S., sometimes practically covering suitable manured areas near the coastal shelf-ice in deep bays, while, inland, three Lichens have been reported from snow-free rocks of the Queen Maud Mountains within 237 nautical miles of the Geographical South Pole. Samples of snow collected hereabouts yielded seven different species of Bacteria; but in general we can describe the interior of Antarctica as almost devoid of macroscopic vegetation, and supporting precious little microscopic growth or even life.

In the wide seas that surround the Antarctic Continent, there are scattered islands and archipelagos whose low summer temperatures and vegetational characteristics indicate polar affinities. They include Kerguelen Island in about lat. 49° S. and long. 70° E., whose barren appearance is widely attributed to very stormy drying winds coupled with the low temperature of the ground. The vegetation is largely dominated by *Azorella selago* and to a lesser extent by *Acaena adscendens*, the former often determining the general appearance of the landscape in sheltered situations in the interior. Thus in otherwise desert-like areas it may form tussocks up to ½ a metre high and 1 metre wide. In some places an almost continuous, swarded tundra of these and other plants may be developed, and some slopes may be more or less green, as may be damp depressions. The prevailing winds being westerly, it is chiefly on the sheltered east-facing slopes that the most luxuriant vegetation develops. Here the *Azorella* tussocks have associated *Acaena*, *Agrostis antarctica*, and *Lycopodium saururus*, which tend to overgrow them chiefly from the eastern side, while blocks of rock may be largely covered with Lichens such as *Neuropogon* spp.—again most luxuriantly on their eastern sides.

In suitable situations on Kerguelen the *Azorella* or other 'cushions' tend to coalesce to form a continuous cover which in the most favoured 'oases' may be replaced by almost pure *Acaena*. Species associated with the *Azorella* are commonly few, though usually some crustaceous Lichens are to be found on the stones, and there may occur such dicotyledonous plants as *Pringlea antiscorbutica*, *Colobanthus kerguelensis*, and *Lyallia kerguelensis*, and the Grasses *Agrostis antarctica* and *Festuca kerguelensis*. Like the dominant *Azorella*, most of these plants are of tussocky growth, as are associated Mosses such as species of *Rhacomitrium* and *Blindia*. *Acaena* forms a more even, if wavy, meadow-like community which from a distance may look like a relatively smooth heathland. Commonly associated with it are the same *Pringlea*, *Galium antarcticum*, *Ranunculus biternatus*, and various Grasses. Apart from *Pringlea*, which may represent a relic from some past age, the plants in the *Azorella* community are all more or less xeromorphic. Those of the *Acaena* community, on the other hand, are more or less hygrophytic in character, lacking any obvious means of protection against the mechanical and desiccating effects of the wind. Thus from the rampant main axes of this dominant, which form a thin-meshed network on the ground, leafy shoots ascend to a height of often 20–50 cm. (about 8–20 in.). In rocky places various Ferns occur, including a Filmy-fern (*Hymenophyllum peltatum*) and forms of the familiar northern Polypody (*Polypodium vulgare* agg.) and Brittle-fern (*Cystopteris fragilis* s.l.). Limited to the salty beaches are *Cotula plumosa* and *Tillaea moschata*.

The vegetation of the other islands of the Kerguelen Group, such as the Crozet and Prince Edward Islands which extend westwards in comparable latitudes to 38° E. longitude, and the nearer but more southerly McDonald and Heard Islands, does not appear to show any important deviations in its general character from that of Kerguelen Island itself. However, McDonald and Heard Islands tend to be particularly barren, presumably owing to their higher latitude (c. 53° S.). Of the thirty species of flowering plants known from the Kerguelen Group, no fewer than six (20 per cent.) are endemic, the *Pringlea* (Kerguelen Cabbage) being the sole known representative of an apparently endemic genus.

Of the islands lying south of New Zealand, Macquarie Island (about 55° S.) is antarctic in character, with few and usually dwarf woody plants (such as *Coprosma repens*, though the taller *Acaena adscendens* and an allied species also occur). Wide stretches of the hills are taken over by the yellowish tussocky grass *Poa foliosa*, between whose tufts occur here and there larger ones of *Stilbocarpa polaris* and silvery rosettes of *Pleurophyllum hookeri* as well as two species of *Acaena*. *Azorella selago* is reported to form large cushions on the wind-blown summits of some of these hills and to harbour other plants as on Kerguelen. On the rocks of the shore are tussocks of *Colobanthus muscoides*, *Tillaea moschata*, and a small endemic Grass besides the more familiar *Festuca erecta*. In swampy as in some drier places *Poa foliosa* is typical, and on the beaches *Cotula plumosa*. The nearest land is 650 km. away, and as it is considered unlikely that any vascular plants survived the severe Pleistocene glaciation on Macquarie Island, it is thought that migrating sea-birds must have been the main agents of importation of the thirty-five species of vascular plants known to grow on the island—*cf.* page 114.

Even though they lack arborescent growth and must be mentioned here, most other ice-free islands of the South that have been investigated appear to be scarcely polar in type. Thus the Falkland Islands near southern South America and the Antipodes Islands near New Zealand support quite large bushes, besides Grasses up to 1·5 metres in height which are apt to grow so closely together as to prevent the entry of other plants. The large island of South Georgia, however, which lies about 1,200 miles east of Tierra del Fuego, is within the zone of pack-ice and has a clearly antarctic character. In spite of persisting glaciation and poverty in species, the vegetation is relatively luxuriant near the shore and in sheltered valleys. Its character is chiefly determined by a few plants, such as the tussocky Grass *Poa flabellata* and the somewhat shrubby rosaceous *Acaena adscendens*, which are often so overwhelmingly dominant that other plants play only a minor role. The *Poa* tufts may be quite tall, the height of a Man being commonly approached by the long and stiff leaves protruding from tussocks that themselves often exceed ½ a metre in height, and that are separated by bare spaces in which, when the area is sloping, water flows away quickly after snow-melt or heavy rain. Such vegetation is largely confined to seaside situations. On rocks near the beach a thick turf and sward may be formed, especially in manured areas, and sometimes overlying deposits of peat. In some places an unbroken grassy tundra may extend to an altitude of 200 or even 300 metres on sheltered north-facing slopes (which in the Far South of course tend to be the most sunny and favourable). Other such slopes, especially where damp, and the banks of brooks, may be covered by the *Acaena*.

Inland areas on South Georgia which have not been so invaded and are not too swampy, often support a meadow-like community of such Grasses as *Festuca erecta*, *Deschampsia antarctica*, and a relative of the European *Phleum alpinum*, often with associated *Acaena adscendens*. Mosses and especially Lichens may here play an important role in the consolidation of the vegetation, ' Reindeer-moss ' Lichens (including a *Cladonia* allied to *C. rangiferina*) and members of the lichen family Stictaceae being often abundant, while *Neuropogon melaxanthus* and allied species may practically cover the rocks in the higher zones. Intermediate situations frequently support mixed cryptogamous carpets, and exposed ones little save scattered Lichens. Low-lying swampy areas, on the other hand, are typically inhabited by a community dominated by *Rostkovia magellanica*, which gives them a characteristic dark-brownish colour. Associated are a few other flowering plants and some Liverworts, and many more Mosses. The freshwater aquatic plants include a Water-starwort (*Callitriche antarctica*), a Buttercup (*Ranunculus biternatus*), and several Bryophytes besides a greater number of Algae.

Vegetation-types of fresh and salt waters, and of snow and ice, wherever they may be developed, will be described in Chapters XV and XVI.

## Further Consideration

The only book devoted to truly arctic vegetation is the present author's *Botany of the Canadian Eastern Arctic, Part III, Vegetation and Ecology* (Department of Mines and Resources, Ottawa, Canada, National Museum Bulletin No. 104, pp. vii + 304 and map, 1948), which gives illustrated descriptions of the vegetation-types recognized in the vast eastern parts of arctic Canada. Otherwise the above account has resulted from perusal of numerous published papers as well as from personal experience in a considerable proportion of the regions involved. Much the same is true of the brief consideration given to high-alpine regions, concerning which the appropriate parts of most of the general as well as regional works cited at the end of Chapter XII may be found helpful if further details are desired. As if in tribute to the enterprise of its authors, the *Journal of Ecology*, published regularly since 1913, is remarkably rich in well-illustrated accounts of the vegetation of various arctic and alpine regions, including some of the most rigorous and difficult of access.

All truly arctic vascular plant species recognized to date, including those mentioned in the above chapter, are described and illustrated in the author's *Circumpolar Arctic Flora* (Clarendon Press, Oxford, pp. xxviii + 514, 1959).

## Chapter XIV

# VEGETATIONAL TYPES OF TROPICAL AND ADJACENT LANDS

In the last two chapters we dealt with the main types of land vegetation found in temperate and polar and some adjacent or allied regions. It now remains for us to complete this survey of vegetational types developed on the land of the world with some consideration of those of tropical and adjacent regions. This consideration will be a mere brief outline that can scarcely do justice to the range of types that includes the most luxuriant, complicated, and often changeable vegetation on earth. Nevertheless one hopes it may help relate some of these types to those of other regions, and at least assist the inhabitant of the latter in his appreciation of what is found in the tropics.

## Tropical Rain Forests

These, especially in equatorial regions, constitute the most luxuriant of all vegetation-types. They occur chiefly where soil conditions are favourable in moist tropical lowlands and where there is scarcely a distinct (or at all events no long and severe) dry season. Their chief development is : (*a*) in the Amazonian region of South America, whence they range northwards in the Caribbean and Gulf of Mexico regions nearly to the Tropic of Cancer, southwards past the Tropic of Capricorn in Brazil, and westwards to the Pacific Ocean coast of Colombia and Ecuador ; (*b*) about the Equator in central and western Africa, extending southwards past the Tropic of Capricorn in eastern Africa and Madagascar ; (*c*) in western India and Ceylon ; and (*d*) in the Malayan region whence they range north to the Himalayas, north-east to Indo-China and the Philippines, and south and east through much of Indonesia and New Guinea to Fiji and adjacent archipelagos of the western Pacific, with an intermittent extension in eastern Australia well past the Tropic of Capricorn. These are the regions in which tropical rain forest appears to be the natural climax under present conditions, although in most of them it is tending to diminish rapidly in area owing to the activities of Man, and in some considerable tracts has disappeared altogether. Replacement is mainly by secondary growth on areas of cultivation. In addition, subtropical rain forests (which seem best treated here) occur widely in central and southern South America, around the Tropic of Cancer in Central and North America and in eastern China, farther north than the tropical rain forest in the Himalayan region and farther south in East Africa, and also in Hawaii and southeastern Australasia.

The country occupied by tropical rain forests is usually flat or rolling, though they may extend up the lower slopes of mountains to an altitude of about 1,000 metres (3,281 feet) or even higher. In some areas rain falls almost every afternoon and night practically throughout the year, in others there are one or two dry seasons[1] of not more than three months each. Often the rain will pour down for days or weeks, and everything becomes soaked in a thick grey mist. The temperature is relatively high and uniform, the annual means being normally around 25–26° C., and the rainfall commonly totals between 200 and 400 cm. annually, though in places there may be much more. The relative humidity also tends to be high, being usually above 80 per cent., though comparatively low values may obtain for short periods. Some notion of what the climate is like may be obtained from the tropical palm houses of botanical gardens. But although the light is dazzling when the sun shines on the upper canopy from its midday position high in the sky, beneath the commonly three storeys of trees a sombre gloom prevails, the atmosphere being humid and close. Nevertheless some rays may penetrate and sun-flecks prevail—and, it seems, be microclimatically and physiologically important.

In these tropical rain forests it is chiefly in the tree-canopy that animal life flourishes—of innumerable and sometimes gaily-coloured[2] Insects, Tree-frogs, Lizards and Snakes, Birds, Squirrels, Monkeys, and so forth, many of which never touch the ground during their lives (I. V. Polunin *voce*). The component plants may lose their leaves individually each year or so ; but there is no regular seasonal change

[1] Professor Paul W. Richards points out (*in litt.*) that although a dry season cannot be adequately defined in terms of months with less than a certain minimum rainfall, dry seasons in these regions may be considered as consisting approximately of those months having less than 4 inches (about 10 cm.) of rain.

[2] In general, however, protective coloration is more characteristic of rain-forest fauna—particularly with the Insects, which tend to be brown or green and to harmonize with their environment (J. A. R. Anderson and I. V. Polunin *in litt.*).

affecting the whole vegetation, flowering and fruiting going on all the time, though with particular species tending to have their own definite seasons in these and some other respects. Thus whereas in some species the different individuals may lose their leaves at entirely different times, more often there is approximate synchronization of this event between them each year—but not between members of different species to nearly such an extent as in most temperate forests. The dormant buds are most often small and unprotected, but frequently develop after several or many years, so giving rise to 'cauliflory' (the formation of flowers on old 'bare' wood), which is particularly common in these regions.

The main plant components of the tropical rain forest are normally the following seven:

1. *The forest trees.* These form the main structural component, sometimes referred to loosely as the 'roof' or 'canopy', which is typically made up of three more or less separate *strata* characterized by different types of trees. These 'storeys' or 'layers', as they are also called, are usually ill-defined and indeed seldom easy to recognize by casual observation, owing to the fact that species of all manner of intermediate heights are commonly present, while upgrowing young trees may be of almost any height up to the stratum to which their kind belongs, and even different component species of a stratum often have different heights. In general, however, there can be distinguished strata consisting of trees whose crowns vary in height about a mean, and commonly there are three such strata in tropical rain forests.

The roof of the forest has usually an irregular profile, the trees of the highest (A) stratum being often more or less widely spaced and rarely forming a continuous layer to which the term 'canopy' may be applied. The second (B) stratum, or sometimes even the third (C), is commonly the highest layer of tree crowns forming a continuous mass. The crowns of the B stratum typically extend from about 15 to 30 metres in height, while the still shorter trees composing the C storey are usually small and slender and have narrow tapering crowns commonly 5–15 metres high. Fig. 141 is a profile diagram of typical mixed rain forest in British Guiana in which the three tree strata are barely recognizable. When, as in this case, the two upper strata are much broken, the third is usually dense; but when the upper ones are dense the third is apt to be much less well developed—as in Fig. 142. In the former circumstances Palms may be prominent, as in the example shown in

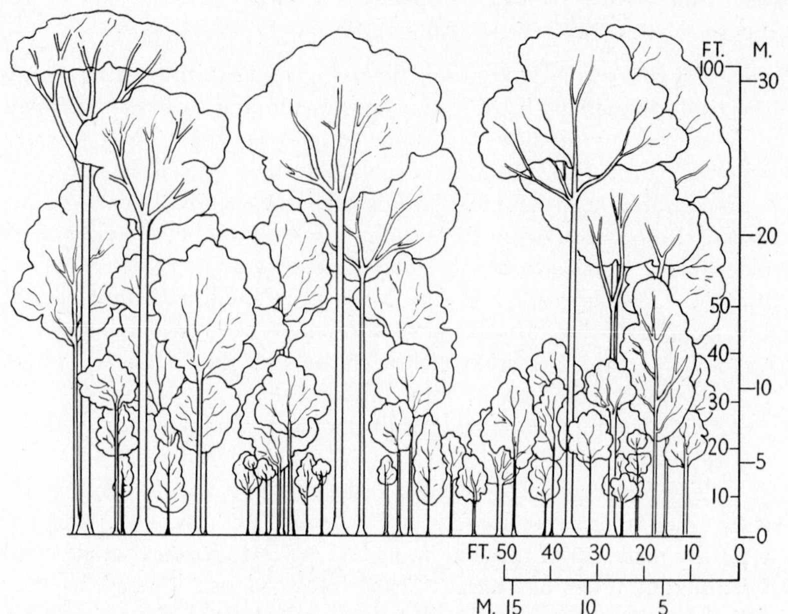


FIG. 141.—Profile diagram of primary mixed tropical rain forest, Moraballi Creek, British Guiana, showing all trees over 4·6 metres high on a strip about 45 metres long and 7·6 metres wide. (After Davis & Richards.)

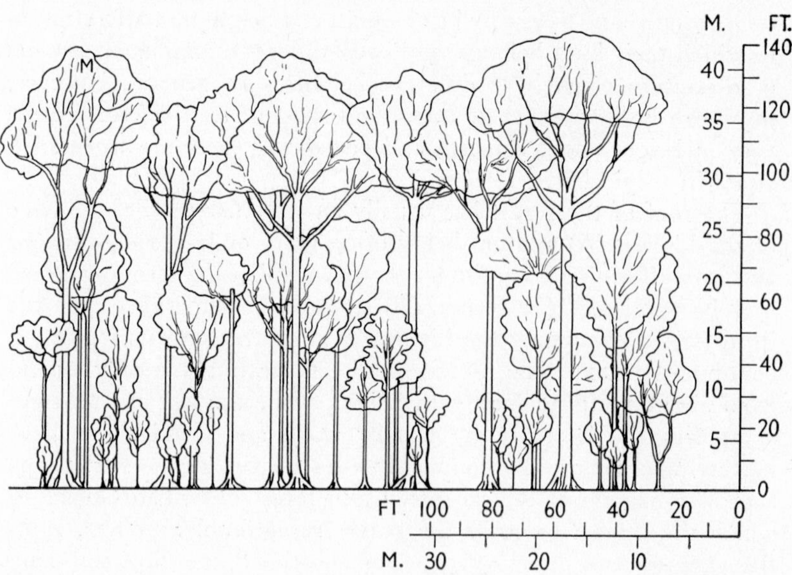


FIG. 142.—Profile diagram of climax evergreen forest in Trinidad, British West Indies. The community is a consociation of Mora (*Mora excelsa*, marked M) up to about 45 metres high. The diagram represents a strip about 65 metres long and 7·6 metres wide. (After Beard.)

Fig. 143, or there may be many tall shrubs. Mostly, however, dicotyledons predominate, the large Palms, Bamboos, and sometimes Tree-ferns being evident chiefly in disturbed areas.

FIG. 143.—Tropical rain forest in the Philippine Islands. Note the different heights of the trees and the feathery leaves of Rattans and other Palms.

The trees of each stratum usually represent numerous different species belonging to various families, a considerable proportion of the lower ones being young members of species that are dominant (or more often co-dominant) above. Indeed one of the striking characteristics of most tropical rain forests is the extremely mixed dominance, so that a species commonly occurs only from one to three times in an acre. Local consociations of single dominance may, however, be developed (Fig. 142), though in real tropical rain forests this appears to be rare. The leaves of the trees are commonly of medium size, having an area of 2,000–18,000 sq. mm. They are usually entire and ' leathery ', and dark-green with glossy surfaces. Thus they belong to the laurel or large-sclerophyll type, being mostly oblong-lanceolate to elliptical in outline, often with extended ' drip-tips '. However, the type of leaf varies considerably with the stratum, drip-tips, for example, being scarcely ever found on leaves of mature trees of the higher strata. In many tropical rain forests, foliage extends almost continuously from the herbs on the ground to the tops of the dominants, and although many large trees are present, this foliage of one sort or another mostly hides their trunks (Fig. 144). In other instances the canopy is exceedingly dense and there is little development of undergrowth and ground-covering, so that the trunks of the trees stand out in the gloom as huge columns. Often they show ' plank ' buttresses as in Fig. 145, where an intermediate amount of ground-vegetation is visible.

Although it is often contended that competition between the trees finds expression chiefly in the struggle towards the light, actually the different strata have each their own species. Normally these individually reach their own particular level before attaining full development and thereafter make no attempt to pass that level. The arborescent species thus seem to fall into groups having a particular height-limit and degree of tolerance to shading by the next stratum above—or, in the case of the topmost stratum, presumably demanding full exposure—the struggle towards the light being mainly in the immature stages. Nor does there appear to be any intense struggle for root-room—a feature that has been confirmed by Dr. R. E. Schultes (*in litt.*), with the rider that it is unexpected and more ought to be made of it.

It should be recalled finally that in these tropical rain forests, not only flowering and fruiting but also the loss and replacement of leaves can take place at any time of the year and in fact normally does take place at all times (considering the vegetation as a whole). Thus in many species the leaves appear to be renewed annually, and individual trees devoid of leaves may be observed in the forest

FIG. 144.—Another scene of tropical rain forest in the Philippines. Note the density of the foliage, which often hides the large tree-trunks.

FIG. 145.—Base of tree-trunk showing exaggeratedly buttressed roots in tropical rain forest.

at any period, though a new crop soon develops on them. In this, as was already indicated on pp. 424–5, particular species tend to have their own special times—for example, members of the genus *Hevea* in South America commonly lose their leaves at the end of the dry season, regularly, each year, just before flowering.

2. *Herbs, etc.* Where the tree strata are not too dense and sufficient light penetrates, there may be a fair development of green ground-vegetation which, like the dominant trees, is independent of external support. Such lower vegetation in moist situations tends to be largely herbaceous, Ferns and Selaginellas being often prominent, whereas on dry ridges it may consist largely of woody plants. In other cases a shrub stratum (D), consisting mainly of tallish woody plants, may be roughly distinguishable, with, below, a ground-layer (E) of herbs and tree-seedlings up to 2 metres in height. The shrub layer often includes some coarse herbs such as Scitamineae (Bananas, Gingers, etc.) which may exceed 5 metres in height. But in general, in spite of the prevailingly warm and humid conditions, herbs and other lowly plants are little developed on the ground owing to the lack of sufficient light. Thus in lowland rain forest any luxuriant herbaceous ground-vegetation is found chiefly in clearings and by streams and openings where illumination is above the average for the level, while in the interior of the forest green herbs—apart of course from epiphytes—are found chiefly as widely scattered individuals or scarcely at all. On steep slopes, however, more light tends to penetrate owing to the angle of the (lateral) rays, and herbaceous vegetation is generally more abundant, though still the number of herbaceous species is liable to be far smaller than that of different trees. Indeed, in contrast to the situation in temperate regions, the herbaceous vegetation in tropical rain forests is almost always far less various than the arborescent, and, with relatively ' open ' conditions, is more apt to form ' families ' of single species. The herbs belong to various (if usually few) systematic groups but typically include members of the Madder family (Rubiaceae) as well as some Grasses and members of the Sedge family (Cyperaceae) in addition to Ferns and Selaginellas, and, in the Amazonian region, Marantaceae and Melastomaceae. Their foliage is usually thin, sometimes variegated, and very variable in shape, in contrast to that of the dominant trees.

3. *Climbers.* We now come to the first of the three groups of plants that, although they are still green, are dependent on external mechanical support and afford the main ' forest furnishings ' ; of

them the climbers or 'vines' are generally the most important. Indeed the woody climbers, also called lianes (or lianas), are apt to be so large and numerous as to afford one of the most impressive features of the tropical rain forest. They may be thin and wire-like or rope-like, or as thick as a man's thigh, vanishing like cables into the mass of foliage overhead, or here and there hanging down in gigantic loops. Often they are unbranched up to the profusely branched crown. Some are said to attain lengths of over 200 metres, ascending one tree, then descending to the ground before ascending another, and so on. Often they pass from tree to tree and link the crowns so firmly that even if a tree is cut through at the base it will not fall.

Lianes are most abundant where the forest has been disturbed, or about its margins—as for example along river banks where they may completely screen the interior of the forest. In addition to the large woody climbers that reach the crowns particularly of the B stratum of trees, there are usually some small, mainly herbaceous ones (including Ferns) that seldom emerge from the shade of the undergrowth. Among the climbers the large lianes comprise, however, by far the more numerous *synusiae* (groups of plants of similar life-form, each filling much the same ecological niche and playing a similar role, and contributing to a biocoenosis—*cf.* p. 321). These large lianes belong to many different families and genera—chiefly of dicotyledons, though Climbing Palms or Rattans are often prominent among them.

The climbers as a whole include twiners which by the revolving movement of their growing tips become wound around their supports; also root-climbers and tendril-climbers which have specialized sensitive roots and tendrils, respectively, for attachment; and scramblers which lack such abilities or organs but scramble over other plants, often being aided passively in their climbing by recurved spines or wide branching. Many species use more than one method. As the crowns of tropical trees tend to be less branched and less leafy than those of temperate trees of similar size, woody climbers help to close the canopy and decrease the penetration of light. They may also mis-shape the crowns or constrict the stems of trees, though such things are more regularly done by stranglers (*see* pp. 435–6).

4. *Epiphytes.* These are plants which grow attached to the trunks, branches, and even living leaves of the trees, shrubs, and lianes, such situations being the only ones available in closed forests for

species of small stature but having high light-requirements. A few of the larger types and many of the small ones grow in the rain-forest undergrowth, being supposedly species that are intolerant of root-competition or smothering by fallen leaves. All have to put up with lack of soil and hence paucity of mineral nutrients, and a more or less precarious water-supply, though in this last connection we should recall the persistently heavy and often daily rainfall in most of their habitats.

Epiphytes do not ordinarily have any ill-effect upon the supporting ' host ', and, though constituting a very characteristic element in the structure of the forest, play only a minor role in its economy. This may even be the case when the epiphytes are so abundant as to form an almost continuous investment of tree-trunks, as they commonly do in uplands where the tree-canopy is thin or relatively simple (*cf.* Fig. 162). They do, however, play an important part in the ecosystem as habitats for animals, and they are further interesting in showing many remarkable structural adaptations. Their number and diversity are great, usually involving a wealth of cryptogams of all lower groups as well as Pteridophytes and flowering plants, including some shrubs. Indeed it is the presence of a wide range of epiphytes which especially distinguishes the tropical rain forest from temperate forest communities, though epiphytes are characteristic also of montane and subtropical rain forests, and may be even more luxuriantly developed therein. Moreover, different species of trees frequently show distinctions in their epiphytic floras, supposedly because of different chemical constituents of rain-wash as well as for the more obvious reasons of shade or bark-texture, etc.

A few of the more striking types of adaptations of epiphytes should be mentioned. Many are constructed so as to collect a substitute soil, which is mainly derived from the dead remains of other plants, being often assembled by Ants which inhabit the plant's own root system that grows into the so-constituted ' vegetable flower-pot ' of these ' nest-epiphytes ' (Fig. 146). Others have to be able to absorb water rapidly and for this purpose often have spongy ' velamen ' roots ; they also have to be able to conserve the water they get, and consequently are often markedly xeromorphic or possessed of special reservoirs (*e.g.* Fig. 147) or storage tissues (in 'tank-epiphyes ').

Three main classes of rain-forest epiphytes may be recognized, corresponding to different microhabitats : (*a*) extreme xerophilous

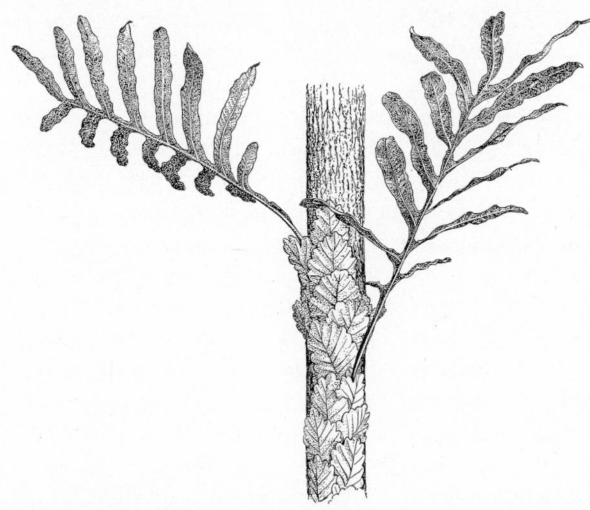

Fig. 146.—An epiphytic Fern (*Drynaria* sp.) which has small humus-gathering leaves and larger photoysnthetic ones that also produce spores. (× about $\frac{1}{12}$).

Fig. 147.—An epiphytic Bromeliad (*Billbergia* sp.) with a mass of fibrous roots investing the branch of the ' host ' tree. Note that the leaves form urn-shaped cups for collecting and holding water, which is absorbed by special hairs on their insides. (× $\frac{1}{9}$.)

epiphytes, living on the topmost branches and twigs of the taller trees, such as some Bromeliads and, remarkably enough, Cacti; (*b*) sun-epiphytes, usually xeromorphic and occurring chiefly in the centres of the crowns and along the larger branches of the upper tree-storeys, and usually comprising the richest of the epiphytic synusiae in both species and individuals; and (*c*) shade-epiphytes, mainly found on the trunks and branches of C-stratum trees, or on the stems of the larger lianes. The shade-epiphyte synusia consists chiefly of Ferns, and most of its members show no trace of xeromorphy. The average vertical ranges of the different synusiae depend on the light factor. Thus they tend to be constant within any one type of forest but differ in different types, being high in forests where the top strata are dense, relatively low in more open types of forest, and still lower on isolated trees or the margins of clearings or rivers.

Further adaptations (or anyway beneficial specializations) widely exhibited by epiphytes are wind-borne spores (such as those of Ferns) or seeds (such as those of Orchids) or fruits, though other seeds and fruits are commonly dispersed by animals. Indeed it is difficult to conceive of epiphytes being able to maintain themselves without some effective means of dispersal of their propagules. Some types, often termed hemi-epiphytes, develop long aerial roots which reach the ground and so link epiphytes with the next group of 'forest furnishings', the stranglers.

The epiphytic vegetation of tropical rain forests often includes abundant Algae, Lichenes, Musci, and Hepaticae; indeed, with the usual absence of the mossy layer on the forest floor, all the Lichens present and almost all of the Algae and Bryophytes are normally epiphytic except occasionally in spots where fallen leaves have not collected. There are, however, all manner of 'associules' on stones, fallen logs, and so forth, as well as on tree-trunks down to ground-level. Otherwise, non-vascular plants contribute widely to the classes of sun- and shade-epiphytes and also grow as 'epiphyllae' on (normally living) leaves—in the last instance mainly in the shady undergrowth. Actually, the most abundant epiphytes of the shade community tend to be Bryophytes, which often carpet the branches of shrubs or hang down in the air, while the epiphytes of the sun community include also many foliose Lichens, the Bryophytes of this synusia tending to be more compact and xeromorphic. The epiphyllae are mainly Algae, Lichens, or leafy Liverworts, and are found chiefly on the upper surface of rather long-lived evergreen leaves of tough consistency. They often have interesting structural modifications which appear to assist their adherence to the substratum, though normally they do not have any appreciable ill-effect on leaves even when they largely cover their surfaces.

5. *Stranglers.* These are plants which begin life as epiphytes but later send down roots to the soil, becoming independent or nearly so, and often killing the tree which originally supported them.

FIG. 148.—Roots of Strangling Fig on a large tree-trunk.

They thus form a synusia which is biologically intermediate between dependent and independent plants. Most familiar and plentiful in both species and individuals are, widely, the Strangling Figs (*Ficus* spp.), which may play a considerable part in the economy as well as physiognomy of the rain forest. The seeds commonly germinate far up in the forks of tall trees and from the epiphytic bush first formed are developed long roots which descend to the ground, those nearest the trunk of the supporting tree branching and anastomosing until it is encased in a strong network (Fig. 148). After a time the original tree usually dies and rots away, leaving the strangler whose crown has meanwhile become large and heavy, as a hollow but independent tree in its place (Fig. 149). Species of *Clusia*, forming large crowns but seldom killing their hosts, are often the most plentiful stranglers in the South American rain forest.

6. *Saprophytes.* These, the plants obtaining their nutriment from

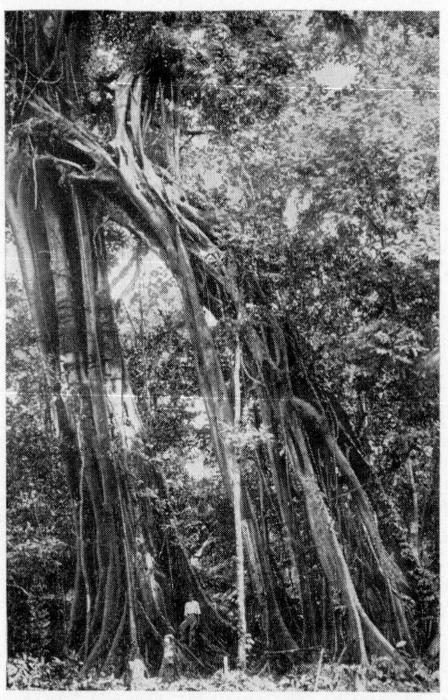

FIG. 149.—An old specimen of Strangling Fig in which the roots serve as trunks, the original 'host' having disappeared.

dead organic matter, together with the parasites, comprise the non-green, heterotrophic components of the tropical rain-forest vegetation. As in temperate woodlands, the vast majority are Fungi and Bacteria which aid in organic breakdown—chiefly near the surface of the soil. There are, however, in addition usually some small associated flowering plants such as certain Orchids and members of the Burmannia family (Burmanniaceae) and the Gentian family (Gentianaceae), as well as others of the Triuridaceae and Balanophoraceae, which contain little or no chlorophyll and live by the same saprophytic means. They are chiefly found in deep shade on areas of the forest floor where dead leaves tend to accumulate to a greater depth than usual—*e.g.* in slight hollows or the angles between the buttresses of trees—but they may be absent from considerable tracts, especially in rain forest with a marked dry season. For in general there is very little humus accumulation in the tropics, owing to the rapidity of decay and breakdown of organic matter. The forest floor normally is barely covered by a thin litter of leaves, and commonly shows through in frequent bald patches, or these last may support cryptogams (*see* p. 434).

FIG. 150.—Flower and buds of *Rafflesia manillana*, a true parasite on the roots of a *Cissus* vine. *Rafflesia* has no regular leaves or stem, and no chlorophyll, the flowers growing directly from the roots of the host; an allied species, *R. arnoldii*, has the largest known flowers (about a metre in diameter).

7. *Parasites.* Of these there are, apart from Fungi and Bacteria, two main synusiae in the tropical rain forest—the root-parasites growing on the ground (Fig. 150) and the semi-parasites (often termed hemiparasites) growing epiphytically on the trees. The former are few and of little importance, comprising two small but remarkable families. On the other hand, the epiphytic semi-parasites all belong to the Mistletoe family (Loranthaceae—Fig. 151) and are numerous in species and often abundant, being met practically throughout the area of the rain forest. They are woody shrubs that in forests of fair density occur on the twigs and branches

of the taller trees, whereas in open types or areas they may descend almost to ground-level. Their vertical distribution thus corresponds with that of the autotrophic sun-epiphytes, and seems to be determined chiefly by intolerance of shade.

In subtropical regions where the rainfall is abundant and well-distributed, rain forests occur which are similar to the tropical ones except for their tendency to be less luxuriant and dominated by fewer species, and to include temperate elements but a smaller total

FIG. 151.—A tropical hemiparasitic Mistletoe, *Viscum orientale*, the root of which forms a single haustorium (absorbing organ).

flora. Often there are fewer lianes and epiphytes as well as, especially, trees; and often the middle (B) tree storey predominates, although traces of both the others may be developed. Examples are found bordering on the tropical rain forests and elsewhere as already indicated above, and include the more luxuriant ' hammocks ' of southern Florida. Such special features as plank-buttressing and cauliflory, characteristic of the tropical rain forest, become less evident or disappear. As temperate regions are approached, these subtropical rain forests pass into the poorer but still evergreen, warm-temperate ones described in Chapter XII. It should also be noted that, in periodically drier areas inhabited by other types of vegetation, there often occur, along rivers, 'fringing forests' which are evergreen and otherwise reminiscent of the rain forest (although usually less luxuriant).

In spite of the widespread destruction wrought by Man particularly during the past century, it has been computed that one or other form of tropical rain forest or 'seasonal' forest (*see* below) still occupies about half of the total forested area of the world.

## Tropical Forests with a Seasonal Rhythm

Where marked dry seasons occur in the otherwise humid tropics and the dominants are dependent upon seasonal rainfall, the vegetation presents a much more varied appearance. Here conditions tend to be so 'critical' that slight differences in the climate or soil may introduce marked changes in the plant formations. Actually, regions with one or sometimes two pronounced dry seasons of several months' duration occupy a much greater area in the tropics than those with a constantly humid climate and luxuriant evergreen vegetation. Such 'seasonal' climates of marked extremes are particularly characteristic of the interiors of continents. When their areas are timbered and tropical or subtropical, they may be classified in the following three main groups of descending water-availability :

1. Widespread though variable are the *monsoon forests* or similar 'seasonal' forests, developed in regions enjoying abundant rainfall during the wet season, but having this alternating with a pronounced drought lasting from four to six months or sometimes longer. The total amount of rainfall is usually less than in tropical rain forests, being commonly between 100 and 200 cm. per annum if we include in this category areas dominated by a rather wide range of deciduous types ; and there are marked daily and seasonal changes in temperature as well as, commonly, strong winds. Often the character of the forest has been changed by human interference, to which its maintenance may even be due, for the dominants are apt to be fire-resistant.

Monsoon or allied forests are found in the areas of the true monsoons in India, Burma, Indo-China, and southwards to northern Australia, as well as on the margins of the tropical rain forest in Africa, Madagascar, Indonesia, and Central and South America. Their vegetation is not as luxuriant as that of the tropical rain forest, though varying in appearance from an impoverished form of the latter down to the savanna-woodland type described below. Thus in comparison with the rain forest, the monsoon forest tends to be more open, with the trees farther apart and no such scramble of all plants for light, while in the dry season (*see* p. 424) most trees shed their leaves and the landscape takes on a ' wintry ' appearance. The degree of defoliation depends, however, on circumstances—particularly on the severity of the season and the proximity of water-courses, along which trees tend to retain their foliage throughout the year. Some evergreen trees persist except when the dry season is particularly rigorous, and indeed there is apt to be relatively poor correlation with the dry season, many species tending to produce young leaves some time before it is over. This dry season is often, moreover, the period of flowering, so that altogether the monsoon forests at this time do not present as lifeless an aspect as do temperate deciduous forests in winter. They do, however, resemble these forests rather than tropical rain forests in that the trees have thick bark, exhibit growth-rings in the wood, lack plank-buttresses, and are usually not more than 12 to, at the most, 35 metres in height.

The trunks of the trees tend to be massive and fairly short, the crowns being usually round and large, spreading widely from often no great height above the ground. The branches are commonly rather stout and gnarled, and the bark is typically fissured or scaly. The community consists of three main tiers—the canopy which is liable to be much interrupted, the undergrowth which tends to be dense but to have small and hard leaves, and the ground or ' field ' layer consisting mainly of more or less lowly herbs. The leaves of the trees are usually thin but may be larger than those of the tropical rain forest, as in the case of Teak (*Tectona grandis*). They function only during the rainy season and so require no particular protection, being commonly hygrophilous (possessed of features characteristic of inhabitants of humid situations). The climbers are fewer and smaller than in the rain forest, being often herbaceous, and vascular epiphytes are normally found only in the canopy. Consequently the undergrowth is often luxuriant, consisting of shrubby thickets (or sometimes of tall tufty Grasses when the forest is immature, though this is rather a feature of savanna-woodland). Bulbous and other geophytes are also commonly present in considerable numbers and flower in the dry season, whereas the shrubs tend to blossom at the onset of the monsoon rains before the leaves appear, and many herbs follow suit during the rainy season. Although the Teak forests may be relatively uniform, a feature of most other types of monsoon forests is the variety of tree-species involved, which may number forty or fifty in a single tract. In general, however, both flora and vegetational luxuriance are markedly poorer than in the tropical rain forest, though the most striking difference lies in the seasonal nature of the monsoon forest.

2. *Savanna-woodlands* or ' parklands ' are often found where the rainless period is more prolonged and the annual rainfall less heavy than in true closed forest. The trees are mostly widely scattered save in favourable situations (such as occur near watercourses), show increasing xerophily and resistance to drought as water-availability decreases, and are often leafless during the dry season. The vegetation is open and park-like, being rich in terrestrial herbs and especially Grasses, but very poor in lianes and epiphytes. Bulbous and other geophytes are often abundant. The trees are commonly stunted to little more than tall shrubs, being usually much less than 20 metres high and sometimes overtopped by tall Grasses during the rainy season. Although normally various, they are most characteristically and widely members of the Pea family (Leguminosae), which frequently dominate alone. Some of the trees may be quite lofty ; but usually they are of lowly stature, often with squat stems and thick fissured bark, the crowns being commonly flattened or umbrella-shaped—allegedly in relation to wind, though this presumption has been questioned. Thus Mr. A. C. Hoyle (*voce*) believes that the causal factors are complicated and include high insolation at times of limited water-supply. The leaves of the trees are usually xeromorphic and their buds well protected, but flowering frequently takes place late in the dry season.

In some places, as for instance in South Africa, it is contended that the more open parkland or ' tree-veld ' is successional, the scattered Acacias and other trees attracting Birds and Mammals that drop seeds around. In this manner a considerable variety of other trees, shrubs, and climbers may be brought in and locally oust the tall Grasses, so that a patchy type of savanna-woodland develops. Even this may not be truly climax but due to edaphic or biotic influences (particularly fire), and indeed it may well be that most savanna-woodland is a fire climax in which the trees become self-selected for fire-resistance.

In these well-lighted, open types of woodlands a few small lianes and epiphytes may occur, though often the latter, particularly, are lacking. On the other hand in favourable situations where the trees grow close together, there may be a fair array of xerophilous epiphytic Bromeliads, Orchids, and Ferns, that seem more properly to belong to the rain forest.

Savanna-woodland of one sort or another is found very widely in tropical and subtropical regions including much of Cuba and elsewhere in the Caribbean, Brazil and northern Argentina, East and central Africa both north and south of the Equator, and occupying much of India and China as well as of northern and eastern Australia.

3. *Thorn-woodlands*, with similar or allied types called tropical thorn-forests, thornwoods, thornbush, caatinga, etc., are usually still more xerophilous, being found in areas of still lower rainfall and more prolonged drought-period than the often poorly-differentiated but usually much more grassy savanna-woodlands. Indeed Grasses are often lacking in the drier thorn-woodlands, or tend to be segregated into clumps separated by areas of bare soil. The present group of vegetation-types are found chiefly where the annual rainfall is between 40 and 90 cm. but variable, with the temperature high all the year round, ranging from 15 to 35° C. The terms quoted are not synonymous in that they are apt to be applied to communities of different physiognomy growing under different circumstances in different regions. And just as the major types dealt with previously in this section grade into one another, as indeed do many vegetation-types elsewhere, so do the present variants intergrade and interdigitate with the savannas and grasslands dealt with below. Moreover, various and even quite different types and sequences may be involved where local water or other conditions change markedly. Thus succulents are often most in evidence in areas of particularly coarse, over-drained soil, and may form distinctive communities alternating with one or another type of thorn-woodland.

The foliage of the dominants of tropical thorn-woodlands is deciduous or markedly xerophilous, or often reduced to mere scales, thorns or prickles being a common feature as the above names imply. Switch-plants with woody photosynthetic stems are also characteristic of the community. The roots of the main plants are much branched, and competition among them for water may be severe. Often they penetrate very deeply, shallow-rooting types such as Grasses having little chance of success. Many of the woody plants store water for the dry season in swollen trunks or roots, as in the case of the Brazilian Bottletree (*Cavanillesia arborea*) whose trunk swells to form an almost barrel-shaped structure. There are also sometimes tracts dominated by arborescent succulents, including giant Spurges (*Euphorbia* spp.) in the Old World and characteristic members of the Cactus family (Cactaceae) in the New World. A few xeromorphic herbs may occur, such as terrestrial Bromeliads with sharp-edged leaves. The accompanying shrubs are no less xeromorphic, being often thorny Acacias or other members of the Pea family, and sometimes forming a grey bushy jungle 3–5 metres high, while a few thin woody climbers may also occur. Epiphytes are usually absent, though Spanish-moss (*Tillandsia* sp.) may be plentiful locally. With the onset of the rainy season the leaves and flowers emerge and vast numbers of geophytic herbs may spring from the soil, the rhythm of life being even more strongly marked than in the monsoon forests.

Tropical thorn-woodlands and -parklands, etc., are widely developed in dry regions: for example, in northeastern Brazil and elsewhere in tropical South America, in the islands of the Caribbean as well as in Central America and Mexico, and in and about the Sudan and regions bordering on the southern Red Sea and the Gulf of Aden. They also occur in southwestern Africa, in India, and in the west and centre and northern hinterland of Australia. Thorn-woodlands and allied types often occupy sandy or limestone soils that are very permeable to water, and alternate with savanna which tends to prevail on the stiffer soils that retain rainwater near the surface. In places where there is a local increase in humidity, as for example in depressions or ravines, this savanna passes to savanna-woodland.

## Tropical and Subtropical Savannas and Other Grasslands

As in other major regions, grasslands in the tropics and subtropics constitute one of the main vegetational types and are usually, but not always, dominated by members of the Grass family (Gramineae). For sometimes grass-like plants of other affinity (particularly of the Sedge family, Cyperaceae), may be the dominants over considerable areas, or plants of quite different types may play a similar role. Savannas are by some considered synonymous with treeless grasslands or steppes but in the present work the term is employed to denote areas which ecologically speaking appear to be true grasslands, in that Grasses or similar herbs seem to be the real dominants, but in which trees or tall bushes (in ‘ bush savanna ’) occur in open formation and give a particular character to the landscape. Normally these tall woody plants are more or less widely scattered except in unusually favourable circumstances such as obtain along water-courses or elsewhere that water is relatively plentiful. The occurrence of more hygrophilous 'meadows' is rare in the tropics and is clearly due to some particular local factor or factors of disturbance.

Although many grasslands in the tropics, as elsewhere, appear to be 'natural' to the extent that they do not owe their existence to direct interference by Man, it now seems clear that there is no such thing as a 'tropical grassland climate' and quite possible that tropical grasslands are not in fact climatic. This may even be the case with the savannas which in one form or another constitute their most common expression, for in the tropics taller woody plants are rarely absent from such areas. Certainly many of these tracts owe their persistence or very existence to fires or browsing animals, or are edaphic climaxes due to local soil conditions, while others appear to be seral. Thus fires often destroy woody and other dicotyledonous plants and Palms without appreciably damaging the underground parts of the Grasses. But whatever their ecological significance may be, these grasslands constitute characteristic types of considerable economic as well as areal importance.

Savannas or their treeless counterparts are very widespread in tropical and subtropical regions, where they often cover vast tracts—though not without considerable local variation within their own areas, as in the cases of many South American 'campos' and 'llanos'. Examples are to be seen in southwestern North America and the West Indies, in Central and South America both north and south of the Amazonian forests, and in very many parts of Africa such as the Sudan and within as well as around the closed forests of the Congo, etc. They also occur in central Madagascar, in disturbed and upland areas of India and elsewhere in Asia, and to the north of the central desert tracts of Australia. The climate is hot, with a moderate range of temperature and a fair rainfall often exceeding 100 cm. annually and well spread over 120 to 190 days, during which 'rainy season' large areas may be constantly under water. On the other hand there is a prolonged drought lasting often for six or seven months of the year, and a tendency to desiccating winds. With such substantial rainfall, more or less xerophilous woodlands are apt to predominate in the absence of disturbance—at least elsewhere in areas of very high temperatures and prolonged rainless periods during the vegetative season. These woodlands may include the savanna-woodlands, which are distinguished by the fact that in them the trees appear to be dominant, although such types grade into savannas, even as these last grade into treeless grasslands.

The savanna presents mostly a park- or orchard-like appearance —a landscape typically of plains of tall Grasses with scattered trees and shrubs. In hollows or swales the trees frequently grow close enough together to form woods, whereas on ridges they are sparse or wholly absent, the vegetation thus constituting a steppe. The Grasses commonly exceed the height of a Man, but range, in different instances, from less than 1 to more than 4 metres high, and form

FIG. 152.—Palm-savanna in southern Florida.

a yellowish straw frequently topped by silvery 'spikes'. They typically grow clustered in dense tufts which exhibit, in the intervals, patches of bare soil often of a reddish or yellowish hue. Low bushes with small and hard evergreen leaves and often prickles or thorns may occur among the Grasses.

The trees which appear at greater or lesser intervals in the savanna are usually stunted and gnarled but sometimes lofty. While many are deciduous, others are evergreen; common heights are 3–6 metres. They belong to characteristic species not usually occurring in the forest, and commonly include Palms (Fig. 152) or other plants of peculiar habit (Fig. 153). Often the fast-growing, coarse and stiff Grasses interpenetrate the lower branches of the trees and remind the ecologist of their tendency to dominate. Elephant Grass (*Pennisetum purpureum*) may exceed 5 metres in height and form an almost impenetrable 'thicket'. The trees typically include some

Acacias and other members of the Pea family (Leguminosae), and, in Africa, the Baobab (*Adansonia digitata*), with its hugely swollen, water-storing trunk. They often have thick and corky, fissured bark and in favourable situations may form groves. In uplands the Grasses tend to be lower and more mixed with forbs, though even in the lowlands some forbs are to be found—both hardy perennials and others having tubers or bulbs, which enable them to burst forth into leaf and flower with the recurrence of the rainy season.

FIG. 153.—Savanna in Australia developed under rainfall of 25–75 cm. annually. (Phot. D. A. Herbert).

Although many present-day savannas and treeless grasslands have probably resulted from clearance of closed forest, they usually experience a longer period of drought each year than do forests. However, they have more frequent rains and usually less permeable soil than the relatively arid thorn-woodlands. Thus the rainwater that falls is readily available for the shallow-rooting, tussocky Grasses whose dead straw also accumulates to form a mulch, and whose close ' felt ' of roots further helps in water-retention. On the other hand, tree-growth is largely restricted to places where the ground-water lies at no great distance from the surface, most of the successful trees having roots penetrating deeply enough to tap this more lasting source. They also tend to have relatively low and compact crowns, often of spreading, umbrella-like shape, allegedly as a result of exposure to winds. But in many areas they are kept at bay or ousted by burning, or by the intensive grazing of herds of wild or domesticated Mammals ; of these, many of the world's largest are inhabitants of the great grassy plains of tropical and subtropical regions.

## Semi-Desert Scrubs

The arid bushlands characterized by scrubby Acacias and other xeromorphic shrubs are often included among deserts, though actually it seems preferable to consider them as transitional between true deserts and savannas or thorn-woodlands. In tropical and subtropical regions they are found particularly on stony or rocky hill-sides, in open rolling country, and on sandy or gravelly areas exposed to the full glare of the sun. Examples may be seen in the southwestern United States and adjacent Mexico, along the foot of the Andes, and in Africa especially bordering on the Sahara. In the East they occur in Arabia and elsewhere near the northern shores of the Indian Ocean, and also in Australia. The climatic conditions supporting these warm-region scrubs lie between those of the desert proper and of thorn-woodlands, the temperatures being variable but high at all seasons, and the rainfalls occasional though seasonal and commonly averaging from 20 to 50 or more cm. annually. Important is the seasonal distribution and general reliability of the rainfall.

Many of the plants are veritable caricatures, such as those that are grotesquely swollen to store water.

The bushes in these semi-deserts are often of fair size and either grow separated or aggregated into a more or less continuous scrub, most often of thorny Acacias. Grasses if present are dwarfed and wiry, and usually reduced to isolated bunches or ragged patches. Other herbs tend to be leathery- or fleshy-leafed, or, in numerous instances, geophytic, with underground storage of food and water. Cacti in the New World and cactus-like Euphorbias in the Old World frequently form a characteristic feature of the usually open vegetation. Like some of the other plants, including the thorny Acacias, they are often beset with prickly spines. Large-leafed Agaves, Aloes, and Yuccas are also characteristic inhabitants, as are smaller succulents. Although some of the shrubs may be fairly dense and exceed the height of a Man, they are rarely close enough together in these semi-desert bush-lands to obscure the entire horizon. Fig. 154 shows a relatively well-vegetated area in Australia.

In some subtropical regions such as occur in southwestern North America, a shrubby climax may be developed where the annual rainfall averages as little as about 8 cm., provided it is reasonably distributed and reliable. The dominants tend to be many-stemmed but sparsely open, with widely-spreading roots. Although the

FIG. 154.—Semi-desert 'bush-land' in Australia.

formation is commonly called 'desert-scrub' it seems best mentioned here, even as its more temperate counterpart, characterized by the Creosote-bush, was described under semi-deserts in Chapter XII. Indeed the southern, subtropical extensions towards Central America have little of a regular nature to distinguish them from the northern type, and much the same is true in other regions. Thus while the dominants tend to be lower, the Creosote-bush being in the South only about a metre high and others (such as Bur-sages, *Franseria* spp.) commonly lower, the transition is normally so gradual that no further type emerges or account need be given here.

## Tropical and Subtropical Deserts

The hot deserts are areas in the tropics and subtropics having such very slight precipitation that they typically support at best only a scanty growth of scattered plants. Even if the nights are cool, with dew and mists occurring especially in central regions, the days are normally blazing hot. The environment is thus severe and the general run of habitats so unfavourable that they can only be colonized by appropriately adapted plants and animals. Bald expanses of flat or rolling plains predominate, all sunbaked and windswept, with wide tracts of yellowish sand-dunes or browner gravels or more rugged rocky floors, and in places broken scarps of naked hills. Sparingly dotted in the less inimical situations may be low and dry, strange-looking plants, or, in the very occasional damper situations, luxuriant but limited oases.

Hot deserts chiefly occur well to the north and south of the equatorial zone, which imaginative generalizers are apt to say is 'hemmed in' by them. Although probably more extensive than they used to be, owing to interference by Man and his domestic animals, they are often not nearly so vast and invariable as is popularly supposed, great areas being occupied by other types which are only relatively speaking 'desertic'. The main examples are the Sahara and Arabian Deserts, occupying, respectively, much of northern Africa and southwestern Asia, whence there are extensions eastwards into northwestern India and northwards and then eastwards into temperate central Asia. Extensive hot desert and near-desert[1] areas also occur in central Australia and the southwestern portions of North America, and smaller ones in southwestern Africa and western South America.

The primary cause of hot deserts is paucity or even perennial absence of rain, though an excessively clear and dry atmosphere, with scorching sun, usually contributes to the general aridity. Thus the relative humidity in the daytime is commonly less than 50 per cent. and may drop as low as 5 per cent. The rainfall usually averages less than 20 cm. per annum, often very much less, while

[1] To many who have experienced the real deserts of, for example, northern Africa and southwestern Asia, it seems unreasonable to refer to the more productive of the so-called deserts of North America as properly desertic—hence the use of this designation here. It was one of the present author's earliest experiences in Iraq to show pictures of such North American 'desert' areas to students who asked 'But, Professor, how can you call those areas desert, when the vegetation is so great?'

in some areas there may be no rain at all for several years on end. Such areas may be wholly devoid of macroscopic plants over some tracts. Intense radiation and considerable changes of temperature are also common, so that where the ground is rocky or clayey it is liable to be much fissured. Often it is gravelly, sandy, loamy, or stony—but none the less arid. Thus although the substratum and even the topography may change greatly in a single desert area, the abiding influence is the paucity of water. Tracts of different type may exhibit different forms and degrees of vegetative development, or sometimes virtually none, but all have the desert character, the stamp of aridity. For example in the western Sahara there are the pebbly-clayey areas with cushion-plants and succulents, the sandy or gravelly beds of dry watercourses populated with Tamarisks (*Tamarix* spp.), the sand-dunes dotted with heath-like bushes and grass-tussocks, and the rocky plateaux, most desolate of all, consisting of split stones and broken rocks with an occasional spiny or other xerophyte anchored in the fissures. In addition there are saline depressions which at best support relatively sparse colonies of dwarfed shrubby halophytes.

Similar ranges of type are found in other deserts, or extremes from absolutely bare moving sand-dunes to fairly dense heathlands characterized by switch-plants. There may even be open miniature woodlands, with or without large bushy succulents. The American near-deserts[1] are remarkable for their giant Cacti such as the Saguaro (or Sahuaro, *Carnegiea gigantea*) and their small pebble-like Pincushion Cacti (*Mammillaria* spp.), as well as for their glutinous Creosote-bushes (*Larrea* spp.) and characteristic Ocotillo (*Fouquiera splendens*) (Fig. 155). The South African desert is famous for the unique gymnospermous Tumboa (*Welwitschia mirabilis*) and the Desert Melon (*Acanthosicyos horrida*), as is the Australian for other highly peculiar plant forms. Thus whereas the desert populations are normally limited to relatively small and scattered plants, many of which are thorny, each area may have its own particular character given by the plants themselves.

Desert plants are adapted in various ways to withstand the adverse conditions under which they have to establish themselves, grow, and ultimately reproduce. Many, particularly among the shrubs and more occasional shrubby trees, have long roots that are said to reach down sometimes to a depth of 10 or more metres (they may certainly exceed 15 metres in length) to subterranean water or at

[1] *See* footnote on preceding page.

least to damp layers deep down in the ground. Regarding the 'extraordinarily deep-penetrating root systems' of Tamarisks, it is even reported that they 'could be followed during the building of the Suez Canal in places to a depth of 50 metres' (transl.).[1] Other desert etc. plants, especially among cryptogams, endure drought by drying up almost entirely without harm to themselves. Yet others are densely tufted or compacted, and often in addition closely

FIG. 155.—Arizona near-desert scene showing the giant Saguaro (or Sahuaro) Cactus (*Carnegiea gigantea*) and bushy Ocotillo (*Fouquiera splendens*). (Phot. F. Shreve.)

invested with hairs and spines, while many, such as Cacti and cactus-like Euphorbias, store water in their massive stems or other swollen organs. Usually these 'succulents' have an extensive system of roots spread out near the surface of the soil and ready to absorb considerable quantities of water when it comes, for most deserts have a short rainy season during which conditions are fairly favourable for plant growth—especially with the aid of the rich nocturnal dew which may occur. At such times annuals spring up and quickly pass through their whole cycle of development,[2] while geophytes, with

[1] K. Rubner, *Neudammer forstliches Lehrbuch* (Neumann, Berlin, 1 Lieferung, p. 180, 1948).

[2] After the heavy rains in central Iraq in the spring of 1957, the author observed small Plantains (*Plantago* spp.) and Grasses (especially of the genus *Schismus*) and

underground bulbous or tuberous storage organs, send up aerial shoots which flower and fruit but die down with the resumption of drought. Hence the ' flowery carpets ' of delicate mesophytes that some of the more seasonally-varying deserts often exhibit between their scattered bushes after adequate rainfall. In contrast to these ephemerals and ' deciduous perennials ', the shrubs commonly have very small evergreen xerophilous leaves, or sometimes larger deciduous ones which are lost after the rainy period ; others may have the leaves reduced to scales, photosynthesis being carried on instead by green twigs or leaf-like or succulent stems.

Most of the desert plants having perennial aerial parts are extremely xeromorphic, exhibiting such features as excessive development of fibrous tissues, thickened or otherwise covered epidermis, sunken and protected stomata, and reduction or ' waxing ' of the transpiring surface. They also commonly exhibit the xerophytic feature of high osmotic value of the cell-sap. Frequently several of these characteristics are shown by a single plant, sometimes to an extraordinary degree. Dispersal of seeds from whole plants detached by the wind and acting as tumble-weeds is fairly common, and often seeds will remain dormant for years on end before germinating when sufficient water becomes available. Even if many xeromorphic desert plants may transpire fairly rapidly when water is plentiful, they are able when necessary, by such features as those already mentioned and by keeping the stomata closed all day, to reduce their water-loss to a minimum and so often survive prolonged drought. They also exhibit considerable resistance to wilting and to injury as a result of water-loss. Thorny shrubs or broom-like switch-plants and other drought-endurers are particularly characteristic of deserts, as are, of course, extreme succulents and many ephemerals, but it is too ' convenient ' to classify desert plants into any such stereotyped categories. A few root-parasites also occur rather widely in deserts. Contrary to popular supposition, the larger succulents are unable to withstand the conditions of the drier deserts.

Where there is a lasting supply of water, as along the banks of rivers whether permanent or seasonal, or where the ground-water rises to near or sometimes above the surface, as in oases, the vegetation is able to demonstrate at once the natural fertility of the soil

other ephemerals in his desert quadrats to grow up, flower, ripen seed, and die down—all within a period of about five weeks, though this is only in the warm-temperate belt. It is, however, possible that germination had taken place before the main rains came, and so closer observations must be made in future. Fig. 156 shows the ' before and after ' effect of heavy rain in a desert area of central Iraq.

A

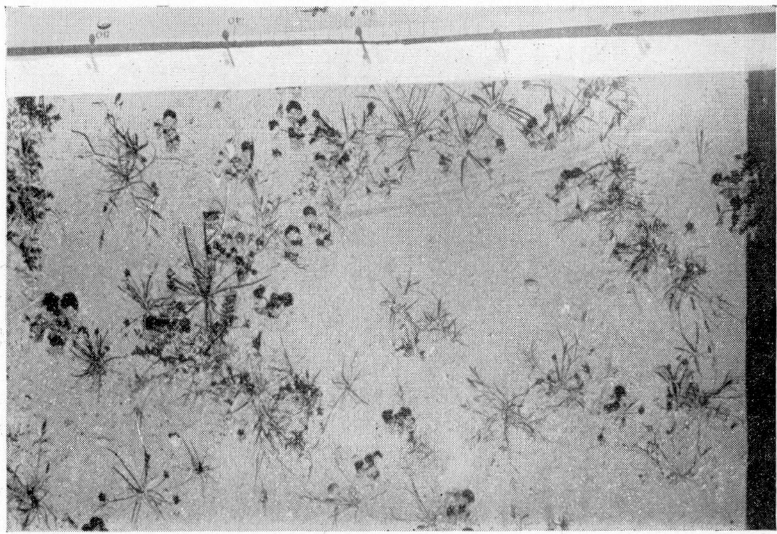

B

Fig. 156.—Tracts of desert in central Iraq. A, metre quadrat showing only 1 small perennial tuft (on right-hand side, about two-thirds of the way back), although numerous tiny seedlings are appearing after heavy rain. B, close-up of an adjacent less gravelly area a very few weeks later, showing species of *Schismus* (slender Grass), *Malva* (broad dark leaves), and *Plantago* (thin rosettes) developed to maturity. The nails projecting from the frame are 10 cm. apart in both A and B.

—provided, of course, that salts are not present to excess. Date Palms (*Phoenix dactylifera*) and attractive gardens can thus be cultivated in otherwise desert areas, and in large oases a fine variety of tropical and subtropical agricultural crops are produced. Wherever there is feed for Mammals, desert forms such as Gazelles are apt to pasture, while for miles around inhabited oases little save poisonous or distasteful plant material is normally left undisturbed. Along dried-up watercourses (*wadis*) the trees may attain large dimensions, though usually remaining small-leafed and thorny, while perennial Grasses, which are otherwise rare, often inhabit the sandy or gravelly beds. Where desert conditions extend into temperate regions, as in the Gobi, the oases are characterized (as mentioned in Chapter XII) by tall Poplars and Willows. Here other vegetation is in keeping with the temperate situation, the crops being such temperate ones as Barley, Wheat, and Plums. On their poleward side such cooler deserts are usually bordered by wide steppes, whereas hot deserts are typically bordered by semi-desert scrub, at least on the equatorial side.

## Mangrove and Other Sea-Shore Vegetation

By far the most characteristic and important vegetation-type of tropical and subtropical sea-shores is the ‘ mangrove ’ or ‘ mangrove-swamp forest ’ developed on mud-flats which are exposed at low tide but otherwise normally covered by salt or brackish water, at least being reached occasionally during the highest tides. Particularly favourable conditions for the development of mangroves are found in creeks and quiet bays ending river estuaries, where tidewaters cause the deposit of river sediment. On the resulting flats and deltas, the water-borne seeds or seedlings of the colonizing plants grow, soon forming the characteristic, rather low and dense forest (Fig. 157). In other cases the mangrove forest in its interior may consist of sizeable trees and be quite lofty (Fig. 158). In Malaya and to a lesser extent in Borneo there are large stretches of uniformly tall, mature mangroves (I. V. Polunin *voce*). Thus in Malaya the ‘ climax ’ mangrove forest consists of relatively few species which tend to be gregarious, producing stands of uniform height, whereas in Borneo the stands are not so pure or uniform (J. A. R. Anderson and I. V. Polunin *in litt.*). Actually, real climax mangrove now scarcely exists in Malaya, owing to felling on a rotation of about 30 years, which leads to a retention of this height-uniformity

FIG. 157.—A typical Mangrove plant, *Rhizophora candelaria*, forming a characteristic marginal 'mangrove' and showing prominent prop-roots below.

FIG. 158.—Interior of Philippine mangrove-swamp forest at low tide, showing, below, the aerating prop-roots and the conical erect aerating roots which project upwards from the mud.

(J. Wyatt-Smith *voce*). Frequently, however, the interior tallness situation is reversed in that the fringe of the mangrove, at least where it does not consist of young pioneer plants, is made up of tall trees, the interior being of much lower or bush-like plants. This is due to the loss of true mangrove conditions and an approach to those of the hinterland forest (J. Wyatt-Smith *voce*).

The abundant strut-like and often arching prop-roots of the mangrove trees or lower dominants, among other features, cause deposition of silt and building up of the surface ; often, new mud-flats are formed and the forest may extend year by year. These prop-roots are well seen in the illustrations, while Fig. 158 shows also numerous slender conical aerating roots growing vertically out of the mud. Both types of roots have ' breathing-pores ' and contain numerous air-spaces that serve for the conduction of oxygen to the underground parts of the system. This function is rendered vitally important by the nature of the substratum and by the usually frequent inundation, and is performed in some cases by knee-like or keeled projections of roots above the surface of the mud. Another function of the ' pneumatophores ', as the aerating roots are called, appears to be to help keep pace with the tendency of the surface level to rise through deposition, for their underground parts frequently bear the fine rootlets on which the tree is dependent for absorption. Different types of mangrove plants bear these different kinds of roots ; and the species may be mixed together or, alternatively, segregated in more or less pure stands. In mangroves in general, and particularly in those of the Indo-Malayan region, there is often to be found a fairly definite succession. The stages of this are usually characterized by different species, and range from the pioneers growing on almost continually submerged surfaces to a mature mangrove forest of often tall trees whose bases may be inundated by only the highest spring tides or, in some instances, scarcely ever reached at all.

Many of the characteristic dominants of mangroves have another feature in common, namely, the ' viviparous ' development of the seeds—that is, their germination while still within the fruits and attached to the parent plant. The typical arrangement, exhibited for example by the Red Mangrove (*Rhizophora mangle*), is for the primary root of the seedling to burst through the hanging fruit and, with adjacent tissues, to grow down as a long and dart-like, slender but bottom-heavy structure (*cf.* Fig. 26, B). Later on the seedling drops—root downwards, so that the tip may be driven into the mud [1] if the tide is out—and forms anchoring lateral roots in a matter of hours, often continuing to grow *in situ*. Actually the seedling is buoyant, so that if the tide is in or for some other reason the root does not stick sufficiently in the mud when it drops, it may be transported by water to some other situation, there to resume normal growth if conditions are favourable. Young seedlings are seen growing in fair numbers among the roots in the foreground in Fig. 158.

Mangroves often extend some distance inland in brackish swamps and lagoons, forming a fairly continuous fringe, or occupying islets between which run the sluggish tidal streams. At high tide they appear like a flooded forest or, about their low and tangled margins, like a mass of green or greyish foliage sitting on the water. Sometimes they are replaced by Palms (such as *Nipa fruticans*) or other large monocotyledonous plants, while near their climatic limits they tend to form dense tall thickets rather than forests. Recession of the tide even in the forested types reveals an ungainly mass of muddy roots and often grotesque boles. Even the trees are liable to be mis-shapen and lowly, while bubbles of stinking gas rise from the rotten mire, and a teeming population of crawling creatures adds to the atmosphere of gloomy squalor.

The climate is usually hot and humid, and conditions are kept monotonous by the tides and salinity, though there may be alternating heavy rainfall and scorching sun. The dominants are evergreen and halophytic, the foliage being leathery, fleshy, and protected by a glossy exterior or woolly covering against excessive transpiration. Their growth is often so manifestly dense as seemingly to prevent the entrance of herbaceous or other vascular plants, though indeed there are few of these which are adapted to the very specialized habitat. A dark coating of Red Algae may occur on the stems and roots submerged by the tides, and some Lichens are usually to be found on the stems well away from the water ; but other epiphytes are rare.

The chief development of mangroves is in southern and eastern Asia, with extensions to northern Australia and the Pacific. Mangroves also occur about Central America, and, to the east, with little variation on both sides of the Atlantic. In areas of low precipitation and general aridity, mangroves and other maritime woodlands are usually lacking or only poorly developed, even as are

[1] According to Dr. Frank E. Egler (*voce*), this happens far less frequently than the text-books imply.

forests inland. Exceptions may be afforded by the mouths of large rivers, where the salt water is diluted with fresh, and conditions of physiological drought are thereby relieved—provided cloudiness reduces insolation and, consequently, transpiration.

Although mangroves are usually seral within themselves, and in the most favourable of tropical rain-forest areas appear to be succeeded by freshwater swamp-forest (*see* pp. 461–3) or perhaps sometimes by tropical rain forest, in other instances there is no certainty that they can develop alone, by mere accumulation of silt or humus, into normal land vegetation or even littoral forest. In such instances the more advanced and stable 'inland' types would seem best considered as edaphic climaxes, that appear likely to persist in the absence of disturbance.

The other vegetation-types of tropical sea-shores are more or less comparable with those of temperate regions. Thus the beach between tide-marks is usually devoid of vegetation on sandy or shingly shores and bears only Algae on rocky ones, while even above high-water mark on exposed coasts the sandy tracts are often poorly vegetated, as are the outermost dunes. However, these last tend to be bound by Grasses such as *Spinifex littoreus*, whose rhizomes give off tufts at intervals, much as do many of the sand-binding Grasses of temperate regions. Many other littoral plants of the tropics adopt a similar trailing habit—including Pes-caprae (*Ipomoea pes-caprae*), which forms a particularly characteristic and widespread vegetation-type. Such plants also have the important faculty of being able to grow out of the sand when covered by its drifting, and in dry climates their areas of prevalence may extend far inland. Some other colonists have prop-roots that grow down and anchor them in the shifting sand, and almost all have a very deep and extensive root system. In more sheltered situations, shrubs often become numerous, as may in time small trees, such as Screw-pines (*Pandanus* spp., Fig. 159, A). Farther back still—or in quiet creeks sometimes near high-tide mark—a closed woodland is typically formed in areas of sufficient rainfall. In subtropical regions, as for instance the extreme southeast of Iraq bordering on the Persian Gulf, there may be salt-marshes reminiscent of those of temperate estuarine flats. An example is seen in Fig. 159, B, where the planted groves of Date Palms (*Phoenix dactylifera*) seen on the horizon afford a characteristic relief.

Littoral woodlands developing out of reach of the highest tides, for example on sandy and gravelly shores that still retain an abnormal

FIG. 159.—A Screw-pine and a subtropical estuarine salt-marsh. A, a Screw-pine (*Pandanus tectorius*) with prop-roots. Such plants are very common along the strand in the eastern tropics and are widely planted for ornamental purposes. ($\times \frac{1}{35}$.) B, a subtropical salt-marsh in the estuary of the Shatt al-Arab, near Fao in the extreme south-east of Iraq bordering on the Persian Gulf, showing, behind, a characteristic grove of planted Date Palms (*Phoenix dactylifera*).

amount of salt, are inclined to be highly characteristic and only gradually, in space or in time, able to take on the aspect of the local hinterland climax. Often they develop as a belt just inland of the mangrove. In other places the forest or scrub even in the tract lying nearest to the sea may be devoid of halophytic species. Where salinity prevails and the littoral forest differs from that of the general hinterland, the sandy or stony soil is often almost bare of dead leaves, and the trunks of the trees are commonly naked ; or they may be beset with epiphytes, both thick-leafed and cryptogamic, and support a mass of thin-stemmed climbers. Where the trees are less close together, there are often dense undergrowths of shrubs and small trees, or patches of coarse Grass. The leaves are usually leathery or succulent, often hairy when young, or hard and sword-like in the cases of Screw-pines and the leaf-segments of Coconut (*Cocos nucifera*) or other Palms. Particularly characteristic trees in such situations in the Old World are species of *Barringtonia*. As the distance from the coast increases, protective measures become less necessary and pronounced, and the forest takes on more and more the appearance and flora of the local climax, containing fewer and fewer species which are not to be found away from the influence of the sea. In other instances the littoral forest may be deciduous, or dominated largely by a single species (such as Ironwood, *Casuarina equisetifolia*). The proximity of the sea is also expressed in the buoyancy of many of the seeds and fruits, which are commonly found in sea-drift, and which help some at least of the characteristic species to attain a very wide distribution. This is said to be the case with the Coconut, plants of which form such a characteristic feature of many tropical sea-shores (Fig. 160).

## Further Seral or Edaphic Communities

Apart from various seral types already mentioned, such as the dunes and, presumably, littoral woodlands dealt with in the last section, and biotic plagioclimaxes which in some respects are of a seral nature, there are yet others to consider in tropical and sub-tropical regions. Outstanding are various types of forested and reedy swamps, secondary scrubs and forests, and weedy communities of many kinds.

Swamps occur chiefly around the edges of quiet bodies of fresh water, in sheltered arms of lakes or sluggish rivers, and in filled or filling hollows where the ground is at least waterlogged and where free water accumulates on the surface for some period or periods of the year. Here, as in temperate regions, there is often a luxuriant development of largely erect monocotyledonous plants, such as Papyrus (*Cyperus papyrus*) or species of Reed (*Phragmites*) or Cattail (*Typha*). These form characteristic reed-swamps, with roots under water or in saturated soil, and with shoots extending more or less high into the air. Whether the inundation is permanent or periodic, and regardless of the water-level being relatively stable or fluctuating, such swamp-plants typically contain air-passages for the aeration of their roots and other covered parts.

FIG. 160.—Coconut Palms along a tropical sea-shore.

In many cases, particularly in the warmer regions, the shallow water is colonized by shrubs or trees, which may have special aerating roots after the manner of mangrove types. Swampy grounds in both the Old and New World tropics are frequently occupied by almost pure stands of certain species of Palms, while even where the forest is mixed it is usually much less rich in species, and particularly in large tree species, than on drier land. These swamp-forest trees usually, but not always, belong to species not normally found in the surrounding forests. They are said in some instances, for example in Burma, to be bare of leaves at the height of the rainy season, when they stand in a metre or more of water. Like tropical rain forest, the swamp-forest may consist of several tiers and may be plentifully supplied with lianes, that in some instances are described as having a short stem which reaches up only to the surface of the water in the rainy season, and from which arise disproportionately long, slender shoots.[1] The numbers of terrestrial herbs depend upon such features as the depth and duration of flooding: often they are few, being chiefly members of the Sedge family (Cyperaceae). However, epiphytic Orchids and Ferns can be plentiful, as can Mosses and Liverworts.

Whereas the swamp vegetation just described is evidently hydroseral, exemplifying stages in the succession, from open water to forest, that appears to take place in the same general manner as in cooler regions, there is one peculiarity in the tropics, where humus does not normally accumulate to any great degree. This is the fact that the majority of tropical swamp soils are not peaty, containing as they do little if any more humus than soils of normal drainage. However, where the water is poor in dissolved mineral matter (oligotrophic) some peat formation can occur, leading to the development of 'moor-forests', which are commonly called the tropical equivalent of the 'highmoors' of cool regions. Corresponding to this on one hand and, on the other, to the normal (non-peaty) swamp soil with a relatively eutrophic water-supply, there thus appear, in the tropics, to be two types of hydrosere leading to different types of climax forest which in both cases are edaphic rather than climatic. For in eutrophic waters the raising of the soil level is due mainly to the accumulation of inorganic sediments, while in oligotrophic waters such raising is chiefly the result of accumulation of plant remains. In both cases the soil level rises scarcely if at all above the height of the highest water-level once this has been reached, as conditions for further substantial accumulation then cease to exist in the tropics where organic breakdown is rapid. Consequently the hydrosere appears to end with the formation of ground in which the water-table is near the surface during at least part of the year. Such ground bears forest more or less like the climatic climax in structure, but different in floristic composition owing to the local water conditions. It is thus an edaphic climax and, like the hydrosere which engenders it, exists in two forms according to whether the soil consists largely of deposited silt or peat.

[1] A similar phenomenon may be observed in some areas of Amazonian rain forest that are subject to periodical inundation (R. E. Schultes *voce*).

Particularly characteristic are the peaty moor-forests originating in oligotrophic waters, which are widespread in the rain-forest region of southeastern Asia, where they are evergreen and dominated by dicotyledonous trees. These last may be as much as 30 metres high on the edge of such areas where the climax has been reached, but often diminish gradually towards the centre where the vegetation typically consists of earlier stages, including dwarf forest and even pools of water. Kneed and other aerating roots may help to make the surface of the ground an ' impenetrable ' jungle even in the mature forest. The dominants are often species peculiar to this type of vegetation ; they are relatively few in number and show a strong tendency to be gregarious, with a single species sometimes forming an almost pure community. Often associated are Palms and Screw-pines, with abundant epiphytes and herbaceous swamp-plants among the furnishings.

In eutrophic waters the early stages clearly consist of free-floating ' sudd ' and communities of submerged aquatics, followed, when the water becomes sufficiently shallow owing to silting, by rooted floating-leaf vegetation consisting of Water-lilies, etc. This prepares the habitat for emergent aquatics that soon constitute the reed-swamp stage, which in turn is succeeded by scrub or low forest. Though it may contain more trees per unit area, the (edaphic) climax canopy tends to be more open than in rain forest, so that light-loving species are commonly included in the undergrowth. Moreover, the total number of species per unit area of this climax tends to be smaller than in the rain forest, but greater than in the seral stages.

It is of interest to note that not only do tropical hydroseres run much the same course as temperate ones, the recognizable stages often having a closely comparable physiognomy, but many of the genera involved are the same in both these main climatic zones, and not a few of the species are closely related or, in some instances, identical. This is especially the case in the early stages in eutrophic waters, when, as in other extreme habitats, only a few co-dominants or even a single dominant may prevail. Thus in Panama the Common Reed (*Phragmites communis* agg.) and/or Narrow-leafed Cattail (*Typha angustifolia*) may largely dominate the reed-swamp stage, as may identical or similar species over much of temperate North America and western Eurasia. Characteristic inhabitants of rocks in rushing water are representatives of the peculiar family Podostemaceae.

Primary xeroseres in the tropics may be observed for example on recently emerged or volcano-devastated areas such as the East Indian island of Krakatoa, where after three years an associes consisting of a lower layer of Blue-green Algae and an upper one of Ferns and other vascular plants was found to clothe the surface of the pumice and ash in some inland places. Eleven years later, in 1897, the interior supported a dense growth of Grasses, with isolated shrubs and fairly numerous forbs as well as Ferns. There were, however, very few lower cryptogams to be seen apart from terrestrial Algae. Nine years later still, the shore supported a belt of well-developed maritime woodland complete with climbers, etc., but the inland savanna persisted. Subsequently this developed into a mixed woodland of fair luxuriance, and came to show every indication of progressing ultimately to the local rain forest (apart from some floristic depauperation and, probably, slowness of succession due to isolation and the consequent difficulties of colonization). Thus the usual sequence, such as we have seen elsewhere, of dominance by cryptogams and then by herbs and finally by trees, holds true in this tropical xerosere, though it should be noted that in rain-forest areas, such as this, there is a preponderance of phanerophytes among the flowering plants—often from quite early stages.

As in the case of the hydrosere, it seems that in the tropical xerosere the number of species goes on increasing to the end, whereas in temperate regions the numbers of species in both hydrosere and xerosere tend to rise to a maximum and then decline as the climax is approached, the decline usually starting when the community becomes closed. Other humid tropical regions appear to have xeroseres of a generally similar nature to that observed on Krakatoa, even if the pioneers in some cases are forbs, Grasses, Sedges, or even woody plants (especially in secondary successions).

The sea-shore and littoral communities outside the normal forest, already dealt with in the last section, are probably indicative of at least potential successions. However, with the factors of the environment as overwhelming as they often are in such situations, it seems unlikely that the successions will become actual as long as the shore-line continues as at present. Rather does it appear that each zone is in equilibrium with its particular environment. This, as we have seen, is apparently the case with many mangroves as well as with the latest stages of tropical hydroseres. But where accumulation can continue, as on some sandy shores, the communities may undergo rapid change and the zones of vegetation be actual stages in continuing successions.

Very widespread in the tropics are ' secondary ' scrubs and forests that form parts of secondary or deflected successions engendered particularly by Man or his domestic animals. When derived from tropical rain forest, such communities are always more or less unstable, whether they consist of weedy herbs, scrub, savanna, forest, or a ' chaotic wilderness of trees, shrubs, herbs and climbers '. When left to themselves and protected from burning, felling, and grazing, they are gradually invaded by primary forest species and proceed towards the climatic climax which with little doubt would ultimately be re-established. But where they are subjected to recurrent fires or persistent grazing, deflected successions set in and lead to biotic plagioclimaxes. Such are, probably, many tropical grasslands and savannas. Even in the forest, according to Professor Paul W. Richards (*in litt. binis*), ' too frequent cultivation, *i.e.* shifting cultivation on too short a rotation, is one of the most important causes of deflected successions ', and, ' especially if accompanied by intermittent burning and grazing, leads to the invasion of forest areas by savanna Grasses and eventually to the establishment of " derived " savanna '.

Shifting cultivation, which is practised by native peoples in nearly all tropical forested areas, is by far the most important cause of forest destruction there. In its course the trees are felled and burned, after which one or more crops are raised before the fertility of the soil is lost by leaching, erosion, and the exposure of humus to the sun, whereupon the plot is abandoned and another cleared. The secondary succession following abandonment usually starts with series or quick-growing herbs and continues with more lasting plants. During such re-establishment of vegetation, soil fertility becomes partially or largely restored, so that after some years the ' secondary ' (or tertiary, etc.) forest may be cleared and cultivated again. The practice is, however, liable to be extremely wasteful —especially when clearing and cultivation are undertaken at too frequent intervals. Less drastic in their effects are the abandonment of plantations and selective exploitation of timber, while strong winds may also fell trees and start secondary successions. On the other hand, shifting cultivation that is not too intense and short in rotation is not necessarily wasteful, and may be preferable to some forms of what is intended to be permanent cultivation, because it is less destructive of soil fertility. It may also be less conducive to erosion.

Secondary forest tends to be lower and to consist of trees of smaller dimensions than does primary forest, the young growth being often remarkably regular in including even-aged stands of one or a few woody species, whereas later on the growth may be extremely haphazard as already indicated. The early dominants are commonly light-demanding and ' weedy ', as are the associated herbs. Such forest may also be recognized by its floristic composition, which usually differs markedly from that of the primary forest, even though there are probably few if any species entirely restricted to the former. Many of the components of the secondary forest are unusually widespread, some often being introduced aliens, while its trees are mostly quick-growing (*e.g.* 12 metres in three years), short-lived, and possessed of efficient means of seed-dispersal. Their leaves tend to be of more various sizes and shapes than those of rain-forest trees. The most shade-intolerant and quickly growing species are, as might be expected, most characteristic of the early stages of the secondary succession.

The secondary forest at least when young is often dominated by a single or small number of species, and usually has a much smaller flora than the primary forest; when very old, however, it may be indistinguishable from virgin forest. On the other hand with long-continued grazing, mowing, or recurrent burning, secondary savanna or grassland is commonly formed, often characterized by species of Lalang Grass (*Imperata*); alternatively, as in temperate grasslands, there may be still further regression with overgrazing, or invasion by Bracken (*Pteridium*). In general, however, secondary successions appear to reproduce in their later stages the changes characterizing natural regeneration of primary forest, in which gaps formed by the death of large old trees are first filled by the easily dispersed and fast-growing dominants of the early stages of secondary forest. The earlier stages in larger clearings commonly include quick-growing Grasses and other weeds which are characteristic of disturbed tropical areas, though they may be even less lasting than their counterparts in cooler regions.

While shrubs may form a stage in the successions occurring in rain-forest areas, often they are omitted, dominance passing directly from herbaceous plants to trees. However, in drier regions shrubs are apt to be important in the secondary successions, sometimes remaining as more or less lasting dominants in what appear to have been previously forested (though ' marginal ') areas. Indeed vegetational differences, such as frequently arise from differences in the soil, tend to be much more marked in the dry districts of the tropics than where rain forest prevails. Outstanding are the laterite soils, typically reddish in colour owing to ferric compounds, which are extremely poor in alkalis and nutritive salts as well as in water-retaining capacity. They are consequently unfavourable to most plants and support relatively poor vegetation—examples being the forests in Burma dominated by Eng (Ira), *Dipterocarpus tuberculatus*, which often forms almost pure consociations and alone grows up well, the other trees being stunted and gnarled. Similar poor forests may also be found on light sands, ' bare ' limestone, and dry ridges of acid-weathering rocks, though these areas often support no more than thorn-woodland or even scrub. Such vegetational poverty is usually in part engendered by the relatively little humus-accumulation, due to rapid breakdown in the tropics. In other cases porous siliceous soils may be occupied by forests having a particular character owing to dominance by particular plants, such as Sal-tree (*Shorea robusta*) or various Bamboos. Communities of these last are often virtually pure, containing no associates apart from small cryptogams, and in many cases apparently owe their origin to cultivation.

## Altitudinal Effects

The vegetation-types of high altitudes above the tree-limit in tropical as well as other regions were covered in a general way in the last chapter, and the communities of fresh and salt waters are treated in Chapters XV and XVI, respectively. But here we must consider briefly the upland types occurring below the timber-line in the tropics and subtropics.

The basal zone of a range of mountains has in general a greater rainfall than the neighbouring lowlands, being consequently often occupied by communities resembling the relatively moisture-loving ones of the lowlands. This is true in tropical regions where, accordingly, rain forest is very widespread and frequently very luxuriant on the lower slopes of mountains. Above comes the montane zone, where the precipitation is often phenomenally high, and which in the equatorial region is still tropical in its lower levels ; but at higher levels here, and throughout its altitudinal range to the north and south, the montane zone is rather temperate in type, with vegetation corresponding more to temperate rain forest. Thus the dominants are often of particularly massive growth and rich branching, but devoid of plank-buttresses ; they are evergreen but tend to have smaller leaves than those of the tropical rain forest. The general foliage, too, is less dense, and commonly only two tree strata are discernible, allowing light to penetrate and plentiful ground-vegetation to develop (Fig. 161). A fair amount of humus may accumulate but stranglers are absent.

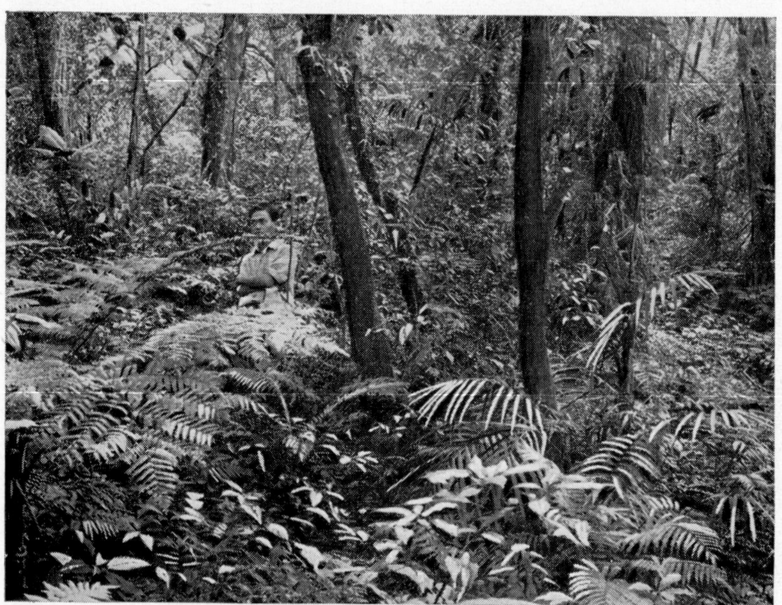

FIG. 161.—Two-storeyed montane rain forest at an altitude of 740 metres in the Philippine Islands.

Although more and more temperate species enter as we ascend in the upper forested zones on tropical mountains, the total flora tends to decrease. But whereas this decrease is particularly marked in the case of trees, it is not accompanied, as it is in unfavourable lowland situations, by any marked tendency to dominance by single species. Leaves in general become fewer in number and usually more slender than at the lower levels, and the epiphytes are usually smaller, almost all herbaceous, and mostly limited to Ferns and Bryophytes or more lowly cryptogams. Small climbers as well as epiphytes are, however, often abundant in the two-storeyed upper montane forest, as shown in Fig. 162. Epiphytic 'mosses' (mostly leafy Liverworts) tend to be particularly numerous and luxuriant where mists prevail in these and any still higher forests, characteristically blanketing the trunks and also hanging from almost every possible point, so that they create far more of a ' show ' than in the three-storeyed rain forest—hence the name of ' mossy forest ' frequently applied to such types.

FIG. 162.—Epiphytes on trunk of tree near upper limit of montane rain forest in the Philippine Islands.

Often the subalpine zone is little marked, except by reduction in the size of the trees and in their foliage which may gradually acquire a more xeromorphic structure, or, in some cases, be deciduous. In time, as we ascend, only a single storey is left, corresponding to the lowest tree one of the tropical rain forest. Often it is exceedingly mossy. As the trunks of the trees become shorter and relatively thicker, the branches tend to enlarge, at least in proportion, until growth becomes irregular as elfin wood is reached. In this the trees are twisted and stunted, being especially low and grotesque in the extreme forms known as ' Krummholz ', though still commonly festooned with Mosses etc. (Fig. 163). This elfin wood and finally Krummholz marks the termination of the forest and the beginning of the treeless alpine zone which is vegetated by scrub, tundra, and heathy or herbaceous vegetation, with ultimately, far above, sparse fell-fields, etc., as described in Chapter XIII. Sometimes, as in the tall mountains of New Guinea, other zones are interpolated.

In tropical and subtropical regions of dry climate, as in temperate lands, forest (or intermediate savanna, etc.) may appear only in the montane zone—or occasionally not at all, as on the western slopes of the Andes in parts of South America, where scrub, steppes, or arid 'punas' characterized by large cushion-plants prevail. Near

FIG. 163.—Mossy elfin forest near summit of mountain, Philippine Islands. Trunks, branches, and aerial roots of trees are covered with festoons of Mosses.

the latitudinal limits of the subtropics, something approaching deciduous summer forest and, above it, forest characterized by evergreen Conifers, may in some places constitute the upper limits of arborescent vegetation and simulate the march into higher latitudes (*cf*. Fig. 83, B). Details also vary elsewhere in many other ways, such as the altitudinal limits involved, though these last tend to become depressed with increasing latitude, proximity to coasts, or exposure to prevailing winds. However, owing to the 'height' of the sun and the wide angle of incidence of its downpouring rays, the influence of aspect tends to be far less marked in tropical than in temperate and polar regions.

## Further Consideration

Although it is in the tropics that the most luxuriant and complicated of all vegetation occurs, most of the pertinent literature is again tiresomely scattered. For such subjects as it covers, however, this is happily remedied by the first book cited below; the others are useful for further details or vivid illustrations:

P. W. Richards. *The Tropical Rain Forest: an Ecological Study* (Cambridge University Press, Cambridge, Eng., pp. xviii + 450, 1952). Brings together the available knowledge concerning tropical rain forests and related topics. *See* also the more general works of Schimper, Faber, Hardy, Campbell, Tansley & Chipp, and Newbigin, cited at the end of Chapter XII.

W. A. Cannon. *Botanical Features of the Algerian Sahara* (Carnegie Institution, Washington, D.C., Publication No. 178, pp. vi + 81 and 36 plates, 1913).

W. A. Cannon. *General and Physiological Features of the Vegetation of the more Arid Portions of Southern Africa, with Notes on the Climatic Environment* (Carnegie Institution, Washington, D.C., Publication No. 354, pp. viii + 159 and 31 plates, 1924).

J. S. Beard. *The Natural Vegetation of Trinidad* (Oxford Forestry Memoirs, No. 20, Clarendon Press, Oxford, map and pp. vi + 7–152, 1946).

G. M. Roseveare. *The Grasslands of Latin America* (Imperial Bureau of Pastures and Field Crops, Aberystwyth, Bulletin No. 36, pp. 1–291, 1948).

R. E. Holttum. *Plant Life in Malaya* (Longmans, London etc., pp. viii + 254, 1954).

Concerning special tropical items or regions there are, in addition to the works already cited, numerous and usually well-illustrated papers in the *Journal of Ecology*, which has been published continuously since 1913, and, almost always in German, in the 26 volumes of *Vegetationsbilder* published between 1904 and 1944 and in the long series of monographs edited by A. Engler & O. Drude and entitled *Die Vegetation der Erde* (Engelmann, Leipzig, 1896 onwards).

## Chapter XV

# VEGETATIONAL TYPES OF FRESH AND INLAND SALINE WATERS

Reed-swamp and other semi-aquatic types of vegetation in which at least half of the plant body is aerial have already been treated in Chapters XII–XIV, dealing with the terrestrial vegetation of different climatic belts. This leaves the more fully aquatic freshwater communities, with some others, to be dealt with in the present chapter, followed by the marine ones in Chapter XVI. Such a separation of aquatic from terrestrial habitats and attendant vegetation seems the more proper when we reflect that whereas on land it is the climatic factors which are of primary importance in determining the distribution of particular vegetation-types, in aquatic media it is rather the chemical composition that is fundamental in this respect. This is particularly the case with salinity, which gives us our primary division into fresh and salt waters. Yet the ecological differences between terrestrial and aquatic habitats are largely matters of degree, chemical and physical conditions in the soil being still extremely important in the former, for example, and light and temperature in the latter. Even the distinction between fresh and salt waters is incomplete, as there are various intermediate 'brackish' waters of varying degrees of salinity and, in addition, inland salt-lakes; these, however, except in such instances as the Caspian Sea which are of marine origin, seem best dealt with in the present chapter, leaving only marine types to be considered in the next.

## Some Features of the Freshwater Aquatic Environment

The temperature and some other conditions vary less in aquatic than in terrestrial habitats, water acting as an effective 'damper' on changes concerning heat. Moreover, major bodies of water exercise an equalizing influence on the temperature of adjacent air. As a result of the minimization of variation in aquatic environments and of the fact that, obviously, they offer no problem of water-supply, aquatic plants and vegetation-types tend to be more widespread than terrestrial ones. However, a marked vertical distribution occurs, the vegetation in sufficiently deep waters being divided into zones according to the different depths. In this delimitation light is usually the main factor, though the temperature of water-masses and the local chemical composition and especially aeration of the water may also be important. The zones, at various depths in water, that are characterized by different forms or abundance of life, largely represent stages of decreasing intensity of light. They range from a relatively bright surface 'euphotic' zone in which the light is sufficient for the normal development of large plants, through a dim 'dysphotic' zone in which photosynthesizing small Algae and even Mosses may still flourish, to a dark and relatively deep 'aphotic' zone in which only non-photosynthesizing organisms can exist. Owing to the varying turbidity of waters, due to suspended particles, and to the different penetration of the sun's rays at different angles, the limits of these zones, which are themselves imprecise, lie at very different depths in different instances.

In summer, lakes in temperate regions experience a marked rise in temperature, particularly on and near the surface, but this is followed by a decrease in autumn. Such fluctuations engender vertical convection currents and eddies which lead ultimately to a temperature of low value throughout, while at the same time they are important in aerating the deeper layers (*see* p. 477, and *cf.* Fig. 165). These last may vary very little (less than 4° C.) in temperature between summer maximum and winter minimum. Tropical lakes may also show a surface temperature fluctuation with changing weather, but here a reduction in temperature of merely 1–2° C. is reported to bring about a circulation similar to that which is effected in cooler regions by a winter cooling of some 20° C.

Limnology is the study of inland waters, including the environment and all inhabiting organisms and their interrelationships. In it a distinction is made between the *benthos* (of organisms growing on or in the bottom material; these may be described as 'benthic'), the freely floating *plankton*, and the swimming *nekton*. The distinction is, however, somewhat artificial as many organisms are border-line cases. The plankton and benthos of inland waters are said to be *limnetic*, in contradistinction to those of the open sea which are said to be *pelagic*. These terms are not much used in limnology, where the region of open water is commonly distinguished as the *pelagial*. In shallow coastal waters the plankton is apt to be mixed with forms belonging to the benthos, and such waters and their plankton may usefully be described as *neritic*.

Halophytes are plants which can tolerate a considerable degree of salinity. But whereas the land halophytes and those of brackish waters are usually *euryhaline* (that is, able to tolerate a wide range of salt-content in different soils), most aquatic halophytes are more *stenohaline* (capable of tolerating only a narrow range of salt-content in different circumstances, their minimum, optimum, and maximum being relatively close together). Similarly, *euryphotic* and *eurythermic* plants are those tolerating a wide range of light and temperature, respectively, and *stenophotic* and *stenothermic* plants are those which tolerate only a narrow amplitude in such respects.

In general the chief boundaries between different types of aquatic vegetation are determined by factors comparable with those operating on land, though the emphasis is often changed. Thus temperature, salinity, and light are of obvious importance in various ways, as are movements due to surf and currents. Light-penetration depends greatly on various factors such as cloudiness of the water (due to suspended bodies whether living or dead) ,reflection from the surface, latitude and the consequent angle of incidence of the sun's rays, and content of dissolved substances. Moving water, besides being better aerated, demands of plants mechanical qualities differing from those required in still water, and, moreover, stagnant fresh water tends to have vegetation of very different composition from running water. Quite apart from this, shelter from currents and waves can be an important factor and even a major necessity in aquatic media. Currents, on the other hand, can disperse plants and improve such conditions as aeration and the potentialities for nutrition. Rainfall tends to be of significance chiefly in affecting the salinity of lagoons, particularly in wet tropical regions. Aquatic plants inhabiting such waters and the mouths of many streams must be widely euryhaline ; thus certain Diatoms living in waters where the salt-content changes widely and rapidly are able both to absorb and let out salt equally quickly, according to the concentration of the medium.

We have seen that light-penetration in water is a very variable factor. This is important because different Algae and other aquatic plants needing light for photosynthesis vary greatly in their actual light-requirements. As explained in the next chapter, this variation is in part associated with the predominating colours of the different groups, but it also exists in fresh waters where Red Algae are usually little in evidence and Brown Algae are practically unknown. Thus different species are differently adjusted as to both wave-length and intensity of light, the green surface-forms flourishing where the intensities are high and red rays plentiful, whereas they are hardly able to utilize the green and blue rays which penetrate deeply into clear waters. (The still shorter-length ultra-violet radiations, which may be lethal, penetrate very little.) Photosynthetic activity of higher plants also diminishes downwards, though the depth at which the daily assimilation just compensates for respiration varies greatly with different species. This ' compensation point ' for the Canadian Water-weed (*Elodea canadensis*) is about 10 metres, whereas for the Moss *Fontinalis* it is about 18 metres under comparable conditions.

Highly important is the physical nature of the substratum, benthic vegetation assuming a very different character according to whether the ' bottom ' is rocky, gravelly, sandy, or muddy—in particular, whether it is hard or soft. Whereas rocky beds are often suitable for attachment of Algae, soft substrata are favoured by most higher plants that have to take root. In the intimacy of smaller bodies of fresh water, the chemical nature of the substratum tends to assume a greater importance than in large and deep lakes. This is because the substances in solution exert an influence largely according to their concentration. Thus, the flora and vegetation often differ markedly according to whether the water is rich or poor in dissolved calcium carbonate and some other salts, while the relative abundance of organic materials or humus may also be important. Ice action is significant on many polar and other frigid lake-shores as well as sea-shores, and even in temperate regions can profoundly affect the nature of the surface and the composition of the marginal flora. Moreover, extensive freezing of water may significantly alter the acidity and nutrient and other chemical content of the underlying medium.

As regards periodic phenomena, temperature in general exhibits far smaller and less rapid fluctuations in water than in the air, and is therefore less influential than on land. But whereas perennial marine Algae even in cold regions may exhibit no period of winter rest, seasonal differences in both quality and quantity of vegetation tend to be well marked in small bodies of inland water. This commonly results from the considerable variation in temperature and easy formation of ice, while especially in boreal and austral regions seasonal variations in light may cause a distinct periodicity. Moreover, the amounts of nitrate and phosphate available in bodies of water may also fluctuate seasonally to a marked extent, which again may be the basis of alterations in the inhabiting population. It is often contended to be as a result of the prevailingly low temperatures that cold-loving Diatoms predominate in the lakes of central Europe in winter and spring, followed by Peridinians in summer and by Cyanophyceae when the temperature has reached 20° C. However, as pointed out by Mr. Robert Ross (*in litt.*), many other Diatoms are by no means cold-loving, and it may well be that the control of this cycle is more chemical than physical, silica depletion for example being very important. Hot springs, having a constantly high temperature, support a largely peculiar and often very limited flora[1]—as do snow and ice at the lower end of the scale of temperatures allowing plant activity (*see* pp. 489–91).

Although the food requirements of Algae and many other water-plants are still but poorly understood, it is clear that the presence or absence of certain mineral salts, derived from the substratum or inflowing currents, is of outstanding importance in helping to determine both the composition and the luxuriance of the vegetation developed. Quite apart from questions of salinity, small freshwater lakes are particularly dependent on the chemical and physical nature of their beds. As already explained in Chapter XI, chemical 'reaction' (acidity, neutrality, or basicity) and especially nutritive salt-content are of fundamental significance in determining details of development of aquatic vegetation—especially plankton—and, of course, also to the dependent animal populations, in bodies of fresh water. Hence the classification of the latter largely on the basis of productivity into 'oligotrophic' (poor in nutrients, with a hard rocky bottom and rapidly deepening water), 'dystrophic' (also poor in nutrients but rich in humus and acidic in reaction), and 'eutrophic' (poor in humus though commonly silted and shallow, rich in nutrients including combined nitrogen, phosphorus, and often calcium). Particularly are the nitrate and phosphate contents of decisive importance in the matter of biological productivity in fresh waters as well as salt ones. Also of great significance are the contents of dissolved oxygen and carbon dioxide, which vary at different depths and in different seasons—*cf.* Fig. 165 for oxygen fluctuations.

In oligotrophic lakes, cold-water Fishes such as Trout are often plentiful; these lakes commonly show succession towards the eutrophic type. Dystrophic lakes, on the other hand, usually lack these

[1] For example in hot springs above 45° C. only Schizophytes appear able to persist, as indicated on p. 499.

deep-dwelling cold-water Fishes and sometimes other types too, their fish-productivity being poor at best, while succession proceeds to peat bog. Eutrophic lakes usually also lack deep-dwelling cold-water Fishes, though they are often suitable for Perch, Pike, Bass, and other warm-water Fishes; succession in them is to swamp or marsh. Oligotrophic and dystrophic waters are often rich in Desmids, eutrophic ones in Diatoms and Blue-green Algae.

Among the various ways in which living organisms alter fresh waters is in the matter of gas-content. In general, green plants (except in non-photosynthetic periods) remove carbon dioxide and add oxygen, while animals do the reverse, so that in the upper, well-lit layers there tends to be a superabundance of oxygen and in the deeper and darker layers more carbon dioxide than above. Such considerations lead to the recognition of two types of waters, namely, those where the gas-content is almost constant in all layers, and those where it decreases markedly in the depths. The former are chiefly masses of water in which vertical currents cause almost constant mixing. In the latter it is common to recognize in summer in temperate regions (1) a wind-stirred and largely homogeneous 'epilimnion' or surface layer rich in oxygen (because of contact with the air as well as photosynthesis), usually extending to a depth of 10–15 metres; (2) a middle 'metalimnion' or 'thermocline' where the temperature and oxygen-content decrease rapidly; and (3) a 'hypolimnion', underneath, where the water is virtually stationary and no oxygen enters from above. Tropical lakes commonly differ from those of temperate regions in that the shallower ones 'only stratify for short periods, if at all, while deeper ones may have cyclical stratification or, if very deep, *e.g.* Nyassa and Tanganyika, may turn over very rarely or not at all' (R. Ross *in litt.*).

It is particularly in lakes sheltered from wind-disturbance in temperate regions that the oxygen stratification tends to follow the bottom contours, and the surface-waters in periods of quiescence are often more alkaline than deeper ones. However, in autumn the surface-waters cool and sink, carrying down dissolved oxygen, and the deeper masses rise to take their place, so getting aerated by a kind of reshuffling each year. The greater the amount of nutrient material and accordingly of organic life in a lake, the faster does the oxygen disappear in the depths during the quiescent period of summer. Carbon dioxide, being complementary in metabolism, exhibits a largely reverse trend, disappearing from the well-lit upper layers but accumulating below. In spite of the relatively small amount in the free atmosphere, which averages about 0.03 per cent. of carbon dioxide, this gas, being easily soluble in water, is widely abundant in lakes. Thus many contain more than 20 c.c. per litre in the depths, although in oligotrophic lakes the content may be as low as 1 c.c. per litre. Oligotrophic lakes may also show little variation in the oxygen content at different depths, in marked contrast to eutrophic ones.

The so-called ' lime ' content (particularly of calcium carbonate and bicarbonate) of freshwater lakes and streams varies greatly, peaty waters being especially lime-poor and ' soft ', whereas those originating in calcareous districts are mostly lime-rich and ' hard '. Variations also occur at different depths and times of the year : thus in summer periods of relative stagnation, living organisms may remove much of the ' lime ' from the upper layers, while the deeper ones, which are already rich in carbon dioxide, actually become enriched in lime. Calcium and allied carbonates and bicarbonates have a marked ' buffering ' effect against changes in the reaction or pH level of a body of water, and as the reaction (or some condition associated with it) is often important in affecting the flora and consequently the vegetation, so are such ' salts ' important. Most favourable is a weakly basic to neutral reaction, markedly acidic waters being biologically unfavourable : hence the limited and peculiar flora of scarcely buffered bog-waters, the acidity of which is associated with marked poverty in lime.

With regard to the impress of the environment as a whole, there is insufficient data as yet to compare the vegetational productivity of different climatic zones. Thus although some tropical inland waters may be more prolific as producers of plant or animal life than some extra-tropical ones, others are practically barren. Many extra-tropical lakes naturally rank extremely high in productivity, and for many which do not so rank a great deal can be done by the addition of fertilizers or by such manuring as is, for example, practised in European carp-ponds. For productivity of lakes is related largely to such factors as chemical content, turbidity, and light. Even in the Arctic the present writer has collected samples from small lakes and ponds that have shown a surprising wealth of algal forms : in one instance of six samples taken in as many small vials from shallow pools and peaty puddles in Baffin Island in July and August, 1936, no less than 179 different species or varieties of Algae were determined. Nearly all of these were microscopic, a large proportion being Desmids. Moreover a considerable number of organisms, such as the familiar planktonic Dinoflagellate *Ceratium hirundinella* and species of the Entomostracan genera *Daphnia* and *Cyclops*, range from the polar regions to the tropics, so suggesting again that at least those conditions which are critical for them are relatively uniform over remarkably wide areas.

## Plankton

Planktonic organisms are those which float freely on or in a body of water ; they may be roughly divided into animal and plant types, constituting, respectively, zooplankton and phytoplankton. The main categories of freshwater plankton are (*i*) the 'limnoplankton' of lakes and ponds ; (*ii*) the 'potamoplankton' of slow streams and rivers ; and (*iii*) the 'cryoplankton' of lasting snow, *névé*, and ice. The cryoplankton is so distinct in habitat and form that it seems best treated separately in the next section. In addition we may distinguish in lakes and ponds (*iv*) the 'tychoplankton' of forms transported from the littoral or from affluents by currents.

Planktonic organisms must be able to remain suspended in water, and this they do either by having the power of active locomotion, particularly by flagella, or, more often, in the case of phytoplankton, by having suitable 'form-resistance'. This latter is commonly expressed in projections from the surface of the usually minute body and, in addition, for success requires a specific gravity near that of the surrounding medium. Thin, light, and flat or curved cell-walls, such as are often found in planktonic Diatoms, help considerably in this connection ; so do gelatinous sheaths possessing almost the same density as water, and light food-reserves of oil, or, of course, still lighter bubbles of gas. Very important is smallness of size, for we all know that large bodies sink more rapidly than small ones of the same material. Also significant is the specific surface area, which is the ratio of the total surface area to the volume of the body ; for the larger the ratio, the greater will be the friction caused during sinking, and consequently the slower this last will be. Hence the frequent provision of spines, horns, ridges, and the like on the outside of planktonic organisms, such as are illustrated in Figs. 5 (note especially the forms of Desmids), 6, and 7. Moreover, owing to the greater viscosity of water as well as protoplasm at low temperatures, the ability of planktonic organisms to float tends to be greater during winter than summer. All such 'flotation-adaptations' are, however, unable to prevent fairly rapid sinking of most except the smallest among the non-motile planktonic organisms if the water is entirely static. Rather is it the turbulence of the water caused by the eddy-diffusion currents that maintains a state of continuous mixing particularly in the epilimnion, and keeps in this upper layer a sufficiency at least for survival of the non-motile phytoplankton which chiefly flourishes here.

Whereas in the sea the differentiation of open-ocean (pelagic) and near-shore (neritic) planktonic organisms is often marked, so that the two communities may be very different, in inland lakes the distinction is relatively poor. Indeed, close relatives of nearly all the species of phytoplankton here occur also in the littoral, whence the open waters of the pelagial were evidently colonized. Moreover, the number of truly planktonic species in lakes is relatively small, a large proportion of the types found being really ' tychoplankton ' (*see* above), which have scarcely more claim to membership of the community than have the particles of inorganic and dead organic suspended matter (' tripton ') present. Still, the numbers of actual ' plankters ' (planktonic individuals) may be great, especially when they exist in highly profuse ' blooms '.

Freshwater plankton communities are composed of (*a*) producers and (*b*) consumers of organic matter, the producers being almost entirely chlorophyll-containing autotrophic plants. The consumers or non-producers, including normal Bacteria and Fungi which make up most of the so-called ' saproplankton ', are dependent upon the carbohydrates and fats and proteins synthesized by the chlorophyll-bearing plankters. In general the phytoplankton is composed not only of the relatively large and obvious types which dominate the so-called ' net-plankton ' and include most of the Diatoms and Dinoflagellates, but also of extremely minute ' nannoplanktonic ' (microplanktonic) species which pass through even very fine nets (of No. 25 silk bolting-cloth) and are usually obtained by centrifuging. In lakes, from one to a very few species commonly predominate and make up the vast bulk of the phytoplankton at any one time, and these may include minute nannoplanktonic types particularly of Peridinians or other flagellates (e.g. *Rhodomonas lacustris*). Bacteria normally contribute only a small proportion of the total ' biomass ', and so may even the large species that dominate the net-phytoplankton. In the zooplankton, on the other hand, such large types as *Daphnia* tend to be most prominent.

In general the most plentiful organisms in freshwater phytoplankton are unicells or small colonies—whether flagellated or non-motile—the Bacteria, Cyanophyceae, Chlorophyceae (including

Desmidiales (Desmids) and unicellular as well as colonial Volvocales), Bacillariophyceae (Diatoms), Dinophyceae (Dinoflagellates), and several other groups of flagellates, etc., being commonly represented. During spring or summer maxima a greenish, yellowish, or brownish ' soupiness ' may be evident to the naked eye, the composition and luxuriance of the community being very variable in time and space. Thus from an aircraft the colours and general appearance of the water of even adjacent tarns may be strikingly different, especially in boreal regions. Except in the tropics where filamentous forms are sometimes dominant (R. Ross *in litt.*), macroscopic plants are commonly lacking in the real plankton, as are Rhodophyceae and Phaeophyceae, though some Fungi may occur.

Continuous investigation of a lake or pond over a period of years is likely to reveal striking changes recurring seasonally in much the same combination and form each year. This variability in type and abundance at different seasons, or periodicity, as it is called, is shown by (1) perennial species which occur in different densities at different times, and (2) ephemeral types which spend the rest of the year in some resistant stage usually on the shore or lake-bottom. The fluctuations are due to interaction between the rates of multiplication and of depletion, the former being dependent on basic biotic influences and the latter largely on natural mortality, predators, and mechanical factors such as sedimentation. Nor do spring forms commonly recur in autumn, owing to the different light and temperature relationships; for in other than tropical regions these two leading factors exhibit marked and important differences in lakes at different seasons.

The circulation of water in winter and early spring brings up nutrients to the surface layers. This often leads to an early ' blooming ' of Diatoms. But with the onset of summer stratification, accompanied by a profuse growth of Green and other Algae, the stock of nutrients cannot be supplemented sufficiently to maintain abundant new growth and reproduction. This is because most of the nitrate and phosphate ions, particularly, have already been removed from the upper layers and stored in the bodies of the organisms that flourish there. Certain Peridinians which can manage with a minimum of inorganic nutrients are then apt to appear in fair numbers. However, in late summer vertical convection gradually extends deeper, causing a replenishment of the upper layers from the nutrient-rich water of the depths, so that population expansion can again take place—*cf.* Fig. 165. The cycle is perennial and more or less perpetual in that the depths are all the time enriched by a ' rain ' of dead bodies containing the all-important nutrients.

It is chiefly in late summer and autumn, when there has been an extensive depletion of mineral nutrients but some replenishment and, meanwhile, a copious increase in organic substances, that water-blooms of Cyanophyceae occur. Then again in autumn there may be another Diatom ' maximum '. To the extent that each new population appears only after the requisite conditions have been provided by its predecessor, there is here a kind of successional sequence, although actually such phytoplanktonic stages are probably all proseral in being non-essential to, or at all events not forming part of, the autogenic main sere.

In connection with the spatial distribution of plant communities which is the mainstay of our subject, we should recall that each physiological activity, such as photosynthesis and reproduction, is greatly affected by various conditions of the environment. Usually with each such ' function ' there is for every pertinent environmental factor a minimum below which, and a maximum above which, there is no activity ; somewhere between lies an optimum at which the function involved is carried on best. These ' cardinal points ', however, may vary with other environmental conditions, even as they do of course with different organisms. With such rare exceptions as perspiration, which generally increases with increasing temperature until death from overheating occurs, each physiological function responds in this manner. So does the organism respond as a whole to change in an external factor—hence the importance of physiological considerations in plant geography. But because several factors normally change at one time, and indeed go on changing all the time, the effects are exceedingly complex and usually difficult to analyse. Moreover the demands and reactions of various types, species, and even lower entities or different stages of plants are themselves extremely various.

In water, as we have already seen, some of the environmental factors which are most variable on land are damped down, but others retain a strong hold, as it were, on plant activity and distribution. Furthermore, the planktonic population depends not merely (and obviously) on the systematic groups present and able to grow and maintain life in the face of often unfavourable conditions, but also on the rate of reproduction and depletion of the component forms. Such depletion may be more rapid than in most other types of plant communities, and numbers may fluctuate greatly because of sinking, death, removal by currents, and consumption by predators.

In lakes there is commonly a marked and steep vertical gradient of phytoplanktonic distribution, especially when the body of water is limited in extent. For example, at the surface we may find an almost continuous investment of often quite large plants such as Duckweeds (*Lemna* spp.), Water-hyacinth (*Eichhornia crassipes*), and the types shown in Fig. 164. Whereas these macroscopic plants might be considered as belonging to the littoral, they often occur as pelagials on ponds and small lakes, especially in warm regions. Such relatively large floating material comprises the *pleuston* (hemi-plankton), which is commonly defined as consisting of macroscopic plants and as including those floating freely within the body of water as well as on its surface. Furthermore, there are some microscopic floating organisms (*neuston*) which stabilize their position upon the surface of quiet water by employing surface-tension. For example, a Green Alga, *Nautococcus* sp., becomes attached to the upper surface-film by means of a flotation disk—thus essentially living as an aerial organism, and forming conspicuous water-blooms of dry (powdery) appearance. Other neuston organisms hang down in the water, from the surface-film.

Within the body of the water, most of the phytoplankton is usually concentrated in the top 10 to 15 metres, its permanent survival being limited to depths where more food material is made by photosynthesis than is used in respiration over an average 24-hour period. This maximum depth is dependent on light-penetration ; even in the clearest alpine lakes the layer of water that is at all densely populated by phytoplankton scarcely exceeds 50 metres in thickness. Indeed in the majority of lakes, at least in the higher latitudes, most of the phytoplanktonic life is concentrated in the uppermost 5 metres (according to Professor G. W. Prescott *in litt.*), while at depths below about 30 metres the numbers of individuals decline to very small values. Yet within these limits different species vary greatly in their preference. Thus more than half of the forms are usually concentrated in the uppermost 10 metres or less, while others attain their maximum concentration at or below a depth of 10 metres. Not a few types, such as Cyanophyceae provided with gas-vacuoles, have a specific gravity of less than unity and so are concentrated at the surface. On the other hand some phytoplanktonic species can have their maximum density at depths greater than 30 metres, an example being the Diatom *Asterionella formosa* in some circumstances in

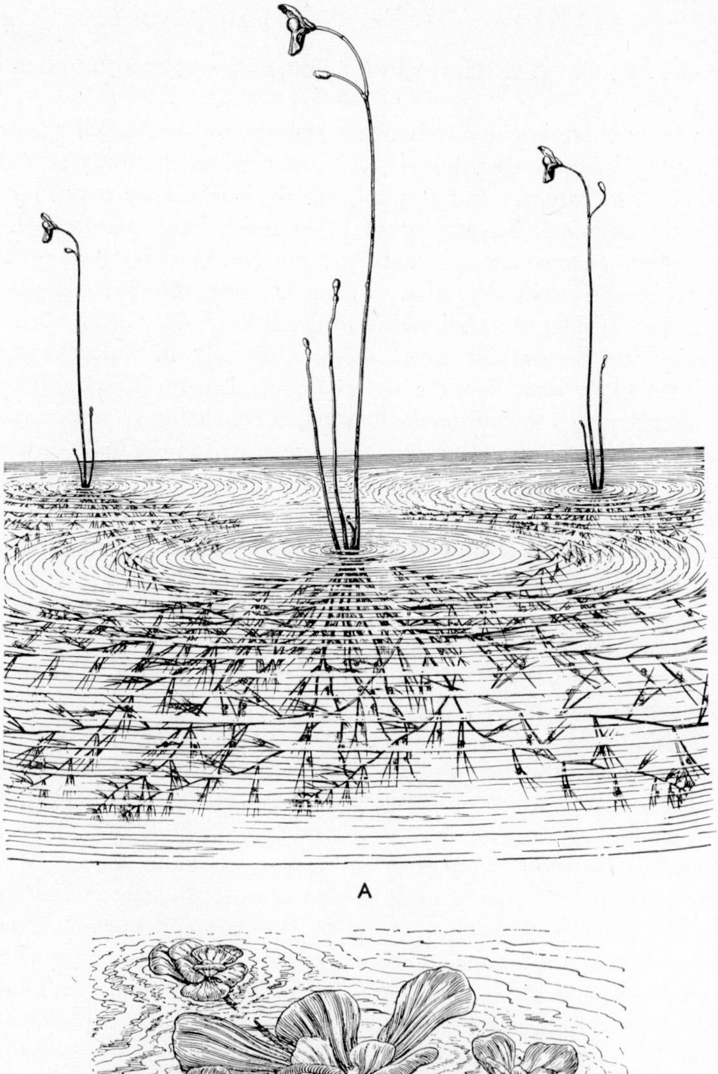

A

B

C

FIG. 164.—Vascular plants floating freely on fresh water. A, a Bladderwort (*Utricularia*), showing underwater branches and leaves bearing bladders which trap minute aquatic organisms. B, another free-floating aquatic plant, *Pistia stratiotes*, that has roots and is very widely distributed in the tropics and subtropics. ($\times \frac{1}{2}$.) C, a 'Batrachian' Ranunculus, *R. aquatilis* s.l., floating in the surface water of a pond near Babylon, Iraq. The finely dissected leaves are immersed but the flowers rise slightly above the surface, being photographed from above.

Europe. Such tendencies result in largely different communities at different depths—even in the same column of water at a particular time. This is illustrated by the diagrams A (representing Algae other than Diatoms) and D (representing Diatoms) in Fig. 165, the numbers being those of organisms per litre in a Wisconsin lake, and the 6 component parts of the figure being taken at approximately monthly intervals during May to October.

The conditions bringing about these varied types of depth-distribution in phytoplankton appear to be those whose cardinal points limit physiological activity, the depth of greatest population-density being that of optimum conditions (the resultant of the factors involved). As we have seen, these optimum conditions vary greatly for different organisms. The issue is, however, rendered uncertain by the operation of mechanical factors such as the dynamics of water. Indeed the most important agent affecting the distribution of plankton in general is the movement of the water—particularly the mixing action of eddy-diffusion currents. Non-motile forms are kept suspended primarily by these, and under conditions of active eddy-diffusion are distributed more or less throughout the zone of turbulence—apart from a tendency to decrease just below the surface,

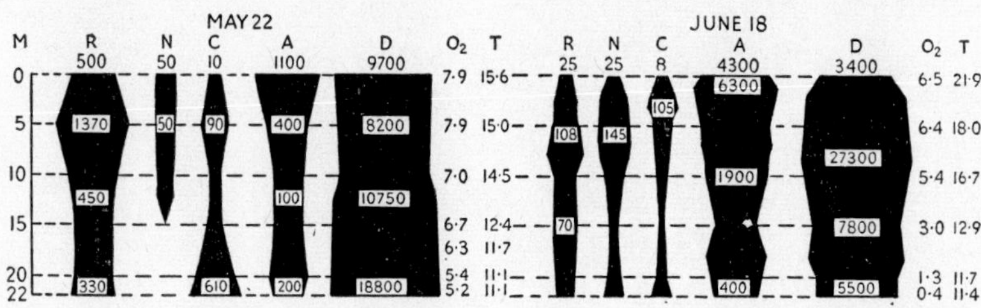


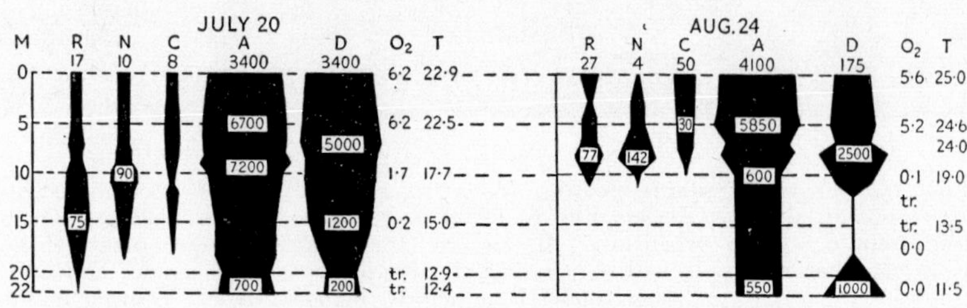


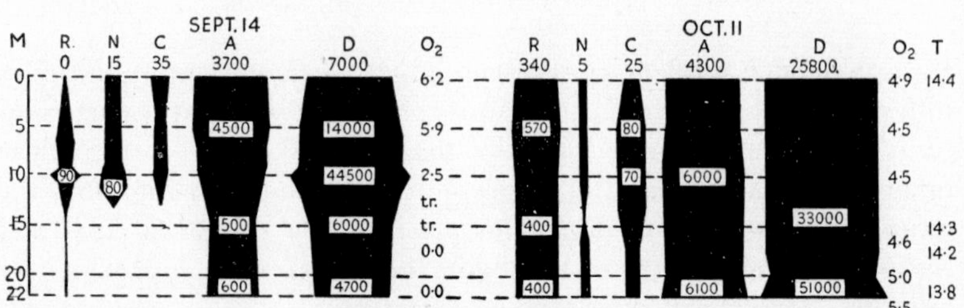


FIG. 165.—Diagrammatic representation of the plankton in a Wisconsin lake during May to October, the numbers being those of organisms per litre. R = Rotifers; N = Nauplii; C = Crustacea; M = depth in metres; A = Algae other than Diatoms; D = Diatoms; $O_2$ = dissolved oxygen in cubic centimetres per litre; T = temperature in degrees Centigrade; tr. = trace. (After Welch.)

where the latter acts as a brake on eddy-diffusion currents and hence allows depletion by sinking. There may also be marked differences on windy and still days, as indicated in Fig. 166 of the representation of a Blue-green Alga of low specific gravity, which accumulates at the surface in calm weather and is then absent below 4 metres (*a*), but in windy weather is plentiful down to much greater depths (*b*). Yet other Blue-green Algae, such as *Aphanizomenon flos-aquae*, can achieve a vertical distribution of 6 metres or more on very calm days (according to Professor G. W. Prescott *in litt.*). However, the really lasting differences in composition occur in and below the thermocline, where the eddy-diffusion currents are curtailed. The latter may, however, extend to considerable depths during the autumn

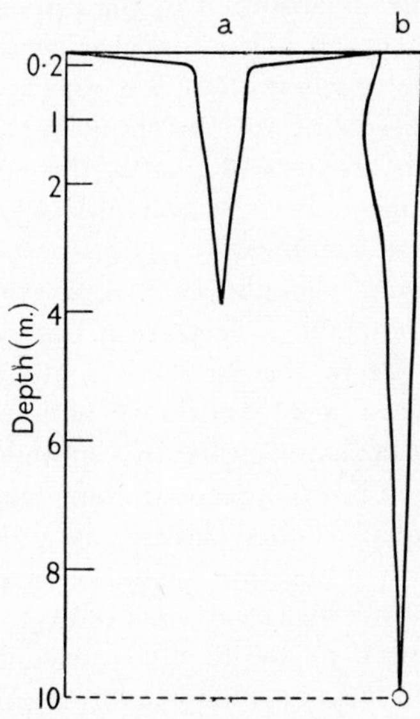


FIG. 166.—Diagram indicating distribution in a European lake of a cyanophycean (*Glosotrichia echinulata*), which is rendered buoyant by included gas-vacuoles : (a) during calm weather, and (b) during windy weather. (After Ruttner, modified.)

circulation, and at such times lead to a virtually uniform distribution of plankton (*cf.* the October section of Fig. 165). Later on, under the winter ice-cover of cool to frigid regions, stratification again appears. Another complicating physical factor influencing stratification is wave action, and yet another is water renewal, during which much of the plankton-rich surface water of lakes is liable to be lost by outflow and commonly replaced by inflowing river or other water poor in plankton.

The biotic factors affecting phytoplankton are far more numerous and complicated than the mechanical ones, and no attempt will be made to analyse them here. They are concerned with such (often interrelated) processes as reproduction, photosynthesis, secretion of external 'envelopes,' parasitism, 'grazing' by animals, and active movement, as well as their various components. All of these can be governed in turn by temperature, light, or the chemical composition of the water as already mentioned. It should be emphasized, however, that temperature differences are less important than many others, being often superseded by such factors as light, the effect of which on photosynthesis in the twilight region (dysphotic zone) is nevertheless in turn influenced by temperature. The long wavelength 'red' radiation is absorbed in the upper layers so that at a depth of commonly 15–20 metres in clear water a vivid 'green' coloration predominates where there are objects to reflect the rays. Absorption and subsequent use for photosynthesis being largely complementary to the colours of plants, the light of these and of greater depths is utilized best by phytoplanktonic organisms that are brownish (such as Diatoms) or reddish (such as the flagellate *Rhodomonas* and certain Cyanophyceae). These brownish and reddish types are often predominant in deep fresh waters, as are Brown and particularly Red Algae in the sea.

Owing apparently to wind and wave action as well as to the mysterious avoidance of shallow water by Entomostraca, the character of the general plankton is often peculiar along lake-shores, where the abundance of phytoplankton may actually be greater than elsewhere owing to turbulence and the low incidence of predation. On the other hand, in deep waters where oxygen tends to be in short supply, the temperature is often so low that few organisms can exist, and, therefore, much less o fthis gas than usual is required for respiration. Finally, in situations where oxygen is definitely deficient, anaerobic (that is, living in the absence of oxygen) Bacteria often abound, including many having a planktonic habit, while below, about the surface of the bottom deposits, numbers of Bacteria computed to be of the order of 100,000 or more per cubic centimetre are frequently found. As well as by such deep-down productivity, the total biomass may also be increased as a result of judicious fertilization (addition of needed materials), an example being the supplying of phosphate to oligotrophic lakes or ponds in which development is not limited by poverty in nitrogen.

In contrast to lakes, running waters are characterized by a true potamoplankton only in those that flow far and gently. Even here the turbulence is not sufficiently reduced to permit much stratification, conditions being much more homogeneous than in lakes. Another difference is the transport of water-masses frequently over vast distances, often involving great changes in ecological conditions and even in climate in different parts of the course. The duration of this transport, depending on speed of current and length of river, determines whether a true potamoplankton is developed ; for most of the planktonic organisms that get carried along in many streams, and particularly in those containing lakes, are merely ' tychoplankton ' washed in from other habitats and doomed to an early death. In effect, a potamoplankton can be developed only when conditions are suitable for the growth and reproduction of ' selected ' species from among those which are washed in. True potamoplankton is thus limited to slowly-flowing rivers of considerable length where the water takes some weeks to reach the sea. On and very near the bottoms of these there is often scarcely any current ; consequently conditions and communities approach those of standing water. Even where the flow is rapid it is remarkable how many free-living Algae such as Diatoms and flagellates are to be found among macroscopic benthic vegetation which is able to benefit by improved conditions introduced by the current (*see* below, especially p. 498).

The planktonic and other aquatic vegetation of ephemeral pools and puddles is extremely various, depending as it does not only on local conditions but, very largely, on chance dispersal. Quite often an extraordinarily rich and seemingly uninhibited development of a single species is found. In saline lakes, fewer and fewer types of organisms persist as salinity increases above that of the oceans (3–4 per cent.), but those which do exist may occur in abundance even at very high concentrations (16–20 per cent.), provided of course no lethal salts are present and the temperature is not too high.

## Cryophytic Communities

The communities developing on snow and ice are in some ways akin to those found in ephemeral pools, which indeed may result from the melting of snow or ice and, initially at least, often harbour the same species. Thus phases of the common arctic and alpine Red Snow Alga *Chlamydomonas* (*Sphaerella*) *nivalis* are frequently abundant in pools of snow-water. This ' species ' may represent a complex of several different ones which undergo a wide range of intergrading morphological changes through growth under different ecological conditions.

In general, the ' cryovegetation ' of snow and ice is greatly influenced by the physical and chemical characteristics of the medium, though, as it lives on or near the surface, it is primarily affected by changes occurring there. Thus variations in salt-content and the pH level of the surface snow or ice and of any liquid water will influence the composition of the vegetation, and so will the nature of the surrounding rock from which inorganic salts are obtained. For substances from wind-borne dust, including particles resulting from erosion, dissolve in any surface moisture after these particles alight on snow or ice, and serve as the source of minerals for microorganisms. Consequently snow-fields and glaciers in the vicinity of acidic rocks, for example, are apt to support very different vegetation from those in limestone districts. In general, acidic environments support red or pink snows and basic ones yield green snows. Red snows, coloured by various organisms, are found in snow-fields practically the world over; the much rarer green and yellow snows occur chiefly in the Arctic and in Europe, although they have been reported also from the United States.

It is perhaps best to refer to the plants growing on snow or ice as 'cryophytes', and the communities they form as cryophytic, for they are scarcely planktonic (that is, free-floating) in such 'habitats'. These cryophytes may be usefully classified according to their preferred environments as growing (1) on ice —*e.g. Mesotaenium berggrenii;* (2) on snow and *névé* (*firn*)—*e.g. Chlamydomonas nivalis;* (3) on both snow and ice—*e.g. Cylindrocystis brebissonii;* and (4) occurring on snow and ice but only after transportation from their normal habitats—*e.g.* various Cyanophyceae including species of *Gloeocapsa*.

Although often a single cryophyte predominates in a particular community, sometimes giving a distinctive colour to the surface of ice as well as snow, usually others are present, the mixture sometimes including a dozen or more species, and, in addition, such animals as Snow-fleas. Dispersal appears to be mainly by wind. Whereas the colour and texture produced vary with the organism and other circumstances, 'red snow' commonly appears in spots scattered over the surface, often involving wide areas, though sometimes the colonizing is more uniform and extends to a depth of 3 or even 5 cm. The 'bloom' developed by organisms growing on ice may also extend for miles, as in the purplish-brown form on the largely snow-free glaciers of southern Alaska and Greenland. This is characterized by filaments of the Alga *Ancyclonema nordenskioldii*, which form bunches up to 2 mm. in diameter on the surface of the ice (but chiefly in small hollows formed by its melting). In addition to such surface inhabitants, according to Professor G. W. Prescott (*in litt.*) 'some organisms are embedded in ice'.

Whereas the majority of recognized land cryophytes belong to the Green Algae—even when they are red, yellow, or brownish in actual colour—or in several cases to the Cyanophyceae or Bacillariophyceae, some Fungi and Bacteria may be associated as parasites. A few moss protonemata have also been found growing on snow or ice, but without developing into leafy plants. The numerous viable but quiescent spores of airborne Bacteria, Fungi, etc., and tufts or scraps of Mosses or other 'land' plants, that are often present on the surface of old snow and ice, can scarcely be considered as elements of its vegetation.[1]

It is on the floating sea-ice of boreal and austral regions, however, that the most plentiful cryovegetation (of a sort) is commonly developed. Here Diatoms, particularly, are often abundant in the pools that result from summer melting, frequently forming considerable aggregations that render the surface brownish; they also occur on the sides and undersurfaces of the floes. Already before the end of the last century, Nansen (*Farthest North*, I, pp. 444–5, 1897) reported from the North Polar Basin:

> 'one-celled lumps of viscous matter, teeming in thousands and millions, on nearly every single floe. . . . When the sun's rays had . . . melted the snow, so that pools were formed, there [were] soon to be seen at the bottom of these pools small yellowish-brown spots. . . . Day by day they increased in size, and absorbing . . . the heat of the sun's rays, they gradually melted the underlying ice and formed round cavities, often several inches deep. These brown spots were . . . algæ and diatoms. They developed speedily in the summer light, and would fill the bottoms of the cavities with a thick layer . . . the water also teemed with swarms of animalcules . . . which subsisted on the plants. I actually found bacteria. . . .'

## Benthos

The vascular plants of semi-aquatic marginal communities have been dealt with earlier in this work and those that comprise the main seral stages of shallow waters are discussed later in the present chapter. Here we must concentrate upon the usually smaller, attached or loose 'bottom' forms of Algae and other organisms which comprise the benthos. For, altogether, these make up a substantial

[1] It is not thought that the living Moss tussock found drifting on an ice-island near the North Pole (p. 109) actually grew on the ice, but this seems possible.

proportion of the biomass of most bodies of fresh, brackish, or inland saline waters. It is chiefly away from the shallowest waters, in which coarse vascular plants usually predominate provided the bed is suitable for their rooting, that these smaller benthic and allied forms are in real evidence, though among the marginal vascular plants there are usually to be found numerous bottom-attached, epiphytic, and unattached Algae or other cryptogams. Indeed a definite gradation can often be traced in the ' microflora ' of smaller forms as one passes from marginal to outer reed-swamps and from the latter to stony or muddy inorganic beds. For example, there are progressive changes in the algal flora associated with modifications in the bottom as it becomes less and less organic in nature, passing from an eutrophic to an oligotrophic condition. This is regardless of the central lake-basin usually being covered with sedimentary ' ooze ' consisting of mixed organic and inorganic matter (*see* pp. 496–7).

The benthic and allied organisms exist about the interface between free water and the usually heterogeneous bottom or its covering, and consequently their relationships are apt to be more complicated than those of plankton. This is furthermore the case because different lake-basins are formed in various ways and are overlain by different materials. Also the basins are variously altered after being filled with water—the shores by wave-action, the bed by deposits of sedimentary ooze—so that, with time, there is normally a progressive decrease in depth. Frequently the form indicated diagrammatically in Fig. 167 develops, in which, on the outermost shore, wave action has created a small cliff and an erosional terrace. To this there is adjoined a usually much wider depositional terrace that consists of sediments, the surface of which is controlled by wave action. This latter, sublittoral terrace may extend 100 metres or more out into the lake before descending more steeply as the infralittoral slope, which, in turn, changes into the central plain of descending or level, deep-water sediments. The water above this central plain is the main region of pure plankton, for the shore terrace, the infralittoral slope, and to some extent often the central plain itself, are all inhabited by benthos and often tychoplankton.

It is convenient here to distinguish as *littoral* that portion of the profile inhabited by photosynthesizing plants, and to subdivide it into the following three zones : (*a*) The *eulittoral*, which is characterized by fluctuating water-levels and hence conditions, being moreover a zone in which wave action on shore-lines may have a considerable effect. (*b*) The usually much more extensive *sublittoral*, which is a zone of shallow water, not fluctuating significantly in level, and bordered on its shoreward side by larger attached plants with leaves reaching the surface. (*c*) The *infralittoral*, which is a deeper region. Beyond this lies (*d*) the *profundal*, in which the light is insufficient for photosynthesis, the only plants normally present being parasitic, saprophytic, or chemosynthetic. Such a sequence is indicated in Fig. 167, though it should be remembered that authorities often differ as to categorization and terminology.

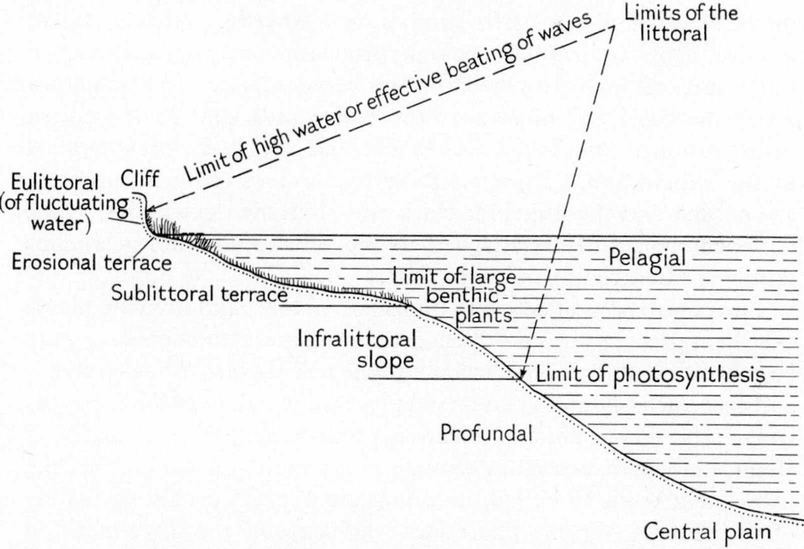


FIG. 167.—Diagrammatic representation of a typical lake-marginal profile. The limit of at all large benthic plants is commonly about the bottom of the sublittoral.

In the shore-terrace and other shallow parts of the littoral, where the bulk and activity of vascular plants and Mosses make seral advance often quite rapid, there are usually abundant associated Algae belonging to the benthos. The higher plants are, so to speak, fugitives from land, the lower ones being ‘ true children of the water ’. But the higher plants themselves often constitute an important part of the habitat of the aquatic microflora and microfauna and of any larger Algae that may be present. Besides firmly attached benthic types, the Algae include ones that are loose-lying (or in some cases crawling) on the bottom or, particularly, among dense higher vegetation. Unlike the situation with higher plants and parasites, the organs of attachment of these lower benthic plants do not normally penetrate the substratum. But these organs are nevertheless effective and, with the watery medium providing almost unlimited possibilities for development, practically all stone or otherwise suitable surfaces within the littoral, including dead or living plants, are more or less thickly populated by attached organisms.

The means of attachment of benthic creatures are many and various, and often have to afford protection against washing away by wave action or currents. They include gelatinous stalks of diverse structure which are sufficient in quiet water and are found in many Diatoms and in such animals as *Vorticella*. Also abundant in both plants and animals are rigid or gelatinous coverings attached to the substratum by tiny stalks or by a broader base. In filamentous Algae the basal cell must bear the entire pull, and so it is often firmly fastened by a lobed attachment-disk which is closely applied to the substratum. In agitated water more resistant attachments are needed and these include thick and shortened gelatinous stalks, flattened thalli broadly attached to the substratum, and gelatinous cushions often reinforced with lime.

The populations attached to underwater stones and to living plants —such as parts of various Potamogetonaceae and Pontederiaceae—are largely different, as is often evident to the naked eye. Thus on stones and rock surfaces, and often on old pieces of wood, crust-like growths frequently of considerable thickness predominate, whereas on living stems and leaves, as well as on such as are rapidly decomposing, the investment tends to be light and flocculent, often consisting mainly of filamentous Algae. The relative lightness of the investment on living and rapidly decomposing substrata appears to be due largely to their more or less transitory nature, so that they support chiefly colonists that must be quick-growing and short-lived. It also seems to be due in part to chemical changes in the immediate environment, brought about by the living or decomposing 'hosts'. A special community is afforded by those Algae and Lichens that penetrate the substratum and hence live partly within the body of stones, etc.—particularly limestone and snail-shells.

In the eulittoral, owing to the fluctuations in water-level and the influence of waves and spray, marked changes in conditions often take place over very small vertical distances, and there may be considerable differences in the composition of the communities from spot to spot. Most of the species that are resistant enough to thrive under the rather extreme conditions here obtaining, grow slowly and can develop only on a firm substratum. In small lakes the eulittoral may be restricted to a zone only a few centimetres high, but which still tends to be well marked and already divisible into belts that are inundated for varying periods in an average year and consequently exposed to rapidly changing temperature and other conditions. Thus in some central European lakes there is often an uppermost ' emersion belt ' that lies above the water for usually more than half the year and is coloured brown by the cyanophycean *Tolypothrix distorta*, which, when dry, can endure temperatures up to 70° C. without injury. Below is typically a ' surf-belt ' of brownish to reddish-yellow, pea-like crusts several millimetres thick and extending to just below the low-water line. This surf-belt is dominated by other Cyanophyceae—particularly by *Rivularia haematites* which forms hemispherical colonies interspersed with stratified layers of lime, and, in the upper portion, by *Calothrix parietina* which resembles flat spots of chocolate. Numerous other forms occur here where moisture is plentiful, including whole hosts of Diatoms and invertebrate animals. Below, the effect of waves becomes weaker with increasing depth—often no more than 10 cm. below the lowest water-level—and the crusts of *Rivularia*, etc., give way to thick grey-green sediments including precipitated ' lime '.

We should mention also the *psammon*, the interesting community inhabiting the wet capillary spaces of sand-bars and sandy shores. This forms a zone as much as 2 to 3 metres wide, extending above high-water mark up to the limit of capillary attraction, and corresponds with the edaphon of the soil but consists mainly of Protozoa and Bacteria, with some Algae near the surface.

The sublittoral, where waves are no longer effective, typically supports a rich growth of plants and animals of many and various forms which are, however, killed by even brief emersion. Frequently the cyanophycean *Schizothrix lacustris* is dominant, characterizing a zone that can extend downwards for several metres if the dominant is not overgrown by filamentous Algae. Here are often freshwater Sponges and other animals coloured green by symbiotic Algae such as *Zoochlorella*. For the water temperature tends to vary little and photosynthesis to be untrammelled, so an especially rich and varied life develops—provided the substratum is suitable for attachment and the composition of the water is not unfavourable.

Deeper down, in the infralittoral, the appearance of the benthos begins to change markedly at depths usually coinciding with the thermocline, for here plant life is drastically influenced by the decreasing temperature and light-intensity. Noticeable in this twilight zone is the marked decline in green types of Algae in favour of Diatoms which here show especially dark-brown coloration. Nevertheless the chlorophycean *Cladophora profunda* and *Dichotomosiphon tuberosus* may still be plentiful. Stones at 10–20 metres' depth are also liable to have a blackish or reddish to violet covering of particular cyanophycean and other forms not found at shallower depths. Here several types of Rhodophyceae such as species of *Hildenbrandia* ('*Hildbrandtia*', etc.) and *Chantransia* may occur, the coloration of which, like the brown of Diatoms, enables them to use for assimilation the short-waved green and allied light-rays that penetrate most deeply. The occasional green plants that persist here and below are often strikingly dark in colour, and their assimilation appears to be favoured either by increases in chlorophyll content or by changes in the proportions of the component pigments in such a way as to aid absorption. In some clear lakes the dysphotic region apparently extends to very considerable depths, fairly frequent plants occurring (sometimes in fair abundance) to 90 metres, and a very few Diatoms, particularly, having been dredged from over 160 metres. It is, however, by no means certain that these forms were actually living and reproducing at such depths—that they had not merely sunk from upper levels.

The depth to which the deeper plant communities extend of course depends on the transparency of the water; but even in the profundal, where photosynthesis is no longer possible, or at all events where a positive assimilation-balance is no longer found, heterotrophic, etc., organisms occur on suitable substrata. In addition to animals and their parasites, the heterotrophs include saprophytic Fungi and Bacteria living, for example, on rotting wood and leaves. There are also some autotrophs in the form of chemosynthetic Bacteria living under particular and often narrowly circumscribed conditions. Quite apart from this, Bacteria and Fungi appear to play much the same role of disease-producing parasites in water as on land, Bacteria more generally attacking animals and Fungi parasitizing many plants as well as animals.

Except on outcrops along steep shores, lake-basins are usually covered by sedimentary ooze which may attain a thickness of many metres. The ooze normally consists of an intricate mixture of organic and inorganic matter that is either *autochthonous* (formed in the lake itself by vital or physico-chemical processes) or *allochthonous* (introduced from outside by inflowing water, falling of dust, etc.). The amount and composition of allochthonous materials will depend on numerous factors such as local physiography and the composition of the rocks whence inflowing waters came; seasonally, pollen grains may form a particularly impressive form of dust. Autochthonous materials are the precipitations (such as 'lime' and 'iron') that take place in water, usually as a result of life-processes, and the sedimentation of plant and animal remains. The so-called 'lime' is mainly calcium carbonate, which is precipitated primarily through the photosynthetic activity of plants that withdraw carbon dioxide or the $HCO_3$–ion from dissolved bicarbonates. Much of it is apt to float as particles in the water and be deposited in shallows as greyish-white marl; at deeper levels, however, the more abundant carbon dioxide commonly redissolves any settling particles which then remain in solution as calcium bicarbonate.

Unlike the situation with lime, the secretion of silicates takes place directly on living organisms—particularly on Diatoms, whose siliceous 'shells', on sinking to the bottom, greatly enrich the ooze with silica. Such sedimentation takes place chiefly in the pelagial region of free and deep water and is the origin not only of currently accumulating diatomaceous deposits but also of the 'diatomaceous earth' in the sediments of long-extinct bodies of fresh and salt waters. Consequently, and in contradistinction to lime, silica tends to be far more plentiful in the sediments of the deep central plains than of the shallow shore-terraces, etc., of lakes—at least when these latter do not contain a large amount of allochthonous quartz material.

The organic components of sediments enable lake-bottoms to be transformed into spheres of often intense vital activity, while even in shallow waters the carbon dioxide produced by respiring organisms can lead to extensive re-dissolving of lime. Humic matter in solution may result in a browning of waters coming in from leached soils and may be flocculated on encountering calcium or other dissolved salts when entering lakes—hence the brownish gelatinous sediment that is commonly found in lakes in boggy regions. Otherwise the organic component results largely from plankton and dust sedimentation, from the sinking of pleuston, and from washing in from the watershed and the littoral zones. Even in temperate regions the total sediment deposited may amount to several thousands of kilograms of dry weight per hectare annually. Herein thrive 'decomposition' Bacteria, particularly, forming such 'end' substances as carbon dioxide, water, ammonia, hydrogen sulphide, and methane. These are thereby returned to circulation, or, in the cases of ammonia and hydrogen sulphide, are subsequently oxidized by chemosynthetic Bacteria which utilize, for carbon-assimilation in the dark (using carbon dioxide as the source), the energy liberated in this oxidation. However, under acidic conditions, as in bogs, cellulose is not broken down to methane, and under *anaerobic* conditions (of lack of free oxygen, such as occur in the profundal of permanently stratified eutrophic lakes) decomposition in general stops short at intermediate organic stages.

In running water, the slower the current the more closely the benthos approaches in type one or another of the communities of standing water. This is seen in streams in which rapids alternate with ' lentic ' stretches having the same substratum; for in the rapids the stones are commonly overgrown by bright-green Algae and Mosses, or in warm waters by thalloid Podostemaceae, but in the stretches of slow current the growth at least of benthic lower plants is liable to be markedly less luxuriant. The difference appears to be due to the fact that whereas in quiet water the organisms are surrounded by a film of liquid that soon becomes depleted of the substances they need, in rapid currents the absorbing surfaces of plants are continually brought into contact with new bodies of water and hence with new sources of materials.

The benthic plants of the so-called torrential communities have to be attached sufficiently strongly to resist the mechanical forces of the current, which may be considerable when it is rapid. Particularly effective and common as a type is the flat thallus applied closely to the substratum. This is well exemplified by many Cyanophyceae and Green Algae as well as by the Red Alga *Hildenbrandia rivularis* and many members of the peculiar dicotyledonous family Podostemaceae. Also prevalent are gelatinous layers and hemispherical colonies such as those found in the surf-belt of lakes; when lime is plentiful they may be held together by it. Attached floating growths must be particularly strong, with powerful holdfasts, as in the cases of tufts or ' streamers ' of Mosses or the larger Algae, while in the more delicate types such as benthic Diatoms the stalks of inhabitants of swift currents tend to be much shorter and thicker than those of their lentic relatives. This keeps them out of the rigours of the main stream. However, since the velocity of a water-current rapidly decreases as the bottom is approached, and at a minute distance from the bottom theoretically becomes zero, the tiniest organisms can easily remain attached to this bottom or even lie loose and undisturbed. Others can, and often in great numbers and variety do, remain protected from the current in tufts of Mosses or Algae.

The nature of the substratum is, as elsewhere, of importance in determining the benthic vegetation of streams and rivers. In general a firm, stony or rocky substratum prevails in rapidly flowing water, because finer particles are washed away, whereas in lentic stretches silty deposits are common and usually copious. Here the rooted vascular plants so important in the hydrosere (as described in the next section) are often prevalent, and the benthos under conditions of slower and slower current approximates more and more closely to that of lake margins.

Temperature may also have a marked influence on the benthos of running as well as of still waters. Thus, for example, the temperature often varies markedly in different parts of the same stream, as well as, of course, in the same place at different seasons—commonly with attendant floristic differences. Accordingly, even in small mountain brooks, the upper part may be dominated (to quote a European example) by *Hildenbrandia* and the lower reaches by another Red Alga, *Lemanea*, while the vernal period may be characterized by the dominance of Diatoms and the aestival by Green Algae, followed by a winter reappearance of the Diatoms. In lakes and ponds, also, there are often three or four seasonal aspects to be distinguished. Lastingly cold springs from deep rock-strata are apt to constitute refugia of cold-stenothermal species, while warm springs lack such types and usually include in their flora specific megathermal forms. Thus whereas at the lowest so-called 'thermal' temperature (30°–35° C.) almost all groups of Algae as well as Mosses and flowering plants are commonly present in favourable alkaline waters, it is only up to about 38° C. that Green Algae survive, and up to 45° C. at the highest that the last Diatoms persist. Above this temperature only Cyanophyceae continue from among these groups, though they persist in fair numbers up to 55° C. A very few species have been found growing above 60° C., but none for certain above 69° C., to which temperature *Synechococcus elongatus* appears able to survive. Bacteria, however, can withstand much higher temperatures, and have been found living in thermal waters up to at least 77·5° C. (In a dormant state some Bacteria can survive one or two boilings at 100° C., and certain Yeasts are capable of enduring a temperature of 114° C.)

A little needs to be added on the subject of algal *epiphytes* (that is, Algae growing attached to other plants). These, in fresh waters, usually grow on higher plants—such as aquatic Grasses, Sedges, Rushes, Horsetails, Water-lilies, Pondweeds, and the like. In temperate regions they may often be roughly divided into communities living (*a*) on submerged plants in very shallow waters, these being mostly Green Algae ; (*b*) on submerged plants at depths of between 1 and 3 metres, these being mostly other Green Algae such as species of *Oedogonium* and *Coleochaete* and, in addition, Diatoms ; and (*c*) on submerged plants at greater depths.

This last category extends down to about 6 metres and commonly includes *Coleochaete*, Diatoms, and Cyanophyceae. Additionally, subdivision of algal epiphytes is often possible in temperate regions into (1) winter annuals, (2) summer and autumn annuals, and (3) perennials. Here the age as well as the nature of the substratum is of great importance ; but whereas there is a general tendency, as might be expected, for older leaves, for example, to be better endowed with epiphytes than younger ones, such a sequence is not always found. There may also be differences in the epiphytic flora of the upper and lower surfaces of leaves, and on different parts of a plant or even organ. Some of these and many other differences appear to be due to differing light-intensities. Moreover, rapid growth, as in the case of most of a leaf (other than its tip), tends to prevent colonization. So far as attachment is concerned, the nature of the ' host ' surface, provided it is large and solid enough, does not appear to matter except to the motile reproductive bodies which tend to come to rest most easily in interstices and depressions. Through germination of such disseminules and subsequent growth, these sheltered situations often become quickly populated with adults of the species concerned.

## Bogs and Saline Waters

Bogs, which abound particularly in the cooler parts of the northern hemisphere, form a special habitat in which the substratum is composed of peat. The peat is usually saturated with water and has lying above it a water-soaked layer of Mosses, particularly of the genus *Sphagnum* (Bog-mosses). Domes of such Mosses are often surrounded by swampy moats ; or species of *Sphagnum* may extend out into the waters of a lake, often ultimately covering it to the centre. Such features are typically characterized by attendant zones of vegetation, the commonly coniferous tree dominants rapidly decreasing in luxuriance and height as they advance into the moat or towards the centre of the bog or margin of the lake. Beyond this zone of often gnarled dwarfs there normally extends one of lowly Heaths, such as species of *Vaccinium* (including Blueberries, Bilberries, Whortleberries, etc.), *Chamaedaphne* (Leather-leaf), *Oxycoccus* (Cranberries), *Andromeda* (Marsh Andromeda), and *Ledum* (Labrador-tea). The flora is liable to be limited by, among other conditions, poor aeration not far down.

The surface is typically of slight mounds or hummocks set in a network of depressions occupied by small shallow puddles. These last are particularly prevalent towards the centre of the bog or persisting lake, where they often coalesce to form larger bog-pools. The vascular plants of these very wet depressions are chiefly hygro-

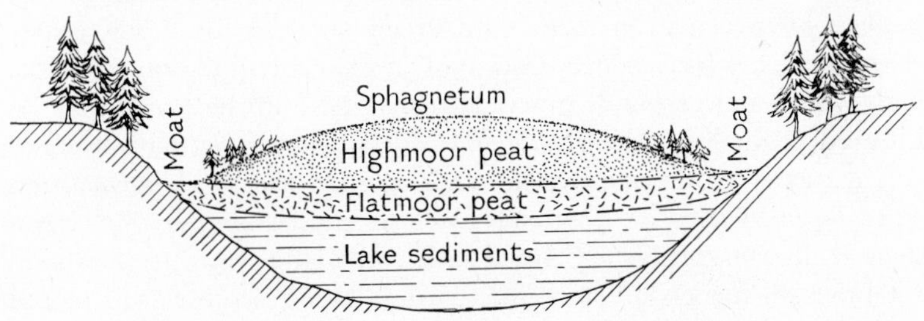


FIG. 168.—Diagram of cross-section through a 'highmoor' bog that has arisen from a small lake, the contours being exaggerated for clarity. (After Ruttner.)

phytic Sedges (*Carex* spp.) and Cotton-grasses (*Eriophorum* spp.), but the zones of recent extension may be of almost pure Mosses. Quaking bogs are those in which such vegetation, owing to extension over waters, in part at least floats like a raft, while hanging bogs are those developed on moist slopes. Fig. 168 shows in diagrammatic form how a lake may become filled by sediments and ultimately by Bog-mosses, etc., to form an extensive bog (Sphagnetum).

The bog-waters, including those of puddles, pools, and embedded lakes, tend to be extremely poor in dissolved salts, strongly acidic in reaction, and possessed of a high content of humic materials which often impart a brownish coloration. Such waters are characterized, from the boreal regions to the mountains of the tropics, by a special microflora of species apparently unable to withstand an alkaline medium. This microflora is particularly rich in Desmids but also contains certain Cyanophyceae such as *Chroococcus turgidus*. Some Diatoms, Peridinians, and other Green Algae also occur, but usually in limited variety compared with the predominant Desmids.

The determining factor appears to be the acidic reaction, coupled with the low salt-content and the abundance of humic colloids in solution.

Saline waters occurring inland vary from faintly brackish to several times the average salinity of the ocean, some being completely saturated with salts. The plants of very salty inland waters, such as are found practically throughout the ice-free land of the world but especially in arid regions, are largely Green Algae, though Diatoms and Cyanophyceae may also occur, with, in addition, higher plants around the shallow margins. These higher plants are usually sea-shore species, so that the communities often resemble some of those already described. *Dunaliella salina* is probably the commonest of the Green Algae inhabiting brine. It and a species of *Stephanoptera* can even form light-green areas on solid salt crusts where the water has a concentration of 33 per cent. of dissolved solids. Such waters in salt ponds practically anywhere in the world may be coloured reddish by the *Dunaliella* and have their bottoms covered with a carpet of Cyanophyceae such as *Microcoleus chthonoplastes*. Quite large species of *Enteromorpha* are known among the Green Algae from salt springs and brine lakes, as well as from fresh waters and brackish lagoons. Here fluctuating salinities often lead to the production of peculiar specimens that are difficult to identify: indeed the characters of several supposed 'species' can be exhibited by different parts of a single thallus! In many brackish waters, such as those near the sea where incoming streams bring fresh water, a wide range of Algae and other plants of both fresh and salt waters often flourish: they are normally species tolerant of varying salinity but, being of different degrees of halophytism, still tend to give populations that vary with the habitat. Thus under only slightly brackish conditions the flora is predominantly a freshwater one, whereas with a close approach to full oceanic salinity it is mainly marine.

## Hydroseres

Apart from the bog succession dealt with above, there are the normal seres occurring in open fresh water—especially around the shallow margins of eutrophic lakes and ponds. Here the different stages characteristically form more or less well-marked zones. Such hydroseres can have their inception in deep waters that gradually become shallower with the deposition of various materials comprising the sedimentary ooze. This last usually includes contributions from the plankton and pleuston which may accordingly be considered part of the sere, though their non-essential nature, provided inorganic sediments are sufficient to build up the bed, makes them rather of proseral significance. Similarly proseral in nature are many of the benthic communities of the profundal and lower infralittoral, though those of the shallower, upper littoral zones commonly form part of the autogenic main sere. These may include the ' Characetum ', which often occupies the floors of bodies of water or shoals chiefly from 8 to 12 metres deep, and is characterized by the curious Green Algae known as Stoneworts (species of the genera *Chara* and *Nitella*), by Bushy-pondweeds or Naiads (*Najas* spp.), and by various aquatic Mosses such as species of *Drepanocladus* and *Fontinalis*. These plants are widely important not only in retaining silt and depositing humus, but also in ' binding ' the surface on which they grow.

The first of what appear to be the normally essential portions of the hydrosere is the ' submerged aquatics ' stage. Although this may to some extent be represented by members of the Characetum, more familiar in the zone expressing this stage in the north-temperate regions are such plants as many of the Pondweeds (*Potamogeton* spp.), Tape-grasses (*Vallisneria* spp.), Water-milfoils (*Myriophyllum* spp.), Horn-worts (*Ceratophyllum* spp.), and Water-weeds (*Elodea* spp.). Most of these are normally rooted, but various lower plants such as the often associated larger Algae and Mosses lack true roots although they may grow attached to the substratum by means of hold-fasts, rhizoids, etc. Some even of the higher plants are normally unattached, floating freely as more or less dense carpets or ' beds ' near the bottom of quiet waters whence they may extend into the general body of the pond or lake. These submerged plants tend to cover slopes down to a depth of about 6 metres, where decreasing light-intensity becomes a limiting factor, though some Mosses may persist more deeply, Spring-moss (*Fontinalis* sp.) being said to form carpets down to depths of about 20 metres in some clear alpine lakes. Stoneworts (Charales), looking like small vascular plants, may grow even deeper down, and a single Moss has been found growing at a reputed 60 metres in Lake Geneva. Fig. 167 showed the relationship of this stage to other early ones of the hydrosere.

These relatively bulky submerged plants collect silt and organic matter produced by other living forms and add this material, together with the results of their own decomposition, to the bed which accordingly becomes built up more quickly. In time it is shallow enough for colonization by other plants which, through long and flexible upgrowing stems and/or leaf-stalks, enable their leaves to reach the surface of the water, so constituting the 'floating-leaf' stage and crowding out most of the submerged aquatics. Examples of such plants with floating leaves are *Potamogeton natans* and some other Pondweeds, some Bur-reeds (*Sparganium* spp.), and most members of the Water-lily family (Nymphaeaceae). In a sense also belonging here is the detached pleuston of Duckweeds (*Lemna*

Fig. 169.—Leaves of Sacred Lotus (*Nelumbo nucifera*) projecting out of the water, and *Pistia stratiotes* floating on the water, in the Philippine Islands.

spp.), *Pistia stratiotes*, Water-hyacinth (*Eichhornia crassipes*), Frog-bit (*Hydrocharis morsus-ranae*), Water Buttercups (*Ranunculus* spp.), etc., which frequently help to consolidate the surface vegetation of this stage. Fig. 169 shows a dense community really belonging to this stage although the leaves of the dominant Sacred Lotus (*Nelumbo nucifera*) project out of the water. Floating freely on the surface are abundant plants of *Pistia* (*cf.* Fig. 164, B). Such prolific aquatic vegetation markedly reduces light-penetration and the turbulence of the water (*cf.* also Fig. 164, C). Various Podostemaceae are particularly characteristic of running warm waters, the vegetation of which may be separated on this and other grounds.

The floating-leaf plants tend to be still more prolific than preceding stages and to build up the bed still more rapidly by their collection of silt, etc., and addition of their own material on death. Consequently in time there can be colonization by swamp plants and emergent hydrophytes of which at least half the body is aerial. These rapidly predominate over the floating-leaf plants, many of which are soon crowded out, and so the reed-swamp stage is attained. Whereas the water is commonly $\frac{1}{2}$–3 metres deep in the floating-leaf stage, in the reed-swamp stage it is usually less than 1 metre deep. Here the main dominants are of such types as the Common Reed (*Phragmites communis* agg.), Bulrush (*Scirpus lacustris*), Reed-maces or Cattails (*Typha* spp.), Water Horsetail (*Equisetum fluviatile*), and various Sedges (*Carex* spp.), or Papyrus (*Cyperus papyrus*) in tropical rivers, one or other of which often forms a practically pure stand. Even within this zone there may be some differentiation, the Bulrushes, for example, occupying the deeper water.

Subsequent events in the hydrosere are outlined and illustrated in Chapter XI; but it should here be remarked that many marsh-plants (*helophytes*, recognizable within the more general category of 'hygrophytes', or plants of moist habitats) and water-plants (*hydrophytes*) are much alike in their morphological and anatomical characteristics. There are, however, some marked differences, as the following characterizations will indicate. In underwater parts the cuticle and other features curtailing transpiration are reduced, stomata being abolished but aerenchyma (*see* below) much developed. Moreover, the vascular tissue even in stems is often arranged centrally when they develop under water, there being no secondary thickening. Such a structure gives tensile strength but allows flexibility, as water affords sufficient support for rigidity to be unnecessary—even though this same water may exert a dangerous pull. In the stems of real marsh-plants, however, the supporting and conducting elements are usually arranged peripherally, as these stems have to stand more or less erect after the manner of those of land plants and meanwhile must have sufficient conducting elements for rapid transpiration. On floating leaves, stomata are usually confined to the upper surface, while submerged leaves are often finely dissected to facilitate the exchange of materials. The same characteristic may, incidentally, save them from being torn by currents.

As it is more difficult to obtain oxygen in water than in air, and still more difficult in waterlogged mud, most aquatic and marsh plants have systems of large air-canals or air-filled cells, constituting the so-called 'aerenchyma', which often dominate their anatomy, extending through their bodies right down to the roots. These last have a particularly difficult problem of aeration for respiration in the oxygen-poor ooze.

Finally, although some annual aquatics occur, such as Naiads (*Najas* spp.), most higher types are perennial, either living through any unfavourable season apparently unchanged or else dying down or, if pleustonic, often descending to the bottom. Even in cool-temperate regions, many shallow-water types appear to continue some photosynthetic activity in winter under the ice—at least as long as this is not covered by a darkening layer of snow.

## Further Consideration

For additional details:

P. S. Welch. *Limnology*, second edition (McGraw-Hill, New York etc., pp. xi + 538, 1952).

F. Ruttner. *Fundamentals of Limnology*, translated by D. G. Frey & F. E. J. Fry (University of Toronto Press, Toronto, Ont., pp. xi + 242, 1953).

F. R. Moulton (ed.). *Problems of Lake Biology* (American Association for the Advancement of Science, Washington, D.C., pp. 1–142, 1939).

Useful accounts of particular aspects are to be found in the appropriate parts of:

A. F. W. Schimper. *Plant-geography upon a Physiological Basis*, transl. and revised edition (Clarendon Press, Oxford, pp. xxx + 839 and maps, 1903). Especially useful in this connection is the 'third' German edition, *Pflanzengeographie auf physiologischer Grundlage*, revised by F. C. von Faber (Fischer, Jena, vol. I, pp. xx + 588, and vol. II, pp. xvi + 589–1613 and maps, 1935).

V. J. Chapman. *An Introduction to the Study of Algae* (Cambridge University Press, Cambridge, Eng., pp. x + 387, 1941).

G. M. Smith (ed.). *Manual of Phycology* (Chronica Botanica, Waltham, Mass., pp. xii + 375, 1951).

K. E. Carpenter. *Life in Inland Waters: with especial reference to animals* (Sidgwick & Jackson, London, pp. xviii + 267, 1928).

G. E. Hutchinson. *A Treatise on Limnology: vol. I, Geography, Physics, and Chemistry* (Wiley, New York, pp. xiv + 1015, 1957).

## Chapter XVI

# VEGETATIONAL TYPES OF SEAS

We have now dealt at least cursorily with each of the main vegetational types of the chief plant habitats, excepting only those of the oceans and salt-seas which, however, occupy between them slightly over 70 per cent. of the surface of the globe. Nevertheless they are relatively uniform over very wide areas and so can be treated fairly briefly. This is especially true of the open ocean and the planktonic communities developing in it. On the other hand, on shallow marine bottoms and particularly around sea-shores, conditions and the attendant plant communities tend to be far more variable, so that altogether we get a set of categories which are largely comparable—for example in their planktonic or, alternatively, benthic nature—with those of fresh waters. But before we deal with each of these in turn, we must consider the sea in general as a habitat for plants.

## Some Features of the Marine Environment

That the marine environment is widely different from the fresh-water one is evidenced by the fact that salt-water plants placed in fresh water, or *vice versa*, almost invariably perish. The light and other physical conditions can be, and often are, much the same in the two media, and temperature fluctuations of the air tend to be similarly ' damped down ', the differences in salinity being commonly the decisive factor so far as inhabiting plants are concerned.

The salt-content of the free oceans is around 3·5 per cent., but in bays and inland seas it may deviate widely from this figure owing to concentration by evaporation or, alternatively, dilution by fresh-water streams. Thus preponderance of evaporation causes the Red Sea to have a salinity of well over 4 per cent. at the surface, while abundant inflow of fresh water makes the salinity of the Baltic Sea in many places less than 1 per cent., and in some only 0·1–0·2 per cent. Such reductions in any particular region—apparently regardless of climatic or other changes—tend to be accompanied by very marked ones in the numbers of species of Green, Brown, and Red Algae present, and in the general luxuriance of the vegetation. At the lower concentrations in middle and high latitudes some of the persisting Brown Algae, particularly, often take on characteristic dwarf forms, and the plankton becomes poor in species and more and more limited to freshwater or brackishwater types. There may also be superimposed layers of waters of different salinities, and supporting different Algae—especially when currents of different origin meet but do not mix.

By far the most abundant solid in solution in sea-water is sodium chloride (common or table salt), which on the average forms nearly 78 per cent. of the total salts present, contributing over 27 grams per litre. It is followed in the scale of abundance by magnesium chloride (nearly 11 per cent.) and magnesium sulphate (nearly 5 per cent.), though salts of calcium and potassium are also fairly plentiful. Sea-water is a ' buffered ' solution, exhibiting resistance to changes in its degree of basicity (the so-called ' reaction ' or ' pH level ', due to the concentration of free hydrogen-ions present). Thus plentiful carbon dioxide is normally available for photosynthesis without disturbance of the buffered state, and the prevailing slight alkalinity enables living organisms to extract calcium carbonate, etc. Especially is this easy in warm seas—hence their numerous large calcareous shells, coral-reefs, and so forth. Containing, as it does, all of the chemical elements essential to the growth and maintenance of protoplasm, sea-water is in general a very appropriate environment for living cells—provided they are adapted to its concentration of salts.

Different Algae vary enormously in their tolerance to variations in the salt-content of the water—from the narrowly stenohaline species requiring the salinity to remain within a narrow range (these are represented by most oceanic forms), to the broadly euryhaline ones that grow in puddles high up on the shore. Here they are bathed in sea-water when the tide comes in or waves reach them, the salinity being often further increased through evaporation ; but after heavy rainfall they may find themselves in almost entirely fresh water. The turgor adjustments involved within the cells in enduring such changes are not fully understood, although it is known that certain Diatoms, living in the mouths of streams where the salinity varies rapidly, are able to take in or let out salt very quickly—according to its concentration in the water.

Owing to the intimacy of aquatic organisms with the medium in which they live, and also to the general stability of the physical characteristics of that medium, slight changes in the environment are apt to be reflected with particular promptness in the plant and animal population, whose components commonly lack the protection their terrestrial counterparts have developed. Moreover the organisms themselves may modify the chemical nature of their environment by withdrawing or adding substances, so that, for example, the surface layers of sea-water often become so impoverished in the essential combined nitrogen and phosphorus as greatly to limit growth and otherwise change the character of the plankton. Such impoverishment is due to absorption by organisms whose dead bodies sink to the depths where they gradually decay, so that replenishment takes place chiefly by vertical convection currents in the cooling period of autumn. This replenishment occurs most actively in temperate and colder seas, and explains the often richer plankton of these regions than of tropical seas where the lastingly warm and light surface waters shut off the deep ones and little vertical convection takes place. Indeed, while tropical seas are estimated to contain on the average 5 planktonic organisms per cubic centimetre, the figure for arctic seas varies from 100 to 500. Nevertheless there is some compensation provided by the greater depth to which the photosynthetic zone extends in the lower latitudes, and still more in the short duration of activity each year in the high latitudes, so that some authorities have recently claimed that there is little or no significant difference in total productivity between the seas of high and low latitudes. But for one reason or another, in spite of the relative uniformity of marine habitats, and the similarity that prevails over vast areas especially in the open ocean, great differences do in fact occur in different regions, which are reflected in their plant as well as animal life.

Among other chemical items it may be presumed that the content of dissolved oxygen and carbon dioxide, and the variable reaction (pH), are all important. Where vertical currents are active in seas, the gas-content and composition of the water will be kept similar in all layers reached by such currents ; but where no such aeration etc. takes place, extreme conditions may occur. Thus in the Black Sea, oxygen is found only to a depth of 183 metres ; below this, normally respiring plants and animals cannot exist, and much the same appears to be true in some tropical lakes. Although the situation with carbon dioxide is substantially reversed through photosynthesis, during which it is absorbed and replaced by oxygen, actually in the surface layer carbon dioxide can be replenished from the air, whereas deep down the preponderant tendency is for it to be given off in respiration and decomposition, oxygen being absorbed. So here again the two gases are largely complementary. During the summer and winter periods of relative stagnation, surface waters tend to be more alkaline than deeper layers, owing to the photosynthetic activity of Algae, which removes the carbonate-ion and leads to a preponderance of hydroxyl-ion.

As regards temperatures, the surface layer of water already shows much smaller variations than the air lying directly upon it. Conversely, water has a regulating effect on the temperature of neighbouring air-masses, and this effect may operate at considerable distances if the air-masses move over land. The temperatures of the surface waters of the sea rarely if ever exceed 31° C.; nor do they fall below the freezing-point of –3·6° C. Deep down in the ocean the temperatures are commonly rather low and uniform—for example, 0·6° C. at 2,000 metres' depth in the Antarctic Sea where the surface was 1·0° C., and 1·6° C. at 3,000 metres in the equatorial part of the Pacific Ocean where the surface was 29° C. But in spite of the relatively small amplitude in this respect, so that perennial marine Algae even in cold regions may exhibit no period of winter rest but carry on vegetative activity in summer and reproduce in winter, while in warm seas the difference in temperature is often no longer effective, the floristic organization of marine vegetation depends substantially upon the temperature of the water. Thus the limits of marine floristic regions tend to coincide with particular isotherms, and this is especially true of plankton, whose latitudinal distribution may be related to local temperatures at particular seasons.

In conjunction with such factors as temperature, the persistence or importation of disseminules is of obvious importance in determining the character of the phytoplanktonic population developing in any one region at various periods of the year. The disseminules may be transported, as adults or otherwise, considerable distances and in quantity by ocean currents, and vast distances will be traversed if a series of generations is involved. Each component type in the plankton has its metabolic requirements adjusted to particular temperature ranges and, having withstood unfavourable seasons elsewhere or in some resistant form, 'blooms' with the return of suitable conditions, different types succeeding one another largely according to their specific requirements. Even in the yearly periodicity in which light plays such an important part, it is clear that temperature may be decisive in favouring the development, for example, of northern species very much farther south than usual in the earlier part of the year, and of southern species northwards when the water warms up in summer. But although the flora tends to be more diverse in warm than cold seas, in the matter of total productivity the reverse may hold—at least of phytoplankton in the upper layers (*see* p. 509).

Light is often the dominant factor in determining the local distribution and extent of aquatic vegetation, being rapidly reduced with increasing depth. The degree to which water allows light to penetrate its depths naturally varies greatly with turbidity and other conditions, but in general the total radiation is reduced to little more than half its surface intensity at a depth of 10 centimetres, and to a little over one-seventieth at 100 metres. Nevertheless in some seas there may be a noticeable effect on a photographic plate as deep down as 1,000 metres. Although photosynthesis doubtless ceases far above such limits, and probably often in the uppermost 100 metres, it still commonly continues to much more considerable depths in seas than in fresh waters, owing to the greater transparency of the former. Thus the euphotic zone in the ocean normally extends down to 80 or more metres, and the dysphotic zone, of dim light and consequently very limited plant production, from the base of the euphotic zone to 200 or more metres. Moreover, because of the greater thickness of the turbulent layer affected by vertical diffusion currents, as well as of this deeper photosynthesis allowed by deeper light-penetration, the habitat of the ' surface plankton ' commonly goes far deeper in oceans than in lakes.

The depth to which photosynthesis extends will naturally vary greatly in different circumstances, being limited markedly by dispersion of light due to suspended particles both living and inert. Moreover, because of the lowering angle of incidence of the sun and consequently reduced penetration of its rays, this depth usually gets shallower and shallower at increasingly high latitudes. It is commonly taken by oceanographers as the dividing-line between the bottom of the infralittoral (also called by some the sublittoral) and the top of the deep-sea system, being often placed at around 200 metres as in the accompanying diagram (Fig. 170). This maximum depth to which photosynthesis extends is also the approximate depth of water at the outer edge of the continental shelf, and separates the neritic (shallow water) province from the oceanic province of what some students term the pelagic division of the sea (their other division being the benthic, comprising the ocean floor and shore). Often the ‘ compensation point ’ (at which the daily accumulation of food as a result of photosynthesis is just balanced by the break-down during respiration of stored materials) is very much less deep, being sometimes only a few metres from the surface, though of course varying with many factors, including the organisms concerned.

It is also convenient to separate an uppermost or ‘ eulittoral ’ zone as extending from the highest to the lowest ‘ normal ’ tide-levels on shores, and a ‘ sublittoral ’ extending from the base of this down to a depth of about 40 to 60 metres, the lower boundary being set at the lowest limit at which the more abundant attached plants grow. It should be noted that some authors continue the eulittoral down to the lower limit of at all abundant attached plants, their so-called sublittoral beginning here and extending down to a total depth of about 200 metres, and so corresponding with what we have here termed the infralittoral. Below the infralittoral is the deep-sea system, divided into an upper ‘ archibenthic zone ’, extending to a depth of between 800 and 1,100 metres, and the lower ‘ abyssal-benthic zone ’, in which conditions are practically uniform. Here the temperatures are always low (– 1° to + 5° C.), solar light is lacking, and there are no seasons. The various zones, etc., are shown diagrammatically in Fig. 170.

The component colours of white light are variously absorbed by sea-water—those of shorter wave-length, such as the very abundant green, being in general less absorbed than the red, and even the blue, though the red may be relatively little affected by stains and suspended matter. This differential absorption of different components of the spectrum seems to be one of the main factors behind the ecological preferences of different Algae for different depths, though details are still not clear. Thus in general Green Algae reign in the uppermost layers where red rays are plentiful, such rays being apparently essential for healthy growth of many of these plants, while Red Algae predominate deeper down where green rays still penetrate, although in each colour-group are species belonging to very different depths. Brown Algae tend to be plentiful at all depths except the deepest inhabited by Algae, where Red Algae commonly predominate.

Apparently both the intensity and the wave-length of the light play a large part in controlling the regional distribution of Algae, the green surface-forms flourishing under conditions of high light-intensity and plentiful red rays, though hardly able to utilize the green rays of the depths. The deep-water Red Algae, on the other hand, are capable of growing under conditions of much lower light-intensity, being able to utilize precisely those deeply penetrating rays of shorter wave-lengths. Only when the light is sufficiently weakened, do many of these deep-water forms appear able to grow well in the red-containing light of the surface. Diatoms tend to flourish best under relatively low light-intensities where the red component is much reduced, often having their maxima at around 10 metres' depth and forming rich growths at 15 to 20 metres where chiefly green and some blue rays prevail.

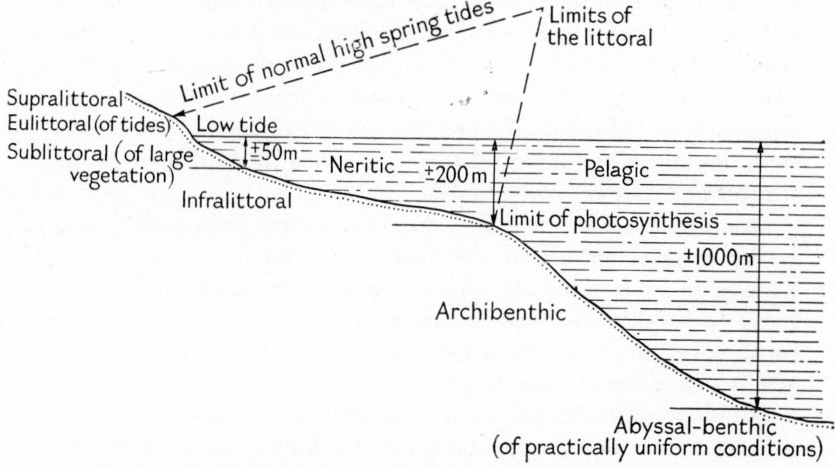


FIG. 170.—Diagrammatic representation of typical sea-marginal profile.

The motion of the water is another factor important to marine vegetation, leading as it does to the occurrence of largely different forms on surf-pounded and sheltered shores. Thus in exposed situations, quite apart from the need for strong holdfasts and 'leathery' thalli to prevent detachment and injury by breakers, the moving water tends to be better aerated than on sheltered shores and consequently to favour increased biological activity. Moreover sea currents, whether regular or irregular, commonly carry Algae, often for consideiable distances, and can be one of their chief agents of dispersal, though for most benthic forms death follows any prolonged period of detachment.

For plankton, although mixing of waters by upwelling or convection or other currents is widely important, a goodly supply of nutrients being necessary for rich development, some degree of stability is also desirable. Thus any surface and other waters of excessive turbulence tend to show only moderate phytoplanktonic populations even when conditions of light and nutrient supply are very favourable. The chief depauperating influence in such circumstances seems to be removal of organisms by descending currents. Horizontal ocean currents, however, are commonly important in bringing in types from other climatic belts, as is evidenced by the widespread distribution of most planktonic species, and even though living conditions may be similar during only limited periods of the year. Neritic types carried seawards by outgoing currents often persist for a while and may even reproduce, though in time they will perish; nor can a population resume existence if the water is persistently devoid of vegetative plants and resting spores of species capable of taking advantage of suitable conditions. This has been suggested as the explanation of the poverty of some off-shore communities where the depth of the water, it is thought, may prohibit the ready 'return' of resting stages.

Also important to the local vegetation, except in very deep water, is the physical nature of the shore or ocean floor—for example, whether it is hard or soft, fixed and rigid or loose and therefore likely to be moved by waves or other influences. Normally bare rock, which on the whole is very inhospitable for land plants, is the best substratum for the larger Algae that form the vast bulk of eulittoral and sublittoral marine vegetation. Especially are such durable rocks as granites suitable for attachment, whereas the softer schists, shales, and sandstones are insufficiently stable for the attachment of large Algae, carrying at best only rather small species. But in general the ocean floor is covered by softish sedimentary deposits that result from weathering and erosion on land or from life in the sea. There is now some reason for supposing that the chemical composition of the substratum may yet hold considerable significance for marine Algae, though this significance is apparently far less than is commonly the case in fresh waters.

In spite of their rather vague and variable separation, the oceanic (pelagic) and neritic provinces are very different. The oceanic province is itself divided into an upper lighted zone and a lower, dark one: its outstanding features when compared with the neritic are its great area and range of depth, its transparency owing to the usual absence of detritus of terrestrial origin, and the consequent deep penetration of light and resultant blueness. In chemical composition these off-shore waters are relatively stable, with salinity almost uniformly high, though the content of plant nutrients may be relatively low in the upper layer, and these may be only slowly replaced.

In the neritic province the chemical constitution is more variable, salinities being usually lower than in the open ocean, and sometimes markedly so. Moreover they are apt to undergo such seasonal or sporadic fluctuations that the inhabitants may have to be euryhaline in nature. However, plant nutrients such as phosphates and nitrates tend to be more readily available in these shallower inshore waters than elsewhere—a fact which is of special importance in the production of Diatoms, the foremost of 'primary sea-foods'. Consequently a unit volume or even unit area of the neritic water is commonly far more productive than a similar unit of oceanic water, though the latter as a whole, because of its extent and depth, provides the bulk of inhabitable space on earth. (The free atmosphere is scarcely to be considered habitable space except very close to the surface of the earth, for the organisms that are found free in it appear to be making only temporary excursions therein, however protracted these excursions may seem.)

## Plankton

It seems best, in dealing with the sea, to consider all phytoplankton together—without separating any macroscopic floating matter as pleuston. Moreover, barring accidental detachment, for example of marine vascular plants, when either death or resettling must soon follow, the 'regular' phytoplanktonic organisms of the sea are all lowly Thallophytes or Schizophytes. Thus under the heading of marine phytoplankton are commonly included all of the floating or drifting forms of plant life of the oceanic and neritic provinces of the sea—as befits the Greek derivation of the world plankton, which means 'wanderer'—whether they be microscopic, as in the vast majority of cases, or quite large, as in the case of Sargasso-weed (*see* p. 521). Although the number of different groups of plants normally represented in plankton is limited, there is no dearth of variety in form, as Fig. 171 indicates.

The general characteristics of phytoplankton were discussed in the last chapter, much of which was devoted to the conditions of life and phytoplanktonic communities of fresh waters. Those of the ocean are again mainly microscopic and so will not be described in detail. They are chiefly Diatoms and Peridinians (Dinoflagellates), or, in some warm seas and brackish lagoons, Blue-green Algae (Cyanophyceae). Examples of typical Diatoms and Peridinians are shown in Figs. 6 and 7, respectively. Thus the brown colora-

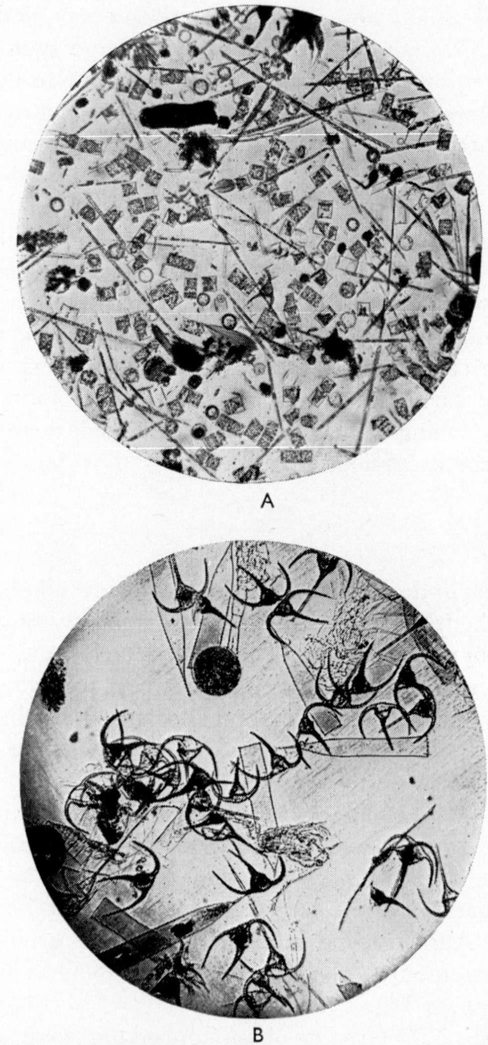


FIG. 171.—Photomicrographs of marine phytoplanktonic communities. A, Early summer 'maximum' of Diatoms off the Atlantic coast of North America. Dominant are *Guinardia* sp. (short and square) and *Rhizosolenia* sp. (long and slender), (× about 35). (Phot. H. B. Bigelow.) B, Late summer 'peak' of Peridinians (anchor-shaped *Ceratium* sp.) and animalcules (pencil-shaped Tintinnids) off the Atlantic coast of North America. (× about 50.) (Phot. H. B. Bigelow.)

tion of many northern waters at certain times of the year is due largely to Diatoms, while the Red Sea owes its name to the red accessory pigment of the planktonic cyanophycean *Trichodesmium erythraeum*. Diatoms are present in all seas and indeed almost everywhere, being usually numerous as regards both forms and individuals; Peridinians are also extremely widespread, but tend to be numerous chiefly in terms of individuals in cold seas and of different forms in warm ones. Green flagellates and Bacteria may also be very abundant in marine plankton—the latter especially near coasts, though there is some doubt as to whether they should be considered truly planktonic (*see* p. 521). Various other greenish, brownish, or yellowish types are also prone to occur—such as, respectively, *Halosphaera viridis*, *Phaeocystis*, and certain Silicoflagellates.

Marine plankton has to remain suspended in water. Consequently the component organisms either swim or are very minute or have some appropriate 'form-resistance', meanwhile employing the seemingly least and lightest possible structural material. This is towards maintaining the specific gravity near the density of the surrounding medium—much as in freshwater types. Such needed buoyancy may be increased by gas-bubbles or, as in the case of Diatoms, by globules of oil. Adhesion of cells together may also increase their tendency to float, though, in general, reduction to small size is highly advantageous. For the rate of sinking of a body heavier than water, as most phytoplankters (phytoplanktonic individuals) are, depends upon the ratio of surplus weight to friction, which is determined mainly by surface area, and the simplest way to obtain a relatively large surface-to-volume ratio is to reduce the absolute size. Thus the smaller the body, the less tendency will it show in general to sink.

Otherwise, if no means of active locomotion or actual flotation is available, reliance has to be placed on an increase in surface area and complexity through structural adaptations involving the external form. This may be as of a bladder, in which much of the relatively large cell is occupied by light fluid, or of a disk, which sinks in zigzag fashion and so covers a greatly increased distance, or of a needle, which sinks slowly when the long axis lies horizontally—as the mechanics of sedimentation make it tend to do. Or the elongated body may be curved or provided with bevelled ends in such a manner that, if displaced, it is soon brought back to the horizontal position, sinking being accomplished in wide circles. Or the cells may be attached in ribbons or chains, or they may be branched or possessed of long spines or other projections to resist sinking. One or more of these features leading to increased form-resistance is commonly found in planktonic Diatoms, which, it is interesting to note, also tend to have lighter cell-walls than their benthic counterparts. Peridinians, in spite of their power of locomotion, may also have a parachute-like or winged form, or may develop marked asymmetry that leads to orientation of the sinking body so that the long axis lies horizontally, accordingly providing the maximum surface and resistance to passive sinking. It is also interesting to note that, in keeping with the reduced viscosity of warmer waters, the summer forms of Diatoms tend to have lighter shells and the southern Peridinians larger projections than their colder-water counterparts.

The majority of marine phytoplanktonic organisms inhabit the euphotic zone, and especially its upper layers. The dysphotic zone is commonly very poor in phytoplankton, and the aphotic zone, except for occasional stray photosynthetic individuals, is limited to saprophytic, parasitic, or chemosynthetic forms. Seasonal variations may also be very marked in marine phytoplankton, often including both spring and autumn maxima when nutrients are plentiful and light and temperatures allow rapid development. Quite apart from this, the seasons may produce a sequence of types favoured by, or able to withstand, particular conditions.

Owing to the minute size of many of the organisms, only a small proportion of the total phytoplanktonic population present is satisfactorily secured by the collecting nets usually employed. Consequently concentration by settling, centrifuging, or filtration is necessary for proper appraisal. The exceedingly minute material thus obtained is called ' nannoplankton ' and includes the smaller Diatoms and Peridinians, Bacteria, numerous flagellates such as Coccolithophores which may be no more than 5 microns in dimensions, and of course the tiniest animalcules.

The composition and density of planktonic vegetation at any particular place and time naturally depend upon the intensity and interaction of various factors. Among the more obvious of these are the rate of reproduction and the rate of removal of individuals by death or sometimes fusion, by consumption by other organisms, or by removal through sinking or in water-currents. There is also a dependence on the rate of growth which itself depends upon the size and type of the parent stock, upon the intensity of the light falling on the surface and reaching the particular depth, and upon the concentration and availability of the elements which are essential for plant growth and photosynthesis—in particular carbon, nitrogen, and phosphorus. Before all comes the question of available stock.

Sometimes the turbidity of the water is such that the compensation point (*see* p. 512) is reached within 5 to 10 metres of the surface, and at times the water is so depleted of certain elements, in particular combined nitrogen and phosphorus (which are taken up by the living organisms), that further development is practically dependent upon replenishment through death and decay, or importation. Paucity of certain metallic elements, particularly iron, also seems to be prone to limit phytoplanktonic growth. Thus fertility may be controlled by the availability of inorganic nutrients, and marine productivity in turn limited by the rate of supply of organic foods—as has been strikingly demonstrated by the extraordinarily increased yield of 'manured' arms of the sea. Here inorganic nutrients were added, that led to an increase in organic food in the form of phytoplankton, which in turn benefited the Fish.

As in fresh waters, replenishment of nutrients by vertical mixing currents takes place in the sea most rapidly in autumn and winter with the cooling and sinking of surface waters, so that in spring there is a relatively large supply available, and the phytoplanktonic population can 'bloom' luxuriantly. It seems that in some of the most actively productive systems of sea-water, almost every atom of phosphorus and nitrogen must be reassimilated several times each year to permit the synthesis of the total organic material observed. The most lastingly productive waters are commonly those where there is continual upwelling from the depths, such as occurs at the boundaries of oceanic currents.

Where conditions fluctuate, the phytoplanktonic crop can develop within a few days of their becoming favourable, whereas a much longer period is required for the development of zooplankton. Nevertheless, owing to animal grazing, to sinking below the lowest level at which they can photosynthesize effectively, to horizontal transport, and to 'indirect factors' such as changes of temperature (quite apart from available nutrients), phytoplanktonic populations tend to vary markedly and often rapidly. Especially is even mild grazing often extremely effective in reducing the population, so that it has been calculated that if only one plant out of every ten in a developing population is eaten, in six divisions 100 plants will produce but 3,400 individuals instead of 6,400—although a mere 413 have been consumed.

The simple cell division of most phytoplanktonic organisms is a very satisfactory and effective method of reproduction that under favourable conditions probably takes place on the average from once to twice every twenty-four hours. It has been calculated that in middle latitudes the increase in total volume of pelagic plants is of the order of 30 per cent. per diem over the year, so that this proportion could die or be removed on the average daily without reducing the plant stock. Whether or not the high latitudes are more prolific than the low ones in the matter of plankton productivity, as used to be contended but is now questioned (*see* p. 509), there seems no doubt that the total photosynthetic activity taking place in the seas, which occupy slightly over 70 per cent. of the earth's surface, is much greater than that taking place on the land-masses of the world. Actually, the average productivity of similar land and ocean *areas* appear to be roughly comparable over the year, being said to be of the order of three tons of dry material per acre, though unit *volumes* of coastal waters are usually many times more productive than those of open ocean waters.

In arctic regions there are apt to be phenomenal outbursts of Diatoms when the sea-ice melts in early summer. Such ' blooming ' may be associated with the rapid germination of spores previously locked in the ice. The population involved tends to be largely neritic, which is not surprising if we recall that the abundant nutrients and variable salinity and other conditions simulate coastal ones. The cryophytic populations developing on the surfaces of melting sea-ice were described in the last chapter, chiefly on pages 489–91, the component organisms being termed ' cryophytes '. When the ' spring ' production of Diatoms has come to a low ebb owing to marked stratification or incipient exhaustion of nutrients, Peridinians (Dinoflagellates) may take over the lead in the matter of organic production in boreal and austral waters—in particular, species of *Ceratium*. Their nutrient requirements are lower than those of Diatoms and their rate of growth is slower; they can continue to propagate in impoverished waters, besides which they have the power of locomotion and consequently of adjustment to the best available conditions. Actually, their daily increase under summer conditions is only 30 to 50 per cent., as compared with about ten times as much for some Diatoms. Somewhat similar sequences may be observed in temperate regions. Thus Fig. 171, A, shows an early summer maximum of Diatoms off the Atlantic coast of North America, and Fig. 171, B, shows the later peak of Peridinians with associated animalcules.

It should be noted that whereas a considerable number of marine Bacteria may be found in the pelagic zone associated with the plankton, they are apparently not truly planktonic but attached to other organisms. Some investigators, however, have claimed that Bacteria are present in relatively small numbers in the body of free water, for example at depths of around 5,000 metres, and to that extent must be considered planktonic. But in any case in the ocean, the main concentration of Bacteria occurs in the uppermost few millimetres of bottom-deposit (*see* below, p. 539).

Of macroscopic marine phytoplanktonic phenomena the most remarkable is the drift of certain higher Brown Algae belonging to the genus *Sargassum.* This familiar genus is predominantly tropical, fairly large, and well differentiated (Fig. 8, H). Although its members occur normally as attached littoral plants, they sometimes become detached and, with the aid of gas-filled bladders, may float far out to sea with the currents. Most benthic Algae even with floats will die in time and disintegrate under this kind of treatment, but two of the species of *Sargassum* grow exclusively (so far as is known) in this free-floating manner, though apparently they are unable to reproduce except by vegetative fragmentation. The species which thrive in this freely-floating state, *Sargassum natans* and *S. fluitans*, exhibit marked elongation of the branches as compared with the normally attached species. With some other seaweeds and animals living attached to or among their branches, they tend to aggregate in one relatively quiet part of the western Atlantic which is accordingly known as the Sargasso Sea, whose surface is largely covered by ' floating meadows ' of these so-called ' Sargasso-weeds ' or ' Gulf-weeds '. In this manner they constitute the only such extensive ' drift ' that is known or likely to occur in the world, fragments of other drifting Algae, such as detached *Fucus*, *Laminaria*, or *Macrocystis*, even though sometimes forming extensive aggregates, being rarely if ever found in a healthy state very far from their shore or ' shallow ' of origin.

## Benthic Environments and Life-Forms

The general features of the marine environment have already been described in the first part of this chapter, but we must here add some which are of particular importance to the attached plants (benthos). These factors are best treated in four groups, namely, physical, chemical, biological, and dynamic.

1. Among physical factors we have dealt in some detail with temperature and illumination, though it should be emphasized that both these can vary greatly between tide-marks and in pools and over shallow bottoms. Temperatures may even be elevated sufficiently to cause death of stenothermic Algae, at least when these are exposed for long periods by low tides, while Professor V. J. Chapman has informed the author that he has witnessed the killing of *Chondrus* at low spring tides by frost. Moreover, seasonal variations can induce 'migration' of Algae from one level to another. Thus in warm regions some of the Algae which in winter occur at high levels are found only at much lower ones in summer, while in the North, owing to the unfavourably low winter temperatures of surface waters, the upward extension of sensitive species occurs instead in summer. Such 'migration' normally takes place through young disseminules becoming established at the desired level (*cf.* p. 524). In unusually favourable circumstances, light may be sufficient to allow Algae to live at depths as great as 200 metres, a depth of 180 metres being reached by quite large numbers off the island of Minorca in the Mediterranean Sea.

Whereas on land the chemical nature of the substratum is commonly important to the rooted plants, in the sea it is its physical nature which usually matters most. For nutrients are furnished through the sea-water in which the plants are immersed, the substratum serving in most instances merely as a place of attachment. Consequently the degree of hardness, or of smoothness or, alternatively, irregularity of the surface, plays the most important role, each taxon being apt to evince some (often exclusive) preference for solid rock, smoothed boulders, gravels, sand, or mud.

Hydraulic pressure, which increases regularly with depth, appears to have little effect upon benthic Algae except in limiting the extension into deep waters of types with gas-filled bladders. Thus in the widespread Brown Alga *Ascophyllum nodosum*, although the increased pressure of unusually high tides can cause escape of gas, the thickness of the bladder-wall is a function of the depth at which these bladders develop, and an individual transported to a much lower depth loses the gas in its bladders and dies.

2. As regards chemical factors, we have dealt with the importance of variations in salinity and noted how a marked lowering thereof, as for example at the mouths of rivers or in such 'continental' seas as the Baltic, is commonly accompanied by marked changes in the algal flora and vegetation. Thus the numbers of species of

benthic Green, Brown, and Red Algae are greatly reduced by the disappearance of stenohaline types, as is the general luxuriance of growth; moreover some of the persisting Brown Algae, particularly, may take on characteristic dwarf forms. On the other hand the remarkably euryhaline Green Alga *Enteromorpha intestinalis*, which is widely familiar in fresh and brackish waters as well as in normal sea-water and brine, is reported to undergo optimum development in diluted sea-water, though it has been suggested that this may be only where there is an influx of nutrient materials such as those contained in sewage. Also liable to be subjected to marked variations in salinity—as well as in temperature, degree of desiccation, and so forth—are the littoral Algae that are exposed to the air for varying periods between tide-marks or that grow in small tidal pools. As might be expected in view of the upward or downward salinity-trends which these pools have to undergo as a result of evaporation, or of rains and the influx of freshwater streams, respectively, these littoral Algae have been demonstrated to display greater tolerance to variations in osmotic pressure than do Algae growing below low-tide mark. In addition to the *Enteromorpha*, *Fucus ceranoides* and species of *Ulva* are known to be widely euryhaline.

In reaction, sea-water is somewhat alkaline, owing to most of its contained carbon dioxide being combined in the form of carbonates and bicarbonates and to the removal, by plants during photosynthesis, of the (acidic) carbon dioxide formed on dissociation of these carbonates and bicarbonates. Especially in tidal pools is the alkalinity apt to be marked, a pH of as much as 10 being sometimes reached after several hours' exposure by the tide. Although most Algae will tolerate a pH of up to at least 9, pH 10 appears to be too high a degree of alkalinity for many 'stenoionic' species (*i.e.* those which are narrow in their tolerance of changes in the relative abundance of free acidic or basic ions), and it has been contended that this is why such Green Algae as *Ulva*, having high photosynthetic rates, are prone to oust the frailer types, such as many Red Algae. However, it should be remembered that evaporation raises the salinity as well as the alkalinity, and so it seems possible that the reason may be rather the failure of the frailer types to respond to increases in the osmotic pressure of the medium.

It has also been suggested that the low concentrations at which saturation of oxygen is attained in warm waters may have some correlation with the less profuse development of Algae in many tropical as compared with cold waters. However, according to

Professor V. J. Chapman (*in litt.*), 'The evidence suggests that it is a matter of the relative ratio between photosynthesis and respiration. In warm waters these are nearly equal and hence there is never a great development. At lower temperatures the respiration rate drops more rapidly than photosynthesis, so that there is a greater excess of photosynthesis over respiration and hence greater growth.' It is to be expected that the nitrate and phosphate content, which are known often to control phytoplanktonic development, have some influence also on benthic Algae ; certainly many of these, such as *Prasiola* on land, are greatly favoured, from the high-arctic regions southwards, by manuring, etc.

3. Among biological factors the successional tendencies are notable, as exhibited in the repopulation of denuded rock surfaces. Here a rapid development of *Enteromorpha* may precede the attachment of eggs of Bladder Wrack (*Fucus vesiculosus*) and, apparently, facilitate the development of young plants of the latter, which later may oust the *Enteromorpha*. Again, the building up of silty banks is often aided by algal growth fostering deposition.

Also important may be the relationships between epiphytic Algae in the sea and the ' hosts ' on which they grow. Thus the epiphyte is often protected by the host against rough seas or excessive illumination ; or the host may benefit from protection provided by the epiphyte ; or the load of epiphytes may be too great and cause the host to be torn away from its point of attachment. In many cases of widely different affinity the epiphyte is reduced to a disk-like form completely adnate to the host, while some epiphytes actually penetrate the host tissues, such penetration usually being accompanied by some degree of parasitism. Much the same relationship exists between many Algae and marine animals, apparently often resulting in symbiosis. Again, browsing by marine animals such as Molluscs—and, in some parts of the world, harvesting by Man—may have a noticeable effect on the algal or other marine vegetation, and may even cause the disappearance of particular species from some localities. Finally, diseases can have much the same effect—as in the case of the ' wasting disease ' of Eel-grass (*Zostera*) off many northern shores.

The migration of Algae into deeper or shallower water at different seasons is chiefly manifested by quick-growing species having more or less continuous reproduction, following which the sporelings only survive and grow in the most favourable zone for the particular time of year.

4. What may be termed dynamic factors tend to be most effective about shores or in shallow waters and consequently to affect the marine benthos quite markedly. Examples are turbulence, due to waves and currents, and emersion, due to variations in water-level particularly as induced by tides. The importance of wave action has already been implied, and is illustrated by the often very different algal flora and vegetation developed on exposed capes and in sheltered bays. The effects are complex but appear to be primarily mechanical, in that the fixation of spores or persistence of fragile Algae is

FIG. 172.—*Postelsia palmaeformis*. Note the strong but flexible axes which are resistant to surf. (× about $\frac{1}{7}$.) (Courtesy of the National Museum of Canada.)

prevented on heavily battered rocks, whereas an absence of turbulence in sheltered situations leads to the deposition of sediment which constitutes an obstacle to the establishment of some Algae. Others, however, are favoured by this muddy substratum; and calm conditions may allow a heating of the water which favours many Algae but leads to the disappearance of some stenothermic species. Some types, such as the Bladder Wrack, when growing in exposed situations may show characteristic features enabling them to resist the tearing action of the waves, while others, such as the surf-loving *Postelsia palmaeformis* (Fig. 172) of the Pacific coast of North America, are favoured by exposure, being at best stunted in sheltered situations.

Particularly marked is the zonation of Algae living in the intertidal belt, on shores that are alternately left uncovered by the ebbing tide and reflooded by the flow. Thus the Algae are regularly emersed and submersed, their conditions of life being subject to drastic fluctuations. Owing to variation in the amplitude of the tides themselves, there are found, above the low-water mark of the lowest spring tides, practically all temporal degrees of emersion ; these take a leading part in determining the localization, at levels where each finds favourable conditions, of different groups of shore Algae. Whereas the Algae of permanently submerged zones below low spring tide-mark are liable to die after short exposure to the air or to diluted sea-water, those living between tide-marks are more resistant, being often able to withstand emergence for many days on end, while some (especially among Blue-green Algae) can lose so much of their water as to become brittle without injury. Again, certain species die if they are kept constantly submerged ; an example is *Pelvetia canaliculata*, which passes most of its life in the air. Yet others are protected by growing among dense mats of larger Algae (such as species of *Fucus*). These Algae exposed to emersion, however, in general have to withstand considerable degrees of desiccation, and, in addition, marked changes in salinity and temperature. It is apparently a combination of these varying factors that produce, on sea-shores, the characteristic zonations in more or less regular horizontal bands of different Algae at particular levels which, however, may vary according to the locality, degree of shelter, and so on. As pointed out by Mr. F. T. Walker (*in litt.*), quantitative variation may be not only seasonal and with depth but also cyclic, over periods of years, while at least for Laminariaceae in Scotland ' decrease in seaweed density has been found to be more the result of a reduction in the number of plants per unit area than of the weight of individual plants '.

Various delimitations and systems of nomenclature have been proposed for the main recognizable zones or belts inhabited by benthic marine Algae. These may be usefully designated, in line with our earlier subdivision of the ocean's margin (Fig. 170), as follows: (1) *Supralittoral zone*, lying between the upper limit of marine vegetation and the high-water mark of ordinary spring tides, the plants being bathed in sea-water only during storms or unusually high or equinox tides, and in Europe characteristically including the Lichen *Verrucaria maura* which may form a continuous black coating on the rocks. (2) *Eulittoral zone*, often called simply ' the littoral ', corresponding to the part of the shore undergoing more or less regular emersion and submersion by tides or surf. This zone varies in width from shores with no noticeable tides, where it includes only the band regularly reached by surf, to those with wide tidal amplitude, where various ecological conditions develop at different levels and it is necessary to subdivide it into ' horizons ' or ' girdles ' (*see* below). (3) *Upper sublittoral zone*, varying with the location but characteristically extending approximately 20 metres downwards from the low-water mark of ordinary spring tides to the lower limit of abundant major benthic vegetation—*i.e.* to where the light-intensity is markedly reduced and where there is little disturbance of the water or rapid variation in the temperature. In temperate regions almost all the Laminariaceae live in this zone ; indeed below it most of the light-demanding species thin out and it is chiefly those characteristic of deeper waters which persist. (4) *Lower sublittoral zone*, extending from the lower limit of the upper sublittoral zone down to the lower limit of at all plentiful benthic vegetation (usually 40–60 metres in total depth), and characterized by relatively constant temperature and other conditions, and weak illumination. (5) *Infralittoral zone*, extending from the lower limit of at all plentiful benthic vegetation right down to the lower limit of photosynthesis.

It may be noted that different belts or girdles of vegetation are commonly discernible within the above main zones, being often designated and named separately, and that it is sometimes useful to recognize, above all the rest, an *adlittoral zone* of constant emersion characterized by halophytes living a normal aerial life but able to endure exceptional waves and sprays during storms. The salt is concentrated by evaporation and may damage or deform ordinary land vegetation. The adlittoral zone, and zones 3 and 4, are not distinguished in the accompanying diagram (Fig. 170).

Gymnosperms, Pteridophytes, and Bryophytes do not live in the sea, and although some Angiosperms occur there, and a greater number of Fungi and Schizophytes, the vast bulk of marine plant-life is made up of Algae of extremely numerous and diverse types. Much as the Raunkiaer system of life-forms (that was outlined, with modifications, in Chapter III) may be useful to give some idea of the physiognomic composition of a terrestrial flora when actual floristic knowledge is lacking, so may a more recently proposed system of biological types of Algae be of service where marine flora is concerned.

In this system the first three of the following (main) categories are annual and the remainder are perennial: *ephemerophyceae* (*e.g. Enteromorpha*), being found throughout the year but often forming several generations; *eclipsiophyceae* (*e.g. Nereia*), being well developed during only one part of the year and passing the remainder as a microscopic vegetative form; *hypnophyceae* (*e.g. Dudresnaya*), differing from these last in that they pass the unfavourable season in a resting stage; *phanerophyceae* (*e.g. Fucus vesiculosus*), having the 'frond' perennial and erect; *chamaephyceae* (*e.g. Lithophyllum*), having the 'frond' reduced to a crust; *hemiphanerophyceae* (*e.g. Sargassum*), having only a part of the erect 'frond' persisting for several years; and *hemicryptophyceae* (*e.g. Acetabularia*), having only the basal creeping portion of the 'frond' persisting.

It is also possible, and sometimes useful, to categorize marine Algae according to their particular ecological needs (such as types living in pounding surf) or gross morphological characteristics (such as encrusting types) or the nature of their substratum (such as *epiliths* attached to rocks, or *pelophiles* growing on mud). They may furthermore be divided according to their temperature requirements into eurytherms and stenotherms, the latter being composed of micro-, meso-, and mega-thermic species characteristic of low, medium, and high temperatures, respectively, while much the same can be done in connection with the factors of illumination and salinity. Finally, not only do Algae show marked periodicity, especially in regions where seasonal changes are pronounced, but the time and duration of development of a species may be different in different parts of the world, while some types which in boreal regions persist throughout the year develop only in winter and spring farther south.

It should be noted that the plants composing the marine benthos are very largely *lithophytes*, attached to rocks or boulders. The more massive forms are fixed to the substratum by strong adhesive disks (in Fucaceae) or crampons (in Laminariaceae), small forms usually having simpler devices. The number of species flourishing on sandy or muddy bottoms is often very limited, such substrata, at least in agitated water, commonly representing virtual desert so far as benthic Algae are concerned, though in calm and shallow bays they may be occupied by Eel-grasses (*Zostera* spp.), or in warm regions sometimes by other rooted Angiosperms or attached Green Algae. The few Algae that flourish in such situations are usually provided with root-like organs of attachment which penetrate the substratum.

## Benthos

Although only about 2 per cent. of the sea area of the world is shallow enough to be occupied by benthic plants, the vegetation-types of the eulittoral and sublittoral are much the most striking and studied of all to which the term marine can be properly applied. Numerous books and papers describe these zones in more or less detail for different parts of the world, so a brief outline of the vegetation will suffice for each of the four main regions, viz., tropical, warm-temperate, cool-temperate, and polar.

1. The marine vegetation of tropical seas is apt to be less luxuriant than that of cooler regions, though some groups of Monocotyledons and Green Algae are largely restricted to warm waters, where reef-Algae may show periodic correlation with the monsoons. Apart from such manifestations as the Sargasso Sea which are, rather, planktonic, and were accordingly treated above as such, Brown Algae tend to be relatively poorly represented in tropical seas whereas Red and Green Algae are abundant. Although Red Algae are particularly characteristic of the sublittoral zone, certain species of this group often form a thick coating of a dirty violet colour on the roots and stem-bases of the mangrove-swamp dominants which form such a characteristic feature of the eulittoral vegetation of tropical shores ; but mangroves, being mainly aerial, were dealt with in Chapter XIV. Small Green Algae also with low light requirements may form a characteristic investment on the soft mud, which is rich in organic material, between the roots of the dominant mangrove trees. In a few instances Brown Algae have been reported to form fairly well-developed littoral communities in the tropics.

Unlike the situation in colder seas where the unstabilized bottoms are often devoid of macroscopic vegetation, the eulittoral and sublittoral in some tropical regions may have sand or gravel beds populated by numerous Green Algae. These may even be found in deep water, many being strongly calcified and in addition accumulating much sediment. Also forming extensive communities in some places are marine Monocotyledons such as species of *Thalassia* and *Cymodocea* which may dominate characteristic consociations or associations down to a depth of some 30 metres. In many parts of the Pacific Ocean the so-called ' coral-reefs ' are largely built up by calcareous Algae—in particular by *Porolithon onkodes*. Such virtually tide-less seas as the Caribbean naturally have practically no inter-tidal vegetation or girdling of Algae, the communities near the surface being determined in each place very largely by the type of substratum.

2. In warm-temperate regions the marine benthic vegetation is very various in different areas such as the Mediterranean and the seas of southernmost Africa and Australia, the differences being supposedly due largely to historical causes. The absence or paucity of *Fucus* and *Laminaria* may give the vegetation a very different aspect from that of most northern seas. In parts of the Mediterranean where the high temperatures of the air and absence of appreciable tides result in reduction of the littoral vegetation, Eel-grasses (*Zostera* spp.) may grow densely in the upper sublittoral where the bottom is muddy. They are accompanied by epiphytic and other Algae, while near-by sandy bottoms may be largely covered with 'meadows' of *Posidonia oceanica*, also a Monocotyledon, as deep down as 60 metres. At 80–100 metres only isolated plants of the *Posidonia* occur, though algal vegetation may still be luxuriant at a depth of 120–130 metres, and, in exceptionally clear water, fair numbers of Algae may persist to at least 180 metres, or, in some cases, to 200 metres.

In rocky places in the Mediterranean the supralittoral zone is characterized by a dark girdle of the Lichen *Verrucaria maura*, or of various Cyanophyceae where the substratum is calcareous, while eulittoral rocks may support a fine girdle of *Rissoella verruculosa* which, though a Red Alga, somewhat resembles the brown Wracks of more northerly shores. The lithophytic vegetation of the sublittoral zones is rather various and rich in different forms, showing distinctions occasioned by differences in illumination—chiefly at different depths but also to some extent according to shadows cast by irregularities of the coast. Thus the shade-species predominating in the depths are chiefly Red Algae, such as species of *Lithothamnium*, while the Brown Algae, such as species of *Cystoseira*, prefer brighter areas, and some of the Green Algae, such as *Acetabularia acetabula* (*A. mediterranea*), favour the very brightest spots. The Red Algae of well-lit places are usually dull in colour; at the other extreme are species so sensitive to light that they are restricted to shaded areas even at considerable depths. In any case the active vegetative season in the Mediterranean largely coincides, near the surface, with the winter and spring, whereas in deeper water the chief activity occurs in the summer and autumn. During early summer, Brown Algae may even prevail over Red Algae in deep water, whereas at other seasons Red Algae predominate in poorly-lighted situations. Some species even exist in different winter- and summer-forms. Moreover, exposed habitats that support luxuriant vegetation during winter may be almost barren in summer.

In South Africa the girdles distinguishable in the eulittoral are, uppermost, of *Porphyra capensis* which in places extends from the upper limit to mid-tide level. Below this is often a 'bare zone' that may be largely devoid of macroscopic vegetation, succeeded by a girdle formed of an association of two species of *Chaetangium* and, farther down, by two or three other characteristic girdles. The sublittoral is often dominated by various Laminariales.

3. The algal vegetation of cool-temperate seas is tolerably well-known and often markedly diverse even in such closely adjacent bodies of water as the North Sea and the Baltic, the former of which is far more productive than the latter. The variation seems to be in accordance with differences in the tides and salinity, which in the North Sea are both very considerable, whereas in the Baltic both are weak, so that its Algae are poor in species and development. Yet in both instances, as in most cool-temperate seas, Brown Algae predominate. They are chiefly represented by species of *Fucus* and *Laminaria* or their allies, though many smaller types also abound. Red Algae are also represented by numerous types, but Green Algae offer less variety, and the only at all widespread marine Angiosperms are Eel-grasses. The eulittoral is much wider in the North Sea than in the Baltic, and in some places bears more abundant vegetation than does the sublittoral, though this is not the case in Scotland (according to Mr. F. T. Walker *in litt.*). Actually, in the Baltic Sea most of the marginal vegetation is commonly in the sublittoral, as the tides are weak and ice frequently grinds against the upper shores which are thereby rendered inhospitable for macroscopic plants.

In most exposed situations away from salt-marshes in cool-temperate seas, macroscopic vegetation in the eulittoral is virtually limited to rocky and bouldery substrata, any shingly, sandy, or muddy beaches being largely barren. This is not, however, necessarily the case low down, or, particularly, in some estuaries and sheltered creeks, where plentiful between-tides vegetation may develop even on 'soft' bottoms. Unlike the situation in warm-temperate regions, in cool-temperate seas the algal vegetation of winter tends to be poorer than that of summer, which for most species is the main period of vegetative activity in the boreal and austral regions (though of course involving antithetic times of the year in the northern and southern hemispheres). Many perennial types, however, reserve their main reproductive activity for winter, a few, such as species of *Fucus*, being in this respect independent of the season, while again relatively few, such as species of the Rhodophycean genus *Polysiphonia*, reproduce mainly in summer. Particularly striking differences between winter and summer states are exhibited by those types which shed their assimilating ' fronds ' at the beginning of the cold season, the frondless residue being often covered with reproductive organs. Others, such as many Laminariales, have an intercalary zone of growth producing a new ' frond ', the old one being cast off as a whole in the spring : this commonly happens at about the same time to all the representatives of a species in a particular region.

The most characteristic sequence on open shores and, for example, in the English Channel, shows a supralittoral zone formed for the most part by Lichens, with girdles of yellow or orange *Xanthoria parietina* and *Caloplaca marina* above, and of blackish *Verrucaria maura* below. The eulittoral is characterized by a series of girdles formed largely by individual Brown Algae—for example, successively from top to bottom, by *Pelvetia canaliculata*, *Fucus spiralis*, *F. vesiculosus*, and *F. serratus*. Lower down, uncovered at most only by the lowest spring tides and forming the upper sublittoral, are girdles of large Kelps (Laminariales). Commonly *Laminaria digitata* is dominant near low-water mark and *L. cloustonii* farther down, or *L. saccharina* may replace the latter where the substratum is more or less sandy. To these normal girdles which have analogies elsewhere, as for example on the Atlantic coast of North America, various facultative ones may be added ; nor is there any exact correlation with tidal level, for, especially on strongly exposed rocks, wave action induces a displacement upwards of the upper girdles to a height roughly corresponding with that attained by the waves.

In some circumstances, various Green Algae can largely take the place of the characteristic tidal girdles of Brown Algae. Ecological factors can also favour the presence of quite a range of other algal communities that are not restricted to such narrow bands and definite levels along the coasts : such are, particularly, the communities of tidal pools and grottoes, and of local run-off areas. Even sandy and muddy shores may be well populated in the upper sublittoral by Eel-grasses accompanied by characteristic epiphytic

Algae. In the lower sublittoral belt, down to some 30 or more metres, gravelly or coarse sandy bottoms are characterized by an abundance of branched and unattached *Lithothamnium calcareum*. Fig. 173 depicts a scene near the base of the girdles of Fuci on a rocky part of the Atlantic coast of temperate North America, showing some tufted Red Algae and large Kelps (Laminariales) at the lower levels, and Fig. 174 is a drawing of a typical Kelp.

FIG. 173.—Scene at low tide on a rocky sea-shore of the eastern United States. Above are seen luxuriant Wracks (Rockweeds, species of *Fucus*), and below are a tufted Red Alga and some large Kelps (Laminariales). (Courtesy of Chicago Museum of Natural History.)

On muddy tidal flats or shallow bottoms in sheltered situations, Blue-green Algae often form a delicate investment which binds the surface, while some forms of *Fucus* can live merely resting on mud without being attached. Often they are partly embedded in the surface and, with some other forms including various Green Algae and halophytic terrestrial Angiosperms, favour estuaries where salinity and other conditions vary markedly, such vegetation-types merging into those of salt-marshes (*see* Chapter XII). The vegetation of inland saline waters ranging from saturated brine to slightly brackish lagoons, etc., was mentioned in Chapter XV.

The Pacific Ocean supports a widely different benthic algal vegetation from the Atlantic, so that the Pacific coast of North America is very different in this respect from the Atlantic coast. For although in the Pacific the eulittoral may be dominated by species of *Fucus* (as well as of *Egregia*), the lowest portion of this zone is characterized by the unique laminarian *Postelsia palmaeformis*

FIG. 174.—A characteristic Kelp, *Alaria dolichorhachis* ($\times \frac{1}{6}$). (After Kjellman.)

(Fig. 172) on rocks exposed to heavy surf, while the sublittoral contains numerous other Laminariales, often of peculiar form and great size. Examples of these are *Macrocystis pyrifera* (Fig. 175) and *Nereocystis*, which are commonly attached on rather deep bottoms 10–30 metres down, and may thus be considered as extending the upper sublittoral downwards. However, they possess such a very long ' stalk ' that the fronds, borne at the summit and often accompanied by air-bladders, can spread out on the surface of the water even at high tide. Such plants thus project their upper parts into the ecological sphere which is most favourable especially in the all-important matter of illumination.

In southern South America and the less frigid of the austral islands, there may be recognized in the eulittoral an uppermost girdle of various drought-resistant Algae, a middle-to-lower one of surf-resistant Red Algae or, in less exposed situations, of various Green and Brown Algae, and a lower surf-girdle of large Brown Algae such as *Durvillea antarctica.* Large Laminariales such as *Macrocystis pyrifera,* and crustose and other Red Algae, together characterize the sublittoral. On the southernmost Australian and New Zealand coasts the benthic vegetation corresponds for the most part to that of southern South America, though Eel-grasses may abound where the bottoms are sandy or muddy. Thus the same

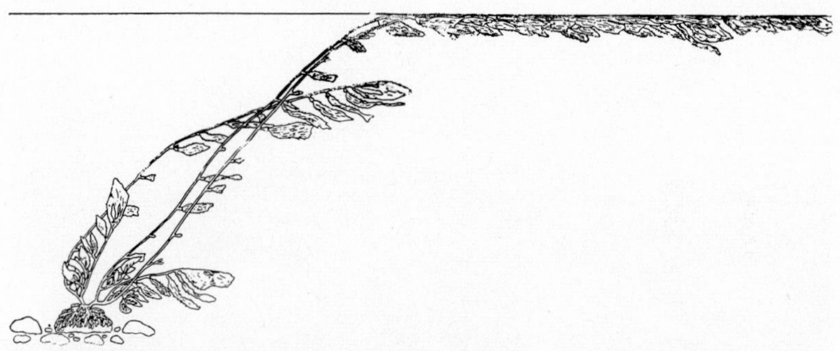

FIG. 175.—A giant Pacific Kelp, *Macrocystis pyrifera.* (× about $\frac{1}{180}$.) (After Skottsberg.)

*Durvillea* is a characteristic component of the flora, and the same *Macrocystis* reaches a reported 60 metres in length (according to recent accounts; old reports that it attains much greater lengths have not been substantiated). It is interesting to note that a Lichen determined and widely cited as *Verrucaria maura,* which characterizes the supralittoral belt of so many shores in the northern hemisphere, plays a similar role in South America and New Zealand.

4. In arctic seas the algal flora is rather limited but the vegetation is sometimes luxuriant. Indeed, in the Arctic and Antarctic it is chiefly in the sea that life abounds, the plant and animal communities on land being of relatively poor development. Particularly robust and abundant are some of the gregarious Brown Algae, such as species of *Laminaria* and *Fucus,* although many Red and some Green Algae usually occur in addition. The vegetation is largely limited to rocky and bouldery substrata, sandy and muddy ones being usually devoid of major growths except in a few situations towards the southern extremity of the Arctic where the common Eel-grass (*Zostera marina*) may form fair 'beds'.

Even on the most rugged rocky shores in the Arctic and much of the Subarctic, the eulittoral zone is poorly vegetated in exposed situations owing to the rigours of the climate and particularly to the tearing and grinding of ice, which tides and breakers keep in motion when once it has broken up in early summer. Thus the eulittoral and immediately adjacent sublittoral tend to be ' polished ' by ice-floes and -pups or splinters of ice which waves and currents carry against exposed shores through much of the growing-season.

FIG. 176.—An arctic foreshore photographed from near low-tide mark, showing eulittoral boulders with sides covered by Brown Algae (chiefly Bladder Wrack, *Fucus vesiculosus*), whereas their exposed upper surfaces have been kept bare by ice-action. Pangnirtung, Cumberland Sound, Baffin Island.

On the other hand in sheltered situations, including bays and the interior (landward) shores of near-by islands, and even the sides of boulders (Fig. 176), where there is protection from the ice, species of *Fucus* may form a luxuriant investment—except in the very Far North where their growth tends to be poor.

It is, however, in the middle and lower sublittoral, out of reach of floe ice and chiefly at depths of 3–25 metres, that benthic plant life really flourishes in the Arctic—provided the bottom is hard. Here giant Laminariales may form extensive ' beds ', species of *Alaria* and

*Agarum* as well as of *Laminaria* abounding, associated with Red Algae such as species of *Lithothamnium* and *Lithophyllum*, and often beset with epiphytes. Even on desolate Akpatok Island in Ungava Bay the present writer has measured specimens of *Laminaria longicruris* up to 47 feet (14·3 metres) in length, and doubtless longer ones occur in the great off-shore beds. Such luxuriant algal vegetation which survives the arctic ice may almost be compared with the Pacific *Macrocystis* that ranges nearly to the tropics. Although the lower limit of the photic region is often placed at only about 36–40 metres in the Arctic, even off far-northern Spitsbergen *Delesseria sinuosa* has been dredged ' quite fresh ' from as deep down as 155 metres and *Ptilota pectinata* has been brought up from a reported 274 metres. Presumably these were detached specimens; but it may be noted that vegetation of *Phycodrys* and *Pantoneura* has been reported from depths down to 118 metres off the indubitably arctic Jan Mayen Island.

The periodicity of arctic Algae appears to be much like that of cool-temperate ones, and indeed many species are common to both regions. However, in conformity with the virtual absence of annuals among the higher plants on most areas of arctic land, none at least of the more massive types of Algae is supposed to be able to complete its cycle of development in less than a year in the Arctic. Also in conformity with the situation in cool-temperate seas, it seems that vegetative activity prevails in summer and reproductive activity in winter for types growing well below low-tide mark, even though the temperature is commonly from $-1°$ to $-2°$ C. during the latter season when darkness largely prevails. Indeed it has been claimed that the richest local algal vegetation may occur at depths where the temperature does not rise above 0° C. at any time of the year.

Owing in part to differences in such conditions as those of temperature and salinity, and in part to factors not yet understood, different arctic seas in spite of their connection with one another are apt to possess distinct algal floras, the dominant Laminariales, for example, being often different in Spitsbergen, Siberia, and arctic America. Beyond this, the benthic flora and vegetation tend to be far poorer in waters of low salinity, such as occur near the heads of fiords into which large streams flow, in Hudson Bay, and off the coast of parts of Siberia near the mouths of great rivers, than they are in waters of more normal marine salinity.

In the Antarctic, again, the vegetation of the eulittoral zone is often very poorly developed because of exposure and ice, which tears plants from the rocks or otherwise prevents them from developing properly. Consequently the types occurring are mostly small, though representatives of Green and Red as well as Brown Algae commonly occur —including, particularly, crustose Corallinaceae. Only these and other calcareous Algae seem to be unaffected by the almost constant surf and rubbing ice-floes of open coasts, though in sheltered pools, lagoons, and coves, the vegetation may be quite luxuriant even in the eulittoral. The sublittoral is again characterized by gregarious Brown Algae of substantial size, commonly including species of *Desmarestia* and *Cystosphaera*, down to a depth of some 30–50 metres, with usually an assortment of associated Red Algae. The larger species among the Brown Algae include *Lessonia simulans* up to $5\frac{1}{2}$ metres long, and the general richness is said to be not inferior to that of the arctic sublittoral. Although doubtless some Red Algae, particularly, grow at greater depths, the examples dredged from hundreds of metres down were evidently not growing there, drifting Algae being commonly encountered in the Antarctic as elsewhere.

As no large rivers exist in the Antarctic, the discharge being chiefly in the form of icebergs which float far before melting appreciably, there is little freshening of the water near the coasts in the manner which apparently impoverishes the algal flora of many boreal seas. On the other hand in both the Arctic and Antarctic, wherever the inland-ice or glaciers extend down and calve into the sea, no eulittoral vegetation can exist and even sublittoral Algae are liable to be injured. Thus vegetation here, and on shores invested with shelf-ice, is chiefly found about stretches of beach that are free from ice in summer. Even on such beaches there is a freezing more or less 'solid' in winter—which does not, however, preclude the existence of large Algae.

## Aphotic Bottoms

The average depth of the oceans being computed at nearly 4,000 metres, most areas of sea-floor are deep and dark, being reached, if by any daylight at all, only by an insufficient amount of it to allow the normal growth of benthic Algae. Phosphorescence is entirely inadequate. Such Algae as have been dredged up on occasion from the aphotic zone have drifted there and, being unable to photosynthesize, will not long persist. Nevertheless, these ocean depths have their flora of saprophytes, parasites, and chemosynthetic organisms, that form vegetation of a sort. This deep-sea-floor vegetation is mainly composed of Bacteria, which occur in great abundance in the upper layers of bottom sediments and, although of course microscopic and scarcely evident in their physical effect, are believed to play significant roles in determining the character of the deposits. Thus they form humus and precipitate compounds of calcium, iron, and manganese. They are mostly motile rods and comma-shaped forms, and are much more often coloured but less frequently spore-forming than is the case with terrestrial types.

The greatest numbers of marine Bacteria have been found in coastal waters where life is most prolific. In the upper waters, and especially within the uppermost 50 metres, there are often a considerable number attached to floating organisms and other particulate matter; but the main concentration is on the bottom—especially just below the mud-water interface. Here as many as an estimated 420,000,000 cells per gram of wet mud have been observed. More or less teeming populations of this nature appear to be practically world-wide, marine Bacteria being capable of development at unusually low temperatures, and ocean depths being relatively stable and not too low in this respect. Thus even in the Arctic Ocean, Bacteria in great numbers may be responsible for the colours of bottom deposits, including those at very considerable depths, and it has been estimated that at latitude 82° 42′ N. in the North Polar Basin there are from $3\frac{1}{2}$ to 7 tons of bacterial matter per cubic kilometre of sea water, while farther south, in Barents Sea, the uppermost 4 cm. of bottom mud are estimated to contain 20 gm. of Bacteria per square metre.

The presence of numerous saprophytic Bacteria attached to the planktonic organisms of the uppermost layers of the ocean, whether or not such Bacteria be considered actually planktonic, results in prompt decomposition of much of the dead material before it can sink to great depths, it being claimed that a considerable proportion of the mineral nutrients are returned to the water within or a little below the euphotic zone. Nevertheless sufficient elaborated material reaches even very deep ocean beds to support a teeming population of, particularly, animals and Bacteria. The Bacteria are chiefly found in a thin layer of surface ooze in which is concentrated a large proportion of the organic detritus—dead bodies and parts thereof—which is constantly sinking and supplying food for them as well as for competing animals. These bottom Bacteria are in general more numerous in fine than coarse deposits, and occur principally near the surface of such deposits. Thus although viable cells have been recovered from a depth of more than 3·5 metres below the surface of marine sediments, their numbers rapidly decrease below the first few millimetres from the interface.

### Further Consideration

There is still no single work adequately covering the topics discussed in the above chapter, although further useful details are to be found in the appropriate parts (almost always obvious from their headings) of such books as those of V. J. Chapman and of G. M. Smith (ed.) cited at the end of Chapter XV. Particularly valuable for accounts of general conditions and phenomena in seas is H. U. Sverdrup, M. W. Johnson, & R. H. Fleming's *The Oceans : their Physics, Chemistry, and General Biology* (Prentice-Hall, New York, pp. x + 1087, 1942), while the 'third' edition of Schimper's *Pflanzengeographie auf physiologischer Grundlage*, revised by F. C. von Faber (Fischer, Jena, vol. II, 1935), gives on pages 1447–98 accounts and illustrations of many of the communities involved.

The individual Algae concerned are usually treated in the volumes of Fritsch cited at the end of Chapter II, and in F. Oltmanns's *Morphologie und Biologie der Algen*, second edition (Fischer, Jena, especially vol. III, pp. vii + 558, 1923), while the marine vegetation of different oceans and stations is described in various works too numerous to mention but often selectively cited in one or more of the above books.

# Chapter XVII

# LANDSCAPES AND VEGETATION

Man's handiwork—as, for example, in the maintenance of particular types of forest or in their clearance to form arable or grass lands—often reveals the potentialities, or even directly demonstrates the productive capacity, of particular areas. Thus the Hazel coppice with Pedunculate Oak 'standards' developed so commonly on heavy soils in England is, when cleared, normally suitable for Wheat, as is much of the mixed deciduous woodland of New England. This is well known to local inhabitants who seek out such terrain. On the other hand, the acidic heathlands found in many areas on both sides of the North Atlantic tend to be too poor for the growth of other than the most meagre of crops, being generally best given over to pasturage. These two examples also illustrate two of the main divisions of landscape—namely, those which are largely forested and those which are not.

Outside of the polar, high-alpine, and desert regions, there are few major land areas in the world that are not substantially covered by plants, or where plants do not 'form the chief embellishment'. Consequently the vegetation largely characterizes the landscape locally, and, being made up of different plants having different requirements and ranges, affords a valuable field of study for interpreting landscapes and predicting the best uses to which various areas may be put.

## Landscapes and Component Landforms

In spite of the general importance of vegetation almost everywhere in the world, the stage for its display, so to speak, is set by the local conformation of the surface of the earth, which exhibits various so-called 'landforms'. These last may be subdivided into constructional and destructional categories.

Constructional landforms of the first order are the continents and ocean basins, and, of the second order, plains (of horizontal structure and low relief), plateaux (of horizontal structure but high relief), mountains (of variously disturbed structure), and volcanoes (of conical structure). The cognate landscapes of these forms of the second order are familiar to us all, at least from illustrations. The vegetation which tends to clothe them normally occupies a secondary, dependent position in the hierarchy of nature. Moreover it is so general in the case of continental plains and plateaux, and so bound up with local features and conditions on mountains, etc., that it would seem in the former instance to be pointless and in the latter fruitless to attempt to describe it here. For plains and plateaux generally have their rocks horizontally-bedded, with their deposits or even igneous extrusions in flat layers, imposing an over-all similarity of conditions and attendant vegetation; contrastingly on mountains the variability is so extreme as to defy brief description.

Far more numerous and liable to be dependent upon vegetational development are the landforms of the third order—the so-called destructional ones. These are produced by the agents of erosion working on the constructional forms, their characteristics being determined in part by the erosional agent and in part by the constructional landform involved. Some of these features, such as river valleys, are produced directly by erosion, the removal of material; others, such as river deltas, are the result of the importation and deposition of sediment; still others, such as natural bridges, are residual, being left after the surrounding material has been removed. Each and every one of these landforms tends to have its own characteristic appearance and to contribute to the various types of landscapes, which indeed are primarily made up of mixed landforms of the second and third orders. Secondarily, they are for the most part veneered with vegetation, which of course varies according to local climatic and other conditions, but nevetheless is often widely comparable and sometimes actually characteristic of a particular landform even throughout regions of very different climate. Thus sand-dunes tend to be colonized by similar, coarse, binding Grasses all the way from the Arctic to the tropics.

As landscapes are primarily made up of various and variously aggregated landforms, each of which indicates much of what has gone on before and also of what may logically be expected to follow—whether naturally or as a result of enlightened disturbance by Man—their study is of both academic interest and applicational value. This interest stems from the manner in which the earth scientist can, from appropriate investigation of the landforms, often tell us much regarding the past history of an area, while the value of such studies is appreciated when, as is often the case, potentialities for future development emerge. As an example of an easily recognized feature we may consider an *esker*, the elongated ridge of gravelly material that is often left after the disappearance of an ice-sheet. The presence of a well-formed esker indicates not only that the area was glaciated in the past but also that the glaciation was of the over-all, ' continental ' type and that the ice was locally stagnant for a considerable time. Knowing that an esker is formed of assorted gravel or sand, we can tell at a glance that it will afford an abundance of good building or road-making material as well as good drainage, though there will probably be plentiful water and fertile outwash plains nearby. An ecologist could probably go farther, and tell us, for example, even if the esker is covered with forest, whether it could be converted into productive pasturage.

## Landforms and Plant Life

It will be appropriate at this point to consider in turn the various destructional landforms that are most common or important and, at the same time, their more characteristic forms of plant life. This consideration may conveniently be given under the headings of the chief agents of erosion, which are *streams*, *glaciers*, *ground-water*, *winds*, and *waves* and *currents*. Each resultant structural group may then be subdivided into (*a*) erosional, (*b*) depositional, and (*c*) residual, landforms or minor features. As already suggested above, the vegetational features of constructional landforms such as plains, plateaux, and mountains tend to be too general (or, in the case of mountains, comparably variable in different instances) to be distinctive and pertinent in this connection, being moreover already considered in our treatment of the main climatic belts of the world.

Erosional features made by streams include, besides *peneplanes* which are too generalized for specific vegetational characterization, various kinds of *valleys* and *gorges*. These, being more sheltered and often much lower than the surrounding uplands, tend to support more luxuriant vegetation. Indeed many plants, for one reason or another, are restricted in a particular region to valley sides or eroded bottoms, and much the same may be the case with whole plant communities—including some of the most important to mankind. Thus, near the northern limit of arborescent growth, trees are largely or entirely restricted to valleys—for example in northern Alaska, Labrador, and Lapland—as they are also in many arid regions where watercourses alone afford sufficient moisture for their growth. Besides the more open and mature valleys, streams may cut narrower *gullies*, *ravines*, *gorges*, and *canyons*, the steep and usually rocky sides of which often afford habitats for plants that are not to be found elsewhere in the vicinity. Consequently such plants may be useful indicators of peculiar conditions—for example of rock crevices or ' open ' soil and lack of competition, of a humid or shaded situation, or sometimes of a particular type of substratum such as is afforded by calcareous rock. Quite frequently valleys with the long axis lying east and west have very different conditions on their north- and south-facing slopes, which may be more clearly indicated by differences of flora and vegetation than by ordinary meteorological observations. These last are, moreover, tedious and often costly to make. And though everybody knows that a south-facing bank in the boreal regions tends to be sunnier and warmer than a north-facing one, it may also be drier and so not necessarily preferable for all cultivational purposes. Here again plants form useful indicators of the immediately local conditions, Ferns for example being characteristic of damp and shady banks whereas succulents occur on dry and sunny ones.

Of depositional features made by streams there are also many—such as *alluvial fans* and *cones*, *flood-plain deposits*, *channel bars*, *deltas*, and *natural levees*. Each of these has its tendency towards supporting a characteristic vegetational type which usually varies markedly in regions of different climate, particularly—although certain plants, such as some Poplars, are widely characteristic, occurring in similar situations in a considerable range of climates. These stream depositional forms, being usually of fine material plentifully supplied with plant nutrients, and commonly situated in sheltered valleys, include some of the most vegetationally (and hence agriculturally) productive terrain. Being low-lying and often damp, they may also produce fine pasturage.

The residual features left by stream erosion are, from the point of view of our present study, relatively minor ; though the vegetation on their area may so bind the surface as to delay their formation, it is usually meagre. Examples are *divides* and *monadnocks*, and, in part, those flat-topped erosion remnants known as *mesas* and *buttes*. Even the residual forms of this category which are fairly extensive, are liable to be rocky and exposed and consequently rather poorly vegetated.

Erosional features made by glaciers somewhat resemble those made by streams, except that the *valleys* are often deeper and U-shaped and their steep sides are usually scoured. The bottoms may be scoured too, and retain so little soil that the vegetation suffers in spite of the favourably sheltered situation. Depressions or deeper troughs are often occupied by water—*finger-lakes*, *paternoster-lakes*, and, especially, *tarns*, being numerous in glaciated territory. These bodies of water vary from oligotrophic and unproductive where the surface material has been scoured away, to eutrophic and productive where comminuted deposits were left and considerable sedimentation has occurred. Here may be extensive reed-swamp and other seral stages. *Cirques*, those rocky amphitheatres where mountain glaciers started in bygone times, are usually so poorly vegetated that they stand out to this day as barren and forlorn.

Of depositional features left by glaciers there are many, such as various types of *moraines* and *glacio-fluvial deposits*. Terminal moraines, located at the ends of glaciers whose margins remained stationary for a long time, usually take the form of hummocky belts of small rounded hills and basins which are irregularly distributed and often enclose lakes or swamps. Their vegetation is consequently very variable from spot to spot, but is usually luxuriant in favourable situations as the unassorted material includes much that is of fine texture and nutritional value. Such areas are often valuable for market-gardening or pasturage. Ground moraine of variable thickness is left by continental glaciers almost everywhere when they recede. Though again of unassorted material and beset by lakes and swamps, and sometimes also by smooth elliptical hills called *drumlins*, ground moraines tend to be flatter and consequently more suitable for large-scale agriculture than terminal moraines. The glacio-fluvial deposits of streams, which carried much of the finer glacial debris out beyond the terminal moraines, are various but individually assorted. Thus the coarser sand and gravel was usually deposited near the terminal moraines but the finer sand and clay tended to be carried and deposited much farther away, the fans often coalescing to form a gently sloping *outwash plain*. Such plains are usually well vegetated and suitable for agricultural development, though they may be beset with *eskers* (*see* p. 543), with conical or other deposits of assorted sand and gravel known as *kames* and widely used for building and road-making material, or with pits known as *kettle-holes*. These last are often filled with water and were left where large blocks of ice had been buried in the moraine or outwash material and subsequently melted, giving an irregular 'thaw-sink' topography. *Erratic boulders* of various shapes, sizes, and provenance constitute a minor depositional feature in many formerly glaciated areas.

The residual features left by glaciers are also various, though commonly exposed, rocky, and very poorly vegetated. Such are both *arêtes* (the 'knife-edge' ridges left between glacial troughs) and *matterhorn peaks*, which latter are left when several cirques have so cut into the different flanks of a mountain as to isolate it and reduce it to a spectacular horn or needle. The vegetation in such instances is almost invariably poor, as befits the lofty exposed situation and rockiness of the substratum; it is often poorer than on constructional mountain surfaces, owing to the instability of the residual ones. In high alpine situations it may consist of little more than Lichens on the rock-faces, crevice plants where they can find a roothold, and tussock or other herbs where soil accumulates (*cf.* Fig. 137, B). In *hanging valleys*, the other important member of this category, the vegetation may be much less poor, owing to the sheltered situation; it is, however, usually less luxuriant than in the associated main valley, at least when compared with the floor of the latter. The *roches moutonnées* or 'sheep rocks', those asymmetric rocky hills smoothed by ice-action which characterize many formerly glaciated areas, are at once erosional *and* residual. As with large erratic boulders, their rock surfaces are often to this day devoid of other than lichen and similarly dwarfed cryptogamic growth. However, in favourably sheltered situations, soil and higher vegetation may largely occupy all but their steeper sides, crevices being especially favoured, while a thick cap of humus, often supporting trees, may cover their domed tops (*cf.* Fig. 92).

Erosional features made by ground-water include *caverns* and *tunnels*, the vegetation of which becomes drastically reduced with decreasing light away from the orifice and, of course, limited to saprophytes, etc., in the dark. Even near the orifice where the light seems fairly strong and green plants prevail, these are chiefly vegetative forms of shade-plants such as various Ferns, the types occurring farthest in being commonly Bryophytes, Algae, and long-drawn-out seedlings utilizing stored food-reserves. *Sinkholes* or *swallow-holes* are funnel-shaped depressions in the surface of the ground in regions of soluble rock, formed either by the collapse of a cavern roof or, directly, by the solvent action of descending surface-water which enlarges cracks or joints. The bottoms of such sinkholes may become choked with sediment, so that water can no longer drain out readily and often a pond develops; or more luxuriant vegetation may grow in the sheltered depression than in surrounding areas. This is especially noticeable on pastured calcareous 'downs' where water percolates away and the general monotony of the short, grassy vegetation may be relieved by sinkholes containing dense shrubby growth or even trees.

Of depositional surface features left by ground-water, *spring deposits* are the most frequent and important, usually appearing as *mounds* or *terraces*—commonly of calcium carbonate though sometimes of siliceous material. The vegetation varies greatly according to local circumstances but is usually distinctive—as is true also of the 'spring flushes'. These are most noticeable on slopes below springs where the irrigating water constantly supplies fresh mineral salts and the ground consequently bears grassy or forbaceous (*i.e.* of herbs other than those of grass type) vegetation that is often bright-green in colour in the midst of brownish acid-tolerant vegetation. Such flushes may be evident even if the spring or surface run-off is not; for they still indicate a local abundance of fresh percolating water.

Residual features left by ground-water are *natural bridges* and *chimneys*, almost invariably of very limited extent. Although they introduce whole series of microclimatic and often local habitat effects, each of which may have its characteristic plant inhabitants, the resulting communities tend to be extremely limited in area and, moreover, similar to the types to be found in comparable habitats about cliffs and steep banks elsewhere.

Erosional features made by winds include *blow-outs*, which are broad and shallow depressions scooped out of soft rock or sand in more or less flat regions, *wind-caves*, due to differential erosion of soft materials on hill-sides, or rarely *blow-holes* extending right through a hill. These last two types occur chiefly in arid regions and, because also of the dynamic and often eroded nature of the surface, tend to be devoid of macroscopic vegetation. Blow-outs may also be practically barren for much the same reasons—for example in deserts, where they may be some miles in length and hundreds of feet in depth. In other instances the lower levels may become occupied by lakes, complete with attendant vegetation; or the soft rock may be colonized by plants, particularly in fissures, and any sand surfaces in time become bound by grassy or other vegetation which may gradually cover the area.

Features due to deposition by wind include *sand-dunes* and *loess*.

Dunes are accumulations of sand and are formed in much the same manner as snow-drifts, being started by some obstruction which causes an eddy in the sand-bearing wind. Once started, each dune provides the obstacle which causes its further growth. Sand-dunes are of very various form and size, ranging from a few square feet up to several square miles in area, and from inches to perhaps 1,000 feet (304·8 metres) in height. Commonly the component sand is well sorted as to size and rounded as to particle-shape. Dunes are apt to be formed wherever there is a source of sand available—for example on a sandy beach or river plain, or where sandstone disintegrates in a dry climate. Unless 'bound' and covered by vegetation, so that many surface particles are held while the wind is slowed down and no longer has full access to the sand, dunes migrate, though rarely at a rate of more than 25 feet a year. This migration takes place through the transfer of sand from the windward to the leeward side of the dune, and in its course may overwhelm roads, farms, and forests. The most effective way of stopping the migration of dunes is to plant on their windward side suitably hardy Grasses and shrubs adapted to sandy soil and capable of binding the surface. Such are Marram Grass (*Ammophila arenaria*), Lyme-grass (*Elymus arenarius* s.l.), Volga Giant-wildrye (*E. giganteus*), and certain members of the Pea family, which are used for this purpose of stabilizing dunes in various parts of the world and may be followed by suitable coniferous and other trees. Even when a climax forest is attained the dune origin is commonly evident—and irksome to the foot-traveller—owing to the intimate topography of ups and downs caused by the bodies of the stabilized dunes. Frequently sand-dunes become stabilized naturally by similar means, the common sequence being that one of the coarse rhizomatous Grasses will pioneer in colonization (*cf.* Fig. 28, A, and Fig. 93), followed by Mosses or Lichens or other 'secondary binders' on the floor, followed in turn by less xeromorphic higher plants (for the sand is usually damp beneath the air-dried surface). These last include shrubs and ultimately trees when the surface has become fully stabilized and sufficient humus has accumulated to form a reasonably nutrient soil (Fig. 177).

Loess is wind-deposited dust; its deposits are usually without special form but may be of great extent and considerable thickness. Its fine texture and content of food-salts make loess a fertile substratum provided sufficient moisture is present and it is not too compacted; it gives an easily worked and agriculturally

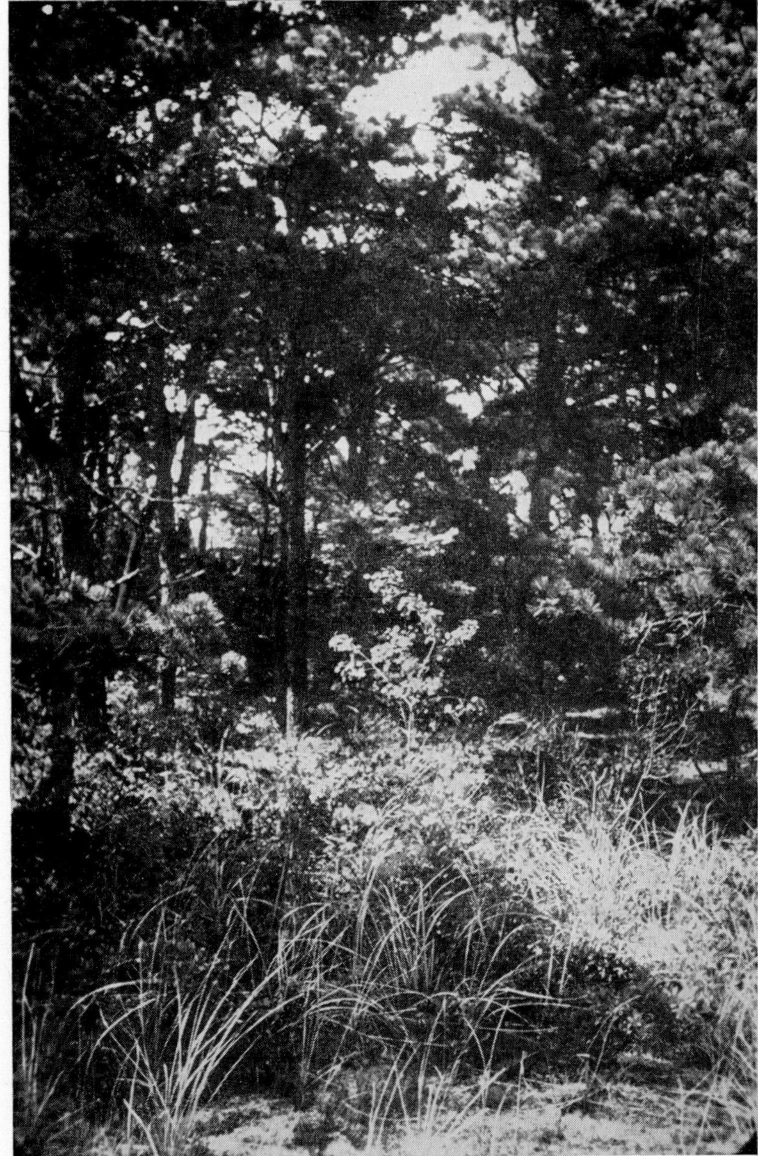

Fig. 177.—Old sand-dune colonized by shrubs and Pitch Pine (*Pinus rigida*) after stabilization by Marram Grass (*Ammophila arenaria,* persisting in foreground). Prout's Neck, Maine.

desirable soil. However, if unprotected by vegetation it is easily eroded.

Residual features left by wind include *mushroom rocks* and some *mesas* and *buttes*: their tops are usually poorly vegetated owing to exposure and dryness, their sides being often barren owing to abrasion and erosion.

Erosional features due to waves and currents include *wave-cut benches*, *cliffed shore-lines*, and *sea-caves*. Of these the benches extend down to the lower limit of wave erosion and tend to be well vegetated by fair-sized Brown and other Algae as indicated in Chapter XVI. The cliffs commonly introduce a host of crevice and other microhabitats and consequently support very various plant communities in different spots and instances, though their exposed and unstable nature usually prevents the attainment of anything approaching the local climax. Deep and narrow inlets and sea-caves are also very variously vegetated according to local conditions, though owing to their rocky nature and the frequently poor light in them, there is considerable limitation of the flora and of sturdy growth. Sometimes, however, where salt water does not reach and a lasting supply of fresh water percolates, so that the atmosphere is continuously damp, a fine growth of Ferns and Bryophytes is developed in the mouths of caverns and as far in as light allows.

Depositional features of waves and currents include *beaches*, *tidal deltas*, and various kinds of *bars*. The beaches are liable to be barren, especially where the surface is exposed and dynamic, though in sheltered situations alongside salt as well as fresh water the surface may be colonized and, where silty, often well vegetated. This is especially true in tidal creeks and about the on-shore periphery of deltas, which in the tropics typically support luxuriant mangrove vegetation of shrubs or trees as described in Chapter XIV. In extra-tropical regions a swarded salt-marsh often develops in such situations. Sand and, especially, mud bars or spits may also be so adorned when formed in sheltered situations such as deep bays; more often, however, they are devoid of higher plants, though in cases of intermediate stability the surface may be bound by a close investment of Schizophyta or lowly Green etc. Algae.

Residual features formed by waves and currents include *stacks* and *arches* which, being cliffed and exposed, tend to be poorly vegetated although they introduce an array of microhabitats comparable with those found about cliffs. Though distinctive and often striking, such features are minor in being uncommon and in occupying very limited areas.

Additional agents of erosion include gravity, giving for example *screes* and *talus-heaps* below cliffs, and animals (including Man), which are constantly producing *new surfaces*, either directly or indirectly, as has repeatedly been indicated in earlier chapters.

## Interpretation and Uses

Landscapes are typically made up of the smaller to medium-size landforms. However, in viewing a landscape in most parts of the world, it is chiefly the clothing vegetation which is seen. This, like all other vegetation, as we have already observed, varies greatly with local conditions. Therefore it affords a ready and evident means of distinguishing the landforms and other local features which make up a landscape, in turn being of assistance in their interpretation and consequently proving of value to the ecologist when he has to decide on the uses to which particular areas may be put. For it has been rightly said that the study of vegetation, especially when it is of established communities and they are mature, affords more reliable indications of the action and interaction of local factors than direct measurements, and is often the best basis for agricultural and allied planning.

To the common question of *what is the explanation of particular plants growing in particular places*, there can scarcely be a satisfactory general answer. To be sure, the presence of, say, a certain tree in a spot is an expression of something more or less definite, and indeed, much of this book has been devoted to consideration of the kind of items that would have to be satisfied before such presence could come about, and of what, in consequence, it implies. But these items vary enormously and complicatedly from instance to instance and even from spot to spot. Thus before we could have any chance of contemplating our tree where it grows, a viable disseminule would have had to be produced and liberated at a suitable place and brought by some means to the relevant point at some time in the past. Moreover, this disseminule would have to be fortunate enough in its circumstances to find sufficient water for germination and for the successful establishment of the resulting plant—which implies also suitable conditions of climate, soil, and so forth for the growth of the plant in that particular spot. Any deficiency or serious deviation at a critical stage might easily have proved fatal. And then, in order for the species to become established in any numbers, it would have to reproduce successfully and withstand predators, diseases, and competitors. Alternatively, Man may have taken a hand, though, as we have often seen, in the case of introductions his continued intervention is commonly necessary for persistence. In any case, a whole complex of circumstances lie behind the arrival of a particular plant in a particular place, and a further complex of conditions has to be satisfied before it can become established and survive there. Furthermore, for anything approaching permanence, we have the many problems involved in successful reproduction. And as both circumstances and conditions are complicated, and it seems safe to conclude that there are very many thousands of different combinations of them favouring the existence of particular species among the hundreds of thousands known on earth, it would seem futile to attempt to treat these matters systematically here. Even a series of specific examples from a particular place would be of little help, unless it were to inhabitants of that one place—especially as in the final analysis a good deal is left to chance.

What the asker of the above question may often have in mind, however, is *what does the presence of a particular plant tell us about the place in which it grows*—especially in terms of practical application? It usually means that the plant involved has found suitable conditions at least for growth and survival, and that the conditions under which we may know it to flourish elsewhere are approximated to here—though we should meanwhile recall that preferences may change (*e.g.* at different stages of the life-cycle), as may of course ecological factors themselves. Although many plants have too wide an ecological amplitude to mean much in this connection, at least as far as present-day knowledge goes, others are exacting in their requirements. Others, again, have specific needs such as the presence (or absence) of particular substances in the soil. Here we think immediately of certain 'indicator' plants or groups of plants which are so called because they require (and therefore indicate) the presence of particular conditions, and may consequently be valuable in demonstrating that these conditions obtain where they grow. For the existence of a particular plant or community in a particular place is an expression within certain limits of a particular combination of actual habitat conditions, among other things, and, where these limits are narrow, or a specific one is finite, we have a ready-made demonstration of the situation obtaining locally.

These ' indicator ' plants, communities, and other signs are prone to vary from one region to another, sometimes even of comparable climate, so that considerable local knowledge is necessary for effective practice of the principles involved. Imparting such local information, even for a single limited area, is beyond the scope of this introductory book : recourse must be had to detailed local floristic and ecological works such as are now available for many parts of the world. But even with much book knowledge, field experience is usually necessary for reliable interpretation and use, as observations have to be analyzed for usable data and synthesized into applicable forms. Thus most of us living on either side of the North Atlantic know that Willows and Poplars like an abundance of water in the soil, yet there are wide variations in this respect between different species of Willows and Poplars, some especially of the latter favouring rather dry habitats. Indeed one species, popularly known as the Trembling Aspen (*Populus tremuloides*), in certain circumstances and places can be a fair indicator of rather arid conditions—which emphasizes the need for specific observations and local knowledge. Moreover, members of an individual species often vary in their needs for water, etc., in different regions, according to other habitat factors and to their particular state, while it must also be remembered that species within a genus are sometimes difficult to tell apart—even to taxonomists, which too many ecologists are not. Still more liable to be confused in our minds are members of lower taxa which may yet exhibit marked ecological preferences or needs, and indeed different habitat preferences may be shown by physiological strains lacking any evident differences in form.

Especially do plants tend to become more limited to conditions expressed by certain habitats as they approach the periphery of their range. This principle should always be borne in mind to avoid mistakes in interpretation. Thus Beech forests in westernmost Europe are largely limited to calcareous soils, in England being commonly associated with chalk, whereas to the east this is no longer the case. The European Beech does, however, seem everywhere to be indicative of fairly dry, well-drained conditions, and it has been suggested that its western association with chalk, especially, is due to the drier conditions usually found thereon as compared with adjacent clayey and other soils.

In view of the local variability of soil and some other conditions, it is only to be expected that individual species of plants are in general unreliable as indicators, being of relatively ' low indicator value' as it is called. Nevertheless many dominants, and some other special instances such as the European Beech or Ash or even beds of Stinging Nettles, may be useful as individual indicators. Far more reliable, however, are groups of species or, preferably, whole communities. These make up vegetation, which, as we have seen, often provides the most characteristic (though variable) surface feature not only of landforms but also of entire landscapes.

Apart from the truism that, in the absence of drastic disturbance, the luxuriance and form of the vegetation developed on an area will give to everyone some indication of its productivity, considerable local knowledge is commonly required to interpret vegetation and use it as a basis for agricultural or forestral planning. Given this local knowledge and some practical experience in its employment, an observant farmer or forester can usually tell more about the uses to which a particular tract of land can be put, from observation of its standing vegetation, than can be determined from much tedious measurement. Nor is this surprising, for it is often not so much this or that particular factor of the environment which is likely to affect the natural vegetation, as the result of interaction of all the factors obtaining locally. Of this composite result the vegetation is, in a sense, a measuring apparatus, and an extraordinarily delicate one. For the type, composition, and degree of luxuriance of the plant communities are apt to be immediately eloquent on the subject of local conditions, and it is inconceivable that any battery of instruments, however complicated and delicate, could ever really emulate natural vegetation in this respect.

Often the vegetation will not only give an indication of minor and unsuspected habitat differences but also emphasize gross ones such as landforms in a landscape. An example of the former is the common persistence of beds of Stinging Nettles (*Urtica dioica*) about the sites of old habitations or areas of loosened soil and, of the latter, the existence of dark clumps of trees in depressions in many grasslands. Yet in other instances vegetation may obscure the local conformation of the earth's surface, including some striking if minor landforms, by its very luxuriance.

To such further questions as 'Where, so far as surface and vegetation features indicate, ought I to build my house and dig my garden', there is again no simple answer: it will depend on the region and various other circumstances. But a close study of the vegetation of likely situations, coupled, perhaps, with observation of the plant growth around already established dwellings in similar habitats, will give many useful pointers, as it will also in such matters as shelter and water-supply, if these have to be considered. For vegetation is often the best indicator of conditions not only in the air but also below the surface of the ground, landscapes being, as we have repeatedly observed, frequently best interpreted through their ' green mantle '. Moreover, the occurrence of similar groups of plants in different spots usually indicates a close similarity of conditions, while the converse usually holds, at least throughout an area of fairly uniform climate. So, altogether, careful and suitably enlightened observation of vegetation can be of the greatest practical value.

In these considerations, whether the emphasis is practical or academic, it should be remembered that vegetation may not only accentuate but also mould or even be responsible for some landforms. For plant growth promotes deposition, as of sand on dunes and silt in water, and increases the accumulation on natural levees of material from flooding rivers. Plants also cause the chemical separation of calcium carbonate which is largely responsible for ' coral ' reefs. Moreover vegetation impedes erosion, conserving the soil and underlying mantle of weathered rock or transported material by reducing or preventing removal by wind or water. With its flow thus retarded, rain-water or snow-melt water is permitted to sink into the ground, the vegetation being in turn favoured in what often becomes a mutually cumulative effect. And as the soil and underlying mantle are protected by vegetation from erosion, so is the bedrock protected from the weathering that precedes erosion (apart, of course, from the small amount of weathering of exposed rock surface that may be caused by plant growth). Thus may parts of landscapes be moulded ; and hence the wide use of vegetation for wind-breaks, shelter-belts, dune-stabilization, and prevention of erosion by excessive run-off and other means. Vegetation, whether natural or planted, is, or should be, not only the main medium but also a leading tool of the conservationist.

## Land-Use Classification

For the all-important practice of the most effective land utilization in an area, intimate familiarity is necessary with the vegetation and other local manifestations. In the words of Dr. Edward H. Graham (in his work cited at the end of the present chapter), this should be

> ' Not the detailed inspection of the micro-biologist or soil analyst, but a consideration of landscape as an ecological complex prescribing the

use which man can make of the land. This involves, before all else . . . Land-use classification [which] should relate to the physical capacity of the land to produce given crops for an indefinite period without exhaustion or waste of the land resource. It does not hold that production of tilled crops is the highest use of the land, but rather that this is true only for certain classes of land. Some land, for example swampy areas, is poorly used if it is not devoted to muskrat or other wildlife production, for efforts to produce more intensive crops only result in a waste of time, labor, and materials.'

In addition there are the areas—amounting for example in the United States to about 2 per cent. of the total land—occupied by roads, towns, and railways, all of which have to be chosen and maintained with the greatest possible knowledge and care. Land classification in the modern sense should therefore include also inventory and over-all planning.

A very general computation has given the following figures for the occupation of the world's land surface *before Man transformed so much of it* : 30 per cent. forest or arborescent scrub, 19 per cent. grassland, 17 per cent. desert, and the remaining 34 per cent. poor mountain or polar areas (*cf.* Fig. 65). Most of the disturbed tracts are considered capable of reinstatement so far as vegetation-type is concerned, and accordingly these figures may also be regarded as at least potential ones for the future. Curiously enough, although many forested areas of past or recent times are considered capable of cultivation, the same proportion of about 30 per cent. of the total land surface of the world is also believed to be cultivable, while another 30 per cent., without being too cold or too dry to support crops, is of poor grazing-land, marsh, waste, or otherwise unsuitable.

Of the many ways of classifying land, perhaps the most practical and valuable is according to use-capabilities. This is based, as it should be for permanence, on natural characteristics such as soil and other biological conditions—ignoring such immediate considerations as financial aspects or the skill of the operating individual. In this system the following eight classes are widely recognized with reference to rural use, though of course urban, industrial, transportational, and recreational areas should also be established with due reference to a scheme of land classification wherever possible. The eight classes are placed in three major groups, namely, A, B, and C.

A. *Suitable for cultivation involving tillage*

I. Without special practices for the prevention of serious erosion or other lasting deterioration, though fertilizers and simple crop-rotations are often used. This land is of very good productivity and, being level or nearly so, is practically free from any possibility of erosion. The soil is easy to work, deep, and at least fairly well supplied with plant nutrients.

II. With simple practices—such as contour cultivation, strip cropping, growing protective cover-crops, or simple water-management. This is good land but not quite as good as that comprising Class I—owing to physical conditions such as the slope, which may be just steep enough to make water run off at a speed that will carry away soil. Or the soil may be so wet as to require drainage, or, alternatively, may be rather dry. In any case there are deficiencies which either limit the use of the land to some extent or require attention year after year.

III. With complex or intensive practices—such as terracing, though usually a combination of remedies is needed. This is moderately good land for cultivation, being more limited than that of Class II by reason of one or more natural features. It can be regularly used for crops only with intensive treatment and employing the best of farming methods. Sometimes the slope demands erosion control, or it may be undesirably dry or, alternatively, so wet as to require drainage.

IV. With intensive practices and limited use—such as cultivation in small plots or on long rotations with only occasional crops. This land is not suitable for regular production of cultivated crops, most often because of steepness and consequent danger of erosion. Commonly it can be cultivated safely perhaps one year in every six; in the other years it is best used for hay or pasturage. Some cases are too dry for dependable cropping without irrigation. It is only fairly good for arable crops but usually affords good grazing or forest land provided the rainfall or other precipitation is adequate.

B. *Suitable for permanent pasture or woodland but not for cultivation*

V. Without special practices—land only slightly susceptible to deterioration when the range is fully grazed or the forest is widely cut. It is usually nearly level and accordingly not subject to erosion, but, because of wetness, climate, or such permanent obstructions as rocky outcrops, is not suitable for cultivation. However, the soil is deep and the land has few limitations for any kind of grazing or for forestry use, which should be entirely successful.

VI. With some restriction in use—land moderately susceptible to deterioration, so grazing must be by rotation and logging only with due care, and there may have to be special conservation practices such as contour furrows across slopes to maintain forage and protect soil. This is quite good land for forestry or grazing but is somewhat limited for these purposes by shallow soil or steep slopes, or by excessive wetness that cannot be remedied by drainage to permit use for crops. Alternatively, in arid or semi-arid regions, there may be limitation through lack of moisture.

FIG. 178.—An example of Class VII land. (Phot. U.S.D.A.)

VII. With severe restriction in use—land highly susceptible to deterioration, so grazing must be only occasional and felling highly selective (Fig. 178). On this land extreme care must be exercised to prevent erosion as a result of pasturing or lumbering.

C. *Suitable for wildlife but not for cultivation, pasture, or woodland*

VIII. With or without special practices—productive of useful wild plants, fur, game Birds, Mammals, or Fish ; generally serving as range for wild or semi-wild animals (Fig. 179). Such land is usually very rough or wet or susceptible to severe erosion. Or it may be so arid or steep as to be unsuitable for grazing and fail to grow trees. Examples include rocky foothills, rough mountain land, bare rock outcrops, coastal sand-dunes, and many swamps and marshes.

FIG. 179.—An example of Class VIII land. (Phot. U.S.D.A.)

Fig. 180 illustrates all eight land-use capability classes. It may readily be seen that farms are concerned largely with group A (Classes I to IV), pasturage and forests primarily with group B (Classes V to VII), and wildlife largely, but by no means exclusively, with group C (Class VIII). Areas of Class VIII may, moreover, have important recreational, aesthetic, or watershed-protection values, as was pointed out by Dr. Edward H. Graham (*in litt.*). They may furthermore be of great scientific interest. Open waters may also be looked upon as belonging to Class VIII, as they are best adapted to the production of undomesticated plants and animals. Actually, neglect can cause even the best and most productive agricultural land to deteriorate, through erosion, practically to the bottom of the scale, as is illustrated in Fig. 181, which should serve as a severe warning to any who might ignore conservation practices or at least reasonable caution.

Within all of the classes except No. I, subclasses may be established according to the nature of the most important character limiting use-intensity. Thus, soils that are subject to erosion are placed in an ' erosion subclass ', indicated by adding an ' e ' to the designation, as, for example, ' Class IVe '. Similarly, soils with a problem primarily of water-control are placed in the ' w ' subclass of the appropriate class. Other usual subclasses are of soil-deficiencies and aridity while salinity adds yet another.

FIG. 180.—Illustration of the eight land-use capability classes. (Courtesy of U.S. Soil Conservation Service.)

The separation of the different land-use capability groups and, particularly, classes, naturally depends on different manifestations and criteria in different regions ; yet to a considerable extent it tends in some circumstances to take account of floristic and vegetational features or effects, and, consequently, to be phytogeographical in basis. For, as we have already observed, the plant life gives us a living expression of the total environment such as nothing else can replace. It even provides us with ready-made experiments on, and something of an interpretation of, what happens beneath the soil surface. Especially where established communities are concerned, suitably enlightened study of the plant life not only affords a more exact indication of the combined action of all site factors than any measurement of individual ones, but it commonly provides the most reliable ecological basis for any agricultural, forestral, or allied planning.

## Further Consideration

Almost any modern work on general physical geography or geology will have some treatment of landforms as such, though the approaches and classification may vary greatly in different works. A useful account, largely along the lines followed in the present chapter, is to be found in Henry D. Thompson's *Fundamentals of Earth Science* (Appleton-Century-Crofts, New York, pp. xiii + 461, 1947). As for the usually far wider, constructional landforms that were deemed to be too variable or, alternatively, too general for useful consideration in any detail here, the mountain ones are well treated in R. Peattie's *Mountain Geography* (Harvard University Press, Cambridge, Mass., pp. xiv + 257, 1936) and the plains and plateaux in M. D. Haviland's *Forest, Steppe and Tundra* (Cambridge University Press, Cambridge, Eng., pp. [xi] + 218, 1926).

For further details about land utilization, including many botanical aspects, reference may be made to Edward H. Graham's *Natural Principles of Land Use* (Oxford University Press, London etc., pp. xiii + 274, 1944). This gives an extensive and valuable annotated bibliography from which any interested reader may select further works to his taste. A very readable introductory book is Paul B. Sears's *Life and Environment* (Teachers College, Columbia University, New York, pp. xx + 175, 1939).

## CHAPTER XVIII

# PLANT ADJUSTMENTS AND APPLICATIONS

Consideration of both (1) the natural ' adaptations ' and (2) the man-made modifications of plants, in each case (*a*) of individual kinds and (*b*) of vegetation, gives us by cross-inference four sets of topics. These are all of peculiar interest and importance, and are exemplified individually by (*i*) evolution (which depends substantially on the favourable modifications or adaptations of individual plants); (*ii*) plant-breeding (in which Man manipulates the characteristics of individual plants); (*iii*) successional change (of natural vegetation); and (*iv*) combating of erosion (for which planted or encouraged vegetation is the best weapon). To the extent that these and allied considerations are often areal, for example in leading to extended ranges, they should be included among the concerns of plant geography. Each is a large subject that can be treated here only in broad outline or with special reference to the example mentioned.

### ' ADAPTATIONS ' OF INDIVIDUALS

However evolution of plants may have come about—and there appear to be many and various causes and mechanisms of evolutionary change—it is clear that the tendency is generally towards forms more suitably adapted to the environment than were their ancestors. Actually it seems that the main single cause of evolution in plants has been—and continues to be—the ' natural selection ' of heritable characteristics that are beneficial in competition and hence advantageous in the general ' struggle for existence '. Most species produce, at least potentially in the form of disseminules, far more individuals than ever survive, and it is the progeny possessing favourable variations in structure or function that tend to persist. When these variations are heritable, they may become ' fixed ' in succeeding generations and benefit the race; for in the intense competition that is characteristic of life on earth, individuals having even slight advantages over their fellows, for example in exhibiting taller or more rapid growth, will have the best chances of success. Altogether, variation is one of the most universal attributes of living things, and the outcome of natural selection upon the varying populations of successive generations is persistence of the forms possessing the most beneficial characters—or, as it is frequently called, 'survival of the fittest'.

Whether or not we accept this explanation of evolution by natural selection approximately as propounded nearly a century ago by Charles Darwin—and most biologists nowadays believe that it is only a partial elucidation of the mechanisms involved—the fact that evolution takes place is now almost universally accepted. Moreover there can be few if any who would deny that the common course of evolution is through forms which, as it proceeds, become more and more closely aligned with the demands of particular habitats or groups of habitats, its outcome being then in races or higher taxa that are more or less closely adapted to the conditions in which they grow. That is the keynote of the plant geographical aspect of the subject; and whereas we could go on explaining and exemplifying *ad nauseam*, it seems best to leave matters here. For there can scarcely be any group of plants that does not afford instances of adaptations to the particular environmental factors under which one or more of its members grow, and which thereby affect its distribution in actuality or potentiality.

On the utilitarian side we should note that, with crops and trees—including Maize in the mid-western United States and Conifers in Scandinavia—it has sometimes been observed that seed from acclimatized local plants gives better results than seed imported from even a relatively short distance away. This 'regional adaptation' tends to be especially marked when the testing-ground lies in an area of unusually diversified climatic or other conditions. The reason appears to be that the 'native' strains have been rendered appropriate to the local conditions through the action of natural selection on a population that was once more mixed genetically. Nature, as it were, is in this way doing the plant breeder's work for him. Yet the basis here is Man's husbandry and, usually, importation of seed in the first instance.

## Man-made Adjustments

When we come to consider Man's direct and deliberate manipulation of certain characteristics of individual plants or, particularly, kinds of plants, we are dealing to a considerable extent with processes of selection which are, instead, artificial. Thus plant-breeders select, from among the variants they observe in nature or can produce by hybridization or other genetical practices, the most desirable tendencies which, when heritable, persist in subsequent generations. Often two or more desirable characteristics exhibited by different strains are combined in one strain by hybridization or other techniques. By such means, through the ages, most of our domestic races of vegetable, cereal, pulse, root, and other crops have come into existence, and by modern methods are being improved all the time in relation to modern conditions and needs. Thus strains of many crops have been developed which are able to overcome obstacles that previously prevented them from being grown successfully in whole regions. Examples of such major feats include the pushing farther and farther north of the wheat belt in Siberia and Canada, and cultivation of hardy strains of other cereals higher and higher up in mountainous areas. Certain fruits, too, are now being produced successfully in increasingly rigorous climes without the aid of costly contrivances such as glasshouses. In addition there is the chemical treatment by various ' plant growth substances ' which is becoming increasingly important in many crop improvement connections. Resistance to disease or frost or drought, promotion of early flowering and rapid fruiting, and all manner of other adjustments which can be made in plants by artificial selection and enlightened breeding or chemical treatment, have greatly affected the potential and often the actual ranges of the crops involved—which again strikes the distributional keynote of our subject.

By such means does Man to a considerable degree mould plants to his needs and extend the area as well as the productivity of his crops. It should, however, be re-emphasized that these ' artificial ' strains of plants are not only commonly incapable of withstanding the competition of native vegetation if this is not kept back by Man, but that Man has also often to modify the habitat even further for success. This he accomplishes by such agricultural, horticultural, or forestral practices as ploughing, fertilizing, mulching, irrigating, draining, and so on. Thus such domesticated plants may, from Nature's point of view, be considered doubly artificial—on one hand in origin and, on the other, in their habitat. But as plant geography deals in a practical way with plant distributions as we see them in the world as a whole, even these ' artificial ' plants are important objects of our study. Indeed Chapter VIII is largely concerned with their modifications and distributions.

## Vegetational Adaptation

Just as different kinds of plants are adapted in form or function for life under particular conditions, and this fact largely limits their distribution on earth, so the communities which plants make up collectively, and which as a whole we term vegetation, are limited in area by local conditions. Thus the general principle of adaptation of plants to particular habitats applies also to vegetation ; and even as evolution has tended in a very general way to be towards better and better adaptation of individuals, so it appears to have been with vegetational change. Most obviously, the dominant species on which so much depends, commonly have their areas prescribed by climatic conditions and, more locally within climatically suitable areas, by edaphic or other immediate considerations. And so it largely is with the rest of a community, though local conditions are often controlled to a considerable degree by the dominants themselves, or by other plants of similar life-form. Nor is the total effect of the community necessarily by any means the same as the sum of the effects of its components if considered individually.

Perhaps the most noteworthy and general tendency to change in natural plant communities is through the process of succession, which was considered in Chapter XI. The progression from one community to another of more efficient energy-utilization which is succession, and which normally involves domination by higher and higher life-forms as the stages succeed one another in an area, is essentially a matter of the changing environmental demands and adaptational attainments of successive colonists. Thus the largely different plants involved in different stages have usually such different habitat requirements that the species of one stage are commonly ousted by those of the next—because they are not suitably adapted to its attendant conditions. These conditions, admittedly, are largely introduced or controlled by the plants themselves ; but the principle nevertheless holds. The immediate plant geographical implication is that successional changes introduce different conditions to which usually very different plants are adapted, and whose distributions are thereby altered, at least potentially. At the same time succession tends to render areas unsuitable for many previous colonists and their ecological analogues, correspondingly limiting the ranges of such organisms. These and allied changes go on continuously in the world today, as Man or other agencies disturb vegetation and initiate or alter successions in various ways. We have, moreover, repeatedly seen how many plants become established in an area only when suitable habitats have been prepared for them by other species ; thus plant distributions, and consequently the local vegetation, are often complicatedly dependent on the successional stage reached, or at least on the establishment of particular plant communities. For conditions which preclude one species or type will commonly favour some other.

Plants vary greatly in the extent to which they can adjust themselves to varying environmental conditions, and the same is true of the communities which they make up. Thus a patch of Fireweed will bloom gloriously in the early years of a forest clearing but thereafter wane and soon disappear as the conditions are changed by colonizing shrubs and saplings ; on the other hand, these woody plants may enter at the same time as the Fireweed and persist right through to the climax stage. All the above and numerous other considerations lie behind the present-day distributions of plants and consequently of vegetational types, as should be abundantly clear from the present work.

## Manipulation of Vegetation

Modern Man is the biotic superdominant of the world, and the changes which he effects in vegetation are among the most striking on earth. Such changes are apt to be of a more or less destructive nature, examples being heavy lumbering and grazing, burning and clearing, and the cultivation of lowly crops in place of lofty forests. Yet many are constructive so far as Man's needs are concerned—hence the whole vast industry of agricultural and related practices. Some are even constructive from the points of view of both Nature and mankind, an example being the stabilization of dunelands by ' binding ' vegetation—particularly by planting such coarse sand-binding grasses as Lyme-grass and Marram Grass. These are often followed by leguminous plants and Heaths, and, in time, by bushes and trees. Or afforestation may be effected by direct planting of young trees in already vegetated areas. Thus stabilization can be effectively carried out by Man's intervention, and frequently leads to luxuriant growth and substantial productivity where there was previously a mere barren waste. Man also in a sense manipulates the vegetation over wide areas by perpetuating such features as fire and grazing ' subclimaxes '.

The above and some other aspects of what may be looked on

as Man's manipulation of vegetation have been at least touched upon elsewhere in this work; many are dealt with in more worthy detail in recent books on conservation and allied topics. Agriculture, horticulture, and forestry themselves are to a large extent dependent upon Man's manipulation of habitats and cognate plant communities, whether the latter consist of individual crops or mixed stands.

The practical value of the concept of plant communities is widely recognized to be considerable in forest, range, and wildlife management—*e.g.* in North America—and in vegetation mapping for land use as often practised elsewhere. Thus in the United States, land utilization and management are happily to a considerable and ever-increasing extent based on the indications afforded by vegetation and on the potentialities of its growth—for example, after the manner outlined in the last chapter. Moreover, many of the most scientifically based and successful practices involve the judicious modification of existing vegetation rather than the creation of new, 'artificial' forms. For such practices the careful recording of the species concerned, as well as of the density and composition of plant communities, is often important. Usually, samples are taken as a basis for estimating the general conditions or productivity of the plant cover over the area of which the samples are representative; comparable sampling elsewhere may also serve as a standard for comparing the vegetation of different areas.

The methods employed in sampling vegetation include the use of *quadrats*, which are test areas (commonly squares, hence the name) of designated size in which the kinds and numbers (or areas) of plants are recorded, and of *transects*, which are cross-sections of vegetation studied along a line or belt. A *line transect* is one in which there are recorded, by names or symbols, the plants touching or overlapping a string stretched along the ground, while a *belt transect* represents a band of vegetation of designated width. In each case the recording should be done on a diagram drawn to scale. A belt transect is essentially an elongated quadrat and is usually far more instructive than a line transect, but it is more tedious to construct and record. Also involving intensive labours is the *bisect*, which is a cross-section of vegetation as it is revealed by a trench extending down to the deepest roots. For the investigation of succession, permanent quadrats may be established and studied from time to time. *Clip quadrats*, in which can be determined the oven-dry weight of the total vegetation clipped from the test area, are valuable to indicate local plant productivity. Exclusion or enclosure of animals may usefully be practised to indicate the extent to which browsers, etc., are modifying the local vegetation. Transplant experiments of plants or whole clumps of vegetation may also be valuable in indicating climatic, edaphic, or biotic impress. Vegetation maps of various types and on various scales, based on the closest possible observation of the composition and boundaries of the communities

FIG. 181.—Part of a maze of gullies which crosses more than an entire county in the southern United States and has 'permanently' destroyed more than a hundred thousand acres of excellent land. The original gully had begun about 70 years previously with a drip from a barn roof. (Courtesy of U.S. Soil Conservation Service.)

involved, and often supplemented by quadrats, transects, or other special methods of study of test areas, are also often prerequisite to successful application of modern agricultural and forestral techniques over wide stretches of country. Much the same is true of soil maps, indicating the type and extent of the main soils of different areas. In these and other ways, the study and understanding of vegetation and its habitats are of fundamental importance to prudent land utilization and, consequently, to humanity.

Conservation, which largely depends on wise treatment of vegetation, is a rapidly developing theme, of the utmost significance to civilization. Prevention is far better than cure, but very often we are too late for the former and sometimes even for the latter. Of this we have already seen instances, a terrible one being indicated in Fig. 181. In other cases remedy may be simple, as illustrated

FIG. 182.—Destructive water-erosional gully in heavily overgrazed pasture in Illinois. (Courtesy of U.S. Soil Conservation Service.)

in Figs. 182 and 183, where bad water-erosion was stopped by simply excluding livestock for two years and so allowing succession to proceed. In yet other cases all that is needed may be a planting of Willows on a stream-bank or of Lyme-grass on the windward slopes of sand-dunes. Yet altogether an appalling proportion of the once-productive land areas of many major countries has been lost to cultivation owing to unwise practices following Man's desecration of vegetation. This has led particularly to devastating erosion, and judicious planting of suitable crops or binders is often the best key to the reclamation of such tracts where this is possible. In the continental United States, for example, the area of cropland that is under either cultivation or rotation cropping is computed to stand at some 478 million acres, or about one-quarter of the total land area. Perhaps another 238 million acres could be added to Classes I to IV lands (*see* Chapter XVII) that are at present neither cultivated nor in rotation cropping but are yet capable of being cropped, especially with intensive practices. But it has been estimated that

FIG. 183.—The same as Fig. 182, two years later. Livestock have been excluded by fencing, whereupon by natural succession a cover of soil-protecting vegetation soon developed and controlled soil loss. Instead of a wasteful and dangerous gully (*cf.* Fig. 181), the area was restored to potential usefulness. (Courtesy of U.S. Soil Conservation Service.)

already some 25 million acres originally suitable for cultivation have been lost through water-erosion and soil-blowing, another ten million acres have been lost through other types of soil deterioration, and more than half of the remaining cropland has been damaged (critically as to 121 million acres and seriously as to 128 million acres) by one or another of these scourges (according to the 1954 figures given out by the U.S. Department of Agriculture's Soil Conservation Service). Other computations have indicated that more than one-third of the productive top-soil of the United States has already gone, and that the water-cycle has been drastically disturbed. This is a most distressing situation to which Professor Paul B. Sears's book *Deserts on the March* drew eloquent attention more than two decades ago. Conservation of soil and other natural resources is above all a way of life, as people have come more and more widely to realize in recent years, though still there is not nearly enough appreciation of its significance, let alone application of effective measures.

## Plant Geographical Study

A plant geographer should have considerable knowledge of ecology on one hand and of taxonomy on the other. His work must be ecologically based in its analysis of environmental factors as an outcome of which he can tell, for example, why such and such a plant community is restricted to such and such an area ; and above all it must rest upon a sufficiently precise taxonomy. Those are the immediate prerequisites of plant geographical study. For sound ecological knowledge some understanding of a wide range of basic sciences even outside of biology is necessary ; as for precise taxonomy, even closely allied and superficially similar plants can have very different reactions to environmental conditions, and so a knowledge of the local flora in the particular area of interest is virtually essential.

The methods of the modern plant geographer must accordingly be as scientifically based and exact as is humanly possible. Admittedly a good deal may be done by merely determining what grows where. For this the main requisite, apart from intensive field investigation, is to know precisely what we are dealing with—namely, the identity of each particular plant in question, coupled with the ability to determine that it is essentially the same ' kind ' throughout the ascertained range. But for interpretation and application of such observations we must have far wider knowledge and biological understanding—or, instead, an empirical system which could scarcely be worked out in sufficient detail for general use.

The ecological reactions of closely-related species or even races of plants can vary markedly, as can, accordingly, their ranges both individually and as components of vegetation, so the plant geographer must be able to recognize both habitat and taxonomic differences. For such ecological items his knowledge of soils and climates and of their component factors is particularly important, while as tools for making taxonomic studies he should have available a good regional 'flora' and a well-arranged herbarium in which are filed accurately-labelled specimens, dried and mounted on paper sheets, of as many as possible of the entities involved. Only with such solid foundations can plant geography really flourish and be of lasting value to mankind.

Different plant geographers work in different ways, and even the same investigator may use widely different methods in different circumstances—according to the current state of knowledge, according to when and where he was trained, according to what he has set out to accomplish, and so on. If, as is often the case, the object is to determine as far as possible the geographical range of a particular plant species, the usual method is to have recourse to a major herbarium. This should be done wherever possible because, although perusal of appropriate literature may give a fair idea of where a particular plant is present and where absent, it is nevertheless desirable to check the range against actual specimens labelled accurately and precisely with the localities in which they were collected. Adequate travel for the purpose of determining the areas of individual plants in the field is usually out of the question—and unnecessary if a good herbarium is available in which the findings of sufficient previous collectors are accumulated. Often, however, it is necessary to visit (or borrow material from) more than one herbarium for this purpose, bearing in mind the importance of checking the identity of every specimen on which a fresh 'locality' is based, for the very best of herbaria will inevitably contain occasional misidentifications and imprecisions.

Concerning plant ranges it should be recalled that negative evidence is insecure at best: because a particular plant species has not been found in (or at least has not been recorded from) a given region, we must not assume that it does not occur there—unless, perhaps, a very limited and well-known area is involved.[1] Nor may we conclude, without detailed trials, that the plant in question is incapable of growing in the area under the conditions obtaining there. Thus, maps indicating the supposed ranges of individual species can be misleading in suggesting absences which may not exist. On the other hand, such maps are valuable especially when showing (by spots) the definitely known stations. For these purposes various outline maps are available; but they must be 'spotted' with

[1] Such instances as that illustrated in Fig. 62 should act as a warning in this connection.

the greatest possible care, and preferably from authenticated specimens in view of the frequency with which literature citations, recollections, previous identifications, and so forth are prone to err. In this, again, all determinations should be checked.

Allied studies of, for example, the dispersal methods of particular species, or the distribution of the more complicated communities which they make up collectively, usually involve *ad hoc* field investigations. Of such studies more and more are needed. In most major populated regions there are nowadays herbaria[1] with staffs who will aid in determining plant specimens, if necessary by correspondence, provided a specimen labelled with the place, date, and collector's name is submitted. It is when we attempt to study the more complex communities which make up vegetation, that lasting personal contact is virtually essential. Yet such study is both instructive and rewarding, as vegetation affords a fine indication of local conditions. This was demonstrated in the last chapter.

## Further Applicational Possibilities

Apart from the practices of agriculture and forestry which to a large extent are ecologically based, conservation of natural resources such as forests and grasslands probably constitutes the most important application of ecology, which itself is to a considerable degree plant-geographical in basis. Modern wildlife and fisheries management should, however, not be forgotten in this connection. Consequently the preservation of natural areas for ecological and allied study is important, and also has its significance for plant geography. With the current disturbance of so many tracts, frequently so drastically that indigenous plant indicators disappear and there may be scarcely any native plants left, it is often only through the ecological or phytogeographical study of 'preserved' areas that the most appropriate schemes of land-utilization and conservation can be worked out and applied. Such areas are, moreover, the 'controls' by which the effects of Man's modification of surrounding tracts can be properly judged. For, to quote Sir Arthur G. Tansley (in R. S. Adamson's *The Vegetation of South Africa*, 1938), 'A knowledge of what nature produces when she is left to herself is one of the indispensable requisites of wise exploitation.'

[1] These are listed, usually with details of staff, etc., for all portions of the world in the *Index Herbariorum* published periodically by the International Association for Plant Taxonomy, Utrecht, Holland, and sent free to all members of that Association.

The introduction of exotics—for crops, mere convenience, or aesthetic or other purposes—is an application of importance. Species introduced into a new region or at all events a new environment may vary in their fate from complete failure of growth to becoming pests and largely ' taking over ' their new locale, after the manner of the Prickly-pear in Australia, though this is usually only where (and not much longer than) there is drastic disturbance by Man. Nevertheless introductions should be effected with care, preferably after appropriate trials have been made. The result may of course greatly extend the area inhabited by the species concerned. Thus many of the finest coniferous forests of Europe are now of Douglas Fir or other western North American species, and some considerable plantations in the eastern United States are of Scots Pine. In making such introductions it is prudent to consider not only the conditions in the lands concerned but also the ecological economy of the individual plants. For example, certain American trees thrive only in mixed stands, and so application in America of the pure-stand tendency of European forestry is liable to be unsuccessful where these species are concerned.

In connection with plant introduction, consideration of what are known as ' agroclimatic analogues ' may be valuable. These are based on the principle that a given variety tends to be very similar in its phenological behaviour (that is, with regard to such weather-affected activities as the times of flowering and fruiting) in areas of similar climatic and latitudinal conditions, the analogues being areas that are sufficiently alike in these features affecting crop production to offer a fair chance for success of plant materials transported among themselves. Elements of comparison in determining these analogues are the mean monthly and yearly temperatures, absolute minimum and maximum temperatures, average monthly, seasonal, and yearly precipitation, precipitation-evaporation ratios, length of frostless periods, and latitudes. In addition, soil and other features have of course to be taken into consideration when making trials. Fig. 184 indicates the application of such comparison to the Ukraine in terms of United States districts, with distinction between year-round analogues (for winter and spring crops, the appropriate State being named in slanting type) and April–October analogues (for spring crops only, the State being named in vertical type). In other such maps available at the American Institute of Crop Ecology, Washington, D.C., the winter and spring crop analogues may be separated. Consideration of latitude and the time of year takes into

FIG. 184.—Map showing positions of meteorological stations of the Ukraine, with indications of their climatic analogues in the United States. (Drawn from data kindly supplied by Office of Foreign Agricultural Relations, U.S. Department of Agriculture.)

account the photoperiodic demands of some plants for a particular length of day for such vital activities as flowering, and the special needs of others for, say, water which in particular regions tends to be available at particular seasons.

This matching of geographical areas on the basis of purely physical data should be verified by biological means, such as are provided by phenological records of similar plants growing in the two or more areas concerned. The plants used for such verification should if possible be pure-line varieties or *clones* (that is, derived vegetatively from a common ancestor); if the phenologies of given varieties of Wheat, Potatoes, etc., are more or less similar in climatically and latitudinally analogous areas, we then have our biological check that these areas are agroclimatic analogues. Such preliminary tests may conveniently be effected by exchange and co-operation among agricultural experiment stations, as may the next desirable stage, namely, establishment of uniform field trials of selected varieties. Nor need there be limitation to two areas in this connection; rather is it desirable to have a world-wide indication of all areas of similar phenology, meteorology, and latitude. This will give no guarantee of successful introduction between the analogous areas, plants and ecological factors being what they are; but it could act as a useful guide and save much time and effort, seed and money, which otherwise can easily be wasted. A simpler device that may already save some disappointment in introduction is the climograph. This is a diagram constructed by plotting the mean monthly temperatures at a point against their precipitation or humidity, and connecting the twelve points for the year by a closed line. If approximately coinciding climographs are given by two regions, at least for critical periods of the year in so far as climate is concerned, it may be considered worth while to try plant introductions from one to the other.

Many countries and states attempt to prevent the spread of plant diseases into new areas by imposing rigid restrictions on the importation of living plant materials, for these often carry diseases. It is particularly in fresh areas, or with species or strains that are unaccustomed to their ravages, that the greatest devastation by plant diseases is likely to take place. A striking example is the virtual extermination of Sweet Chestnut trees from eastern North America by a blight introduced from China where it has long attacked with far less effect a different but related species. Much the same principles obtain, and quarantine or other restrictions are imposed, in connection with human and domestic animals' diseases, so many of which are caused by Bacteria.

In wildlife management the most effective activity for increasing numbers is often improvement of the habitat, and in fresh waters the effect of adding fertilizer or manure (as in European carp-ponds) may be remarkable. The same can be true in salt waters, as was demonstrated during World War II in Scottish fiords where the addition of nutrients led to the extraordinarily rapid growth of Plaice and other Fishes. Many agricultural, horticultural, and forestral practices are comparable with this to the extent that the habitat is commonly prepared for some particular crop or other plant—which is usually an exotic form and, very often, unable to persist without the maintenance of some special man-made habitat. With this principle of habitat preparation and maintenance, with cultivation and tillage, we are already familiar ; but it should be re-emphasized here as it is largely applicational and, moreover, can and does lead to vast extensions in the ranges—albeit artificial—of many plants. As an extreme case Man is able, with the knowledge born of sufficient experimentation, to create in the laboratory or greenhouse almost any environment anywhere, so long as he cares to pay the necessary price.

Particular plants or vegetation-types often give a useful indication of the geological substrata on which they grow. For example, faults in various rocks or different strata of sandstone can exhibit marked floristic or vegetational differences. This may extend to questions of presence or absence of valuable minerals and, where no other than floristic or vegetational changes are visible at the surface, may be of obvious use in prospecting. In general, however, this subject has been little stressed except in particular instances and places, so that the field lies wide open for more precise observation and application.

Of indicator plants—or, better, groups of plants—there are many that can be valuable for agricultural or other planning. Examples include the Cacti and ' desert ' shrubs that indicate overgrazing in many parts of the American south-west, or the Sheep Sorrel and other small weeds that indicate a similar condition in many cool-temperate areas. Further indicators of similar or other conditions are mentioned in almost any modern ecological or allied textbook, and especially in the works of Clements cited at the end of this chapter. Indeed, most of the important habitat conditions have their plant indicators—even though we may not think of them in that light, and they may be only local as emphasized in the next paragraph.

If, as we often do when walking over a meadow, we come upon a clump of coarse Rushes, this is a strong indication of damp conditions ; if the Rushes are in a temperate region and accompanied by such hygrophytes as Marsh-marigold (*Caltha palustris* agg.), this combination can be taken as a sure sign of lasting percolation or of a water-table near the surface. Conversely, certain Heaths and Lichens are indicative of dry conditions, and certain forbs of a calcareous substratum—at least in many parts of the world. Whereas a single indicator species may be usefully suggestive, it is far better to have a group of them, which with suitable experience may be taken as virtually infallible. But even as the flora and vegetation change in different areas, so may such indications, which individually are chiefly of local use ; consequently precise local knowledge is needed for their application.

Accordingly it would seem superfluous in this very general treatise to multiply the examples. Suffice it to repeat that land-use science, employing such methods as plant indicators, can be of very great importance to the modern world.

Of other plant geographical or, often, primarily ecological principles and findings that have wide applicational value there are very many —as indicated, for example, in the concluding sections of Professor H. J. Oosting's work cited at the end of this chapter, though the examples he gives are mainly North American. These principles include many that are widely employed : in horticulture, for cultivated plants are as subject as any others to ecological laws ; in agriculture, where so many of the practices, however familiar and widespread, are basically ecological ; in pisciculture, where the feeding and maintenance of a rich phytoplankton is all-important ; in silviculture, *e.g.* towards deciding whether to maintain temporary forests of a successional nature or to let the stands develop naturally towards the climax ; in reforestation of suitable areas (after deciding which areas are suitable) and revegetation of exposed soils, where special autecological and local synecological knowledge are normally essential for success ; in range management, which is largely applied ecology, though it should be recalled that the most effective practices are in general those which least disturb the natural balance between the grassland and its environment ; in pasture and various cropland choice and treatment, *e.g.* in relation to suitable indicators and rotations ; in general land-management, which raises the questions of whether our single-cropping and maintenance for it of open-soil conditions is really sound, involving as it commonly does the destruction of soil structure by deep ploughing ; in weed and disease control, where autecological studies suggest the possible effectiveness of more judicious land management as well as application of selective herbicides ; in conservation, where vegetative cover is the most effective means of checking erosion ; in water-supply and wildlife management, where the ecological problems are almost endless ; in landscaping, where knowledge of the habitat requirements of the species concerned is fundamental ; and so on—almost *ad infinitum.* Indeed we may suggest without serious fear of contradiction that it is largely, and perhaps in the long run only, through the enlightened application of effective research in the plant sciences *sensu latissimo* that Man can continue to keep abreast of population increases and feed and clothe the world's teeming millions.

It may be claimed with good reason that this is the age for the biological scientist : for whereas the physical sciences have already achieved a high degree of consistency, in the life sciences our knowledge is often still no more than meagre and our understanding rudimentary (yet the importance of learning more and more is enormous, as indicated above). And so it is that in plant geography and some of its relatives, our analytical perception is often poor and many fundamental principles doubtless still await discovery. Whether, indeed, with the changing drifts of life, this situation will ever be fully remedied, remains to be seen. But already there is a vast body of pertinent information which is being added to all the time, and the present book has as its main object the sifting of this knowledge and introduction to the principles that emerge.

## Additional Reading

It has been customary to conclude previous chapters with lists of pertinent works or suggestions for further reading. In the present instance any good modern textbook of genetics and plant breeding, such as E. W. Sinnott, L. C. Dunn & T. Dobzhansky's *Principles of Genetics*, fifth edition (McGraw-Hill, New York etc., pp. xiv + 459, 1958), or M. B. Crane & W. J. C. Lawrence's *The Genetics of Garden Plants*, fourth edition (Macmillan, London, pp. xvii + 301, 1952), should suffice to give the needful student some background to the cognate facts and principles on which we have (barely) touched.

The ecological items were dealt with in Chapters X and XI, at the ends of which further reading was suggested. Concerning erosion and its control, such works as H. H. Bennett's *Elements of Soil Conservation* second edition (McGraw-Hill, New York etc., pp. x + 358, 1955) and Paul B. Sears's *Deserts on the March*, revised edition (Routledge & Kegan Paul, London, pp. xi + 181, 1949) are to be recommended as both vivid and readable, while John D. Black's more recent *Biological Conservation* (Blakiston, New York & Toronto, pp. xiv + 328, 1954) deals with other practical aspects and has a useful annotated bibliography.

On the subject of indicators, F. E. Clements's *Plant Indicators* (Carnegie Institution, Washington, D.C., Publication No. 290, pp. xvi + 388, 1920 is still the standard work, although an abridged version appears in his *Plant Succession and Indicators* (Wilson, New York, pp. xvi + 453, 1928). Chemical control of plant growth, etc., is dealt with in L. J. Audus's *Plant Growth Substances*, second edition (Leonard Hill, London, pp. xxii + 553, 1959), and applied ecology in H. J. Oosting's *The Study of Plant Communities*, second edition (Freeman, San Francisco, Calif., pp. viii + 440, 1956)

Additional reading on particular topics has been suggested at the end of almost all previous chapters under the heading of 'Further Consideration'.

# INDEX

References in **heavy type** are to illustrations. For international understanding and accuracy, scientific (*italicized Latin*) plant names are chiefly used, the English or other equivalents being cross-referenced to them. The full extent of such vernacular names is indicated in both text and index by Capitalization of Initial Letters, the name-sequence being retained in the index — usually without cross-referencing. Thus ' Mountain Sorrel ' will be found so listed (and there referred to its Latin name, *Oxyria digyna*), and not under ' Sorrel, Mountain '. Other listings are generally treated similarly. To obviate the need of a glossary, technical terms are listed in the index and explained in the text—usually on introduction. Often, too, they are illustrated.